P9-DBQ-732

Applying educational psychology

Fifth Edition

Myron H. Dembo
University of Southern California

YORK COLLEGE
PENNSYLVANIA
Servire est vivere
LIBRARY

Longman
New York & London

Applying Educational Psychology, fifth edition

Copyright © 1994, 1991, 1988 by Longman Publishing Group.
All rights reserved.
No part of this publication may be reproduced, stored in a retrieval system, or transmitted in any form or by any means, electronic, mechanical, photocopying, recording, or otherwise, without the prior permission of the publisher.

Longman, 10 Bank Street, White Plains, N.Y. 10606

Associated companies:
Longman Group Ltd., London
Longman Cheshire Pty., Melbourne
Longman Paul Pty., Auckland
Copp Clark Pitman, Toronto

Senior acquisitions editor: Laura McKenna
Development editor: Virginia L. Blanford
Production editor: Halley Gatenby
Text and cover designs: Circa 86
Cover photo: Lorne/Explorer
Text art: Vantage
Photo research: Circa 86

Copyright acknowledgments follow the indexes at the back of this book.

Library of Congress Cataloging-in-Publication Data

Dembo, Myron H.
Applying educational psychology by Myron H. Dembo,—5th ed.
P. cm.
Includes bibliographical references and index.
ISBN 0-8013-1398-8
1. Educational psychology. 2. Learning, Psychology of 3. Classroom management. I. Title.
L81051 . D369 1991
370 . 15—dc20 93-13375
CIP

2 3 4 5 6 7 8 9 10-DO-97969594

In memory of my mother and father
Lillian and Harry Guy Dembo
and
To my aunts and uncles
Sylvia and Sol Miller
Mildred and Lou Resnick
Pinky and Irving Rudolph
Who always loved me like their own son

16/1/97-62.55-BNA

Contents Overview

Contents

PART 2 Learning and Motivation: Instructional Applications 35

PART 3 Preparing for Effective Teaching 234

Classroom Applications

Debate Forums

Foreword

Teacher education is in the midst of a far-reaching revolution, a revolution based on research about teachers—how they think; make decisions; integrate their knowledge of content with knowledge about teaching, management, learning, development, and motivation; and how they act. This research draws heavily on a general cognitive psychological framework reflecting how individuals think and learn in complex situations. One finding that continues to emerge is that learners do not passively accumulate facts and concepts to be used at some later date, but rather that they actively construct meaning from a wide array of information including prior knowledge and specific, contextual information. This constructivist perspective rejects the assumption that teaching is just the application of already acquired knowledge, and therefore that teacher education is the "filling-up" of novice teachers with appropriate knowledge. As Myron Dembo points out in the first chapter of *Applying Educational Psychology*, Fifth Edition, teaching is not an algorithmic of prior knowledge; rather, it is a complex problem-solving activity.

This model of teaching as decision-making may not comfort those prospective teachers who only want to know, "What do I do in my classroom on Monday morning?" *Successful* teaching is very difficult, fraught with unpredictable practical and ethical issues. Nevertheless, current views of teaching and teacher education ask you, the prospective teacher, to accept this uncertainty as an inherent aspect of teaching. No educational psychology textbook can provide you with the "silver bullet"—the one *best* way to teach—and no textbook should try.

But you need not go off to teach unprepared, armed only with beliefs and ideas constructed from your own educational experiences. Educational psychology in general, and *Applying Educational Psychology*, Fifth Edition, in particular, can help you develop the necessary conceptual framework for understanding the teaching-learning process. The conceptual framework that Dembo provides, modeled in Figure 1.1, is an excellent heuristic for organizing the knowledge base of educational psychology and understanding how it intersects with other domains of knowledge in curriculum and instruction. Dembo continually revisits this model throughout the text, showing how the content knowledge of each chapter fits into the overall framework, and how it applies to the problems of teaching.

Educational psychology texts are often seen as compilations of research, lacking an integrative and applied framework. In contrast, *Applying Educational Psychology* and the framework it provides should help you begin to integrate different content knowledge into a coherent way of looking at teaching. In addition, by focusing continually on this teaching-learning process, Dembo encourages you to link this content with real classroom problems, rather than simply to memorize (and probably forget) the topical knowledge. This focus on application is maintained by various elements in the text, including the vignettes that open every chapter, the "Reflecting On..." problem that end each chapter, and the Part Syntheses and integrating questions that end each part and tie several chapters together

Besides this general framework, educational psychology does offer specific, useful tools for understanding student thinking, learning, and motivation. The framework is not content-free—nor should it be, given current research. The days are long gone when educational psychologists generalized from simple experiments on animals to the complexities of the classroom. We now know a great deal about how real students learn in real classrooms, and this knowledge can be very useful. The specific concepts provided in *Applying Educational Psychology*, Fifth Edition, represent important knowledge about learning and teaching—concepts that sometimes parallel, but in other cases contradict, common beliefs.

For example, prospective teachers sometimes believe that students either have the ability to do academic tasks (called "intelligence") or do not. Yet recent research supports the idea that cognitive and metacognitive strategies that enable students to improve their performances dramatically can be taught and learned. Studies also suggest that intelligence is comprised not of some monolithic entity but of a multiplicity of knowledge, skills, and abilities. Research on the tenacity of student misconceptions—especially in math and science—also contradicts common wisdom that "covering" the material in a well-organized lecture is effective teaching. Finally, recent research on student motivation suggests that, while student interest is important, motivation includes a number of other beliefs that influence learning. Accordingly, contrary to common belief, it is not enough for teachers to be enthusiastic and interesting; they must also think carefully about the types of assignments they give and how they evaluate and provide feedback on them. Dembo provides excellent explorations of current research on the cognitive psychology of student learning and motivation that should dispel some of the more simplistic and common views of teaching and learning.

Applying Educational Psychology, Fifth Edition, comprises one important component of an educational psychology course. It develops a conceptual framework for thinking about the teaching-learning process and provides the most recent and applicable research on learning, cognition, and motivation. It is a valuable tool for both faculty and students in educational psychology. In addition, given the power of the framework and approach, this text should be particularly useful in courses that integrate educational psychology with students' actual field experience, or with other coursework in education. Taken together, the components of this text will help prospective teachers become better learners, better decision-makers, and better teachers—the ultimate goal for all teacher education programs.

Paul R. Pintrich
The University of Michigan, Ann Arbor

Preface

Welcome to educational psychology! My primary purpose in writing this text is to help you become a better learner, as well as a better teacher. To achieve this, I will provide you with coverage of important theory and research in educational psychology while focusing on how you can *apply* this knowledge, both inside and outside the classroom. As you read, you will find many questions, issues, and exercises that encourage you to reflect and think critically about both teaching and learning. I believe that if you use educational psychology to improve your own learning, you may be more motivated to use the same principles in your own teaching.

I have been teaching both undergraduate and graduate educational psychology for more than 25 years. Before that, I taught junior high school. And before that (of course!) I was a college and graduate student, like you. Whether as a public school teacher or a college professor, I have always had a strong belief that future teachers need to learn how to bridge theory and practice. We urge teachers to emphasize critical thinking, but for some reason we seem hesitant to involve them in that same critical thinking while they are being trained to become teachers. My students have made that clear to me.

I owe my students a great deal. They consistently discuss in class how theories of learning and motivation can be related to the ways they approach their other college courses, how understanding personal and social development provides better understanding of their own family experiences, and even how understanding individual differences and methods of behavioral change helps those who are parents deal with their own children. It is these concerns that I have tried to address throughout the life of this textbook.

How is this accomplished?

EMPHASIS ON LEARNING HOW TO LEARN

In this book, unlike most educational psychology texts, the section on learning theory comes *first*. By confronting the learning theories explored in Chapters 2 through 5 (and especially in Chapter 3, "Cognitive Approaches to Learning"), you will begin to comprehend your own learning processes and construct your own knowledge of educational psychology.

You will cover the material on cognitive psychology later in the course if your instructor chooses to begin with the development chapters. You will still be able to improve your own learning strategies by reacting to the various pedagogical elements in the text that encourage you to become an active learner:

- *Advance organizers* for each chapter—graphic models, chapter outlines, and chapter objectives—allow you to preview material and call up associations, experiences, and prior knowledge of the topics to be presented. Research suggests that these elements increase your comprehension and retention of the information presented.
- *Vignettes* provide snapshots of how the material in each chapter plays out in real life. Such "stories" offer structures for factual information that aid memory.
- *Focus questions* scattered throughout the chapters help you identify key points. By focusing on main ideas, you will solidify your conceptual grasp of the content.
- *Debate Forums* encourage you to think critically about current controversies in the teaching-learning process. Critical thinking is a higher-order mental skill that enhances deeper understanding.
- *Reflecting On...* questions and experiential exercises at the end of each chapter encourage you to stop and mull over the material you have just read. Such pauses support the learning process, allow you to check comprehension, help you integrate the main ideas of the chapter, and—most important—provide an opportunity for you to *apply* your knowledge.
- *Part Syntheses with integrating questions* at the end of each part suggest how theories, models, and information discussed in several different chapters may interact in real classrooms. This unique feature encourages you to retrieve information from a variety of sources in order to make real decisions and solve real problems.

In addition to these in-text elements, the student *Study Guide* designed to accompany this text is *integrated* with the text in its emphasis on you as current learner as well as prospective teacher. Unlike most study guides that accompany educational psychology texts, this goes beyond fill-in-the-blanks, definitions, and multiple-choice questions. All crucial specific textbook material is reviewed—including sample tests for each chapter—but the primary function of the *Study Guide* is to reinforce the content of the text in helping you become a more effective learner. Each chapter includes a section on *using learning strategies*, with integrating questions involving higher-level thinking. Exercises are designed to encourage you to apply educational psychology to your current courses, as well as to your current or future roles as teachers and parents. By completing the exercises in the *Study Guide*, you will acquire a deeper level of learning that should, in turn, improve your academic performance and teaching expertise.

EMPHASIS ON APPLYING THEORY TO INSTRUCTION

This textbook has always included numerous Classroom Applications, but this edition contains many more: an average of almost three per chapter. The applications in this text include explanations about *why* a particular strategy is recommended, and the strategies are described in sufficient detail that you can actually use them in teaching situations.

These applications are color-coded in green and teal blue for easy identification. Teal headings with the applications "apple" icon also introduce text sections including instructional implications of theory, so that you can readily find all the material that relates theory to actual practice. A complete list of the Classroom Applications follows the table of contents.

In addition, Part Three of the text provides clear, practical guidance for planning and managing classroom instruction. The principles of learning and motivation presented in Chapters 6 and 7 are based on and linked to the learning theories presented in Part Two, and a variety of specific strategies is provided, including sample lesson plans for direct instruction, discovery learning, and cooperative learning.

EMPHASIS ON COGNITION, CULTURE, AND SOCIAL ISSUES

Virtually all the feedback I received on earlier editions of this text from both students and colleagues called for expanded coverage of cognitive learning theory, culture, and the new reality of classroom diversity. In response, Part Two has been significantly revised and expanded, with a primary emphasis on cognitive learning theories in Chapter 3, and on cognitive perspectives on motivation in Chapter 4.

Part Four explores these areas in even greater depth. Chapter 8 has been revised to include the sociocultural approach to intelligence. Chapter 9, "Cognition, Culture, and Language," was applauded in the previous edition as ground-breaking by some instructors; I have revised and expanded it to emphasize some of the most pressing issues in education today, including culture and ethnicity, the new demographics of the classroom, and the explanations that various learning theorists provide for low academic performance by students from different cultural backgrounds. Chapter 10, which moves from Erikson's theory of development to the critical social and developmental issues of today, includes new material on gender differences, self-concept, child abuse, and student stress, as well as a discussion of various family socialization concerns. Chapter 11 provides a broad picture of current issues in special education and individual differences, including an update on legislation in this important area.

EMPHASIS ON PARENTING AND PARENT-TEACHER INTERACTION

I have changed the title of this book in this edition from *Applying Educational Psychology in the Classroom* to simply *Applying Educational Psychology*, in recognition of the fact that these concepts and principles are useful in "real life" as well as in a classroom context. In keeping with this, I have focused in particular on parents—both by providing material to help teachers and parents interact more successfully, and by providing information for present and prospective parents interested in helping their own children become more successful learners. See, for example, approaches to discipline and how parents and teachers can work together to improve classroom behavior (Chapter 7); ideas for using the knowledge and skills of parents from multicultural backgrounds in the classroom (Chapter 9); recommendations for monitoring children's television viewing, the effects of different parenting styles on children's development, and the advantages and disadvantages of children working during high school (Chapter 10); raising exceptional children (Chapter 11); and conferencing with teachers (Chapter 13).

IN SHORT. . .

The major focus of this textbook is on you as *both* learner and teacher, and the content, organization, and pedagogical format of the book are all driven by that focus. You will find here a taxonomy of learning strategies that is a *useful* way to organize your own concepts of how to learn and how to teach. You will also find a treatment of cultural diversity that far exceeds that of most educational psychology textbooks. If you use all the elements provided in this text, you will find yourself encouraged to be an *active learner* as you confront critical issues in educational psychology, and as you apply your knowledge to your own learning and teaching.

ACKNOWLEDGMENTS

I would like to thank the graduate students at the University of Southern California who provided help with the manuscript:

Dan Bronkhurst wrote the drafts for the scenarios that introduce each chapter and completed the Author Index.
Anne Josephson reviewed the page proofs.
Martin Eaton helped research materials for Chapter 3.
Matt Nelson researched and wrote draft material for certain sections of Chapter 10.
Marjorie Faulstich-Orellana researched and wrote draft material for Chapter 9.

I also appreciate the insight I received from colleagues in the Department of Educational Psychology, Robert Rueda and Richard Clark.

My writing was influenced by thoughtful reviews from the following individuals:

Kay Alderman, University of Akron
Carole Ames, Michigan State University
Carolyn Anderson, University of Cincinnati
Douglas Beed, University of Montana
Curtis Jay Bonk, Indiana University
Susan Christ, Southern Illinois University

Anne C. Diver-Stamnes, Humboldt State University
Thomas Fetsco, Northern Arizona University
Gay Goodman, University of Houston
Cathy W. Hall, East Carolina University
Eunsook Hong, University of Nevada, Las Vegas
Richard Hovey, Black Hills State College, South Dakota
Frederick C. Howe, Buffalo State College
Lawrence Kavich, University of Northern Iowa
Pamela Laughon, University of North Carolina, Asheville
Sharon McNeely, Northeastern Illinois University
Joel Milgram, University of Cincinnati
Fayneese Miller, Brown University
Wayne A. Nelson, University of Illinois, Edwardsville
Peggy Perkins, University of Nevada, Las Vegas
Jean Pierce, Northern Illinois University
Paul Pintrich, University of Michigan
Gregory Schraw, University of Nebraska, Lincoln
Thomassine Sellers, San Francisco State University
Gary Stainback, East Carolina University
Robert J. Stevens, Pennsylvania State University
Shirley Walters, West Chester University
Victor L. Willson, Texas A & M University
Jane A. Wolfle, Bowling Green State University

A special note of thanks to Paul Pintrich of the University of Michigan at Ann Arbor, who not only reviewed this manuscript during development but also contributed the foreword. Dr. Pintrich shares my enthusiasm for encouraging students to take command of their own learning.

Finally, I owe a special thank you to Virginia Blanford, developmental editor; to Laura McKenna, senior acquisitions editor, who made important recommendations for improving the quality of the book; and to Halley Gatenby, managing editor, who also served as this book's production editor and helped transform the manuscript into a finished text.

I would greatly appreciate your reactions to this book. I welcome your praise and your criticism. Please use the page at the end of this book to send me your comments, so that I can construct the next edition of this text with your help.

Part one

Applying Educational Psychology

As the author of this textbook, I have two important responsibilities. The first is to help you become an effective *learner*, and the second is to help you become an effective *teacher*. Sometimes educational psychology students are so concerned with applying their knowledge to teaching that they neglect to consider how they can improve their own learning in this and other courses in which they are enrolled.

My emphasis on the importance of improving your learning has influenced the content organization of this book. After the introductory chapter, we move directly to the study of learning and motivation. You will learn how to make decisions about learning *both* as a student and as a teacher. The information on motivation will help you understand the motivational processes related to successful learning. You will be encouraged to analyze your present study strategies and motivation to learn.

In the following chapter, we will explore the related but independent processes of teaching and learning. You will be introduced to the teaching-learning model around which this text is organized, and which will provide you with a touchstone for the variety of decisions you will need to make in determining your own instructional beliefs. This introductory chapter provides a brief overview of the model itself, and of the decision-making roles played in the instructional process by both learners and teachers. It also underlines the importance of research in understanding how learning takes place by incorporating a substantial research base into the text itself. At the end of the chapter, you will find an appendix that describes the research process in more detail and provides a clear guide to resources in educational psychology that may prove helpful to you as both learner and teacher.

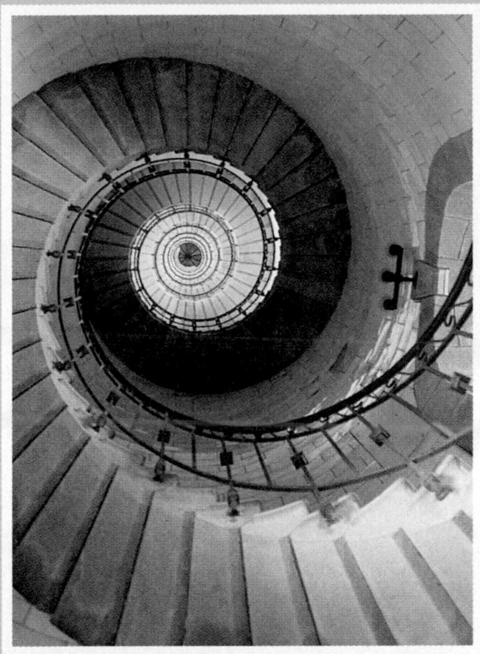

Throughout the book I will ask you to think about your own educational experiences and the teachers who taught you. When you visit classrooms you may be surprised to note that they look different from the ones you experienced. They are definitely different from the public school classrooms I taught in when I began my teaching career. And the classroom of 2000 will look significantly different from the one you are sitting in, or teaching in, today. Your students may or may not speak English as a first or second language. Many of them—often more than half of them—will be children of color. Their families may include two parents—both of whom may be the same sex, or one of whom may be a stepparent—or one parent. Or they may live with a grandparent or an aunt. Their families may include sisters, brothers, stepbrothers, cousins, or other children whose relationship is even less clear.

What difference will all of this make to you as as teacher? How will this dramatic diversity in your classroom impact your teaching—and your learning how to teach? I am going to help you answer these questions as you read the research, theory, and classroom applications in the book. Let's get started . . .

Chapter 1

The Teacher as Decision Maker

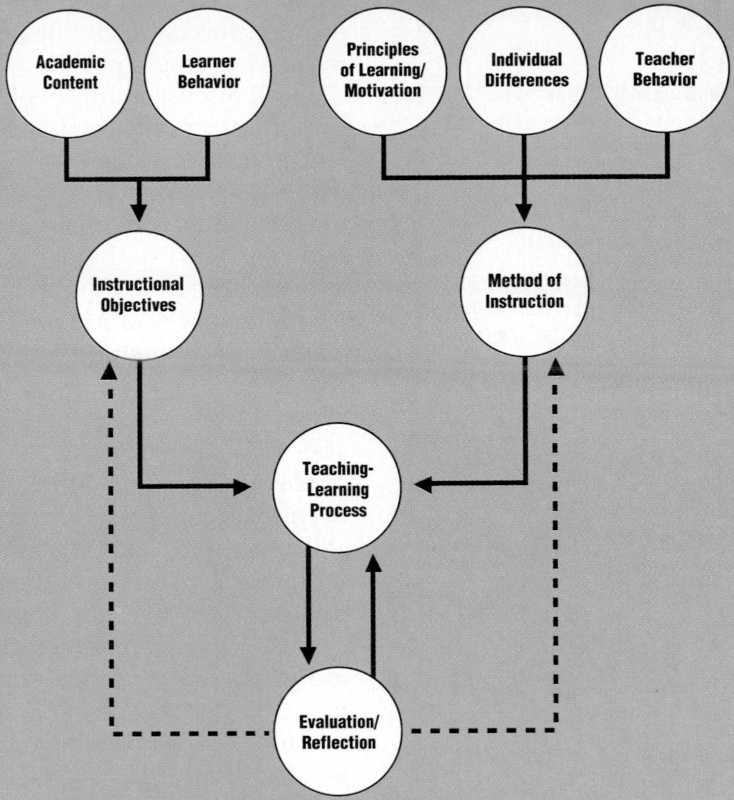

OBJECTIVES

After mastering the material in this chapter you will be able to:

- Use a model of the teaching-learning process to analyze a teacher's instructional behavior.
- Identify how students' beliefs and self-perceptions influence their learning.
- Observe student behavior in classrooms.

Orientation

teaching. A system of actions intended to induce learning.

learning. A process by which behavior is either modified or changed through experience or training.

behavioral learning theories. Theories of learning that focus on external events and tend to ignore internal factors in learning.

cognitive learning theories. Explanations for learning that focus on the role of the learner's mental processing of information.

Teaching and **learning** are related but independent processes. Sometimes teaching leads to learning—but not always. Although the teacher may facilitate learning, each student must take charge of his or her own learning. Smith (1960) defines teaching as a "system of actions intended to induce learning" (p. 230).

I will discuss in this book two different approaches to learning that have important implications for teaching. **Behavioral learning theories** view learning as a process by which behavior is either modified or changed through experience or training. **Cognitive learning theories** emphasize the acquisition or construction of knowledge and how it can be organized and connected so that it can be retrieved. Cognitive theories view learning as a mental activity that is inferred based on behavior (Schunk, 1991b).

Weinstein and Mayer (1986) emphasize the active roles of both the teacher and the student in the teaching-learning process. They point out that teachers enter the classroom with two different kinds of goals: (1) goals concerning the products of learning—what students should be able to do or perform as the result of learning; and (2) goals concerning the process of learning—the strategies students use to learn. Thus, teachers need to be concerned with both *what* students learn and *how* they learn.

To facilitate learning in others, you must learn the major factors that influence the success of the teaching-learning process. This is no easy task, for the classroom is a complex meshing of simultaneous activities and events. I have organized this book around an instructional model that identifies some important decisions a teacher must make during the instructional process so that you, the teacher, will better understand the relation between teaching and learning. Shavelson (1973) has emphasized the importance of teachers' decisions during instruction by stating, "Any teaching act is the result of a decision, either conscious or unconscious . . . *the* basic teaching skill is decision making" (p. 144).

This introductory chapter explains the model and discusses the ways you can use psychological content to improve your teaching effectiveness. The major goals of this book are to help you

- become an effective learner
- examine the effects of your decisions on your students' learning
- examine your personal beliefs about the teaching-learning process
- evaluate your beliefs and practices so that you can modify your teaching behavior and become a more effective teacher
- understand how student beliefs and self-perceptions influence their motivation and achievement behavior

? How do teachers' beliefs influence their teaching decisions?

Teachers espouse hypotheses, or beliefs, about the nature of the teaching-learning process that influence their classroom behavior. These beliefs lead them to make important decisions that set the conditions for behaviors under which students live and learn at school (Greenwood & Parkay, 1989; Mayer, 1985a). For example, if teachers believe that teaching reading is best accomplished by emphasizing the pronunciation of letters and words, they may have difficulty switching to a different type of program that emphasizes comprehension and high-level thinking skills (e.g., analysis and inference) (Richardson et al., 1991). Teachers' beliefs also have been shown to be related to their decisions regarding grade retention (Tomchin & Impara, 1992), classroom discipline (Woolfolk, Rosoff, & Hoy, 1990), teaching low-achieving students (Dembo & Gibson, 1985), and adolescents (Eccles, 1991).

Careful observation of teacher practices in the classroom can provide insights into a teacher's belief system and will reveal that not all teaching decisions are supported by empirical research or are consistent with sound educational theory or practice.

Let's look at a comment from a student observer who questioned a teacher about a particular teaching behavior:

> She reads to the class because she feels that lecturing "over their heads" is not good and that they will learn nothing from it. She feels that if students understand what she says, they will learn much better. After reading to the class, she asks questions to test their comprehension.

This teacher's beliefs about learning prompted her to read to the class. What classroom experiences led her to this decision? If she had lectured "over their heads" in the past, what was the cause of her behavior? Did the students not understand important information? Was her vocabulary too difficult for the students' level of development? The answers to these questions should help to explain why her lecturing was ineffective. Although she feels that her students will learn better by being read to than by being lectured at, the solution to the problem may prove to be as ineffective as her original strategy.

McDonald (1965) provides a good example of how a teacher's decisions can shape what students will learn:

> A fourth-grade teacher was introducing a unit on "Pioneer Life." He asked the students what they wanted to study about "Pioneer Life" and what kinds of questions they should raise concerning the subject. As the discussion proceeded, the children suggested the usual categories for studying a history unit—namely, the pioneer's food, shelter, and clothing. One child mentioned that he had seen a Western movie in which a man accused of horse stealing was immediately hanged. This comment on the movie evoked considerable interest in the group, and one of the children asked why the man was hanged right away. The teacher dismissed this question as irrelevant to a discussion on pioneer life. The decision not to utilize this question in effect set the stage for the kinds of things that the pupils would talk about. Had the teacher chosen to capitalize upon this question, topics concerning pioneer conceptions of justice and due process of law, the function of law-enforcing bodies, and the validity of citizens' arrests could have been developed. These topics

> did not emerge in the ensuing discussion, nor were they included as relevant points in the outline of topics to be studied under the headline of "Pioneer Life." The teacher's decisions at this point, then, determined the character of what the children could learn. (pp. 63–64)

McDonald asks whether this teacher would have profited by examining his decisions in the light of his teaching hypotheses.

These examples illustrate the importance of examining and testing teaching hypotheses, or beliefs, so that you can make necessary modifications in educational procedures and practices. Teachers must learn to ask questions about their own teaching practices in order to monitor their own behavior. Most important, they must determine how their students perceive classroom events, since their beliefs and self-perceptions also influence their classroom behavior (Schunk & Meece, 1992).

THE STUDENT AS DECISION MAKER

> ? In what way can the student be considered a decision maker?

Up to this point, I have focused on the role of the teacher in the teaching-learning process. Although some teachers require students to make many decisions determining what and how they will learn, most students don't make the same type of decisions that teachers make about instruction. However, research has determined that students are active information processors and influence classroom events as much as they are affected by them (Pintrich et al., 1986).

Paris and Newman (1990) believe that students actually develop different "theories of schooling" that influence their classroom behavior in terms of their motivation, study habits, learning strategies, and interests. Understanding these theories and beliefs can provide the teacher with helpful information as to why students behave as they do.

A good example of how students' theories can influence their decision making was identified by Dweck (1986), who showed that children can have two different perspectives about intelligence. Some children believe that learning is incremental; others believe that the ability to learn is static. *Incremental theorists* believe that intelligence is modifiable through effort. If one works harder, one can become more able. *Entity theorists* believe that individuals have a fixed amount of intelligence or ability that is not modifiable by the degree of effort. When students with both beliefs are given difficult tasks to complete, entity theorists are more likely to give up sooner and state that they don't have the ability, while incremental theorists persist on the task and demonstrate greater effort when tasks become more difficult.

A wide variety of students' beliefs and self-perceptions guide their behavior. It is clear that students can't be perceived as "empty vessels" whom teachers simply fill with knowledge. Paris and Newman (1990) believe that it is important for teachers to have class discussions about classroom activities so that they can "see" what their students are thinking: "Children need to express their theories about what they tried to do, how they tried to reach their goals, what they did when they faced obstacles, and what they should do if faced with similar problems in the future" (p. 98). An important aspect of teaching from a cognitive psychology perspective is to understand how students construct or make sense of their knowledge.

THE TEACHER AS DECISION MAKER

?

How do the major components in the teaching-learning process impact the effectiveness of instruction?

Before studying the teaching-learning process, you should understand its major components. The use of an instructional model best accomplishes this purpose. Figure 1.1 is an instructional model that has been adapted from Hunter (1971), who has applied it to the education of both preservice and inservice teachers.

An important aspect of this model for teachers is that it integrates the important components in the teaching-learning process: the students

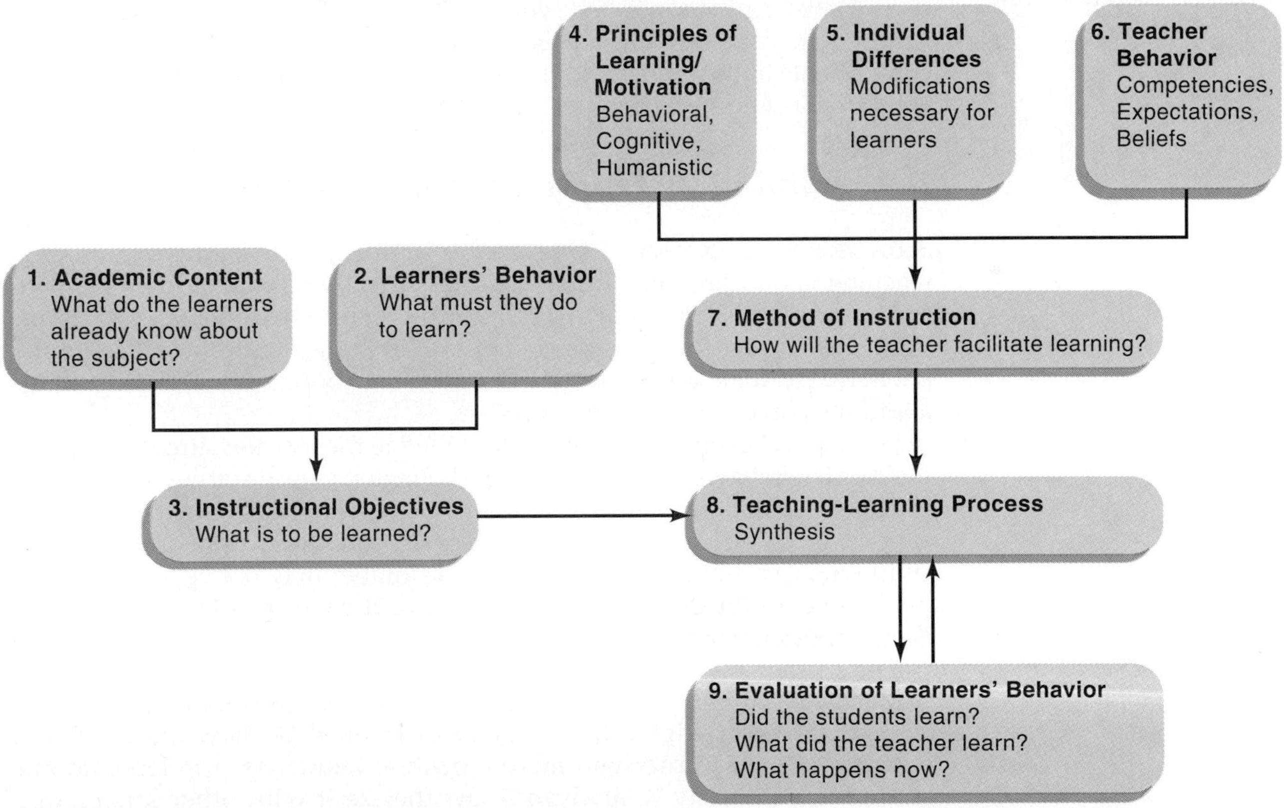

Figure 1.1 The Decisions That Make Up the Teaching-Learning Process.
Source: Adapted from Hunter, 1971, in Allen and Seifman.

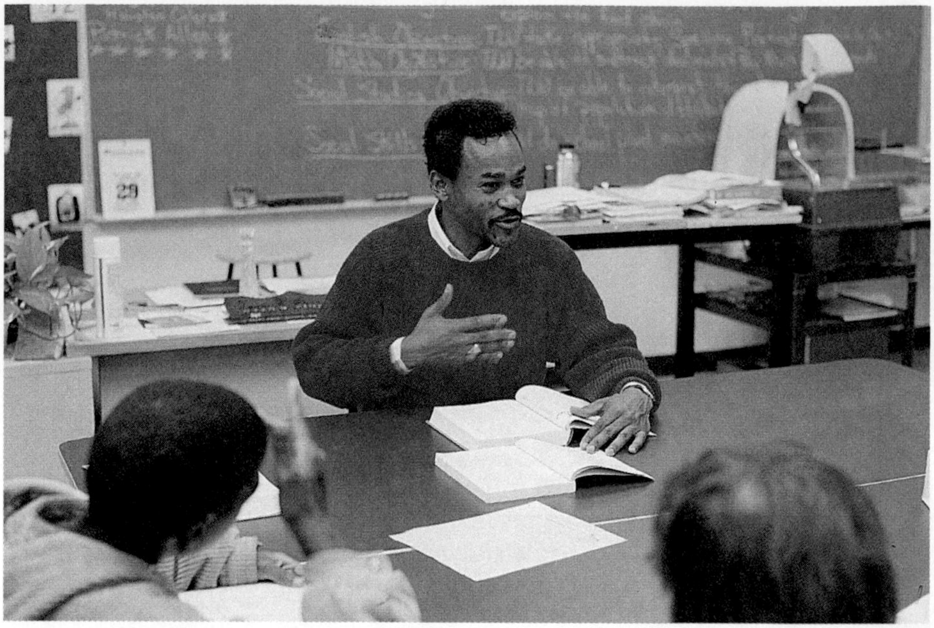

Effective teaching involves many decisions before a teacher begins teaching a lesson.

instructional objectives. Statements regarding the specific changes educators intend to produce in student behavior.

entry behavior. The knowledge, skills, or attitudes that a learner brings into a new learning situation.

whom they teach, the objectives they hope to attain with them, and the methods and behaviors they use to accomplish their objectives. Because each component is separated, you can study each one and relate research findings to your teaching decisions during instruction. Let's look at the components in the model and the decisions that a teacher must make. Each component is numbered for easy identification.

Determining Instructional Objectives

Academic Content. One of the important decisions to make in teaching is deciding on an **instructional objective.** What is to be learned? (See circle no. 3 in Figure 1.1.) A number of earlier decisions must intervene during this process. Teachers' familiarity with the content area, particularly their ability to determine what the learners already know about the content, impacts this process.

Some psychologists refer to the knowledge the learners already know as their **entry behavior.** Assessing entry behavior requires at least two kinds of measurement, according to Hunter (1971). The first is the continuum—easy to more difficult—that exists in most content areas. For example, a child who can multiply by a single-digit number may not be able to multiply by two- or three-digit numbers. Starting at the proper level of difficulty is an important condition of any instructional program.

The second measure of a learning task is its level of complexity. The *Taxonomy of Educational Objectives: Cognitive Domain* (Bloom et al., 1956) categorizes knowledge into a number of levels that allow the teacher to determine if the learner will merely possess knowledge, understand and summarize it, apply it, analyze it, synthesize it with other knowledge, evaluate it, or some combination of these.

THE BEHAVIOR OF THE LEARNER. Before determining the instructional objective, you must also consider the behavior of the learners (circle no. 2). What must they do in order to learn—read, write, list, conclude, analyze? The behavior must be relevant to the objective (students can't learn to debate merely by reading books on debating, nor can they solve chemistry problems simply by memorizing formulas). And the behavior must be relevant to the learner. If a child is a poor reader, your reliance solely on a social studies textbook for factual material is not an appropriate teaching behavior.

The synthesis of the first two teaching decisions—what the students will learn and how they will learn it—constitutes the *instructional objective* of a lesson (circle no. 3). The determination of this objective will help you to decide later whether you have been successful in changing the learners' behaviors.

The model in Figure 1.1 identifies some important responsibilities for you to consider before you even begin teaching a lesson. Too often, teachers start out with instructional techniques or strategies before they know what they are trying to teach, or they identify objectives before they analyze the individual abilities of the students. Planning objectives without first assessing the needs and abilities of the learners is a risky procedure that often leads to inappropriate, irrelevant, or unnecessary teaching.

declarative knowledge. Knowledge about things.

procedural knowledge. Knowledge about how to do things.

Determining Instructional Methods

Another major decision is answering the "how" question in the instructional process (circle no. 7). How will you facilitate learning? Teachers differ greatly in their styles of teaching. These differences involve the degree of planning, the amount of control of student behaviors, the method of presentation of material, the types of grouping, and so forth.

Figure 1.1 identifies a number of factors that should influence a teacher's instructional methodology, including theories and principles of learning and motivation (circle no. 4), individual differences of students (circle no. 5), and teacher behavior (circle no. 6).

PRINCIPLES OF LEARNING AND MOTIVATION. Principles of learning and motivation (circle no. 4) can help you determine the conditions that will help students improve their performances. R. Gagné (1985) points out that not all learning is the same and that the instructor needs to teach differently to effect different kinds of learning. Repetition is an important principle in learning multiplication tables, but it is less useful in learning to solve mathematical equations. Another way to view learning is to determine whether one is attempting to teach **declarative knowledge** or **procedural knowledge** (Anderson, 1985). Declarative knowledge is information about things such as a date, a friend's address, and the information in a textbook. Procedural knowledge is knowledge about how to do things such as solve a math problem, drive a car, and tie a shoelace. As you will learn in Chapter 3, the conditions for learning declarative knowledge are different from those for learning procedural knowledge.

Knowledge of the theories and principles of learning and motivation, then, can improve your decisions in selecting appropriate teaching methodologies. Such knowledge will also help you better understand the assumptions that lie behind various educational procedures and practices and determine how best to motivate students to learn.

INDIVIDUAL DIFFERENCES AMONG STUDENTS. Another component to consider in deciding *how* to teach is the individual differences of students (circle no. 5). (I pointed out earlier that this information is also important when deciding what is to be learned [circle no. 3]). Teachers need to make some modifications in response to their students' level of attention, memory and language development, and motivational differences (Short & Weissberg-Benchell, 1989). With experience, teachers sometimes discover that procedures effective at one grade level are less effective at another. Many differences abound, even among students of the same age or stage of development. Teachers are facing new challenges in the 1990s. For example, it is not uncommon to have students in class who were exposed prenatally to drugs and/or alcohol, or have HIV–related developmental difficulties, or are homeless, or face violence on a regular basis.

One of the major concerns today is the apparent inequality of educational experiences for students of different ethnic and cultural backgrounds. For example, the Census Bureau reported in 1992 that 33 percent of all Americans between 15 and 17 years of age are high school dropouts or at least one grade level behind. In addition, the achievement gap between white students and African Americans and Latinos begins in elementary school and widens as students get older. While the dropout or failure rate for whites is 32 percent, it is about 48 percent for African Americans and Latinos. Teaching students from different cultural back-

One of the important challenges in teaching is dealing with student differences in the classroom.

grounds is an important dimension of successful teaching. (The challenges of instruction in a culturally and linguistically diverse classroom are explored in depth in Chapter 9.)

TEACHER BEHAVIOR. The third component influencing how to teach is teacher behavior (circle no. 6). Like students, teachers also differ greatly in their teaching styles, personalities, personal concerns and adequacy, expectations, and so on. The literature of teaching effectiveness has confirmed the relationship between specific teacher variables and student achievement within several domains of teacher behavior—classroom management, instructional organization, and lesson presentations. However, teacher behaviors must be appropriately matched to student differences if they are to have their intended effects. Some teaching methods work successfully for some objectives or for some types of students but are less effective for other objectives and students (Englert, 1984).

Teachers hold differing expectations for students (Good & Brophy, 1991). They do not treat all students alike in the classroom. Some students are called on more frequently, asked more thought-provoking questions, or reinforced more often. If a teacher expects a student to achieve at a lower level than another student, this expectation affects the teacher's behavior toward both students.

Classroom management is another important component of teacher behavior. Lemlech (1988) views classroom management as the orchestration of classroom life: planning curriculum, organizing procedures and resources, arranging the environment for working efficiency, maintaining student progress, and anticipating potential problems. Research indicates that teachers who are good classroom managers also tend to produce more student learning (Good & Grouws, 1975; McDonald & Elias, 1976; Rosenshine & Berliner, 1978).

Evaluating and Reflecting

Although evaluation/reflection (circle no. 9) is a separate component, it is manifested during the planning of objectives and continues throughout the instructional process. As a teacher, you must know how to measure student behavior at various points before the start of instruction (to organize an appropriate instructional program for students), during each segment of instruction (to facilitate student progress), and at the end of instruction (to determine how well instructional objectives were met and to decide where to go from there).

You should pay particular attention to the evaluation of learning outcomes at the end of instruction. Did the students learn anything from the instructional lesson or unit? If you failed to develop any specific objectives at the beginning of the lesson, you may be hard pressed to answer the question. When the expected does not occur, you must reflect on your own behavior as well as that of your students: What went wrong? Were the objectives appropriate for the students? Was my teaching method appropriate for the objectives? Should I reteach all or part of the lesson? Should the class move on to another topic? With this self-questioning technique, a teacher can properly evaluate the students' learning and revise different components of the teaching-learning process.

DECISIONS, DECISIONS

Using the teaching-learning model, we can now summarize the major decisions according to the six components that make the teaching-learning process work. Keep in mind that each decision does not operate independently but interacts with the others in an on-going manner (Hunter, 1971):

Individual differences: What learning task can the student handle at the entry stage of learning? What learner behavior and characteristics are relevant to the task and to the learner's characteristics? What modifications does a particular learner require?

Instructional objective: What is the primary instructional objective of the lesson?

Learning and motivation principles: What principle(s) of learning and motivation can a teacher apply to the learning task?

Teacher behavior: How can the teacher's own beliefs and behavior be used to translate teaching decisions into effective action?

Method of instruction: What is the best instructional method to attain the instructional objective? How will the teacher synthesize the preceding decisions into the teaching-learning process?

Evaluation/reflection: How successful was the teaching-learning process? What happens now?

THE ROLE OF EDUCATIONAL PSYCHOLOGY

? How can the study of educational psychology help a teacher become a more effective instructor?

The discipline of educational psychology provides theory and research findings on each of the six components in the teaching-learning model to guide your teaching decisions. Throughout the text I will emphasize the linkages between and among these components. This is why I often refer to discussion in other chapters while I am dealing with a particular topic. For example, suppose a teacher believes that students must assume responsibility for their own learning. This belief should influence the teacher's approach to motivation and classroom management and discipline. However, sometimes teachers' practices are inconsistent with their beliefs. For example, the teacher who wants students to be responsible learners may develop a management system that fails to teach students how to take responsibility for their own behavior. In this situation, the teacher needs to reevaluate how his or her beliefs can be best implemented. This example is an important issue that I will discuss in more detail in Chapter 7 (Classroom Management and Discipline).

Another important point about learning educational psychology is that some people believe that the more psychological knowledge teachers possess, the more effective they will be in the classroom. Cohen (1973) discusses this belief as "to know good is to do good" (or the "mythstake"). Unfortunately, research studies have failed to demonstrate a relationship between measures of classroom teaching behaviors and the teacher's knowledge of psychological information (Aspy, 1972; Silverman & Kimmel, 1972). Perhaps one reason for this finding is that many teachers simply memorize psychological material without attempting to internalize and apply it in any meaningful way. Surely, we would be dissatisfied with an attorney who knew the law but had difficulty defending clients because of the ambiguities in the law.

Although you will read research conducted by educational psychologists concerning various aspects of teaching and learning, you also need to consider the role of *teacher as researcher.* A researcher identifies problem areas, raises questions, and determines what research procedures are best to answer the identified questions. In a similar manner, teachers need to reflect on their experiences and seek answers to their own questions through reading, observing, and talking to students. In this way, the teacher also acts as a researcher (Schubert & Ayres, 1992).

Teaching is not an exact science. Teachers apply personal knowledge to the complex world of the classroom and make decisions that lead to improved student performance. Teaching will then lead to learning.

To help you internalize the psychological information presented in this book, I have interspersed questions throughout the text and provided synthesizing learning activities at the end of each unit with suggestions for further reading. Take time to consider the questions and activities, and discuss them with your classmates. Avoid the tendency to be a passive learner by simply underlining sentences. Remember, in a short time you will have to apply educational psychology in the classroom. Why not begin now? Finally, please read the preface to this book if you skipped it earlier, especially the section on the special features of the text. This information is important in helping you to use the book successfully.

USING THE TEACHING-LEARNING MODEL TO ANALYZE INSTRUCTION

Let's look at two different teaching incidents to give you an opportunity to use the teaching-learning model in analyzing classroom instruction. As you read each incident, identify the components (i.e., instructional objectives, principles of learning and motivation, individual differences, teacher behavior, methods of instruction, and evaluation/reflection) that influence the amount of learning in the classroom. Identify the types of decisions made by teachers and the students' perceptions of events in their classrooms. I will comment on each incident at the end.

An Elementary School Classroom

Mr. Walker is a fourth-grade teacher whose class was observed during the first month of school. The lesson is part of a unit on the history of Los Angeles.

Teacher: *Math time is over. Quietly go back to your regular seats, and put away your math books.* (There is much noise in the classroom. Some children stop right away; others keep working in their books.)

Aaron: (Walking over to Carl's desk) *I saw a great movie last night.*

Teacher: (In a loud, threatening voice) *Aaron, what do you think this is, time to play with friends? Did I say go visit a neighbor and talk?*

Aaron: (No response.)

Teacher: *You're holding up the entire class.* (By now most of the class has settled down; some students are still quietly talking.)

Teacher: *Now, will everyone please take out the social studies book.*

Julie: *What social studies book?*

Teacher: *The books I passed out yesterday—the history of Los Angeles.*

Julie: *Oh, I didn't know that was social studies.*

Teacher: *Well, if you spent a little more time listening instead of talking to Susan, maybe you would learn something.*

Adam: *I can't find my book.*

Teacher: *Well, you'd better find it because I don't have any more, and these books need to be used next year. We waste so much time changing subjects. When we change, there should be no talking. You don't need to visit with a neighbor or sharpen your pencil. Now, open your books to page fifty and read the chapter to yourself.*

Phil: (To Steve after 10 minutes) *I've already finished. Where are you?*

Steve: (Whispering) *I'm almost finished.*

Teacher: *Phil, Steve, stop talking* (at this point they had already stopped). *Phil, you're a good student, but you need to learn to control your mouth.* (To the class) *Has everyone finished reading?* (Students respond yes and no.)

Teacher: *Okay, let's get started. Who can tell me a main point from the chapter?* (Many hands go up, and students begin whispering for attention.) *There is no need for sound effects.*

Lisa: (Calling out) *They were telling about prehistoric animals.*

Teacher: *Good. What kind of animals?*

Tom: (Calling out) *Dinosaurs.*

Teacher: *No, there weren't any dinosaurs in Los Angeles, at least we haven't found any dinosaur bones yet. What other animals did they have?*

Pam: *Elephants.*

Ralph: *Camels.*

Teacher: *Right. Did the camels look like the camels today?*

Class: *No-o-o!*

Teacher: *How many humps did they have?*

George: *Two.*

Teacher: *Wrong. Don't you pay attention to what you read? They had one. What other animals were there?* (Wesley drops his pencil box.)

Jimmy: *Hawks.*

Teacher: *Wesley! What do you think you're doing? What did I just say? What kind of prehistoric animals did we have in Los Angeles?*
Wesley: *Dinosaurs.*
Teacher: *You haven't listened to a thing I've said all morning.*
Bill: (Raises hand) *Mr. Walker? Mr. Walker?*
Teacher: *What is it?*
Bill: *I just wanted to tell you about hawks.*
Teacher: *Let me finish with Wesley, then we'll talk about it.* (Many students are fidgeting and appear to be daydreaming. No hands are raised. Mr. Walker glances at the clock and realizes it's time for lunch.) *It's lunch time. We'll have to finish tomorrow.*

What do you think it was like being a student in Mr. Walker's class? How do you think students were affected by his feedback to questions? Would you be motivated to become involved in the discussion?

Mr. Walker's general goal was to teach his students what life was like in Los Angeles many years ago. More specifically, he wanted the students to identify the kinds of prehistoric animals that lived in Los Angeles (*instructional objective*). However, he failed to tell his students the objective before they began reading the textbook. In addition, he didn't prepare them for the lesson by evoking their curiosity or interest in the topic, nor did he consider the *individual differences* in reading speed and comprehension. After the class observed how he responded to incorrect answers, the students did not appear eager to respond. When one of the students thought that dinosaurs had lived in Los Angeles, he could have used this response as an opportunity to explain about the discovery of bones and the kind of bones that were found. He also could have led a discussion concerning why there were no dinosaurs in Los Angeles (*methods of instruction*). Instead, he told the student he was wrong.

A major problem was Mr. Walker's classroom management (*teacher behavior*). Effective classroom managers develop concise procedures in the classroom that reduce the possibility of problems during transition from one subject to another. It is clear that Mr. Walker had not established any rules or procedures, and in fact, he mentioned to the class that they were unruly during transition periods. Yet, he did nothing to help them improve their behavior. Instead of using positive reinforcement to change his students' behavior, he used ridicule and criticism, which are not good *learning and motivational principles* to change behavior.

A Secondary School Classroom

Mr. Barratt's ninth-grade class has been studying the functions and decisions of the Supreme Court to help students identify and analyze factual and value problems using our legal-ethical framework.[1] *To accomplish this purpose, he selects a contemporary issue for class discussion. This morning he has rewritten a newspaper article for his students to read.*

[1]This incident was written by Johanna Lemlech of the University of Southern California

Teacher: *Okay, folks, let me give you an overview of what we're going to do this morning and, in fact, most of this week. First, we're going to read about the Fort Lauderdale senior citizen who was sentenced to prison for murder. Then, we will review our chart on American legal-ethical values, and later, we will begin our discussion and research.*

Mr. Barratt passes out the article, and the students begin to read silently. He moves around the room and helps several students with unfamiliar words. The news story is about a 76-year-old man, Roswell Gilbert, who has been sentenced to life imprisonment in Florida with no possibility of parole for 25 years. Mr. Gilbert had shot his wife, to whom he had been married for 51 years. His wife had Alzheimer's disease and osteoporosis (a bone disease) and was in a great deal of pain all the time. Gilbert knew that he was breaking the law, but he could no longer stand to see his wife in pain. His neighbors testified at the trial that his wife had begged him to kill her and end her suffering. Florida governor Bob Graham asked his cabinet for "an act of mercy" to free Gilbert while he appealed the decision. A member of the governor's cabinet responded to the governor, "I don't want to send a message that it's all right to take a person's life because that person is ill." At the time this incident was presented in class, Gilbert was in prison and his daughter feared that he would die there.

Teacher: *What are the issues here? What are the facts of this case?*
Susan: *The man killed his wife.*
Bill: *He knew he was breaking the law.*
Bennett: *The jury found him guilty of murder.*
Ann: *His wife was sick and wouldn't get better.*
Sam: *Hey, we don't know that a cure wouldn't be found.*
Ann: *Well, she was in a lot of pain. Maybe he couldn't stand that.*
Bob: *There aren't any cures for Alzheimer's disease; everybody knows that.*
Teacher: *We're straying from the facts now. Remember, our task right now is just to identify the facts of the case. We'll discuss the conflicts later. Are there some additional facts?*
Gilbert: *We know that his neighbors testified for him that his wife begged him to end her suffering.*
Ann: *The governor asked for an "act of mercy."*
Teacher: *Why don't we move ahead? Using our chart to help us remember our legal-ethical framework, begin to identify values and value conflicts.*
Jared: *Well, the law says murder is wrong, so the big issue is the rule of law.*
Teacher: *Good thinking, but what are some other basic values at stake?*
Maria: *Well, I think due process is an issue.*
Bill: *Why? I don't understand that.*
Todd: *Well, lots of times even supposed murderers are allowed out on bail. He wasn't some kind of kook or mass murderer; he should be allowed out on bail. He is being treated differently from others.*
Teacher: *Todd, do you know for a fact that other murderers are allowed out on bail to appeal their cases?*
Todd: *Well, no. But I do know that it is awfully unusual for someone who is not a menace to society to be imprisoned for twenty-five years without bail.*

Jan: *Mr. Barratt, isn't the issue whether or not there is evil intent? His motive wasn't evil.*

Teacher: *Interesting point. Are you saying that there is a difference between his motive and that of other murderers?*

Jan: *Yes, I guess so. He believed that he was acting in a moral way.*

Teacher: *It's all right to kill someone, then, if you claim to be moral?*

Jan: *Well, I don't know.*

Teacher: *Does anyone else want to respond to that point?*

Jared: *I do. I heard my parents talking about this case. Isn't he saying that there is a higher authority than Man for certain acts, that some laws have to be broken if you are a moral person?*

Teacher: *Do you think that our legal system should be responsive to moral values?*

Sharon: *Well, it isn't fair that he should go to jail for mercy killing.*

Sam: *Do you mean anyone can decide when someone else should die?*

Teacher: *It sounds like we are ready to take a position and discuss the consequences. Who can identify the value conflict in this issue?* (Mr. Barratt continues by helping the students to focus on the value conflicts pertaining to the issue and asks them to prepare for a debate on the issue in two days.*)*

What differences in student perceptions do you think existed in Mr. Walker's and Mr. Barratt's classes? How do you think students' thinking processes were affected in each class? How could the teachers' behavior influence students' perceptions of their ability? How did the two instructors differ in their beliefs about learning and motivation?

Mr. Barratt clearly was involved in some long–term planning in his class. He stated that the students would read, review prior material, discuss, and research the topic. The primary *objective* was to identify value conflicts. He rewrote the newspaper article for his students to read and moved around the class to monitor the reading activity (*individual differences*). As the instruction began, he guided the discussion through planned questions (*teacher behavior and instructional methodology*). He told the students that the initial discussion should focus on "facts." By remaining silent, he encouraged multiple responses. When the students began to stray from the immediate objective of identifying facts, he reminded them and asked if there were some additional facts. He then used Sam's statement as a cue that the next phase of the lesson should begin. He brought out the chart of American legal-ethical values and value conflicts. At no time did Mr. Barratt respond with a personal opinion. He continued to probe and guide the inquiry—for example, "It's all right to kill someone, then, if you claim to be moral?"

Mr. Barratt planned distinct phases of his lesson. The students first read the prepared material and were encouraged to identify the facts and, then, the value conflicts. Later, he asked students to *evaluate* and synthesize their discussion into two conflicting positions and to do group research to prepare for a class debate (these phases were not reported in the brief transcript you read).

You have read brief descriptions of two teachers with different instructional skills. Although the secondary school teacher appeared to be more successful in attaining his goal, I could have easily presented a situation in which an elementary school teacher used a similar teaching strategy with great success. I mention this because I don't want you to think that teaching effectiveness is related to any particular level of instruction. I will present examples of effective and ineffective teaching at all levels in school.

A Final Comment on the Model

? What are the different perspectives on how teachers can best be educated?

Before we leave this introduction, it is important that I clarify my position on a crucial issue in teacher education. The education literature is filled with debates regarding the best way to educate teachers. Some experts believe that any attempts to quantify and sequence teaching as a predictable step-by-step process are doomed to failure (see Costa, 1984; Eisner, 1983). The critics of this approach believe that focusing on the holistic, or total, aspect of teaching is a more effective method of educating teachers. For example, Eisner (1983) states, "Teachers are more like orchestra conductors than technicians. They need rules of thumb and educational imagination, not scientific prescriptions" (p. 5). My position is that beginning teachers need help in identifying the major variables relating to the teaching-learning process. In this way, they will have a better understanding and awareness of that process. As teachers develop greater awareness of the variables influencing learning, there can be more emphasis on the "big picture." Although variables initially are discussed here in a linear fashion to help you better understand the teaching-learning process, you need to recognize that in the real world of teaching, everything happens at once!

Another related issue in teacher education is whether teaching is more an art than a science. At one extreme of this continuum are those who believe that "good teachers are born, not made." This position relies on intuition as a basis of action. At the opposite end of the continuum are those who believe that good teaching is based on a science of instruction whereby teachers learn effective teaching behaviors. I find it difficult to subscribe totally to either perspective. There may be certain natural traits or abilities in people that make them good teachers. Yet I am convinced that there are important teaching skills that can be learned to enhance teaching effectiveness. I also believe that a sound empirical data base will improve the artful teacher's performance. Thus, I believe that good teaching involves both art and science.

Finally, some teacher educators have used this particular teaching-learning model (Figure 1.1) in a rigid manner, believing that only one type or method of teaching should be used in all situations. I believe that the use of the model doesn't prevent the teacher from using a variety of methods and approaches in the classroom.

THE COMPLEXITY OF CLASSROOM LIFE

Good and Brophy (1991) have pointed out the complexity of classroom life and have explained why teachers are unaware of or misinterpret classroom behavior. They attribute lack of awareness to three factors:

- So much happens so rapidly that it is difficult to be aware of all events.
- There is no formal system to provide teachers with information on how to behave in the classroom.
- Some teachers do not acquire the observational skills for analyzing and labeling classroom behavior in their teacher education programs.

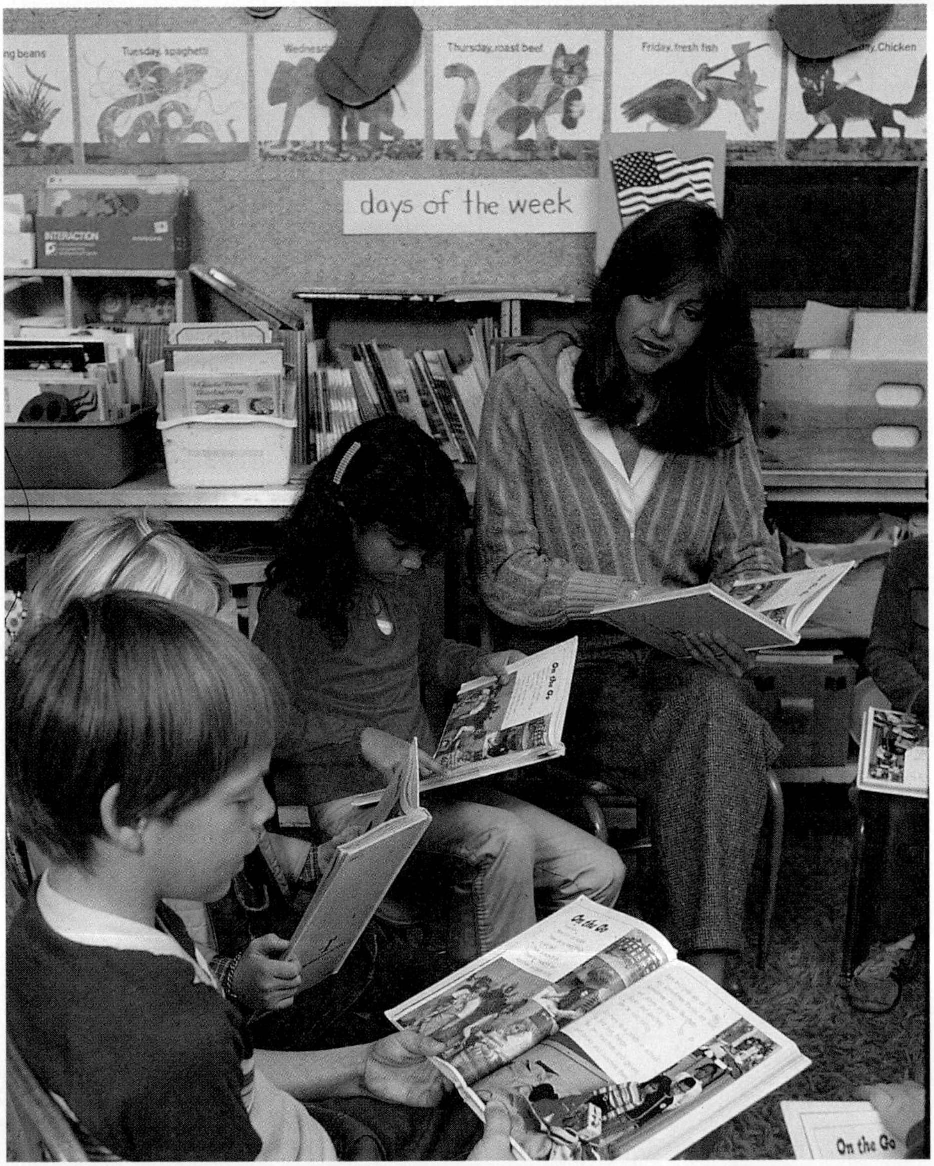

Teachers collect important information about students by observing their behavior throughout the school day.

CLASSROOM Application

OBSERVING IN THE CLASSROOM

Teachers need to learn as much as possible about individual students in the classroom. Observation of student behavior is an important method of collecting information. Keen observation of all important classroom events is not an easy task since, in one single day, a teacher may engage in more than a thousand interpersonal exchanges with students (Jackson, 1968). To make matters even more difficult, teachers also have to *interpret* complex behavior as it happens. A teacher cannot become a skilled observer in one day or one week. A teacher must learn the skills of observation and practice them over a long time.

Almy (1969) identifies three aspects of observation: *descriptions, feelings,* and *inferences*. First, descriptions refer to how we look and to what we say or do. Second, our own feelings and emotions about what we observe influence what we see and hear. Finally, we infer what the behavior means from what we see and hear and from what we feel and know from past experiences. Almy points out that when teachers study students to get to know them better, they need to discriminate between actual behavior of the students and their own feelings and emotions, which influence the interpretations of that behavior. This distinction helps the teacher to see behavior more clearly and to reach conclusions about a student that are more likely to be based on factual evidence.

If a student has a history of problems in the classroom and becomes involved in an altercation with another student, the teacher may infer from observation that the "problem" student was responsible for the disagreement. Another observer who knows nothing about the students involved may interpret the situation differently. If two students of different abilities complain about a homework assignment, a teacher's reaction to the lower achiever may be more negative than the reaction to the same comments made by the higher–achieving student.

Think about how your past experience with a friend, family member, or classmate has influenced how you interpreted something that person has recently said.

In summary, accurate observation is crucial to making appropriate classroom decisions. Yet it is very easy for an observer to misinterpret classroom behavior. The observer's past experiences, biases, and prejudices can lead to incorrect interpretations. Consequently, a classroom observer has to examine and become aware of any personal perceptual blinders. You need to learn to observe behavior as accurately as possible before interpreting what you *think* you see. If you don't observe or listen objectively, you may end up finding exactly what you expected to find, making an invalid inference, and allowing that to lead to inappropriate decision making.

Many different types of observation can be made in the classroom. One of the most useful types of observation is the *anecdote*—a narrative account of a situation as seen by an observer. The following are some guidelines to keep in mind while observing students (Good & Brophy, 1991):

- *Decide what you want to observe.* Focus on one area at a time—social interaction, behavior during seatwork, progress in reading, and so on. Knowing your purpose allows you to observe students in appropriate situations and obtain adequate samples of their behavior.
- *Consider the factors that could influence behavior.* Choose an appropriate time of day. Think about what subjects students like and dislike, the size of the instructional group, and other factors that might influence student behavior.
- *Observe both inside and outside of the classroom.* John Holt (1982), in *How Children Fail*, reminds teachers: "If we look at children only to see whether they are doing what we want or don't want them to do, we are likely to miss all the things about them that are the most interesting and important" (p. 36).
- *Keep a running log.* Make sure your observations are dated and distinct from one another. Divide your page into two columns and note observations on the left-hand side, and inferences or interpretations on the right. Remember that interpretations often change as more information is collected.
- *Note specific behaviors—body language, facial expressions, and posture, as well as overt actions.*
- *Avoid interpretations that are not supported by fact.*
- *Identify patterns, and look for places where expected patterns did not occur.*

PROBLEMS ENCOUNTERED BY BEGINNING TEACHERS

? What problems do beginning teachers commonly confront?

All teachers are faced with problems. Bluming and Dembo (1973) state that teachers rarely leave their profession as a result of inadequate training in their discipline. However, many do leave because they are discouraged by aggravations that interfere with normal teaching situations and find themselves unable to make effective decisions about the problems that arise in their classrooms.

What are the concerns of a beginning teacher? Veenman's (1984) review of literature on the topic indicates eight problems—classroom discipline, motivating students, dealing with individual differences, assessing students' work, relationship with parents, organization of classwork, insufficient and/or inadequate teaching materials and supplies, and dealing with problems of individual students. He finds that the problems of elementary and secondary teachers are similar. This textbook will deal with all the problems Veenman found except those regarding teaching materials and supplies.

Ryan (1970) describes the first year of teaching in a book with an interesting title, *Don't Smile until Christmas.* He points out that the novice teacher faces many situations and events without adequate preparation.

> They find high school students are hard to reach; they underestimate the difficulty of motivating them and overestimate their own skills as disciplinarians. They do not anticipate the amount of time and work necessary to keep up with students. The volume of administrative tasks surprises them. They are unprepared to handle classes *and* take roll, write tardy slips, read notices from the office, and execute the dozens of ever-present administrative details. The emotional and physical drain of teaching five periods a day leaves them little energy for anything else. . . . Of course, the first year of teaching is not always unpleasant. Some beginners are tremendously relieved to discover that their fantasies of failure do not come true. They are surprised to find out that they can teach, that they like what they are doing, and that students do respect them. For some, anticipated sources of trouble turn out to be their strengths; they *do* have a good command of their subject matter; they *can* be fair to all the students and avoid playing favorites. . . . But whether the first year of teaching is a sad one or a joyous one, it is a year of intense learning for all. (pp. 172–173)

Fuller and Bown (1975) divide teacher concerns into three phases: survival concerns, situation concerns, and pupil concerns. The first, or entry, phase of teaching—the "survival phase"—is marked by anxiety and trepidation because the teacher is concerned with personal adequacy: Do my students like me? What do other teachers think of me? Does my principal think I am doing a good job? Preservice teachers have more concerns of this type than inservice teachers do. These survival concerns may cause some beginning teachers to concentrate much of their time on developing positive interpersonal relations with students, befriending rather than teaching them; while other teachers may be more concerned with maintaining student control rather than making academic progress (Rosenholtz, 1989). Hoy (1967; Hoy & Woolfolk, 1990) has shown that some beginning teachers actually become more impersonal and authoritarian during their initial orientation to the real world of teaching. He believes that this change is due to the socialization processes in schools where teachers are expected to manage well-behaved and controlled students. As a result, beginning teachers want to become good classroom managers and tend to become less humanistic in accomplishing this goal.

I was reminded of the strong effects of teacher socialization when I visited the classroom of a teacher who had been in my educational psychology course a few years earlier. The student was one of the more "nontraditional" students I had in the class. He often spoke of the radical changes that needed to occur in the classroom and mentioned that he would take steps to ensure that his classroom would be different. He would teach students effective learning strategies, would de-emphasize rote learning, and would involve parents in the learning process—all excellent teaching practices! However, when I observed his classroom, it appeared that he either had modified his beliefs or had found it difficult to practice what he believed, because his classroom was one of the more traditional ones in the school! Could the desire to succeed during the "survival phase" of teaching alter his teaching beliefs and practices?

When teachers feel that they are surviving the demands of teaching, they become more concerned with student achievement and enter phase two, the phase of teacher situation concerns. These concerns pertain to the frustration and limitations regarding teaching various subject areas. Concerns about class size, time pressures, and lack of instructional materials are examples of frustrations evoked by various teaching situations. Inservice teachers have more concerns of this type than preservice teachers do.

Until the first two phases have been dealt with adequately, teachers don't appear to aspire to the third, which Fuller and Bown (1975) identify as the phase of concern about pupils (e.g., recognizing the social and emotional needs of children at different developmental levels, identifying individual differences in the classroom, and realizing the inappropriateness of some material for certain students). Based on Fuller and Bown's findings, it is not surprising that some teachers are not able to deal with individual student needs. In fact, Cruickshank and Callahan (1983) believe that some teachers never get to phase three because they leave the profession psychologically defeated, or they struggle for years in phase two, "preoccupied with themselves and with what they teach" (p. 254). The important implication of Fuller and Bown's work is that beginning teachers need to be concerned about their own personal development and how their own needs may influence both awareness and interaction in the classroom.

The following excerpt from "Diary of a Beginning Teacher" (Morris, 1968) records the personal concerns of a teacher in the early teaching phase. As you read the diary, make a list of the various topics mentioned and discuss them with students in your class. What problems might give you the most trouble?

September 7. I'm exhausted today. I gave them all back their papers which, thank goodness, took up part of the class time. I also assigned them four questions to do for homework. I didn't write the questions on the board, which was a mistake; I ended up repeating everything five or six times.

I feel so pushed, preparing and correcting papers; hope things calm down soon.

September 9. I tried playing a game with them in class today. It didn't go very well. One of the biggest problems was that I didn't have a firm enough control over the class to do it. I had them asking each other questions. They were divided into two teams and all that. I even set up a panel of judges who decided whether the answer to a question was right.

I also gave them a pop quiz at the beginning of the period. I tried it in one class at the end, but that didn't work as well; they were too excited from the game to settle down.

One real catastrophe today. The map fell on my head during fourth period. The class went wild; luckily the assistant principal was right outside the room and came in and rescued me.

September 13. I gave the quiz today and they did pretty well and then I finished up discussing geography—I hope. I only gave them twenty of the spelling words and left off the longest and most difficult. They were very upset because they said they had all learned that one. The day has finally come. Despite all of the work and how tired I am, I think I am really going to like teaching.

September 26. I'm having a problem getting the classes to keep quiet now. For a while they were pretty good, but now they're beginning to get to me. Even the good students are starting to talk during class. I don't think it's because they're not interested because the talk is almost always about what I'm discussing, but still they're talking without permission. If it was only a little I wouldn't mind, but it's beginning to get to the point where I can't go on because of the talking.

September 27. The assistant principal came and visited one of my classes today. Before class I was talking at my desk with one student and all of a sudden I heard this deathly silence hit the class. (I guess that's not the right way to say it, but anyway) I looked up and there he was. I started the class. I'd ask a question and there was absolute silence. Nothing. It was terrible! It's bad when they're all talking at once, but it's horrible when they're afraid to move.

September 29. I've been getting bored, teaching the same thing over and over and so today I did different things in different classes. I discussed with some, gave some a quiz and had others writing. I tried discussing with my sixth-period class, but they're just impossible after about ten minutes. I got really mad at them and told them to take out their books and study quietly for ten minutes and then I would give them a quiz. While they studied, I made up the quiz and it was a dilly—

only four people passed. I suppose it isn't good educational psychology to do that, but it made me feel much better, and at that point it was either them or me.

October 14. I have now firmly and purposely gotten my classes separated. That is, I am no longer doing the same thing five times a day. At first it was a big help being able to prepare only one lesson each night. But I realized that it was terribly boring for me, and my boredom would be reflected in the kids. Once I felt that I had my bearings, I decided to change all that. Well, it's taken me this long to carry out my plan. Although I use much of the same material in all of my classes, I do not use it all at the same time or in the same manner. I can really see the difference in the classes.

October 19. Tonight was the PTA open house. I was pleased at how well it went. I guess that parents are not really ogres after all. But it was an awfully long day. I really do love teaching and I look forward to all of my classes, but I often feel that I am not doing my best for these kids. Teach and learn—and have I learned a lot in these seven weeks.

November 4. Teacher's Convention—WHAT A FARCE!

November 9. Every day I learn so much. I hope that the children are learning some too, but they couldn't possibly learn more than a fraction of what I have. I think there is hope for me yet. I already know so much more than I did in September. Sometimes I feel the huge mountain of things yet to learn pressing down on me, but I think I've made a significant dent in the mountain. I may live through the year. But then again, it seems overwhelming.

December 8. Ugliness! Nothing went well at all. Jabber, jabber, jabber—I don't know. Sometimes I get so upset and depressed it's horrible. They don't listen or follow instructions, or learn anything. I guess it's a normal feeling for new teachers.

December 12. Almost the end of the period before vacation. I guess not really but it seems like it must be. Happiness!! They announced that all evaluation meetings are cancelled until after Christmas. Hurray! Except for the faculty meeting Thursday.

The diary provides some good examples of typical problems faced by a beginning teacher. Ryan (1970) describes the first year of teaching as an emotional roller coaster. Did you detect the swings in the teacher's emotions as she progressed throughout the semester? Your first impressions of this teacher might lead you to the conclusion that all is lost! However, if you return to the teaching-learning model you will see that her problems can be identified. There are three obvious areas that are causing problems: *teacher behavior* (particularly management problems—failing to write questions on the board, classroom control, questioning, and maintaining attention); *evaluation/reflection* (constructing a poor test and using evaluation as a discipline technique); and *methods of instruction* (lack of variability in lessons). After identifying these problems, she could take steps to acquire information and skills to alleviate them. Think about the type of advice you would give her as you read about the variables composing the teaching-learning process.

Summary

THE STUDENT AND THE TEACHER AS DECISION MAKERS

1. All teachers have personal hypotheses or beliefs about the teaching-learning process even if they are not consciously aware of them.
2. Teachers' beliefs lead them to make important classroom decisions that affect how students learn in school.
3. Students' beliefs and self-perceptions influence their motivation and achievement behavior.
4. Teachers need to (a) examine the effects of their decisions on learning, (b) examine their personal beliefs about the teaching-learning process, (c) evaluate the effectiveness of beliefs and practices, and (d) modify teaching behavior when necessary.

THE ROLE OF EDUCATIONAL PSYCHOLOGY AND USING THE TEACHING-LEARNING MODEL

5. Educational psychology includes content that the teacher can use to formulate and test personal beliefs about teaching and learning.
6. An instructional model that identifies the major components in the teaching-learning process includes instructional objectives, individual differences, teacher behavior, theories and principles of learning and motivation, teaching methods, and evaluation of student behavior.
7. Teachers need to learn to analyze their problems so they can put their knowledge of educational psychology to use. Thus, teachers must both *understand* and *apply* psychological knowledge.
8. Beginning teachers appear to be most concerned with their personal adequacy in meeting the demand of teaching. Other concerns involve classroom discipline, motivating students, dealing with individual differences, assessing student work, handling relationships with parents, and organizing the classroom. Understanding educational psychology can help in all these areas.

Reflecting on the Teacher as Decision Maker

1. Analyze Common Myths about Teaching

Combs (1979) believes that myths are the greatest source of failure in the schools. Since people behave in terms of their beliefs, behavior based on false or inaccurate information often results in false or inaccurate outcomes.

Read each of the following statements and determine whether you agree, disagree, or are not sure about the accuracy of each statement. After identifying your beliefs, discuss how they might lead to certain teaching or classroom practices.

	Tend to Agree	Tend to Disagree	Not Sure
1. A person needs to feel some pressure to be motivated to learn.	________	________	________
2. Children have a natural desire to learn.	________	________	________
3. Younger children need more structure than older children.	________	________	________
4. Competition is a great motivator.	________	________	________
5. Human intelligence is fixed by the time a child begins school.	________	________	________
6. Failure is helpful in motivating students.	________	________	________

2. Think about Teaching Problems

Discuss some teaching problems that your previous teachers have had. Did they realize that a problem existed? What strategies did they use to attempt to solve the problem? What types of teaching problems do you think will give you the most trouble? Why do you feel this way?

3. Use Library Reference Sources to Identify Information about Teaching and Learning

Use *Psychological Abstracts, Resources in Education*, or *Current Index to Journals in Education* to locate articles on a topic or issue of interest (see Appendix: Using Library Reference Sources and Reading Journal Articles). If an article includes ideas about methods and techniques in teaching, summarize it and mention how you might use the ideas discussed in the article. Don't hesitate to criticize the author if you disagree with the ideas presented in the article. If the paper reports a research investigation, write an abstract of the article following the outline below:

- Author(s)
- Title of article
- Journal in which article appears (include date, volume number, and pages)
- Purpose of the study (found in the first few paragraphs)
- Subjects
- Procedures (or methods)
- Results
- Conclusions

4. Analyze the Teaching-Learning Process

Make arrangements to observe a teacher presenting a lesson. Keep detailed notes on both the teacher's and the students' behavior during the lesson, and analyze the lesson by answering the following questions (Hunter, 1973):

a. Was there a perceivable objective? Did the teaching focus on a particular learning target, or did it include a little bit of everything or anything?
b. Was the objective appropriate for this group of learners? Had the objective already been achieved by the learners, or was it so difficult that there was little possibility of achieving it?
c. Was the objective achieved? Was there evidence of progression toward advancement or attainment of the objective?
d. What did the teacher do that facilitated learning?
e. What did the teacher do that interfered with learning?
f. What problems arose during the lesson? How did the teacher handle these problems?
g. What suggestions do you have for improving the lesson?

Key Terms

teaching, p. 4
learning, p. 4
behavioral learning theories, p. 4
cognitive learning theories, p. 4
instructional objectives, p. 8
entry behavior, p. 8
declarative knowledge, p. 9
procedural knowledge, p. 9
experimental research, p. 32
control group, p. 32
experimental group, p. 32
hypothesis, p. 32
independent variable, p. 33
dependent variable, p. 33
significant difference, p. 33
correlation, p. 33

Suggestions for Further Reading

Boyer, E. L. (1983). *High school: A report on secondary education in America.* New York: Harper & Row. This book discusses the results of a major study of the American high school.

Bullough, R. V. (1989). *First-year teacher.* New York: Teachers College Press. An in-depth case study of the first year-and-a-half of a seventh–grade teacher's experience. Three appendixes include advice on selecting a school and surviving the year.

Emmers, A. P. (1981). *After the lesson plan: Realities of high school teaching.* New York: Teachers College Press. The author provides helpful insights into secondary teaching.

Goodlad, J. (1984). *A place called school: Prospects for the future.* New York: McGraw-Hill. An excellent description of classroom instruction. It provides proposals for improving the effectiveness of schools.

Greenwood, G. E., & Parkay, F. W. (1989). *Case studies for teacher decision making.* New York: Random House. The book provides typical teaching situations for students to develop their decision-making skills.

Holt, J. (1982). *How children fail* (rev. ed.). New York: Delta. An insightful analysis of student learning and failure in the classroom.

Kowalski, T., Weaver, R. A., & Henson, K. T. (1989). *Case studies on teaching*. White Plains, NY: Longman. This book presents cases on first-year teachers that provide insight into the major problems facing them.

Schubert, W. H., & Ayers, W. C. (1992). *Teacher lore: Learning from our own experience*. White Plains, NY: Longman. Experienced teachers provide their insights about teaching.

The following references are good sources for developing observational skills in the classroom:

Almy, M., & Genishi, C. (1979). *Ways of studying children: An observation manual for early childhood teachers*. New York: Teachers College Press.

Boehm, A., & Weinberg, R. A. (1987). *The classroom observer: Developing skills in early childhood education*. New York: Teachers College Press.

Borich, G. D. (1990). *Observation skills for effective teaching*. Columbus, OH: Merrill.

Cartwright, C. A., & Cartwright, G. P. (1984). *Developing observation skills* (2nd ed.). New York: McGraw-Hill.

Cohen, D. H., Stern, V., & Balaban, N. (1983). *Observing and recording the behavior of young children* (3rd ed.). New York: Teachers College Press.

Good, T. L., & Brophy, J. E. (1991). *Looking in classrooms* (5th ed.). New York: Harper & Row.

Appendix: Using Library Reference Sources and Reading Journal Articles

It is important for you to get acquainted with the library facilities at your college or university. Reading books and journal articles will help you keep up with developments in your field long after you attain your degree. The following reference sources can be useful in locating research and applied articles in your field of specialization: *Psychological Abstracts, Resources in Education,* and *Current Index to Journals in Education.*

Most colleges have resources to complete a computer search of literature. It still is useful to begin looking at reference journals to get a better idea of the topic and related descriptors for your search. *Descriptors* are short descriptions or names that could be used to search a topic. Once you are sure what topic you want to search, ask your librarian for information and assistance for completing a computer search of the literature.

PSYCHOLOGICAL ABSTRACTS

Psychological Abstracts is published monthly by the American Psychological Association and contains abstracts of articles appearing in more than 500 journals in psychology and related areas. Each issue has sections covering various topics of psychology. The section on child development and adolescence and the section on educational psychology, which include abstracts in areas such as attitude and adjustment, testing, special education, counseling and guidance, school learning and achievement, and curriculum programs, are most relevant for the teacher.

Every December issue contains both an author index and a subject index of all articles in the previous 11 issues of the year. A semiannual index is also available. When using cumulative indexes, check the subject index for articles pertaining to the topic. The subject of the article appears in a concise form. After the description of the subject, you will find one or more numbers referring to the abstract included during the preceding year. The information will help you find the abstract in the appropriate monthly issue.

RESOURCES IN EDUCATION

Another important reference source has been established by the Office of Education, the Educational Resources Information Center (ERIC), which collects, stores, and disseminates information on education. ERIC abstracts include papers presented at educational conferences, reports of research in progress, final reports of federally funded studies, and abstracts of some documents listed in *Psychological Abstracts.* The advantage of the ERIC system is that it includes many documents not usually published in journals and provides the best compilation of current educational research.

All the abstracts in ERIC appear in a monthly publication called *Resources in Education.* Each abstract is classified by subject area, author, and institutional and accession (identification) number. To locate an abstract, first select key research terms in your area of interest. If you are interested in teaching procedures, you might look under teaching methods, educational strategies, or teaching techniques.

To help identify appropriate search terms, ERIC has published the *Thesaurus of ERIC Descriptors.* This publication includes all terms used to classify ERIC documents. Once the key search terms have been identified, you should then examine the semiannual or annual cumulative indexes for the titles or pertinent references and locate the abstract in a monthly issue of *Resources in Education.*

Most educational libraries have the ERIC collection on microfiche (small sheets of microfilm that require special readers to enlarge the image to normal page size). Therefore, once you identify the accession number of the document from *Resources in Education* (e.g., ED 013 371), you can locate the corresponding numbered microfiche of the complete article. If you wish to obtain a copy of the document, you can order it through the ERIC Document Reproduction Services.

CURRENT INDEX TO JOURNALS IN EDUCATION

Another important resource is the monthly journal *Current Index to Journals in Education* (CIJE), compiled by specialists of the ERIC system. Articles from more than 500 journals are classified and listed according to the same system developed in the ERIC *Thesaurus.*

The CIJE is divided into four sections: subject index, author index, journal contents index, and main entry section. The procedures for selecting an entry are similar to those for *Resources in Education.* Locate articles in the main entry section by checking the subject index to find the titles and numbers of the articles. If the title of an article is not sufficient to convey the main meaning of the article, the CIJE staff provides a brief annotation under the title.

JOURNALS IN PSYCHOLOGY AND EDUCATION

As you locate educational journals, you will see that they fall into various categories. Some journals include only research articles; other journals include papers on general issues in education and some research articles. Specialized journals are available in specific teaching areas and focus on teaching techniques and research reports. *Psychological Abstracts* focuses on journals reporting research investigations, and the *Current Index to Journals in Education* includes research and applied journals. Some journals have articles listed in both reference sources. *Resources in Education* includes papers presented at conferences and special reports that are not listed in the other two reference sources.

The following are examples of types of journals. Refer to the listing of journals included in the CIJE for a *complete* list of available journals in education and psychology.

Research Journals

American Educational Research Journal
Child Development
Developmental Psychology
Journal of Applied Behavioral Analysis
Journal of Educational Psychology
Journal of Educational Research
Journal of Experimental Education
Psychology in the Schools

General Journals

Educational Leadership
Elementary School Journal
Journal of General Education
Phi Delta Kappan
Teachers College Record
Theory into Practice

Specialized Journals

American Biology Teacher
American Business Educator
American Music Teacher
Arithmetic Teacher
Art Education

experimental research. An investigation that explores cause-and-effect relationships.

control group. A group in an experimental study that receives no special treatment.

experimental group. A group receiving special treatment in an experimental study.

hypothesis. A statement about the relationship among variables.

Coach and Athlete
Educational Theatre Journal
Elementary English
German Review
Journal of Reading
Journal of Secondary Education
Mathematics Teacher
Physical Education
School Science and Mathematics
Social Education

READING RESEARCH ARTICLES

There are many types of research studies conducted in educational psychology. A detailed discussion of research methodology is beyond the scope of this textbook. However, two major methodologies are classified as *qualitative* and *quantitative*. Qualitative research method is used to describe a number of research strategies that have roots in anthropology and sociology. The terms *case study*, *field study*, and *ethnography* are used to describe different qualitative methods.

Qualitative research methods have several distinct characteristics (Hittleman & Simon, 1992). First, they involve such methodologies as observing, questioning, and reading diaries of individuals in their natural setting. Second, the data collected are generally verbal, not numerical. Third, qualitative researchers tend to focus on the process of an activity rather than only its outcomes. Understanding how a classroom climate or environment develops from the first day of school is an example of studying process. A researcher more interested in the outcome or product of classroom climate might want to study how learning differs in classrooms with different climates. Finally, qualitative researchers analyze the data verbally rather than use statistics as a basis for their conclusions. I discuss a number of research findings in Chapter 9 (Cognition, Culture, and Language) using qualitative methodology. One such study involved observations of how American Indian children learn differently at home and at school (Philips, 1983).

Quantitative research is the more traditional methodology used in educational psychology. The basis of quantitative research involves assigning numerical values to variables so they can be analyzed statistically. Some researchers explore the statistical relationship between variables, while others are more interested in the cause-and-effect relationship between variables. Of course, it is possible for researchers to use both quantitative and qualitative methodologies in the same investigation.

The following is some terminology you will need to become familiar with in reading quantitative research. In **experimental research** (studies that explore cause-and-effect relationships), the researcher uses **control groups** and **experimental groups** to test hypotheses. A **hypothesis** is a statement about the relationship among variables in a study. An example of such a statement is, "If students participate in cooperative learning, they will develop more positive attitudes about mathematics." In some investigations, researchers will identify questions that they want to answer rather than use a hypothesis. For example, does cooperative learning improve attitudes toward mathematics? The experimental group(s) use the particular method or technique that the researcher wants to investigate (cooperative learning), and the control group(s) use the normal, or typical, learning method for learning mathematics (e.g., the lecture-discussion method).

Two other terms usually found in research articles are **independent variables** and **dependent variables**. The independent variable is the variable that the experimenter is manipulating. In the foregoing example, it is a method of instruction—cooperative learning. The dependent variable is the variable that the researcher uses to measure the effect of the independent variable. The dependent variable in the study on cooperative learning could be an instrument measuring attitude toward mathematics that is given to the subjects in the study before and after the investigation.

independent variable. A variable that is manipulated or modified in an experimental study.

dependent variable. A variable in an experimental study that may change as a result of the manipulation of the independent variable.

significant difference. A difference based on a level of probability established before an investigation begins.

correlation. A measure of the degree of relationship between two variables.

To test whether or not a hypothesis has been confirmed, researchers use various statistics based on the laws of probability. For example, suppose that at the beginning of the study the control and experimental groups have the same average score on their attitude toward mathematics—let's say, 85.4. However, at the end of the study the control subjects score 90.4 and the experimental subjects 95.7. Is this difference large enough to confirm the hypothesis? The only way to determine this is by a statistical test. Thus, when you read about a researcher identifying a **significant difference**, the term refers to a statistical probability determined before the study. Common levels of significance established in research studies are $p < .01$ or $p < .05$. These probability levels can be interpreted as follows: A probability of less than .05 means that for a finding to be significant, it can happen by chance only 5 times out of 100. Stating this finding in another way, if the investigation were conducted 100 times, the size of the difference in attitude scores between the control and experimental groups would likely occur 95 times out of 100. If the statistical test indicates that the probability is greater than .05, the researcher would then state that there was no significant difference between the groups. As a result, the hypothesis could not be confirmed.

Even if you do not understand the statistical tests used in a research article, you will be able to determine whether significant results were attained by reading the text or tables in which significant differences are identified by the probability levels for each statistical test.

Some studies use correlational methods to investigate educational issues. A **correlation** between two variables is a statistical indication of their relationship. It is determined by a mathematical formula. Because correlations are used extensively in educational research, it is important that you be able to interpret the meaning of a correlation.

If two variables increase proportionately (e.g., children's age and weight), their correlation is positive. A negative correlation signifies that as one variable increases, the other decreases (e.g., a car's increase in age and decrease in price).

The symbol used to denote a correlation is r, which ranges from -1 to $+1$. The closer r is to -1 or $+1$, the higher the correlation. The closer r is to zero, the smaller the correlation. We almost never obtain a perfect negative or positive correlation (-1 or $+1$), but we do find that variables correlate to some degree.

For example, we might refer to $r = .50$ as a moderately positive correlation, to $r = .95$ as a high positive correlation, and to $r = -.91$ as a high negative correlation. Correlations near zero denote no or minimal relationships between the variables. If no sign (+ or –) is present in front of the correlation, it is assumed to be positive.

Finally, correlations do not imply causality. That is, two variables may correlate (e.g., smoking and lung cancer), but one variable is not necessarily the cause of the other. There is a high positive correlation between the number of liquor stores and churches in urban areas. I would hope that one is not the cause of the other!

When you take courses in research design and statistics, you will learn more about the different ways to conduct research education. In the meantime, this brief introduction will get you started reading research articles. For more information, locate books on introduction to research, such as *Educational Research: An Introduction* (Borg & Gall, 1993) and *Interpreting Educational Research: An Introduction for Consumers of Research* (Hittleman & Simon, 1992). For information specifically on qualitative methodology read *Becoming Qualitative Researchers* (Glesne & Peshkin, 1992) and *Doing the Ethnography of Schooling* (Spindler, 1982).

Although the format of quantitative research articles varies depending on the particular journal, some common components can be identified:

- *Abstract.* This section is found on the first page of the article and briefly reviews the purpose, procedures, results, and conclusions in fewer than 150 words. By reading the abstract, you can quickly determine whether you are interested in the article. Some research journals do not include an abstract.
- *Introduction* (often not labeled). The first few paragraphs of a research article review previous literature on the topic to provide a rationale for why the investigation was undertaken. The last paragraph in this section usually includes the questions or hypotheses to be investigated.
- *Method.* This section describes how the study was conducted and includes a number of subsections—for example, the subjects, procedures, and instrumentation used in the investigation.
- *Results.* This section summarizes the data collected, describes the statistical tests used to test the hypotheses, and reports whether or not the hypotheses were confirmed or rejected. The format of this section is likely to be different in qualitative research reports where researchers tend to provide examples of verbatim comments from the individuals they interviewed.
- *Discussion.* This section examines and interprets the results of the investigation. The author usually discusses the conclusions reached and the implications for future research. Some research articles combine the results and discussion sections.

Part two

Learning and Motivation: Instructional Applications

The primary responsibility of teachers is to help students learn. Teachers' selection of educational goals, instructional procedures, and classroom organization and behavior are based in part on their conceptualization of the teaching-learning process. In this section you will learn how teachers' beliefs about the role they play can have an important impact on instructional decisions.

All teachers have beliefs or theories about learning that form the very fabric of their teaching strategy. By watching teachers behave in the classroom, we can usually infer their basic assumptions about the teaching-learning process, even though those teachers may not be able to articulate their beliefs. For example, the teacher who directs and controls all student activities is operating under a set of beliefs different from those of the teacher who establishes conditions under which students make many of their own decisions about how they will learn.

I believe that one of the objectives of teacher education is to help teachers see the relationship between beliefs and practices.

Throughout the history of education, practices have changed as we have learned more about the learning process. Years ago teachers had it drummed into their heads that the best way to ensure learning was through repetition, a principle from behavioral learning theory that dominated educational thinking for some time. Students spent their time copying spelling words, historical information, and mathematical formulas over and over again until they learned the information. Teachers began to change some of their methods when they were confronted with views based on research findings that repetition was not the best strategy for attaining higher-level learning objectives.

Before proceeding, let's identify some of your beliefs about learning. Check whether you agree or disagree with the following statements (adapted in part from Seaberg, 1974, pp. 7–8):

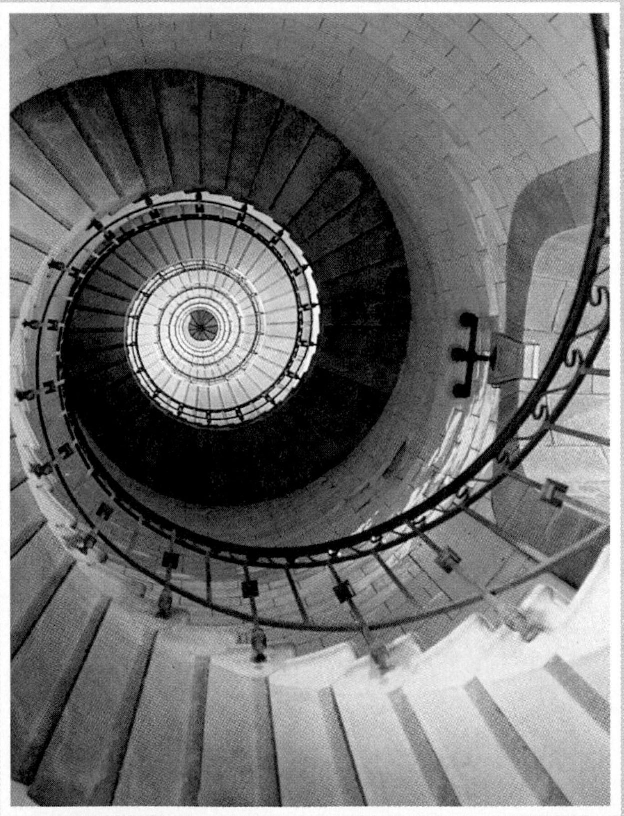

Agree	Disagree	I believe that:
____	____	1. Learners need grades, gold stars, and other incentives as motivation to learn and to accomplish school requirements.
____	____	2. Learners can be trusted to find their own goals and should have some options or choices in what they learn in school.
____	____	3. Teachers need to determine what students are thinking about while solving math problems.
____	____	4. Students should be graded according to uniform standards of achievement, which the teacher sets for the class.
____	____	5. Students should set their own individual standards and should evaluate their own work.
____	____	6. Curriculum should be organized along subject matter lines that are carefully sequenced.
____	____	7. The teacher should help students to monitor and control their own learning behavior.
____	____	8. The school experience should help students to develop positive relations with peers.

For the most part, statements 1, 4, and 6 would be supported most strongly by behavioral psychologists, statements 3 and 7 by cognitive psychologists, and statements 2, 5, and 8 by humanistic psychologists. Did your responses fall into any particular pattern? Let's briefly review each of these theoretical positions.

Contemporary *behaviorists* view environmental factors in terms of *stimuli* and resultant behavior in terms of *responses.* They attempt to demonstrate that behavior is controlled by environmental contingencies of external reward or reinforcement, which are links between behavioral responses and their effects (or stimuli). Teachers who accept the behavioral perspective assume that the behavior of students is a response to their past and present environment and that all behavior is learned. For example, classroom troublemakers "learn" to be disruptive because of the attention (reinforcement) they get from peers; withdrawn students "learn" that their environment does not reinforce gregariousness, and they become reserved and silent. As a result, any behavior can be analyzed in terms of its reinforcement history. The logical extension of the behavioral principle of learning is a method to change or modify behavior. The teacher's responsibility, therefore, is to construct an environment in which the probability of reinforcing students for correct or proper behavior is maximized. This goal is best attained by carefully organizing and presenting information in a designed sequence.

In contrast to the behavioral perspective, *cognitive psychologists* focus more on the learner as an active participant in the teaching-learning process. Those who adhere to this perspective believe that teachers can be more effective if they know what knowledge the learner already has acquired and what the learner is thinking about during instruction. More specifically, the cognitive approach tries to understand how information is processed and structured in an individual's memory. Many cognitive psychologists believe that teachers should instruct students in ways to use techniques or strategies to learn more effectively. Weinstein and Mayer (1985) state that effective instruction "includes teaching students how to learn, how to remember, how to think, and how to motivate themselves" (p. 315).

Humanistic psychologists believe that how a person "feels" is as important as how the person behaves or thinks. They describe behavior from the standpoint of the believer rather than of the observer, and they are especially concerned with "self-actualization"—the growth of persons in whatever area they choose. The humanistic teacher is interested in creating an educational environment that fosters self-development, cooperation, and positive communication, because of the belief that these conditions will foster greater learning.

In the next four chapters we investigate theories of learning and motivation, and their instructional applications in educational settings. Keep the following three points in mind while you are reading the chapters in this part of the book:

1. There is no *one* behavioral, cognitive, or humanistic theory. Individuals within each of these systems differ on various points.
2. Not all educational practices are backed by one specific theory. In fact, more recently, there have been attempts to integrate various orientations that incorporate cognitive-humanistic or cognitive-behavioral methods.
3. You need to learn *when* to use ideas from various perspectives because each has strengths and weaknesses, depending on the particular purpose you may have in mind.

Chapter 2

Behavioral Approaches to Learning

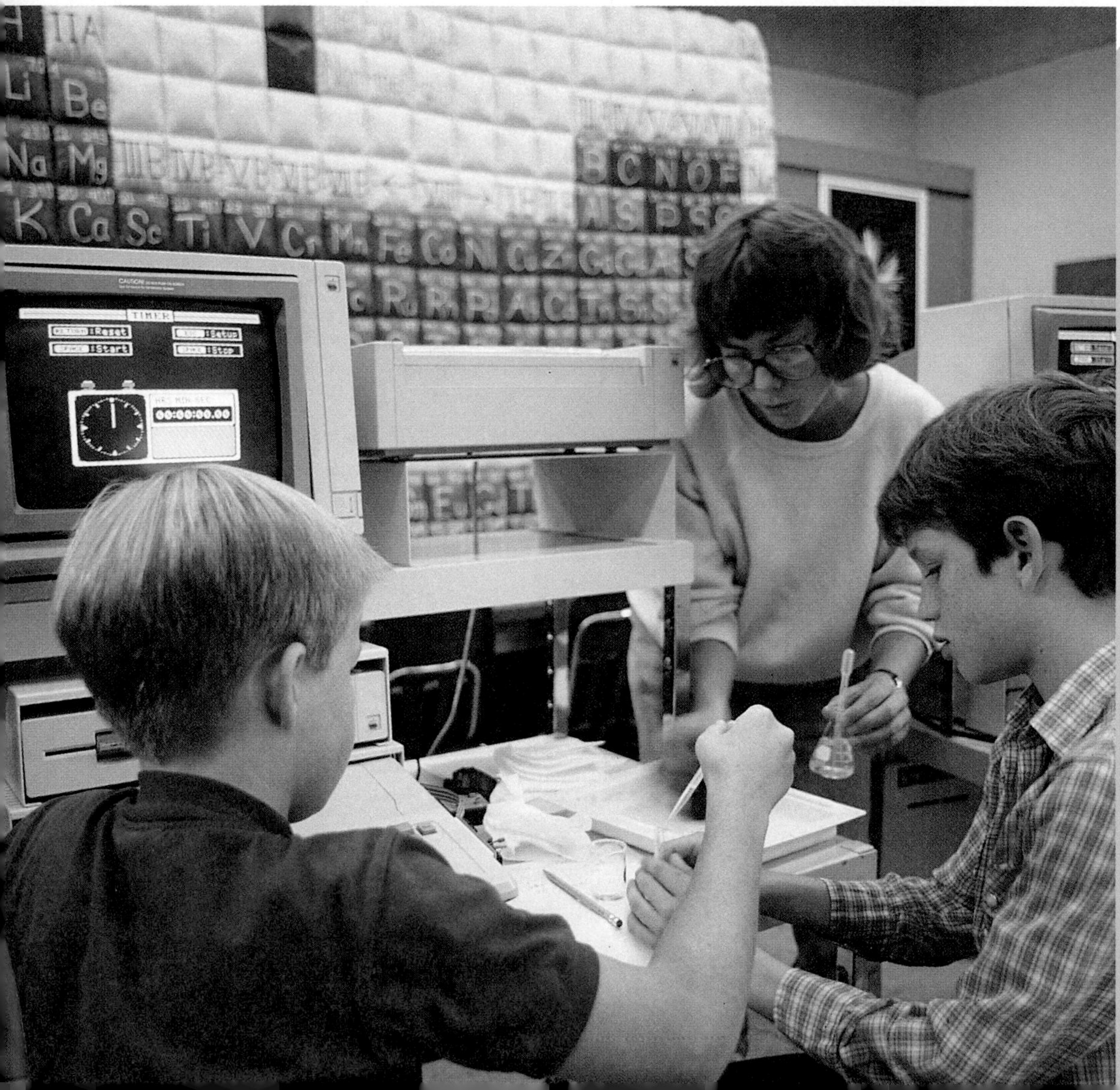

Classical Conditioning
- Pavlov
- Watson

Applied Behavior Analysis
- Early Developments—Thorndike
- Skinner
- Discrimination, Stimulus Control, and Generalization
- Consequent Stimuli
- Schedules of Reinforcement
- Extinction
- Shaping—A Method for Developing New Behaviors

Social Cognitive Theory
- Types of Modeling
- Processes in Observational Learning
- Social Learning in the Classroom

Cognitive Behavior Modification
- Self-Management
- Self-Verbalization

Instructional Applications of Behavioral Learning Principles
- Programmed Instruction
- Computer-Assisted Instruction (CAI)
- Computer Competence
- Research on CAI

Debate Forum: Do Media Influence Learning?

Mastery Learning

Classroom Application: Developing and Implementing a Mastery Learning Program

Personalized System of Instruction (PSI)

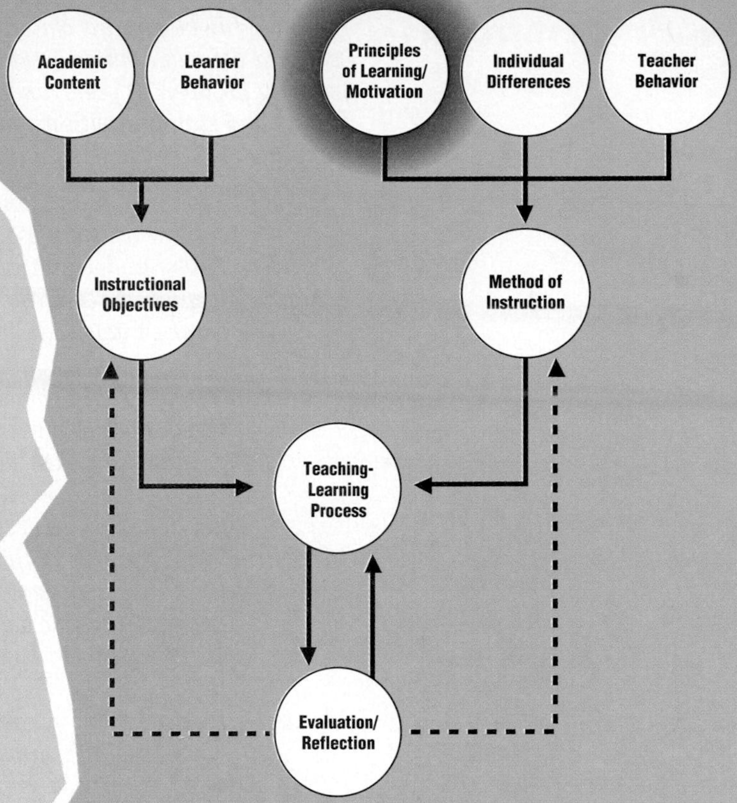

OBJECTIVES

After mastering the material in this chapter you will be able to:

- Describe the procedures used in applied behavior analysis for modifying behavior.
- Use shaping to develop complex behaviors.
- Use behavioral principles in designing a lesson.
- Develop and implement a mastery learning program.

Orientation

In her 3 years of teaching fourth grade, Jackie Chi had never had a student as disruptive as Bobby Hanford. She couldn't remember a day when she hadn't had to reprimand Bobby for his classroom behavior. She decided to seek the advice of a seasoned veteran of these "student wars," Marion Howe. Marion had been teaching for over 20 years, and she had a fine reputation, not only among the faculty and staff but with parents and students as well. What follows is a brief sampling of their conversation about Bobby:

Jackie: *Marion, I can't stand it! This kid is driving me absolutely crazy, and I can't teach the class anything. I spend all of my time trying to get Bobby under control.*

Marion: *It might be easier for me to help if I knew what a typical interaction between you and Bobby would be like.*

Jackie: *Let's see. On a typical day, I'll just get the class started on the daily lesson, when Bobby will start to laugh loudly, or talk very loudly. When I ask him to stop, he'll begin to slam his book down on the desk, or mumble under his breath. Of course, I can't let this happen in the class, so I go over to his desk and tell him that the next time he makes a noise, he'll be in deep trouble.*

Marion: *What happens at that point?*

Jackie: *It's almost like he wants to push me to the limit, Marion, like he really enjoys seeing me get upset. At that point he will do one more thing that always seems to send me through the roof. By that point, I'm fit to be tied.*

Marion: *Jackie, I think you hit it on the head when you said it seems like he enjoys seeing you react like that. Sounds to me like Bobby enjoys the attention you're giving him. When he's being reprimanded in front of the class, he's in control, isn't he? Doesn't it feel like he's the one deciding how the day will go?*

Jackie: *That's exactly how it feels, and I hate it! I can't let this nine-year-old ruin my career.*

Marion: *That's not going to happen. You need to realize that his behavior is designed to get your attention and to make you react as you have been. You have control over this child, Jackie. Your response to his behavior is under your control, not his. How could you respond differently to Bobby when he does the same things in class?*

Jackie: *Well, it sounds ridiculous, but I could ignore him when he's disruptive, and pay attention to him when he behaves appropriately.*

Marion: *Exactly, Jackie!*

The principles of behavioral psychology are used both in designing instruction and in behavior therapy in treating numerous personal and social problems such as anxiety, fear, aggression, and depression. In this chapter, we will explore behavioral learning principles and focus on their use in an instructional setting. In Chapter 7 (Classroom Management and Discipline), we will look at how these principles can be used more directly in managing classroom behavior.

In this chapter, you will see how behavioral psychology moved from working with only observable behavior to the incorporation of cognitive processes (e.g., thoughts, beliefs) within its framework. You need to realize that behavioral psychologists view the role of the teacher as a manager of instruction. They are strong proponents of using specific objectives and of sequencing instruction on the basis of presenting basic facts first, moving then to more complex information. Behaviorists believe that if teachers properly present and sequence information, students will learn more.

I have emphasized that individual differences should influence a teacher's instructional decisions. The principles of behavioral psychology have been applied successfully with many kinds of learners in a variety of learning situations. Various forms of individualized instruction have been used extensively to deal with student diversity in the classroom, especially with low-achieving students.

Most forms of technology in education (e.g., computers) are based on behavioral learning principles. The incorporation of this technology in the curriculum may produce changes in your instructional role. You need to be prepared for these changes because you will not always present information to students. Instead, you may be spending more time diagnosing students' learning problems and deciding on alternative learning methods. These decisions are as important as deciding how material should be presented in the first place. Do not reject technological developments simply because they are unfamiliar. School districts are now providing opportunities for teachers to learn more about how they can use technological developments in the classroom.

CLASSICAL CONDITIONING

Pavlov

A Russian physiologist, Ivan Pavlov (1849–1936), accidentally came upon an interesting learning phenomenon while working with dogs in his laboratory. If a bell was sounded a few seconds before a hungry dog was presented with food, after several trials the dog would salivate simply at the sound of the bell. Pavlov identified the food as an **unconditioned stimulus** and salivation as an **unconditioned response** (an example of a stimulus that produces some observable response without prior learning). The bell, which originally had no particular meaning for the dog, took on meaning, or became a **conditioned stimulus,** because of its association, or pairing, with the food, which elicited a **conditioned response**—salivation.

This kind of learning is called **classical conditioning,** or stimulus substitution, because the conditioned stimulus, after being paired with the unconditioned stimulus often enough, can then be substituted for it. Figure 2.1 is a schematic representation of classical conditioning.

Pavlov found that when a dog was conditioned to salivate at the sound of a bell, it would also salivate at other similar sounds, such as that of a siren, even though the new stimuli were never used in training. Once a particular conditioned stimulus was associated with a response, other similar stimuli also were able to elicit the response. He called this phenomenon **stimulus generalization.**

unconditioned stimulus. A stimulus that naturally elicits a particular response.

unconditioned response. The unlearned, biological reaction evoked by an unconditioned stimulus.

conditioned stimulus. A stimulus that does not initially elicit a response but through its pairing with an unconditioned stimulus acquires the capability of eliciting the same response as the latter.

conditioned response. A response elicited by a conditioned stimulus.

classical conditioning. A procedure in which the conditioned stimulus, after being paired with the unconditioned stimulus often enough, can then be substituted for it.

stimulus generalization. A process whereby once a particular conditioned stimulus is associated with a response, other similar stimuli are able to elicit the response.

Before conditioning
CS (bell) → no response or irrelevant response
US (food) → UR (salivation)
During conditioning
CS (bell)
US (food) → UR (salivation)
After conditioning
CS (bell) → CR (salivation)

Figure 2.1 A Schematic Representation of Classical Conditioning.

extinction. In operant conditioning, the gradual disappearance of reinforcing events that maintain a behavior.

connectionism. A term used by Thorndike to explain learning that is concerned with the formation of bonds between stimuli and responses.

Watson

John B. Watson (1878–1958) was the first psychologist in the United States to use Pavlov's research findings as a basis for a learning theory. Watson believed that learning is a process of conditioning reflexes (responses) through the substitution of one stimulus for another. According to Watson, humans are born with a few reflexes and the emotional reactions of fear, love, and rage. All other behavior is established by building new stimulus-response (S-R) connections through conditioning.

In one of his most famous experiments, Watson conditioned an 11-month-old child to fear a white rat that he had made friends with. Watson made a loud noise (unconditioned stimulus, or US) whenever the rat was presented to the boy, which resulted in a fear response (unconditioned response, or UR). Within a short time, the boy became fearful (conditioned response, or CR) at the sight of the rat (conditioned stimulus, or CS).

Watson also demonstrated that the boy's fear could be unlearned by the process called **extinction**. This is accomplished by repeating the CS without following it up with the US: presenting the rat without making the loud noise.

Many students' attitudes are learned through classical conditioning. For instance, they may learn to acquire negative attitudes toward foreign languages because they associate these languages with the unpleasant experience of being asked to translate sentences aloud in class. Being asked difficult questions in class (US) elicits anxiety (UR). Students who are conditioned to fear foreign languages may generalize their fear to blanket other subjects of the school's curriculum or the institution of school. The same learning process operates in other school experiences.

APPLIED BEHAVIOR ANALYSIS

Early Developments—Thorndike

For the first several decades of this century, the learning theory of E. L. Thorndike (1874–1949) dominated educational practice in the United States. His theory became known as **connectionism** because he posited that learning was a process of "stamping in," or forming, connections between a stimulus and a response.

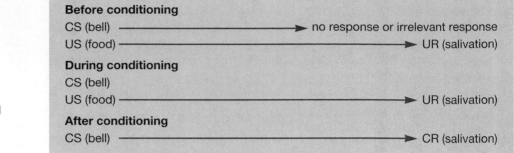

law of effect. Thorndike's finding that the connections between stimuli and responses are strengthened by satisfying outcomes.

reward. An object, stimulus, or outcome that is perceived as being pleasant and may be reinforcing.

law of exercise. Thorndike's finding that the repetition of a learned response strengthens the bond between the stimulus situation and the response.

Thorndike developed his theory from extensive research on the effect of reward on the behavior of various animals. One of his major studies used cats that he placed in a "puzzle box"—a small cage with a door that would open if the cat pulled a string hanging inside the cage. The cat's task was to get out of the cage to obtain food (reward) placed outside the cage. Usually the cat went through the process of walking around, clawing at the floor, jumping at the sides of the cage, and other similar movements until, by chance, he pulled the string opening the door of the cage. Thorndike repeated the experiment several times. The cat still stalked around his cage but pulled the string much sooner. After several trials the cat centered his behavior around the string, eventually pulled the string immediately, and collected his reward (food).

Thorndike explained the process of learning as follows: After the cat hit upon the correct response and was rewarded for it, a connection was gradually strengthened between the situation (stimulus) and the response.

From animal learning, it was only a step upward (maybe more!) to human learning, which Thorndike saw as comprising the same elements. His research with various animals gave him his most important principle of learning, the **law of effect** (Thorndike, 1913):

> When a modifiable connection is made between a situation and a response and is accompanied or followed by a satisfying state of affairs, the strength of that connection is increased. When an annoying state of affairs goes with or follows a connection, the strength of that connection is decreased. (p. 71)

The main factor influencing all learning is **reward,** or a "satisfying state of affairs." In his later writings, Thorndike eliminated the negative or "annoying" part of the law of effect because he found that punishment did not necessarily weaken bonds and its effect was not the opposite of reward.

The **law of exercise** was his second important learning principle. In general, it stated that the more an S-R connection is practiced or used, the stronger it will become; the less it is used, the weaker it will become. He also modified this law in his later writings because he found that practice without reward was ineffective. Connections were strengthened only by rewarded practice.

Thorndike's (1913) learning theory led to a number of educational practices. His general advice for teachers was, "Put together and exercise what should go together, and reward desirable connections" (p. 70).

Thorndike showed one bond between stimulus and response that occurred in mathematics. Constant repetition of multiplication tables with the teacher providing the reward formed bonds between the stimulus (What is 7 × 7?) and the response (49). In reading, repetition was also emphasized by having students learn the most frequently used words at various grade levels.

The more S-R bonds subjects had, the more intelligent they were considered to be, because they had more bonds at their disposal in problem

respondent. A response that is elicited by a known stimulus and requires no previous learning.

operant. A term used by Skinner to describe responses not elicited by any known stimulus.

situations. The law of effect led to the use of concrete rewards such as gold stars placed on students' papers and emphasis on verbal praise. The law of exercise led to much repetition, practice, and drill for all subjects.

So far in our discussion of behavioral psychologists, we have viewed learning from the perspective of forming connections, or associations, between a stimulus and a response. I have identified two vantage points in this approach: learning through the simultaneous occurrence of stimulus and response (Pavlov and Watson) and learning through the act of being rewarded (Thorndike).

Since the early explanations of learning by these psychologists, many individuals have contributed to these perspectives. Few have made as much impact on educational practice as B. F. Skinner (1904–1990).

Skinner

? How does Skinner's view of learning differ from that of other behaviorists?

Like Thorndike, Skinner viewed reward, or reinforcement, as the most important element in the learning process. We tend to learn a response if it is immediately followed by reinforcement. Skinner preferred the term *reinforcement* to *reward* because *reward* is a subjective interpretation of behavior associated with a pleasurable event, whereas *reinforcement* is a neutral term, defined simply as an effect that increases the probability of a response. The use of *reinforcement* removes any subjective interpretation from the concept and, like Skinner's other concepts, is discussed in terms of observable and measurable events. Skinner (1986) states: "A reward is compensation or remuneration for services performed and is seldom immediately contingent on behavior. We reward people; we reinforce behavior" (p. 106). His purpose was to establish relationships between behavior and environmental stimuli that would lead to a science of human behavior. Skinner called his approach the *experimental analysis of behavior.*

Skinner believed that the purpose of psychology is to predict and control behavior. Because all behavior is learned, it follows that a teacher or psychologist can apply the same principles of learning to change behavior (Skinner, 1953).

Skinner identified two types of response in the learning process: **respondents** and **operants.** Respondents are elicited by specific stimuli such as Pavlov's bell. Earlier we read about Pavlov's classical conditioning theory and found that an individual can learn by the pairing of association of stimuli. In a respondent situation, an individual learns merely by being in the situation, by responding to the environment.

Although humans learn some behavior by classical conditioning, Skinner argues that most human behavior takes the form of operant responses that the individual emits. Such behaviors as writing a letter, picking up a book, and driving a car are operants—responses that an individual makes to no known stimuli.

Initially, an individual's responses in a given situation are random, but after a time certain responses (operants) become more dominant than others because of selective reinforcement. Skinner called this process **operant conditioning**—a learning situation in which a response is made more probable or frequent as the result of immediate reinforcement. A kindergarten student during the first week of school emits a number of responses: talking with other students, paying attention to the teacher, walking around the room, and bothering other students. As the teacher begins reinforcing certain responses—by smiling when the student pays attention, for example—some of the responses begin to occur more frequently. Of all possible responses that could be emitted in a given situation, some responses become more dominant than others.

operant conditioning. A type of learning that involves an increase in the probability that a response will occur as a function of reinforcement.

Reinforcement is a powerful procedure for encouraging appropriate behavior.

applied behavior analysis. A scientific method of behavioral change using principles of *operant conditioning.*

baseline. The natural occurrence of a behavior before intervention.

? What is the difference between classical and operant conditioning?

An important difference between Pavlov's classical conditioning and Skinner's operant conditioning is that in classical conditioning the consequences of a behavior carry no weight in the learning of that behavior. Reinforcement is unnecessary because the stimuli bring about the desired response.

Operant conditioning, although closer to Thorndike's theory than to Pavlov's, is different from Thorndike's explanation of learning. Thorndike felt that reward strengthens a bond that exists between a stimulus and a response, whereas Skinner believed that what is strengthened is not an S-R bond but the probability that the same response will occur again.

FROM OPERANT CONDITIONING TO APPLIED BEHAVIOR ANALYSIS. Skinner initially developed the principles of operant conditioning with animals—rats and pigeons. Later in his career he wrote about the generalizability of operant principles and their applicability to complex behavior. *Walden Two* (Skinner, 1948) is a novel about a utopian society based upon operant principles. In *Science and Human Behavior* (Skinner, 1953) he pointed out how these same principles functioned in social institutions like government, law, religion, economics, and education.

By the early 1960s psychologists began using operant principles for clinical purposes in shaping or modifying human behavior in applied settings. They worked in hospitals, schools, prisons, and other institutions. This major change in emphasis from basic laboratory research with animals to applied applications led to the formal acknowledgment of what is now called **applied behavior analysis.** A major development in the formal recognition of applied behavior analysis as a separate research entity was the appearance in 1968 of a new journal, the *Journal of Applied Behavior Analysis*, which served as an outlet for research and defined the field. In the journal's first article, Baer, Wolf, and Risley (1968) defined *applied behavior analysis* by stating that the research is *applied* if it was directed toward clinically or socially significant behavior and the psychologist attempted to bring about behavior change of applied significance. Teaching a mentally retarded individual to cook and live independently or teaching a delinquent youth to interview for a job are examples of socially significant behaviors.

Whether the research constitutes *behavior analysis* is determined by the methodological approach in implementing and evaluating treatment interventions. This methodology is marked by a distinct approach toward assessment, experimental design, and data evaluation (Kazdin, 1978). Assessment in applied behavior analysis is conducted by the objective evaluation of overt responses. This means that the psychologist must identify the specific behavior to be changed and determine the frequency or duration of the response before the intervention begins. This level of responding is called the **baseline.** Behavior change is measured by comparing the baseline behavior with behavior after the intervention. The psychologist then attempts to demonstrate that the change is the result of the specific intervention (e.g., reinforcement) rather than some other factor. This plan for demonstrating the cause of the change is called the *experimental design.*

One of the many types of designs used is to alternate the environmental contingencies over time. The absence of the intervention is called the *baseline* (or A) *phase,* while the intervention is called the *experimental* (or B) *phase*. One of many different designs used is ABAB, because A and B phases alternate (see Figure 2.2). After the behavior in one phase is stabilized (i.e., it is relatively uniform), the psychologist moves to the next phase. The final step in applied behavior analysis is data evaluation, the determination of whether a change in behavior was made. The purpose of moving back to the baseline phase is to ensure that a cause-and-effect relationship exists between the behavior and reinforcement. If the researcher stopped after the initial intervention, he or she could not be sure that the change in behavior was the result of reinforcement. The behavior could be attributed to some other environmental condition.

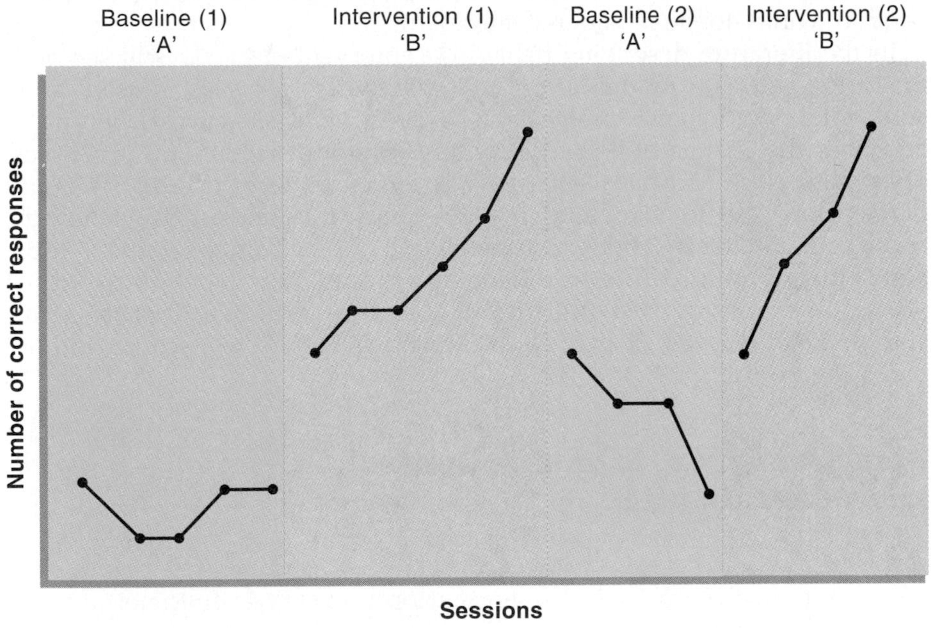

Figure 2.2 Reversal Design Demonstrating a Functional Relation between Variables. *Note:* At Baseline (2) the reinforcement is stopped and begun again at Intervention (2).

An example of the use of the ABAB design is illustrated by the teacher who wanted her high school students to clean up the classroom without being told. She began her intervention program by recording how many times during each class period she saw students picking up paper from the floor (baseline). After two weeks she placed different signs around the room encouraging students to take pride in their room by keeping it clean. She continued to record the number of times paper was picked up from the floor (experimental). She found that papers were picked up at a higher

behavior modification. Interventions designed to change behavior in a precisely measurable manner.

discriminative stimulus (S^D). A stimulus (S^D) in the presence of which a given response is likely to be reinforced.

reinforcing stimulus (S^R). A stimulus that increases or maintains the behavior upon which it is contingent.

rate. She then removed the signs and found that, in a week, the pickup rate returned close to the initial rate (baseline). After two weeks, she replaced the signs and noticed that the pickup rate increased (experimental). This short experiment indicated that the signs were the major factor influencing the students' behavior.

I recommend that teachers using applied behavior analysis employ the two-phase AB design: the baseline (A) and intervention phase (B). Although the design has weaknesses in demonstrating a definite cause-and-effect relationship, it provides the teacher with a relatively easy way of comparing behavior before and after some intervention. Furthermore, I don't feel it is appropriate for the classroom teacher to halt a successful intervention that works.

Two important criteria are used to evaluate the success of applied behavior analysis: experimental and therapeutic. The change agent must show that the client's behavior during the treatment phase is significantly different from that at the baseline phase. Finally, the change agent must report on the importance of the change in behavior. For example, did the reduction in aggressive behavior by a student allow him or her to function successfully in the classroom? If the aggressive behavior was reduced, but not enough to allow the individual to function in the classroom, the intervention would not be considered successful.

In the literature describing behavioral interventions, you will see both the terms **behavior modification** and *applied behavior analysis* used. Most behavioral psychologists prefer the term *applied behavior analysis*, because it describes the change of behavior by application of behavioral principles. They argue that *behavior modification* is a general term to identify many procedures used to change behavior, including hypnosis, drug therapy, and electroconvulsive shock treatments (Alberto & Troutman, 1990). Most behaviorists would like to dissociate themselves from these other procedures. Yet you will still find books with titles like *Behavior Modification: What It Is and How to Do It* (Martin & Pear, 1988), whose authors prefer that term.

Discrimination, Stimulus Control, and Generalization

? What is the role of discrimination training in instruction?

Operant conditioning can be adequately explained without the presence of a stimulus initiating a response. However, we can talk about a response being brought under the control of a **discriminative stimulus** (S^D), a cue or signal that increases the probability of a response. This situation is best illustrated in Skinner's early research with rats placed in a small apparatus called a *Skinner box*, which is equipped with a lever, light, food tray, and food-releasing mechanism. By providing a **reinforcing stimulus** (S^R), food, the researcher can train a rat to push the lever only when the light (S^D) is turned on. If the rat pushes the lever when the light is off, it receives no reinforcement. The light is a cue that makes the response of lever pushing more likely to occur. Later the rat can be taught to push the lever only when the light is off. People, also, respond differently to different stimuli. For example, college students often use different language around their friends than they use at home with their parents. Behavior is said to be under stimulus control when the response varies depending on what stimulus is present.

Earlier I discussed stimulus generalization in classical conditioning. We also can identify stimulus generalization in operant conditioning. Sometimes behavior learned in one situation will be performed in other, similar situations even though the behavior is not reinforced in the new situations. For example, stimulus generalization occurs when a child responds politely to a teacher in the same way he responds to his parents. The behavioral psychologist who teaches a child to use appropriate social behaviors in a clinic is interested in the transfer or generalization of these same behaviors with peers, at home, and in school.

discrimination learning. The restriction of responding to certain stimulus situations but not others.

response generalization. A condition whereby a behavior becomes more probable in the presence of a stimulus or situation as a result of a similar behavior having been strengthened in the presence of that stimulus or situation.

Events occurring before and after a student makes a response can determine when and where that response will occur. The teacher wants students to learn certain responses under specific conditions. When a student receives the stimulus (4 + 3 =) and responds (7), reinforcement follows. We say that **discrimination learning** has taken place. An important part of teaching is to present stimuli so specific that only one response is correct. If reinforcement is contingent upon only the correct response, more learning transpires. Another type of generalization involves responses rather than stimulus situations. Changing one response can inadvertently influence other responses. The term **response generalization** describes this condition. For example, adolescents who are taught to reduce their physical aggression when they get mad might also learn to speak in a lower voice and be more patient with others.

The following examples illustrate the stimulus-response processes in learning:

Teacher Presents Stimulus (S^D)	**Child Responds**	**Teacher Presents Consequent Stimulus (S^R)**
"Who was the first president of the United States?"	"Washington."	"Good."
"How many times will four go into sixteen?"	"Three."	"No, that's wrong."
Teacher shows the letter *B* and asks: "What sound is this?"	No response	No consequence
Teacher then says, "This is *Bbbb*, say '*Bbbb*.' "	"Bbbb."	"Good, that's much better."

positive reinforcement. A procedure that maintains or increases the rate of a response by presenting a stimulus following the response.

negative reinforcement. The termination of an unpleasant condition following a desired response.

punishment. A procedure in which an aversive stimulus is presented immediately following a response, resulting in a reduction in the rate of response.

APPLIED BEHAVIOR ANALYSIS IN TEACHING. The basis of applied behavior analysis in teaching is to ensure responses to stimuli. Unless the learner emits responses to stimuli, it is impossible to guide his or her behavior toward a behavioral goal. Teachers play an important role in the classroom by controlling and directing the learning activities. Behaviorists urge the use of instructional objectives (i.e., objectives stated in terms of actual behaviors such as *list, recite,* and *compare*) because teachers must know what they are trying to accomplish before they plan a sequence of behaviors directed toward a goal. After identifying the objective, the teacher would determine the most logical order of presenting the material in small steps (Chapter 6 includes a discussion on how to write behavioral objectives and plan a sequence of instruction) and then provide reinforcement immediately after the learner responds. The following teaching practices would be encouraged by behaviorists:

- returning and discussing all exams promptly
- questioning students regularly and reinforcing correct answers
- checking student work continually
- generally making an attempt to reinforce all behavior conducive to the development of good attitudes toward learning

Consequent Stimuli

? What is the difference between negative reinforcement and punishment?

A number of consequences occurring after a response are discussed in this chapter. Table 2.1 presents a four-cell classification identifying types of reinforcement and punishment. We have already discussed **positive reinforcement**—the presentation of a stimulus that, when added to a situation, increases the probability of a response occurring (cell A). Second, an individual can receive **negative reinforcement**—the termination of an unpleasant stimulus (such as isolation) that, when taken away from a situation, also increases the probability of a response occurring (cell B). In the case of isolation, it may be maintained until the student promises to cease misbehaving. In another example of negative reinforcement, a child becomes sick just as the teacher hands out an examination. The sickness results in removal from class. Thus the response of getting sick has been followed by a negative reinforcer because it discontinued the test, an aversive (unpleasant) stimulus. We might expect "sickness" behavior to increase in frequency in similar test situations. Third, a child can receive **punishment**—the presentation of an unpleasant stimulus (such as contradiction or reprimand) that decreases the probability that a response will occur at all (cell C). Another form of punishment attempts to decrease behavior by taking away a pleasant or reinforcing stimulus (cell D). This type of punishment is used by teachers when they remove students from class activities or even from the class itself, until the students are ready to demonstrate proper behavior. The procedure is called **time-out** and will be discussed in Chapter 7 (Classroom Management and Discipline). Note that positive and negative reinforcement seek to *increase* the probability of a response, whereas punishment aims to *suppress* the response.

time-out. A behavioral control method that involves removal of a disruptive student from the classroom or to an isolated part of the classroom.

primary reinforcement. A stimulus, such as food or water, that satisfies a basic need.

secondary reinforcement. A process that uses a stimulus that is not originally reinforcing but that acquires reinforcing properties when paired with a primary reinforcer.

Premack's principle. A principle that contingent access to preferred activities serves as a reinforcer for the performance of low-frequency behaviors.

TABLE 2.1 TYPES OF REINFORCEMENT AND PUNISHMENT

	Present Stimulus	Remove Stimulus
Response Increase	A **Positive Reinforcement** *Example:* "Great job on your term paper!"	B **Negative Reinforcement** *Example* "Okay, you don't feel well, you don't have to take the examination today."
Response Decrease	C **Punishment 1** *Example:* "Will you please shut up?"	D **Punishment 2 (Time-out)** *Example:* "Fred, we can't tolerate your talking—move your seat to the study area for ten minutes."

In the studies of operant conditioning with animals, **primary reinforcement** (food or water) is a factor. These reinforcing stimuli work toward the satisfaction of the animals' physiological needs. Most reinforcement in educational environments is **secondary reinforcement**—learned. It is reinforcing because it has been paired with (or is exchangeable for) a primary reinforcer. Money, for instance, is not reinforcing to an infant, but later it becomes influential in affecting behavior when the child learns that it can be exchanged for candy.

Behaviorists identify three classes of secondary reinforcers: *social reinforcers* (social acceptance, smiles), *tokens* (physical objects like money, grades, prizes, points), and *activities* (free play, listening to music, trips). The premise behind using activities is **Premack's principle** (Premack, 1959): Given two activities, the more preferred may be used to increase the rate of the less preferred. In other words, an interesting activity on which a person spends a good deal of time can reinforce behavior in an activity in which the person is less interested and on which the person spends less time. If a child likes to build model airplanes but does not like to read, telling the child he can work on his project after he successfully completes his reading assignment accomplishes reinforcement of the reading behavior.

Havighurst (1970) points out that people react differently to various types of reinforcers. Some students are motivated by being praised verbally in front of their peers; others shun such attention. A reinforcing event is not inherently effective, so it is wise for a teacher to make a list of possible reinforcers for various students in the class. The expression "different strokes for different folks" best summarizes this point.

Teachers who learn about applied behavior analysis invariably ask, "How do I know what will be reinforcing to a student?" The only sure

Teachers can use tokens as secondary reinforcers. In this photo, the teacher is giving slips of paper to students for appropriate behavior. These slips are worth points that can be traded for classroom privileges.

way is to observe the student and to recognize which stimuli increase the frequency of the response that follows. In a class of 30 or more students, the burden is staggering. Instead, ask the students to fill out a questionnaire that includes such questions as: What special things do you like to work with or play with in the classroom? What are three jobs in this classroom that you like to do most? If you went to a store to buy three games that you like, what would they be? You can modify these questions for the age level of the students in the classroom.

Age difference should be a factor in the teacher's selection of a reinforcer. You can use a five-cent eraser as a reinforcer for a young child, but an adolescent demands a reinforcer of greater value. Activities like helping the teacher, using a tape recorder, or doing puzzles are potentially reinforcing for elementary students; for junior high and high school students, more appropriate reinforcing activities are talking to a friend, playing video games, reading a magazine, or listening to music. Make a list of some potential reinforcing stimuli and events for the age level of students you will be working with.

Schedules of Reinforcement

A *schedule of reinforcement* refers to when or how often a response is reinforced. Through experiments with rats, pigeons, and then humans, Skinner was able to identify some important relationships between the way in which reinforcement is administered and the rates of learning, response, and extinction.

Reinforcement can be continuous or intermittent; the teacher reinforces correct responses each time or periodically. An experimenter or teacher using an intermittent schedule of reinforcement has two choices: reinforcing a proportion of responses (a ratio schedule) or reinforcing responses following a lapse of time from the previous reinforcement (an interval schedule). There are two types of ratio and interval schedules: fixed and variable (see Figure 2.3).

A **fixed-ratio schedule** is based on presenting the subject with a reinforcer after the subject emits a specified number of responses. In a 4:1 ratio, for example, the subject is reinforced after each set of four responses. The teacher who tells the students that they can go to recess after completing four more problems is using a fixed-ratio schedule of reinforcement.

A **variable-ratio schedule** is based on presenting the subject with a reinforcer after an average number of responses. The exact number of responses may vary, from one reinforcer after every 3 responses to one reinforcer after every 20 responses. In this schedule the subject never knows the exact number of responses required for reinforcement. Outside the realm of education we find another example: Slot machines work on a variable-ratio schedule of reinforcement.

As noted, interval schedules are also fixed or variable. A **fixed-interval schedule** is based on a constant unit of time between reinforcements. Grading students on a 10-week period is an example of a fixed-interval schedule of reinforcement.

A **variable-interval schedule** provides reinforcement following the first correct response after a lapse of time. As in the variable-ratio schedule, the subject never knows when the next reinforcer is due. The student might be reinforced for remaining in her seat according to the following sequence: after 5 minutes of appropriate behavior, 3 minutes, 10 minutes, and 2 minutes. This reinforcement schedule is based on a variable interval, with an average of 5 minutes.

fixed-ratio schedule. A reinforcement schedule in which a subject is reinforced after a specified number of responses.

variable-ratio schedule. A schedule of reinforcement in which a predetermined number of responses, varied from one time to another, must occur between each reinforced response.

fixed-interval schedule. A reinforcement schedule in which a predetermined, fixed-time interval must occur between each reinforced response.

variable-interval schedule. A schedule providing reinforcement following the first correct response after different lapses of time.

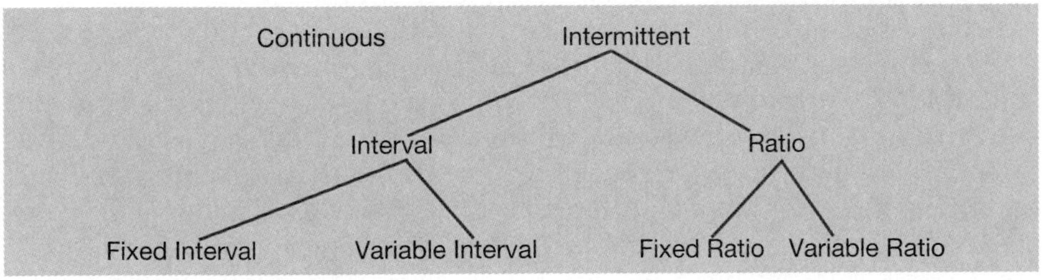

Figure 2.3 Types of Reinforcement Schedules in Operant Conditioning.

Each of the different schedules produces its own patterns of response. The continuous schedule of reinforcement is most effective in teaching new responses. Lower response rates accompany fixed-interval schedules because of the time lapse involved. The response rate picks up at the end of the time interval, as confirmed by college students' cramming for their final examinations. Fixed-ratio schedules are more conducive to constant response rates, and variable-ratio schedules are most effective for maintaining constant and high response rates.

Undesirable behavior is often unwittingly reinforced. When a teacher occasionally gives in to students' pleading for certain activities, the teacher is reinforcing them intermittently, a practice that contributes to the perpetuation of the behavior. The students learn that if they keep pleading, the teacher will eventually give them their way.

Here are some reinforcement rules to keep in mind:

- In teaching a new task, reinforce immediately rather than permit a delay between response and reinforcement.
- In the early stages of a task, reinforce every correct response. As learning occurs, require more correct responses prior to reinforcement; gradually shift to intermittent reinforcement.
- Reinforce improvements or steps in the right direction. Do not insist on perfect performance on the first try.
- Do not reinforce undesirable behavior.

Extinction

? Can you weaken behavior without using punishment?

Yes, it is possible to weaken behavior by removing the reinforcing events that maintain the behavior. For example, one teacher allowed his students to earn extra recess time by completing additional assignments in mathematics, science, and reading. After a few weeks he noticed that the students were doing all the extra work in science and not doing any work in reading or mathematics. He then changed the rule so that no extra recess time was given for additional work in science. In a short time, the students were doing less science and more mathematics and reading assignments. In this case, extinction was applied by removing the reinforcer for competing science assignments (Jenson, Sloane, & Young, 1988).

Behaviorists recommend that extinction be used in conjunction with other techniques. Clarizio (1980) details the use of extinction with modeling and social reinforcement. A second-grade teacher faced a problem with overanxious children who continually blurted out answers without raising their hands. The teacher ignored all called-out answers and acknowledged only those children who raised their hands, with such comments as, "Roberto has his hand up and is waiting to answer the question," or "Karen has her hand up and is being considerate to the class." The teacher soon noticed a marked increase in hand-raising behavior. In addition, many students who had not participated in class discussions began raising their hands and had more opportunities to contribute to the class discussion.

Many teachers find extinction difficult to use because they must learn to ignore certain misbehaviors. Sometimes they admonish students about the improper behavior (this attention is reinforcing to many students) and then ignore the behavior for the remaining time. On an intermittent schedule of reinforcement, the teacher's behavior is likely to cause the misbehavior to occur at a higher level than if extinction had not been attempted. Of course, there are many types of behavior teachers cannot ignore, especially behavior that is injurious to students. If the misbehavior consistently occurs, extinction procedures may not be advisable. Extinction works primarily when the reinforcement is attention. If a student is getting attention elsewhere, say, from peers, other changes in teacher-student interaction will have to discourage the behavior.

Another factor to consider is that even after the problem behavior has lessened, it may suddenly reappear. Such **spontaneous recovery** (or re-emergence) can cause difficulty for teachers if they are caught off guard and inadvertently reinforce the student for the inappropriate behavior. Students often will test to see if the teacher will pay attention to their inappropriate behavior. Don't conclude that the procedure failed and revert to your previous behavior. The re-emergence of inappropriate behavior can be quickly terminated once again by ignoring it. However, if you don't ignore the behavior, the result may lead to rapid relearning on the part of the student (Alberto & Troutman, 1990).

spontaneous recovery. The re-emergence of behavior after a period of extinction.

shaping. A technique whereby individuals are taught to perform complex behaviors that were not previously in their repertoire.

Last, keep in mind that during the early stages of extinction, misbehavior may worsen before it improves. Kindergarten students who get their way with their teacher by throwing tantrums will become extremely frustrated when the teacher pays no attention to their behavior. However, they will quickly get the message.

The message for teachers regarding the use of extinction is: Be consistent, ignore certain misbehavior, and combine extinction with other methods such as reinforcement of appropriate behavior. Finally, choose behaviors for extinction in situations where you can tolerate the initial rise in intensity and frequency of the misbehavior.

Shaping—A Method for Developing New Behaviors

? Why is shaping needed in behavior change programs?

We have learned thus far that the key to learning is the immediate reinforcement of desired behavior. But what happens if the desired behavior is not part of students' behavioral repertoire? For example, how can you reinforce students for doing their homework if they don't take their books home? How can you reinforce students for performing complex behaviors if they never perform them? To solve this problem, behaviorists use a procedure called **shaping**, or *successive approximations*, in which reinforcement is applied to responses that successively approximate (or become increasingly closer to) the desired behavior.

Walker and Shea (1988) provide the following example of shaping:

> Jeff, a severely handicapped child, was having great difficulty interacting appropriately on the playground during circle or ball games requiring running from one specific location to another. When he was required to engage in a game of this type, he ran about at random, dashing here and there, jumping up and down, and in general confusing himself and his playmates.

prompting. The presentation of an additional stimulus to increase the probability that an appropriate response will be made in the presence of a discriminative stimulus.

fading. The gradual removal of prompting so that the learner can respond to a discriminative stimulus without additional assistance.

Mr. Speer, the physical education teacher, wished to modify this behavior. He realized he had to start the change process with the behavior presently being manifested by Jeff. He determined that Jeff did attend to the action of the game and attempted to play by the rules. In his effort to help Jeff, Mr. Speer modified the rules of the game; he established a "new rule" in which all team members ran hand-in-hand in pairs from one location to another. Jeff was Mr. Speer's partner until he was conditioned to the new running pattern. The game was played by the traditional rules after Jeff developed acceptable skills. (p. 97)

Frazier (1969) reported the use of shaping to improve the academic achievement in a residence home for children. The steps needed to attain this goal were broken down into the following components:

- Coming to class on time
- Participating in studying behavior and responding to the teacher
- Performing well on tests
- Completing homework
- Improving performance as time progressed

The students earned points for exhibiting each of these behaviors. Students exchanged their accumulated points for various toys and prizes in a store set up for this purpose. Students who earned enough points could participate in the many preferred activities available.

This behavior modification program increased the level of school attendance from about 50 percent to 86 percent after a few months. More important, the students became more cooperative in class and used their study time more effectively.

Students often need help responding appropriately at the lower or prerequisite levels in shaping behavior. This special help—whether physical, visual, or verbal—is called **prompting**. Basically, it is an additional stimulus that increases the probability that an appropriate response will be made in the presence of the discriminative stimulus (S^D). A teacher who holds up a picture of a president after providing biographical information on his life is providing a visual prompt. Another teacher might use a rule as a verbal prompt and define a verb, then present students with sentences and ask: "Is the underlined word a verb?" (S^D). "Does the word describe an action? Then it is a verb" (prompt). "Right, Susan, it's a verb" (Alberto & Troutman, 1990). Although prompts are effective ways to increase the probability of success, they should be withdrawn gradually, or faded, as instruction progress. Behaviorists use the term **fading** to describe the gradual removal of a prompt.

You need to consider the following in developing shaping procedures:

- If you are not sure about the desired behavior, you will have difficulty determining the prerequisite behavior, or steps necessary to get there.
- You need to determine where to start. The students must be able to perform the prerequisite behavior you select so that shaping can begin.

- You need to consider the size of the steps. If they are too small, you will be wasting a great deal of time; if the steps are too large, the students' behavior will not be reinforced and the desired behavior will not be learned.
- You need to be sure that the behavior at one level is acquired before you move to the next level.

modeling. A type of learning in which individuals observe and then imitate the behavior of others.

social cognitive theory. Bandura's theory that explains how individuals acquire complex skills and abilities through observing the behavior of others.

reciprocal determinism. The mutual influence of the individual and the environment on each other.

SOCIAL COGNITIVE THEORY

Since the early 1940s, behavioral psychologists have been interested in how children acquire social behaviors. These behaviors include cooperative, competitive, affiliative, assertive, aggressive, moral-ethical, and other social responses. Social responses are learned primarily from observing the behavior of others and are referred to as **modeling**, or observational learning.

Numerous behavioral explanations have been advanced based primarily on modifications of reinforcement theory (e.g., Baer, Peterson, & Sherman, 1967; Miller & Dollard, 1941; Mowrer, 1960). All of these theories have been criticized because they don't satisfactorily explain all forms of modeling. First, they don't account for the fact that children are usually selective in what they model; children don't imitate all behavior that has been reinforced. Second, children sometimes imitate models with whom they have had no previous interaction. A third problem is that the theories don't adequately explain why children first model new behavior days or weeks after their initial observation without being reinforced for the behavior and without seeing the model reinforced for the behavior.

In 1963 Bandura and Walters, in *Social Learning and Personality Development,* first stated that an individual could model behavior simply by observing the behavior of another person. They departed from the traditional operant conditioning explanation that the individual must perform and be reinforced for his or her responses in order for learning to occur. Later, Bandura (1969, 1977) proposed the most comprehensive and widely accepted theory of modeling, which he initially called *social learning theory;* it is now identified as **social cognitive theory**. According to Bandura, children learn social behaviors by observing the actions of important people in their lives—their parents, siblings, teachers, peers, and television heroes. These observations are stored in the form of mental images and other symbolic representations that help them imitate behavior.

Bandura (1977) rejected the unidirectional view of the effects of the environment on the individual, the major premise of the behavioral perspective. Instead, his central theme is **reciprocal determinism**, a process by which personal factors, environmental factors, and behavior all operate as "interlocking determinants of each other" (p. 10). In social cognitive theory, both behavior and the environment are changeable, and neither is the primary determinant of behavioral change. For example, aggressive children expect other children to react hostilely toward them. This expectation causes the aggressive child to act aggressively. The consequence is that other children respond to the child's aggressive behavior more aggres-

inhibitory-disinhibitory effect.. A type of imitative behavior resulting either in the suppression or the appearance of previously acquired behavior.

eliciting effect. Imitative behavior in which the observer does not copy the model's responses but simply behaves in a related manner.

sively, thereby strengthening the child's initial expectation (Bell-Gredler, 1986). "Aggressive children thus create through their actions a hostile environment, while children who favor friendly modes of response generate an amicable social milieu" (Bandura, 1977, p. 198).

Bandura's (1977) work helped bridge the behavioral and cognitive perspectives and contributed greatly to the practice of cognitive-behavior therapy. He studied the ways individuals can learn to control their own behavior (see the section on cognitive behavior modification later in this chapter) (Bandura & Kupers, 1964; Bandura & Perloff, 1967) and how modeling can be used to treat phobias (Bandura, Grusec, & Menlove, 1967). Today, self-control procedures and modeling are used in many programs to treat a variety of children's and adolescents' social and emotional problems.

Types of Modeling

Bandura (1969) has organized modeling behavior into three categories: the **inhibitory-disinhibitory effect**, the **eliciting effect**, and the *modeling effect.* The inhibitory-disinhibitory effect makes a response less frequent or allows it to occur by influencing the response consequences of a model. Generally, we become inhibited when we observe others experience unpleasant consequences for engaging in behavior similar to ours. Bandura (1967) demonstrated how children could disinhibit their fear of dogs. He had children watch a film in which a child who did not fear dogs was playing with a dog in a party setting. He found that the children lost their fear after viewing the film.

A model can also have an eliciting effect on an observer by facilitating a response repertoire already present in the observer. Facilitation occurs when an unlikely response becomes more probable: Observing a friend donate time to collect for the annual cancer drive in your community may motivate you to volunteer your services for various charitable activities.

The final category, modeling effects, develops new responses through the observation of a model. This category has important implications for education. Children learn much new behavior from observing the behavior of parents, siblings, or peers. The small boy who watches his older brother move a kitchen chair to the cupboard to reach a cookie will probably attempt the same behavior later on.

Processes in Observational Learning

? How are cognitive processes used in observational learning?

Bandura (1977) identified four components of observational learning: The student must *attend* to the various aspects of the modeling situation; *retain* what has been learned from observing the modeling situation; *motorically reproduce*, or match, what has been observed in the modeling situation; and be *motivated* to perform the behavior observed.

self-efficacy. The belief that one can successfully execute the behavior required to produce a particular outcome.

ATTENTIONAL PROCESSES. Modeling will not take place unless the learner attends to and accurately perceives the behavior of the model. Several characteristics of the model and observer determine the extent of observational learning. Observers are more likely to attend to models who are similar to them and are perceived to be competent, warm, and powerful. Observers who are dependent, have lower self-concepts, and/or are anxious are more likely to model behavior. In general, individuals are influenced by the probability of reinforcement (or outcome expectancies) as they determine who and what they observe.

RETENTION PROCESSES. Individuals will not be influenced by observation if they don't remember what they see. Observed behavior is represented in memory in symbolic form. Individuals use two representational systems—*imaginal* and *verbal.* Individuals store sensory images of what they see and use verbal coding to remember the information. For instance, an individual learns, retains, and later reproduces the correct route to a store more accurately by converting the visual information into a verbal code describing the correct series of left and right turns (e.g., RRLR) than by using only the visual imagery of the route. In addition to symbolic coding, rehearsal (e.g., repeating RRLR to oneself) serves as an important memory aid. An observer can increase proficiency and retention by visualizing and/or practicing the observed behavior.

MOTOR REPRODUCTION PROCESSES. The third component of modeling involves converting symbolic representations into appropriate actions. The individual must (1) select and organize the response elements and (2) refine the response on the basis of informative feedback. Thus Little Leaguers who try to model the swing of their favorite major league baseball players will not become good batters unless they practice and receive corrective feedback on their swing. An important factor influencing accomplished performance is the learner's **self-efficacy**—the belief that one can successfully execute the behavior required to produce a particular outcome. If learners don't believe they can master a task, they will not continue working on the task.

? What is the difference in the role of reinforcement in operant conditioning and Bandura's social cognitive theory?

MOTIVATIONAL PROCESSES. Social learning theory distinguishes between acquisition and performance because individuals do not model everything they learn. This situation led Bandura to employ a mediational interpretation of the effect of reinforcing consequences on behavior:

vicarious reinforcement. Observation of positive consequences received by another person or model that leads to matching behavior by the learner.

self-reinforcement. A procedure in which individuals reinforce their own behavior.

"Reinforcement does play a role in observational learning but mainly as an antecedent rather than a consequent influence" (1977, p. 37). Thus reinforcement is important not as a strengthener of behavior but as a source of information and an incentive. The anticipation of reinforcement influences attentiveness to the model's action and enhances retention of what was observed by motivating the observer to code and rehearse modeled, valued behavior.

While direct reinforcement to the observer or model is one way to increase modeling behavior, direct reinforcement is not a necessary component for observational learning. Bandura identifies two other systems: **vicarious reinforcement** and **self-reinforcement**. In vicarious reinforcement, the model is reinforced for some appropriate behavior and the observer's performance of the same behavior increases in frequency even though the observer is not directly reinforced. An example is a teacher who reinforces a student for helping behavior and, as a result, the rest of the students in the class spend more time helping one another. A second function of vicarious reinforcement is the arousal of emotional responses. When an actor or actress does a TV commercial asking you to use a certain cologne or perfume and walks away with a handsome or attractive individual, the reinforcement to you is vicarious—if you intuit or experience the pleasure the actor or actress receives from the attention. The company manufacturing the item hopes that the reinforcement is sufficient for you to purchase the product. Vicarious reinforcement can have the same effect as direct reinforcement or an even stronger effect (Bandura, 1986).

Both direct and vicarious reinforcement involve consequences delivered by the environment. Self-reinforcement, on the other hand, is independent of the consequences delivered by society. It is consciously cultivated by individuals who develop performance standards for themselves and tend

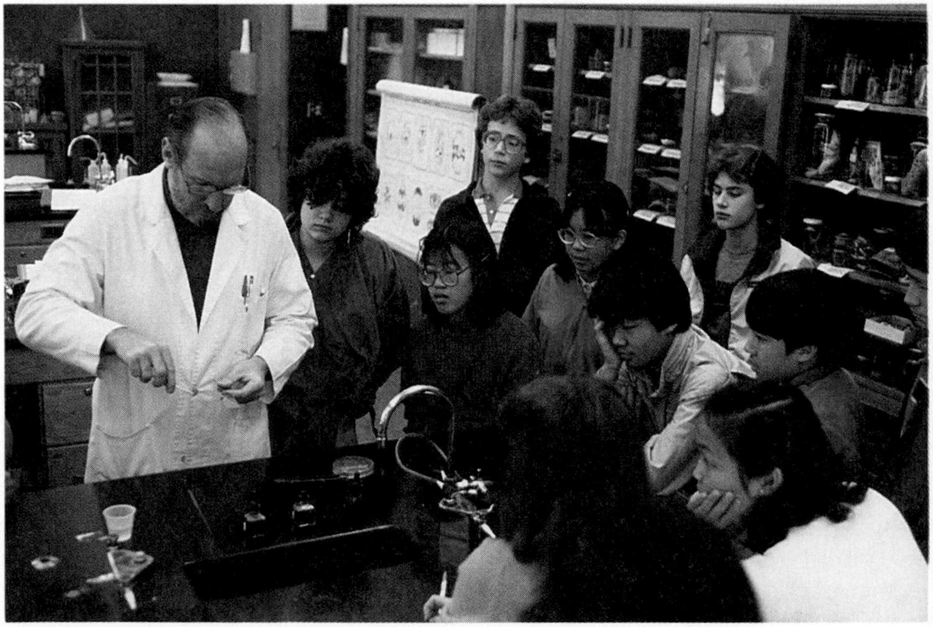

Modeling is an effective procedure for teaching complex skills.

to respond to their behavior in self-rewarding ways if their performance matches or exceeds a standard. Thus students who take an extra year of a language establish performance standards for themselves and respond to their own behavior in self-rewarding or self-criticizing ways, depending upon the evaluation of their performance.

Do you have a hobby or interest that you pursue that is self-reinforcing? Do people have to tell you when your work in this special activity is at a high level of proficiency, or do you set your own standards?

Social Learning in the Classroom

Children learn a great deal from observation in the classroom. The most obvious use of observation is instruction in new skills (e.g., math problems, art projects, science experiments). Other ways teachers can use modeling are to demonstrate logical thinking and problem-solving behavior by thinking out loud as they solve problems on the chalkboard and by displaying intellectual curiosity, emotional control, respect for and interest in others, and good listening and communication habits. Teachers who model such characteristics tend to induce those same qualities in students. However, teachers who exhibit negative social behaviors also induce the same qualities in students (Good & Brophy, 1987).

Clarizio (1980) provides an excellent example of how a teacher used modeling to develop students' interest in English literature. The teacher made it a practice to be reading an interesting book as the students entered the room. Sometimes he laughed out loud, frowned, smiled, or exhibited other behaviors that conveyed interest in the book. Some student always commented about the teacher's interest in the book. The teacher reinforced the student's interest by telling the class a little bit about the book or by reading some of the more humorous or exciting passages. He also asked students to talk about interesting books they had recently read. As an English teacher, he not only talked about the pleasure gained from reading but also demonstrated his own enjoyment and interest in reading. Can you think of other ways for a teacher to model important learning behaviors?

A good deal of classroom behavior is learned by vicariously experienced rewards and punishments. Kounin (1970) has found that interaction between a teacher and a student has an impact on other students who view the incident. When the teacher reprimands a student for inappropriate behavior, the whole class experiences the effect. You can encourage social control by discussing how one should behave in the classroom and pointing out how individual students and groups help to maintain this behavior. The identification and reinforcement of positive models provide clues for other class members. However, this same learning process works against the teacher if students see others getting away with misbehavior.

? When is modeling a more effective approach to instruction than shaping?

cognitive behavior modification. A technique that changes behavior by modifying an individual's inner, self-directive speech.

Modeling can be used to teach academic and motor skills and can have a strong effect on learning. It is especially useful when reliance on operant learning procedures would be less efficient or even dangerous. Would you want to be in a car in which the instructor was using a trial-and-error method of learning, waiting to reinforce the driver's correct response? In teaching by modeling, the instructor demonstrates how to perform the task or skill; the student observes this behavior and attempts to imitate the teacher or model. The student often is able to learn complete sequences of behavior in a much shorter time by modeling than by shaping.

Bandura (1977) states that the "failure of an observer to match the behavior of a model may result from any of the following: not observing the relevant activities, inadequately coding modeled events for memory representation, failing to retain what was learned, physical inability to perform, or experiencing insufficient incentives" (p. 29). Can you relate any of these factors to a specific instance in which an instructor's demonstration failed to result in learning? How does social cognitive theory help you suggest modifications in the instructor's approach?

COGNITIVE BEHAVIOR MODIFICATION

The latest development in behavioral psychology is the incorporation of various cognitive processes (i.e., thoughts, perceptions, expectancies, self-statements) within the behavioral framework. The theory behind these approaches is that children and adolescents have deficient cognitive processes that guide or control their behavior. If the cognitions that direct or control behavior can be altered, behavioral change will follow. These approaches are called **cognitive behavior modification**, *cognitive-behavioral therapy*, or *self-control.* As mentioned earlier, Bandura's (1977) social cognitive theory provided much of the theoretical support for the use of these approaches in the treatment of behavioral, emotional, and academic problems.

Self-Management

? How does cognitive behavior modification differ from traditional behavioral change procedures?

Several self-management or self-control therapies were developed in the 1960s and 1970s. Although early self-control procedures were based on operant principles of learning, developments during the 1970s led to more cognitive-oriented self-control procedures (Kendall & Braswell, 1985). In the traditional approach to applied behavioral analysis, the classroom teacher uses positive reinforcement and other procedures (e.g., modeling) to improve student behavior. Once the desired behavior changes are attained, a transfer of control is made from the teacher (external) to the student (self-regulation). The procedure involves *self-assessment,* whereby students determine whether they have performed specific behaviors; *self-monitoring,* whereby students monitor and record their performance of certain behaviors, keeping a record of how often and to what extent they engage in some activity (e.g., how many times they talk without permission); and *self-reinforcement,* whereby students give themselves reinforcement when they behave appropriately. After a period of time, the procedures permitting students to reinforce themselves for appropriate behavior are slowly removed, and control is shifted to reinforcers in the students' natural environment, like grades, social status, and achievement feedback (Workman, 1982).

Some of you may be thinking: "Can a teacher actually trust students to record information honestly and reinforce themselves?" Several studies indicate that students can be effectively trained to monitor their own behavior. In the early stages of this training, students are told that their individual assessments will be observed by the teacher. Self-monitoring accuracy does improve when individuals are informed that their accuracy is being assessed by someone else (Mace & Kratochwill, 1988). In fact, there is evidence that self-reinforcement procedures are generally as effective as teacher-administered consequences (Workman & Hector, 1978).

Today, more cognitively oriented self-control techniques are used. One way individuals have been taught to control their own behavior is through self-instruction, a type of self-control that is based on the work of Luria (1961) and Vygotsky (1962). Luria found that as children get older, they are able to inhibit behavior not only by following adult instructions but also by responding to their own self-directed instructions. Vygotsky described a progression from overt language to "internalized talking" and finally to silence. He pointed out that self-talk is important because it provides self-guidance.

Self-Verbalization

? How can self-verbalization modify behavior?

The theory behind self-verbalization training is that an individual's inner speech influences cognition (thinking) and guides behavior. Some children have inappropriate self-verbalizations and, therefore, act in an inappropriate manner. Thus if more appropriate self-verbalizations are introduced, behavior can be changed.

Meichenbaum and Goodman (1971) developed a cognitive modification program called *self-instructional training* to teach impulsive children to work more slowly and carefully. Each child observed a model who performed a task and simultaneously verbalized the procedures used. The model then verbally instructed the child while the child performed the task. Next, the child performed the task while instructing himself or herself and then tried the task while whispering the instruction to himself or herself. Finally, the child performed the task silently (using covert self-instruction).

The following is the verbalization produced by the model (Meichenbaum & Goodman, 1971); the purposes of particular statements are in parentheses:

> Okay, what is it I have to do (*problem definition*)? You want me to copy the picture with the different lines. I have to go slowly and carefully. Okay, draw the line down, down, good; then to the right, that's it; now down some more and to the left (*focusing attention and response guidance*). Good, I'm doing fine so far (*self-reinforcement*). Remember, go slowly. Now back up again. No, I was supposed to go down. That's okay. Just erase the line carefully . . . . Good. Even if I make an error, I can go on slowly and carefully (*self-evaluative coping skills and error-correcting options*). I have to go down now. Finished. I did it! (p. 117)

Initially, psychologists used cognitive behavior modification to help children in clinical settings with various behavior problems (e.g., impulsiveness, hyperactivity, aggression, and anxiety) to develop better self-control. More recent applications of self-verbalization training have been in cognitive learning, to help students develop cognitive strategies in academically relevant tasks (see Meichenbaum & Asarnow, 1979; Schunk, 1986, for a review of this literature).

Meichenbaum and Asarnow (1979) describe a self-verbalization training program in an academic area. The study was designed to increase junior high school children's reading comprehension. The researchers began by using task analysis to determine the specific strategies that poor readers needed to complete in order to read effectively. They were guided by the following questions: What should poor readers say to themselves before, during, and after reading a selection that would help to enhance understanding? What should they say when trying to answer questions about the reading?

By the last training session (Meichenbaum & Asarnow, 1979) the poor reader's internal dialogue was similar to the dialogue in the following modeled passage:

> Well, I've learned three big things to keep in mind before I read a story and while I read it. One is to ask myself what the main idea of the story is. What is the story about? A second is to learn important details of the story as I go along. The order of the main events or their sequence is an especially important detail. A third is to know how the characters feel and why. So get the main idea. Watch sequences. And learn how the characters feel and why.
>
> While I'm reading I should pause now and then. I should think of what I'm doing. And I should listen to what I'm saying to myself. Am I saying the right things?
>
> Remember, don't worry about mistakes. Just try again. Keep calm, and relaxed. Be proud of yourself when you succeed. Have a blast! (pp. 18–19)

The researchers reported an improvement in the reading skills of students who received this training as compared with a control group who did not receive self-verbalization training.

programmed instruction. An instructional procedure in which material is arranged in a particular sequence and in small steps.

teaching machine. A mechanical device incorporating a programmed learning format.

linear program. Programmed material presented in a manner so that all learners progress through the material in the same order.

INSTRUCTIONAL APPLICATIONS OF BEHAVIORAL LEARNING PRINCIPLES

A number of instructional programs have been developed from behavioral learning principles. As you read the material, see how each of the following behavioral principles is incorporated into the program:

- Identification of behavioral objectives
- Opportunities for frequent responding or practice
- Careful planning of the organization and sequencing of content
- Active student participation
- Immediate feedback and reinforcement

? How do programmed instruction and computer-assisted instruction employ behavioral principles of learning?

Programmed Instruction

In 1954, Skinner published a paper, "The Science of Learning and the Art of Teaching," about his laboratory techniques that modified the behavior of both animals and humans. He stated in detail the principles of operant conditioning and described methods for automating instruction to improve human learning in school settings. This paper provided the theoretical basis and provoked the enthusiasm for **programmed instruction**.

Programmed instruction works as a self-instructional package that presents a topic in a carefully planned sequence and requires the learner to respond to questions or statements by filling in blanks, selecting from a series of answers, or solving a problem. Immediate feedback occurs after each response, and students can work at their own rate. The program can be incorporated into books, **teaching machines**, or computers. (The next section of this chapter discusses computer-assisted instruction.) Those who advocate programmed instruction stress that it can improve classroom learning, presenting even the most difficult subjects in small steps so that all students can succeed at their own rates. Figures 2.4 and 2.5 illustrate two types of programs. Figure 2.4 presents a **linear program**, in which the programmer lays out the route or sequence of frames for all students to follow in completing the program. To avoid any error, each frame or segment of the program includes a small piece of knowledge. The frames in linear programs rarely include more than one or two sentences.

Sentence to Be Completed	Word to Be Supplied
1. The important parts of a flashlight are the battery and the bulb. When we "turn on" a flashlight, we close a switch which connects the battery with the ____________.	bulb
2. When we turn on a flashlight, an electric current flows through the fine wire in the ____________ and causes it to grow hot.	bulb
3. When the hot wire glows brightly, we say that it gives off or sends out heat and ____________.	light
4. The fine wire in the bulb is called a filament. The bulb "lights up" when the filament is heated up by the passage of a(n) ____________ current.	electric
5. When a weak battery produces little current, the fine wire, or ____________, does not get very hot.	filament
6. A filament which is *less* hot sends out or gives off ____________ light.	less
7. "Emit" means "send out." The amount of light sent out, or "emitted," by a filament depends on how ____________ the filament is.	hot

Figure 2.4 Part of a Linear Program in High School Physics.
Source: Skinner, 1958.

branching program. Programmed material that presents a variety of alternative routes through the material.

Figure 2.5 represents a **branching program**, in which a student's responses determine the route followed. Alternative routes, called "branches," are predictors of the problems the student may have in completing the program. These branches allow the student who has answered a question incorrectly to go back and review pertinent information about a concept and find out why the response was not correct. Students who do not make mistakes never see these frames and can skip to later frames in the program. The branching program typically presents more information per frame than the linear program: two or three paragraphs per frame, rather than one or two sentences per frame. Last, branching programs tend to use multiple-choice questions as the method of eliciting student responses. Students recognize the correct answer instead of constructing the response, as Skinner requires in his linear program. Each response to a question is keyed to a different page or frame in the program.

Programmed materials are not limited to pure linear or branching formats. For example, some branching programs can be modified for intelligence or achievement test scores. There are even "discovery programs," which present an experiment or problem followed by a multiple-choice question that calls for the student to derive a conclusion, hypothesis, or generalization.

Skinner (1954, 1986) points out why teaching machines are needed in the classroom: First, a long time between a response and its reinforcement is common. If you accept the premise that the immediacy of reinforcement is an important variable in learning, then handing back test papers two or three weeks after the examination or being unable to answer students' questions is a serious instructional problem that needs modification. Second, he criticizes the relative infrequency of the use of reinforcement in many classrooms. Finally, there is a lack of organized instructional

Page 6: A course *description* tells you something about the content and procedures of a course; a course *objective* describes a desired outcome of a course.

Whereas an objective tells what the learner is to be like as a result of some learning experiences, the course description tells only what the course is about.

The distinction is quite important, because a course description does not explain what will be accepted as adequate achievement; it does not confide to the learner the rules of the game. Though a course description might tell the learner which field he will be playing on, it doesn't tell him where the foul lines are, where the goalposts are located, or how he will know when he has scored.

It is useful to be able to recognize the difference between an objective and a description, so try an example.

Which of the statements below looks most like an *objective?*

To be able to explain the *principles for developing reading readiness in the primary grades . . .* **turn to page 7.**

Discusses principles, techniques, and procedures in developing reading readiness in the primary grades . . . **turn to page 8.**

Page 7: You said "To be able to explain the principles of reading readiness in the primary grades" was a statement of an objective.

You are correct! The statement describes an *aim* rather than a course. It doesn't do a very good job of it, but at least it does attempt to describe a goal rather than a process.

Now let us move on. **TURN TO PAGE 10**

Page 8: Oh, come on now! The collection of words that led you to this page is a piece of a course description, and not a very good description at that. I hope you are not being misled by the fact that college catalogs are composed of such phrases. They are *not* statements of intended learning outcomes and they are *not* what we are concerned with here.

Let me try to explain the difference this way. A course description describes various aspects of a PROCESS known as a "course." A course objective, on the other hand, is a description of a PRODUCT, of what the learner is supposed to be like as a *result* of the process.

Return to page 6 and read the material again.

Figure 2.5 Part of a Branching Program on Instructional Objectives.
Source: Mager, 1984.

sequence in the teaching of complex skills. Teachers do not carefully arrange material (stimuli to shape the learner's behavior) toward instructional objectives. Skinner believes that teaching machines deal with these concerns.

The research on programmed instruction has not been positive (see Rothrock, 1982). Although the results of different studies vary somewhat, the general conclusion is that programmed instruction has not lived up to the expectations of its proponents. Attention is now directed to computer-assisted instruction, which uses the same basic learning principles.

computer-assisted instruction (CAI). The use of a computer as tutor to present information, give students opportunities to practice what they learn, evaluate student achievement, and provide additional instruction.

Computer-Assisted Instruction (CAI)

The rapid development and dissemination of the microcomputer in the schools has created the opportunity for the use of these machines for individualizing instruction. **Computer-assisted instruction (CAI)** is an attempt to use the computer as a tutor to present information, give students opportunities to practice what they learn, evaluate student achievement, and provide additional instruction when needed. In many ways, CAI seeks to apply behavioral principles in a more efficient way than traditional programmed instruction.

computer-managed instruction (CMI). The use of a computer for managerial purposes in instruction.

In addition to instructional activities, the computer can be used for managerial purposes, such as determining error rates, student progress, class averages, and making assignments based on the diagnosis of student weaknesses. These functions all fall under the heading of **computer-managed instruction (CMI)**.

Vargas (1986) identified three major uses of CAI in schools: (1) *drill and practice,* (2) *simulation,* and (3) *tutoring.* The key to the effectiveness of CAI is the quality of the software (the programs that run the computer). Poorly developed software, like a disorganized lecture, will lead to little learning.

DRILL AND PRACTICE ACTIVITIES. The predominant use of CAI has been with drill and practice activities in the basic skill areas. Such programs are used with skills already learned in order to improve speed or accuracy. Many programs attempt to motivate students with gamelike formats and graphics presented as reinforcers. One commercially available drill and practice series of programs is Milliken's *Math Sequences.* These programs cover the range of mathematical computation skills for grades 1 through 8. The CAI part of the program provides the student with practice in basic skills. This practice gives the student one or more chances to answer the question correctly. If the student fails to answer the problem correctly, the computer provides prompts that guide the student to the correct response. When the student responds correctly, a graphic representation of a cartoon animal praises the student, and the program moves to the next problem. When the student successfully completes the assignment, the student is again praised by the computer and is moved to the next level of the program. The CMI features of the Milliken programs allow the teacher to make individual and class assignments, review individual and class performance, set individual performance levels for each student, and provide a printed record of student performance. These functions performed by the computer free the teacher to work on higher-level skills. Vargas (1986) points out that some drill and practice programs subvert their own goals by preventing students from working at top speed. The reason is that students are forced to wait until the visual and auditory entertainment (i.e., the "reinforcement") is completed before the next problem is presented.

SIMULATIONS. Simulations are programs that attempt to simulate or imitate an actual experience to provide students with opportunities to learn specific skills or improve decision-making or problem-solving processes. For example, there are simulations available to learn how to fly an airplane, run a business, respond to a crisis situation. There is a simulation program available for elementary students, called *Lemonade,* in which students manage a lemonade stand and earn or lose money on the basis of various decisions they are asked to make. A simulation for high school students, *Revolutions Past, Present, and Future,* is designed to teach students the development of revolutionary movements. Students use information from the American, French, and Russian revolutions to build a model of events leading up to a revolution. As more use is made of software that focuses on problem-solving skills in school, computers may contribute to the development of higher-level thinking as well as to practice in basic skills (Patterson & Smith, 1986). Vargas (1986) points out that simulations used properly can be an excellent teaching technique. However, it is often difficult to find a simulation to meet the particular instructional needs of the teacher. In addition, some programs may imitate very little of the actual events or decisions involved in a real-world situation.

TUTORIALS. The third category of CAI is tutorials, which are designed to teach new subject matter. These programs often consist of several screens of textual material, followed by exercises or questions. They are available in almost any subject area. Most tutorial systems can adapt instruction by using students' prior performance in the program to determine what material to present, its difficulty, and the rate of presentation. Vargas (1986) points out that many tutorials present several screens of text before calling for a student response, and that often they do not break down a skill into small steps that would be easier for the student to master.

Computer Competence

Martinez and Mead (1988) reported on the status of computer competence or computer literacy among school-age children in the United States. This evaluation involved African American, white, and Latino male and female students in grades 3, 7, and 11 from different geographical regions around the country. The items on the questionnaire included information on computer background (e.g., exposure to computers, courses taken, and other

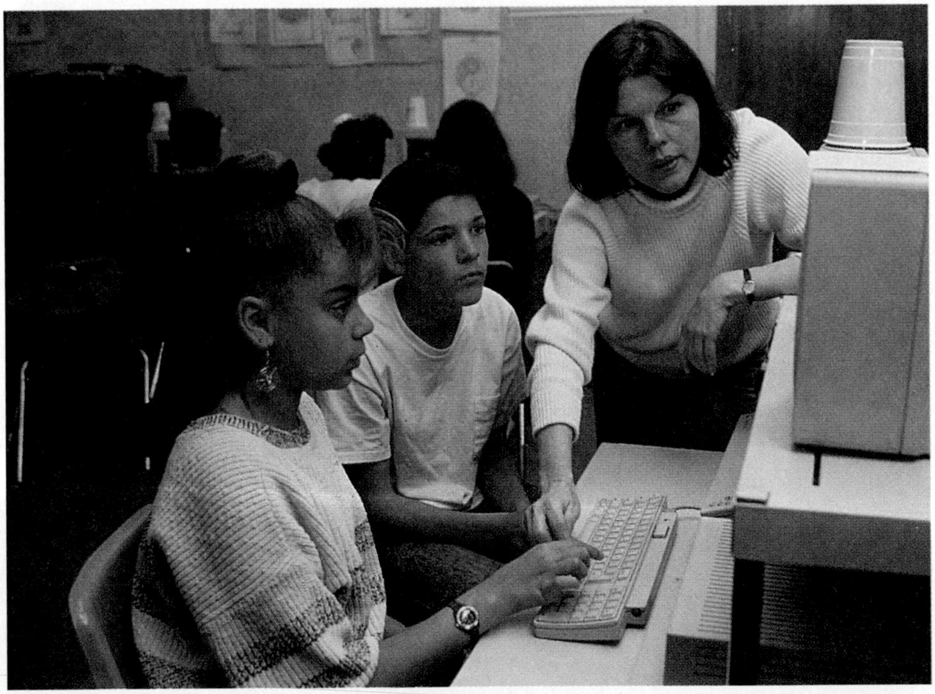

It is important that all students develop computer competence.

general computer-related information) and attitudes regarding computer use, computer knowledge, computer applications, and computer science/programming. The data indicated that most children had some familiarity with and practical knowledge of computers. However, only a small fraction of the students were able to answer questions about important computer applications or about programming (no grade averaged at least 50 percent of the items correct). Table 2.2 identifies student responses to the frequency of computer use in subject areas. The data indicate that computers are seldom used in the students' academic courses. When the machines are used, they are mainly confined to computing classes.

TABLE 2.2 FREQUENCY OF COMPUTER USE IN SUBJECT AREAS

How Often Do You Use a Computer to:	Almost Every Day	Several Times a Week	About Once a Week	Less Than Once a Week	Never
	Frequency—Grade 7				
Practice math	5.7%	4.7%	9.8%	17.5%	62.3%
Practice reading	3.1	3.8	5.9	8.8	78.4
Practice spelling	2.8	3.3	7.8	10.0	76.1
Do science problems	1.9	2.9	3.1	6.8	85.3
Learn and make music	2.4	3.0	6.2	10.3	78.1
Play games	19.4	15.4	16.3	24.6	24.3
	Frequency—Grade 11				
Practice math	3.4%	3.0%	3.6%	12.1%	77.9%
Practice reading	1.8	2.1	2.0	6.9	87.2
Practice spelling	1.4	1.6	2.8	6.7	87.5
Do science problems	0.8	1.5	1.9	8.6	87.2
Learn and make music	1.4	1.7	2.2	9.0	85.6
Play games	8.5	9.8	14.0	33.9	33.8

Source: Martinez and Mead, 1988.

The following are important additional findings of the evaluation (Martinez & Mead, 1988):

- Most students like using computers and want greater access to them.
- Much learning about computers takes place outside of school and independent of formal instruction.
- Males, in general, demonstrate a slightly higher level of computer competence than females.
- There are clear racial/ethnic differences in computer competence, favoring White students over African American and Latino students.
- Students whose parents are college graduates and from high socioeconomic backgrounds are more likely to have used a computer, to be studying computers in school, and to have a computer at home.

- Many computer coordinators have minimal training in computer studies and rate themselves mediocre in their ability to use computers. (p. 6)

The evaluators were concerned with the equity issue relating to computer competence. That is, as knowledge and use of computers becomes increasingly important in the workplace, minority students will be at a serious disadvantage when they seek employment. As a result, it is important that educators develop policies to ensure that all students have equal access to computers and develop competency in their use.

Research on CAI

In general, traditional computer-assisted instruction (i.e., the computer used as a personal tutor) has a moderately positive effect on student achievement (Bangert-Drowns, Kulik, & Kulik, 1985; Kulik, Kulik, & Bangert-Drowns, 1985). However, there is limited research on other uses of computers. CAI is more successful when it supplements the regular classroom instruction than when it is used to replace classroom instruction entirely. The positive effects of CAI appear to be greatest for elementary and secondary students and less effective for college students (Tobias, 1985). As yet, we cannot determine the total impact of computers on students (Lepper & Gurtner, 1989).

It appears that the computer revolution is years away. Two major problems limit the use of computers in the classroom: the availability of appropriate software and cost considerations. Most teachers are fortunate if they have one or two computers in their classrooms. Even in classes with as many as eight computers, students spend a great deal of time waiting for a turn at the computer (Center for Social Organization, 1984).

In the 1950s and 1960s some educators believed that programmed instruction would replace teachers. Similar claims were made for motion pictures and instructional television. Today we hear that computers will revolutionize education because they have the ability to *interact* with students by allowing them to learn at their own rate and giving them practice on needed skills. Vargas (1986) states that computers have the ability to teach effectively if the programmers writing the software use features that are necessary for learning: "a high rate of relevant responding, appropriate stimulus control, immediate feedback, and techniques of successive approximations" (p. 744). All of these components are basic behavioral principles identified by Skinner decades ago.

With the vast amount of CAI software on the market, it is important that you carefully evaluate the effectiveness of software before making any purchase (see Lillie, Hannum, & Stuck, 1989, and Sloane et al., 1989, for some helpful hints). The evaluation checklist in Figure 2.6 identifies important questions for you to consider. In addition, there are several magazines that evaluate software, such as *Electronic Learning*. Also, many large school districts have computer centers where teachers can try out various computers and educational programs before ordering them for the classroom.

______ 1. Will the program run on the computer(s) you have available?
______ 2. Do the objectives of the program match your classroom objectives?
______ 3. Is the content accurate and at the appropriate level for your students?
______ 4. Are instructions clear and easy to understand?
______ 5. Do screen graphics enhance rather than interfere with learning?
______ 6. Does the program encourage and allow students to work at their own rate of speed?
______ 7. Are students required to decide between at least two responses when presented with a question?
______ 8. Does the program provide accurate and corrective feedback?
______ 9. Are students able to see their progress on a daily basis?
______ 10. Does the program adjust to the performance level of the students?
______ 11. Does the program handle student errors adequately?
______ 12. Can the program keep records of student and class progress?
______ 13. Is it possible for the teacher to add to the content of the program?
______ 14. Is support or help available to the teacher through either the distributor or manufacturer?

Figure 2.6 Evaluation Checklist for Educational Software.
Source: Electronic Learning's Inservice Workshop, 1983, and Vargas, 1986.

DEBATE FORUM

Do Media Influence Learning?

In 1983, Richard Clark wrote an article reviewing the effectiveness of media in education.

Argument: No evidence suggests that students learn more from new electronic media (e.g., television, films, computers) than they would from reading a textbook or listening to a presentation by a teacher. In Clark's words: "The best current evidence is that media are mere vehicles that deliver instruction but do not influence student achievement any more than the truck that delivers our groceries causes changes in our nutrition" (p. 445). Clark argues that media may make learning quicker and more economical, and make knowledge more accessible to learners—all excellent reasons for using electronic delivery systems over others (e.g., teachers and books)—but that media have not been proved more or less *instructionally effective.*

Counterargument: The medium itself does not influence learning, but certain attributes of media influence the development of certain thinking processes (Kozma, 1991; Salomon, 1979). *Media attributes* include the ability of television and movies to "zoom" into detail or to reflect three-dimensional objectives. New media like interactive videodisc technology (which allows viewers not only to see and hear but also to interact with computer-controlled programs) provide "unique mixes" of attributes that do make original contribu-

Mastery Learning

mastery learning. An instructional strategy that allows students to study material until they master it.

In 1968, Bloom and Keller published important articles describing methods for increasing student mastery over content in a regular class or course. Bloom emphasized the importance of improving the achievement of students in elementary and secondary schools. Although the roots for his system of **mastery learning** initially came from the writings of John Carroll (1963), the implementation of his system uses operant conditioning principles.

Mastery learning is a type of instruction that emphasizes student mastery of specific learning objectives and uses corrective instruction to achieve that goal. Mastery learning assumes that virtually all students can learn what is taught in school if their "instruction is approached systematically, if students are helped when and where they have learning difficulties, if they are given sufficient time to achieve mastery, and if there is some clear criterion of what constitutes mastery" (Bloom, 1974, p. 6).

tions to learning (Kozma, 1991). An example would be the teacher's ability to visually simulate very complex and time-consuming experiments in chemistry in a very short time span.

Response: "No one media attribute has a unique cognitive effect," since there are "a variety of equally effective ways to highlight details" other than "zooming" (Clark, 1991, p. 35).

Counterargument: Media research indicates that computer-assisted instruction leads to greater achievement when compared with traditional forms of instruction.

Response: When computers show an increase over traditional methods of instruction, "it is not the computer [itself] but the teaching methods built into [it] that accounts for the learning gains" (Clark, 1991, p. 36). In experiments where the same group of teachers design a CAI presentation *and* a live teaching presentation, no achievement differences are found between the CAI and teacher-taught students. Only when different teachers design CAI and live presentations do achievement gains favor the computer. Clark claims that, in such studies, the computer group achievement is due to the fact that more time and money are provided for investment in CAI design than in traditional teaching presentations.

What do you think? What is your experience learning from different media? Do you think there are some special advantages of using media? When would you use media in instruction? How could you learn about the effectiveness of a particular type of media?

Although the roots of mastery learning can be found in the writings of many educators as far back as the 1920s, Carroll is credited with providing the theoretical background and Benjamin Bloom with designing the basic instructional process for mastery learning (Guskey, 1985). In 1963, Carroll published an article entitled "A Model of School Learning," in which he challenged the traditional view that student aptitude determined how much knowledge would be learned in a given course. Carroll pointed out that student aptitude reflected an index of learning rate. That is, most students have the ability to learn what is presented in school, but they differ in the time it takes them to learn the material. When aptitude is viewed as an indicator of learning rate, youngsters are not viewed as good or poor students but rather as fast or slow learners.

Carroll proposed a model of school learning based on the belief that if each student were allowed the time needed to learn the material, and the time was spent appropriately, then the student would be able to achieve the specified learning objectives. However, if all students were given the same time to learn the material, many students would not attain the level of knowledge expected by the instructor. Carroll expressed the degree of learning attained by a student in the following equation:

$$\text{Degree of learning} = f\,(\text{time spent}/\text{time needed})$$

That is, the degree of learning is a function of the amount of time spent learning, relative to the amount of time the student needs to spend to learn the material.

Bloom (1968, 1974) was impressed by Carroll's perspective on teaching and learning. If aptitude were related to the time a student needed to learn, then it would be possible to modify the nature of instruction to ensure that almost all students mastered the material presented in a given course.

Bloom noted that in traditional methods, teachers organized instruction into units that usually corresponded to chapters in a textbook. After the instruction, teachers tested students to determine how much knowledge they had acquired. Because of the cumulative nature of the knowledge, students who failed to master the material in the first unit were likely to have problems mastering the material in the second, third, and succeeding units. Thus, as the course proceeded, some students mastered less material and got further behind the rest of the class.

Bloom believed that dividing the instruction into small units and checking on learning progress at the end of each unit were useful instructional techniques. However, although the quizzes or tests at the end of the unit helped the teacher and students to determine what had been learned, the tests were of little value to the students in helping them to master more knowledge.

Bloom set out to develop an instructional approach that would produce better results. What was needed, he believed, was some type of feedback and corrective process that would diagnose individual learning difficulties (feedback) and prescribe specific remediation procedures (correctives) to help students learn the material.

In the section that follows on **Personalized System of Instruction (PSI)**, I identify an *individually based, student-paced* program in which students typically learn independently of their classmates. Bloom wanted to develop a system that was a *group-based, teacher-paced* approach to instruction, in which students learn, for the most part, cooperatively with their classmates (Guskey, 1985).

Personalized System of Instruction (PSI). An individually based, student-paced form of mastery learning developed by Keller.

formative test. The measurement of student achievement before or during instruction.

summative test. The measurement of student achievement at the end of an instructional unit.

? How does mastery learning attempt to improve student learning?

Bloom outlined his innovative teaching-learning strategy as follows: The content is divided into small learning units comprising one to two weeks of instructional time. After the material from the unit is presented, a **formative test** is administered to determine each student's progress and to identify areas in which more instruction is needed. A high level of performance is required (usually 80–90 percent correct) on each formative test for the student to move to enrichment activities or another unit of instruction. Students who have not mastered the material are engaged in corrective work for a class period or two following the formative test. Students are provided with alternative learning resources such as additional lectures, small-group instruction, different textbooks, filmstrips, study guides, or worksheets. Then they are administered another formative test to ensure that they have mastered the unit before moving on to the next unit. The students who demonstrate that they have mastered the material are given special enrichment activities to expand their knowledge. At the end of a series of units, the teacher evaluates the final competence of students by giving a **summative test** covering the objectives in the units. If the program is successful, almost all the students should attain a high score on the examination and would be more similar in their achievement levels as compared with traditional instructional programs. In addition to improved achievement, Bloom (1971) believed that mastery learning would lead to many important affective outcomes such as improved attitude toward the subject matter and a more positive academic self-concept.

CRITICISMS OF MASTERY LEARNING. Arlin (1984) has raised an important issue regarding the use of instructional time in mastery learning. He argues that there is a time-achievement dilemma involved in mastery learning programs. By this he means that low achievers in group-based mastery learning do better because of corrective instruction, but faster students may be slowed down waiting for the other students to catch up. Arlin argues that the time needed to bring slow learners up to mastery must come from somewhere. If the corrective procedures are done during regular class time, then content coverage may be reduced. Cox and Dunn (1979) raise additional concerns about the implementation of mastery learning: First, not all teachers have the ability to identify prerequisite skills and begin instruction at the proper level. Second, some students may actually develop poor study habits from recycling by using the "principle of least effort," whereby they may risk failure on the first examination to

CLASSROOM Application

DEVELOPING AND IMPLEMENTING A MASTERY LEARNING PROGRAM

Block and Anderson (1975) recommend the following procedures for developing and implementing mastery learning in the classroom:

- *Develop instructional objectives* from your textbook using the *Taxonomy of Educational Objectives: Cognitive Domain* to ensure that the objectives cover various levels of complexity (the Taxonomy of Educational Objectives is discussed in Chapter 6). The chapter headings and subheadings of your textbook can be used as a guide in determining course objectives.
- *Construct the final examination* on the basis of the objectives of the course. The test results should be based on each student's mastery of the objectives (called *criterion-referenced measurement*; see Chapter 12) rather than on how much each has learned relative to other students in the class. It is useful to write test items on separate 3-by-5 index cards for each objective in the course.
- *Select a mastery performance standard* that reflects the level of performance on the test that you would be willing to accept as indicating mastery over the course objectives. There are no specific guidelines for making this decision. Many teachers set the criterion for mastery at the percentage of correct answers needed to obtain a grade of A, which is usually 90 percent. In some cases, a teacher may establish mastery performance standards for different parts of the test that cover objectives of varied importance. If some students' performance is not indicative of mastery, you need to decide whether to give no grade or a grade of incomplete. If this cannot be done in your school district, then establish levels for B through F work. Discuss these standards with the students before implementing the mastery program.
- *Break the course into a series of units* of instruction and decide how you will teach the material in each unit. In most cases, whole-class instruction will be used.
- *Develop formative and summative quizzes* to determine student progress in meeting the objectives of the units. The quizzes should be parallel in that they should measure the same content, be of the same level of difficulty, and not take more than 15 to 20 minutes to complete.

- *Give students either corrective instruction or enrichment activities,* depending on the results of the formative quiz. Providing corrective instruction for those students who did not attain mastery is the most important aspect of mastery learning. The corrective instruction can be given outside the regular instructional time, either during the school day or after school. This is one way to deal with the time problem raised by the critics of mastery learning.
- *Give enrichment activities* to students who have mastered the material as demonstrated by their scores on the formative test. These activities should broaden the students' understanding of the material and may involve special reading assignments, writing essays in an area of interest, and other types of independent research.

Block and Anderson characterize different follow-up activities according to whether they can be used for (1) *individual* students or (2) a *group* of students, and whether they focus on different ways of (3) *presenting* the content or (4) *involving* students in learning the material. Table 2.3 summarizes the types of instructional materials and activities that can be used in the classroom.

- *Present the summative quiz and report the scores to students* when you feel that the corrective instruction has been sufficient to remediate learning difficulties. If certain students still have not attained the specified mastery level, you can repeat the corrective instruction–summative test cycle.
- *Grade students for mastery* at the end of the course and evaluate the effectiveness of the program. Determine what changes need to be made before the next semester. Check the Suggestions for Further Reading at the end of this chapter for additional references on establishing a mastery learning program.

TABLE 2..3 EXAMPLES OF FOLLOW-UP ACTIVITIES USED FOR DIFFERENT INSTRUCTIONAL PURPOSES

Instructional Procedure	Individual Students	Groups	Focus on Presenting Content	Focus on Involving Students
Alternative textbooks to give students a different presentation of the material	X		X	
Workbooks to give students more familiarity with the text-book material	X		X	

continued

TABLE 2..3 CONTINUED

Instructional Procedure	Individual Students	Groups	Focus on Presenting Content	Focus on Involving Students
Flash cards to give students repeated exposure to the material	X		X	
Reteaching to review material by using examples or illustrations different from those first used		X	X	
Audiovisual aids to provide instruction focusing on the visual or sensory modalities	X	X	X	
Token economies to stimulate interest by giving students tokens or points in exchange for a particular level of academic performance (see Chapter 7)	X			X
Academic games to create interest among students who have similar learning problems		X		X
Group affective exercises to deal with students' feelings and attitudes (see discussion of values clarification in Chapter 5)		X		X
Programmed instruction to provide a simplified presentation of the material	X		X	X
Tutoring to involve students who have mastered the material as classroom aides; can also use older students working with younger students	X		X	X
Small-group study sessions to enable students to discuss material that is giving them problems		X	X	X

Source: Adapted from Block and Anderson, 1975.

discover the minimal knowledge that must be learned to pass the second examination. Also, constant recycling among slower students may cause them to develop negative self-concepts—exactly the opposite of what the proponents state mastery learning will eliminate! Third, if the teacher believes that mastery learning can solve most or all the problems of individual differences with a group of students who lack the intellectual skills and/or cognitive strategies to learn the material, the teacher may be taking on an unreasonable responsibility. Cox and Dunn state:

> Certain instructional objectives have a higher probability of achievement for some learners than for others. Obviously, time and resources for recycling and building of the missing prerequisites are not unlimited. So it naturally follows that some objectives or sequences of objectives differ in their appropriateness for various learners. (p. 28)

Fourth, there is a difference between earning an A in the course and attaining mastery of the material. Students may be led to believe that they know more than they really do because the criteria selected for mastery are low. In summary, the proponents of mastery learning believe that individual differences in achievement can be reduced or minimized by carefully designing instruction. Critics of the system believe that the proponents underestimate the difficulties of implementing the system in a class with diverse individual abilities and feel that time limitations prevent all or most students from mastering the same objectives without a decrease in content coverage.

RESEARCH ON MASTERY LEARNING. Since 1968, many school districts have implemented different types of mastery learning programs, and researchers have conducted numerous investigations concerning the effectiveness of these programs (see Block, Efthim, & Burns, 1989). When reviewing research on mastery learning, it is important that you determine how the program is organized and implemented before you reach any conclusions regarding the effectiveness of the programs. For example, one major variable in the effectiveness of programs is the amount of time that is allotted to corrective instruction. Few differences have been found in evaluations of mastery and nonmastery programs when the instructional time was the same (Kersh, 1972; Slavin & Karweit, 1984).

One of the first major reviews of mastery learning was conducted by Block and Burns (1976), who found positive effects of the programs but not as large as mastery learning advocates often indicate. Almost all programs produced more learning and less variability in achievement than nonmastery approaches. In addition, the researchers found positive effects in the affective domain (i.e., students' attitudes toward the subject and how they felt about themselves as learners). Guskey and Gates (1986) completed an analysis of the research on group-based mastery learning in both elementary and secondary classrooms. Although they substantiated earlier findings of positive achievement gains compared with nonmastery approaches, they reported wide differences in gains from study to study.

More recently, Slavin (1987) completed a review of group-based mastery learning that was more critical than any of the past reviews. He found that long-term experiments lasting four weeks to months were not as effective as shorter studies of four weeks or less. The implication is that researchers need to show significant gains over longer periods of time to support interventions in schools. He also reported that standardized achievement tests showed fewer gains than did experimenter-made tests. This result may be caused by the fact that the experimenter-made tests emphasized the material in the mastery learning curriculum more than that in the conventionally taught curriculum. Finally, his data supported Arlin's (1984) criticism that slower-learning students are helped at the expense of faster-learning students.

Personalized System of Instruction (PSI)

Keller (1968) established an individually based, student-paced form of mastery learning. Although there are many variations of Keller's program in use, most courses include the following five features: *self-pacing, unit mastery,* a *minimum of lectures,* an emphasis on *written assignments,* and the use of *undergraduate or graduate proctors* (Johnson & Ruskin, 1977).

Self-pacing. The students are given course assignments divided into small units of homework. The number and size of the units vary depending on the discipline and the instructor. Students work at their own rate and decide when to complete their course assignments. Thus they take exams on material when they are ready—not when the instructor decides to give an exam!

Unit mastery. Students proceed to new course material only after demonstrating mastery of the previous unit or assignment. They are able to take tests as many times as necessary until mastery (as identified by each instructor before the course begins) is reached. In the original PSI courses, Keller graded students by the number of units they completed (75 percent of final grade) and their score on a final examination (25 percent of final grade).

Lectures. Lectures in PSI are not used as the main vehicle for information dissemination. In fact, students are not even required to attend lectures (. . . now you're getting more interested in this section!). Lectures are used as a motivational device to present new and interesting material not covered in the individual units. Students who complete specified units are permitted to attend, and no examinations are given on the material.

Written assignments. Rather than passively listening to lectures, the students are actively reading, studying, and writing on their own. Study guides, prepared by the instructor and keyed to a specific text or supplemental readings, provide the goals or objectives for each unit, include an introduction section explaining how the new material relates to material already learned, suggest strategies for mastering the material, and often include sample quizzes for self-assessment to ensure mastery of the material.

Proctors. An important feature of PSI is the use of proctors who have passed the course with an A grade. In the early formulation of the course, Keller assigned 10 students to each undergraduate proctor. Today graduate student proctors also are used in most PSI courses. They maintain regular office hours and meet weekly with the instructor to discuss the course organization. In most PSI courses the proctor (1) scores and evaluates each student's quizzes over the units, (2) points out areas on the quizzes where material has not been mastered, (3) suggests ways to improve study skills, and (4) encourages consistent progress throughout the course.

CRITICISMS OF PSI. In general, PSI has received positive reactions among college students. However, some students (see Gasper, 1980) would like more group discussions and interaction among students. Other students complain that the program demands more self-discipline than they are willing or able to exert. There is also concern that the program best fits courses with highly structured content, such as mathematics, chemistry, and engineering, but is less useful in courses like literature, history, and philosophy, in which analysis and evaluation activities are stressed. Jaynes (1975) expressed his dismay with PSI when he stated:

> I object to the too arrogant standardization that it imposes upon the mind. . . . What the Keller Method in complex subjects does is to grind down the individual student's particular style of going over things. It rebukes his wish to insert his own importances. (p. 631)

RESEARCH ON PSI. Kulik, Kulik, and Cohen (1979) compared 75 courses taught both conventionally and by PSI and found that "PSI produces superior student achievement, less variation in achievement, and high student ratings on college courses, but does not affect course withdrawal or student study time in these courses" (p. 307). Most students enrolled in PSI courses appear to like the self-paced arrangements, the availability for personal tutoring, and the ability to obtain a high grade if specific requirements are met. However, the PSI format works best for students who have the self-discipline and motivation to learn independently (Johnson & Ruskin, 1977).

Would you like to take a mastery learning or PSI course? What factors seem most appealing to you? What factors would you be most concerned about? Think about these questions from the role of both a teacher and a student.

Summary

CLASSICAL AND OPERANT CONDITIONING

1. Early behavioral psychologists viewed learning as forming connections or associations between a stimulus and a response.
2. Skinner believes that all behavior is learned. Most learning occurs because of operant conditioning—a situation in which a response is made more probable or frequent as the result of immediate reinforcement.

APPLIED BEHAVIOR ANALYSIS

3. Applied behavior analysis is the extension of operant conditioning principles to change the behavior of humans in natural settings. It is based on specific methodology and evaluation procedures.
4. The basis of applied behavior analysis in teaching involves (a) specifying the desired instructional objective, structuring lessons in small steps, and presenting the steps in a sequence; (b) providing for involvement in a lesson by encouraging students to respond to various questions and problems; (c) providing immediate feedback to student responses to all questions, quizzes, and homework assignments; and (d) reinforcing students for correct answers, proper study habits, and other desirable classroom behavior.
5. Students may respond differently to various types of reinforcements.
6. Behavior is influenced by different schedules of reinforcement—fixed and variable ratio, and fixed and variable interval.
7. In attempting to reinforce behavior, you should reinforce behavior immediately. Start by reinforcing appropriate behavior continuously, and then move to a variable schedule to maintain the behavior. Be sure not to reinforce undesired behavior.
8. Shaping and modeling are important procedures for developing new behaviors.

SOCIAL COGNITIVE THEORY

9. Observational learning can occur without any immediate reinforcement.
10. There are four important processes in observational learning: attention, retention, motor reproduction, and motivation.
11. Reinforcement in social cognitive theory is viewed as a source of information and an incentive rather than as a consequent condition of behavior.
12. Vicarious reinforcement and self-reinforcement can be effective alternatives to direct reinforcement.
13. Cognitive processes can be incorporated in behavioral approaches to help individuals guide or control their own behavior.

INSTRUCTIONAL APPLICATIONS OF BEHAVIORAL LEARNING PRINCIPLES

14. Programmed instruction and computer-assisted instruction (CAI) use the principles of operant conditioning in presenting information to students.
15. Students seldom use computers in their academic courses.
16. Much learning about computers takes place outside of school and independent of formal instruction. African American and Latino students may have less access to computers than white students do.
17. Teachers need to evaluate the effectiveness of all computer software.
18. When comparing the use of media with traditional instructional methods, researchers disagree over whether media are more effective or simply more efficient.
19. Mastery learning programs can be established to ensure higher levels of learning for most students.
20. Personalized System of Instruction (PSI) is an individually based, student-paced form of mastery learning.

Reflecting on Behavioral Approaches to Learning

1. Evaluate the Impact of Operant Conditioning

According to Skinner, we are all products of operant conditioning. We learn appropriate and inappropriate behavior according to the same principles. To what extent do you agree with this statement? Can you use operant conditioning principles to explain some of your own behavior (both positive and negative)?

2. Identify Appropriate Reinforcers

The importance of choosing appropriate reinforcers was emphasized in the chapter. Assume that someone is going to reinforce one of your behaviors. Select two or three reinforcers that you believe would be effective in modifying your behavior.

3. Use Shaping to Change Behavior

Identify an individual with whom you have had contact (e.g., a sibling or friend). Specify a behavior you would like to develop by using a shaping procedure. Outline the starting point you would select and the successive approximations you would go through (Martin & Pear, 1988).

4. Discuss the Usefulness of Teaching Machines, Computers, and/or Programmed Textbooks

How do you regard the use of teaching machines, computers, and programmed textbooks? Do they adequately solve the problem of providing efficient individualized instruction? In what situations would you prefer to be taught by a machine or a program rather than a teacher? What factors would influence your decisions?

5. Plan a Lesson Using Applied Behavior Analysis

Plan a lesson, and point out how you can use principles of operant conditioning to improve learning. Be specific in identifying the principles used in your lesson.

Key Terms

unconditioned stimulus, p. 41
unconditioned response, p. 41
conditioned stimulus, p. 41
conditioned response, p. 41
classical conditioning, p. 41
stimulus generalization, p. 41
extinction, p. 42
connectionism, p. 42
law of effect, p. 43
reward, p. 43
law of exercise, p. 43
respondent, p. 44
operant, p. 44
operant conditioning, p. 45
applied behavior analysis, p. 46
baseline, p. 46
behavior modification, p. 48
discriminative stimulus, p. 48
reinforcing stimulus, p. 48
discrimination learning, p. 49
response generalization, p. 49
positive reinforcement, p. 50
negative reinforcement, p. 50
punishment, p. 50
time-out, p. 51
primary reinforcement, p. 51
secondary reinforcement, p. 51
Premack's principle, p. 51
fixed-ratio schedule, p. 53
variable-ratio schedule, p. 53
fixed-interval schedule, p. 53
variable-interval schedule, p. 53
spontaneous recovery, p. 55
shaping, p. 55
prompting, p. 56
fading, p. 56
modeling , p. 57
social cognitive theory, p. 57
reciprocal determinism, p. 57
inhibitory-disinhibitory effect, p. 58
eliciting effect, p. 58
self-efficacy, p. 59
vicarious reinforcement, p. 60
self-reinforcement, p. 60
cognitive behavior modification, p. 62
programmed instruction, p. 65
teaching machine, p. 65
linear program, p. 65
branching program, p. 66
computer-assisted instruction (CAI), p. 67
computer-managed instruction (CMI), p. 68
mastery learning, p. 73
Personalized System of Instruction (PSI), p. 75
formative test, p. 75
summative test, p. 75

Suggestions for Further Reading

Hughes, J. N. (1988). *Cognitive behavior therapy with children in schools.* New York: Pergamon. An excellent discussion of cognitive-behavioral approaches for helping children who display emotional and behavioral problems.

Jenson, W. R., Sloane, H. N., & Young, K. R. (1988). *Applied analysis in education: A structured teaching approach.* Englewood Cliffs, NJ: Prentice-Hall. A good reference for how behavioral principles are used in instruction.

Kazdin, A. E. (1978). *History of behavior modification: Experimental foundations of contemporary research.* Baltimore: University Park Press. Provides a comprehensive review of the history of behavioral psychology.

Witt, J. C., Elliott, S. N., & Gresham, F. M. (1988). *Handbook of behavior therapy in education.* New York: Plenum. A detailed discussion of behavioral analysis and intervention in educational settings.

To learn more about Skinner's theory of learning:

Skinner, B. F. (1948). *Walden two.* New York: Macmillan. The novel in which Skinner conceives of a utopia based on the application of science to human behavior.

Skinner, B. F. (1968). *The technology of teaching.* New York: Appleton-Century-Crofts. Includes some of Skinner's most important writings.

Skinner, B. F. (1971). *Beyond freedom and dignity.* New York: Knopf. Skinner asserts that we are not free to choose because our choices are made on the basis of what has happened to us in the past.

The following books describe how to organize and implement a mastery learning program:

Block, J. H., & Anderson, L. W. (1975). *Mastery learning in classroom instruction.* New York: Macmillan.

Block, J. H., Efthim, H. E., & Burns, R. B. (1989). *Building effective mastery learning schools.* White Plains, NY: Longman.

Guskey, T. R. (1985). *Implementing mastery learning.* Belmont, CA: Wadsworth.

Issues regarding the use of computers in education are discussed in the following:

Lillie, D. L., Hannum, W. H., & Stuck, G. B. (1989). *Computers and effective instruction.* White Plains, NY: Longman. Includes a guide for assessing software.

Savas, S. D., & Savas, E. S. (1985). *Teaching children to use computers: A friendly guide.* New York: Teachers College Press. A clearly written introduction to programming.

Sloane, H. N., Gordon, H. M., Gunn, C., & Mickelsen, V. G. (1989). *Evaluating educational software: A guide for teachers.* Englewood Cliffs, NJ: Prentice-Hall. Offers guidelines for assessing student needs, evaluating instructional software, and evaluating the adequacy of a program.

White, C. S., & Hubbard, G. (1988). *Computers and education.* New York: Macmillan. A small book on the basics of computer uses in education.

Chapter 3

Cognitive Approaches to Learning

Acquiring and Using Learning Strategies

The Information-Processing System

Short-Term Sensory Store

Working Memory

Long-Term Memory

Executive Control—Metacognition

Learning: Cognition and Metacognition

Basic and Complex Knowledge

Cognitive Strategies: Declarative Knowledge

Rehearsal

Elaboration

Organization

Classroom Application: Using Cognitive Strategies in an Educational Psychology Course

Instructional Procedures to Aid Elaboration and Organization

Classroom Application: Applying Cognitive Psychology to Learning and Teaching

Cognitive Strategies: Procedural Knowledge

Pattern-Recognition Knowledge

Action-Sequence Knowledge

Thinking Skills

Debate Forum: How Should Thinking Skills Be Taught?

Teaching for Thinking

Classroom Application: Learning Strategies for Reading Comprehension

Classroom Application: Learning Strategies for Writing

Classroom Application: Learning Strategies for Mathematics

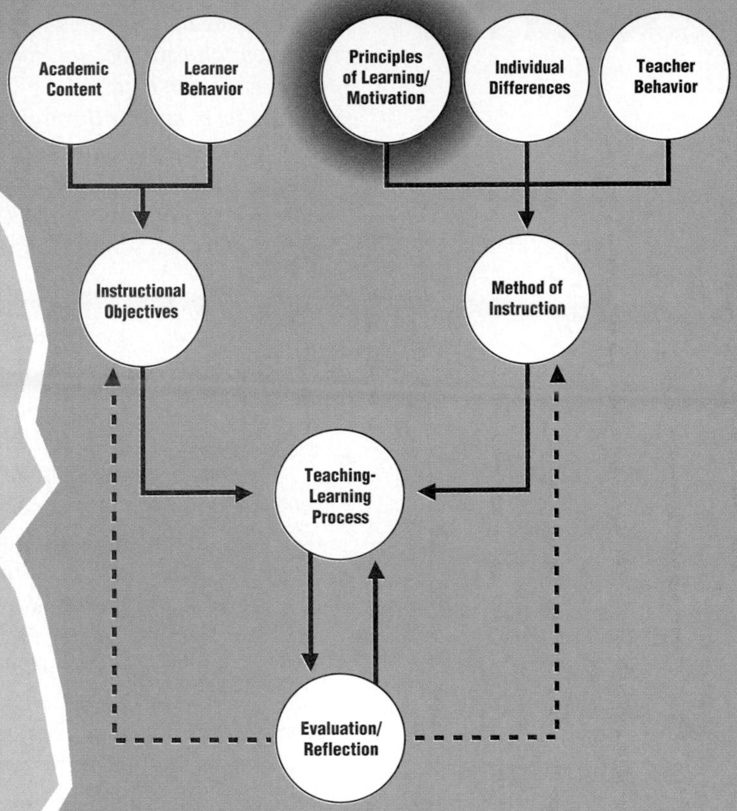

OBJECTIVES

After mastering the material in this chapter you will be able to:

- Identify how the information processing system influences learning.
- Use learning strategies to become a more effective learner.
- Plan and implement lessons based on declarative and procedural learning tasks.
- Teach students learning strategies to make them more effective learners.

Orientation

Barry Park had decided to take Mr. Johnson's "America Goes to War" class as an elective in his senior year. He had always been interested in wars and the military and thought that this class would probably be easy. As he soon discovered, however, Bob Johnson took his course seriously and expected that his students would do the same. He required a great deal of research on the part of his students, and his tests were known throughout the school as being very challenging.

As the first examination date approached, Barry realized that he needed to organize the material and to develop better study techniques. Fortunately for Barry, Mary Washington was taking the class, and she offered to be his study partner. Here is a glimpse of their first study session:

Barry: *We have a week, Mary, to study for this test. What's the first thing we need to do?*

Mary: *We know he's going to ask us about the ten major wars in America's history, so the first thing we need to do is memorize them. I took another class with Mr. Johnson, and he showed us how to use different study methods to learn new material.*

Barry: *What do you want me to do, now?*

Mary: *Well, why don't you make a list of the wars from the beginning.*

Barry: *Okay, if we write them down, in order, they would be the Revolutionary War . . . then the War of 1812 . . . the Mexican War . . . followed by the Civil War . . . and the Spanish American . . . then World War One . . . Two . . . and Korea . . . Vietnam, and finally the Persian Gulf. Now how do we memorize these?*

Mary: *If we use the first letter of each war, we can make a little saying like we did when we were taking music lessons from Mrs. Jones, remember?*

Barry: *And she wanted us to memorize the lines and spaces.*

Mary: *Right.*

Barry: *Okay, let's see . . .* R,W,M,C,S,W,W,K,V,P.

Mary: *Well, we could make the 'R' into Robert, and tell a story about Robert. . . .*

Barry: *I've got it! Robert Was Making something, but what? . . . Cookies! Robert Was Making Cookies and . . . Suzie Was . . . Wiping Kitty Vomit . . . Puddles! That would work!* Robert Was Making Cookies, Suzie Was Wiping Kitty Vomit Puddles. *It's sort of gross, but at least we'll remember it.*

Mary: *We sure will, Barry. Now, what else did he say that he would ask us?*

Barry: *He wants us to be able to answer twenty multiple-choice questions on the Revolutionary War.*

Mary: *Okay, we know that since they're going to be multiple-choice, he will probably ask us either "Who? What? When? or Where?" What can we do to study for these kinds of questions?*

Barry: *I've got it! I can use the "word cluster" thing that Mr. Watkins taught us last year. I can put the word* Revolution *in a circle and then list all the People (Who), Terms (What), Dates (When), and Places (Where), in surrounding circles. Then if I use my highlighting pens, I can use different colors for each type of question.*

learning strategies. Techniques or methods students use to acquire information.

Cognitive psychology offers an approach to instruction different from that of behavioral psychology. Behavioral psychologists use reinforcement to motivate students to maintain task persistence. Although cognitive psychologists also are interested in engaging students in instruction, they are more interested in what students are doing or thinking *while* they are so engaged. Also, cognitive psychologists do not believe that stimulus, response, and reinforcement adequately explain the learning process. They believe that behavior is always based on cognition, an act of knowing or thinking about the situation in which the behavior occurs. As a result, they are concerned with the organization of knowledge, information processing, and decision-making behavior—aspects of the cognitive realm.

The cognitive approach offers a different conception of the teaching-learning process. Where the behavioral approach emphasizes the role of the teacher in presenting information, the cognitive approach views the learner as a more active participant in the learning process. The amount of learning in the cognitive approach depends both on how teachers present the material and on how the student processes it.

The role of the teacher is also different in the two learning perspectives. Behaviorists view the teacher as an executive whose primary role is to manage student behavior and make instructional decisions that direct student activities. Cognitive psychologists are more likely to view the role of the teacher as a mediator or facilitator, one who helps students to select appropriate **learning strategies**,[1] monitors their understanding, and makes decisions for future learning. This is not to say that behavioral approaches do not involve any of these functions, only that they do not emphasize them.

Finally, behavioral psychologists approach instruction by emphasizing the importance of clearly identifying what students are to learn, carefully planning the organization and sequence of content, and providing immediate feedback and reinforcement to student responses. From the cognitive perspective, one of the major goals of instruction is to help students manage and control their own learning. If students do not have the strategies needed to learn, the teaching goal must be to help them acquire these strategies.

ACQUIRING AND USING LEARNING STRATEGIES

Recently, a small pipe under my sink sprang a leak. I tried to tighten the loose nut that was causing the leak but I didn't have a wrench that would fit into this small area. I did not panic. Fortunately, my neighbor is a plumber. We have a nice arrangement: When I can't attend football games, I give my tickets to him, and he lends me tools. When he opens his tool kit, I am always amazed at the number of different wrenches he owns. As an

[1] Rapid developments in cognitive psychology have led to differences in terminology. In this book, I am using the terminology developed by Paul Pintrich at the University of Michigan; *learning strategy* is a general term that refers to the use of cognitive and metacognitive strategies. Some researchers refer to cognitive strategies as *learning strategies* or *learning tactics*.

cognitive strategies. Behaviors and thoughts that influence the learning process so that information can be retrieved more efficiently from memory.

metacognitive strategies. Procedures used to plan, monitor, and regulate one's thinking.

expert plumber, he not only possesses a large number of different tools but also knows how and when to use them. If he didn't have these tools, he couldn't remain in business. I have three basic tools: a hammer, a screwdriver, and a wrench. You can understand why I'm not very successful in completing the variety of tasks required of a homeowner!

If you think about school tasks, successful learners also use a large number of "tools" to make schoolwork easier and increase the probability of their success. Educational psychologists call these tools learning strategies. Table 3.1 summarizes a number of important learning strategies that will be included in my discussion of cognitive psychology: **cognitive strategies** to help you learn, remember, and understand course material; and **metacognitive strategies** to help you plan, monitor, and regulate your cognition (thinking). These strategies will help you learn and teach more effectively.

TABLE 3.1 A TAXONOMY OF LEARNING STRATEGIES

Cognitive Strategies	Basic Tasks (e.g., memory for lists)	Complex Tasks (e.g., text learning)
Rehearsal strategies	Reciting list	Copying material Verbatim note taking Underlining text
Elaboration strategies	Mnemonics Imagery	Paraphrasing Summarizing Note making Creating analogies Answering questions
Organizational strategies	Clustering Mnemonics	Selecting main idea Outlining Mapping
Metacognitive Strategies		**All Tasks**
Planning strategies		Setting goals Skimming Generating questions
Monitoring strategies		Self-testing Focusing attention Monitoring comprehension Using test-taking strategies
Regulating strategies		Adjusting reading rate Rereading Reviewing Using test-taking strategies

Source: Adapted from McKeachie et al., 1990.

Many students who have difficulty learning in school attribute their problem to a lack of ability when their actual problem is that they have never been taught how to learn. In fact, it is not enough for students to know about different learning strategies; they must also learn how and when to use the strategies appropriately, and be willing (motivated) to use them (Paris, Lipson, & Wixson, 1983; Zimmerman & Schunk, 1989).

Students must be taught learning strategies so they can become self-directed learners.

Some students use one or two major learning strategies for all tasks in all courses. These students often don't have the necessary tools to learn the complex material they encounter in the courses they are required to take. For example, simply taking verbatim notes at a lecture is not going to be helpful if the professor asks questions requiring analysis of the material. Students who know how to take notes in classes that focus on higher-level thinking can better use their notes to prepare for the type of learning and testing in the course.

Each semester students come into my office to discuss a poor performance on an examination and tell me that they were prepared for the examination because they read each chapter two or three times. Obviously, these students have not learned to check their understanding. Weinstein and Stone (1992) refer to this situation as the "illusion of knowing." Students think they understand but don't do anything to test themselves to confirm or deny their belief. Instead, they wait for the examination for feedback that they don't know the material. The instructor's responsibility is to teach students how to monitor their knowledge *before* the examination, or before they hand in papers, so they can make changes in their learning strategies to increase the probability of success on the task.

Let's return once more to my plumbing problem to illustrate the important relationship between knowledge and willingness to try different strategies. I'm going to admit something: I don't have confidence in my ability to do many household chores. Therefore, I procrastinate, fail to purchase tools that could help me complete tasks, and don't pay much attention when my friend tries to explain how I can be a successful handyman. Therefore, even if I had the tools, I might not attempt to complete the job myself! In many ways, my behavior as a "handyman" is not much different from what cognitive psychologists are learning about the relationship between motivation and learning: Even if one has knowledge of a learning strategy, he or she may not be motivated to use it!

self-regulated learning. Learning in which students are actively involved in motivating themselves and using appropriate learning strategies.

information-processing system (IPS). The cognitive structure through which information flows during the process of learning.

short-term sensory store (STSS). The part of the information-processing system that briefly stores information from the senses.

Think about how your perceptions of ability influence your motivation and achievement behavior in different classes. Do you tend to change learning strategies when you have difficulty learning, or do you use the same ineffective strategy over and over again?

A major goal of cognitive psychologists is to encourage **self-regulated learning**. Zimmerman (1989) points out that many of the educational reforms of the past focused on what schools and teachers could do for students to help them learn. Self-regulated learning theories take the position that students can do a great deal to promote their own learning through the use of different learning and motivational strategies. These theorists believe that "learning is not something that happens *to* students; it is something that happens *by* students" (p. 22). Self-regulated learners are active learners rather than passive learners. When given a learning task, they monitor and control their behavior by setting management goals, using their prior knowledge, considering alternative strategies, developing a plan of attack, and considering contingency plans when they run into trouble. Educational research studies report that self-regulated or active learners have more effective strategies for selecting and attending to important information in text and lectures, and have the ability to organize material in a more efficient manner than passive learners do (E. Gagné, 1985).

As you read this chapter, I am going to ask you a number of questions to help you think about and evaluate your own learning. Most important, I want you to consider how *you* can become a more active learner by using the learning and motivational strategies discussed in the next two chapters.

THE INFORMATION-PROCESSING SYSTEM

? How does the human mind acquire information?

Cognitive psychologists have developed information-processing models to identify how humans obtain, transform, store, and apply information. I will first present an **information-processing system (IPS)** (see Figure 3.1) and then explain how cognitive and metacognitive strategies can be used to aid in the learning and retention of knowledge in this system.

Short-Term Sensory Store

As shown in Figure 3.1, the flow of information begins with input from the environment, such as the visual perception of words in a text. This information enters the **short-term sensory store (STSS)**, referred to in some models as the *sensory register*. Information in the STSS is stored briefly until it can be attended to by the working memory (sometimes called short-term memory). Information that does not enter working memory is quickly lost, usually in a fraction of a second. If the student does not attend to informa-

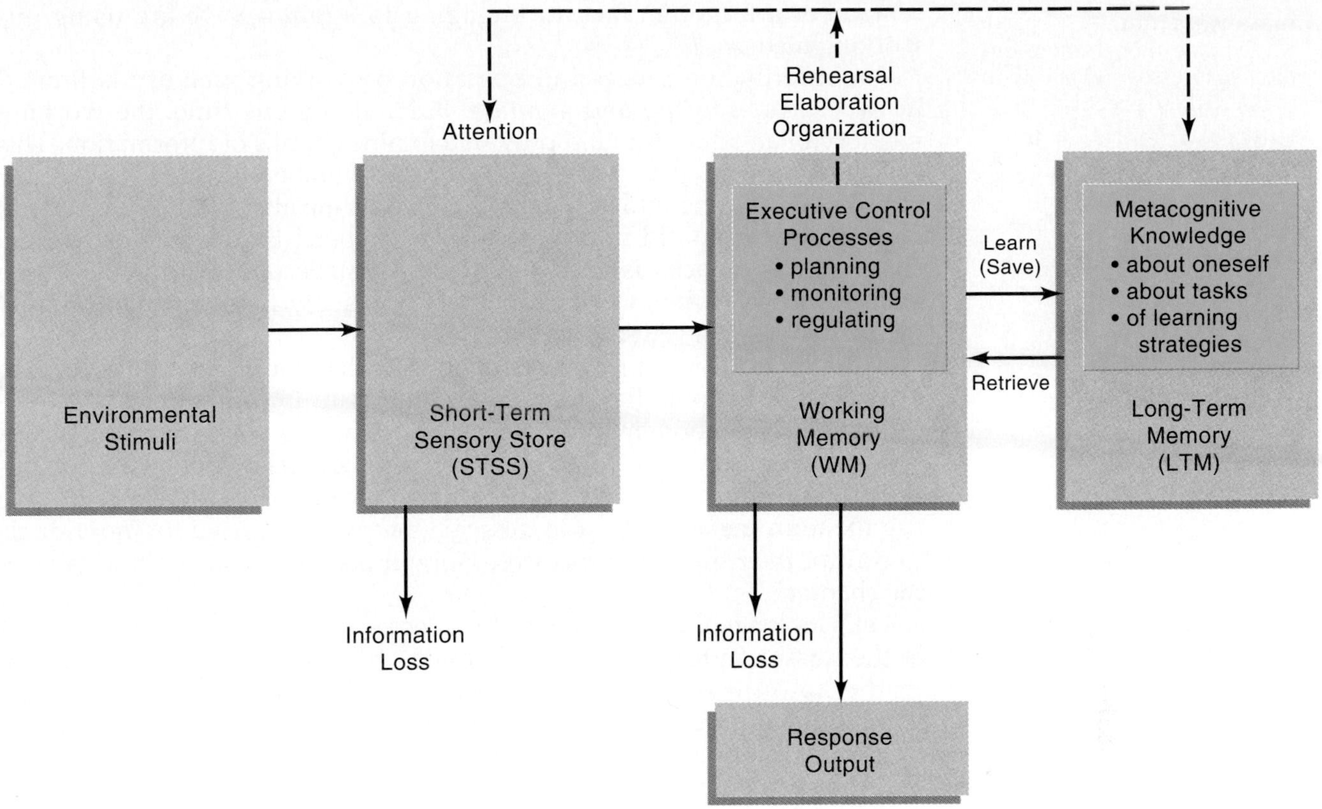

FIGURE 3.1 An Information-Processing Model of Learning.

tion, there is little concern about retention or retrieval because no information will have been acquired. Thus the importance of attention cannot be overestimated in any model of information processing.

> **working memory (WM).** A store for the performance of mental operations such as solving math problems; also for temporary storage.

Working Memory

> **?** Why is some information remembered and other information soon forgotten?

In moving from the short-term sensory store to **working memory (WM)**, information is changed to a verbal form involving a name coding. For example, shortly after seeing A, the student will no longer retain the visual pattern but instead will keep in working memory the verbal name of the pattern, the letter *A*. Similarly, TREEHOUSE will be held in working memory as *tree* and *house*. Working memory is the active part of our memory system and has been described as the center of consciousness in the IPS. Whenever we are consciously thinking about something, actively trying to

metacognition. Knowledge of one's own cognitive processes and ability to regulate these processes.

chunking. Grouping of data so that a greater amount of information may be retained in working memory.

rehearsal strategies. The process of repeating information over and over in working memory in order to retain it.

remember a forgotten fact, or engaging in a fantasy, we are using our working memory.

The information processing operation of working memory is limited in two ways—*capacity* and *duration*. First, at any one time, the working memory of an adult can hold only five to nine chunks of information. This condition is referred to as the "7 ± 2 Magic Number" (Miller, 1956). New information coming into WM will, if it catches the attention of the student, tend to crowd out old information already there. For elementary school children, this capacity is even less (Case, 1985). Second, without an active effort from the learner, working memory holds information for only a brief time, often less than 30 seconds.

A number of control processes operate at the working memory level to provide it with some flexibility in dealing with information. These processes focus attention, manipulate information, and organize and assist in retrieval of information. Some of these control processes operate automatically; others are subject to conscious voluntary control (Mayer, 1988). We use the term **metacognition** to describe the processes used by individuals to control their thinking processes. We will discuss metacognition later in the chapter.

Let's look at some of the control processes that are of particular interest to the classroom teacher. As I mentioned, the working memory is limited in the amount of information it can deal with at any given time. **Chunking**, or grouping, information is one way of keeping more than nine (7 ± 2) pieces of information in working memory. For example, it is usually easier to remember a number such as "194781235" if the numbers are grouped in threes (194 781 235), because the original nine units are reduced to three chunks. When we read a word, we think of it as a single unit rather than as a collection of separate letters. A sentence can be thought of as a single unit, or chunk, instead of a series of letters and words. The working memory can handle more information when it is organized into larger units of information because the organization reduces our memory load. Although the working memory uses various chunking strategies automatically and unconsciously, these strategies also can be taught. The important implication for teaching is to minimize the load placed on a student's working memory when you are trying to teach new information.

Working memory holds information for only a brief time. The information entering the WM is quickly bumped out by new information, or it fades away. The longer information remains in WM, the more likely it will be properly organized and retrieved when it is needed. **Rehearsal strategies** are used to retain information for longer periods. They involve repeating or rehearsing the information we have in our WM. For example, after receiving directions on how to get to a location, a motorist may repeat "left-left-right-left" while driving down the road. In another situation, a person might try to visualize objects again after they have faded away (disappeared from the WM). Researchers are interested in studying the effectiveness of the kinds of rehearsal strategies that can be helpful to learners.

Long-Term Memory

> **?** What factors determine if information will be retrieved from long-term memory?

Long-term memory (LTM) stores all the information we possess but are not immediately using. It is generally assumed that storage of information in the LTM is permanent. That is, the information neither fades from long-term memory, nor is it ever lost except perhaps as a result of senility or some other physical malfunction. Thus cognitive psychologists view the problem of forgetting as the *inability to retrieve or locate information* from memory rather than the loss of information.

Information enters the LTM through the working memory. While information must be repeated or rehearsed to stay in working memory, it must be "elaborated" to be put into LTM. That is, it must be classified, organized, connected, and stored with information already in LTM. Once in LTM, the flow of information does not stop. It proceeds in two directions. Working memory nearly always calls up data stored in the LTM. For example, when we learn something new about representational government, working memory will call up our previously acquired knowledge, such as our understanding of the concepts "democracy" and "republic." Stored data also are called up as part of a problem-solving process—for instance, a student remembers a relevant theorem when performing a geometric proof. Also, information in LTM, as well as in WM, controls the ultimate output of the student's behavior. Certain behaviors are mastered to the point of **automaticity**. That is, they may be conducted without conscious thought. An example of such behavior in school is the **decoding** of words in text by expert readers. The advanced reader grasps the meaning of words or whole phrases without having to decode the sound of each letter.

Encoding is the process of transforming new information for integration into memory. The way in which new information is encoded and integrated into memory, as well as the depth and breadth of integration, affects the ease with which the information is retrieved. Information in the long-term memory is encoded for storage in one of two forms, episodic or semantic. **Episodic memory** is the recall of events in our lives. It allows us to recall images of what happened and what was said during these events, much like a videotape that we can replay for ourselves. **Semantic memory**, as the name implies, stores "meaning." Andre and Phye (1986) state that semantic memory "contains the generalizations we have drawn and acquired from experience" (p. 7). It contains our knowledge of concepts, rules, principles, and skills. Thus, when we read a sentence in a book, it is the meaning of the sentence that we save, not the particular words or grammatical characteristics of the sentence.

Anderson (1985) believes that semantic memory contains two types of knowledge: knowledge about things (called declarative knowledge) and

long-term memory (LTM). The part of the information-processing system that retains encoded information for long periods.

automaticity. The result of overlearning behaviors to the point that they can be carried out without conscious thought.

decoding. The process of translating a symbol back into its original form.

encoding. The working memory process of transforming incoming information into episodic or semantic form and associating it with old knowledge for storage in long-term memory.

episodic memory. Information in long-term memory that is stored in the form of images.

semantic memory. Verbal information stored in long-term memory.

executive processes. The part of the information-processing system that controls the flow of information and implements cognitive strategies to reach a learning goal.

knowledge about how to do things (called procedural knowledge). As I mentioned in Chapter 1, there are different learning strategies for different types of knowledge. In the words of Sharon Derry (1990): "There are different learning tools for different learning jobs" (p. 350).

You now have some idea as to how information flows in the information processing system. Beginning with the environment, information flows to the short-term sensory store. The information that is attended to proceeds to the working memory, where it may be encoded and stored permanently in the long-term memory. Information then flows from the working memory to direct behavior. The purpose of learning strategies is to help learners control the information processing system so that they can better store and retrieve information. Helping students establish relevant connections among knowledge is an important teaching goal.

Executive Control—Metacognition

? Why is it important to develop metacognitive skills?

We need to discuss in more depth the control, or **executive processes**, of the IPS. These processes monitor and direct the cognitive activities in progress. The skills are responsible for assessing a learning problem, determining learning strategies to solve the problem, evaluating the effectiveness of the chosen strategy, and changing strategies to improve learning effectiveness.

The functioning of the executive processes is based on metacognition, which has two separate but related aspects: (1) knowledge and beliefs about cognitive phenomena (stored in long-term memory) and (2) the regulation and control of cognitive behavior (stored in working memory). Flavell (1976) states:

> "Metacognition" refers to one's knowledge concerning one's own cognitive processes and products or anything related to them, e.g., the learning-relevant properties of information or data . . . . Metacognition refers, among other things, to the active monitoring and consequent regulation and orchestration of these processes in relation to the cognitive objectives on which they bear, usually in the service of some concrete goal or objective. (p. 232)

The knowledge aspect of metacognition refers to *knowledge about oneself* as a learner (e.g., one's preferences, strengths, weaknesses, interests, study habits), *knowledge about tasks* (i.e., information about the difficulty of various tasks and the different demands of academic tasks), and *knowledge of learning strategies* and how to use them. Holt's (1982) observations of student learning in classrooms provide an excellent example of the importance of such awareness:

> Part of being a good student is learning to be aware of the state of one's own mind and the degree of one's own understanding. The good student may be one who often says that he does not understand, simply because he keeps a constant check on his understanding. The poor student, who does not, so to speak, watch himself trying to understand, does not know most of the time whether he understands or not. Thus, the problem is not to get students to ask us what they don't know; the problem is to make them aware of the difference between what they know and what they don't. (p. 17)

The second aspect of metacognition, the regulation and control of our cognitive behavior, directs our thinking processes during the learning situation. As mentioned earlier, these control processes operate in one's working memory. Three general types of metacognitive control or self-regulation are *planning, monitoring,* and *regulating* (see Table 3.1) (Pintrich & Schrauben, 1992; Zimmerman & Martinez-Pons, 1986).

PLANNING STRATEGIES. Planning involves setting goals for studying, skimming reading material, generating questions to be answered, and analyzing how to attack the learning task. I view planning for learning as similar to the manner in which a football coach develops a "game plan" for the opposing team. After watching films of the opposition's previous games, the coaching staff decides on both offensive and defensive strategies. For example, if the team has a weak defensive secondary, the coach may decide to emphasize passing over running. The coaches work with each player to make sure that he understands his responsibility in carrying out the team's game plan. In a similar manner, a student should have a general game plan for learning in each course as well as specific plans for completing assignments and studying for tests. Successful students don't just show up for class, take notes, and wait for the instructor to announce examination dates. They anticipate how much time is needed to complete assignments, obtain information for papers before writing, review notes well before exams, organize study groups when necessary, and use a variety of other self-regulated behaviors. In other words, successful students are active learners rather than passive learners.

MONITORING STRATEGIES. Monitoring strategies include tracking of attention while reading a text, asking oneself questions about the material, and monitoring one's speed and time taking an examination. These strategies alert the learner to possible problems in attention or comprehension so that they can be "fixed" or repaired. While studying for an examination, you ask yourself questions and realize that you don't understand certain sections in your biology book. Your method of reading and note taking is not working for these sections. You need to try some other learning strategy.

Comprehension Monitoring. A special type of monitoring is comprehension monitoring. Skilled readers start this process at the beginning of a reading assignment and continue it until the assignment is completed (Brown, 1980). The skilled reader has a comprehension goal in mind, such as finding a particular fact or determining the main ideas of a text. Such a reader's strategy might then be to skim the text for the fact or read the text for the main ideas. Following execution of this strategy, if the important fact has been located or the main ideas grasped, the skilled reader will experience satisfaction at reaching the goal. However, the reader's experience might instead be one of frustration at not finding the fact, or one of confusion caused by not understanding the passage. If comprehension monitoring shows that the goal has not been reached, then a remedial step would be taken, such as reskimming the material or perhaps reading the text more carefully.

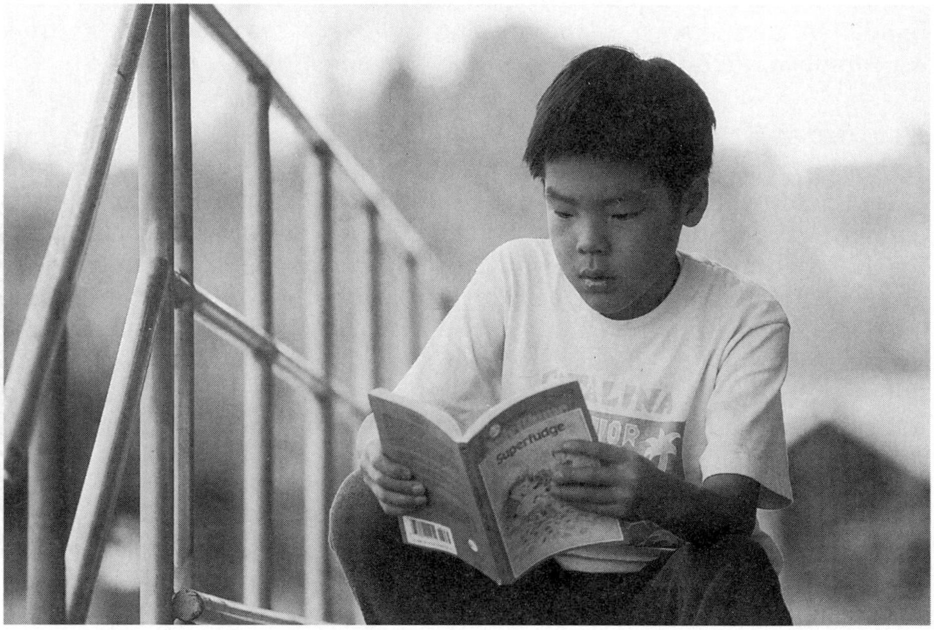

Effective readers have good metacognitive skills, allowing them to monitor their understanding.

Researchers have found that many young children as well as college students are deficient in comprehension-monitoring skills. Many students continue to rely on repetition (e.g., rereading, copying notes, using flash cards) as their major strategy in attempting to learn new knowledge from a textbook or lecture. To help such students, Devine (1987) suggests that they practice the following strategies for monitoring and improving comprehension of text:

- Change rate of reading to accommodate for differences in the comprehensibility of the text. Speed up for easier sections to quickly get an idea of the author's overall plan, but slow down for more difficult sections.
- Suspend judgment. If something is not clear, continue to read. The author will probably fill in the gaps, add more information, or clarify points in the text.

- Hypothesize. When something being read is not clear, make it a habit to hypothesize about the meaning of the unclear passage and read along to see if your guess makes sense.
- Reread difficult passages. This simple strategy can often be effective, particularly when information appears contradictory or ambiguous.

Focusing Attention. The classroom environment frequently makes it difficult for some students to filter out appealing distractions and focus instead on educational tasks. Teachers often complain that students who have trouble maintaining attention in the classroom are immature, have an attention deficit, or are unmotivated to learn. Unfortunately, using different labels to describe students with attentional problems does little to improve their learning. Corno (1987) views attentional concerns as a self-management problem because the students have difficulty planning and controlling their learning. She believes that students need to be taught to self-manage or self-regulate their behavior by learning strategies to handle distractions, as follows:

- Keep objectives focal: "Pay attention to what you're doing."
- Set reward contingencies: "If I finish this, I'll get to . . ."
- Avoid visual contact with distractor.
- Isolate self: "I'd better go to the learning center."
- Protest: "Please, I'm trying to concentrate here!"
- Enlist help from teacher or other task-oriented peers. (p. 257)

Many psychologists believe that students lack knowledge about attention in the same way that they lack knowledge about mathematics or scientific concepts. If they can be taught techniques to monitor and self-regulate their attention, the teacher no longer needs to be totally responsible for the attention of all the students in the class. The students can use these skills both at home and at school to improve their learning. What do you do to self-regulate and control your attention?

Knowledge of the information-processing system also can be helpful to the teacher concerned with student attention. Information available in the short-term sensory store will be lost if it is not attended to in working memory. Therefore, the first thing a successful teacher must do is to get students to attend to important material. The teacher can do this by helping students to pick out important material, motivating them to attend to it, reducing distractions, and teaching them the skills to cope with distractions that do occur.

Efficiently picking out the important information in text or lecture material involves the use of a strategy on the part of the learner. It has been shown that faster learners have better methods for selecting the right information on which to focus (Thorndyke & Stasz, 1980).

Several strategies may be used by the teacher or student to determine which information is important. Teachers can use instructional objectives to inform students of lesson goals. Students who are told at the beginning of a lesson what the goals and objectives of the lesson are attend to and retain verbatim information better than students without this advantage (Hamilton, 1985).

Many students determine what is important in a lesson by anticipating the kinds of questions that will be asked on the next exam. This skill has been shown to lead to increased attention to relevant material (Rothkopf & Billington, 1979). Teachers generally hold students responsible for learning more information than they actually test for, because tests only sample information in a particular area. Teachers do not want to "give away" exact test questions because if they did, students would learn only that material. Untested but important material would be ignored. However, teachers can reveal what kind of question (e.g., multiple-choice or essay) will be on a test and what general areas of the subject will be covered. This allows the students to determine, for example, whether to study for recall of specific facts or to strive for an understanding of general concepts. Certainly, the teacher can tell students which material is less important so that they can more efficiently use their study time.

REGULATION STRATEGIES. Regulation strategies are related to monitoring strategies. For example, when learners realize that they don't understand a portion of the text, they go back and reread the difficult section, slow their reading pace through difficult or unfamiliar material, review course material that they don't understand, and skip certain questions on an examination, returning to them after easier questions are answered. Regulation strategies help students modify their study behavior and allow them to repair deficits in their understanding (Pintrich & Schrauben, 1992). Students need to be taught "fix-up" strategies to remedy learning problems.

The following is an example of metacognitive strategies in action. Suppose the task is to read a chapter in American history. A student, Robert, realizes that knowledge of this material will be assessed by means of an essay test. Using his metacognitive abilities, Robert assesses his own knowledge of the subject and decides it is necessary to plan out a study approach in order to gain a general understanding of the main ideas and to be able to recall the most important facts. Therefore, he paraphrases each section of the chapter, underlines the important facts, and monitors his own progress during study. He realizes that he has difficulty comparing and contrasting some of the battles discussed in class. Therefore, he decides to develop and write responses to short-answer essay questions he thinks may be on the test. The ability to change or modify one's behavior by disregarding strategies that don't work for strategies that do work is an important characteristic of successful students!

Metacognitive strategies work in conjunction with cognitive strategies (e.g., outlining and note taking). One can't plan, monitor, and self-regulate successfully if one doesn't have the skill and will to use available cognitive strategies.

How would you rate your metacognitive skills thus far in this course? What have you learned about yourself as you take notes and read the book? How have you decided to learn the material in the course? How difficult is the content? What action plan have you developed to be a successful student in this course? In what ways have you monitored and regulated your reading or studying behavior since you started the course? Some of my students have found it useful to keep a log of their planning, monitoring, and regulating behavior in some course they are taking. In this way, they can report on the different strategies they use to become more successful students.

LEARNING: COGNITION AND METACOGNITION

As you can see, metacognitive processes are important in helping us gauge the extent of our learning as well as in deciding how to learn. Now we need to learn more about the tools or strategies we can use to help us learn. In terms of the information-processing system, these cognitive strategies help us to prepare new information for integration with known information and for storage in our long-term memory. Therefore, our metacognitive and cognitive strategies must work together. The cognitive strategies (e.g., underlining and paraphrasing) are necessary tools to learn content, but the metacognitive strategies provide the monitoring and direction for their use. In other words, students can be taught to use many different cognitive strategies, but if they don't have the necessary metacognitive skills to help determine which strategy to use in a given situation, or to change strategies, they will not be successful learners.

Keep in mind that very young children do not have the ability to think about their own thought processes. By first grade, however, students know that some learning tasks will be more difficult than others. Students in the third grade usually know when they have failed to comprehend something. However, these young students are limited in their ability to do anything about this knowledge. It is not until late childhood or early adolescence that students become capable of assessing a learning problem, devising a strategy to solve the problem, and evaluating their success (Flavell, 1985). This does not mean that the individual learning strategies discussed in this chapter are not important for the young learner, only that you will have to determine which strategies are most useful considering the developmental level of the learner.

In discussing declarative and procedural knowledge and the instructional procedures that are appropriate to each, we will follow the instructional decisions of two teachers, Mrs. Jones and Mr. Oliva. Mrs. Jones teaches junior high science and is applying cognitive principles in developing instructional lessons in a life science course. Mr. Oliva teaches fifth grade and is applying cognitive principles in teaching mathematics. Later in the chapter, I often refer to Tables 3.2 and 3.3, which illustrate the instructional objective, the type of knowledge each objective represents, the learning conditions appropriate to promoting each type of knowledge, and examples of relevant instructional techniques that include various learning strategies.

In the remainder of this chapter, we will explore how different cognitive strategies can be used with different learning tasks, and we will discuss thinking skills. The types of knowledge are interrelated. If students are performing a laboratory procedure in chemistry (procedural knowledge), they must know information about different chemicals (declarative knowl-

TABLE 3.2 CONDITIONS PROMOTING LEARNING THE INSTRUCTIONAL OBJECTIVES IN MR. OLIVA'S MATHEMATICS CLASS

Learning Objective	Type of Knowledge	Conditions Promoting Learning
Students will associate Roman numbers *V*, *X*, and *C* with *5*, *10*, and *100*.	Declarative	Rehearsal: Spaced and frequent practice associating Roman and decimal numbers to overlearning. Elaboration: Explanation of some Roman numbers as originating from counting on fingers.
Students will identify finite sets.	Procedural—Pattern Recognition	Provide a definition: "A finite set is one in which the members of the set are countable." Provide varied true examples: {5, 10, 15}, the set of all people in the world, the set of all grains of sand in the world, all even numbers below 100. Provide matched nonexamples: {5, 10, 15 . . . }, the set of all odd numbers above 100.
Students will divide fractional numbers using reciprocals.	Procedural—Action Sequence	Provide a written description of steps: "Invert the divisor, and multiply." Check prerequisite knowledge: Does student understand "invert"? Can student identify the divisor? Can student correctly multiply fractions? Provide practice: Frequent, spaced practice can make this procedure almost automatic. Provide corrective feedback: Use students' verbal self-reports or error analyses to analyze source of errors. See Table 3.4

TABLE 3.3 CONDITIONS PROMOTING LEARNING THE INSTRUCTIONAL OBJECTIVES IN MRS. JONES'S LIFE SCIENCES CLASS

Learning Objective	Type of Knowledge	Conditions Promoting Learning
Students will definite the metric terms *kilo, deca, deci, centi, milli.*	Declarative	Rehearsal: Spaced and frequent practice in associating each term with its meaning promotes overlearning. Elaboration: Using mnemonic and associating terms with familiar words.
Students will recall the eight life processes: food getting, respiration, excretion, response, secretion, growth, reproduction, movement.	Declarative	Elaboration: Encourage students to take notes, paraphrasing definitions of each life process. Prompt students to think about how they carry out each life process. Organization: Activate schema. Prompt students to relate each function to their own respective body parts.
Students will classify living and nonliving objects.	Procedural—Pattern Recognition	Definition: Living things carry out all the life processes. Provide varied true examples: Demonstrate how diverse organisms (e.g., protozoa, mammals, plants) carry out the life processes. Provide matched nonexamples: Compare living organisms with things that show only some of the life processes—for example, crystals that grow but do not get food, respirate, respond, secrete, reproduce, or move.
Students will follow the scientific method in investigating a self-chosen question.	Procedural—Action Sequence	Provide a written list of steps—see Figure 3.8 Provide practice: Have students describe each step they will take, and why, in investigating some life phenomenon. Provide corrective feedback.

Determine learning objective → Classify objective as to type of knowledge involved (e.g., declarative versus procedural knowledge) → Recall conditions necessary to learning this type of knowledge → Apply appropriate learning strategy

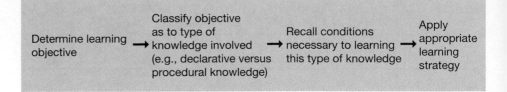

Figure 3.2 Process for Determining Learning Strategy Appropriate to Learning Objective.

edge). When they attempt to solve a problem in chemistry, both declarative and procedural knowledge are needed. Figure 3.2 identifies the decisions that need to be made in instruction.

distributed practice. Learning trials divided among short and frequent periods.

massed practice. Practice that is grouped into extended periods.

Basic and Complex Knowledge

? What are some methods that students can learn to increase their retention of basic knowledge?

The process of knowledge acquisition can be viewed on a continuum from basic to complex. Basic learning involves such things as recalling names and dates, associating a word in English to its equivalent in Spanish, and listing chronologically the events leading up to the Civil War. More complex learning involves understanding the main ideas in a story, solving verbal problems in algebra, or comparing and contrasting the poems of two different authors. Some of the strategies effective for memorizing basic tasks may not be useful for learning more complex tasks. The successful learner attempts to process meaningful information so that it will be stored in long-term memory and retrieved when it is needed. One of the major problems in cramming for examinations is that students don't learn the material in a way that makes sense to them and don't attempt to relate the information to what they already know. The result is that 24 hours after the exams, nothing, or very little information, is retained. What strategies have you used that lead to poor or good retention and retrieval of information?

When we think of basic learning, our image is of having information drilled into us through endless repetition. Whether memorizing a song or learning the capitals of each state in the United States, we have been told by our teachers that we must practice, practice, practice. But does it matter how we practice? Cognitive psychologists offer some advice as to how practice can be made more effective. Research has shown that **distributed practice** among frequent and short periods is more effective than a smaller number of sessions of **massed practice** (Underwood, 1961). If you want students to remember the presidents of the United States without error, they should practice for many short sessions, reading the list and saying the names over and over. The classic "all-nighter," of which I must admit I experienced a few during my undergraduate days, is the best example of massed practice. Although this practice method may be effective in learning a large amount of information in a short time, it is a poor method of learning *if* retention of information is the goal. Think about the examinations on which you used massed practice. How much of the content did you remember a few days after the examination?

In memorizing a list, you should be aware of the **serial position effect**, which results from the particular placement of information within a list. In general, a person is more likely to remember information placed at the beginning (*primacy effect*) or the end (*recency effect*) of a list than information placed in the middle.

Most people have difficulty learning a long list at one time and find it easier to break the list into smaller groups. This is **part learning**. This method is appropriate, for instance, in teaching the multiplication tables. Students can start with the 2s table and work upward. Part learning is also useful in teaching the symbols for chemical elements.

Forgetting is an overwhelming impediment to learning. A widely accepted explanation of this phenomenon is that interference from previous or subsequent learning occurs. When previous (early) learning interferes with subsequent (later) learning, **proactive inhibition** occurs. **Retroactive inhibition** takes place when subsequent learning interferes with previous learning. The child who has learned to spell *relief* may later experience proactive interference when learning to spell *receive*. In another situation, our ability to recall and use metric measurements can be hampered by our familiarity with the English measurement system. An example of retroactive interference is the difficulty experienced by a student who finds that learning in a second-period French class interferes with learning in a first-period Spanish class. Learning a second programming language, such as FORTRAN, may inhibit our ability to recall the commands and format of previously learned BASIC.

The chance of interference in basic learning is high. One means of reducing the effects on basic learning is the proper sequencing, variation, and organization of material so that interference can be minimized. For example, similar concepts should not be taught too closely in time. In teaching kindergarten children the alphabet, the letter *b* should be totally familiar to them before the letter *d* is introduced. When the letter *d* is introduced, the differences between the two letters should be pointed out. Research has shown that **overlearning** reduces the effects of interference on the learning of basic material (Underwood & Ekstrand, 1966). Overlearning occurs when practice or drill continues after the student reaches the desired level of performance.

For the most part, teachers deal with more complex knowledge that is connected or interrelated, such as information from textbooks and lectures. Such knowledge gets its meaningfulness from our ability to relate the ideas of the text or lecture to knowledge we have stored in long-term memory. When we gain new information about something, such as "Columbus explored the Virgin Islands in 1493," what we store is the meaning, or main ideas, contained in the text. Unless we specifically attempt to encode it, information such as the grammatical structure of the preceding sentence is lost. In long-term memory we connect this knowledge with other things we know about America and Columbus. This makes it meaningful to us.

serial position effect. The process by which the position of material in a list affects the ease with which the material can be recalled.

part learning. The process of breaking up a large learning task into smaller segments for easier learning.

proactive inhibition. An explanation for the forgetting that takes place when previous learning interferes with the retention of new information.

retroactive inhibition. The interference of new material with the retention of previously learned material.

overlearning. Continuing practice or drill after a student reaches the desired level of performance.

elaboration strategies. Integration of meaningful declarative knowledge into long-term memory through adding detail, creating examples, making associations with other ideas, and drawing inferences.

organizational strategies. Learning strategies that impose structure on material via hierarchial and other relationships among the material's parts.

COGNITIVE STRATEGIES: DECLARATIVE KNOWLEDGE

Let's now turn to the three cognitive strategies that can facilitate the storage of ideas in long-term memory: *rehearsal*, **elaboration**, and **organizational**.

Rehearsal

BASIC TASKS. I first mentioned the importance of rehearsal in describing how information, when repeated or rehearsed, can be retained when it enters working memory. The rehearsal is performed by repeating the information to oneself subvocally or out loud. When looking up a phone number, we often repeat it out loud until we have completed dialing. We do the same when learning the combination to a padlock.

? What strategies can I use to improve my recall of text material?

COMPLEX TASKS. Rehearsal strategies for more complex tasks such as learning material from a textbook include saying the material aloud as one reads, taking notes from the reading, and underlining or highlighting material in the text.

Underlining allows students to quickly locate and review important information in a text. Studies have shown that students learn more from a text if they underline important and relevant ideas in it (Fowler & Barker, 1974; Snowman, 1984). Rickards and August (1975) compared recall under different types of underlining conditions. They found that students told to underline any sentence in each paragraph recalled more than did students told to underline the most important sentence in each paragraph. Apparently, the free underlining condition allowed students to connect the passage to existing knowledge structures. It is important that students use underlining sparingly and underline only the information that they find important. How many times have you seen a student in a college course underline almost every sentence in the book with a Magic Marker? How is this underlining helpful?

Studies have found that underlining irrelevant information reduces recall of important data (Smart & Bruning, 1973). Because students below the sixth grade cannot reliably determine which information is important (Brown & Smiley, 1977), it is best to encourage underlining for older children only. An alternative is to teach underlining to younger students and older students who do not know how to underline. Such a program should begin with an explanation of what is important in a passage, such as the topic sentence. Younger or less able students may not have the knowledge structures necessary to allow them to underline freely. The next step would be to teach students to underline sparingly, perhaps only one or two sentences in a paragraph. Finally, students should be taught to review and paraphrase those passages underlined.

In some situations underlining alone is not an effective way to learn the material because it doesn't provide an opportunity to think about the material. Therefore, using marginal notations with underlining can be a more useful method. Figure 3.3 identifies various types of annotation used in marking a political science textbook chapter. Compare the suggested types of annotation with the annotation you are currently using while reading this textbook. What improvements can you make in your own annotation?

Types of Annotation	***Example***
Circling unknown words	. . . redressing the apparent (asymmetry) of their relationship
Marking definitions	*def* [To say that the balance of power favors one party over another is to introduce a disequilibrium.
Marking examples	*ex* [. . . concessions may include negative sanctions, trade agreements . . .
Numbering lists of ideas, causes, reasons, or events	components of power include (1) self-image, (2) population, (3) natural resources, and (4) geography
Placing asterisks next to important passages	* [Power comes from three primary sources . . .
Putting questions marks next to confusing passages	?→ war prevention occurs through institutionalization of mediation . . .
Making notes to yourself	*check def in soc text* power is the ability of an actor on the international stage to . . .
Marking possible test items	T There are several key features in the relationship . . .
Drawing arrows to show relationships	. . . natural resources . . . , . . . control of industrial manufacture capacity
Writing comments, noting disagreements and similarities	*can terrorism be prevented through similar balance?* war prevention through balance of power is . . .
Marking summary statements	*sum* [the greater the degree of conflict, the more intricate will be . . .

Figure 3.3 Marginal Annotation. Source: McWhorter, 1992.

? I spend a great deal of time underlining my texts and memorizing important material. Why am I having difficulty in some of my courses?

Rehearsal strategies play a limited role in learning. They influence attention and encoding of information in the information-processing system, but they don't help you construct meaning from the information and relate the information to what you already know. This is why rehearsal strategies generally are ineffective tools to help in long-term memory. Many college

mnemonics. Techniques that impose a useful link between new data and visual images or semantic knowledge.

loci method. A mnemonic involving the association of each item to be learned with a particular location in a mental image created by the learner.

acronyms. Mnemonics that use the first letter in each word of a list to form a word.

peg-word method. The formation of a mnemonic by the association of a series of cue words and visual images.

key-word method. A method of associating new words or concepts with similar-sounding cue words through the use of visual imagery.

students use *only* rehearsal strategies to learn content. Rehearsal strategies need to be supplemented by the use of other learning strategies that assist the learner in organizing and integrating information in long-term memory (McKeachie et al., 1990; Weinstein & Mayer, 1986). These additional strategies are elaboration and organization.

Elaboration

BASIC TASKS. Elaboration strategies help learners store information into long-term memory by building internal connections between items of information to be learned (Weinstein & Mayer, 1986). For basic learning, **mnemonics** can be useful elaboration techniques that impose a linkage between new data and visual images or semantic knowledge (Belleza, 1981; Schneider & Pressley, 1989). They can be very useful for improving recall of names, categories, sequences, or groups of items.

Some popular mnemonics include the loci method, acronyms, and the peg-word method. With the **loci method**, used since classical Greek times, the student creates a mental image of a familiar place, such as the classroom. In this image, several easily identifiable locations are determined. The student then associates each individual item on the list with a particular location in the image. A student studying the presidents might visualize George Washington sitting in the first seat inside the door of the classroom. Farther into the classroom would be John Adams, then Thomas Jefferson, and so on. Then, during recall, the student imagines walking through the room, visualizing each president in his place. In this way, the list of presidents, in its proper order, is made more meaningful through the association with a visual image.

Acronyms use the first letter in each word to form a mnemonic. "ROY G. BIV" is an acronym that gives the order of the colors of the rainbow: *R*ed, *O*range, *Y*ellow, *G*reen, *B*lue, *I*ndigo, and *V*iolet. Similar to an acronym is the sentence mnemonic that uses the first letter of each term as the first letter of each word of a sentence. "*M*y *v*ery *e*fficient *m*other *j*ust *s*at *u*p *n*ear *p*op" gives the planets in order from the sun: Mercury, Venus, Earth, Mars, Jupiter, Saturn, Uranus, Neptune, Pluto. Another kind of acronym involves taking the first letters of a series of words to describe steps in a procedure. For example, the initial letters of the words *d*ad, *m*om, *s*ister, *b*rother can be used to help students remember the four steps in long division: *d*ivide, *m*ultiply, *s*ubtract, and *b*ring down.

The **peg-word method** uses visual imagery and semantic associations in remembering serial data. For instance, items in a list are associated, as in a visual image, with each phrase in a chant: "One is a bun, two is a shoe, three is a tree," and so on. The student who is studying a series of items imagines the first item stuck between the halves of the bun, the second item stuck in a shoe, the third item hanging in a tree, and so on.

A useful mnemonic for learning foreign language vocabulary is the **key-word method** (Atkinson, 1975), which involves the creation of an image that relates the English to the foreign word. For example, the Spanish word for *postal letter* is *carta*. An appropriate image might involve a huge postal letter being transported to the post office in a shopping cart. Thus the word *carta* would be encoded both as an idea and as an image. The student's subsequent attempts to recall the Spanish word for *postal letter* would stimulate the image of the letter in the cart, providing a concrete cue to the correct word. This method has been shown to have significant success in teaching foreign vocabulary (Atkinson, 1975).

COMPLEX TASKS. Elaboration strategies for more complex learning from texts include paraphrasing, summarizing, creating analogies, writing notes in one's own words, explaining, asking questions, and answering them (Weinstein & Mayer, 1986). When someone asks us to elaborate on an idea we have expressed in discussion, they want us to add more information to what we have said to provide detail, give examples, make connections to other issues, or draw inferences from the data. The additional information makes our point more meaningful to the listener and also is likely to make the point easier to remember.

> ? I can memorize facts, but I have trouble learning more complex material. How can I learn complex material?

We can elaborate for ourselves when learning more complex information. As information enters working memory, the efficient learner thinks about the information: What does this new information mean? How does it relate to other ideas in the text and other information already learned? The learner may create examples that demonstrate the new knowledge. Thus, when encoding the information that Switzerland is politically neutral in international relations, the advanced learner might relate this to Switzerland's history of noninvolvement in the wars of the past several centuries. The learner may also draw conclusions as to the relationship of this neutrality to Switzerland's role as world banker.

A social studies lesson provides a second example of elaboration. A student learning that ancient Egyptian society depended on slavery may elaborate on this fact by adding details, making connections with other information, or drawing inferences. By way of providing detail, the student may notice that Egyptian slaves were largely prisoners of war. The student may connect the concept of Egyptian slavery with what is known of antebellum American slavery, noting similarities and differences. The student may infer that life for an Egyptian slave was hard and held cheaply by Egyptian society at large. In this way, the efficient learner integrates the new ideas into long-term memory by associating the new data with the old knowledge (Bransford, 1979). This procedure leads to improved understanding of the material and to an increased probability that the data will be remembered at a later time.

> ? How can I improve my note taking?

NOTE TAKING AND NOTE MAKING. Note taking is discussed here under elaboration because taking notes can do far more than create an external store of information for review. It can also encourage elaboration and integration of the new information. Some students don't realize that there are two steps to note taking: writing information from a lecture and then making sense of what one wrote. Stopping at the first step is not a useful strategy for learning.

The kinds of notes taken affect the way in which the information is integrated and organized. Taking verbatim notes encourages encoding of verbatim data and amounts to little more than rehearsal. Taking summary notes encourages reorganization and integration (Anderson & Armbruster, 1984). Take brief notes, in your own words, that organize and summarize the important points of the lecture so that the notes make sense to you (some individuals call this second step *note making*).

McWhorter (1992) suggests a method of note making that can be helpful for studying. This procedure includes the following steps:

1. Leave a 2-inch margin at the left side of each page of notes.
2. Keep the margin blank while you are taking notes.
3. After you have edited your notes, fill in the left margin with words and phrases that briefly summarize the notes. (pp. 166–167)

These *recall clues* should be words that will trigger your memory and help you recall the complete information in your notes. These clues function as memory tags. They help you retrieve information that is labeled with these tags. A variation of this system is to write questions rather than summary words and phrases in the margin. The questions help to remind you of the information in your notes. Also, with the questions, you can evaluate your understanding of the material for the examination.

Attending class and taking notes is only the beginning phase of learning. Analyzing and organizing lecture notes after class is the key to retention and retrieval of information.

matrix notes. A system of note taking in which the student fills in information in the cells created by vertical and horizontal headings.

Although taking notes does help the encoding process, the most efficient and effective use of notes includes reviewing them. Students who take their own notes and review them learn more than do students (1) who take notes but do not review them, and (2) who review notes taken by another person (Kiewra, 1989b). Part of the benefit of reviewing notes is that it allows further elaboration and integration of the material at that time. Therefore, you should be encouraged not simply to read over your notes but to think actively about the ideas in the notes and relate them to other information you already have. Also, the research supports the benefit of borrowing notes from a friend if you miss a lecture. You will benefit from reviewing a friend's notes.

In a review of note taking, Kiewra (1985) found that the types of notes taken affected the manner in which the information was encoded. You should be encouraged to take conceptual notes that stress the main ideas of the lecture. Detailed notes are also related to performance and should be taken to supplement the lecture's main ideas.

Kiewra (1989b) believes that teachers can improve students' note taking and review behaviors and, consequently, their achievement in the following ways:

- Lecture at a slower rate.
- Repeat complex subject material.
- Present cues for note taking.
- Write important information on the board.
- Provide students with a complete set of notes to review.
- Provide structural support for note taking such as a skeletal outline (e.g., provide the students with topic headings under which they have to place major ideas) or a matrix framework.

A good method of taking notes for comparing and contrasting information is to use **matrix notes**, a system in which notes are written in matrix form. Figure 3.4 provides an example of this system for a lecture passage on the topic moths and butterflies. As you can see in Figure 3.4, notes written in matrix form list major topics of information in the lecture (i.e., moths, butterflies) as vertical column headings, and the subtopics (e.g., growth, wings) as horizontal column headings. Cells within the matrix contain ideas representing the intersection of the headings. Kiewra (1989a) states that matrix notes have several advantages over other forms of notes (e.g., linear), including organizing lecture material for easier recall, integrating ideas within and across categories of information, and making it easier to identify missing information from lectures (e.g., the lecture failed to mention anything about the cocoons of butterflies). Kiewra suggests using matrix notes whenever two or more topics with several subordinate ideas are discussed. Did any instructor in high school or college teach you to take notes? Would you benefit from improved note-taking skills?

A final word about note taking: Not all students may benefit from taking notes. Note taking may be less productive for students of lower ability (Kiewra, 1989b) or for students who have difficulty processing aural information (information they hear). Such students might do better if encouraged to listen carefully to a lecture and review notes provided by the teacher.

LECTURE PASSAGE:

Moths and Butterflies

A moth has two sets of wings. It folds the wings down over its body when it rests. The moth has feathery antennae and spins a fuzzy cocoon. The moth goes through four stages of development. A butterfly also goes through four stages of growth and has two sets of wings. Its antennae, however, are long and thin with knobs at the ends. When a butterfly rests, its wings are straight up like outstretched hands.

MATRIX NOTES BASED ON LECTURE PASSAGE:

	Moths	Butterflies
Similarities		
Growth	4 stages	4 stages
Wings	2 sets	2 sets
Differences		
Antennae	feathery	long and thin with knobs
Rest	wings over body	wings outstretched
Cocoon	fuzzy	?

Figure 3.4 Matrix Notes for a Lecture Passage on Moths and Butterflies. Source: Kiewra 1989a.

clustering. The organization of items into groups on the basis of shared characteristics or attributes.

In summary, as compared with students who simply study material verbatim, students who elaborate while studying tend to understand the information better and are better able to recall important concepts later when it is required (Derry, 1990). Evaluate your study behavior to determine how you might use more elaboration strategies.

Organization

BASIC TASKS. A method for increasing the meaningfulness of basic knowledge is to provide an organizational structure or **clustering** of terms (Weinstein & Mayer, 1986). This type of organization reflects what some researchers believe is the hierarchical organization of information stored in long-term memory (Collins & Quillian, 1969). For example, students find it easier to recall the different types of rock when studying geology if an organizational structure is imposed. Learning the names of rocks can be difficult, as demonstrated by this list: granite, gabbro, peridotite, syenite, felsite, basalt, pumice, obsidian, shale, sandstone, conglomerate, limestone, dolomite, evaporite, organic limestone, coal, slate, schist, phyllite, gneiss, quartzite, marble, and anthracite. Figure 3.5, however, shows how this list can be reorganized in a hierarchical fashion. Such organization has been shown to improve subsequent recall (Frase, 1973).

You have a large number of important terms in this chapter. Consider clustering the terms under headings to help you learn their definition and use.

Mr. Oliva has taken several steps in designing instruction on Roman numeration that reflect the cognitive principles of basic instruction. First, he has provided daily periods of instruction so that students have frequent opportunity to rehearse

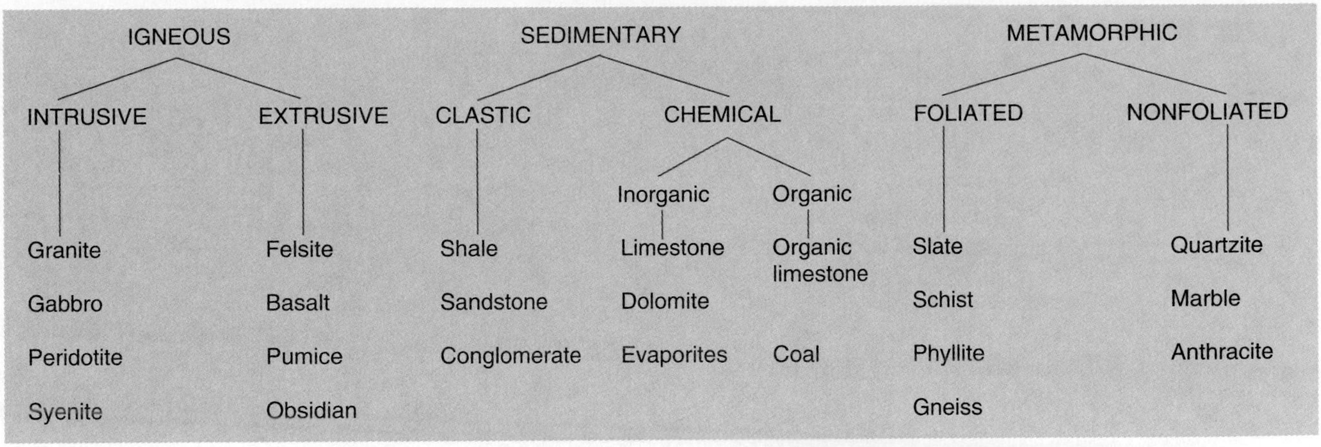

Figure 3.5 Hierarchical Organization of Rock Types.

the association of Roman and decimal numbers. To aid in elaboration, Mr. Oliva shows how some of the Roman numbers are related to counting on one's fingers. The V stands for the open hand (5 fingers), and X represents two open hands (10 fingers). The other symbols are more difficult to associate in this way. However, C can be remembered as cent *(100).*

Mrs. Jones's basic objective involves associating the decimal terms kilo, deca, deci, centi, *and* milli *with their appropriate meaning. In addition to frequent rehearsal of this material, Mrs. Jones aids elaboration by use of mnemonics. First, to aid in encoding the descending order of value of terms, she devised the following sentence using the first few letters of each term in a word: "*Kil*ling* de*finitely* dec*eases* cent*ipedes and* mill*ipedes." Further, Mrs. Jones associates several of the similar terms with familiar words that help to distinguish them. Thus* deca *is associated with* decade*—10 years—and* deci *is associated with* deci*mals.*

? What strategies are effective for organizing and linking information so that it will be remembered?

COMPLEX TASKS. As was the case for basic learning, new complex information is easier to learn and remember if it is presented in an organized format, especially if the format is hierarchically arranged. Having a well-organized body of knowledge in long-term memory is characteristic of experts in any field; chess and science are examples. This organization allows the expert to manage data more efficiently in working memory and to quickly locate needed information stored in long-term memory.

Derry (1990) provides the following example of how an organized idea network can help with retrieval of information:

> Consider a test question that requires students to identify the author of a certain piece of "period poetry." Student A has organized her knowl-

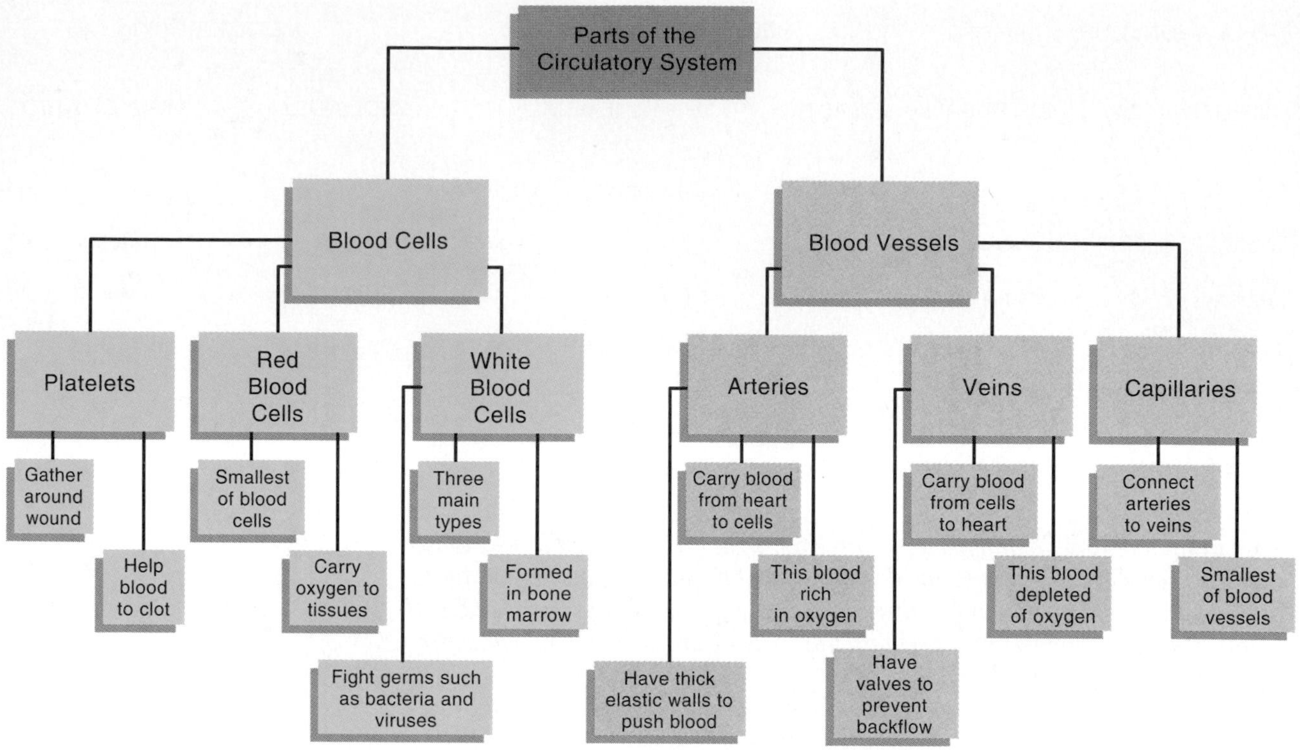

Figure 3.6 An Example of a Concept Map. Source: Peresich, Meadows, and Sinatra, 1990.

> **mapping.** A way of representing ideas in texts in the form of a diagram.

edge about poets within a structure that groups poets according to the time periods in which they wrote. Thus, she accesses the name *Matthew Arnold* by first considering evidence that the author is from the Victorian era, and then by searching only through her knowledge about the poets in that period. Student B, whose knowledge structure reflects only his personal preferences in poets, may have to search randomly and extensively through a larger set of poets in order to answer the test question. The absence of a well-differentiated hierarchical structure precludes the possibility of a controlled search. (p. 354)

Weinstein and Mayer (1986) suggest that outlining and **mapping** can be useful organizational strategies. These are techniques to better understand text material by helping the learner analyze the text structure. Mapping information is a process of drawing a diagram to picture how ideas are connected. Outlining is a strategy where major and minor ideas are written in abbreviated form using important words and phrases.

Teachers can teach outlining skills by giving students an example of a well-developed outline of a lecture or chapter in a textbook and explaining how the material follows the outline. Next, the teacher can give the class incomplete outlines in which students are given (1) an almost complete outline with a few supporting details left blank for them to fill in while listening or reading, (2) an outline with main topics where all supporting

CLASSROOM
Application

USING COGNITIVE STRATEGIES IN AN EDUCATIONAL PSYCHOLOGY COURSE

I asked students in my own educational psychology course to report on methods they used to help them understand the material in this chapter. The following examples are some of their reported cognitive strategies.

OUTLINE

Sid Ellis handed in the following outline of the material in the first part of this chapter. He pointed out that he finds it useful to include one or two descriptor words next to certain items in the outline:

1. Information-Processing System
   A. Short-term sensory store (one second duration)
   B. Working memory (7 ± 2)
   C. Long-term memory (storage center)
   D. Executive control (metacognition)
      1. Knowledge and beliefs about
         a) oneself
         b) task
         c) learning strategies
      2. Regulating cognition
         a) planning
         b) monitoring (attention, comprehension)
         c) regulating

continued

details need to be filled in, and (3) an outline with supporting details but missing main ideas. Students can learn to write good outlines if they are given proper practice (Devine, 1987).

Mapping can serve as a substitute for note taking and outlining. You should first identify the main idea of the text, then identify the secondary ideas or parts supporting the main idea. After labeling these parts, you can then connect these secondary ideas with the main idea. The end product is a map with the main idea at the center and the supporting ideas around the main idea (Van Patten, Chao, & Reigeluth, 1986). See Figure 3.6, illustrating a concept map for parts of the circulatory system, and the map in

2. Cognitive strategies
   A. Declarative knowledge (about things)
      1. Rehearsal (repeating information)
      2. Elaboration (relate information to prior knowledge)
      3. Organization (increase meaningfulness)
   B. Cognitive instruction
      1. Schemata (cognitive structures)
      2. Advance organizers (material presented at a higher level of conceptualization)

MAPPING

Lisa Davis completed a map to link the major material in the chapter:

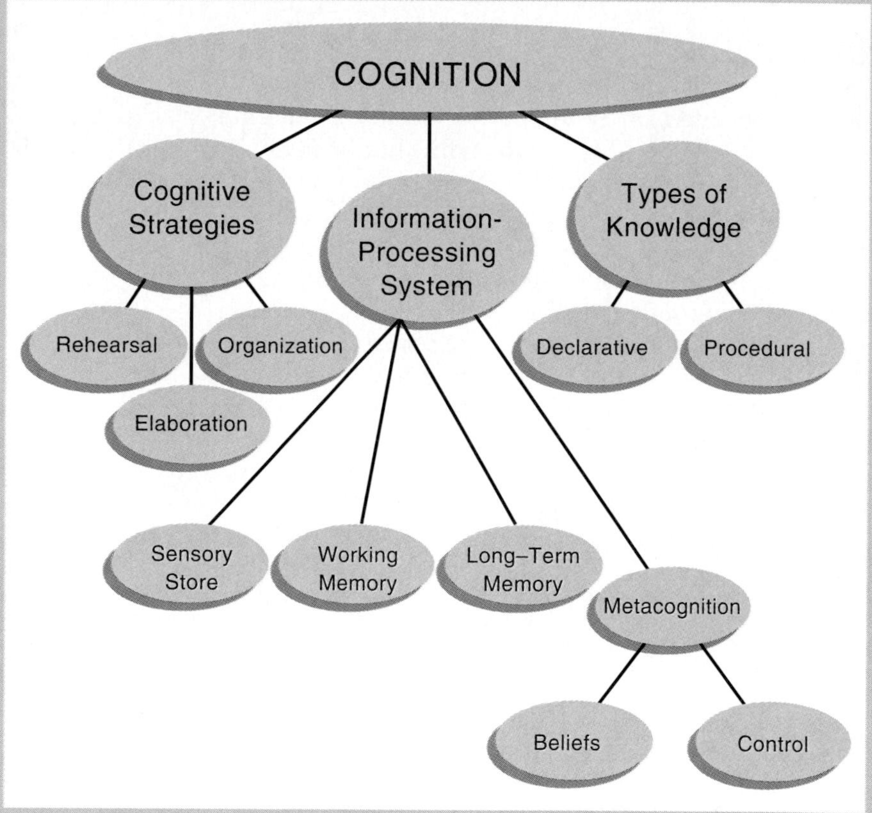

the next application section that one of my own students developed for the information-processing system.

Textual material often provides cues regarding organization. Scanning text for chapter, section, and subsection titles has been recommended for many years as a preliminary reading technique for determining the organization of the material. Have you carefully analyzed how the instructional components of this book can help you learn more effectively: teaching-

IMAGERY

Tony Gonzales reported that he used imagery to help him understand how elaboration and organization help retrieve information in long-term memory: "I view long-term memory like a well-organized closet where there is a place for shirts, sweaters, jackets, pants, and so on. When I need something, my categorization and organization help me to find it quickly. If I just threw clothes into my closet, I would spend more time trying to recall what items I had and spend more time locating them." Students who just memorize material and fail to elaborate or organize it have difficulty retrieving information when it is needed.

MATRIX NOTES

Ellen Chin used matrix notes to analyze the instructional implications of behavioral and cognitive psychology:

	Behavioral Psychology	Cognitive Psychology
Teacher's Role	Manager	Facilitator
Student's Role	Passive	Active
Motivation	External	Internal
Learning	Change in Behavior	Processing of Information

learning model, objectives, orientation, running glossary, application and research section, and summary?

I would like you to analyze the learning strategies you use in your college courses. To what extent can they be categorized under rehearsal strategies rather than elaboration and organizational strategies? Consider how you can use more elaboration and organizational strategies in your own learning.

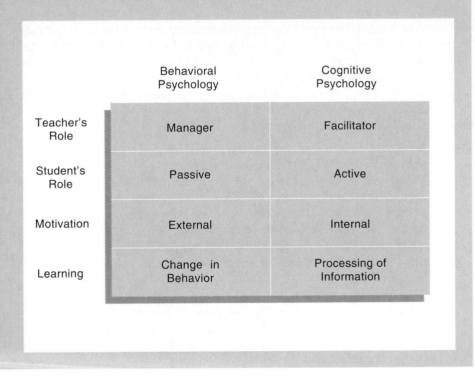

schemata. Cognitive structures created through the abstraction of previous experience.

Instructional Procedures to Aid Elaboration and Organization

The manner in which a teacher presents and organizes knowledge can have an important impact on student learning. The following discussion includes two ways in which teachers can help students remember and retrieve information.

? How do schemata help me recall information?

SCHEMATA. Some researchers have investigated the use of **schemata** in comprehension monitoring and problem solving. *Schemata* (plural for *schema*) are cognitive structures that may be created through the abstraction of previous experiences or acquired through instruction. Schemata make learning easier by giving incoming information meaning and reducing the number of things to which we must attend. They do this in two ways. First, schemata provide an organizational structure into which new information can be fitted. Hierarchical organizations of knowledge, as in the geology example discussed earlier, demonstrate this function. Second, schemata help get information into long-term memory because they elaborate new information into a meaningful structure. As a result, they let us know what to expect from incoming information. For example, we know that a story will normally have at least one character, a conflict, a beginning, a climax, and a resolution. Gordon and Braun (1985) have developed a series of schema-related questions to help students improve their reading comprehension:

- *Setting:* Where and when did the story take place? Who was in it?
- *Main goal:* What is the main goal?
- *Starter event:* What started the chain of events in the story (first episode)?
- *Inner response:* What does the character think, feel, or want?
- *Action:* What does the main character do?
- *Reaction:* What are the reactions of the characters?
- *Outcome:* What happened as a result of the main character's action? or reaction? (p. 70)

Armbruster (1986) identifies another type of schema—content schema—that involves knowledge of objects, events, and situations. Content schemata are generic characterizations of what we know about the world and, as such, help us to interpret new information. One way they do this is by providing an analogy or comparison by which new information can be understood. Armbruster (1986) provides an example by comparing the workings of a bread factory to the process of photosynthesis in a leaf:

> Have you ever been to a bread factory to see how bread is made? First, the materials needed to make the bread—flour, milk, and other ingredients—are transported to the factory. Then they are mixed together

to form dough. Next, the dough is baked in ovens. In the ovens, heat energy is used to change the dough into the final product—bread.

The leaf of a green plant is much like a bread factory. Just as flour and milk must be transported to a bread factory, so must water and carbon dioxide be transported to the leaf factory. Heat energy is used to make bread in the bread factory, while sunlight provides the energy to make the product in the leaf factory. Bread is the final product of a bread factory, and sugar, the food for green plants, is the final product of the leaf factory. The process by which green plants make their own food is called photosynthesis. (p. 262)

generative teaching. A method of improving comprehension in which students are trained to generate analogies and images of what they read.

Using content schemata as a basis for interpreting new knowledge is an effective strategy for teachers to employ in designing lessons.

Mrs. Jones wants to design a lesson on the eight life processes, the functions all living things must fulfill: food getting, respiration, excretion, growth, movement, response, secretion, reproduction. As Table 3.3 shows, this objective involves declarative knowledge. Consequently, the use of a relevant content schema may help in effectively teaching this material. To do this, Mrs. Jones will make use of a schema that all the students possess; she will prompt them to call up an image of their own bodies in thinking about each of the life processes. The familiar functions of their bodies can serve as a basis for understanding more general life processes. For example, when considering the life process "food getting," students will be prompted to think about how their bodies go about getting food, such as going to a restaurant, cooking their own dinner, or even growing food in a backyard garden. By calling up this schema of their own bodies, the students have something to which the new information can be "attached." Students will then be asked to elaborate on food getting by thinking of what they eat, how it is important in staying alive, and what hunger is and why it is important. By integrating food getting with other concepts, such as hunger or nutritional value, they add additional meaning to the concept and make additional connections with previously learned information. These additional connections help in retention and subsequent recall of this information (Anderson, 1985; E. Gagné, 1985).

? How can I summarize information so that I can better understand it and relate it to other information in a course?

Generative Teaching. Wittrock (1991) has extended schema theory into an instructional procedure called **generative teaching**. He has shown that when students are trained to generate analogies and images of what they read, their comprehension increases. These images may involve graphs, pictures, tables, and diagrams. The important aspect of this approach is that you need to take an active approach to your learning. You must change your perception of learning from simply recording and memorizing information to generating understanding by relating what you learn in class to your own knowledge and experiences.

advance organizers. Introductory information providing a framework and organization for material to be learned.

Have you ever noticed that when you "study" verbatim material from the text, you may not really understand what you are studying? For example, you may prepare for an examination on this chapter by studying the definition of terms in bold. When your instructor asks questions that slightly alter the information, will you be able to answer the questions? You are more likely to answer the questions correctly if you do more than study information verbatim from the text: Begin by rephrasing the definitions in your own words and think of examples. In this way, you are better able to check your understanding (metacognitive strategies).

Wittrock (1991) provides some good ideas for developing summaries of what has been read. Instead of taking a sentence in a book and slightly altering it, generate a sentence that (1) does *not* appear in the text, (2) relates important information from two or more sentences in that paragraph, and (3) uses your own words.

? How do advance organizers facilitate learning?

ADVANCE ORGANIZERS. Another way in which schemata have proved useful in promoting comprehension is through the use of **advance organizers** (Ausubel, 1968). Advance organizers present information before a lesson to make the lesson content more meaningful and easier to understand.The information in an advance organizer is presented at a higher level of abstraction and generality than the lesson content to aid the learner in subsuming or integrating the new material. I already have stated that one of the conditions for meaningful learning is that the learners have relevant ideas in their cognitive structure to which they can relate the new material. An advance organizer serves this function. According to Joyce and Weil (1972):

> The organizer can be a statement, a descriptive paragraph, a question, a demonstration, or even a film. It might be one section or it might be an entire lesson which precedes the other lessons in a unit of work. The form of the organizer is less important than the fact that its solution must be clearly understood and continuously related to the material it is organizing.
>
> The instructor can use organizers at many stages throughout the lesson or unit. As the learner moves to new material, new organizers provide a framework for relating new ideas to information already studied. In this manner, the learner has a framework to organize his information, and relate and differentiate the many ideas he has learned. (p. 175)

Before students begin studying the caste system in India, for example, a brief presentation of *social stratification* as an organizer will help them to understand the nature and purpose of the caste system. This more abstract discussion is an organizing outline for relevant information in the lesson. In mathematics, teaching the number line before proceeding to the addition and subtraction of negative numbers is another example of the effec-

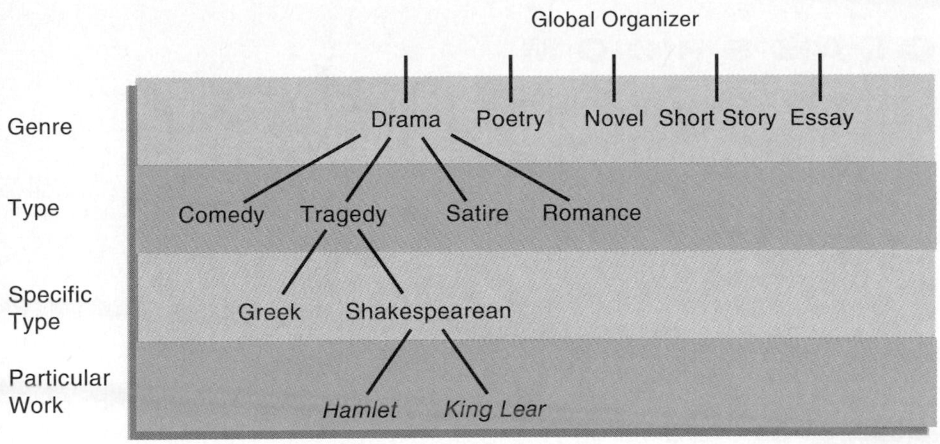

Figure 3.7 Possible Model for a General Organizer in Literature.
Source: F. Robinson, 1970.

tive use of an organizer. In teaching literature, the model shown in Figure 3.7 can be presented as an organizer to explain the derivation of the similarities and differences in various literary forms or to explain the interrelationships of forms within any of the main subdivisions of literature.

> ? How is an advance organizer different from an introduction or summary of what is to be learned?

It is important to realize that typical introductions or summaries of content presented before a lecture, a chapter in a book, or a film are not examples of advance organizers. The purpose of introductions and summaries is to orient students to the new material. In addition, they are typically presented at the same level of abstraction or generality as the new material. As a result, they do not provide the same framework as advance organizers do in helping students better organize and integrate new information.

There has been considerable discussion regarding the effectiveness of advance organizers for different types of learning as well as the conditions under which they should be used (see Barnes & Clawson, 1975; Lawton & Wanska, 1977; Mayer, 1979a, 1979b). Advance organizers do not always increase the amount of learning. They appear to be most useful when the information is poorly organized or when the learners lack prerequisite knowledge or abilities.

Mayer (1987) has used advance organizers in the form of concrete models or analogies to effectively teach concrete representations for the main components in a computer system. For example, objects such as a scoreboard, a window, and a scratch pad are used to explain how the memory functions of a computer operate. Students who have been given these models prior to instruction about computers have done better in solving both familiar and novel computer problems than students who have not had the benefit of the models. This effect has been particularly strong for low-ability learners, which suggests to Mayer that more skilled learners can invent their own models.

YORK COLLEGE PENNSYLVANIA Servire est vivere LIBRARY

CLASSROOM
Application

APPLYING COGNITIVE PSYCHOLOGY TO LEARNING AND TEACHING

The following are examples of instructional activities that can encourage students to use learning strategies. These activities serve different purposes and need not be used all the time. Assess your instructional objectives and decide which activities to use. Modify the activity for the grade level of the students you are teaching. Finally, consider how *you* can make use of the following information this semester!

Attention-Focusing Strategies

1. Make modifications in the physical environment to reduce distractions.
2. Inform students of the learning goals of the lesson.
3. Tell students the important points in a presentation.
4. Teach students self-monitoring and self-control techniques so they can handle distractions.

Rehearsal Strategies

1. Identify the basic terms and facts students should memorize.
2. Have students list the important new terms in the course.
3. Teach students to take notes and underline important information.
4. Teach students mnemonic techniques that you have found helpful and encourage them to make up their own devices.

Elaboration Strategies

1. Ask students questions that reflect the level of thinking presented in class objectives and tested in exams.
2. Have students summarize your lectures.

3. Have students study a reading assignment in pairs and take turns summarizing and explaining paragraphs (or larger units) to one another.
4. Provide time at the end of each class for students to review and elaborate their notes and ask clarifying questions of one another and the instructor.
5. Encourage your students to ask themselves and answer each of the following four questions at the end of a class presentation:

    a. What was the main point of the lesson?
    b. What in the lesson did I find most interesting?
    c. What is one probable test question that will come out of the lesson?
    d. What one question do I most want to ask of my instructor?

Organization Strategies

1. Provide a written assignment that requires students to use organizational skills (e.g., have the student outline part of a chapter in a text).
2. Explain how the material you present builds to broader concepts later in the course.
3. Tell students to skim a chapter to see how it is organized before they begin reading in depth.
4. Have students discuss why they felt something was important enough to include in their notes.
5. Encourage students to develop concept maps.
6. Use advance organizers to help students connect new material with prior knowledge.

Metacognitive Strategies

1. Encourage students to set specific goals for themselves for each assignment or study period.
2. Encourage students to monitor their reading.
3. Have the students describe the steps they used in solving a problem.
4. For each class session, require the students to keep a log of the main points they understood and the items and topics that were unclear to them.
5. Have the students describe the processes they are using to complete an assignment.

Source: Adapted in part from Johnson et al., 1991.

pattern-recognition knowledge. Procedural knowledge having to do with the recognition of patterns of stimuli.

It's a good time to pause and think about how you can use different strategies to improve your learning as well as your students' learning. The Classroom Application on pp. 122–123 provides some excellent guidelines.

COGNITIVE STRATEGIES: PROCEDURAL KNOWLEDGE

? How is teaching procedural knowledge different from teaching declarative knowledge?

Up to this time we have focused on declarative knowledge (knowledge about things), which is a major aspect of school learning. We now turn to ways to facilitate procedural learning, another important category of school learning.

Procedural knowledge tells us how to do something. To know how to do something, we need to know not only the *steps* in the procedure but also the *conditions* under which the steps are to be taken. Procedural knowledge can therefore be thought of as being composed of conditional if-then statements, which take the form: *if* certain conditions apply, *then* a specific action is to be taken. An example of an arithmetic procedure occurs in dividing by fractions: *If* dividing by a fraction, *then* invert the divisor and multiply. An *if-then* statement can be one step in a procedure, and many such steps can be chained together into quite complex procedures, because each step results in the necessary conditions for the next step in the chain. Long division of large numbers represents such a chain of conditional statements.

Procedural knowledge is used to transform information—in the foregoing example, transforming information about a divisor and a dividend into a quotient. As can be readily seen, procedural knowledge is essential for the basic skills of school and independent living. Basic to any success in school is the ability to execute successfully the procedures that transform numbers into other numbers (arithmetic) and symbols into meaning (reading). To succeed in independent living, the number of procedures the competent adult must master is innumerable: paying bills, cooking meals, shopping for food and clothing, solving problems, and so on. Procedural knowledge takes one of two forms: *pattern-recognition knowledge* or *action-sequence knowledge.*

Pattern-Recognition Knowledge

? How do you teach a concept?

Pattern-recognition knowledge pertains to the ability to recognize and classify patterns of stimuli. One important instance of pattern recognition is the ability to identify new incidents of a concept, or **concept learning**. A *concept* represents a group of ideas or things that share some common characteristics and have the same name (Merrill, 1983). Recognizing that a platypus is a mammal because it is a furred animal that suckles its young is an incident of a pattern-recognition skill. A second important incident of pattern recognition is identifying the conditions calling for a certain behavior or the application of a particular rule, such as when to "invert and multiply" (Anderson, 1985; R. M. Gagné, 1985).

concept learning. The acquisition of pattern-recognition knowledge involving the learning of a rule or rules for classifying a number of objects into mutually exclusive categories.

Concepts and other pattern-recognition procedures are learned through a process of generalization and discrimination (E. Gagné, 1985). As an infant learns language, he or she often labels objects inappropriately because they share some nondefining characteristic. The child may learn to call the household pet "doggy" and then proceed to call all four-legged animals "doggy." The child has overgeneralized the concept "doggy" and will eventually learn to apply this label only to animals more like Fido. This process of reducing the range of situations to which the concept applies, based on some defining characteristic of the concept, is called *discrimination*.

Generalization is the process of broadening the situations to which a concept or pattern-recognition procedure is appropriate. For example, a child, after examining many animals classified as mammals, may come to hold a conception of a mammal as an animal with fur that suckles its young and bears its young live. If the child is subsequently told that the platypus is a furry mammal that suckles its young but lays eggs, the concept of "mammal" will generalize to include the platypus by dropping that part of the concept concerning how the young are born.

In teaching children concepts and pattern-recognition procedures, the teacher defines the concept and gives examples that promote accurate application of the procedure. By *accurate* I mean that the children will be able to apply the concept or procedure in all the appropriate situations and refrain from applying the concept in inappropriate situations. In other words, the teacher strives for accurate generalization and discrimination.

Two conditions promote accurate generalization. The first is the presentation of true examples of the concept that are similar on the defining attributes but greatly different on irrelevant attributes. The example of mammals meets these conditions because the attributes of furriness and suckling of the young were constant, and the irrelevant attribute of manner of birth was varied. The second condition is the successive presentation of examples so that they may be held in working memory simultaneously (Tennyson & Park, 1980). Thus, when teaching the concept of "mammal," it would be desirable to present successive examples of not only the platypus but also horses, dogs, humans, mice, and other mammals.

Accurate discrimination is stimulated when a known procedure does not work (E. Gagné, 1985), as in the previous example of the child incorrectly labeling all animals "doggy." The conditions promoting accurate discrimination are the simultaneous presentation of examples and matched nonexamples. The matched nonexamples share relevant and irrelevant attributes but vary on at least one relevant attribute.

action sequence. A sequence of behaviors or cognitive actions to be taken to reach a goal.

Mr. Oliva wants to teach his class the concept of finite set. He defines a finite set as one in which the members can be counted. To promote generalization, Mr. Oliva provides his class with the following examples of finite sets that vary on the irrelevant attribute of size of set:

- *{5, 10, 15}*
- *Even numbers of less than 100*
- *All people in the world*
- *All grains of sand in the world*

Some of these sets are very large, but they are, at least in theory, countable. To promote discrimination, Mr. Oliva provides his class with the following matched nonexamples:

- *{5, 10, 15, . . . }*
- *odd numbers greater than 100*

*Mrs. Jones also has an objective involving pattern-recognition learning. She wants students to be able to classify living and nonliving objects accurately. To do this, students will have to use the declarative knowledge regarding the eight life processes they learned earlier. The conditional statement representing the procedure the students will be learning is "*If *an object carries out all eight life processes,* then *it is alive." Generalization will be promoted through the use of varied examples of living organisms such as protozoa, fish, mammals, and plants. Mrs. Jones will show how each example carries out the eight life processes. To promote discrimination, Mrs. Jones will provide matched nonexamples, such as crystals, that grow but do not carry out other processes such as movement, respiration, and response.*

Action-Sequence Knowledge

? What procedures need to be taught for acquiring action-sequence knowledge?

The second type of procedural knowledge refers to knowledge of action sequences. An **action sequence** is simply a sequence of behaviors or cognitive actions to be taken to reach some goal (E. Gagné, 1985). The actual procedure of regrouping, or borrowing, in subtraction is an example of an action sequence.

Action sequences are first learned as a list of steps composing some procedure (Anderson, 1982). For example, the steps in a physical activity, such as starting a car, may first be learned as a series of instructions. The learner consciously proceeds through each step, one at a time, until the procedure is complete. For example, in starting a car, the learner might begin by thinking, "First, if the car door is closed, then open the door; second, if the car door is open, then sit in the driver's seat; third, close the door; fourth, put on the seat belt; and fifth, insert the key into the ignition."

As you can see, if each step had to be consciously thought out before execution, very little work would be done. With practice, however, the procedures become almost automatic, and the driver carries them out with little thought. This frees working memory to perform other tasks, such as conversing with a passenger while starting the car. When procedures have been learned to the point of automaticity, however, another source of errors is introduced—the **set effect**. The set effect results when carrying out an automatic action sequence leads to a failure to process important information, which results in inefficient or incorrect performance. To continue the example, when driving home from work, how many times have you forgotten to make a special stop at a store to pick up something? Once the action sequence for driving home from work has been triggered, it can be difficult to interrupt. The benefit we get from making this procedure automatic is that it frees working memory for other tasks. We can ruminate on the happenings in the classroom or staff cafeteria while driving home. It often seems that we have to drive all the way home, however, and then make a special trip to the market.

set effect. The failure to process important information as a result of the automatic executive of an action sequence.

task analysis. The identification of the subordinate skills and knowledge that learners must acquire to achieve an educational objective.

There are two major roadblocks to learning a procedure. First is the limited capacity of working memory, especially troublesome in learning long and complex procedures. Any procedure that requires more than nine steps (remember the 7 ± 2 rule presented earlier in this chapter) usually is too long to keep in working memory. To overcome this limit, memory supports can be used. Instead of requiring the student to memorize the steps of a procedure, provide a written list of the steps. After all, it is the successful execution of the procedure that is important, not the memorizing of the steps.

A second potential problem in learning a procedure is the absence of prerequisite knowledge. It is essential to ensure that students already have the knowledge and skills necessary to learn the procedure. For example, it is difficult for a student to solve a geometric proof if the necessary axioms and theorems have not been mastered. The use of **task analysis** (see Chapter 6) is helpful here. Through task analysis, necessary subordinate skills are identified. The teacher can then assess the students' abilities on the subordinate skills. If necessary, the teacher should provide remedial lessons on skills in which students are deficient before teaching the skill itself.

When you teach action sequences, take care to avoid errors caused by the set effect. The simplest remedy for the set effect is to promote automaticity of only those procedures unlikely to be changed and those used often enough so that increased speed is valued (E. Gagné, 1985). Basic academic skills, such as reading, arithmetic, and writing, are important candidates for automatic responses. When action sequences such as letter and word decoding become automatic, working memory is freed for other important tasks, such as comprehending what is decoded.

We all know how difficult some tasks can seem when we are first learning them and how easy these same tasks can become with practice, but good execution comes with good practice. Practice of incorrect procedures only leads to incorrect execution of those procedures. Therefore, feedback must indicate not only whether a response is right or wrong but, if it is wrong, how it can be corrected (Elawar & Corno, 1985).

A particular procedure that Mr. Oliva is teaching in his fifth-grade math class is division by fractional numbers (see Table 3.2). His instructional program has four aspects. First, the procedure is written out for the students in the text: "Invert the divisor and multiply." Second, Mr. Oliva gives a pretest to assess the students' prerequisite knowledge. Students must know several things to be able to follow this procedure. They must know the meaning of invert *and* divisor, *and they must know how to multiply fractions. After modeling the procedure for the students, Mr. Oliva ensures that division by fractional numbers is practiced for a short time each day. Finally, following this practice, Mr. Oliva gives students corrective feedback.*

To determine where students make errors, Mr. Oliva has three alternatives. First, he can ask students to explain how they arrived at an incorrect answer by orally describing each step taken in attempting to solve the problem. Similarly, Mr. Oliva can ask students to show all their work. Either of these two methods will allow Mr. Oliva to pinpoint and correct the faulty step in a student's procedure.

These procedures often are not possible, as when Mr. Oliva is correcting papers after class or when students fail to show all their work. In such cases, Mr. Oliva can resort to error analysis, which is the examination of student errors to determine where mistakes were made. Table 3.4 shows several types of errors and their probable causes. It is important that Mr. Oliva give this feedback to his students as soon as feasible so that they do not continue to practice the procedure incorrectly.

TABLE 3.4 TYPICAL ERRORS IN DIVISION OF FRACTIONAL NUMBERS AND THEIR PROBABLE CAUSES

Error	Cause
(a) $\frac{1}{2} \div \frac{1}{2} = \frac{1}{4}$	Student failed to invert the divisor before multiplying. Check student's understanding of *invert* and *divisor.* Also check whether student recognizes that " ÷ " means *divide.*
(b) $\frac{1}{4} \div \frac{3}{8} = 1\frac{1}{2}$	Student inverted the dividend. Check the student's understanding of *divisor.*
(c) $\frac{5}{8} \div \frac{2}{3} = \frac{15}{18}$	Student multiplied incorrectly.
(d) $\frac{7}{8} \div \frac{1}{8} = \frac{3}{4}$	Student did not recognize problem as one calling for division. Student subtracted instead.

Although Mrs. Jones's teaching field is a content area (life sciences) rather than a basic skill and usually involves more declarative knowledge, she must also teach some action sequences. One such procedure is the scientific method. Like Mr. Oliva, Mrs. Jones provides a written list of steps in the scientific method in the form of the flowchart in Figure 3.8. Mrs. Jones will also assess prerequisite knowledge by checking the students' understanding of basic vocabulary, such as hypothesis, experiment, *and* theory. *Some practice will be given in using the scientific method by having students carry out investigations of issues of their own choosing. However, as automaticity is neither necessary nor desired, frequent practice is not required. More important for Mrs. Jones's purposes is that students appreciate the purpose and importance of each step of the scientific method.*

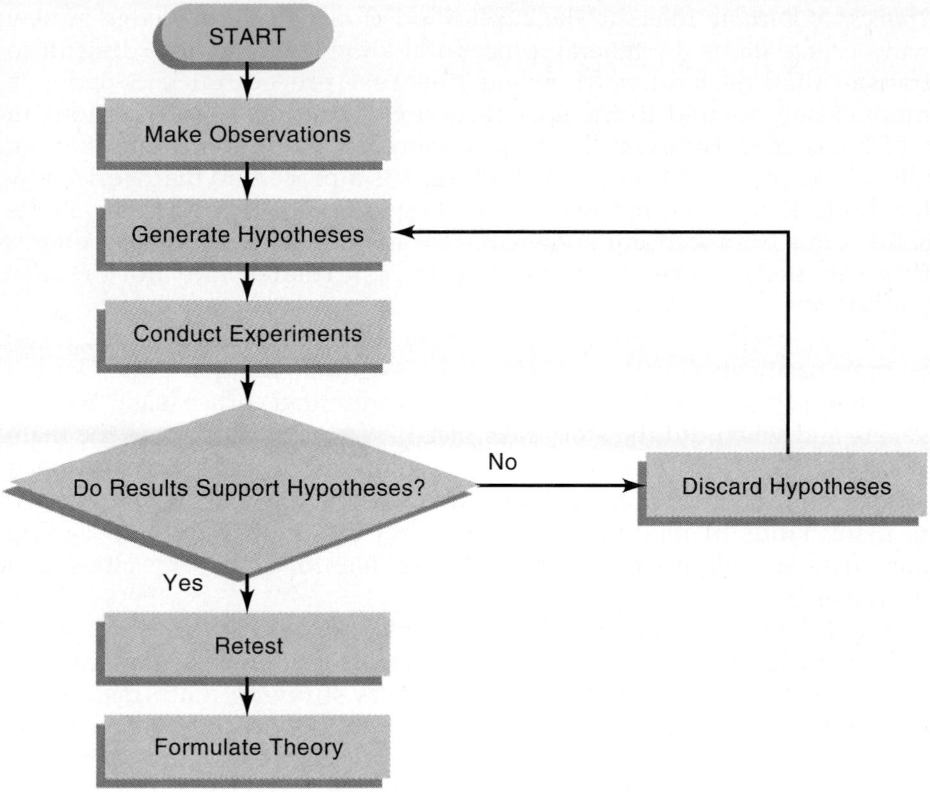

Figure 3.8 Flow Chart of Steps in Following the Scientific Method.

Although pattern-recognition and action-sequence procedures have been discussed separately, they seldom function that way. The correct use of an action sequence requires recognition of the proper conditions that call for it. Recognizing the conditions is a pattern-recognition process. For example, in subtraction, one must be able to recognize the pattern of numbers that call for regrouping if one is to execute this procedure correctly. In Table 3.4, error *d*, the student failed to recognize the stimulus pattern calling for division and mistakenly subtracted the numbers.

Procedural and declarative knowledge also interact. Declarative knowledge often provides data needed for a procedure. Comprehending the conditions calling for a procedure requires declarative knowledge. Mr. Oliva's students must know the meaning of *divisor*, *invert*, and ÷ to carry out this procedure successfully. To use again the example of regrouping, students must know that the upper number is less than the lower number in order to know that regrouping is required. Mrs. Jones's students must know the eight life processes before they can classify objects as living or inanimate.

THE TRANSFER CHARACTERISTICS OF PROCEDURAL AND DECLARATIVE KNOWLEDGE. In helping students generalize new learning, it is important to understand that procedural and declarative knowledge differ in their *transfer* characteristics (Gick & Holyoak, 1987).

critical thinking. Thinking that is focused on deciding what to believe or do.

problem solving. Finding solutions to problems for which solution methods are not immediately clear.

Transfer of learning refers to the application of skills or knowledge in new ways or situations. In general, procedural knowledge is more difficult to transfer than declarative knowledge because procedural knowledge is more closely related to the specific context, problems, or situations in which it is used. For example, the procedure for dividing fractions that Mr. Oliva is teaching his fifth-grade math class is a procedure that works only for this task. It would not work for adding or subtracting fractions. While some forms of procedural knowledge are more generalizable than others, this knowledge is nevertheless highly task related and not broadly applicable.

Because declarative knowledge is more conceptual and abstract, it can be more easily applied to a variety of contexts and situations. The Gordon and Braun (1985) schema-related questions presented earlier (e.g., "Setting: Where and when did the story take place?" "Action: What does the main character do?") illustrate this point. These questions, which are designed to aid comprehension, elicit declarative knowledge that can be applied to many kinds of reading situations. They can be used when reading fairy tales as well as other forms of fiction like folk tales, mysteries, and short stories.

The differences in the transfer characteristics of declarative and procedural knowledge can have important consequences for classroom learning (Schoenfeld, 1989). For example, researchers studying math instruction have noted that many teachers overemphasize the learning of procedural skill in math, while de-emphasizing the development of more conceptual math knowledge. The result is that students become skilled at manipulating numbers but not at solving real-world problems. Students need both procedural and declarative knowledge if they are to apply successfully what they have learned.

THINKING SKILLS

? What is the difference between critical thinking and problem solving?

In recent years many educators have become concerned with the fact that schools focus too heavily on basic facts and fail to emphasize thinking skills. Two different categories of thinking skills are critical thinking and problem solving. **Critical thinking** is defined by Ennis (1985) as "reasonable, reflective thinking that is focused on deciding what to believe or do" (p. 46). The following are some examples of critical thinking skills: focusing on a question, analyzing arguments, judging the credibility of a source, understanding logic (including inference, deduction, and induction), identifying assumptions, and deciding on a course of action. **Problem solving** is finding solutions to problems for which solution methods are not immediately clear (Nickerson, Perkins, & Smith, 1985).

The teaching of critical thinking is an important educational goal. However, not all educators agree as to how this goal can best be attained.

Seifert (1991) believes that the major difference between the two categories of thinking is a matter of emphasis: critical thinking refers more to the *process* of thinking (e.g., using deduction to analyze a dilemma), whereas problem solving pertains to the outcomes or *products* of thinking (e.g., solving a mathematics or chemistry problem). Sometimes both critical thinking and problem solving involve both processes and products.

Many school districts now incorporate the teaching of thinking in their curriculum. Beyer (1991) published a book, *Teaching Thinking Skills*, in which he explains how the following critical thinking skills can be taught: observing, comparing, predicting, problem solving, sequencing, and conceptualizing. In another book, *Developing Minds*, Costa (1985) lists over 15 different programs to select from, including Feuerstein's (1980) Instrumental Enrichment, Lipman's (1985) Philosophy for Children, and de Bono's (1985) CoRT (Cognitive Research Trust).

Instrumental Enrichment is designed for junior high students and is presented as a separate curriculum in which students are trained with classroom and individual paper-and-pencil exercises. These exercises, called *instruments*, give students practice in abstract and logical thinking, analytical and abstract reasoning, and problem-analysis skills. The goal of Instrumental Enrichment is to help students develop insight into their own intellectual processes and to make them more active thinkers. An important aspect of this program is the use of *bridging*, which relates skills taught in the program to real-world problems.

Philosophy for Children also teaches problem-solving skills, but does so within the context of short stories. The stories are based on different philosophical topics or issues that describe the activities of young children as

DEBATE FORUM

How Should Thinking Skills Be Taught?

Few educators disagree with the idea that thinking can be taught. The disagreement, however, is based on how best to teach these skills.

Argument: Thinking skills can be taught explicitly, by identifying the skill and developing a series of exercises or activities especially designed to improve that skill. For example, Beyer (1991) describes exercises to teach the thinking skill of comparing. De Bono's (1985) CoRT method is another example of the skills approach. For the most part, proponents of this approach believe that thinking ability can be improved independent of the subject matter curriculum.

Counterargument: Over 100 thinking programs on the market today claim that they can improve students' thinking. Unfortunately, there is little research to support many of the programs' claims (Nickerson, 1988). Considerable evidence suggests that thinking skills *can* be improved (Maclure & Davies, 1991; Nickerson, 1988), but controversy abounds as to the best methods and procedures to use. One problem: There are many definitions of "thinking skills"—and different approaches satisfy different definitions.

Thinking skills can best be taught within the context of the regular school curriculum (see next Classroom Application section). For example, one teaches how to think mathematically in math classes, not in "thinking programs"; one teaches problem solving dealing with social issues in a government class, not in a course using special exercises on the topic!

What do you think? Have you had any experience with special programs to help improve your thinking skills? What is your evaluation of such programs? How would you research this topic?

they apply thinking to everyday problems and situations. A major assumption of this program is that children are naturally interested in philosophical problems in the area of values and ethics and can develop the thinking skills necessary to deal with these subjects.

The CoRT program shows 9- to 11-year-old students how to develop original solutions to problems by teaching them to change their perceptions of problems that they will face outside of school. Students are taught to consider the aims, goals, and objectives in a situation and consider new ideas without immediately judging them as good or bad, right or wrong.

TEACHING FOR THINKING

Teaching students to improve their thinking takes time and effort, but the research indicates that such instruction can make a difference in helping many unsuccessful learners achieve academic success. You already have learned about the importance of teaching students such strategies as note taking, underlining, summarizing, memorizing, and outlining, as well as techniques for improving reading comprehension. Information on learning strategies in content areas (e.g., science, social studies, literature) is available (see Hyde & Bizar, 1989; Jones et al., 1987; Resnick & Klopfer, 1989). Refer to the references cited in this section as well as the Suggestions for Further Reading at the end of the chapter for more detailed study of specific learning strategies. Consider developing your own learning strategies curriculum.

Pressley et al. (1989) provide excellent resources for learning more about learning strategies and outline important steps in the implementation of strategic learning in the classroom. They recommend that the teacher start by finding out what strategies are available, selecting a few general strategies that can be used across subject areas, and then moving to more specific strategies that are more domain specific (i.e., unique to a certain field or specialization) and motivating students to use the strategies.

Winograd and Hare (1988) provide the following recommendations for teaching learning strategies:

- *What the strategy is.* Teachers should describe critical, known features of the strategy or provide a definition/description of the strategy.
- *Why the strategy should be learned.* Teachers should tell students why they are learning about the strategy. Explaining the purpose of the lesson and its potential benefits seems to be a necessary step for moving from teacher control to student self-control.
- *How to use the strategy.* Here, teachers break down the strategy, or reenact a task analysis for students, explaining each component of the strategy as clearly and as articulately as possible and showing the logical relationships among the various components.
- *When and where the strategy is to be used.* Teachers should delineate appropriate circumstances under which the strategy may be employed. . . . Teachers may also describe inappropriate instances for using the strategy.
- *How to evaluate use of the strategy.* Teachers should show students how to evaluate their successful/unsuccessful use of the strategy, including suggestions for fix-up strategies to resolve remaining problems. (pp. 123–124)

The following Classroom Applications are intended to provide you with additional information for teaching students learning strategies so they can improve their thinking skills.

CLASSROOM
Application

LEARNING STRATEGIES FOR READING COMPREHENSION

Many students believe that the key to reading is learning how to decode words. The result is that they often don't learn how to comprehend what they read, make inferences, generate questions, answer questions, and paraphrase material as they read (Pressley et al., 1989). In other words, many students don't realize that they must be active participants in the reading process. The following is an example of a strategy to help students improve their reading comprehension.

Roehler and Duffy (1984) believe that teachers who work with poor readers should explain explicitly the mental processing associated with strategies used by good readers. Direct explanation emphasizes the teacher's role in explaining the *process* of reading to students. The teacher using this approach explains to students how to implement the strategy, discusses the effects produced by the strategy, and describes when and where to use the strategy.

Duffy and Roehler (1987) provide the following examples of direct explanation of reading skills. The first example includes teaching word meaning; the second example includes teaching how to combine prior knowledge with current information in a text to make predictions.

Skill: Assessing word meanings

"My pillow is made from the *down* of geese."

T: What word is confusing in there?

S: Down.

T: Down. Okay, what are you going to do to figure that out?

S: It's like going down, or downstairs.

T: All right. Going downstairs. You've already realized that that doesn't make sense. Now, what's next?

S: Look for clues.

T: Good. Are there any clues?

S: Pillows and geese.

T: All right. We looked for clues. Now we've got to think about what those clues tell us. The pillow is made from something of the geese. In your experience what would a pillow be made of?

S: Feathers.
T: How are you going to know if you're right or wrong, George?
S: Read the sentence with the word in it.
T: All right. Try it, George.
S: My pillow is made from the feathers of geese.
T: Does that make sense?
S: Yes.
T: Good. (p. 519)

Skill: Combining prior knowledge with current text to make predictions

T: What do you think is going to happen next here? I mean, you're reading the story. What'll happen next, Candy?
S: (responds)
T: Oh, okay. What do you think, Mark?
S: (responds)
T: Interesting. Why do you think what you think? How can you make these predictions like this? How can you predict what's going to happen next in the story?
S: I thought about the story and Roberto and his problem.
T: Yes, but how did you use that to predict? Did you use your own experience?
S: Yea. I thought about what I thought would probably happen.
T: That's right. Because you've been thinking about the story and you've been thinking about Roberto and his problem. And that's part of what reading is. It's making predictions about what's going to happen next. (p. 519)

Helping students become strategic readers requires explicit explanations about the mental processing involved. However, these explanations may be difficult to provide. It's necessary for teachers to decide how their students are reasoning and what the associated explanations should be. Duffy and Roehler (1989) don't believe that the techniques can be proceduralized, since the dialogue unfolds in unpredictable ways depending upon how students restructure what their teachers say. As a result, direct explanation is a process that involves spontaneous and fluid interactional exchanges. See Duffy and Roehler (1990) for lesson plans for teaching various learning strategies in reading.

CLASSROOM Application

LEARNING STRATEGIES FOR WRITING

Several national studies indicate that students in the United States have inadequate writing skills (Boyer, 1983; National Assessment of Educational Progress, 1986). Teachers find that students need assistance in each of the three stages in the writing process—generating content, organizing, and revising (Beal, 1989). Students complain that they can't think of enough material to include in a paper, have difficulty planning and organizing the paper, and don't know what to do when they are asked to revise their writing.

Cognitive psychologists have found that *metacognitive processes* play an important role in writing. As a result, cognitive strategies have been developed to help students better understand the writing process and the procedures for regulating writing performance.

The following cognitive strategies for writing can be applied in many different settings (adapted from Beal, 1989):

Generating Content

- Select topics that are exciting or emotionally arousing.
- Help children set up a "future topics" file, to store information that is not appropriate for a present writing assignment but may be relevant for a future assignment.

CLASSROOM Application

LEARNING STRATEGIES FOR MATHEMATICS

For many students mathematics involves memorizing rote techniques for getting correct answers without learning how to think and prob-

- Train students to list single words on a topic to help them write more.
- Ask questions about stories.
- Give students cards with sentence openers such as "For example," or "Also," or "That's why" to use as they begin each sentence.
- Require students to use a "dialogue" style of writing, in which the characters tell the story through conversation.

Planning and Organizing Text

- Provide students with prepared "templates" for different text structures, with slots that can be filled in. For example, a "class news" article might have slots for the title and for *who, where, when*, and so on.
- Provide students with part of a narrative and ask them to complete it.

Evaluating and Revising Text

- Provide a guide to tell children precisely what to do while revising. For example, use advice printed on index cards that tells the child first to review a sentence and then to select an appropriate action.
- Help students question themselves about the comprehensibility and meaning of written material.
- Provide students with examples of different types of text problems and help them locate such problems in other written material.
- Provide the students with written text and model the revision process. Illustrate specific examples of additions, deletions, substitutions, and text rearrangement.

lem solve. Did you "understand" the mathematical concepts and principles of algebra, geometry, or calculus? Did you learn how to be an effective problem solver in mathematics? Many students are more concerned with "getting through" a course by memorizing mathematical procedures than with understanding what they are doing.

Mathematics educators have identified many inappropriate processes and strategies commonly used by students and have recommended learning strategies that can be used to help students become more successful learners. Standards recently defined by the National Council of Teachers of Mathematics emphasize problem solving as the most critical of mathematics skills.

continued

PROCESS MONITORING

Math students often appear not to monitor their own cognitive behavior (Romberg & Carpenter, 1986). Schoenfeld (1983) has found that expert problem solvers are "vigilant managers" who monitor their problem-solving performance, but that novices are often unaware of their own thinking processes.

Lester and Garofalo (1986) suggest that mathematics teachers help students develop metacognitive knowledge by asking questions that require them to reflect upon their own mathematical thinking. You can serve as a reactor and provide feedback to your students' responses. Questions like the following can be asked:

- Think of everything you do when you practice solving math problems. Why do you do all these things?
- What things can you do to solve more problems correctly? Why? Do you usually do these things?
- What kinds of errors do you usually make? Why do you think you make these errors? What can you do about this?
- What kinds of things do you forget to do when solving math problems?
- What kinds of problems are you best at? Why? What kinds of problems are you worst at? Why? What can you do to get better at these? (pp. 12–13)

Schoenfeld (1985) suggests two methods of group problem solving during which you can function as manager or consultant in promoting students' awareness of their cognitive problem-solving processes.

First, pose a problem for the class and ask for suggestions as to possible solutions. To encourage students to speak up, avoid evaluating their suggestions during this brainstorming session. Once all suggestions are in, ask the class to evaluate the reasonableness of each suggestion. Act as manager in encouraging students to examine all aspects of a problem and all student suggestions for arriving at a solution. The purpose of this type of management is

Summary

ACQUIRING AND USING LEARNING STRATEGIES

1. Successful learners use a large number of "tools" or learning strategies to make schoolwork easier and increase the probability of their success.
2. Students must be motivated to use learning strategies. Two important categories of learning strategies are cognitive and metacognitive strategies.

to demonstrate to students, through the classroom discussion, the *metacognitive processes* of assessing a problem, selecting a solution strategy, and evaluating the strategy's effectiveness.

Schoenfeld's (1985) second strategy involves small-group discussions of a problem that you pose. Act as consultant with these groups by asking a series of questions:

- What (exactly) are you doing? (Can you describe it precisely?)
- Why are you doing it? (How does it fit into the solution?)
- How does it help you? (What will you do with the outcome when you obtain it?) (p. 374)

These questions are designed to promote the students' awareness of their cognitive processes and to stimulate their development of metacognitive skills.

Derry and Murphy (1986) recommend a third approach to teaching math by providing instruction in general problem-solving models and supplementing the instruction with domain-specific strategies. They used such an approach in an arithmetic program, Training in Arithmetic Problem-Solving Skills (TAPS), which incorporates a general problem-solving model called the Four C's: Clarification, Choosing a solution, Carrying out the solution, and Checking the results. Once students learn the general model, they are instructed in specific subroutines for each step:

- *Clarification.* Teach students to classify word problems into "problem schemata" to identify the goal of a problem, and to eliminate irrelevant information.
- *Choosing* a solution. Teach students word problem heuristics, such as working backward, breaking up the problem into smaller segments and setting up subgoals.
- *Carrying out* the strategy. Demonstrate the value of persistence, strategy, and careful work.
- *Checking* the results. Teach estimation, and then ask important questions about each step of the procedure to locate errors.

THE INFORMATION-PROCESSING SYSTEM

3. The information-processing system (IPS) is a model that cognitive psychologists use to identify how individuals obtain, transform, store, and apply information. It comprises the short-term sensory store, working memory, and the long-term memory.
4. The flow of information through the IPS is monitored by control or executive processes (metacognition).
5. Metacognitive knowledge is the process by which individuals think about their thinking. It involves both knowledge about one's cognitive processes and the active planning, monitoring, and regulation of these processes.

6. Comprehension monitoring helps readers decide whether they have understood what they have read at a level necessary to reach their reading goal.
7. Self-verbalization can be used to help students monitor and control their attention.

COGNITIVE STRATEGIES: DECLARATIVE KNOWLEDGE

8. Two types of knowledge are declarative and procedural. Different learning strategies are used to learn different types of knowledge.
9. Learning declarative knowledge is aided by rehearsal, elaboration, and organization strategies.
10. It is easier to retrieve information if one's knowledge network is well elaborated and organized.
11. Mnemonics are elaborative techniques that help us remember information by connecting it to visual images or semantic knowledge. This connection makes the information more meaningful and thus easier to remember.
12. Although note taking helps the encoding process, notes can be even more effective when reviewed, as review promotes further elaboration and integration of the material to be learned.
13. Many students use only rehearsal strategies in learning. As a result, they have difficulty understanding and recalling complex information.
14. Outlining or mapping text or lecture material helps learners manage information more efficiently in working memory, because it helps to organize knowledge. Having a well-organized body of knowledge in long-term memory is characteristic of experts in any field.
15. Schemata are cognitive structures that help learners to organize and process information efficiently by providing an organizational structure into which new information can be fitted and by helping us to know what to expect from new incoming information.
16. Students must change their perceptions of their role in learning from simply recording and memorizing information to generating understanding of the information.
17. Advance organizers can be used either to activate students' present cognitive structure or to equip students with the necessary cognitive structure they do not have.

COGNITIVE STRATEGIES: PROCEDURAL KNOWLEDGE

18. Procedural skills are likely to be accessed and used spontaneously only if they have been properly practiced and the learner knows the conditions under which they should be used.
19. Pattern-recognition skills are involved in concept learning and in knowing when to execute an action sequence.
20. Pattern recognition is learned through the processes of generalization and discrimination.
21. Barriers to learning action sequences are limited working memory and the lack of prerequisite skills.
22. Problem-solving strategies demonstrate the interaction of declarative and procedural knowledge.
23. Procedural knowledge is more difficult to transfer than declarative knowledge.

THINKING SKILLS

24. Some thinking skills programs are more effective than others. As a result, it is important that you carefully evaluate available programs before deciding to implement a program.
25. There are learning strategies specific to different content areas that help students learn more effectively.

Reflecting on Cognitive Approaches to Learning

1. Teach Students to Think

A common complaint among teachers is that some students refuse to think. They attempt to memorize information, easily forget concepts taught earlier in the course, and fail to relate previous learning to present situations. Holt (1982) illustrates his concern for this problem in the following description of one of his students:

> What she needs is a broom to sweep out her mind. She has so much junk in there, her filing systems are in such a mess that she can never find anything, and the file drawers and old trunks must be emptied out before they can be put into any kind of order. If she could only forget completely about nine-tenths of the facts and rules she has all mixed up in her head, she might begin to learn something. (p. 186)

How does this problem begin? Does the problem improve or get worse when students reach college? What advice would each of the learning theorists you have studied propose?

2. Think about Learning Strategies

Think about the learning strategies you used in school. How did you memorize rote material? How did you learn concepts in history, chemistry, and mathematics? If you had to do it over again, how would you improve your learning strategies in high school? Did you change your learning strategies in college?

Analyze the way you deal with problems of attention according to the following skills: monitoring your current attentional state, analyzing the attentional demands of the task, selecting an attentional strategy, and evaluating the attentional strategy. What would you teach your students to improve their attentional skills?

3. Plan a Lesson Using Learning Strategies

Develop a lesson in your teaching specialty. Describe how you would use the information in Table 3.1 to increase your students' learning. If you developed a lesson plan in an earlier chapter, describe how you could use cognitive psychology to improve the lesson.

4. Lead a Discussion to Explore Students' Thinking

Lead a discussion with your students about some important issue in your field. Structure the discussion according to the ideas discussed by Schoenfeld (1985) or Lester and Garofalo (1986) in the previous Classroom Application. Closely observe how your students respond to this type of exercise: Which students participated and which did not? How enthusiastic were the students in exploring their own thought processes? Did the students have difficulty? Why? What did you learn about the students' knowledge of the topic?

5. Help Students Improve Their Metacognitive Skills

Ask students to keep a daily learning log in which they write about material they don't understand, generate questions they would like to discuss in class, summarize insights learned from a lesson or reading assignments, and identify any other aspects of their learning (Bondy, 1984). Discuss the information in the logs with students at the end of the week and have other students or yourself model effective learning strategies raised from the information in the logs. Provide students with examples of what they might place in the logs before they begin.

Key Terms

learning strategies, p. 89
cognitive strategies, p. 90
metacognitive strategies, p. 90
self-regulated learning, p. 92
information-processing system (IPS), p. 92
short-term sensory store (STSS), p. 92
working memory (WM), p. 93
metacognition, p. 94
chunking, p. 94
rehearsal strategies, p. 94
long-term memory (LTM), p. 95
automaticity, p. 95
decoding, p. 95
encoding, p. 95
episodic memory, p. 95
semantic memory, p. 95
executive processes, p. 96
distributed practice, p. 104
massed practice, p. 104
serial position effect, p. 105
part learning, p. 105
proactive inhibition, p. 105
retroactive inhibition, p. 105
overlearning, p. 105
elaboration strategies, p. 106
organizational strategies, p. 106
mnemonics, p. 108
loci method, p. 108
acronyms, p. 108
peg-word method, p. 108
key-word method, p. 108
matrix notes, p. 111
clustering, p. 112
mapping, p. 114
schemata, p. 118
generative teaching, p. 119
advance organizers, p. 120
pattern-recognition knowledge, p. 124
concept learning, p. 125
action sequence, p. 126
set effect, p. 127
task analysis, p. 127
critical thinking, p. 130
problem solving, p. 130

Suggestions for Further Reading

Beyer, B. K. (1987). *Practical strategies for the teaching of thinking*. Needham Heights, MA: Allyn & Bacon. A guide for the teaching of thinking skills, K–12.

Beyer, B. K. (1988). *Developing a thinking skills program*. Needham Heights, MA: Allyn & Bacon. Provides ideas on how to develop and implement a thinking skills program.

Chance, P. (1985). *Thinking in the classroom: A survey of programs*. New York: Teachers College Press. Describes eight curriculum programs and instructional strategies intended to develop thinking abilities.

Farnham-Diggory, S. (1992). *Cognitive processes in education* (2nd ed.). New York: HarperCollins. The author demonstrates how cognitive and developmental principles can be applied to teaching different content areas.

Gagné, E. D., Yekovich, C. W., & Yekovich, F. R. (1993). *The cognitive psychology of school learning* (2nd ed.). New York: HarperCollins. Discusses how recent developments in cognitive instructional psychology are applied to the teaching of academic subjects.

Glover, J., Ronning, R., & Bruning, R. (1990). *Cognitive psychology for teachers*. Columbus, OH: Merrill. A good overview for how teachers can use cognitive psychology in their instruction.

Levin, J. R., & Pressley, M. (Eds.). (1986). Learning strategies [Special issue]. *Educational Psychologist*, 21 (1, 2).

Mastropieri, M. A., & Scruggs, T. E. (1991). *Teaching students ways to remember: Strategies for learning mnemonically*. Cambridge, MA: Brookline. A detailed discussion with examples of how mnemonics instruction can be applied to the curriculum.

Pressley, M., Goodchild, F., Fleet, J., Zajchowski, R., & Evans, E. D. (1989). The challenges of classroom strategy instruction. *Elementary School Journal, 89*, 301–342. An excellent review article for learning strategies.

Pressley, M., et al. (1991). *Cognitive instruction that really improves children's academic performance*. Cambridge, MA: Brookline. A book filled with excellent examples for teaching students learning strategies in reading comprehension, vocabulary, spelling, writing, and mathematics.

Tiedt, I. M., et al. (1989). *Teaching thinking in K–12 classrooms: Ideas, activities, and resources*. Needham Heights, MA: Allyn & Bacon. Provides strategies that can be incorporated in your regular lesson plans and provides over 70 lesson plans.

For review of research on teaching thinking:

Adams, M. J. (1989). Thinking skills curricula: Their promise and progress. *Educational Psychologist*, *24*, 25–77.

Gick, M. L. (1986). Problem-solving strategies. *Educational Psychologist, 21*, 99–120.

McCormick, C. B., Miller, G. E., & Pressley, M. (Eds.). (1989). *Cognitive strategy research: From basic research to educational applications*. New York: Springer-Verlag.

Nickerson, R. S., Perkins, D. N., & Smith, E.E. (1985). *The teaching of thinking*. Hillsdale, NJ: Erlbaum.

Schneider, W., & Pressley, M. (1989). *Memory development between 2 and 20*. New York: Springer-Verlag.

Chapter 4

Motivation and Learning

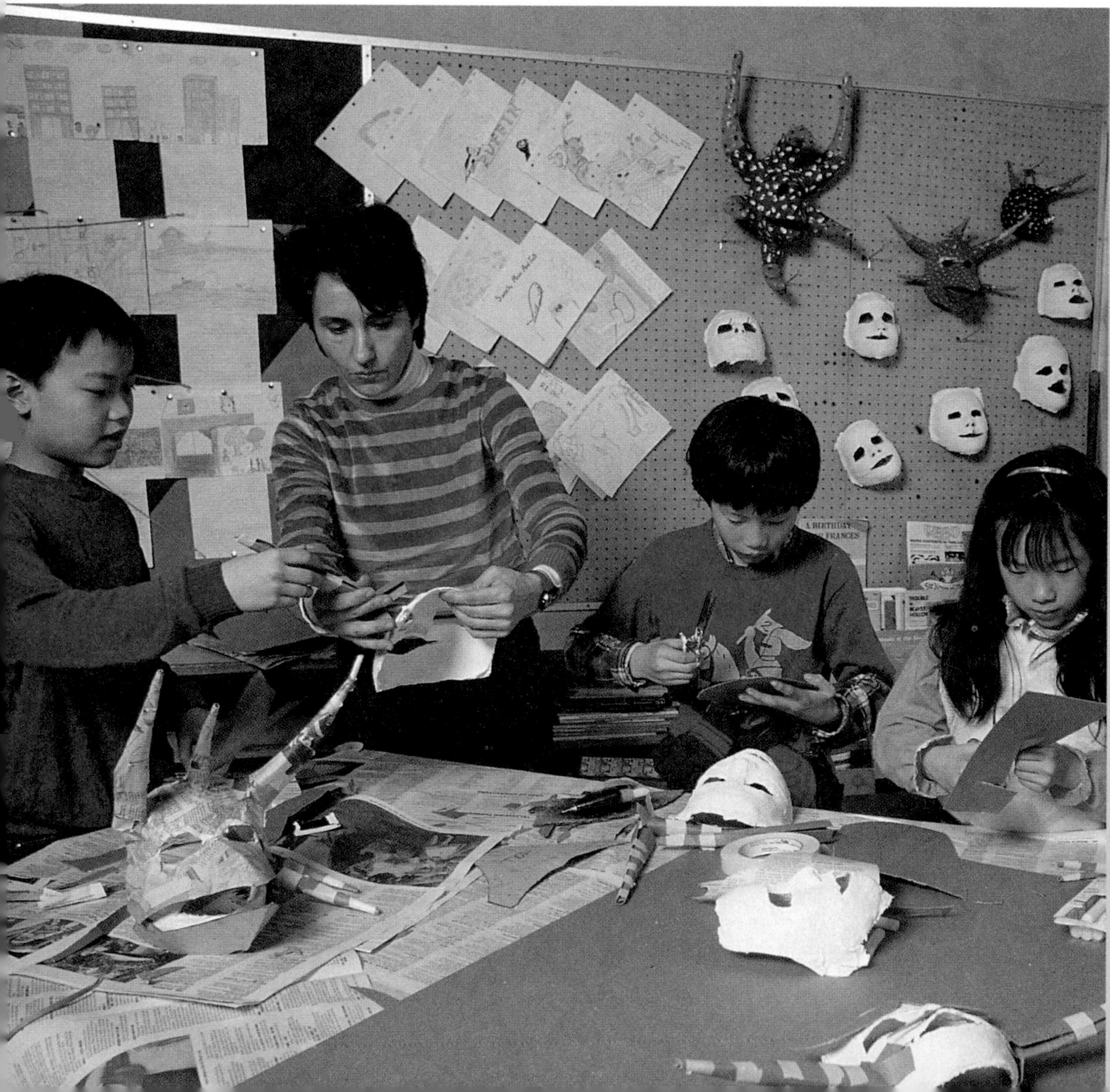

Personal Factors Influencing Motivation

Value Component: "Why Am I Doing This Task?"

Expectancy Component: "Can I Do This Task?"

Affective Component: "How Do I Feel about This Task?"

Classroom Organizational Factors Influencing Motivation

Task Dimension

Authority Dimension

Recognition Dimension

Grouping Dimension

Evaluation Dimension

Classroom Application: Preparing Students for Cooperative Learning

Time Dimension

Debate Forum: Is Ability Grouping an Effective Way to Deal with Student Differences?

Teacher Behavior

Teachers' Sense of Efficacy

Classroom Application: Motivating Students to Learn by Developing a Mastery Orientation

Teachers' Expectations as Self-Fulfilling Prophecies

Debate Forum: Are Junior High School Students Unmotivated?

Appropriate Teacher Expectations

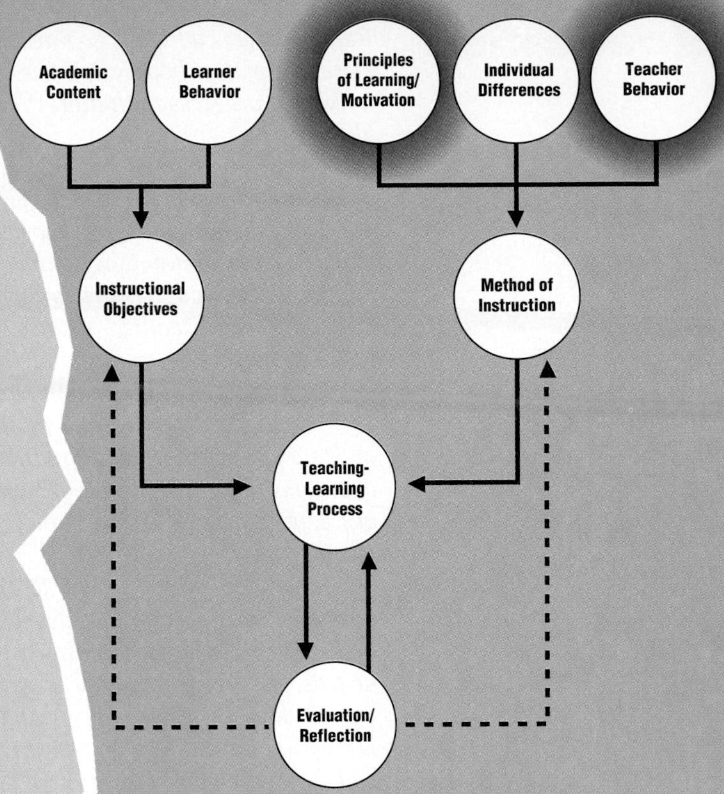

OBJECTIVES

After mastering the material in this chapter you will be able to:

- Describe how self-perceptions influence the use of learning strategies.
- Identify the different personal, classroom organizational, and teacher behavior factors that influence student motivation to learn.
- Describe how a teacher can make changes in classroom instruction to enhance student motivation and academic achievement.

Orientation

Many teachers have had a student who is bright and has all the potential in the world, but who seems to fall short when it comes to succeeding academically. Ralph Engel is a high school teacher who experienced this problem in his health class. No matter how Ralph tried to motivate Ryan Smith, he just couldn't seem to make any progress with him. What follows is Ralph's account of what he learned about Ryan:

"I knew Ryan from football, and he was one of those kids who never really gave one hundred percent. He made an effort, but only as much as necessary to stay on the team. That attitude used to keep him off of the field when we were in a clutch game, and unfortunately Ryan doesn't seem to have learned the lesson. He's still making only enough effort to 'stay on the team.' Here's a kid who could be getting A's and B's if he wanted, yet he consistently winds up with C's and occasionally D's. I'm frustrated, and I know that his parents are frustrated too.

"I got a chance to talk with Mr. and Mrs. Smith about Ryan. During the course of our conversation, I found that Ryan's father was a starting wide receiver at State University. I'm a graduate of State myself, so we naturally began to talk about our alma mater and, of course, our mutual love for football. As a result of our conversation, I began to piece together what I felt might be an explanation for Ryan's lack of motivation.

"Since elementary school, Ryan was expected to follow in his dad's footsteps, at least athletically. Ryan has developed the belief that in order for him to be accepted by his father, he must maintain a certain level of performance in athletics. When he was younger it was easy to give his best performance, knowing that his parents were feeling his sense of pride and were proud of his accomplishments on the field. Unfortunately, all of this ended when Ryan's younger brother, Josh, began to play ball.

"Ryan has to work twice as hard to accomplish the same task on the field that Josh seems to be able to achieve with minimum effort. Over the years, Ryan's father has slowly shifted his attention, and sense of gratification, from Ryan to his younger son. It is Josh who is now bringing home 'A' report cards and is receiving trophies as 'Outstanding Player' of the game.

"After spending the better part of two hours talking with Mr. and Mrs. Smith, I realized how parental expectation can influence student motivation."

Teachers experience many different motivational problems in the classroom. Some students are more concerned with avoiding failure than with trying to learn; others don't believe anything they do will lead to success; some students are so anxious that they can't concentrate on tasks; and other students have the ability to succeed but don't contribute in class because they lack self-confidence in their ability. Motivational theory and research helps teachers understand the different factors influencing achievement behavior in the classroom.

Two orientations have dominated teachers' traditional thinking about motivation. The behavioral approach views motivation in terms of intensity and duration of behavior. The student who works harder and longer on a task is perceived as more motivated than the student who fails to expend similar energy and persistence. (See Chapter 2 for extensive coverage of this approach in the discussion of operant conditioning.) Finding appropriate incentives or reinforcers to maintain task behavior is an important aspect of this approach.

The second orientation derives from the work by Atkinson (1964) and McClelland (1965), who view motivation as an unconscious drive or need that is socialized early in a child's life. This view closely aligns motivation with the study of personality. From this perspective, responsibility for increased academic involvement rests with students. Since motivation is strongly influenced by child-rearing experiences, teachers are limited in what they can do to change achievement motivation. Teachers often complain about students' family backgrounds and lament: "I don't know how to turn this student on!"

Maehr (1978) points out the inherent problem with this perspective: "If one assumes that motivational change only comes through personality change, one inevitably accepts a certain fatalistic outlook as a teacher. How many personality changes can a teacher—or even the best special education program—affect in a given year?" (pp. 223–224).

In this chapter, we will explore developments in a third approach—the *cognitive* view of motivation (see Ames & Ames, 1984, 1989), in which the teacher is concerned with *cognitive-mediational processes*—the personal explanations for success and failure and informational processing that occur in instructional settings. As a result, motivation is reflected in how students think about their goals, the task, and their feelings about completing the task. This approach seeks to understand *why* students choose to engage in academic tasks rather than what they do or how long they spend doing so. The fundamental principle is: If you want to change students' motivation, you will need to change their beliefs or self-perceptions.

As we saw in Chapter 1, both teacher and student beliefs influence teachers' classroom decisions and students' engagement in academic activities. How teachers view motivation will influence their perceptions of what they can do or should do to establish a classroom environment that will enhance student motivation. The cognitive view of motivation provides important insights for understanding, diagnosing, and remediating motivational deficiencies. Thus, I strongly believe that if teachers realize how much student motivation is influenced by students' self-perceptions that are *changeable,* rather than by personality characteristics that are less likely to be changed, they will assume more responsibility for the way students behave. This responsibility can encourage teachers to make modifications in classroom organization and instruction that increase student motivation to learn.

Pintrich and Garcia (1992) argue that motivational beliefs help students form an *intention to learn,* while cognitive strategies are used to enact learning. This important statement emphasizes the interaction between motivation and cognition that I first mentioned in the orientation section of the last chapter.

Teachers do not have to wait for students to become motivated to learn. As a teacher, you have the ability to influence the type of motivation displayed in the classroom through a variety of teaching decisions. Many of the factors that can contribute to a negative motivation pattern are identified in the teaching-learning model: student characteristics, teacher behavior, instructional procedures (including goals and tasks), and evaluation processes. I have divided this chapter into three sections: the personal beliefs and perceptions that influence student motivation, specific classroom practices, and the teacher behaviors that influence student motivation.

PERSONAL FACTORS INFLUENCING MOTIVATION

Our model for understanding personal factors influencing motivation is based on the work of Pintrich and DeGroot (1990), who identified three motivational components related to self-regulated behavior: a *value component*, which includes students' goals and beliefs about the importance and interest of the task ("Why am I doing this task?"), an *expectancy component*, which includes students' beliefs about their ability to perform the task ("Can I do this task?"), and an *affective component,* which includes students' emotional reactions to the task ("How do I feel about this task?").

Research on the three components indicates the following:

- Students who become involved in a task with the purpose of mastering it, who find it interesting, and who like academic challenges are likely to engage in more cognitive and metacognitive strategies (value component) (Ames & Archer, 1988; Paris & Oka, 1986).
- Students who believe that they are capable of completing a task engage in more cognitive and metacognitive strategies and persist at the task longer than students who believe they are less capable (expectancy component) (Paris & Oka, 1986; Schunk, 1989).
- Students who have test anxiety and/or feelings of disgust or shame because of their inability to complete a task successfully tend to be ineffective learners and often do not use appropriate learning strategies (affective component) (Benjamin et al., 1981; Covington, 1992).

You can learn a great deal about students' motivation by observing their behavior and learning about their beliefs and self-perceptions regarding academic tasks.

Value Component: "Why Am I Doing This Task?"

? How do students' goal orientations influence their motivation to learn?

Goal theory is one of the most recent approaches to the understanding of achievement motivation in schools (Weiner, 1990). Goal setting controls behavior by influencing future behavior. Goals motivate individuals and provide them with information about their abilities as they attain or fail to attain their goals. More important, achievement goals determine patterns of motivation that determine how learners think about and engage in different academic activities (Ames, 1992).

One perspective on goals distinguishes between mastery (don't confuse this term with mastery learning) versus performance goals (Dweck, 1985). A **mastery goal** is oriented toward learning as much as possible for the purpose of self-improvement, irrespective of the performance of others. A **performance goal** focuses on social comparison and competition, with the main purpose of outperforming others on the task. A similar dichotomy used by researchers is **intrinsic** and **extrinsic motivation.** Intrinsic motivation refers to doing an activity "for its own sake," or for the personal enjoyment and satisfaction of completing a task. Extrinsic motivation refers to behavior influenced by external events such as grades, points, or money. It is not uncommon for students to have multiple goals in school when they behave differently in different classes or pursue different goals in the same class (Wentzel, 1991). Table 4.1 summarizes the behaviors elicited by mastery and performance goal orientations.

mastery goal. Learning as much as possible for the purpose of self-improvement, irrespective of the performance of others.

performance goal. An orientation toward learning in which outperforming others is a major concern.

intrinsic motivation. Motivation influenced by personal factors such as satisfaction or enjoyment.

extrinsic motivation. Motivation influenced by external events such as grades, points, or money.

TABLE 4.1 TWO DEFINITIONS OF SCHOOLING

	Mastery	Performance
Success defined as . . .	improvement, progress, mastery, innovation, creativity	high grades, high performance compared with others, relative achievement on standardized measures
Value placed on . . .	effort, academic venturesomeness	demonstrating high performance relative to others
Basis for satisfaction . . .	progress, challenge, mastery	doing better than others, success relative to effort
School/classroom oriented toward . . .	how all students are learning, progressing	students' relative performance levels
Focus . . .	the student as a continual learner	periodic demonstration of achievements relative to others
Reasons for effort . . .	learn something new	high grades, demonstrated ability
Evaluation criteria . . .	absolute criteria; evidence of progress	norms; social comparisons
Type of involvement . . .	all participate; high degree of choice	differential participation by ability; low choice
Errors viewed as . . .	part of the learning process, informational	failure, evidence of lack of ability
Ability viewed as . . .	developing through effort	fixed

Source: Maehr, 1992.

Parents have a positive influence on a child's motivation to learn when they communicate high expectations, encourage a high degree of effort, and provide a supportive home environment.

Using the distinction between mastery and performance goals, we can understand how students define schooling and learning in different ways. The goal orientation that students adopt influences the effort they exhibit in learning tasks and the type of learning strategies they use. Thus, when students adopt a mastery goal orientation, they are more likely to have a positive attitude toward the task (even outside the classroom), to monitor their own comprehension, to use elaboration and organizational cognitive strategies, and to relate newly learned material with previously learned material. In contrast, students who adopt a performance orientation tend to focus on memorization and rehearsal strategies and often do not engage in problem solving and critical thinking. In general, they don't think about what they learn, but rather look for shortcuts and quick payoffs (Maehr & Anderman, 1993).

Maehr (1992) suggests that it shouldn't be surprising that students with different goal orientations behave differently in class:

> If a student's view of the purpose of learning is to be judged more able than other students, then why should she bother to engage in deep processing strategies (e.g., elaboration and organization) which often are time consuming and do not lead to immediate results? Why should she strive for a deep level of understanding if the "bottom" line is the score on a test of definitions of terms? Why should a student be curious about *why* hydrogen and oxygen make up water molecules, when in order to succeed, she merely needs to report that water consists of such molecules? (p. 2)

Different research investigations on students' goal orientation and learning processes in the classroom have produced consistent results: A mastery or intrinsic orientation for learning leads to higher levels of cognitive engagement or involvement in subject matter (Ames & Archer, 1988; Nolan, 1988; Pintrich & Garcia, 1992). In other words, students who adopt a mastery or intrinsic goal orientation use learning strategies such as elaboration and organization, and more metacognitive strategies than students who have a performance or extrinsic orientation. This research is an excellent example of the important interaction between motivation and learning. As I mentioned before, students may know about many different learning strategies, but may not choose to use them. Therefore, it appears important to learn about your students' learning goals.

GOAL SETTING AND MOTIVATION. Schunk (1991a) points out that the effects of goals on behavior depend on three properties: *specificity, proximity,* and *difficulty level*. Goals that set specific performance standards are more likely to increase motivation than are general goals such as "Do your best." Specific goals help the learner determine the amount of effort required for success and lead to feelings of satisfaction when the goal is attained. As a result, learners come to believe they have a greater self-efficacy regarding the task.

Goals also can be identified by the extent to which they extend into the future. Proximal goals are close at hand and result in greater motivation directed toward attainment than more distant goals. Pursuing proximal goals also conveys reliable information about one's capabilities. When students perceive they are making progress toward a proximal goal, they are apt to feel more efficacious and maintain their motivation. Since it is harder to evaluate progress toward distant goals, learners have more difficulty judging their capabilities even if they perform well.

Student perceptions of the difficulty of a task influence the amount of effort they believe is necessary to attain the task. If they believe they have the ability and knowledge, learners will work harder to attain difficult goals than when the standards are lower. As they work and attain difficult goals, they develop beliefs in their competence. However, if they don't believe they have the ability to attain a goal, they are likely to have low expectations for success and not become involved in the task. This is why it is important for teachers to give students easier goals in the beginning of a unit so they experience success and develop confidence in their ability for further learning.

The best example for this discussion is to think about how student motivation is influenced by the goals established by two different teachers. The first teacher simply tells students to write a term paper and hand it in on a certain date. The second teacher breaks the assignment down into different phases—prewriting (e.g., choose a topic; find, read, and take notes on three sources; use correct bibliographic notation), drafting (e.g., develop thesis statement, identify subtopics, draft subtopics), revising, editing, and submission (e.g., review and revise full document, prepare bibliography and table of contents). He provides his students with a checklist of all the activities under each phase, identifying the date each activity is due. He explains the criteria for each activity and provides feedback when it is handed in (Spaulding, 1992). Think about how the specificity, proximity, and difficulty level in goal setting in each class impact student motivation and perceptions of ability.

A final point about goals: Allowing learners to set their own goals may encourage greater interest in attaining them. Thus, setting conferences

locus of control.
Individuals' perception of who or what is responsible for the outcome of events and behavior in their lives.

learned helplessness.
A situation in which individuals learn over time, through constant failure, that they cannot control the outcome of events affecting their lives.

with students to discuss individual classroom goals or establishing contracts for completing academic tasks can help students take more responsibility for their learning and develop greater self-efficacy (Schunk, 1991a).

Expectancy Component: "Can I Do This Task?"

? How does perception of control influence motivation to learn?

CONTROL BELIEFS. The notion that individuals' perception of control influences their behavior has been discussed by many psychologists (deCharms, 1981; Deci, 1975; Rotter, 1966). Some students blame someone or something else for their poor performance: a poor test, a confusing book, or an incoherent teacher. These students believe external aspects of their environment wield control over their downfall (or over their success). They see themselves as powerless to counteract this trend. DeCharms used the terms *origins* and *pawns* to describe students who believe they can control their behavior and students who believe that others control their behavior.

Much of the conceptualization and research in this area stems from the social-learning theory of Rotter (1966), who used the term **locus of control** with two dimensions—*external locus of control* and *internal locus of control*. An "external" person perceives having little control over fate and fails to perceive a cause-and-effect relationship between actions and their consequences. An "internal" person holds the reins of fate securely and understands that effort and reward are correlated.

Students' control orientation is extremely important. If they do not anticipate teachers' approval as a response to their efforts, they will be less disposed to strive for success. Children will work harder at tasks if they believe they (rather than chance or the teacher) are responsible for the success they achieve (Lefcourt, 1966; Rotter, 1966). As they work harder and achieve success, they acquire better self-concepts of their ability.

Learned helplessness is one of the worst conditions that can develop when students learn over time that they have no control over the outcome of events (Abramson, Seligman, & Teasdale, 1978). That is, they see no relation between effort and the attainment of goals. As a result, they quickly abandon the use of learning strategies rather than attempt to modify their approach to learning.

Diener and Dweck (1978) completed an interesting investigation demonstrating the differences in motivation and use of learning strategies between "helpless" and successful students. Both groups of students were trained to solve a series of tasks. At the end of training, they were equally successful. In the second phase of the study, the researchers presented similar but unsolvable tasks to the students and asked them to verbalize their thoughts as they worked. As soon as the students began failing, the helpless children acted as if their prior successes had never occurred. They failed to use any reasonable learning strategies to solve the task and said such things as, "Nothing I do makes a difference" or "I don't have the ability to solve these tasks" or "I never did have a good memory." In general, their verbalizations (self-talk) were irrelevant to solving the problems. In contrast, during this failure stage, success-oriented students used the same learning strategies they had employed during the first stage of the study and tended to attribute failure to a lack of effort or to the difficulty of the task. Most important, their verbalizations served as self-monitoring statements: "I should slow down and try to figure this out" or "The harder it gets, the harder I have to try" or "I almost got it now."

SELF-EFFICACY BELIEFS. *Self-efficacy* is an individual's evaluation that he or she has specific performance capabilities on a particular type of task (Bandura, 1982). Efficacy perceptions are different from locus of control or outcome expectations. It is possible for a person to believe that a successful performance will lead to a desired outcome, for example, a good term paper will lead to a high grade (locus of control). Yet the person might not believe that he or she has the necessary knowledge or skill to perform well (self-efficacy). Thus, self-efficacy is a judgment about one's confidence in his or her ability to achieve a particular task. One way to determine self-efficacy concerning a task is to ask students a question like: How many of the following math problems do you think you can solve?

Perceived efficacy can influence motivation. Students with a high sense of efficacy are more likely to choose difficult tasks, expend greater effort, persist longer, apply appropriate problem-solving strategies on tasks, and have less fear and anxiety regarding tasks than are students with a low sense of efficacy for a task (Schunk, 1989).

Think about your beliefs and behavior regarding an assignment in a particular course that you believed you could complete and another assignment in which you doubted your competency. You may have procrastinated or attempted to avoid the task that you believed exceeded your abilities and might result in a low sense of efficacy. On the other hand, when you believed you had the skill to master tasks, you were probably eager to get started, worked hard, and gained further confidence in your ability when the task was successfully completed.

An investigation by Collins (1982) illustrates how self-efficacy beliefs impact achievement behavior. Collins selected students who were high, average, and low in mathematical ability and identified those students who had high and low mathematical self-efficacy. He found that within each ability group, those students who had high efficacy solved more problems correctly and were willing to redo problems they missed than were students low in self-efficacy. Self-efficacy was more predictive of achievement behavior than the students' actual ability levels.

Observing a similar peer successfully performing a task well can promote a sense of efficacy in the observer. For example, if a low-achieving

attribution. An individual's perception of the causes of his or her own success or failure.

student observes another low-achieving student successfully completing a math problem at the chalkboard, the observer is likely to believe that he or she also could learn to solve the problem. The effectiveness of the model can be enhanced if the model describes to the class how he or she studied, persisted at the task, or overcame any difficulty learning the task (Schunk, 1991a). Using culturally different students as peer models can also be an effective way to increase their classroom status and perceived competence by other students in the classroom.

> ? Why do students interpret success and failure differently and how does this interpretation influence motivation to learn?

ATTRIBUTION BELIEFS. One of the early theories of achievement motivation was developed in the 1950s and 1960s by David McClelland (1965) and John Atkinson (1964) and focused on motivation as a learned behavior. According to the theory, achievement behavior is based on the resolution of two competing needs—the need to achieve versus the need to avoid failure. Some students work hard for success without seriously worrying about the possibility of failure; other students think less about succeeding than about avoiding failure. Atkinson and Feather (1966) found that persons in whom motivations to achieve are stronger than motivations to avoid failure set goals of intermediate difficulty, whereas persons with the opposite motivational tendency avoid tasks of intermediate difficulty and prefer easier or more difficult tasks in which their efforts are either doomed to failure or guaranteed success. Avoiders of failure like very easy or difficult tasks because they are certain of succeeding at an easy task and they can rationalize failing a difficult task—either way they can't lose!

In the early 1970s Bernard Weiner and his associates (Weiner, 1972; Weiner et al., 1971) proposed a reinterpretation of Atkinson's theory. Weiner's research has shown that individuals' beliefs about the causes of their successes and failures are important in understanding achievement-related behavior. He has proposed an attributional model to explain achievement that includes the locus-of-control dimension. An **attribution** is the inference that an individual makes about the cause of behavior. Weiner's model deals with four major perceived causes of success and failure in achievement situations: *ability, effort, task difficulty,* and *luck.*

Table 4.2 shows that the attributions can be classified into two dimensions–stability and locus of control. Two of these attributions (ability and task difficulty) are stable in nature, whereas the others (luck and effort) change. This means that if a person were asked to repeat the same task, it is likely that the perception of ability and the difficulty of the task would remain the same. However, the perception of the role of luck and effort is likely to change from one time to another. The other dimension—locus of control—refers to whether a person's achievements are seen as being

TABLE 4.2 DETERMINANTS OF ACHIEVEMENT BEHAVIOR

Locus of Control	Success or Failure Attributed to Stability Factors	
	Stable	**Unstable**
Internal	**Ability** *"I'm good (bad) in science."*	**Effort** *"I studied hard for the test (I didn't study enough)."*
External	**Task Difficulty** *"The test was easy (hard)."*	**Luck** *"I guessed right (wrong)."*

under the person's own control (ability or effort) or are seen as being caused by forces external to the person (task difficulty or luck).

Let's look at some examples to understand how individuals assign causes to their performance and how these explanations affect subsequent achievement. Consider two students who have received a high score on an English test. The first student attributes success to superior ability, whereas the second student attributes success to luck. For the first student, success will likely increase self-confidence, since he attributed success to his own skills. For the second student, however, the impact of success will be less meaningful, since he takes no credit for it.

Attributions also affect future expectations in failure conditions. A person who fails an English test and attributes the failure to lack of effort may believe that she could do better next time if she tries harder, but the person who views failure as being due to a lack of ability will hold less hope for doing better in the future. For this reason, Weiner believes that the stability dimension (ability and task difficulty) is more predictive of future performance than the locus of control dimension (effort and luck).

Attribution beliefs can influence self-efficacy. For example, students who attribute academic problems to low ability are likely to have a low sense of efficacy and not try very hard to succeed. However, self-efficacy theorists argue that efficacy judgments, rather than attributions, are the major determiners of achievement behavior and affect (Ames, 1987).

Covington and Beery (1976) discuss attributions among success-oriented and failure-avoiding students. The most extreme case of failure avoidance is represented by learned helplessness. Success-oriented students tend to believe that they can handle most academic challenges. As a result, their ability is not viewed as an important issue in learning. Therefore, these students view success and failure as related to the quality of their efforts. The research clearly points out that success-oriented students tend to attribute success to ability and effort, and failure to lack of proper effort (see Bar-Tal, 1978). These explanations are helpful to the individual because success inspires further confidence as a sign of one's ability to do well, whereas failure signals the need to try harder. The success-oriented individual is not threatened by failure when it does occur, because it doesn't reflect on the individual's ability. This explanation also helps to understand why failure can be used to motivate already successful students.

Failure-avoiding students generally have a different set of attributions. They tend to attribute their failures to a lack of ability and attribute their successes to external factors such as luck or an easy task (Weiner & Kukla, 1970). It is difficult to imagine a more distressing situation—the students blame themselves for failure but take little or no credit for success. They feel that they have little control over their academic destiny so they minimize pain by trying to avoid failure.

If success is so important to a positive self-esteem, why do these students fail to take responsibility for their success? Covington and Beery (1976) believe that success implies an obligation to do well the next time. Students who find it difficult to live up to this expectation believe that success is not of their own making. Aronson and Carlsmith (1962) found that such individuals sometimes sabotage their own effort when they find themselves in danger of succeeding!

The attribution literature suggests that it is incorrect to assume that low-achieving students are always unmotivated. On the contrary, they appear to be extremely motivated—to avoid failure, rather than to succeed. Teachers need to spend more time learning about their students' beliefs about the causes of their success and failure.

There are some other considerations about the emphasis on effort you need to consider (Ames, 1990):

- Some students may already believe that they are working as hard as they can. If you convince these students that poor effort is the primary cause of their academic problems, they may decrease their sense of efficacy regarding the task. The reasoning may be as follows: If I try hard and still can't solve the problems, then I must lack ability.
- If you continually emphasize the importance of sustaining a maximal effort on tasks, some students may conclude that they don't want to work so hard to succeed.

The implication is that you need to (1) know how your students attribute the causes for their successes and failures, and (2) encourage both reasonable effort attributions and the use of appropriate learning strategies so that students can learn more effectively and efficiently.

All three of the self-perceptions discussed in this section—control, self-efficacy, and attributions—have been shown to influence the use of learning strategies. Research (see Schunk & Meece, 1992) shows that students who are high rather than low in internal control report they are better managers of their study time, their study environment, and their actual effort in the face of boring or difficult tasks. Students who feel more efficacious about their ability to do well in a course or on a task, and who believe that their behavior and effort influence their performance, are more likely to use different learning strategies than students who feel less efficacious about their ability and don't believe increased effort will make a difference in their achievement results.

? Why are resource management strategies necessary to become a successful learner?

resource management strategies. Strategies that assist students in managing the environment and the resources available.

Table 4.3, on page 158, identifies resource management strategies that can be added to the Taxonomy of Learning Strategies with cognitive and metacognitive strategies. **Resource management strategies** help students in managing their environment and available resources. These resources include planning the time available for studying and organizing time for other activities in one's life; establishing a study environment free of distractions; managing oneself in terms of effort, mood, self-talk, self-reinforcement; and seeking help from others. All of these resource management strategies have an impact on student motivation. Successful students use these strategies to help them adapt to the environment as well as modify the environment to fit their needs (McKeachie et al., 1990).

Think about the resource management skills that are necessary each semester at your college or university. One of the first things successful students learn if they live in dorms is how to plan their study schedule and find a quiet location to study. Students also must learn how to register for classes they want, how to get into courses taught by certain professors, how to get help from professors and teaching assistants, how to deal with the "blues" when they feel bad about a poor test result, how to self-motivate when they would rather party than study for an examination, and how to organize study teams when it is beneficial to study with others. Self-management is an important part of motivation. I have seen many bright students who were not successful in school because they had difficulty managing themselves to meet the requirements and demands of school. Assess your resource management strategies by analyzing each of the areas listed in Table 4.3. What are your areas of strength and weakness?

Affective Component: "How Do I Feel about This Task?"

? How are emotions related to causal explanations of success and failure? How can causal attributions of students and teachers conflict?

COVINGTON'S SELF-WORTH THEORY. The self-worth theory of achievement motivation (Covington, 1984, 1992; Covington & Beery, 1976) incorporates a motivational component with the causal perceptions of success and failure. According to self-worth theory, an individual learns that in our society one is valued because of one's accomplishments. The key factor to achievement motivation can be explained by how a person attempts to maintain positive ability perceptions that are the basis of self-worth.

Table 4.3 A TAXONOMY OF LEARNING STRATEGIES

Cognitive Strategies	Basic Tasks (e.g., memory for lists)	Complex Tasks (e.g., text learning)
Rehearsal strategies	Reciting list	Copying material Verbatim note taking Underlining text
Elaboration strategies	Mnemonics Imagery	Paraphrasing Summarizing Note making Creating analogies Answering questions
Organizational strategies	Clustering Mnemonics	Selecting main idea Outlining Mapping
Metacognitive Strategies		**All Tasks**
Planning strategies		Setting goals Skimming Generating questions
Monitoring strategies		Self-testing Focusing attention Comprehension monitoring Using test-taking strategies
Regulating strategies		Adjusting reading rate Rereading Reviewing Using test-taking strategies
Resource Management Strategies		**All Tasks**
Time management		Scheduling Setting goals
Study environment management		Finding defined area Finding quiet area Finding organized area
Effort management		Attributions to effort Dealing with mood Using self-talk Showing persistence Using self-reinforcement
Support of others		Seeking help from teacher Seeking help from peers Using peer/group learning Obtaining tutoring

Source: Adapted from McKeachie et al., 1990.

If a person fails at a task, the feedback evokes the possibility of a lack of ability. In addition, failure creates feelings of unworthiness and self-rejection. As a result, when individuals are faced with the possibility of failure, they will avoid the situation or develop strategies to protect against any inferences as to the lack of ability.

A problem that teachers must deal with is that children's perceptions of their academic abilities decline as they proceed through school (Nicholls, 1984). When children first enter school, they believe that effort is the most important student attribute. In fact, young children generally believe that students who work hard are brighter than those who do not try (i.e., ability and effort are perceived as synonymous). They also believe that working harder can actually cause an increase in ability. By working hard they can please their teacher and develop the positive image of a "good" student (Covington, 1984). The result of such perceptions is that young children do not feel bad when they fail.

By ages 11 and 12, students have considerably lower self-perceptions of competence. This change is due to the fact that, as students get older and perceive the social comparison in the classroom (e.g., grades, ability grouping), their sense of worth begins to depend on doing better than someone else. The consequence of social comparison information for most students leads to the realization that effort does not compensate entirely for ability. Thus, the belief that "I may not be as smart as I thought" begins to emerge as students progress through the elementary grades. Ames and Felker (1979) have shown that competition tends to magnify the positive affect associated with success (pride) and the negative affect associated with failure (shame or guilt).

Another factor related to changes in self-perceptions is that while young children believe that trying hard leads to improvement in ability, trying hard takes on negative characteristics for older children (by age 12). As these children make greater distinctions between effort and ability, they come to realize that success with a good deal of effort indicates lower ability. As a result, high effort becomes an indicator of low ability (Paris & Byrnes, 1989).

Holt (1982) provides a good example to illustrate how evaluation by others influences our behavior. The next time you are around an infant, observe her motivation in trying to succeed at a new task. The infant is like a scientist, always observing and experimenting. Even when the infant fails, she continues to try to make sense out of the environment. An infant does not react to failure as does a child or adolescent. "She has not yet been made to feel that failure is shame, disgrace, a crime. Unlike her elders, she is not concerned with protecting herself against everything that is not easy and familiar; she reaches out to experience, she embraces life" (Holt, 1982, p. 112).

If we examine the role of effort from both teachers' and students' perspectives, we will find that in some cases teachers and students operate at cross-purposes. Although teachers highly value achievement, they often reward (or punish) some students more than others for exactly the same level of performance. Students who are perceived as having expended effort (regardless of their ability) tend to be rewarded more and punished less than students who do not try (Weiner & Kukla, 1970).

However, Covington and Omelich (1979) found that students experienced greatest shame with a combination of high effort and failure and least shame with low effort and failure. This research helps to explain why failure-avoiding students often do not try! Expending effort and still failing poses a serious threat to one's self-esteem. The student who does not try but fails can always rationalize that success could have been achieved through proper effort, thus maintaining a reasonable level of self-esteem. Teachers, however, tend to reinforce students who demonstrate effort and punish those who do not. Understanding the perspectives of both the teacher and the student helps to see how effort can become a "double-edged sword" for many students. They must walk the tightrope between the threatening extremes of high effort and no effort at all. They must demonstrate some effort to avoid negative sanctions from their teachers—but not enough to risk shame should they try hard and fail. Some students use excuses to maintain a balance between these extremes. A popular tactic is to try hard but to use excuses (external factors) to explain why trying did not help. Such behavior avoids any inference as to low ability (Covington & Omelich, 1979). Covington (1983) summarizes the safe strategy of many students: "Try, or at least appear to try, but not too energetically and with excuses always at hand" (p. 149).

I can remember a friend in college who was a bright but anxious student. He always told everyone that he never had enough time to study before an exam. Everyone was impressed by the success he gained with little apparent effort. It was not until years later that I learned that he had always found time to study regularly during the term. If he did not do well on an exam, he always had his previously announced excuse that he had not crammed for the exam!

? How do students who are motivated to avoid failure behave in the classroom?

STRATEGIES FOR AVOIDING FAILURE. What strategies have you used to protect yourself from the possibilities of failure? Have you ever raised your hand early in a class period to answer a question, knowing that the instructor might not call on you later? Have you remained silent when asked a question by an instructor, hoping that if you paused long enough the instructor would rephrase the question once or twice until either the answer was given to you or someone else was called on? Have you ever entered a class when you had read only part of the assignment and raised a question early in the discussion, hoping that the instructor would not call on you again? If you stop to think about it, you will probably recall numerous incidents of classroom strategies that you used to protect yourself from failing.

I can identify with the following situation, and it may be uncomfortably familiar to you, too: A common practice in language classes is to require students to take turns translating sentences into English. As the instructor moves down the row asking one student after another to translate, anxious students are not paying attention to each translation. Instead, they are counting down the row to locate the sentence they will have to translate and begin covertly practicing the task. During this time they have missed the translations of all the previous sentences. Learning all the sentences is vital to the content of the particular lesson, but some students are more motivated to avoid failure than to learn the lesson.

Here is another example from elementary school: A student knows that the teacher does not collect seatwork, or if the teacher does collect it, it will not be corrected. If the assignment requires yes/no answers, multiple-choice, or >, <, = equations, the student need only pattern answers so that they look legitimate. The assignment gets "done," and the student is not hassled by the teacher to keep busy. Unfortunately, nothing is learned but how to avoid completing an assignment.

During the past few years, I have asked college students to provide examples of strategies they have used to avoid failure or to reduce personal responsibility for their achievement. The following are samples from my collection:

- Fail to show up for class when you're not prepared.
- If you fail to complete your assignment, tell the instructor at the *beginning* of the class that you left the assignment at home and will bring it in the next day. The instructor will be impressed with your honesty and usually will allow you the extra day.
- Remain anonymous to the instructor and class to avoid getting involved, and thus avoid the responsibility of participation.
- To avoid being called on, look at the instructor, then look down at your open book and flip through the pages as if you're looking for something. The instructor thinks you're looking for the answer, so he won't call on you.
- Study everything else but what you are supposed to study. When you run out of time, you can rationalize, "But I studied as much as I could, I really tried, I just didn't have enough time."
- Take your notes and books wherever you go (i.e., beach, meals, home). This lessens the guilt of wasting time.
- If you have no idea as to what is going on in class, and the big final is coming up, call for a study session and make sure all the smart people are present so they can "share their knowledge."

Do public school teachers and college instructors contribute to failure-avoiding strategies? If so, in what way? Discuss your opinions (diplomatically, of course!) with your instructor. What about procrastinators? How do students who study only at the last minute protect their self-worth?

? How does anxiety interfere with learning?

ANXIETY. Researchers have indicated that for some students small amounts of anxiety can facilitate learning (Sieber, O'Neil, & Tobias, 1977). If you feel confident and prepared for an examination, a little anxiety can serve as motivation to excel. However, if you have a high level of anxiety, it can be detrimental in achievement settings (Stipek, 1988).

The type and degree of anxiety differ widely among students. For some, anxiety is a generalized fear of the total school situation and, for others, a fear of specific aspects of the school environment such as teachers, peers, particular subject areas, or tests. In extreme cases (as in school phobias), the fear is so great that the child may refuse to go to school.

Some school subjects evoke more anxiety than others. For example, Tobias (1980) has written about math anxiety, pointing out that "math-anxious" and "math-avoiding" individuals do not trust their problem-solving abilities and experience a high level of stress when asked to use them. These anxious feelings about math can lead to lower grades and to the avoidance of math and math courses (Hackett, 1985; Hutton & Levitt, 1987). The sources of anxiety in math classes stem from time pressures to complete work, humiliation by being called on to perform in front of the class (remember the feeling when you were asked to put a homework problem on the board and were not prepared), and emphasis on right answers.

Test Anxiety. Test anxiety is a specific form of anxiety about academic and ability evaluation. Hill and Wigfield (1984) state: "Test anxiety is one of the most important aspects of negative motivation and has direct debilitating effects on school performance" (p. 106). Educators are especially concerned about this type of anxiety because it increases through the elementary grades to high school and becomes more strongly (i.e., negatively) related to indexes of intellectual and academic performance (Hembree, 1988; Wigfield & Eccles, 1989). As students proceed through school, the higher their anxiety is, the more likely it is that their achievement will be lower. There is also a negative correlation between anxiety and intelligence test scores: the higher the test anxiety, the lower the IQ score. To the argument that people with high anxiety are also less intelligent, and as a result, score lower on IQ tests, Gaudry and Spielberger (1971) respond: Highly anxious students perform as well as students with low anxiety on nonstressful and more structured tasks. Other researchers have found a more plausible explanation: Highly anxious students react to a normal intelligence test situation as they would to any regular examination seen as a stressful situation, but when intelligence tests or learning tasks are presented under "nontest" situations, highly anxious students perform as well as or better than students with low anxiety (Sarason et al., 1960; Wrightsman, 1962).

Recent research has focused on the relative independence of two dimensions of test anxiety—worry versus emotionality. Worry reflects the cognitive aspects of anxiety—the negative beliefs, troubling thoughts, and poor decisions. Emotionality refers to the unpleasant affective reactions such as tension and nervousness. Although both dimensions can have a debilitating effect on students, the worry dimension has a stronger negative relationship with academic performance than the emotional dimension. One reason for this finding is that emotionality tends to decrease once a student begins a test, while worrisome thoughts often continue throughout the test and may be experienced for a period of time in advance of the examination. Also, achievement suffers because attention is affected during test taking when students must remember, or retrieve, what was learned (Covington, 1992).

Covington (1992) has recently proposed an interaction model of achievement anxiety where he shows the effects of anxiety at three stages—appraisal, preparation, and test taking. Students' motivation to succeed or to avoid failure is determined in the test appraisal stage by whether they judge the upcoming test to be a challenge or a threat. In the test preparation stage, students begin studying while thinking about such things as their ability, expectation, and the futility and effectiveness of their study. Students threatened by failure may become involved in avoidance behaviors such as irrational goal setting or procrastination that will further erode their study effectiveness. Finally, in the test-taking stage, students attempt to retrieve what they have learned, sometimes in the face of great physical tension and worry. Anxiety, at this stage, interferes with the retrieval of information.

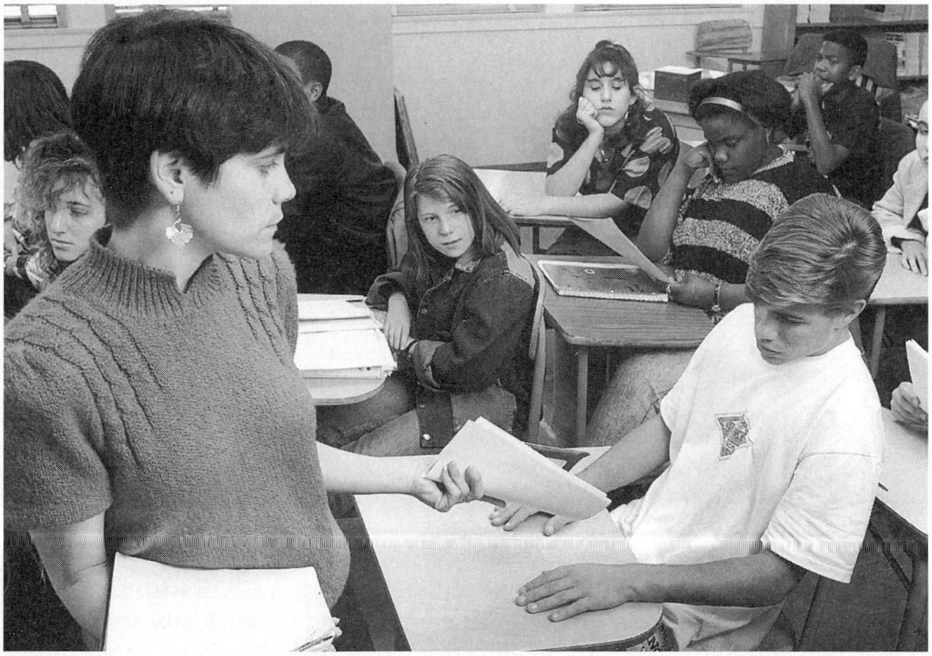

There are many anxiety-producing situations in a classroom. Can you relate to the student in this photo?

CLASSROOM ORGANIZATIONAL FACTORS INFLUENCING MOTIVATION

? How can a teacher modify the classroom environment to enhance students' motivation to learn?

In the previous section of this chapter I identified students' beliefs and perceptions that influence their motivation to learn. I also indicated that a mastery orientation toward learning is beneficial to academic success. The characteristics of mastery-oriented students identified in Table 4.1 include interest in improving their knowledge, willingness to take risks, enjoyment of academic challenges, belief that errors are part of the learning process, and belief that ability can be improved through exhibiting greater effort. One of the most important findings I discussed was that mastery-oriented students were more likely to use more complex learning strategies in their approach to learning.

Certain teacher behaviors and classroom instructional organizational factors are more likely to elicit a mastery goal orientation, thus changing students' motivational perceptions (Ames, 1992a). Six specific steps can be taken in the classroom to attain a mastery orientation. These steps—actually dimensions—were first identified and described by Epstein (1988) and are now being implemented by Ames (1992a) and Maehr (1992). The acronym TARGET represents the six interrelated dimensions: task, authority, recognition, grouping, evaluation, and time (see Figure 4.1).

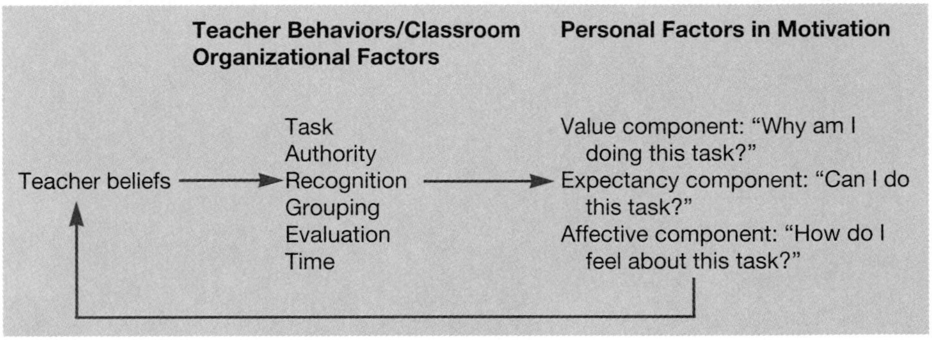

Figure 4.1 A Framework for Enhancing Student Motivation to Learn.

Task Dimension

The task dimension focuses on designing learning activities, tasks, and assignments that increase student interest and involvement in learning. For example, having students complete dittos comprising boring exercises or using the class period to have students look up answers to text questions are not learning activities designed to stimulate curiosity or interest in learning. Teachers need to develop tasks that make learning more interesting and involve variety and personal challenge (Brophy, 1986).

Teachers also need to think about how they present assignments and whether the assignments challenge students to become involved in the subject matter. Brophy et al. (1983) found that students were less likely to become involved in a task when the teacher introduced it in a negative fashion (i.e., suggesting the task was boring or pointless, or that they would find it difficult or frustrating). You can probably remember the attitudes of students in a class when a teacher said something like, "I really don't want to teach this, but the school district requires it," or "This section is the least interesting of the course."

UNIDIMENSIONAL VERSUS MULTIDIMENSIONAL CLASSROOMS. The manner in which tasks are defined can influence students' perceptions of their own and others' ability. Rosenholtz and Simpson (1984) found that some teachers develop a unidimensional classroom, where all students tend to use the same materials and are given the same assignments, and there is a single standard for success. These teachers constantly reinforce the notion that some students are smarter than others, and they behave in ways that support this belief (for example, constantly talking about the "top" or "smarter" students).

Other teachers develop a multidimensional classroom where students work on different assignments and tasks and have less opportunity to compare their performance with others. These teachers often communicate to their students how much everyone in the class is learning and that there are many different ways to succeed. In addition, these teachers point out that all students have different strengths and weaknesses. The advantage of this classroom climate is that students develop a sense of their own ability that is not dependent on the comparison of ability with others (Ames, 1992a).

Finally, teachers need to compare the tasks they give to low-achieving and high-achieving students. Let's take reading as an example. Poor readers spend less time reading aloud, read fewer pages and books, and receive less emphasis on higher-order comprehension or thinking skills. Poor readers spend most of their reading time on isolated drill and practice activities, particularly letter-sound relationships and word pronunciation. Good readers spend more time trying to comprehend what they read (Allington, 1991). Why should it be surprising, then, that poor readers continue to read less well, when they are less likely to be given tasks that will make them better readers?

Ames (personal communication, July 10, 1992) believes that low-achieving students are asked to spend more time doing drill and practice tasks that put them further behind their classmates. Therefore, they actually spend more time doing what they are not good at—which only reinforces their self-beliefs that they aren't able. In contrast, high achievers spend time doing what they are good at, which reinforces their beliefs that they are able. Over time, the academic achievement of the two groups becomes magnified.

Throughout this book I recommend teaching practices to help students learn more effectively— cooperative learning, mastery learning, computer-assisted instruction, and a variety of learning strategies. These teaching and learning methods are not only for high achievers. *Both* high and low achievers benefit from stimulating and varied tasks.

As you observe in classrooms, consider the nature of instruction given to high and low achievers as well as students from different ethnic and racial groups. Consider your next reaction to someone who states: "This task, activity, or method won't work with these students!"

Authority Dimension

The authority dimension involves how much opportunity students are given to take their own initiative and responsibility for their learning. Your beliefs regarding how motivation should be viewed influences classroom organization. If you believe that students have little inclination to learn in school and need to be encouraged to learn through external incentives, you are more likely to be influenced by procedures that emphasize more teacher control over learning activities. If you believe that children are naturally curious and that learning is a process of self-discovery such that motivation comes from within the person, you are likely to establish a different type of classroom situation. You do not have to take a position at either extreme. Some educators believe that intrinsic motivation can be used to guide much of classroom learning and that students may need some external incentives to learn material they are less interested in.

An important issue regarding intrinsic versus extrinsic motivation is how teachers can maintain student involvement in learning activities that are not very interesting or exciting to students, without alienating them from learning or having a negative effect on their self-concepts or independence (Ryan, Connell, & Deci, 1985). This issue is especially important because there appears to be a steady decrease in students' intrinsic motivation for learning as they progress through school (deCharms, 1981; Harter, 1981).

The way you organize the classroom environment can have considerable impact on students' motivation and their view of themselves. Two investigations reported by Ryan, Connell, and Deci (1985) further illustrate this point.

Deci, Nezlek, and Sheinman (1981) explored the relationship between a teacher's orientation to students' intrinsic motivation and self-esteem. They identified autonomy- and control-oriented teachers. *Autonomy-oriented teachers* are likely to support students in solving their own problems and pursuing their own interests. *Control-oriented teachers* are likely to motivate students with rewards and to use subtle control procedures. The researchers found that students' motivation and perceived competence were strongly related to the orientation of the teachers. In particular, belief in the ability to achieve individually and in self-worth was greater in classrooms of autonomy oriented teachers than in classrooms of control-oriented teachers.

In another investigation, Ryan and Grolnick (1984) determined the extent to which students viewed their classrooms to be autonomy oriented versus control oriented. The data indicated that students who perceived their classrooms as more autonomy oriented were higher on intrinsic motivation and perceived cognitive competence, and reported higher levels of self-esteem than did the students who perceived their classrooms as more control oriented.

continuing motivation. The tendency to return to and continue working on tasks away from the classroom without the supervision or control of the teacher.

Researchers also have found that teachers can undermine intrinsic motivation and learning by too much emphasis on external rewards or incentives (see Lepper & Hodell, 1989, for a detailed discussion of this literature). It appears that when students already enjoy an activity and receive rewards for participating in the activity, they will be less likely to return to the activity than students with the same interest who didn't receive any rewards for participation.

This result seems contrary to what you have already learned about reinforcement theory. Could it be that too much reward is not good? Let's look at one explanation of this phenomenon: When students receive a reward for doing something, they attribute the reward as the reason for engaging in the activity even if, without the reward, they would have been intrinsically motivated to complete the task. Once they perceive the extrinsic reward as the reason for participating in the activity, they will engage in the activity if the reward is given. Another way of explaining this result is that the students discount their initial interest in the task as the reason for doing the task. Instead, the more powerful extrinsic reward is perceived to be the cause (Stipek, 1988).

This research doesn't suggest that rewards are bad or that teachers should not reinforce students. You need to differentiate between using rewards to involve students in activities that they don't want to pursue (such as completing homework assignments) and using rewards in situations in which students already enjoy the assigned activity. Don't worry about undermining intrinsic motivation in the former case; it is only when the activity may be interesting or enjoyable where you need to omit or reduce the use of rewards for students. Stipek (1988) suggests: "When extrinsic rewards are used to prod students into initially engaging in a task, every effort should be made to shift students' attention away from the extrinsic reward and toward the importance of the task and the feelings of competence that derive from mastery" (p. 67).

? Does it make a difference how teachers motivate students?

CONTINUING MOTIVATION. Maehr (1976) has cautioned teachers to be concerned about students' **continuing motivation**—that is, the tendency to return to and to continue working on tasks away from the classroom without the supervision or control of the teacher. These questions pertain to continuing motivation: Will students read during vacations? Will students visit scientific exhibits and museums? Will students follow current events? Will young adults vote? The point is that although teachers have power and control over students while they are in the classroom and can make them follow directions and complete academic tasks, some of the methods they use to attain these short-term objectives (e.g., punishment, threats, and criticism) may be detrimental to the students' continuing motivation in the subject area. Inappropriate classroom experiences can make today's highly motivated students tomorrow's unmotivated students. Pascarella et al. (1981) found that although teacher control was positively related to science achievement in high school, it was negatively related to a number of behavioral indicators of continuing motivation.

Finally, an important motivational factor is the degree of freedom in selecting the task or assignment. In general, giving students some options as to the type of assignment they can complete is related to continuing motivation. Maehr (1984) believes a choice of assignments can affect the meaning or purpose of the task and result in greater personal investment. However, if the teacher strongly emphasizes social comparison, student choices may be based on completing the selected task successfully (i.e., to protect one's perceptions of ability) rather than selecting the task because of interest (Ames, 1990).

Recognition Dimension

The recognition dimension concerns the formal and informal use of rewards, incentives, and praise in the classroom. These factors have important consequences for students' interest in learning as well as their feelings of self-worth and satisfaction with their learning (Ames, 1992a). The problem, however, is that many classrooms are managed under the false assumption that competition motivates students to achieve. The result is a scarcity of rewards, the majority of which go to the best students in the

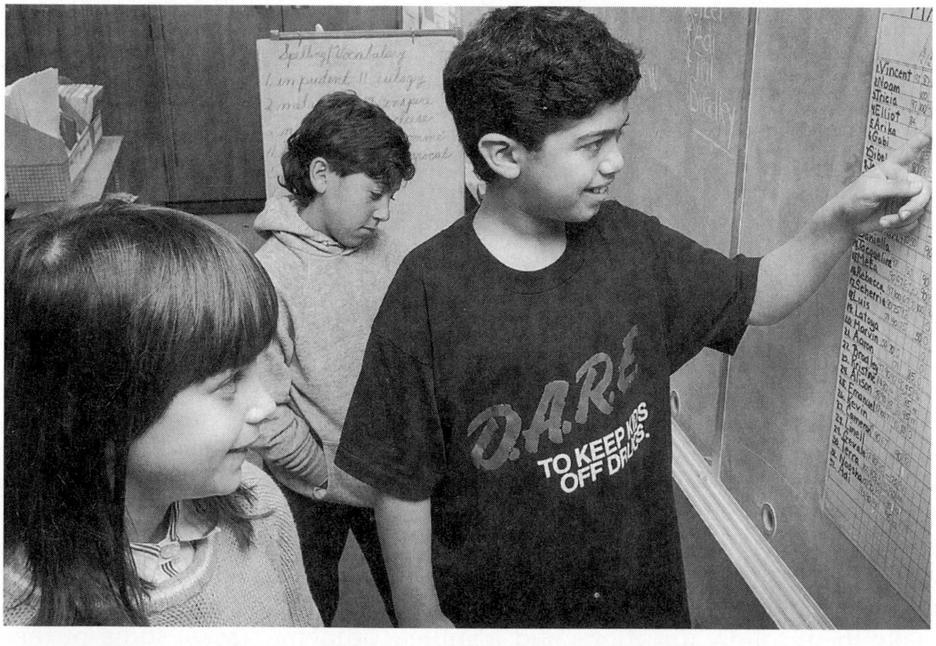

Classroom charts and graphs identifying student progress do not motivate all students to excel.

class. Less-capable students have a more difficult time being recognized for their achievement or accomplishments in these classrooms. Can you think of some ways to recognize more students for their accomplishments in the classroom? What were some of the methods used by some of your teachers in school? What practices would you implement, and what practices would you avoid?

There are situations in which a limited amount of competition can be effective (e.g., motivating a group of bored students to complete an assignment, or motivating a group of learners of similar ability to work harder). However, competition doesn't motivate low-achieving or failure-avoiding students to become more involved in academic tasks (Covington, 1992). It sometimes does the opposite by causing students to withdraw from classroom activities and take fewer risks!

I used to play tennis with a friend who made the ball spin all over the court while I ran from side to side attempting to return it. One day, when he said: "Next Tuesday at the same time?" I replied that I was busy and would get back to him. I neither enjoyed the competition nor did it make me want to practice my tennis skills because I perceived that I had no chance of success. Can you think of examples in your own life when competition had positive and negative effects on your motivation *and* behavior?

? How can the improper use of praise have a negative impact on students?

THE USE AND MISUSE OF PRAISE. There is no question that teachers need to find more opportunities to reinforce and praise students for their accomplishments. However, *how* praise is given appears to be an important factor in its impact on students. Teachers need to reconsider the common strategy of finding opportunities to constantly praise students for all types of behavior and academic performance. You may be thinking: "What's wrong with praising students? Isn't this a good way to communicate high expectations and reinforce good behavior at the same time?" Brophy (1981) has pointed out how the incorrect use of praise can undermine achievement behavior. When teachers try to find something good in the work of low-achieving students to encourage them, the praise is often for some irrelevant or unimportant aspect of completing the task. For example, if the task is to complete math problems, commenting on a student's neat homework paper is not likely to have the positive effect on the student that the teacher intended. What happens is that the student often discounts the praise. What's worse is that the student often interprets the praise to be unrelated to effort or performance, but as evidence of lack of ability. The result is a negative effect on self-efficacy. The student may be thinking the following about the teacher: "He must really think I'm dumb, if he praised me for that," or "How could she say that paper looks good, I know it's lousy."

cooperative learning. Instructional procedures that depend on students helping one another to learn in small groups.

The effect of praise also must be considered in terms of the students' stage of development. For young students who view effort and ability similarly, praise can enhance their perceptions of their competence. However, for older students who view ability and effort differently, praising their effort may be interpreted as having low expectation for their ability (Ames, 1990).

Brophy (1981) provides guidelines for the effective use of praise. Included in his advice is

- praising genuine progress or accomplishment
- making it contingent upon objective accomplishment
- specifying the reasons why it is given
- making it private (so as not to embarrass the student)
- attributing success to effort and ability

Grouping Dimension

? How does cooperative learning enhance student motivation to learn?

Grouping focuses on students' ability to work cooperatively with others rather than competitively on school tasks. As we discussed in the previous section, using competition extensively does not necessarily produce the intended motivational effects. As a result, teachers are turning more to **cooperative learning.**

Let's look quickly first at what cooperative learning is *not* (Johnson & Johnson, 1987):

- assigning individual projects and allowing students to interact so they can check their progress or ask questions of other students
- assigning a group project with one student doing most of the work
- having students sit together as they do their own homework assignments

Johnson and Johnson (1989) describe what cooperative learning *is*. Five basic elements that need to be included for a lesson to be cooperative are:

- *Positive interdependence.* Students must perceive that they "sink or swim" together. This means that they must share goals, divide the tasks, share resources and information, assume responsibility for different roles, and, most important, receive rewards based on their group performance.
- *Face-to-face interaction.* Students discuss the nature of the task, decide how they can best work together, and explain to one another how to solve problems. The importance of helping others is emphasized.
- *Individual accountability for learning the assigned material.* Each student must develop a sense of personal responsibility to the group. A key to

success in cooperative learning is for each member to master material so that he or she can help other members of the group achieve success.
- *Collaborative skills.* Obviously, placing students in groups and telling them to work cooperatively without teaching them the necessary social skills will not lead to compatible working relationships within the group.
- *Group processing.* Students discuss and evaluate their progress and maintain effective working relationships among members.

jigsaw method. A procedure that emphasizes and reinforces cooperation among students.

In cooperative learning, students work together in small (four- to six-member) teams that remain stable in composition for many weeks. There are many ways to organize cooperative learning in classrooms. We will focus on five of the most widely used and researched techniques: Teams-Games-Tournaments (TGT), Student Teams–Achievement Divisions (STAD), Jigsaw, Group Investigation, and Team-Assisted Individualization (TAI).

TEAMS-GAMES-TOURNAMENTS (TGT). In TGT, students of different ability, race, and gender are assigned to four- to five-member teams. After the teacher presents the material for the day, the teams complete worksheets, quiz one another, and study together in preparation for a tournament, which is usually held once each week. In the tournament, students are assigned to three-person "tournament tables" where they compete with students of similar ability (based on the previous week's outcomes). As a result, the lowest-achieving students in each group have the same opportunity to earn points for their teams as the highest-achieving students.

The tournaments consist of students' taking turns picking cards and answering corresponding questions on the material studied during the week. At the end of the tournament, the teacher prepares a newsletter that recognizes successful teams and the top scores (similar to the results in a bowling league!). Although team membership stays the same, tournament table assignments are changed on the basis of the performance of individual students. Low achievers, who initially compete against students of similar ability, can compete against high achievers as they become more competent.

STUDENT TEAMS–ACHIEVEMENT DIVISIONS (STAD). STAD uses the same four- to five-member teams used in TGT but replaces the tournament with 15-minute quizzes, which students take after studying with their teams. The quiz scores are translated into team scores, with top scores receiving more points than lower scores. An "improvement score" also has been used

JIGSAW. In the **jigsaw method,** students are assigned to small, heterogeneous teams. The academic material is divided among the members of the team, and students study their parts or sections with members of other teams who have the same material to learn. Next, they go back to their groups and teach their sections to team members. Finally, all the group members are tested on the entire body of information. For example, suppose a teacher established an objective that required the students to learn biographical information on Martin Luther King, Jr. The teacher would divide the biographical information into four or five parts depending on the number of students in the groups. The students would study with members of other groups who had been given the same section of the biography. Then they would go back and teach their section to the rest of their own group. The goal is to have each group learn the complete biographical information. Student scores can be determined by a variety of procedures. One approach records grades for individual students only. In another approach, quiz scores are used to establish team scores.

GROUP INVESTIGATION. Group Investigation is a method of cooperative learning in which students work in small groups to complete various class projects. Each team breaks the task into subtopics with individual students carrying out the activities needed to achieve their group goal. Each group makes a presentation about its research to the class. In group investigation, rewards or points are not given; instead, students are asked to work together to achieve group goals.

Sharon et al. (1984) described the following six steps of the Group Investigation approach:

1. *Topic selection.* Students choose specific subtopics within a general problem area, usually delineated by the teacher. Students then organize into small two- to six- member task-oriented groups. Group composition is academically and ethnically heterogeneous.
2. *Cooperative planning.* Students and teacher plan specific learning procedures, tasks, and goals consistent with the subtopics of the problem selected in Step 1.
3. *Implementation.* Pupils carry out the plan formulated in Step 2. Learning should involve a wide variety of activities and skills and should lead students to different kinds of sources both inside and outside the school. The teacher closely follows the progress of each group and offers assistance when needed.
4. *Analysis and synthesis.* Pupils analyze and evaluate information obtained during Step 3 and plan how it can be summarized in some interesting fashion for possible display or presentation to classmates.
5. *Presentation of final product.* Some or all of the groups in the class give an interesting presentation of the topics studied in order to get classmates involved in each other's work and to achieve a broad perspective on the topic. Group presentations are coordinated by the teacher.
6. *Evaluation.* In cases where groups pursue different aspects of the same topic, pupils and teachers evaluate each group's contribution to the work of the class as a whole. Evaluation can include either individual or group assessment, or both. (pp. 4–5)

TEAM-ASSISTED INDIVIDUALIZATION (TAI). TAI is an excellent example of how behavioral and humanistic principles are combined to teach mathematics in a cooperative learning format (Slavin, 1985). In this approach, students are assigned to four- to- five- member, mixed-ability learning teams, as well as skill-level groups on the basis of a placement test. Students proceed through a specific hierarchy of skills. Teachers work with the skill-level groups on different mathematics concepts and skills, after which students return to their teams and work on self-instructional materials. Group members check one another's work against answer sheets, help with difficult problems, and prepare one another for quizzes. Students who achieve mastery scores on quizzes add points to their teams' scores. At the end of each week, groups that exceed a pre-established criterion for completing units of material can earn certificates or other rewards. Students who do not achieve at a mastery level are given special help.

RESEARCH ON COOPERATIVE LEARNING. Investigations on cooperative learning have found that in most cases it has a positive effect on academic achievement. It also increases students' cooperative and altruistic behaviors and students' liking of others. In addition, it can improve race relations and the social acceptance of mainstreamed students in regular classrooms. Finally, there is evidence that cooperative learning can improve thinking skills (Johnson & Johnson, 1987; Slavin, 1990). On the basis of positive research findings, it appears that cooperative learning can be an effective instructional method for attaining many of your classroom instructional objectives.

Research on cooperative learning indicates that it can have a positive effect on both academic achievement and interpersonal relations.

? How do individual differences influence group functioning?

Group Interaction. Webb (1985, 1987) has reviewed the research on helping behaviors that contribute to successful learning in cooperative groups. She has reported that it is important to differentiate between giving help and receiving help as well as to distinguish between different kinds of help. Help that a student gives to others in his or her group can be categorized as *explanations* or as *terminal help*. Explanations consist of step-by-step descriptions of how to solve a problem or how to correct an error. An example of an explanation given during a unit on scientific notation is: "Okay, look. 63,000,000 times 8,500,000. This is 63 with 6 zeros. So in parentheses, 63 times 10 to the sixth and then 85 times 10 to the fifth . . ." (Webb, 1982, p. 646). Terminal help, on the other hand, consists of brief responses such as "No, that's not right," or "No, I got 45,000,000." The following are findings from Webb's reviews:

- Not all kinds of help are equally effective.
- How often students give and receive help is not important for learning.
- Giving and receiving explanations are beneficial to learning.
- Giving and receiving terminal help are not beneficial to learning.
- Exchanging information is not effective for learning (e.g., "The answer to number 4 is 36.78" or "That's not right. I got 23.5.")
- Receiving no response to one's question is detrimental to learning.
- High-ability students are most likely to give explanations to others.
- Extroverted students are more successful than introverted students in obtaining explanations when they ask questions.
- Boys may be more successful than girls in obtaining help.
- Groups with only students of *medium* ability spend more time explaining, and all students participate in group discussions.
- Heterogeneous groups with a moderate range of ability demonstrate a high level of explaining.
- Groups with only low-ability or high-ability students do little explaining.
- In groups with a wide range of ability, the high-ability students often explain to the low-ability students while ignoring the middle-ability students.
- In groups with an equal number of boys and girls, all students are able to obtain help when asked.
- In groups where boys outnumber girls or girls outnumber boys, the boys are more successful than the girls in obtaining help.
- In groups of mostly girls, the girls direct many of their questions to the boy who is not likely to answer all of their questions.
- White students tend to be more active and influential in groups than minority students.

Webb (1987) suggests that the teacher who initiates cooperative learning should begin first by assigning an equal number of boys and girls to a group, forming groups in which students have "medium" ability or in which there is a moderate range of ability, and avoiding group compositions with only one boy or one girl, or all low- or high-ability students. In addition, students need to be taught when and how to ask for help, and how to give help.

Seeking Help. Certain students are more likely to ask for help. Table 4.3 identified help-seeking as an important resource management skill. Newman (1991) states: "Seeking help from a knowledgeable other person can be more beneficial than giving up prematurely, more appropriate than waiting passively, and more efficient than persisting unsuccessfully on one's own" (p. 154). Yet not all students seek help when they need it. The research indicates that children who perceive themselves to be academically competent, who feel in control of their academic success, and who have a mastery orientation view help-seeking as an effective learning strategy and are more likely to seek help (Newman & Schwager, 1992).

The research indicates that low-achieving students, who need help the most, often are less likely to seek it. Sometimes the reason for not seeking help rests on the students' attitudes or perceptions about help; that is, they won't get help from teachers or peers if they ask, will get a negative reaction from peers, or feel too embarrassed to ask. Also, the classroom climate and structure of activities influence help-seeking behavior. Classes that emphasize the importance of cooperative learning and are based on a mastery orientation are more likely to encourage help-seeking behavior (Newman, 1991).

Cultural and Racial Factors in Group Interaction. Cohen (1982, 1986) has been concerned with improving group interaction in multiracial groups where white students dominate minority students. This condition

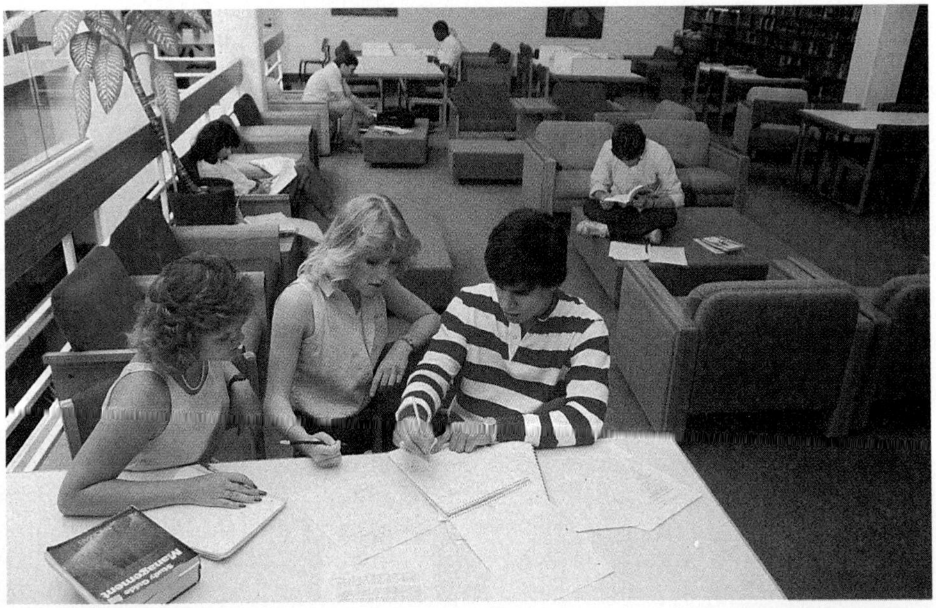

Successful students know when to seek help from others.

is likely to occur even when minority students have more ability than white students. Cohen attributes this behavior to status differences between the two groups of students. The white students talk more often and their suggestions are used more often by the group. In evaluations after group work, the white students are seen as having better ideas and are viewed as the leaders of the group. The problem is that students sometimes act as if race or ethnicity (and sometimes gender) were itself an indicator of competence. Unless someone shows them otherwise, they will tend to use these false indicators to guide their behavior.

While it is often difficult to change students' perceptions of one another, Cohen and her colleagues (see Cohen, 1982) have found some success by altering students' expectations about one another's competence. They gave minority students special training on tasks and asked them to tutor white students on the tasks. When groups of white and minority students were formed, the white students no longer dominated the group interaction.

Cohen (1986) also thinks that providing opportunities for all group members to experience different assigned roles may help to change competence expectations held for low-status students. Students are assigned to the roles of facilitator (to see that everyone in the group gets the help she or he needs), checker (to make sure that everyone finishes his or her work), and reporter (to present what the group found during each work session). This approach led to greater interaction among students but did not eliminate the impact of all status influence in the groups.

Be aware of status differences in group interaction. If certain students believe that other students are not capable of helping them, they may not ask for assistance, offer to help them, or even work cooperatively with them. Thus, while educators are excited about the outcomes of cooperative learning, we must realize that simply placing students in groups will not lead to greater learning for all students unless the teacher deals directly with the factors that contribute to unequal or inappropriate group interaction.

Evaluation Dimension

The evaluation dimension of enhancing motivation involves the classroom procedures used to assess and monitor student learning. (Many of the following comments are also related to the recognition dimension.) Evidence suggests that student motivation can be undermined by the evaluation procedures used in class (Covington, 1992). In developing a mastery orientation, students need to feel that mistakes are a normal part of the learning process, and that opportunities will be available to improve their work. In this way, students are more likely to feel that effort pays off (Ames, 1992).

Many activities in school are competitive—a circumstance that often emphasizes social comparison and eventually leads to a performance orientation rather than a mastery orientation. Ames (1992a) states: "Children are more likely to adopt a mastery goal orientation when evaluation is based on personal improvement, progress toward individual goals, participation and effort" (p. 341). She recommends that teachers focus on the

CLASSROOM

Application

PREPARING STUDENTS FOR COOPERATIVE LEARNING

I have spoken to many teachers who say that they have tried cooperative learning but that it did not work. After further discussion, it was apparent that their students had little experience with and preparation for group learning. Remember that students spend most of their school experiences competing with one another and often find it difficult to abandon their competitive approach to learning.

The success of cooperative learning depends a great deal on the ability of students to interact appropriately in group settings. Johnson et al. (1984) identify a number of interpersonal skills necessary for success in cooperative settings:

Forming skills are needed for organizing the group and for establishing minimum norms of appropriate behavior. Such skills include being able to move into and out of groups with a minimum of noise and disruption, working quietly and actively while in the group (i.e., staying on task), encouraging everyone to participate, and interacting with group members in a courteous way. One of the most important behaviors that teachers need to stress is that put-downs are not a part of effective group functioning.

Functioning skills are the second level of cooperative skills. They involve the managing and implementation of the group's efforts to achieve tasks and to maintain effective working relationships among members. Such skills include expressing support and acceptance for the contribution of group members, knowing

continued

comparison between students' current performances and their earlier performances on the same or similar tasks, or on comparison between the students' current performance and some set of predetermined criteria for successfully completing the assignment rather than on comparisons with other students.

Teachers frequently post grades on tests or quizzes. This kind of public evaluation fosters social comparison processes that also can lead to a performance orientation. Next time you are in a classroom, notice who looks at the charts and graphs that are used to report student progress. In my experience, it is the students on top rather than those on the bottom of the chart who are most interested in the class ranking. Do you think that the

when and how to ask for help or clarification about what is being said or done, offering to explain or clarify another student's position, and motivating the group with new ideas or suggestions when enthusiasm wanes.

Formulating skills are directed at helping students to understand and remember the material being studied in the group. Such skills include encouraging group members to summarize aloud what was covered, adding important information when something is left out of the summary, reviewing important information, and using learning strategies to remember important ideas.

Fermenting skills are used to stimulate academic controversy so that students will rethink and challenge one another's positions, ideas, and reasoning. Examples of such skills include knowing how to criticize ideas but not people, knowing how to formulate a coherent and defensible position on an issue, and knowing how to probe for and elicit information for achieving answers and solutions to problems. The major concern at this level is to teach the group members not to stop investigation when the first solution is presented. Sometimes the first answer or the quickest solution is not the best solution. Students need to learn how to stimulate the thinking and intellectual curiosity of group members.

In review, students need to be taught *forming skills* to maintain good classroom management and to ensure that group members develop a positive attitude toward work in the group; *functioning skills* to interact effectively in the group; *formulating skills* to ensure that the highest-quality thinking and decision making are made in the group; and *fermenting skills* (often the most difficult to teach) to ensure that students learn how to deal with controversy and deal openly with intellectual disagreements.

To teach these skills, Johnson et al. (1984, quoted material from p. 49) suggest the following five steps:

1. "*Ensure that students see the need for the skill.*" Some teachers use bulletin boards or posters to identify important group

low achievers are motivated to do better when they see their names at the bottom of the chart?

Time Dimension

The time dimension concerns the appropriateness of the tasks, the pace of instruction, and the time allotted for completing learning activities and assignments. In Chapter 2, we learned how to establish a mastery learning program. We also noted that a normal distribution of achievement results is likely to occur when students are given the *same* amount of time to com-

behaviors. These behaviors can be introduced during the first few days of school when you are introducing students to the rules and procedures in your classroom. Start with a few basic rules of group behavior and discuss their importance with your class.

2. *"Ensure that students understand what the skill is and when it should be used."* Students need to model and practice basic classroom rules (see Chapter 7). Observing appropriate group behavior and having an opportunity to practice the skills are important procedures in learning how to behave appropriately in a group.
3. *"Set up practice situations and encourage mastery of skills."* You can assign and alternate different roles to group members, such as encourager, summarizer, and elaboration seeker; evaluate with the class how these roles were played in the group. Often students will recommend helpful tips that can be incorporated into the suggested behaviors or procedures for group interaction.
4. *"Ensure that students have the time and the needed procedures for discussing (and receiving feedback on) how well they are using the skill."* You need to help each group evaluate their functioning. One way is to develop a questionnaire with such questions as, "Did you feel that you had an opportunity to contribute to the group discussion?" "Did the group members listen to your contribution?" "How effective was your group in working toward a solution to the problem?" The answers to these types of questions can be helpful indicators of the groups' interaction.
5. *"Ensure that the students persevere in practicing the skill until the skill seems a natural action."* Remember that it takes time to learn new skills. Some skills will be learned quickly while others will need constant practice over a long period of time. When the day comes that students can move quickly into their group, begin their task, and interact effectively, you will realize that the time and energy spent teaching appropriate group behaviors and procedures were well worth it. Check the suggested readings list for additional information on working with classroom groups.

plete academic tasks. Since mastery programs adjust time requirements for students and allow them to plan their own schedules, they can be effective in motivating students to learn.

The amount of time provided to complete an examination has been found to have negative effects on students who become anxious when taking tests. Evidence indicates that the achievement test scores of highly anxious students are similar to scores of low-anxiety students when the testing procedures are changed. Two major factors are changing time limits and modifying instructions—telling students not to worry about difficult items and to do their best. An important implication of the investigations

DEBATE FORUM

Is Ability Grouping an Effective Way to Deal with Student Differences?

Ability grouping is the placement of students in different academic subjects according to their ability level. In some schools, students are placed in the same ability groups for all subject areas; in other schools, a student may be in the high-ability level in mathematics but in the low-ability level in English.

Argument: Grouping is an effective way to deal with the individual differences of students. High-ability students need special programs to fully develop their talents, and low-ability students need to be educated together to avoid the stress of trying to keep up with their more talented peers.

Counterargument: Ability grouping has little benefit for high-ability students and locks low-ability students into programs and classes where they are stereotyped as weaker students and given an inferior education (Oakes, 1987). Teachers of low-ability classes often do not cover as much material, are less enthusiastic, and are less organized than teachers of high-ability classes. Also, labeling or stigmatizing students assigned to lower-ability classes in school is a major problem. Students in these classes tend to believe that they are

in this area is that current testing programs may be underestimating the achievement and ability of highly anxious students (Hill & Wigfield,1984).

Hill and Wigfield (1984) suggest that school districts should consider giving certain tests in standard ways as well as in optimizing ones. Teachers also need to consider how they present regular classroom tests to students, and whether they are allowing sufficient time for highly anxious students to complete the test.

Ames (1992a) describes how the time structure is closely related to other TARGET areas such as task (how much children are expected to accomplish in a class period), authority (whether children or the teacher determine the time and schedule of activities), grouping (whether students in all groups are given equal time to complete assignments), and evaluation (time pressures on tests). You need to ask: Can students handle the daily work load? Are some students more interested in quantity rather than quality of work? Do students perceive that they have some control over their work schedule? Student answers to these questions will affect their motivation to learn.

less capable, and often they are treated differently by teachers and other students in school. Finally, they are more likely to drop out of school and become delinquent than are students in higher-ability classes (Slavin, 1991).

Response: Thus far the discussion has focused on *between-class ability grouping*. The research on *within-class ability grouping* tends to be more positive (Slavin, 1991). One reason is that within-class grouping is usually more flexible, whereas between-class grouping tends to be more rigid. For example, if a high school student is assigned to a low-ability class, the probability of being moved to another class during the year is small, whereas the student placed in a low group within a class is more likely to be assigned to a higher group if the teacher observes an increase in achievement. Another factor contributing to greater success of within-class as opposed to between-class grouping is the opportunity for students in within-class grouping to participate in different types of ability groups during the day. A student who may be in a lower group in mathematics may be in a higher group in reading. This opportunity reduces the possibility of negative feelings about being in a low-ability group.

What do you think? What is your experience with ability grouping? How do you feel about between- and within-class grouping? What did you notice about the behavior of students in low-ability groups in elementary or high school? How did other students in your class or school treat these students?

TEACHER BEHAVIOR

Teacher behavior and interaction with students appeared as influential factors in motivation throughout the discussion of the TARGET dimensions. However, two aspects of teacher behavior deserve special attention: teacher efficacy and teacher expectations.

Teachers' Sense of Efficacy

? What are important differences between high and low efficacious teachers?

High expectations for student achievement appear to be related to a pattern of attitudes, beliefs, and behaviors identifying teachers and schools that maximize gains in student achievement (Brophy & Evertson, 1976).

CLASSROOM Application

MOTIVATING STUDENTS TO LEARN BY DEVELOPING A MASTERY ORIENTATION

TASK DIMENSION

Provoke Curiosity

Provoke curiosity in students before stating a topic by pointing up a problem or conflict, or giving a pretest to make them realize what they don't know about the topic. Arouse surprise and a feeling of contradiction in students by presenting a phenomenon that violates their expectations or runs counter to their experience and former training, for example, plants that live without sunlight or chlorophyll (fungi). Arouse doubt, uncertainty, bafflement by giving students a problem with no indications for its solution, for example, how to find one's position (latitude and longitude) in the middle of the desert.

Arouse Attention

Arouse attention in students by starting a class with something novel, different, unusual, such as a brainstorming demonstration or a copy of an old newspaper in history. Maintain attention and interest through variety and change; never start a class the same way day after day.

Promote Differential Goals

Provide for different levels of goals among students by encouraging them to strive for levels of performance in keeping with their abilities

teacher efficacy. The belief by teachers that they have the ability to educate all types of students.

For example, Brookover et al. (1978) investigated variables in school climate that influenced achievement and found that teachers in high-achieving schools spent more time on instruction and demonstrated greater concern for and commitment to their students' achievement.

Recently, researchers have explored **teacher efficacy**—teachers' belief in their own ability to affect student learning (Ashton & Webb, 1986; Gibson & Dembo, 1984). A number of investigations have indicated that teachers who have a greater sense of efficacy produce higher achievement gains in their students. The measure of teacher efficacy was originally determined

and by having differentiated materials, activities, and projects available for students of different ability and aspiration levels. Independent study programs are a good example of such an approach.

With individual ability levels in mind, set standards and provide tasks of intermediate difficulty that are within the reach of students but still offer some challenge. Provide easier tasks for students who are discouraged because of low or failing grades. Mastering easier tasks will help them set realistic—and gradually higher—levels of aspiration for their work.

AUTHORITY DIMENSION

Increase Involvement in Learning

Give students opportunities to select activities, assignments, due dates, and those with whom they want to work, as well as their own methods and pace of learning. Involve them in relating the curriculum material to their own experiences and problems. Students need to perceive choices as equally attractive and difficult so they don't select simple tasks just to succeed. Involvement in learning also can be enhanced through games, small-group teaching, cooperative learning, and class discussions.

RECOGNITION DIMENSION

Use Reinforcement

Use praise and encouragement appropriately, particularly for average and slower students and those who are more introverted and lack self-assurance. Give personal, encouraging comments on tests and other work rather than just a grade. Inform students regularly on how they are doing in a course, the sooner after a test or assignment the better.

Promote Beliefs in Competence

On occasion, try to increase the basic achievement motivation of some students through talking with them, having them read about

continued

by teachers' responses on a scale from 1 (strongly disagreed) to 7 (strongly agreed) to two items: (1) "When it comes right down to it, a teacher really can't do much because most of a student's motivation and performance depends on his or her home environment," and (2) "If I really try hard, I can get through to even the most difficult or unmotivated students."

Efficacy beliefs also have been found to be related to teachers' beliefs about managing students. Woolfolk, Rosoff, and Hoy (1990) found that teachers who had a high sense of efficacy favored a more humanistic approach to discipline (i.e., more discussion, self-discipline, solving

highly motivated persons, putting them in a group of highly motivated students, and so forth. Make students aware of their successes and the satisfaction those successes bring them through comments such as, "You really did well in that," "Didn't it feel good to get so many right?" Try to divert students' attention away from their failures by not threatening or punishing them or dwelling on their errors.

Encourage Students' Effort Attributions

Give students individual feedback when they fail, and show them concrete steps they can take to improve. Model how success is attributed to effort by describing personal experiences in which they accomplished tasks by trying hard to succeed. Students might read stories and biographies describing individuals who have accomplished goals through effort, and discuss individually or in groups the reasons why people succeed or fail. The discussion should focus on how attitudes, interests, and efforts are related to succeeding. Along with emphasis on the importance of effort, teach students the necessary learning strategies so they have the competencies and skills to succeed.

GROUPING DIMENSION

Provide Opportunities for Cooperative Learning

Use varied procedures for grouping students according to shared interest, similar ability levels, friendship patterns, and at random, for example. They should have time to talk to one another about personal affairs as well as academic tasks. Games or activities that require team effort also help students satisfy their needs for affiliation and belonging.

problems through cooperative interaction) and supported student autonomy in solving classroom problems. Teachers who believed that students must be controlled and can't be trusted were also likely to believe that extrinsic rewards are important factors in motivating students.

What causes differences in teachers' sense of efficacy? Dembo and Gibson (1985) believe that it results primarily from environmental factors. For example, teachers who are properly trained to deal with the diversity of students found in the classroom, who are supported by their principals, who develop collegial relations with their fellow teachers, and who work

EVALUATION DIMENSION

Reduce Social Comparison and Competition in the Classroom

Social comparison can be reduced by having students work toward individually prescribed or group goals. Limit the use of charts, posting of grades, public pronouncements of high and low scores, and other strategies that lead to excessive emphasis on comparing successful and unsuccessful students. Competition should be geared to the ability levels of the students so that all have a chance to succeed, and students should focus on their own past performance as they set new goals for themselves, rather than on what others are doing or have done.

Reduce Anxiety in Achievement Situations

Give students sufficient time to complete assignments, tests, and other work so they do not worry about them. Clearly identify what is expected in assignments and help students develop a plan to accomplish tasks.

Since anxious students have trouble memorizing information as well as retrieving information that has been learned previously, the use of diagrams, outlines, and other methods for organizing information can help to reduce anxiety. Finally, use relaxation training (Chapter 10) and teach test-taking skills (Chapter 12) when needed.

TIME DIMENSION

Adjust Requirements

Adjust task or time requirements for students who have difficulty completing their work, and allow students opportunities to plan their schedules and progress at an optimal rate.

Material in this Classroom Application is quoted in part from Gorman (1974, pp. 127–128), Hudgins et al. (1983, pp. 424–427), Ames and Ames (1991), and Ames (1992).

cooperatively with parents are more likely to develop the belief that they can solve teaching problems and help students to learn. Unfortunately, there are teachers with a low sense of efficacy who do not have these positive experiences. As a result, they are less likely to believe that they can help certain students to learn.

I believe that research in the area of teacher efficacy raises important concerns about the professional development of teachers. The most crucial of these is: How can teachers continue to develop their teaching skills and maintain their enthusiasm for teaching during the difficult early years of teaching? Reread the "Diary of a Beginning Teacher" in Chapter 1 and notice the frustration expressed by the teacher. Regardless of whether or not additional inservice training and other support are provided at the school where you teach, you need to take responsibility for your own career development. Find someone in the school to whom you can relate, ask questions, share ideas with other teachers, and seek ways to involve parents in some of the activities of the class. One of the most important factors relating to a low sense of efficacy in teaching is *isolation*—the feeling that you are the only one facing teaching problems. The fact is that most teachers have problems, but most do not talk about them to other teachers. Don't judge yourself too harshly as you begin to practice the methods and techniques you learned during your teacher education.

PEER COACHING. One approach to professional development is to foster collegial relationships so that teachers learn to work together rather than individually in improving their teaching skills. Some school districts have initiated "coaching teams" whereby teachers help one another learn to use new teaching methods. The basic notion behind this concept is that teachers, like athletes, need specific guidance or coaching to apply new methods or skills. Joyce, Weil, and Showers (1992) describe three major functions of coaching:

- *Provision of companionship.* The coaching team can involve two or more individuals who check their perceptions and share frustrations and successes as they watch and comment on one another's teaching. This interchange is important in developing a sense of companionship in school.
- *Analysis of application.* The team discusses the curriculum, so that decisions on when to use certain methods of instruction can be made.
- *Adaptation to the students.* Methods of instruction can be modified for individual students.

Lemlech and Hertzog-Foliart (1992) have extended this concept of coaching to student teaching. In order to develop companionship or collegiality, they pair elementary student teachers for two semesters. Partners teach in the same classroom, plan together, observe each other, and provide written and oral feedback to each other. These teacher educators believe that the development of collegiality in teaching must begin during student teaching.

Teachers' Expectations as Self-Fulfilling Prophecies

? How can teacher expectations influence student motivation and achievement behavior?

teacher expectations. Inferences made by teachers about their students' present and future academic achievement and classroom behavior.

Teachers often have different interactions with different types of students. (Recall our discussion earlier in this chapter about teaching reading to students at different ability levels.) In some instances, these differences affect **teacher expectations** (i.e., beliefs about students' present and future achievement and behavior). These expectations can lead to self-fulfilling prophecies, a process in which teacher expectations determine the ways students are treated. Over time, the expectations influence how the students behave in the classroom and how much they learn. Race, social class, personality, and gender are most likely to influence teacher expectancies (Dusek & Joseph, 1985). That is to say, some teachers tend to have greater expectancies for success for white rather than African American and other minority students, and for high- rather than low-socioeconomic-status students, and prefer more conforming and docile students rather than independent and assertive students.

Rosenthal and Jacobson's (1968) *Pygmalion in the Classroom* stimulated a great deal of interest and controversy about teacher expectations. In their study, Rosenthal and Jacobson administered a nonverbal intelligence test to all children in an elementary school. The test was disguised as one designed to predict academic "blooming," or intellectual gain, during the school year. Rosenthal and Jacobson provided each teacher with the names of children in the class who had encouraging scores on the test of intellectual blooming. Actually, these children were selected randomly from the teachers' class lists, not on the basis of any test. There was no real reason to expect unusual gain from the children on the investigators' list. Eight months later all children in the school were retested with the same IQ test, and the designated "bloomers" *did* demonstrate significant intellectual growth. The effects showed up more strongly in the first two grades.

Many subsequent studies attempting to induce similar teacher expectations failed to show any impact on student behavior (e.g., Claiborn, 1969; Fleming & Anttonen, 1971). Although the findings of *Pygmalion in the Classroom* have been widely publicized and discussed, many individuals have criticized the methodology of the study (see Rosenthal, 1985, for a review of these criticisms). Good and Brophy (1990) have pointed out that studies that attempt to induce teacher expectations by providing teachers with phony information have generally not yielded significant results. However, naturalistic studies (observing actual teacher behavior in the classroom) do show the effects of expectancy.

Good and Brophy (1978) present a model to explain how teachers' naturalistic expectations for students can lead to differential patterns of teacher-student interaction, as follows:

1. The teacher expects specific behavior and achievement from particular students.
2. Because of these different expectations, the teacher behaves differently toward the different students.
3. This teacher treatment tells each student what behavior and achievement the teacher expects from him and affects his self-concept, achievement motivation, and level of aspiration.

DEBATE FORUM

Are Junior High School Students Unmotivated?

Argument: When sixth-grade students move to a junior high school building, they tend to show a decline in general interest in school, decreased intrinsic motivation, and decline in self-esteem and confidence in some academic disciplines. Thus it appears that for many students, the early adolescent period marks the beginning of negative educational experiences that often lead to academic failure and school dropout (e.g., Eccles, 1991; Epstein & McPartland, 1976). Many teachers believe that early adolescence is a difficult stage in development that impacts students' attitudes and academic motivation.

Counterargument: Midgley, Feldlaufer, and Eccles (1988) compared the beliefs of 107 teachers who taught the last year of elementary school mathematics with the beliefs of 64 teachers who taught the same students mathematics in the first year of junior high school. Seventh-grade teachers reported greater need to control their students, rated them less trustworthy, and perceived themselves to be less efficacious than sixth-grade teachers, despite the fact that the junior high teachers were more likely to teach in their specialty. In

4. If this teacher treatment is consistent over time, and if the student does not actively resist or change it in some way, it will tend to shape his achievement and behavior. High-expectation students will be led to achieve at high levels, while the achievement of low-expectation students will decline.
5. With time, the student's achievement and behavior will conform more and more closely to that originally expected of him. (p. 12)

This model charts a course for teacher expectations to be self-fulfilling: They must be translated into behavior that will communicate the expectations to the student and shape behavior in the expected direction. This process does not always happen because the teacher either may not form concise expectations about a student or may continually change those expectations. Even when a teacher does have a consistent expectation for a particular student, if that expectation is not communicated to the student, the expectation cannot be self-fulfilling. In still another situation, students who reject teachers' conception of themselves will act in ways that force the teachers to change their behavior toward them. Teacher expectations about students have no direct impact on their behavior unless the expectations are communicated to students and ultimately shape their behavior.

addition, the seventh-grade teachers were viewed as less supportive, friendly, and fair than the sixth-grade teachers by both students and adult observers.

The researchers believe that stereotypes about early adolescents encourage junior high school teachers to believe that their students are unmotivated and must be controlled. Furthermore, they question whether the junior high school environment (with larger classes, more emphasis on teacher control and discipline, a less positive teacher-student relationship, more social comparison among students, and fewer opportunities for decision making and self-management) is the best environment for early adolescents.

The researchers argue that some "motivational problems" of early adolescents result from a mismatch between the environment and the developmental needs of students (i.e, desire for autonomy, peer orientation, self-focus and self-consciousness), and they conclude that the structure of the junior high school may create an environment in which the students are more likely to act in accord with the stereotypes than they would if they were in other more facilitative environments (such as a middle school with grades 6–8).

What do you think? Why do you think the seventh-grade teachers had different beliefs about students and their own efficacy in teaching mathematics than the sixth-grade teachers? Could it be that seventh-grade students are unfairly criticized for their attitudes and behaviors in school? Can a school's culture impact student motivation?

Individual differences of students influence the effects of teacher expectations. For example, students who are more sensitive to subtle communication cues, more dependent or "other-directed," heavily dependent upon the teacher for information, and more disruptive are more susceptible to expectations effects than other students are (Brophy, 1985a).

Brophy (1985a) has summarized the research on how teachers may behave differentially toward students in the class:

1. Wait less time for lows [low-expectation students] to answer.
2. Give lows the answer or call on someone else rather than trying to improve lows' responses by giving clues or repeating or rephrasing the question.
3. Inappropriate reinforcement rewarding inappropriate behavior or incorrect answers by lows.
4. Criticizing lows more often for failure.
5. Praising lows less frequently than highs for success.
6. Failure to give feedback to the public responses of lows.
7. Generally paying less attention to lows or interacting with them less frequently.
8. Calling on lows less often to respond to questions.

9. Seating lows farther away from the teacher.
10. Demanding less from lows.
11. General differences in type and initiation of individualized interactions with students; teachers interact with lows more privately than publicly and monitor and structure their activities more closely.
12. Differential administration or grading of tests or assignments, in which highs but not lows are given the benefit of the doubt in borderline cases.
13. Less friendly interaction with lows including less smiling and other nonverbal indicators of support.
14. Briefer and less informative feedback to the questions of lows. (pp. 309–310)

In reviewing the research on teacher-student interaction relating to teacher expectation for student achievement, Brophy (1985a) points out that high achievers are likely to be more responsive in class, to complete their assignments, and to cooperate more with their teacher than are low achievers. Because teacher expectations are generally accurate, the high-expectation students in a classroom *are* actually the high achievers and the low-expectation students *are* actually the low achievers. Brophy points out that one should not judge all differences in interaction between high and low achievers as a result of teacher expectations.

Can you think of incidents in your schooling when teacher expectations led to self-fulfilling prophecies? Identify the behaviors under each of the following categories: How were they formed? How were they communicated? What type of behavior was exhibited?

The important aspect of teachers' expectations is that they influence the development of children's expectations for their own learning. Students can accurately report differences in the ways that teachers work with high and low achievers. More importantly, teacher practices provide clues about student ability. For example (Weinstein, 1989), children read clues about their relative smartness in the differentiation of

- assignments of tasks to students ("one person will be doing harder work")
- patterns used to group students ("I wanted Miss ——— to put me in a smarter group")
- motivational strategies used for instruction (highs could "read any book they want," lows "can't choose what they read because they need it")
- responsibilities given to learners ("The way you know a person is smart, Miss ——— always picks them to go different places")
- quality of teacher-student relationships ("You can really tell just by the way she treats people who are doing well") (p. 203)

Appropriate Teacher Expectations

Now that you know that *some* teachers have low expectations for particular students, you may conclude that the best teaching strategy is to have no expectations or only positive expectations for student behavior and performance. Good and Brophy (1990) argue that neither of these is a viable alternative. First, expectations cannot be suppressed or avoided. We all develop expectations from our interaction with individuals that tend to stay with us. Even if teachers attempted to avoid other sources of information about their students, they would still develop expectations. Moreover, it probably would be worse to avoid information that could help to plan more effective instructional programs. Second, while teachers need to believe that all students can achieve, this attitude must not be carried to the point of distorting reality by setting unrealistically high standards that some students cannot reach. This strategy can lead to student frustration and failure.

Good and Brophy (1990) suggest that teachers need to develop appropriate expectations by establishing goals *and* moving students along at a pace that they can handle. It is important that teachers monitor their treatment of individual students to ensure that they do not act in a detrimental manner toward certain students and that they change their response as the student changes. As Brophy (1985b) states, "The probability of self-fulfilling prophecy effects does not depend so much on the initial accuracy of expectations as on the degree of rigidity with which they are held and the degree to which they are taken into account in planning and decision making about instruction" (p. 179). In summary, according to Good and Brophy (1987), teachers can deal with expectations:

> By keeping a general focus on instruction as their main task, and by training themselves to observe students systematically with an eye toward their present progress and needs, teachers can maintain a generally appropriate orientation to the classroom. They can reinforce this by learning to recognize and evaluate the attitudes and expectations that they form spontaneously in daily interaction with students. This will enable them to correct inaccuracies and to use accurate information in planning individualized treatment. (p. 161)

Summary

PERSONAL FACTORS INFLUENCING MOTIVATION

1. Teachers can make instructional decisions that can enhance student motivation.
2. Students' beliefs and self-perceptions influence their motivational behavior.

3. Three interrelated components of students' motivational beliefs are value ("Why am I doing this task?"), expectancy ("Can I do this task?"), and affect ("How do I feel about this task?").
4. Motivation and cognition are interrelated. Motivational beliefs help students form an intention to learn, while cognitive strategies are used to enact learning.
5. Resource management strategies help students in managing their environment and available resources.
6. Achievement goals determine patterns of motivation that determine how learners think about and engage in different academic activities.
7. A mastery goal orientation is more likely to lead to the use of more learning strategies than a performance goal orientation is.
8. Goals that are specific and proximal are more likely to motivate students than general goals.
9. Allowing students to set their own goals can encourage greater interest in attaining them.
10. Observing a similar peer model successfully complete a task can enhance the self-efficacy of the observer.
11. Students' perceptions of control and self-efficacy influence the use of learning strategies.
12. Learned helpless students don't see any relation between effort and achievement outcomes.
13. An individual's beliefs (attributions) about the causes of success and failure are important in understanding achievement-related behaviors.
14. The attributions of success-oriented and failure-oriented students differ.
15. Many students develop strategies to avoid failure to protect their sense of worth.
16. Anxiety has two dimensions—worry and emotionality. Each dimension can have different effects on students. Worry has the strongest negative relationship with achievement because it interferes with retrieval of information.
17. Students' use of learning strategies is related to their academic goals, values, beliefs about schooling, and beliefs about themselves in terms of their perceptions of ability, control, and self-efficacy.

CLASSROOM ORGANIZATIONAL FACTORS INFLUENCING MOTIVATION

18. A mastery goal orientation can be enhanced by changing the classroom climate in six (TARGET) areas: task, authority, recognition, grouping, evaluation, and time.
19. Students' perceptions of a task can influence the extent to which students become involved in it.
20. Students' motivation can be influenced by the manner in which teachers introduce assignments.
21. Teachers' control practices can determine the extent to which intrinsic or extrinsic motivation is developed.
22. Certain control measures effective in maintaining students' present performance may contribute negatively to their continuing motivation.

23. Praise can be used ineffectively in the classroom.
24. Cooperative learning can have a positive effect on student achievement and interpersonal relations.
25. The most beneficial behavior in small groups is giving and receiving explanations.
26. Children who perceive themselves to be academically competent, who feel in control of their academic success, and who have a mastery orientation view help-seeking as an effective learning strategy.
27. Teachers should consider gender, ability, and racial or ethnic differences when forming groups, since these characteristics can influence students' perceptions and behavior in the group.
28. Excessive public evaluation and social comparison can have a detrimental effect on student motivation.
29. Teachers need to consider the impact of the time structure of tests and activities on student motivation.

TEACHER BEHAVIOR

30. The development of a high sense of teacher efficacy appears to be related to environmental factors such as effective teacher training and positive collegial and parent-teacher relations.
31. Teachers' expectations can determine how much students learn.
32. Teachers' expectations can lead to self-fulfilling prophecies for students.

Reflecting on Motivation and Learning

1. Become an Active Learner

The following activity is adapted from a exercise developed by Claire Weinstein at the University of Texas. It involves using a learning strategy (Table 4.3) to plan some action or change to make you a more successful learner.

Learning Strategy Analysis

SELECTION (Describe your learning goal and the strategy to be used)

LEARNING STRATEGY TAXONOMY (Check one or more)

Cognitive Strategies	Metacognitive Strategies	Resource Management Strategies
____ Rehearsal	____ Planning	____ Time management
____ Elaboration	____ Monitoring	____ Study environment management
____ Organization	____ Regulating	____ Effort management
		____ Support of others

RATIONALE (Why will this strategy be helpful?)

IMPLEMENTATION AND MONITORING (When and where did you actually use this strategy?)

Date(s)

MODIFICATION (At this point of your action plan, would you choose to modify this strategy? Justify your decision.)

EVALUATION (Did using this strategy help you to achieve your short-term goal? Why or why not?)

You might try a new method of taking notes, organizing your time, or planning your activities. Be specific in setting your goal and explain why the action should prove successful. Record the dates of the implementation of the strategy and evaluate its success. Finally, note modifications you made. Your action analysis strategy can last from one to three weeks.

2. Analyze How You Use Your Time

Time management presents a problem for many college students. There is always too much to do in a short period of time. What activities take up much of your time? How do you plan your time? How much time do you waste? Identify some action you can take to eliminate wasting time.

3. Consider Factors That Influence Student Motivation

Many factors influence the level and kind of motivation exhibited by students in class. From your own experience in school and/or your observations in classrooms, identify factors that enhance or inhibit student motivation in school in each of the following categories:

a. The nature of the learning task
b. The characteristics of the individual learner
c. The classroom environment
d. The behavior of the teacher
e. The grading or evaluation procedures used in class

4. Observe a Classroom

Focus on a few students (perhaps two high achievers and two low achievers) and keep a record of their interaction with the teacher and their participation in the class. It might be interesting to include in your report the following type of information (Good & Brophy, 1991):

1. How often do they raise their hands?
2. Do all students approach the teacher to receive help, or do some seldom approach the teacher?
3. How long does each reading group last?
4. Are the students involved in their work? How long do they work independently at their desks?
5. How often are students in different groups praised? (p. 61)

5. Explore Anxiety-Producing Situations in School

The term *school anxiety* covers anxiety stemming from all situations in school—peer relations, authority relations, test situations, and other in-school, anxiety-arousing transactions. Discuss your school experiences and identify situations that you found anxiety-producing.

The following are common thoughts and worries expressed by individuals who have test anxiety (Smith, 1982, p. 179). Check those with which you can identify the most, and then add additional thoughts you have experienced. Compare your thoughts with those of other students in your class.

a. Worry about Performance

____ I should have reviewed more. I'll never get through.
____ My mind is blank, I'll never get the answer. I must really be stupid.
____ I knew this stuff yesterday. What is wrong with me?
____ I can't remember a thing. This always happens to me.
____
____

b. Worry about Bodily Reactions

____ I'm sick. I'll never get through.
____ I'm sweating all over—it's really hot in here.
____ My stomach is going crazy, churning and jumping all over.
____ Here it comes—I'm getting really tense again. Normal people just don't get like this.
____
____

c. Worry about How Others Are Doing

____ I know everyone's doing better than I am.
____ I must be the dumbest one in the group.
____ I am going to be the last one done again. I must really be stupid.
____ No one else seems to be having trouble. Am I the only one?
____
____

d. Worry about the Possible Negative Consequences
___ If I fail this test, I'll never get into the program.
___ I'll never graduate.
___ I'll think less of myself.
___ I'll be embarrassed.
___
___

6. Remember Your Teachers

Students have diverse experiences with teachers during their school career. They remember some teachers with excitement and fondness and others with resentment and hate. Think about the teachers who had the greatest impact on you (either positive or negative) and examine their behavior. Tell your class or group about these teachers.

Key Terms

mastery goal, p. 149
performance goal, p. 149
intrinsic motivation, p. 149
extrinsic motivation, p. 149
locus of control, p. 152
learned helplessness, p. 152
attribution, p. 154
resource management strategies, p. 157
continuing motivation, p. 167
cooperative learning, p. 170
jigsaw method, p. 171
teacher efficacy, p. 182
teacher expectations, p. 187

Suggestions for Further Reading

Dusek, J. (Ed.). (1985). *Teacher expectancies.* Hillsdale, NJ: Erlbaum. An excellent source of research findings in teacher expectations.

Nicholls, J. G. (1989). *The competitive ethos and democratic education.* Cambridge, MA: Harvard University Press. A discussion of the impact of competition on students.

The following books provide the most comprehensive review of theory and research available regarding motivation in education:

Ames, C., & Ames, R. (Eds.). (1985). *Research on motivation in education: Vol. 2. The classroom milieu.* Orlando, FL: Academic Press.

Ames, C., & Ames, R. (Eds). (1989). *Research on motivation in education: Vol. 3. Goals and cognitions.* San Diego: Academic Press.

Ames, R., & Ames, C. (Eds.). (1984). *Research on motivation in education: Vol. 1. Student motivation.* Orlando, FL: Academic Press.

Spaulding, C. L. (1992). *Motivation in the classroom.* New York: McGraw-Hill

Stipek, D. J. (1993). *Motivation to learn: From theory to practice* (2nd ed.). Englewood Cliffs, NJ: Prentice-Hall. A concise book on motivational problems in education.

These books are helpful in implementing cooperative learning in the classroom:

Cohen, E. G. (1986). *Designing groupwork: Strategies for the heterogeneous classroom.* New York: Teachers College Press.

Johnson, D. W., & Johnson, R. T. (1991). *Joining together: Group theory and group skills* (4th ed.). Englewood Cliffs, NJ: Prentice-Hall. Includes exercises to develop collaborative skills among group members.

Johnson, D. W., & Johnson, R. T. (1991). *Learning together and alone: Cooperation, competition, and individualization* (3rd ed.). Englewood Cliffs, NJ: Prentice-Hall.

Johnson, D. W., Johnson, R. T., Holubec, E. J., & Roy, P. (1986). *Circles of learning: Cooperation in the classroom* (rev. ed.). Alexandria, VA: Association for Supervision and Curriculum Development.

Johnson, R. T., Johnson, D. W., & Holubec, E. (Eds.). (1987). *Structuring cooperative learning: Lesson plans for teachers.* Edina, MN: Interaction.

Slavin, R. E. (1978). *Using student team learning.* Baltimore: Johns Hopkins University Press.

Slavin, R. E. (1990). *Cooperative learning: Theory, research, and practice.* Englewood Cliffs, NJ: Prentice-Hall.

Chapter 5

The Humanistic Perspective

Humanistic Psychology

Combs

Maslow

Rogers

Instructional Applications of Humanistic Psychology

Moral/Character Education

Classroom Application: Using Values Clarification

Debate Forum: Are There Gender Differences in Moral Reasoning?

Classroom Application: Leading a Discussion on a Moral Dilemma

Debate Forum: Values Education: What Values? Whose Values?

Open Education

Criticisms of Humanistic Education

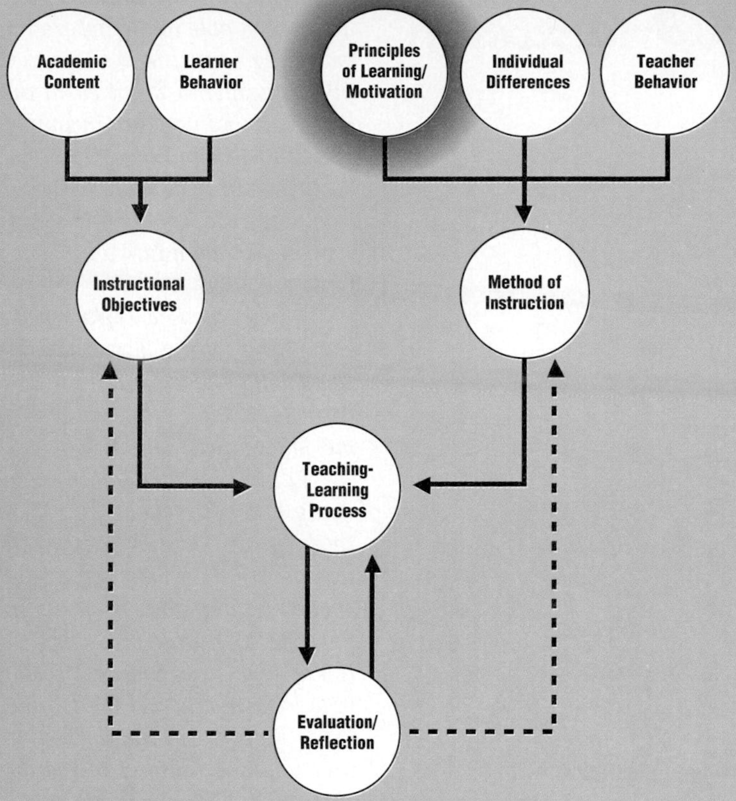

OBJECTIVES

After mastering the material in this chapter you will be able to:

- Use humanistic principles to facilitate learning and human development.
- Lead a class discussion on a moral dilemma.
- Use value clarification exercises to help students better understand their own values.
- Develop an open classroom.

Orientation

Gregory had been acting very depressed for days, and his seventh-grade English teacher, Diane Lewanski, felt that he needed to talk. Greg is a shy, self-effacing youngster, able to attract friends primarily through his self-deprecating humor. It was Greg's routine to say something negative about himself, particularly regarding his academic abilities, at the beginning of almost every class period, and then it was almost nonstop throughout the remainder of the period.

"I'm so stupid," or "I sure hope the class's extra credit doesn't depend on me, or we are all in trouble," were typical of the types of responses that Diane had heard from Greg since he had transferred to the school. Taking Greg aside one day after school, she had a talk with him. What follows is Greg's account of that conversation:

"When Ms. Lewanski asked me to stay after school, I was afraid that I had done something wrong. I was always doing dumb things in her class, and I knew that eventually she was going to call me on the carpet about it. Fortunately for me, instead of being mad, she was really nice and acted like she wanted to get to know me, since I was new in school.

"I didn't feel like talking, especially about having to move to a new city and going to a new school. You know, I never would have talked to another adult about those things, because they would give me advice, or lecture me, but Ms. Lewanski was different. All she did was keep asking me questions about how I felt. If I talked about moving away from my friends back home, she would ask me how that made me feel. It's funny, but when I was answering her questions I would sort of begin to see why I was feeling a certain way. It's almost like I was able to understand how I was really feeling about things, rather than always being angry. I guess the thing I am most afraid of is that people won't want to be friends with me. That's pretty hard to admit, but without even thinking, I had told Ms. Lewanski what I was really feeling. It's almost like I was telling her before I even knew what I was feeling.

"All I know is that the woman knows how to talk to kids. Some teachers act like they could care less about how you feel about things, but Ms. Lewanski lets you know she cares. She doesn't even say anything, really, it's just that talking to her brings out the real person inside, the one who really feels things. I'm glad she asked to talk to me."

The learning theories explored thus far have emphasized the role of environmental and cognitive factors in the teaching-learning process. Although learning is clearly affected by how students think and act, it is also apparent that students are influenced and guided by the personal meanings and feelings they attach to their learning experiences.

In this chapter, we investigate humanistic psychology and its influence on educational thought and practice. Humanistic psychologists maintain that (1) the behavior of individuals is primarily determined by how they perceive themselves and the world around them; and (2) individuals are not solely the products of their environment, as the behaviorists would have us believe, but are internally directed, having free choice, motivated by the desire to "self-actualize," or fulfill their unique potential as human beings.

Ryan (1986) states: "The role of the school is not simply to make children smart, but to make them smart *and* good. We must help them to live well and that will enable the common good to flourish. For schools and teachers to do only half the job puts the individual child and all the rest of us in danger" (p. 233). Kohn (1991) argues for the importance of teaching children to care, to help others, to be more generous and kind. Would our communities benefit from educating students with these values?

In the 1960s and 1970s humanistic psychology flourished in education. Many humanistic educators believed that all we have to do is create a humanistic climate, and children will learn. The research simply did not support this contention. Humanistic education became less influential in the 1980s. However, as crime, delinquency, AIDS, teenage pregnancies, and other social problems explode in our society, questions are once again being raised about the role schools should play in developing caring and concerned citizens.

Humanistic educators believe that education must be made more responsive to the affective needs of students. *Affective needs* are related to students' emotions, feelings, values, attitudes, predispositions, and morals (Beane, 1985/1986). Combs (1981) describes the major goals of humanistic education:

- To accept the learner's needs and purposes and create educational experiences and programs for the development of the learner's unique potential.
- To facilitate the learner's self-actualization and feelings of personal adequacy.
- To foster the acquisition of basic skills and competencies (e.g., academic, personal, interpersonal, communicative, and economic) for living in a multicultured society.
- To personalize educational decisions and practices.
- To recognize the importance of human feelings, values, and perceptions in the educational process.
- To provide a learning climate that is challenging, understanding, supportive, exciting, and free from threat.
- To develop in learners a genuine concern and respect for the worth of others and skill in resolving conflicts.

As you read this chapter, you will see how the goals and objectives of humanistic education have been incorporated into a number of instructional programs. These approaches, although differing in certain respects, have in common the ideal of making education a more human, personal, and student-centered endeavor, as opposed to more traditional, teacher-centered schooling. (In Chapter 7, you will see how humanistic techniques can be used to help students *and* teachers deal more effectively with problems of communication, interpersonal relations, social skills, and discipline.) The humanist perspective offers insights on how teacher treatment of students and the development of a supportive classroom environment can be important factors influencing learning.

It is important to keep in mind that although humanistic education emphasizes the value of learning that is personal and affective, it does not ignore or deny the importance of acquiring basic knowledge and skills. As Combs (1982) argues:

> Humanistic education does not require the surrender of traditional goals and objectives. Quite the contrary. It is a way of making certain that students achieve them. I am not a humanist because I just want to go about being nice to people. I am a humanist because I know that when I apply humanist thinking to my teaching, students will learn anything better. (p. 135)

HUMANISTIC PSYCHOLOGY

> How do different humanistic psychologists view learning? What classroom practices do they encourage?

During the late 1940s, a new psychological perspective emerged from the work of persons engaged in the application of psychology—clinical psychologists, social workers, and counselors—rather than from the work of those researching the learning process. The movement that grew out of this perspective became known as *humanistic, existential, perceptual,* or *phenomenological* psychology, and its members attempted to understand behavior from the point of view of the behaver rather than that of the observer.

To gain a better understanding of the principles of humanistic psychology and how they apply to the learning process, let's first examine the views of three of its major proponents: Arthur Combs, Abraham H. Maslow, and Carl R. Rogers.

Combs

> To understand human behavior . . . it is necessary to understand the behaver's perceptual world, how things seem from his point of view. This calls for a different understanding of what the "facts" are that we need in order to deal with human behavior; it is not the external facts that are important in understanding behavior, but the meaning of the facts to the behaver. To change another person's behavior it is necessary somehow to modify his beliefs or perception. When he sees things differently, he will behave differently. (Combs et al., 1974, p. 15)

This statement is one of the credos of the humanists' concern for the individual's feelings, perceptions, beliefs, and purposes—the inner behaviors that make people different from one another. To understand another person, we need to see the world as the behaver does, to determine how the behaver thinks and feels about herself and her world.

To understand the behavior of a student, you must determine how that student perceives the way he or she acts in a situation. What appears to be strange or unusual behavior to you may not be so from the behaver's (student's) perspective. To the teacher, a student's wanton destruction of school material is inexplicable. To the student who cannot achieve recognition, status, or prestige in school, the behavior (although improper) is a purposeful act that may bring recognition from peers.

This is why perceptual psychologists state that to change behavior, we must change an individual's perception. Combs, Avila, and Purkey (1971) suggest that misbehavior is "the result of not wanting to do what one knows he should do because something else is more personally satisfying" (p. 96). When teachers complain that students are not motivated, what they really mean is that students are not motivated to do what the *teachers* want them to do. Yet if the teachers selected different activities, they might find totally different reactions on the part of the students.

Now let's see how a student's internal perspective relates directly to the learning process. Humanists see two parts to learning: the acquisition of new information, and the individual's personalization of this information. Teachers make the mistake of assuming that students will learn if subject matter is properly organized and presented. But meaning is not inherent in the subject matter; it is the individual who instills subject matter with its meaning (Combs et al., 1971). The dilemma in teaching is not how to present subject matter, but how to help students derive personal meaning from the subject matter. If they can relate it in some way to their lives, you will have succeeded.

Combs et al. (1971) explain the dominance of personal meaning over a person's information retention through the diagram in Figure 5.1. The farther events are from the center of the inner circle, the less they will influence the individual. The closer events are perceived to be to the self, the more they will affect behavior. Now you may understand why so many of the things that we learn are soon forgotten: They have little relation to the self!

For example, suppose you hear on television the recent statistics on unemployment (Figure 5.1: D). Will this information affect your behavior?

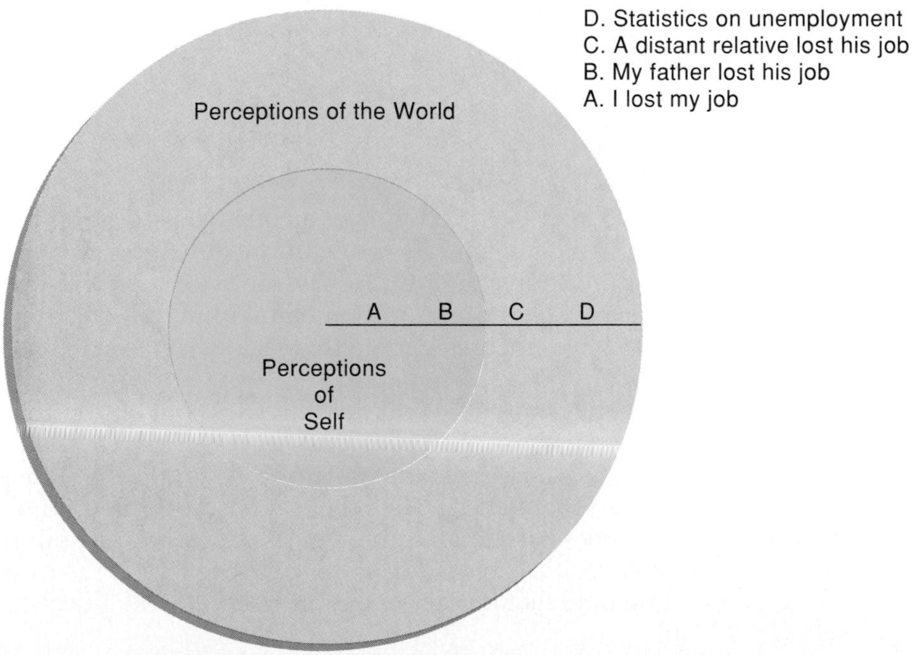

Figure 5.1 Meaning and the Self.
Source: Adapted from Combs et al., 1971.

Probably not, especially if you are currently employed. Now, suppose you learn that a relative in another state was laid off from work (C). The event is now closer to you. You might now pay more attention to the information about unemployment insurance. Let's get even more personal. Suppose your father recently lost his job (B). This information now has much more personal meaning and affects your behavior in many specific ways. You might call your father to discuss the matter with him. Now, let's get even more personal. Suppose you lost your job (A)! You might read as much as you could about unemployment insurance, or even call your local unemployment office for information. Now, indeed, your behavior is strongly affected.

I often ask my students to write down main ideas from each of their courses of the previous semester. Every semester many students admit that their list is going to be a brief one because they cannot remember many worthwhile ideas from certain courses. Think about your own learning. Do you find a relationship between the amount of your learning and the degree of personal meaning you found in the subject?

IMPLICATIONS OF COMBS'S VIEWS FOR INSTRUCTION. Combs et al. (1974) emphasize a perceptual view of effective teaching. The following represents Combs's description of effective teachers: They have a strong knowledge base in their teaching subject; they have accurate perceptions about students and their behavior; they feel competent about their abilities to help students; and they believe that all students can be successful learners. His position on effective methods of instruction is as follows:

> The teacher-education program must help each student find the methods best suited to him, to his purposes, his task, and the particular populations and problems with which he must deal on the job. This is not so much a matter of *teaching* methods as one of helping students to *discover* methods. It is a question of finding the methods right for the teacher rather than right for teaching. (p. 26)

Maslow

Abraham Maslow has long been recognized as one of the leading proponents of humanistic psychology. His work on gratification of needs is extremely influential in understanding human motivation. An important part of his theory is based on the assumption that within us are both forces that seek growth and forces that resist growth. Maslow (1968) states:

> One set [of forces] clings to safety and defensiveness out of fear, tending to regress backward, hanging on to the past, *afraid* to grow . . . *afraid* to take chances, *afraid* to jeopardize what he already has, *afraid* of independence, freedom and separateness. The other set of forces impels him forward toward wholeness of self and uniqueness of self, toward full functioning of all his capacities, toward confidence in the face of the external world at the same time that he can accept his deepest, real, unconscious self. (pp. 45–46)

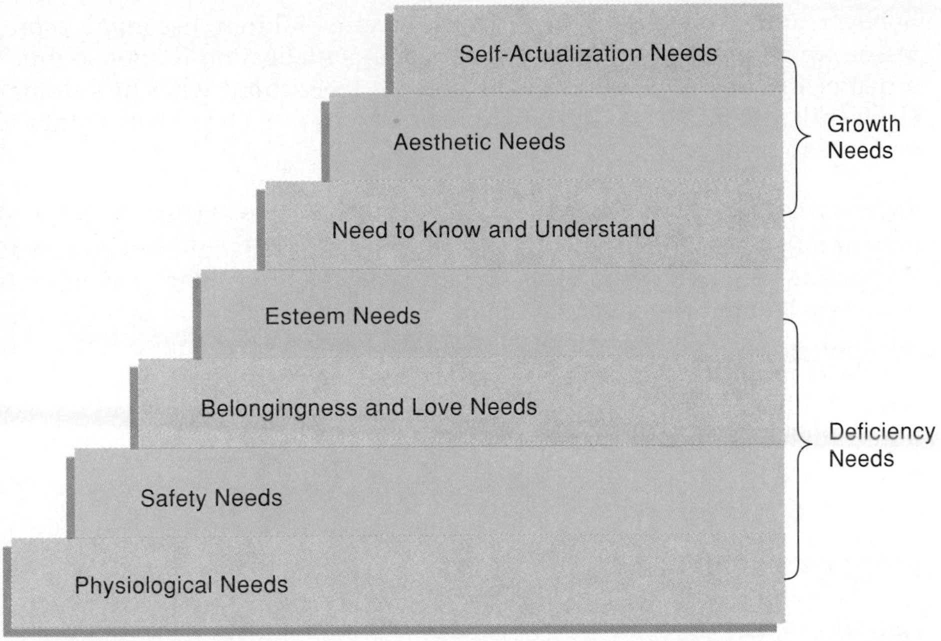

Figure 5.2 Maslow's Hierarchy of Needs.

hierarchy of needs. Maslow's classification of human needs.

self-actualization. Maslow's term for the psychological need to develop one's capabilities and potential in order to enhance personal growth.

Think about these forces as they relate to an important decision that you made in the past or are presently contemplating. What feelings relate to safety, and what feelings relate to growth? Maslow's **hierarchy of needs** (Figure 5.2) is helpful in understanding need gratification. Maslow believes that some human needs, especially physiological needs, are basic to others and that certain needs must be satisfied before the individual becomes concerned with higher needs.

He distinguished the first four needs in the hierarchy from the later ones. He identified the former as *deficiency* needs and the latter as *growth* needs. Generally, the gratification of deficiency needs depends on other people, whereas gratification of growth needs depends more on one's self.

According to Maslow, *physiological* needs (food, water, sleep) are the most demanding of satisfaction. Once these needs have been satisfied, needs at the next level emerge. These are *safety* needs—the desire for good health and for security from harm and danger. Satisfaction of safety needs is followed by motivation for *belonging and love*—to have friends and family, and to belong to a group. An inability to love and belong may motivate a person to behave in different ways to gain such acceptance. For example, some people attempt to use achievement as a substitute for love. The next need on the hierarchy is the need for *esteem*—the desire to have the respect, confidence, and admiration of others, and to gain self-respect.

The next need on the hierarchy is *to know and to understand*—to satisfy curiosity, seek knowledge, and gain understanding. Then, Maslow proposed that some individuals have *aesthetic* needs—for order, symmetry, closure, and the completion of an act. Finally, Maslow assumes that if an individual has been able to satisfy all other needs on the hierarchy, then motivation is directed toward **self-actualization**—the need to develop potential, to become what one is capable of becoming. The manner in which self-actualization surfaces in people varies greatly. Developing a hobby, reading a book, driving a truck, raising children, becoming a professor are all paths to self-actualization. Self-actualization is "not so much a matter of what a person does, as how he feels about what he's doing" (Kolesnik, 1975, p. 42). In the choice of action, each person wants to improve in some way.

IMPLICATIONS OF MASLOW'S VIEWS FOR INSTRUCTION. As a teacher, you may have difficulty understanding why certain children do not do homework, are restless in class, or are completely uninterested in class activities. You may assume that the desire to learn is an important need for all children. But Maslow suggests that interest or motivation to learn may not develop until other basic needs have been met. Children who come to school without breakfast or sufficient sleep, or with personal family problems, anxieties, or fears, are not interested in becoming self-actualized individuals.

Rogers

> According to Rogers, what conditions must be present for learning to occur?

Carl Rogers (1969, 1983) was a humanistic psychologist whose ideas have been influential in educational thought and practice. Through such popular books as *Freedom to Learn* and *Freedom to Learn for the 80's,* he advocated an educational approach that tries to make learning and teaching more humanistic and thus more personal and meaningful.

BASIC PRINCIPLES. Rogers's approach can best be understood from an examination of some of the important humanistic learning principles that he has identified as central to his educational philosophy.

The Desire to Learn. Foremost among Rogers's beliefs is that human beings have a natural desire to learn. This desire is easily verified, says Rogers, by watching the curiosity and eagerness of young children as they explore their environment. The inherent eagerness of children to learn is a basic assumption in humanistic education. In the humanistic classroom, children are given the freedom to satisfy their curiosity, to pursue their interests unabated, and to discover for themselves what is important and meaningful about the world around them. This orientation is in sharp contrast to traditional classrooms, in which the teacher or the curriculum determines what children should learn.

Significant Learning. The second humanistic learning principle that Rogers has identified is that significant or meaningful learning occurs when it is perceived by students as being relevant to their own needs and purposes. As we saw earlier in our discussion of Combs, humanists consider learning to be a two-part process, involving both the acquisition of new information and the personalization of it. Students learn best and most rapidly, humanists feel, when learning is personally significant.

Examples of this kind of learning are not hard to find. Think of the student who quickly learns to operate a computer in order to enjoy a favorite game, or the student who rapidly learns to count change in order to buy a favorite toy. In both instances, learning is purposeful and certainly motivated by the need to know.

Learning without Threat. Another principle identified by Rogers is that learning is best acquired and retained in an environment free from threat. The process of learning is enhanced when students can test their abilities, try new experiences, or even make mistakes without experiencing the sting of criticism and ridicule.

Self-Initiated Learning. For the humanists, learning is most significant and pervasive when it is self-initiated and when it involves both the feelings and mind of the learner. Being able to choose the direction of one's own learning is highly motivating and gives the student the opportunity to *learn how to learn*. The mastering of subject matter is no doubt important but no more so than acquiring the ability to discover resources, formulate problems, test hypotheses, and evaluate the outcomes. Self-initiated learning focuses the student's attention on the process of learning as well as on the product.

Experiential learning is an important process for humanistic educators.

person-centered education. An approach to instruction, favored by Rogers, that focuses on individual feelings, attitudes, and values.

Self-initiated learning also teaches students to be independent and self-reliant. When students learn on their own, they have an opportunity to make judgments, choices, and evaluations. They come to depend more on themselves and less on the evaluations of others.

In addition to being self-initiated, learning should involve all aspects of the person, cognitive as well as affective. Rogers and other humanists call this type of learning (i.e., learning from the "gut" rather than just from the neck up) *whole-person learning*. Humanists believe that if learning is personal and affective, it will induce feelings of belonging in the student. The student will feel more personally involved in learning, more excited over accomplishments, and, most important, more motivated to continue learning.

Learning and Change. The last principle that Rogers has identified is that the most socially useful learning is learning about the process of learning. Rogers notes that in the past, students could get by with learning a static set of facts and ideas. The world was slow to change and what people learned in school was adequate to meet the demands of the time. Today, however, change is a central fact of life. Knowledge is in a constant state of flux. Yesterday's learning is no longer adequate to enable one to function successfully in the modern world. What is needed now, according to Rogers, are individuals who are capable of learning in a changing environment.

IMPLICATIONS OF ROGERS'S VIEWS FOR INSTRUCTION. The learning principles and teacher characteristics that Rogers has identified as central to his educational philosophy have been incorporated into an approach that he calls **person-centered education.** He feels that this approach results in learning that is deeper and that can be acquired more rapidly and pervasively than learning that occurs under traditional classroom approaches. Rogers, like many humanistic educators, is not overly concerned with teaching methodology. The value of curricular planning, the scholarly expertise of the teacher, or the use of technology is not as important for the facilitation of learning as is responsiveness to the student's feelings or the quality of the interaction between students and teachers. Nevertheless, Rogers (1983) feels that certain instructional strategies and methods may be helpful in promoting humanistic learning:

- *Provide students with a variety of resources* that can support and guide their learning experiences. Resources can include such typical instructional materials as books, reference guides, and electronic aids (e.g., computers and calculators) as well as less typical ones, such as building materials, tools, cooking utensils, and the like. Resources can also include people, such as members of the community who may have an area of interest or expertise that they would be willing to share with students. Teachers can serve as resources by making their knowledge, skills, and experience available to students when requested.
- *Use peer tutoring*—students teaching one another—to benefit both the student doing the teaching and the student receiving the help (Devin-Sheehan, Feldman, & Allen, 1976).

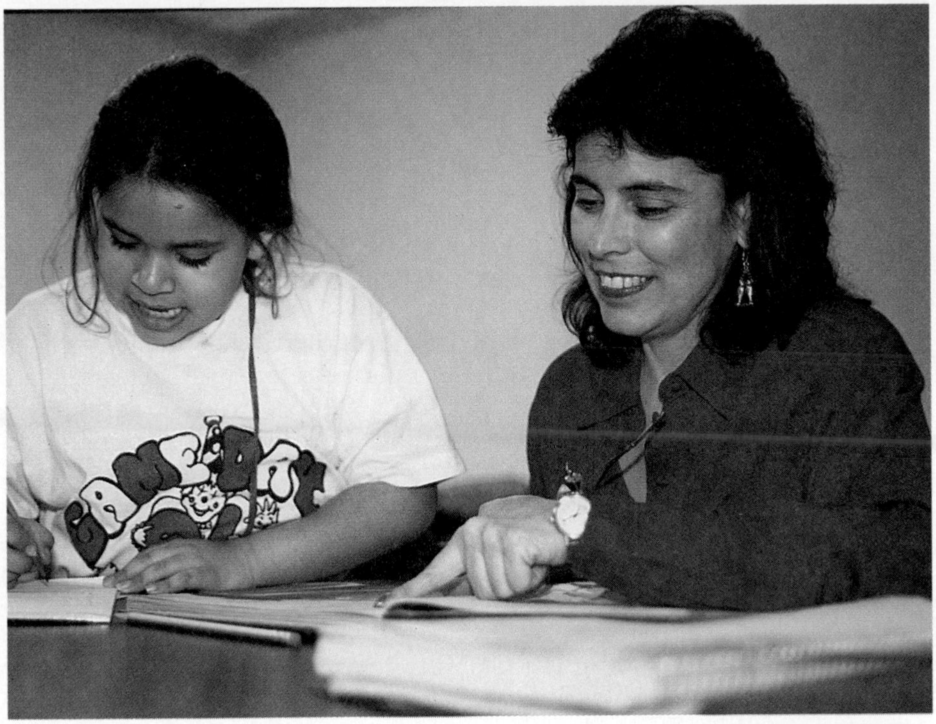

Supportive and caring teachers promote both student learning and personal growth.

- *Use discovery learning* to allow students to seek answers to real questions, make autonomous discoveries, and become engaged in self-directed learning.

The Humanistic Teacher. The humanistic principles that Rogers has identified focus primarily on the learning experiences of the student. However, Rogers's philosophy of education also gives attention to the role of the teacher. Humanistic education is only as successful as the teacher who implements it, and that success is largely dependent upon certain human qualities that the teacher brings to the classroom.

According to Rogers, the teacher in a humanistic classroom is primarily a *facilitator of learning.* In contrast to the traditional teacher who assumes full responsibility for the learning process, the humanistic teacher shares the responsibility for learning with students. Rather than tell students what to do or study, the facilitative teacher acts as a guide and model, helping students to decide what and how they will learn and providing them with the resources to do so. If, for example, students are interested in learning to program a computer, facilitative teachers may respond by providing instruction themselves or by helping students to find other sources of information or expertise.

Rogers has identified a number of personal qualities or attitudes that seem to enhance the teacher's role as a facilitator of learning. These include realness, trust, and empathic understanding.

Realness, or *genuineness,* refers to the degree to which teachers are honest in their relationships with students. Rogers believes that if teachers are to be effective, they must clearly and openly communicate their feelings and beliefs. In other words, they must be real people. As Rogers (1983) states:

empathic understanding. Sensitivity to and awareness of the feelings, motives, attitudes, and values of others.

open education. A type of teaching in which students have a great deal of choice about what work to do and about when and how they do the work.

> When the facilitator is a real person, being what she is, entering into a relationship with the learner without presenting a front or a facade, she is much more likely to be effective. This means that the feelings that she is experiencing are available to her, available to her awareness, that she is able to live these feelings, be them, and able to communicate them if appropriate. (p. 121)

Humanists believe that being real with students encourages open communication in the classroom and helps students to become more connected with their own feelings.

Trust is a basic confidence or faith in the student's potentiality for self-actualization, a conviction that students will naturally "wish to learn, want to grow, seek to discover, endeavor to master, desire to create, move toward self-discipline" (Rogers, 1983, p. 127). This quality is also characterized by an honest acceptance of students as unique individuals, as individuals worthy of respect, and as persons who are fundamentally trustworthy.

By communicating trust and acceptance, teachers convey to students that they are free to take risks in their development as learners and human beings. They can explore, take chances, or even fail without the risk of losing the teacher's support and approval.

Empathic understanding is the ability to view the world through the students' eyes, to understand what the process of learning and education mean personally to the students.

Rogers (1983) observes that empathic understanding is seldom practiced in the traditional classroom. Instead, teachers tend to use an evaluative type of understanding that is often expressed as, "I understand what is wrong with you." This is understanding from the teacher's point of view, not the student's. On the other hand, when the teacher is empathic with how the student feels, the student's reaction is likely to be, "At last someone understands how it feels and seems to be *me* without wanting to analyze me or judge me. Now I can blossom and grow and learn" (p. 125).

INSTRUCTIONAL APPLICATIONS OF HUMANISTIC PSYCHOLOGY

Thus far in this chapter I have discussed how prominent humanistic psychologists view teaching and learning, and the teacher's role in teaching and learning. This section focuses on some specific applications of how humanistic psychologists have attempted to merge the traditional emphasis on skills and cognitive information with the affective area of feelings, values, and interpersonal behavior. The two programs discussed in this section are moral education and **open education** (also called *open classrooms*). Additional humanistic approaches—effective communication, interpersonal relations, and social skills training—are discussed in Chapter 7 because they relate to classroom management and discipline.

This discussion by no means covers the total field of humanistic education. It is intended simply to identify some of the most important and useful concepts for teaching and learning. The Suggestions for Further Reading at the end of the chapter are a good source for additional study in these areas.

socioeconomic status (SES). A ranking to determine social position in a society.

Moral/Character Education

At one time the responsibility for moral education (sometimes called *character education, values education,* or *citizenship education*) was taken by organized religion and the family. Today many people believe the school can and should play an important role in moral education. If so, where should moral education be taught? As part of a special curriculum? Included within the regular school curriculum? How should it be taught, directly or indirectly? These are some of the issues we will explore in this section.

Values impact behavior. Hanson and Ginsburg (1988) found that adolescents were likely to have high academic achievement when they placed a high value on education and had parents who were concerned about their activities and well-being. In fact, the researchers found that even when **socioeconomic status** was taken into consideration, values had a greater impact on school achievement than did socioeconomic status.

Davis (1984) argues that it is impossible for schools to avoid teaching values even if there is no formal curriculum. For example, values are apparent when schools address the following issues: Should evolution and creation be taught in science? What facts about human reproduction should we teach in biology? Should we ignore or include facts related to pregnancy, venereal disease, AIDS, and other sexual problems among teenagers? Living in the classroom environment also involves civic or citizenship issues: Are classroom rules fair? Is there a good balance between cooperation and competition? Are individual responsibility and community responsibility both emphasized? Do students learn respect for self and others?

A National Study of the Moral Behavior of Youth. In a national study of the moral behavior of 9,000 young people and adults, Josephson (1992) reported the following:

- Thirty-three percent of all high school students and 16 percent of college students admitted they had stolen something from a store within the past year.
- Over one-third of all high school and college students said they would lie on a résumé or job application to get a job, and 16 percent of the high schoolers and 18 percent of the collegians said they already had done so at least once.
- Sixty-one percent of high school students and 32 percent of college students admitted they cheated on an exam in the past year.
- Thirty-nine percent of the college students said they lied to their boss, and 35 percent said they lied to a customer within the past 12 months.

Josephson states that although it is difficult to determine whether the present 15- to 30-year-old generation is more likely to engage in dishonest behavior than previous generations, the present data indicate that extensive unethical conduct is exhibited today. He also argues that (a) teaching young people ethical values is the responsibility of families, communities, schools, young people themselves, and human service organizations; and (b) direct instruction on ethics is necessary along with consistent modeling of ethical behavior at the high school and college levels.

> Should schools become more involved in character education?

CHARACTER EDUCATION AND CLINICAL INTERVENTION. London (1987) believes that there must be a major change in the way society sees the role of schools in the development of citizens. At one time the responsibility of children's personal development, including mental health, fell on the home. Today, he argues, we are faced with a psychosocial epidemic affecting millions of schoolchildren—substance abuse, pregnancy, abortion, parenting among teenagers, low self-esteem, depression, and suicide. At the same time, we are seeing greater family disruption and an increase in the incidence of divorce and the number of single parents. Since young

How do you think students can best learn to be good citizens and exhibit moral behavior?

people are the main victims of this epidemic, and schools are where young people spend much of their time, schools are the logical place for major intervention to help promote healthy child development. Thus schools are pressured to assume a broader approach to character development than they have in the past.

London (1987) describes two components of character education: training in *citizenship,* including such topics as the duties of citizens in a democracy, personal integrity as the basis of citizenship, the notion of equality, and the concern for caring for others; and education in *personal adjustment,* the qualities that enable children and youth to become productive citizens. He belives that achievement, self-control, and self-esteem are essential ingredients for character development: "Children who, in the battle against boredom, fear, loneliness, drink or drug themselves or get pregnant cannot very well practice the virtues they have learned. It is a wonder that any of them can learn to read, master arithmetic, or pass exams in schools" (p. 672).

Since the family can no longer perform all the functions needed for character development, other agencies must assist in the task. London argues that, by viewing the adjustment problems of students as roadblocks to the development of character, educators and mental health professionals (social workers, counselors, physicians) should subsume the health care and social service delivery systems under the educational system. This approach would shift the focus of mental health from hospitals, clinics, and private offices to schools. One important implication of this approach would be to change the schools' focus on dealing only with the individual as the primary unit of concern toward attending to families as well (Moynihan, 1986).

What do you think about this approach? Are you convinced such steps need to be taken? Should health clinics provide contraception information? Should the schools get involved in counseling services for students and their families? Would the schools be taking on more than they could handle? What social and political forces need to be considered for such a reorganization of human services? What are the alternatives?

INDIRECT APPROACHES TO MORAL EDUCATION. Indirect approaches to character education tend to encourage students to define their own values and the moral perspectives that support those values. The two most widely used indirect approaches are discussed below.

Values Clarification. Sidney Simon has developed a program called **values clarification**, based on the premise that many young people do not know clearly what their values are. He believes that young people need help in examining their values to direct their insights into how they view choices and make decisions. Simon contends that values clarification does not focus on the content of a person's values but rather on the *process* of valuing.

values clarification. A humanistic approach to moral education designed to help individuals to understand the relationship between their beliefs and their behavior and to become more aware of their values.

Criticisms of Values Clarification. Although the technique of values clarification has been used widely in schools throughout the country, crit-

CLASSROOM Application

USING VALUES CLARIFICATION

Simon, Howe, and Kirschenbaum (1972) propose that teachers use special exercises to involve students in discussion and help them clarify their values. One of the first exercises in their book is designed to help individuals identify the activities they enjoy and whether they are finding time to participate in them. Why don't you try this exercise as I explain it?

1. Make a list of 10 or 15 things that give you great pleasure or joy.
2. Write after the name of each pleasure the date you last experienced it.
3. Place a dollar sign after each activity that costs more than $5.
4. Now go through the list again, and place a *P* after those activities that usually require considerable planning.
5. Review your list, and place an *S* after activities that you share with others.

ics of the approach raise issues about the *ethical relativism* of the program, that is, communicating to students that no one set of values is better than another. Many educators believe that it is important to teach students a particular moral or value system. For example, both abortion rights advocates and anti-abortion groups state that they value life. Thus the same value can be used to support contradictory actions. In this case, developing a value would apparently not provide a clear guide to behavior—a goal of values clarification (Hersh, Miller, & Fielding, 1980).

What happens if the teacher has certain rules about cheating, and some students indicate that cheating is acceptable on tests? Does the teacher accept the values of these students or tell them that they must conform to his value system? Should teachers limit discussion of values that conflict with their idea of how things should be run?

Another issue is whether students discuss what they really feel or instead make statements that are socially acceptable to their peers. Some critics question whether students actually explore their value systems in depth, as the proponents of values clarification feel that they do.

Kohlberg's Theory of Moral Reasoning. During the course of instruction, particularly in the humanities and social sciences, a teacher has

6. Last, place an *A* after those activities that you do alone.

What does this activity tell you about yourself? Using this exercise can lead a discussion into many areas: What are the activities people value? Why is it that some people find time to do the things they enjoy when others do not? What kinds of activities do people enjoy? Why? Do students feel that their values will change or remain the same? What steps can be taken to change the ways in which individuals use their time?

Another series of exercises uses incomplete sentences to evoke discussion about aspirations, attitudes, feelings, and beliefs. Some examples follow:

- I'd like to . . .
- When I grow up . . .
- In about 10 years . . .
- I'm for . . .
- In my opinion . . .
- I really enjoy reading about . . .
- I get angry when . . .

Another approach is to take a controversial issue and place opinions at each end of a continuum. Then ask the students to mark their position on the continuum and discuss the reasons for their selections. This activity is useful in dealing with such issues as sexual behavior, drugs, and other issues of interest to students.

moral dilemmas. Problem situations that require individuals to make decisions that are used to assess their level of moral development.

opportunities to raise questions about ethical or moral situations or to respond to moral issues identified by students in the class. It is important to realize that students differ in their reasoning about these issues. Lawrence Kohlberg (1964) developed a theory of moral reasoning that can help teachers to identify students' level of reasoning and to stimulate students' moral growth.

Traditionally, morality has been equated with character or behavior. However, Kohlberg believes that morality is a set of rational principles for making judgments about how to behave. His basic principle is justice: the regard for the dignity and worth of all persons. According to Kohlberg, children proceed through a series of stages during which they refine their concept of justice. The stages are organized systems of thought through which individuals proceed in a specified sequence.

Kohlberg developed his theory by analyzing **moral dilemmas** presented to children at various age levels. The diagnosis of each child's stage is based on the child's reasons for believing, rather than the behavior itself. A person's stage of moral reasoning cannot be determined on the basis of responses to a single dilemma, because a person may apply more advanced reasoning to some situations than to others. The following is an example of a moral dilemma (Kohlberg, 1976):

Kohlberg's stages of moral reasoning. A theory of moral development based on three levels of moral reasoning.

> In Europe, a woman was near death from a rare form of cancer. There was one drug that the doctors thought might save her, a form of radium that a druggist in the same town had recently discovered. The druggist was charging $2,000, ten times what the drug cost to make. The sick woman's husband, Heinz, went to everyone he knew to borrow the money, but he could only get together about half of what [the drug] cost. He told the druggist that his wife was dying and asked him to sell it cheaper or let him pay later. But the druggist said, "No." So Heinz got desperate and broke into the man's store to steal the drug for his wife. (pp. 41–42)

Table 5.1 presents **Kohlberg's stages of moral reasoning**. Three levels of moral reasoning represent three possible perspectives an individual can take in relation to society's moral norms. A person at the *preconventional level* (Level I) deals with a moral issue from the viewpoint of the specific interest of the individuals involved. Rather than being interested in society's laws, she is concerned with the consequences she would face in deciding upon a particular action. A person at the *conventional level* (Level II) deals with a moral issue from the perception of a law-abiding citizen in society and is concerned with what society views as right or just. A person at the *postconventional, or principled, level* (Level III) deals with a moral issue from a perspective beyond the given laws of that person's own society and asks: "What are the principles upon which any good society is based?"

The first level characterizes children's moral reasoning but can represent adolescent or adult reasoning as well. The second level develops during adolescence and remains as the dominant level of thinking of most adults. The third level is rare; it begins, if at all, during adolescence or early adulthood, and it represents the moral reasoning of only a few adults (Hersh, Paolitto, & Reimer, 1979).

As teachers, we need to be aware that students can choose the same resolution for a dilemma for entirely different reasons. Suppose students were asked whether they would loot a store during a riot. Four different students may state that they would not—all for different reasons! One student might refrain for fear of being shot by the police (Stage 1, "punishment-and-obedience orientation"). Another student might decide not to loot because he wanted a summer job at the store and might be afraid that the store would close down. This student is reasoning at Stage 2, "self-benefit orientation." A student at Stage 3 might be worried about how his friends would view his unlawful act ("good-boy, nice-girl orientation"), and a student at Stage 4 ("law-and-order") believes that a society cannot function effectively if individuals take advantage of social turmoil by participating in unlawful acts. All the students made a decision not to loot, but the reasons for their decision, not the decision itself, determine their placement at four different stages (Mattox, 1975).

Kohlberg (1976) has found that discussing issues at one stage above a person's present level of moral reasoning is most effective in raising moral judgments. Thus, if a student is reasoning at Stage 2, hearing arguments at Stage 3 is more effective than hearing arguments at Stage 2 or Stage 4.

Numerous evaluations of moral education programs using Kohlberg's theory have indicated that such programs can be effective in promoting

Table 5.1 KOHLBERG'S STAGES OF MORAL REASONING

Stage	Description	Example
Level I	***Preconventional level:*** Children at this level reason in terms of their own needs. Answers to moral dilemmas are based on what they can get away with. Moral values reside in good and bad acts, not people or standards. Cultural rules and labels of good or bad, right or wrong, are interpreted in terms of punishment, reward, exchange of favors, or the physical power of those who advocate the rules and labels. Children are concerned about external, concrete consequences to themselves.	
Stage 1	***Punishment-and-obedience orientation:*** Children worry about avoiding punishment by adults or people with superior power and prestige. They are aware of rules and the consequences for breaking them. The physical consequences of an action determine its goodness or badness: "might makes right."	Heinz should not steal, because he would be punished by authorities.
Stage 2	***Instrumental-relativist orientation:*** Children want to satisfy their own needs (and occasionally the needs of others) if they can get away with it. They are motivated by self-interest and aware that relationships are dominated by concrete reciprocity (you scratch my back and I'll scratch yours), not loyalty, gratitude, or justice. They assume that everyone has to look out for himself and is obligated only to those who help him.	Heinz should steal, because he is worried about his wife and he will feel better if she isn't sick.
Level II	***Conventional level:*** Moral value resides in performing good and right roles. Children are concerned with meeting external social expectations; they value meeting the expectations of family, group, or nation by conforming to the expectations of significant people and the social order. There is active support and justification of conventional rules and roles.	
Stage 3	***Interpersonal concordance orientation:*** Children earn approval by being "nice." They are concerned about living up to "good boy" and "good girl" stereotypes. Good behavior is what pleases or helps others and what is approved of by them. Children are aware of the need to consider the intentions and feelings of others; cooperation is seen in terms of the golden rule.	Heinz should steal, because good husbands care about their wives. Other people would disapprove if he let his wife die.
Stage 4	***Authority-maintaining orientation:*** Children are motivated by a sense of duty or obligation to live up to socially defined roles, and to maintain the existing social order for the good of all. They are aware that there is a larger social system which regulates the behavior of the people within it. They assume that the social order is the source of mortality and that laws should be maintained, even at personal expense.	Heinz should not steal, because stealing is against the law and the laws must be maintained even at the expense of personal loss.
Level III	***Postconventional autonomous, or principled, level:*** Children make a clear effort to define moral rules and principles that have validity and application apart from the authority of groups or individuals and apart from their own identifications. There is a concern for fidelity to self-chosen moral principles. Moral value resides in conformity to shared standards, rights, and duties.	
Stage 5	***Social-contract, legalistic orientation:*** Right actions tend to be defined in terms of general individual rights and standards that have been critically examined and agreed on by the whole society. There is an emphasis on procedural rules for reaching consensus because of awareness of the relativism of personal values and opinions. Aside from what society agrees on, there is the possibility of changing the law in terms of rational considerations of social utility. Outside the legal realm, free agreement and contract are the binding elements of obligation.	Heinz should steal, because society places more value on the right to have medicine than on the right to make a large profit. Everyone has the right to get medicine if he or she needs it badly, regardless of the law against stealing.
Stage 6	***Universal ethical orientation:*** The person defines right by decisions of conscience in accord with self-chosen ethical principles that appeal to logical comprehensiveness, universality, and consistency. These principles are abstract and ethical; at heart they are universal principles of justice, of the reciprocity and equality of human rights, and of respect for the dignity of human beings as individuals. There is an orientation of letting one's conscience be a directing agent and of letting mutual respect and trust dominate interpersonal relationships.	Heinz should steal the drug, because a human life takes precedence over any other moral or legal value, whatever it is. A human life has inherent value whether or not it is valued by a particular person—Heinz's wife's life has inherent value whether or not it is valued by the druggist.

Source: Johnson, 1979.

moral judgment (Enright, Lapsley, & Levy, 1983; Leming, 1981; Lockwood, 1978), especially if the program lasts more than a few weeks and if the intervention involves students in discussion of controversial moral dilemmas (Schlaefli, Rest, & Thoma, 1985). A question often asked is whether the training influences *moral behavior.* Unfortunately, *there is no evidence to suggest that changes produced by values clarification or Kohlberg's programs bring about subsequent changes in actual moral behavior.* Rest (1983) explains the lack of such change by pointing out that moral judgment is but one of four components influencing the production of moral behavior, as follows:

- *Moral sensitivity*—the individual realizes that a situation exists that involves a decision to act and that the action has some consequences for the welfare and interests of others.
- *Moral judgment*—the individual must make a decision that involves a course of action (this is the process that the dilemmas measure).
- *Moral motivation*—the individual must act on personal judgment.
- *Moral character*—the individual must have sufficient persistence to implement strategies to behave morally.

It is clear that most educational programs do not deal with all the necessary components. However, it is argued that if programs deal with moral sensitivity and judgment (the first two components), it may be possible to stimulate the development of the last two processes—moral motivation and character. The main point here is that students may *talk* about responsible behavior in such areas as sexuality or drugs but may not *act* appropriately.

Criticisms of Kohlberg's Theory. Kohlberg's theory of moral reasoning is one of the major approaches to moral development, but he is not without his critics. Some of the major criticisms include the following:

- Kohlberg underestimates the importance of Stage 3 reasoning, the "good-boy, nice-girl" orientation. Although postconventional morality (Stages 5 and 6) is a worthwhile goal, Kohlberg has found few individuals who have reached this level. Thus a society will benefit if most of its citizens have respect for law and order. As a result, more emphasis should be placed on Stage 3 reasoning by helping children to understand the importance of rules in maintaining society.
- Kohlberg has a narrow perception of morality in emphasizing justice. He fails to recognize the role of the affective side of morality in terms of such moral emotions as guilt, concern for others, and remorse.
- Although Kohlberg presents research in nine different cultures supporting the universality of his stages, he should not conclude that his description of moral development holds true for all people in all cultures.
- The theory places unrealistic demands on teachers. According to Kohlberg, a teacher should present a moral argument one stage above the student's present level of reasoning. This requirement produces

DEBATE FORUM

Are There Gender Differences in Moral Reasoning?

Argument: Carol Gilligan (1982; Gilligan & Attanucci, 1988) argues that Kohlberg's theory was developed on the basis of his investigation with males and that the description of criteria for each of the stages may be more appropriate for the development of moral reasoning in males than in females. She asserts that women follow a different path to complex moral reasoning and that their development is based, in part, on a different set of values. For example, a woman who would solve a moral dilemma based on a concern for the people involved (i.e., a care perspective or focus) might not score as high as a male who might resolve the same dilemma on the basis of a theme of universal justice.

Using the Heinz dilemma you just read about, individuals with a justice orientation see the problem as a conflict between his desire to save his wife and the druggist's right to carry on his business. Individuals with a caring orientation, in contrast, view the dilemma differently: The question is not one of right to property versus other rights, but why the druggist is not responsive to the needs of another person.

Counterargument: Research using Kohlberg's methodology finds no sex differences in moral reasoning (Gibbs, Arnold, & Burkhart, 1984; Walker, 1984, 1989). When presented with traditional moral problems or asked to identify personal moral problems, males and females indicated *both* a morality of caring and a concern with justice.

Response: Even though males and females respond to moral dilemmas using both orientations (caring vs. justice), females appear to have a preference for the care orientation (Gilligan & Attanucci, 1988). Also, Gilligan's major point is that two paths to morality exist, and that principles of caring and justice are needed to resolve the moral issues we experience in our daily lives.

What do you think? Do you think that males and females differ in the way they reason about moral issues? What other differences do you notice in males and females? Do you know if there is any research to support or refute your notions? (See Chapter 10 for a discussion of gender issues.)

CLASSROOM

Application

LEADING A DISCUSSION ON A MORAL DILEMMA

You can play an important role in the enhancement of moral reasoning by leading discussions on moral dilemmas and creating opportunities for students to think about the issues in increasingly complex ways. Various types of instructional material can be used to raise the issue of moral dilemmas: *hypothetical situations* like the "Heinz" case (see Hersh, Paolitto, & Reimer, 1979; Howe & Howe, 1975; Mattox, 1975); *content-specific issues* stemming from curriculum content, such as America's participation in the Vietnam War or the responsibility of chemical companies to protect the environment; problems of *real or practical concern*, such as classroom situations ("Would you report a friend who was cheating on a test?") or community events.

There are two phases of questioning: *initial* and *in-depth* strategies. In the initial phase, your role is to ensure that students understand the moral dilemma, to help students confront the various moral aspects of the issue, to elicit students' rationale for their point of view, and to encourage students to discuss their point of view with one another. Table 5.2 summarizes the strategies for the initial phase.

TABLE 5.2 INITIAL QUESTIONING STRATEGIES FOR MORAL DILEMMAS

Strategy	Purpose	Questions
Highlight moral issues	Encourage students to take a stand	Should Heinz steal the drug? Should a husband commit a crime in order to save the life of his wife?
Ask "why" questions	Encourage students to defend their positions	Why do you think your solution to the dilemma is a good one?
	Reveal differing reasons for taking the same stand	Why did you reach that conclusion?
Complicate the circumstances	Encourage students to see other points of view	Suppose Heinz's wife asked him to (or not to) steal the drug. Would your position be different?
	Prevent students from avoiding to take a stand by trying to change the dilemma	Suppose there wasn't any other drug that could be used?

Source: Hersh, Paolitto, and Reimer, 1979.

After students have identified the moral dilemma and have exchanged points of view, the teacher moves into the second phase of the discussion by asking in-depth questions that encourage students to deal with different points of view. These advanced strategies include asking refining questions, highlighting contiguous-stage arguments, clarifying and summarizing, and using role-playing.

Refining questions help to extend the various positions taken on the issue and can take many forms. A teacher can ask students to

- explain ambiguous terms that they use in discussion ("What kind of *trouble* would you get your friend into if you reported the cheating?")
- explore one moral issue related to the dilemma, such as authority, contract obligations, and the value of life ("Do you have any obligations to a stranger?" "What is the difference between an obligation to a member of one's family and to a stranger?")
- assume the perspective of a different person in the conflict contrary to the student's position. ("What do you think the teacher ought to do in a situation in which a student is cheating?" "Would your parents think you should report your friend?")
- consider what would happen if everyone followed his or her reasoning on the moral dilemma ("How could teachers run classrooms if everyone cheated on tests?" "What would happen if everyone stole from other people to save the life of someone they knew?")

A second in-depth questioning strategy is to highlight arguments at various stages of moral reasoning. For example, "John, your approach to this problem is different from Peter's. Could you tell us why you think your solution was a good one? How is it different from what Peter said?" If everyone in class provides the same perspective on an issue, the teacher should pose arguments at the next higher stage: "I noticed that no one mentioned that the law states ——— based on the reasoning that ———. Does anyone have an opinion about this legal point of view?"

Another in-depth strategy involves a change in the teacher's role from that of initiating questions to clarifying and summarizing students' statements. After listening to a discussion about whether to report a friend who was cheating on a test, the teacher might state: "I hear a couple of things. Some of you are concerned that classroom rules should not be broken. Others feel that a close personal friendship is more important than any regulation. Finally, some people believe that a close friendship can still be maintained if the student were reported to the teacher."

Finally, the teacher can ask role-taking questions and use strategies designed to stimulate students to take different points of view, such as holding debates or viewing films that depict controversial issues. The teacher will find these strategies most effective when the students are asked to reason from another's point of view.

some problems because very few people reach Stage 5 or 6. Therefore, some teachers may interact with students who reason at stages higher than their own! How will teachers help these students? Another related problem is the difficulty some teachers will have in attempting to lead a class discussion on a dilemma with students who are at different levels and responding appropriately each time at one stage higher than the students' level of reasoning (Fraenkel, 1976; Peters, 1975).

? What is the controversy concerning direct and indirect approaches to moral or character development?

DIRECT APPROACHES TO MORAL EDUCATION. A number of educators criticize indirect approaches to moral education because of their preoccupation with how students think about moral issues rather than how they behave (Ryan, 1986; Wynne, 1988). The critics indicate the ineffectiveness of these approaches by pointing out that they have done little to deal with the moral problems in schools (e.g., poor discipline, vandalism, and physical abuse of students and of teachers) and in society. In addition, in both values clarification and Kohlberg's theory of moral development, the teacher plays a relatively neutral role. Teachers present critical situations and serve as group facilitators but never give their opinion concerning right and wrong in what students say. Today there appears to be more concern that teachers and the schools play a more direct role in developing standards and teaching moral behavior. For example, a former U.S. secretary of education, William Bennett (1986), suggested that schools should develop discipline codes, explain to children and their parents what the schools expect from them, and enforce the rules.

Lickona (1988) provides the following advice on how teachers can be more actively involved in moral education:

- Serve as moral models and mentors for children, providing examples of respect and caring by the way they treat their children and offering corrective moral feedback when students act insensitively toward others.
- Develop a cohesive classroom community in which students know each other, care about each other, and feel part of the group.
- Hold students accountable to high standards of academic responsibility in order to teach the value of work as a way to develop oneself and contribute to the human community.
- Handle discipline in a way that develops moral reasoning and encourage students to discipline themselves and to voluntarily comply with rules.
- Provide opportunities, such as class meeting, for participatory decision making and shared responsibility.
- Teach the skills of cooperation through cooperative learning and practice in reasoned conflict resolution.

- Develop students' capacity for moral reflection through discussion and debate of moral issues drawn from the traditional subject areas.
- Use inspirational role models from current events and history to help students admire and identify with good character. (p. 9)

Wynne (1988) is especially interested in service activities. He states that it is easy to fool oneself into believing that even though students' behavior is inappropriate, their moral thinking or reasoning is good. He believes that character is demonstrated through conduct. Thus, if educators want to help students develop character, they need to organize experiences that generate good conduct. He points to the "For Character" school recognition program in Chicago as an example of what schools need to do. Students are given recognition for participating in such activities as

- tutoring peers or students in other grades
- serving as crossing guards
- taking part in dramatic, musical, or athletic activities
- raising funds for school or community
- helping on service projects with the school or community
- taking part in academic group projects
- visiting patients in hospitals
- helping care for children in nursery school or kindergarten

In 1992 Maryland became the first state in the nation to require public school students to perform community service to graduate. The plan passed by the state board of education requires students to complete 75 hours of community service.

A POSSIBLE RECONCILIATION. Benninga (1988) believes that we can reconcile the issue of direct versus indirect approaches to moral education. He advocates that schools should teach certain values that few individuals would question: justice, persistence, generosity, loyalty, social cooperation, and fairness. When issues arise concerning the application of these values, structured discussions would be the preferable teaching method. He uses the example of how we teach students the principle of free speech and expression as identified in the First Amendment. Yet the Supreme Court of the United States constantly hears cases by litigants who wish to redefine what free speech means. For example, the re-examination of free speech and expression by the Court in 1989 and 1990 made it legal for protestors to burn the United States flag. Benninga's point is that we can and should teach young people the important values of one's community and Western culture. However, we should deal with controversy in moral perceptions and behavior within the framework of open discussion and dialogue.

In addition to formal instruction and discussion, students can have opportunities to become involved in their community whereby they can experience the consequences of positive social behavior. Helping others can be a good place to begin.

DEBATE FORUM — Values Education: What Values? Whose Values?

As I write this sentence, south central Los Angeles is burning. The city has risen up in outrage because four police officers have been acquitted of all charges relating to a videotaped beating of an African American named Rodney King.

During the same month, Vice President Dan Quayle criticized the fictional television character Murphy Brown for choosing to have a child out of wedlock and thereby, in his opinion, glamorizing single motherhood.

The summer of 1992 brought an outpouring of soul-searching among many Americans. What has happened to "traditional" American values? What moral shifts have allowed the unbridled growth of American indebtedness, both personally and nationally? The breakup of the American family? The vicious debates over abortion rights and capital punishment? We are at a time in American history when the country as a whole is re-evaluating its moral underpinnings.

Argument: "It is essential for us to support the family in teaching our students a number of traditional civic and moral values that most parents, educators, and community members agree are essential for democracy" (Kirschenbaum, 1992, p. 776).

Open Education

? How are humanistic principles used in the open classroom?

The apparent success of the British primary schools and the publication of the Plowden Report (1967), a study advocating the development of the open classroom as a model for elementary education in England, have been catalysts in the spread of open education in the United States.

Advocates of *open education* claim that it is both a philosophy of education and the application of Piaget's theory of cognitive development (see Chapter 8). Because of the confusion over what exactly is involved in open education, Walberg and Thomas (1972) have reviewed relevant literature, broken it down into components, and then sought to verify their descriptions with prominent advocates of open education. They have evolved a list of eight themes, paraphrased as follows:

Counterargument: Schools can teach students the process of establishing values but cannot and should not teach them an intact system of values, because no single set of values represents "right" or "good."

Response: *Newsweek* (1992) described a number of values-based educational programs already in place in some schools.

- A new teacher-directed magazine, *Teaching for Tolerance,* focuses on how to foster racial harmony among students.
- Many schools now require community volunteer work as a prerequisite to graduation.
- A program called *Facing History and Ourselves* encourages students to examine racism, prejudice, and anti-Semitism by studying twentieth-century genocide.
- The Child Development Project in California sends specialists into schools to help teachers create environments in which students can become more caring and responsible by using cooperative learning, literature that stimulates discussion and provides examples of empathic behavior, community service projects, and schoolwide activities for whole families.

What Do You Think? Do you believe that teachers should be more actively involved in promoting community values or even the core values of Western society? Is there a danger of indoctrination? Can educators agree as to what values should be taught? Is there greater danger of doing nothing because of the fear that consensus can't be reached?

1. *Provisions for learning*. Manipulative materials supplied in great diversity and range. Children move freely around room. Talking encouraged. No grouping by ability using test scores.
2. *Humaneness, respect, openness, and warmth*. Use of student-made material. Teacher deals with behavior problems by communicating with child, without involving the group.
3. *Diagnosis of learning events.* Students correct their own work. Teacher observes and asks questions.
4. *Instruction.* Individualized. No texts or workbooks.
5. *Evaluation*. Teacher takes notes. Individualized. Few formal tests.
6. *Search for opportunities for professional growth.* Teacher uses assistance of someone else. Teacher works with colleague.
7. *Self-perception of teacher*. Teacher tries to keep all children within sight to monitor their work.
8. *Assumptions about children and the learning process.* Classroom climate warm and accepting. Children involved in what they are doing.

An example of an open classroom environment in the first grade.

Walberg and Thomas found that open classes differ from traditional classes on five of the eight criteria: provisions, humaneness, diagnosis, instruction, and evaluation.

Barth (1971) has investigated the eighth criterion—assumptions about children and the learning process—and suggests that before jumping on the bandwagon, teachers should examine whether their assumptions are attuned to those of successful open educators in the United States and England. (Remember the importance of linking beliefs and practices, discussed in Chapter 1.) The following is a partial list of these assumptions. Read each and determine the degree to which you agree with it.

Learning

- Children are innately curious and will explore their environment without adult intervention.
- Children will display natural exploratory behavior if they are not threatened.
- Play is not distinguished from work as the predominant mode of learning in early childhood.
- Children will be likely to learn if they are given considerable choice in the selection of the materials they wish to work with and in the questions they wish to pursue with respect to those materials.

Intellectual Development

- Concept formation proceeds slowly.
- Children pass through similar stages of intellectual development, each in his own way and at his own rate and in his own time.

- Verbal abstractions should follow direct experience with objects and ideas, not precede them or substitute for them.

Evaluation

- Errors are necessarily a part of the learning process. They are to be expected and even desired, for they contain information essential for further learning.
- Those qualities of a person's learning that can be carefully measured are not necessarily the most important.
- The best way of evaluating the effect of the school experience on the child is to observe the student over a long period.

Knowledge

- Knowledge is a function of one's personal integration of experience and therefore does not fall neatly into categories or "disciplines."
- There is little or no knowledge that is essential for everyone to acquire. (pp. 97–99)

The Walberg and Thomas (1972) list of themes suggests that, although open educators support students' freedom to move around the room and to select their own learning activities, teacher guidance throughout the process is in evidence. Proponents of open education present this fact to some critics who characterize open education as simply "doing your own thing."

One of the most salient features of an open classroom is the physical environment of the room, in which students work individually or in small groups. Most of the individualized instruction is provided by learning or activity centers in the classroom that allow students to explore particular subject areas, topics, skills, or interests. These centers have the advantages of posting explicit directions for proceeding on a topic without the presence of the teacher and of recording the student's participation and progress for later discussion with the teacher.

RESEARCH ON OPEN EDUCATION. Evaluations of open education programs (Giaconia & Hedges, 1982; Peterson, 1979) generally show that these approaches are slightly more effective than traditional education in improving affective but not academic outcomes. In reviewing a large number of studies comparing open and traditional classrooms, Giaconia and Hedges found that open classrooms were moderately more successful in improving cooperation, creativity, achievement motivation, and independence. However, on measures of academic achievement, traditional classrooms were clearly superior.

Interestingly, Giaconia and Hedges also found that when open classes did improve affective outcomes, it was often at the expense of student progress in language, math, and reading. They also noted that certain features differentiated the more effective open education programs from the less effective, including greater emphasis on the role of the children in determining their own learning, greater use of evaluation focusing on students' specific strengths and weaknesses, more individualized instruction, and the presence of manipulative materials.

It appears that other forms of instruction that are based in part on humanistic principles (e.g., cooperative learning) have been more successful in producing academic gains as well as affective outcomes. Slavin (1988) summarizes the research on open classrooms by stating: "The experience of the open-schools movement does suggest that there are limits to self-directed learning by students, particularly when they are learning the basic skills on which so much later learning depends" (p. 303).

In a recent review of the open classroom, Rothenberg (1989) urged educators to reconsider its use. He pointed out that important cognitive and affective outcomes can be attained through the use of open classrooms and that educators should consider more *structure* in organizing open classrooms. This structure would include more frequent monitoring of student work so that basic skills are not neglected.

CRITICISMS OF HUMANISTIC EDUCATION

Much of the criticism of humanistic education attacks the belief that students will learn if they are freed from teacher-directed pressure and are allowed to decide what they want to do in the classroom. Skinner (1973) feels that too many educators delude themselves about what constitutes "freedom": Students are not free simply because their teacher chooses not to exert control over their behavior. He states, "They [students] then simply come under the control of other conditions, and we must look at those conditions and their effects if we are to improve teaching" (p. 13). The teacher who understands the behavioral process, says Skinner, can help students *learn* to be free and happy. This will occur because students will acquire the knowledge and the skills of productive and creative individuals.

Although a proponent of humanistic education, Kozol (1972), in his book *Free Schools,* points out that some teachers seek to *force* freedom on students. From his vantage point he sees that although conscious, or structured, teaching is not always necessary for learning, it is wrong to assume that learning is *never* the result of conscious teaching. (Carl Rogers's writings about teaching have sometimes been so interpreted.) Kozol maintains that when conscious teaching is necessary but "in the name of Joy and Freedom it is not undertaken," parents whose children fail to learn have good reasons to be disturbed with school and with teachers who have let them down.

Beane (1985/1986) identifies a number of additional criticisms of affective, or humanistic, educational programs. First, there is often an absence of clear direction or purpose. Some affective programs are based on vague goals such as "enhancing self-worth" or "developing the total individual." Investigations of affective programs indicate that there is weak support for their ability to bring about changes in self-esteem or attitude toward school (Baskin & Hess, 1980; Strein, 1988). Second, there often is a lack of thoroughness in program planning. Many programs are based on short, experiential activities that lack organization and any theoretical orientation to support the approach. As a result, many programs have little impact on students. Third, inadequate measurement and evaluation are used in affective programs. As a result, educators have less understanding of the factors that influence affective behavior and development than they do in the cognitive domain. Finally, there is inconsistency among components of the affective school program. Many teachers attempt to develop various affective programs so that students can develop their own values and beliefs. However, when these values or beliefs conflict with institutional or community values, some teachers "end up insisting on specific conclusions through gentle coercion or systematic persuasion" (Beane, 1985/1986, p. 29).

More recent writings by the proponents of humanistic education emphasize the successes of cooperative learning and recommend more structure and specific goals for open and moral education. As a result, we may see an increased emphasis on different types of humanistic programs throughout the 1990s.

Summary

HUMANISTIC PSYCHOLOGY

1. Humanistic educators value educational goals that help students to learn more about themselves, relate to others, and make independent decisions. They prefer learning situations that are student centered and oriented toward discovery methods of teaching and learning.
2. Humanistic psychologists are concerned with individuals' feelings and perceptions as clues to their actions.
3. Humanistic psychologists believe that persons determine their own behavior.
4. Humanistic psychologists identify two parts in learning: the acquisition of new information and the individual's personalization of this information.
5. Combs believes that the way individuals perceive their actions is the key to understanding their behavior. In addition, the closer to themselves individuals perceive events to be, the more likely it is that they will react to those events.
6. Maslow sees a person's motivational tendency as moving toward self-actualization, or self-fulfillment. He places the satisfaction of lower-order needs such as food and safety before people's motivation to develop their individuality or to realize their potential.
7. Rogers believes that individuals have a desire to learn and are more likely to learn when they perceive that the learning is relevant to their own needs and purposes and when it is self-initiated. He points out that threat can diminish learning.
8. Rogers points out that the teacher's role as a facilitator of learning can be enhanced if the teacher is real or genuine with students, displays trust or confidence in students' potential for self-actualization, and communicates empathic understanding.

INSTRUCTIONAL APPLICATIONS OF HUMANISTIC PSYCHOLOGY

9. Recent changes in society require that the school assume more responsibility for character development, which includes training both for citizenship and for personal adjustment.
10. An important issue in moral/character education is the effectiveness of direct and indirect approaches.
11. Values clarification aids students in examining their value system so that they can arrive at better decisions.
12. Kohlberg's stages of moral reasoning can be used to classify individuals' responses to moral dilemmas into one of six stages representing different ways of thinking about moral issues.
13. Kohlberg has found that discussing issues one stage above a person's present level of moral reasoning is most effective in raising the level of moral judgments.
14. Open education gives students freedom to select their activities and encourages the teacher to act more as an assistant or facilitator of learning than as one who possesses all the knowledge.
15. Open classrooms are moderately more successful in attaining affective goals (e.g., cooperation and independence) than traditional classrooms. However, on measures of academic achievement, traditional classrooms are superior.

Reflecting on the Humanistic Perspective

1. Remember Your Teachers

Select a teacher you had who used humanistic principles in interacting with students and another whose behavior tended toward the opposite. How successful were they in motivating and gaining respect from students, attaining educational objectives, and encouraging independent learning?

2. Think about the School's Role in Teaching Values

Select one of the following statements that comes closest to your point of view, and defend the reasons for your support of the statement:

a. The schools should help students to develop their own value system through the process of continuous questioning of beliefs. Through this process, students will develop their own value system and become productive and caring citizens.
b. Our society is based on a number of fundamental values. If we want our society to flourish, it is important that the schools teach specific values. If the schools take a position that one value is as good as another, the public will continue to witness inappropriate and destructive behavior among its citizens.

3. Consider Alternative Approaches to Motivation

What new ideas did you learn in this chapter about student motivation? How can you use the ideas from humanistic psychologists to increase student motivation in your class?

Key terms

heirarchy of needs, p. 205
self-actualization, p. 205
person-centered education, p. 208
empathic understanding, p. 210
open education, p. 210
socioeconomic status, p. 211
values clarification, p. 213
moral dilemmas, p. 215
Kohlberg's stages of moral reasoning, p. 216

Suggestions for Further Reading

The following books provide detailed discussions by some of the major humanistic theorists:

Combs, A. W., & Avila, D. L. (1985). *Helping relationships: Basic concepts for the helping professions* (3rd ed.). Boston: Allyn & Bacon.
Maslow, A. (1962). *Toward a psychology of being*. New York: Van Nostrand.
Rogers, C. R. (1983). *Freedom to learn for the 80's.* Columbus, OH: Merrill.
Simpson, E. L. (1976). *Humanistic education: An interpretation.* Cambridge, MA: Ballinger. Defines humanistic education and presents numerous examples of classroom practices.

For suggestions for using values clarification exercises consult:

Raths, L. B., Harmin, M., & Simon, S. B. (1966). *Values and teaching: Working with values in the classroom.* Columbus, OH: Merrill.
Simon, S. B., Howe, L. W., & Kirschenbaum, H. (1989). *Values clarification: A handbook of practical strategies for teachers and students* (rev. ed.). Hadley, MA: Values Associates.

Read the following references for specific information on the open classroom:

Blitz, B. (1973). *The open classroom: Making it work.* Boston: Allyn & Bacon.
Stephens, L. S. (1974). *The teacher's guide to open education.* New York: Holt, Rinehart & Winston.

The following books discuss the teaching of values and character education in school:

Benninga, J. S. (1991). *Moral, character, and civic education in the elementary school.* New York: Teachers College Press.
Likona, T. (1992). *Educating for character: How our schools can teach respect and responsibility*. New York: Bantam.

Part 2 Synthesis

The motivational and instructional methods covered in Chapters 2 through 5 were organized by conceptual orientation—behaviorism, cognitivism, and humanism—to better untangle the "pure" assumptions of each theory that underlie common educational procedures. However, the classification of methods under particular theories of learning does not irrevocably wed these methods to one theory. Cooperative learning uses ideas from all three theoretical positions. For example, in cooperative learning, interpersonal relations and positive communication (humanistic goals) are given high priority. In addition, group rewards provide an incentive for group members to help one another, and individual accountability can be achieved by calculating group scores based on individual achievement (behavioral principles). Finally, group members must identify their task and select appropriate learning strategies to achieve their objectives (cognitive principles). My point is that some teaching methods can be used simultaneously for different objectives and can be claimed by more than one theoretical position.

In analyzing learning theories and instructional applications, we must be careful not to make simplistic or incorrect distinctions among them. For example, one of my students attempted to summarize the differences between humanism and behaviorism as follows: "The humanists are the 'good' guys who are concerned about students, while the behaviorists are the 'bad' guys who are more interested in technology and control than in understanding people." Behaviorists would take issue with this conceptualization by pointing out that they are not against a teacher's being warm and friendly and that they are strongly people oriented. However, they do not believe that these characteristics are sufficient for effective instruction. Likewise, although humanists are less interested than behaviorists in the sequencing of content for instruction, they are not necessarily opposed to planning and using specific teaching techniques.

A great deal of research has focused on the effectiveness of various types of instruction. One of the major issues in the literature deals with the effectiveness of direct, or structured, methods of instruction versus unstructured, or open, methods. The research findings indicate that, in general, direct instruction is superior to unstructured methods for producing mastery of basic skills (Brophy, 1979; Good, 1979). However, mastering basic skills or learning how to learn should not be the only objectives in the classroom. When the educational goals are to promote cooperation, positive attitudes toward the subject area, and personal development, direct instruction may *not* be the best approach. Unstructured teaching methods can be effective in helping students to attain many educational objectives. For example, Peterson (1979) found that open teaching was somewhat more effective than structured teaching in developing independence and curiosity among students. This does not mean that unstructured methods are the only way to attain affective goals. The research on mastery learning and other forms of individualized instruction indicate that positive affective outcomes also can be achieved through structured methods of teaching.

Humanistic psychologists are more closely aligned with cognitive psychologists in their view of the teacher as a facilitator or mediator of learning than they are with behavioral psychologists who view the teacher more as a director or manager of learning. One of the implications of using various teaching methods is to realize that diverse teacher behaviors often are necessary to implement various methods of instruction successfully.

Before you leave this part of the book, I would like you to reflect on how the various theories of learning and motivation discussed in the last five chapters might help you deal with different learning situations. Use information from educational psychology that can help you diagnose the problem and recommend possible solutions. Compare your responses with those of another student in your class. There is no one approach or solution to each of the incidents.

1. Adeidra Wilson, a history teacher, finds that her students do poorly on certain aspects of her tests. Students are able to learn the dates and facts presented in her lectures and in the text, but they do poorly on essay exams when she asks them to become involved in higher levels of thinking, such as comparing and contrasting political candidates or different causes of conflict.
2. Bill Davis is a good student who attends class regularly and has good study habits, but he doesn't have much confidence in his ability. Unfortunately, he is failing elementary algebra and his teacher doesn't know what to do about it. He seems to understand the material, since he completes his homework problems successfully.
3. Frank Barrera was recently hired to teach biology at a school with a large number of low-achieving students. He wants to organize his class and subject matter to make the class interesting and motivate his students to succeed, but he is not sure what to do.
4. Susan Reilly is a Spanish teacher who finds that her students are not interested in learning verb conjugations or other basic aspects of the language. When she attempts to present drill-and-practice exercises, the students simply talk among themselves in class. Yet she does find them using short Spanish phrases in their interaction before and after class.
5. Edwin Rolf is concerned that many of his students come to class angry and upset each day. He has difficulty settling them down to learn and is frustrated that he can't keep their attention for more than 10 minutes.

Part three

Preparing for Effective Teaching

My goals in this section of the book are to help you acquire relevant *knowledge* about effective teaching strategies and develop the *competencies* to perform successfully in the classroom—in other words, to apply in the classroom the principles explored in the preceding chapters.

There are many different ways to teach. The teaching-learning model used in this book indicates that four factors should be considered in this decision—instructional objectives, principles of learning/motivation, individual differences, and teacher behavior. In the first five chapters of this book, we focused primarily on principles of learning/motivation and introduced certain aspects of teacher behavior. In Part Three, we will focus on writing objectives, demonstrate how different lessons can be implemented using different learning and motivational theories and principles, and continue to explore teacher behavior, especially classroom management strategies. In the final two parts of the book, we will add the last two important factors in the teaching-learning process—individual differences and evaluation.

Parts Three and Four syntheses (page 336 and pages 539–543, respectively) give you an opportunity to integrate material from different parts of the book. Take time now to look at these exercises before you continue. Put yourself in the role of teacher for a moment and identify some of the thoughts you may have about working with 30 or more students: "Am I sufficiently prepared for the students? Do I know what I want to teach? How should I teach the lesson? What do I do if they are not motivated to learn? Will they listen to me? How should I manage the classroom? Should I act tough or be nice? How should I handle discipline problems?" These are just a few of the many concerns that a teacher could raise about classroom instruction. I am sure that you could expand this short list to include many more concerns.

Chapter 6

Planning for Instruction

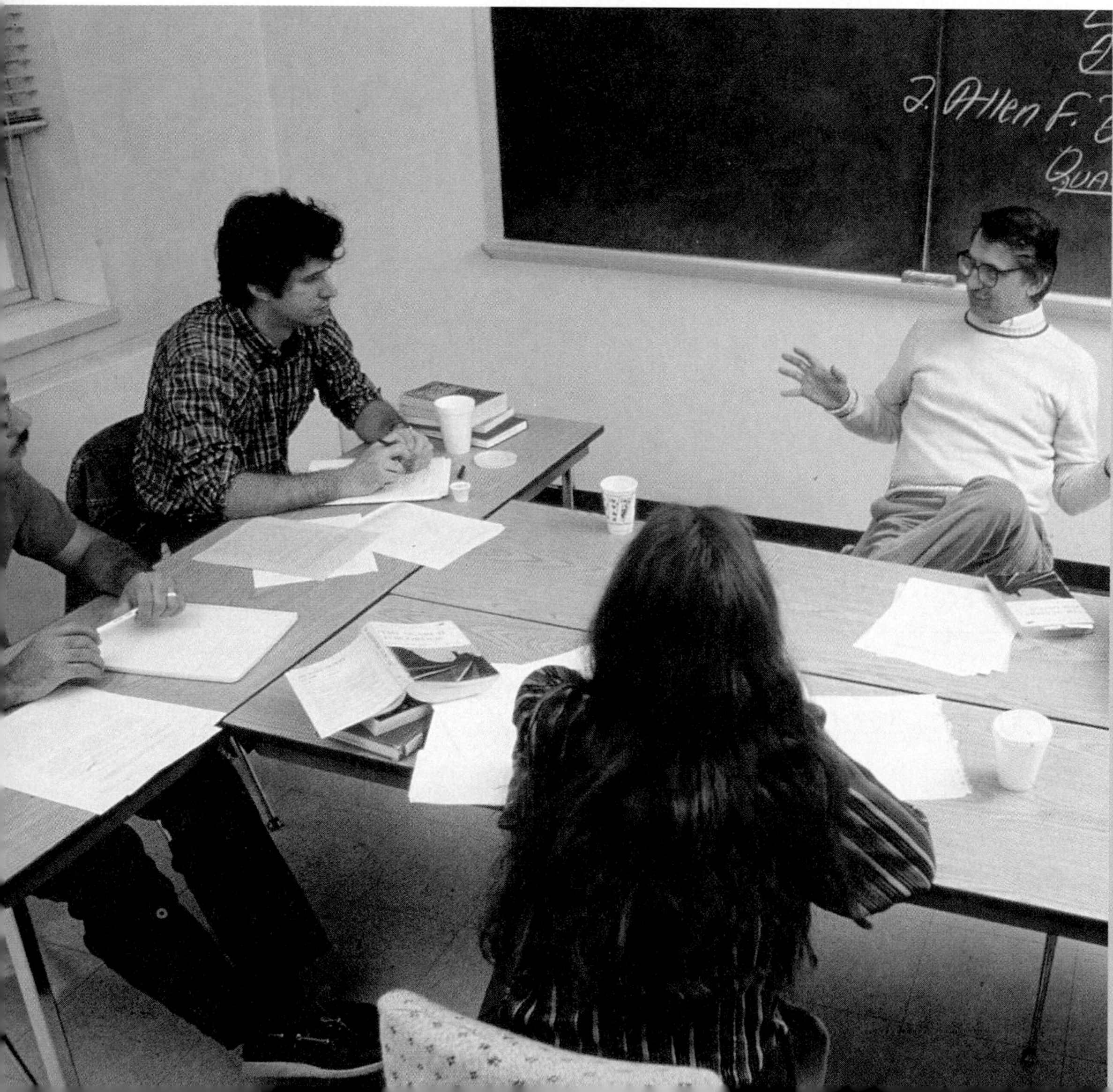

What Should Students Learn in School?

How Specific Should Educational Objectives Be?

The Value of Instructional Objectives

Classroom Application: Writing Instructional Objectives

Can Teachers Plan for Instruction without Using Instructional Objectives?

Developing Objectives for Instruction

Academic Content

Classroom Application: Completing a Task Analysis

Classroom Application: Using the Taxonomy of Educational Objectives

Planning for Instruction

Homework

Classroom Application: Establishing Homework Policy Guidelines

Debate Forum: Does Reducing Class Size Affect Achievement?

Developing a Lesson Plan

Direct Instruction

Classroom Application: Developing a Lesson Plan Using Direct Instruction

Discovery Learning

Classroom Application: Developing a Lesson Plan Using Discovery Learning

Cooperative Learning

Classroom Application: Developing a Lesson Plan Using Cooperative Learning

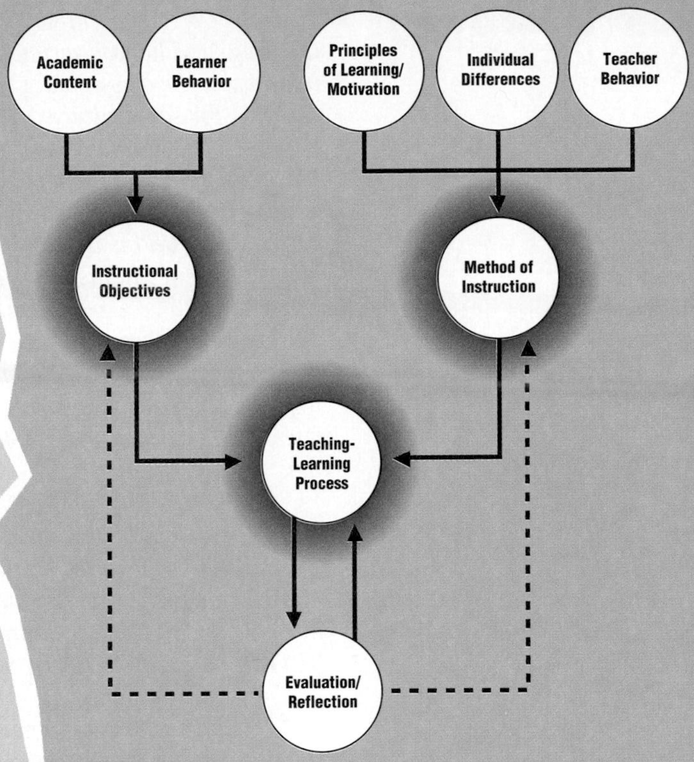

OBJECTIVES

After mastering the material in this chapter you will be able to:

- Write behavioral objectives using the *Taxonomy of Educational Objectives*.
- Construct a task analysis.
- Develop unit lesson plans.
- Develop daily lesson plans for direct instruction, cooperative learning, and discovery learning.
- Establish homework policy.

Orientation

Paul Martin was experiencing a great deal of difficulty with his classes in World History. The students were unruly, and most of his time was spent dealing with disruptive behavior rather than academic material. This was his third year of teaching, and he was seriously considering leaving the profession if things didn't improve in the classroom. One day, Paul decided to ask the department chair, Walt Coombs, for some advice. What follows is Walt's account of how he helped Paul improve his classroom instruction:

"I knew that Paul was having problems with his students, but I didn't realize how difficult a time he was having until he came to me for some advice. He was devastated with his inability to gain control over his classroom, and he had very little confidence in his abilities as a teacher. I knew he had the desire, ability, and personality to be a wonderful teacher, but something was missing. I decided to find out what that something was.

"I observed one of Paul's history classes for three days. Within five minutes of my first observation, it was obvious to me what Paul's problem was, and I also knew how he could solve it. Let me give you a brief sketch of the agenda for that first day:

10:15—Class begins with teacher taking roll
10:20—Teacher tries to gain control of class
10:35—Teacher passes out a worksheet, students have until the end of the period to complete and return it.
11:05—Teacher collects the worksheets.

"The lessons for the remainder of the week were very similar, with slight variations, but it was apparent to both the students and me that Paul did not have well-planned lessons. I determined, at that moment, that Paul's problems would be remedied if he were to create an overall unit plan, covering a period of two to three weeks, and then design specific daily lessons intended to lead to tangible instructional objectives. I worked with him on both the unit lesson, in this case dealing with causes of war, and the individual lessons, which were focused upon militarism, nationalism, alliances, and imperialism. Using a calendar, we outlined a two-week period of time devoted to our unit, and each day was well planned to ensure that daily objectives were identified and that an appropriate instructional strategy was used to meet those objectives.

"By the end of the two-week unit, Paul was beginning to regain his sense of confidence as a teacher. Discipline problems were minimal, and the class average on the unit test was close to a B. What happened to explain this change? The fact that this teacher took time to prepare for his classes by identifying what he wanted his students to learn, and then implemented a plan that would accomplish the objective, gave structure to the class."

From time to time, you have probably gone for a drive in your car or taken a walk with no particular destination in mind. Sometimes you wind up in unexpected places! Taking some college courses can be a similar experience. I am sure that at times during your college career you have asked the following questions: "Where is this instructor taking me?" "What is this class about?" "What am I supposed to be learning in this class?" One important aspect of a teacher's decision making is, first, to determine what is to be learned and, then, to communicate this information to the students. To accomplish this task it is necessary that the teacher take the time to plan for instruction.

All individuals who want to become competent in their chosen field of specialization spend time planning their work-related tasks. For example, can you imagine a defense attorney beginning a trial without studying the evidence against the client or without selecting a defense strategy? Can you imagine a surgeon beginning an operation without having studied the patient's X rays? Does a football coach send a team out to play without a game plan? Competent individuals in any area realize that if they do not take the time to plan, the results will be ineffective or disastrous (Jacobsen, Eggen, & Kauchak, 1989).

Although ineffective planning in teaching does not usually lead to immediate life-and-death situations, it can ultimately lead to disastrous classroom experiences for both the teacher and the students. Effective planning in teaching involves formulating a course of action for implementing instruction over the school year, semester, month, day, and lesson (Clark & Peterson, 1985). Although planning does not always ensure success, it can help to increase the probability of success. Think about some of your present professors or the teachers you had in elementary and high school. Can you identify differences in their teaching that may have been related to their planning for class? Some instructors do get by without spending much time planning for instruction. Many of them simply follow the textbook and as test material use duplicated sheets that students complete by finding the answers to rote questions from the material in the textbook.

It is not always easy for a student to determine on a daily basis whether an instructor is prepared to teach. Some instructors learn how to "wing it" or get by when they are not prepared. For example, it is often difficult to determine whether the instructor who asks, "What do you want to talk about today?" actually has a lesson plan to teach a particular idea or simply has not prepared any lesson for the day.

WHAT SHOULD STUDENTS LEARN IN SCHOOL?

? How does a teacher decide what should be taught?

Before you can decide *how* to teach, you must determine *what* to teach, or the goals of instruction. Instructional goals come from several sources—the student, society, and academic discipline (Jacobsen et al., 1989). The student as a source of goals derives partly from the concern that the school can help the student grow emotionally, intellectually, and physically. Special attention is given to the developmental level of the student. Objectives focusing on health to help students understand their bodies and

TABLE 6.1 SEQUENTIAL EXAMPLES OF EDUCATIONAL, IMPLICIT INSTRUCTIONAL, AND EXPLICIT INSTRUCTIONAL OBJECTIVES

Type and Level of Objective	Examples
Educational Objectives	The student should be able to read well. The student should be able to spell correctly. The student should know about American history. The student should understand addition.
Implicit Instructional Objectives	The student will learn how to read with comprehension. The student will develop appropriate spelling skills. The student will learn about the American Revolution. The student will know how to solve addition problems.
Explicit Instructional (Behavioral or Performance) Objectives	Given a brief paragraph from a newspaper article, the student will be able to identify the main idea. Given a list of 20 incorrectly spelled words, the student will be able to identify and correct the misspelled words with 90 percent accuracy. The student will be able to list five American Revolutionary heroes and describe their respective roles in history. Given 10 addition problems involving pairs of 3-digit numbers, the student will be able to calculate the correct answer with 85 percent accuracy.

THE VALUE OF INSTRUCTIONAL OBJECTIVES

Proponents of instructional objectives believe that they enable teachers to know exactly what student behavior is desired upon the completion of a lesson. Teachers are then in a better position to select appropriate teaching methods for the designated student outcome. Knowing the type of expected outcome is important in making decisions that will help to direct students to that outcome.

Instructional objectives help teachers during evaluation because the teachers can construct test questions directly from their objectives. Constructing tests in this manner takes the guesswork out of the evaluation process.

Finally, evidence suggests that if teachers initially give students the objectives of a lesson or course, the students will spend more time focusing on the designated outcomes (Hamaker, 1986; Mayer, 1987). Hamilton (1985) reviewed studies that investigated the use of different degrees of explicit objectives as an aid to prose learning (e.g., objectives before the presentation of reading material). He found that the different forms of objectives had important effects on the retention of verbal information. The implication of his findings is that it may not matter how objectives are written as long as they identify the information to be learned.

CLASSROOM **Application**

WRITING INSTRUCTIONAL OBJECTIVES

There are a number of ways to write instructional objectives. The instructional objectives in Table 6.1 include one approach, recommended by Mager (1978), that uses three major components:

1. The *behavioral term,* which expresses the type of task required of the student ("write," "list," "solve").
2. The *situation,* or *condition,* under which the behavior is to be performed ("given a reference manual," "without the aid of references," "without the use of tables or a slide rule").
3. The *criterion,* or *level of performance,* which will be used to evaluate the success of the performance or product ("no grammatical or spelling errors," "at least five major steps," "90 percent").

THE BEHAVIORAL TERM

The most important component of an instructional objective is the *action verb* that describes the observable act the student is to perform. Mager (1978) cautions that many words used in writing objectives are open to a wide range of interpretations; teachers should strive for *precision,* as indicated in the right-hand column below.

Ambiguous	**Precise**
to know	to write
to understand	to recite
to really understand	to identify
to appreciate	to differentiate
to fully appreciate	to solve
to grasp the significance of	to construct
to enjoy	to list
to believe	to compare
to have faith in	to contrast

What do teachers mean when they state that they want students to "know" something? Do they want the students to remember certain information, to solve problems, to create new ideas? To "know" can mean many things. The same holds true for such words as *appreciate* or *grasp the significance of.* How do we determine whether students appreciate or grasp the significance of some information or

continued

value? Until we describe specifically what the students will be *doing* to demonstrate that they appreciate or grasp the significance of, we really do not know exactly what the student is to learn from the experience. The more we use words similar to those in the right-hand column of the foregoing list, the more we communicate to the students the exact behavior expected of them. The following statements provide concise information on student outcomes:

- The student *presents* an impromptu speech.
- The student *draws* a diagram of the combustion engine.
- The student *writes* the name of each of the states.

THE SITUATION OR CONDITION

This component describes the "givens," limitations, or restrictions that are imposed on students as they strive for the learning outcome. Following are examples of some conditions that narrow the focus of instructional objectives:

- Given a map of the United States
- Without the use of notes
- After reading Chapter 4 in the textbook
- After viewing *Hamlet*

THE CRITERION OR LEVEL OF PERFORMANCE

This component is a statement of the minimal level of performance that will be accepted as evidence that the learner has achieved the objective. The following are some levels of performance that further delineate an instructional objective:

- All four steps stated in the textbook
- Without an error
- At least 90 percent correct
- Must include three of the four reasons
- Must be correct to the nearest percentage point
- Must be completed within 30 minutes

Now try to write an instructional objective for teaching students to determine the area of a square. The exact wording will vary, but you should have written something like the following: "Given a square with the length of one side marked, the student will determine its area using the formula $A = s^2$"

Try writing another objective for teaching students the correct use of colons in writing. (Don't read on until you have written the objective.) You should have written something like the following: "Given a set of rules for the use of colons and a set of sentences that require colon insertion, the student will place each colon properly without any errors."

The following are additional examples of instructional objectives in different subject areas:

Science: Given a diagram of a cell, the student will be able to identify the major components of the cell and state their functions.

Geography: Given a map of the United States, the student will be able to locate and name each of the original 13 colonies.

French: After studying Chapter 1, the student will be able to conjugate the verb *avoir*.

AN ALTERNATIVE APPROACH TO WRITING INSTRUCTIONAL OBJECTIVES

Some educators believe that it is not always necessary to describe the situation or condition for every objective, especially if a unit of instruction is based on material from a textbook. Also, sometimes the explicit statement of the criterion can be difficult to determine and appears artificial. Gronlund (1991) believes that the three components of behavioral objectives described in the preceding sections—situation, performance, and criterion—can result in long, cumbersome lists of objectives that restrict the freedom of teachers. Instead, Gronlund recommends that teachers should first state the general instructional objective and then clarify the objective by listing a *sample* of the specific types of student performance they are willing to accept as evidence of the attainment of that objective. For example:

1. Understands the meaning of technical terms.
   1.1 Defines the term in own words.
   1.2 Identifies the meaning of the term when used in context.
   1.3 Distinguishes between terms that are similar in meaning. (p. 7)

The objective "Given a drawing of a flower, the student will label in writing at least four of the five parts shown" can be restated as, "Identifies the parts of a given plant structure." In the restated objective, teachers would be free to use real plants, pictures, diagrams, or slides. Also, the students could respond orally, in writing, or by pointing to a specific part of the flower. Last, because the specific standard or criterion is not stated, teachers can vary the standard without rewriting the objective. Teachers may want to have different standards for different groups of children or have lower standards at the beginning of a unit and higher standards at the end of the unit. In summary, if objectives are to help teachers plan for instruction, then any system that helps teachers while reducing the amount of work needed to write objectives should be carefully considered. Take time to try different systems until you feel comfortable with some method.

expressive objectives. Eisner's approach in which teachers define learning activities for students but do not specify exactly what the students might learn.

Can Teachers Plan for Instruction without Using Instructional Objectives?

? What are the advantages and disadvantages of using behavioral objectives?

When objectives were first introduced in education, many proponents argued that *all* teaching goals should be translated into explicit objectives. In rethinking the role of objectives, some educators have raised questions about the need for precision in stating every objective. It may not be necessary to develop long lists of objectives for each unit of instruction. Gage and Berliner (1988) believe that objectives should act as a road map: "And just like a road map, to be useful, need not specify every town and creek, so objectives for a unit of instruction need not specify every change in student behavior" (p. 40).

Some educators argue that the use of instructional objectives can lead to emphasizing outcomes that can be easily measured, and that unanticipated outcomes in education are often the most important. The proponents of instructional objectives respond that teachers can be trained to write objectives at higher levels of thinking. In response to the issue of the importance of unanticipated outcomes, some proponents point out that they do not believe that every outcome of instruction must be specified in advance. However, the decision to spend time in unplanned activities or discussions can better be made if the teacher has some specific objectives in mind. The alternative to not having any objectives is constant wandering throughout the curriculum.

Eisner (1969), one of the critics of the behavioral objectives movement, argues for the legitimacy of what he calls **expressive objectives**. According to Eisner, an expressive objective

> identifies a situation in which children are to work; a problem in which they are to engage; but it does not specify what from that encounter, situation, problem, or task they are to learn. An expressive objective provides both the teacher and the student with an invitation to explore, defer, or focus on issues that are of particular interest or import to the inquirer (pp. 15–16).

A teacher who wants to take a class to the zoo for no purpose other than to allow the students to explore the environment knows that each student will achieve different learning outcomes from the experience. In this situation, the teacher is more concerned with an expressive objective than with an instructional objective.

There is some empirical support for Eisner's concern that activities be considered a legitimate form of planning (see Borko & Shavelson, 1990, for a review of this literature). For example, Zahorik (1975) asked teachers to list in writing the decisions they made prior to teaching and to indicate the

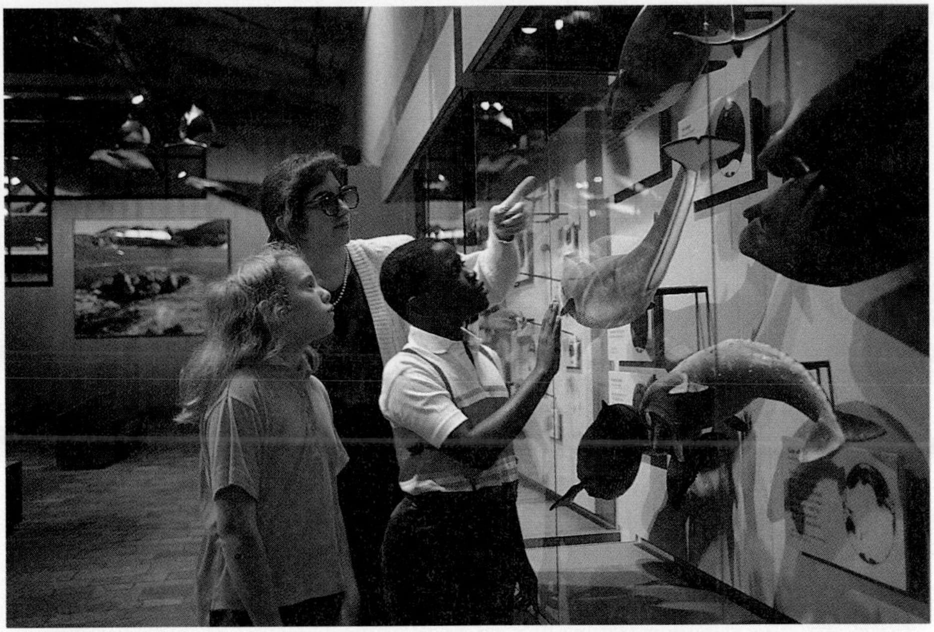

Sometimes it is difficult to determine the specific educational outcome of an educational experience.

order in which they made them. He found that teachers made decisions about objectives, content, pupil activities, materials, diagnosis, evaluation, instruction, and organization. Most important, he found that the type of decision mentioned by the largest number of teachers (81 percent) concerned pupil activities. This was followed by content (51 percent) and learning objectives (28 percent). Other researchers (e.g., Goodlad & Klein, 1970; Peterson, Marx, & Clark, 1978) have reported similar findings. The results of these investigations indicate that many experienced teachers do not use instructional objectives in planning! Although researchers have reported planning strategies used by classroom teachers that do not involve instructional objectives (see Clark & Peterson, 1985), there is no evidence to indicate that more effective teaching results from these alternative strategies.

At this time, you may be thinking: "If many experienced teachers do not use objectives in planning, why am I reading this material?" I have three responses to this question:

1. Beginning teachers need a formalized method of planning as a point of departure. They then can develop alternative strategies as they experiment with various procedures.
2. On the basis of research evidence, planning by objectives is one approach that can help teachers and students.
3. Although I realize that planning by objectives is not the only approach—and may not even be the best—educational psychologists have not adequately prescribed alternative approaches.

This is my position. You should discuss this controversial issue with other educators to gain more insight into the various points of view regarding the use of objectives. Try using them in planning lessons, and evaluate their effectiveness. Then you will be able to draw your own conclusions about their usefulness.

DEVELOPING OBJECTIVES FOR INSTRUCTION

Before you decide what you are going to teach, you should consider three major variables—information about the major goals of the instructional program at the school, the content to be included in your course, and the entry level of your students. Most school districts publish lists of educational goals for students. These goals often are translated into more specific objectives for students at different grade levels and in different courses in documents called *curriculum guides*. These guides are helpful in long-term and lesson planning. Decisions about the course content will depend on your knowledge of the subject area and the textbooks used. In addition, your colleagues can be a useful resource as you begin the process of developing your own courses.

As you are selecting major course goals and selecting content related to these goals, you must also consider the students' abilities, knowledge, and motivation. Ascertaining an individual's entry behavior and teaching that person accordingly is one of the most important factors in effective instruction. It is possible to generate lists of objectives for a course without considering what the students already know. But what good is it to develop objectives if students do not have the necessary skills or knowledge to strive for those objectives? In such situations, it is better to establish objectives at a lower level of difficulty—objectives that the students can reach within a reasonable time.

Academic Content

Academic content provides important raw material for developing implicit or explicit instructional objectives. There are a number of ways in which to view academic content. The first is the type of learning involved. In Chapter 3 you learned about the difference between declarative and procedural learning. Teaching a student to follow certain procedures in solving mathematical or scientific problems involves a type of planning and instruction different from teaching a student basic concepts in these academic areas.

LEVEL OF DIFFICULTY. Another way to view subject matter is in terms of its level of difficulty. Students must be able to count before they can add; they must be able to add before they can multiply. Reading a paragraph depends upon reading a sentence, which depends upon understanding the meaning of words, which depends upon identifying letters. Identifying the subskills according to a hierarchy is called *task analysis*. The outline of the subskills is an important aspect of planning the order of content in a lesson, because without this planned sequence the teacher may omit important knowledge and leave students confused.

CLASSROOM Application

COMPLETING A TASK ANALYSIS

In completing a task analysis, a teacher should ask: "What is it I want my students to do? What do they need to know to do it?" Once the terminal objective emerges, the teacher works backward to delineate which capabilities students must possess to reach the terminal objective. Remember that some students in the class will need more time on certain subskills, whereas others can skip one or more of the subskills. Take the following steps to complete a task analysis and instruct students:

1. State the learning task or objective in behavioral terms.
2. Break the task down into prerequisite skills or subtasks.
3. Determine the relationship between the prerequisite skills and the logical order in which they should be learned.
4. Determine procedures for teaching each of the subtasks.
5. Provide feedback to the students about their performance as each of the subtasks and the final objective are achieved.

Let's take a concrete example to illustrate the importance of knowing the subskills involved in teaching a task: "The student will divide any real numbers (including decimal fractions) up to four digits with 90 percent accuracy when presented in the form $NN.N\overline{)ddd.d}$" (Packard, 1975, p. 224).

1. The first step is to move the decimal point to the proper place.

$$15.2\overline{)1862.4}$$

2. Then the student estimates the first digit of the quotient and writes the number above the line and the appropriate digit.

$$\begin{array}{r} 1 \\ 152\overline{)18624} \end{array}$$

3. The third step is to multiply the divisor by the estimated quotient (1×152) and write the product below the problem, as shown here.

$$\begin{array}{r} 1 \\ 152\overline{)18624} \\ 152 \end{array}$$

continued

4. Then the student subtracts the product from part of the dividend and enters the difference below these numbers.

```
          1
152 )18624
     152
      34
```

5. The fifth step is to "bring down" the next digit in the number being divided.

```
          1
152 )18624
     152
      342
```

After Step 5 the student recommences the procedure of estimating a digit of the answer and multiplying and subtracting until the desired degree of accuracy is reached.

This outline presumes that the student can discriminate numbers, subtract, and divide. These behaviors are part of the student's entering abilities. If they are not, they will have to be taught before the student can successfully attain the objective. Teachers often overlook important subskills in their teaching and, as a result, find that their students have difficulty meeting requirements.

In many subject areas, subskills cannot be taught at random; some of them are prerequisite to others. In the division problem, addition and subtraction must be taught before multiplication. However, teaching the student to adjust the decimal point or to bring down another number from the dividend can take place at any time because none of the other skills depends on either.

Developing a task analysis for lessons takes practice. In the process you must estimate the students' entry behavior. If you know which skills they have already mastered before instruction, you will not have to teach them these skills. Sometimes teachers find that their task analysis is not detailed enough because they erroneously assumed that students had certain entry behavior. By pretesting and making modifications in the original task analysis, they can develop a better instructional sequence. In analyzing the total task, Packard (1975) suggests, "You decide, on the basis of what you already know about the students, what skills they probably already have, categorizing these as entry or prerequisite behaviors. Then you categorize all the other component skills as intermediate objectives leading to your terminal objective" (p. 230). Another example of a task analysis is presented in Figure 6.1.

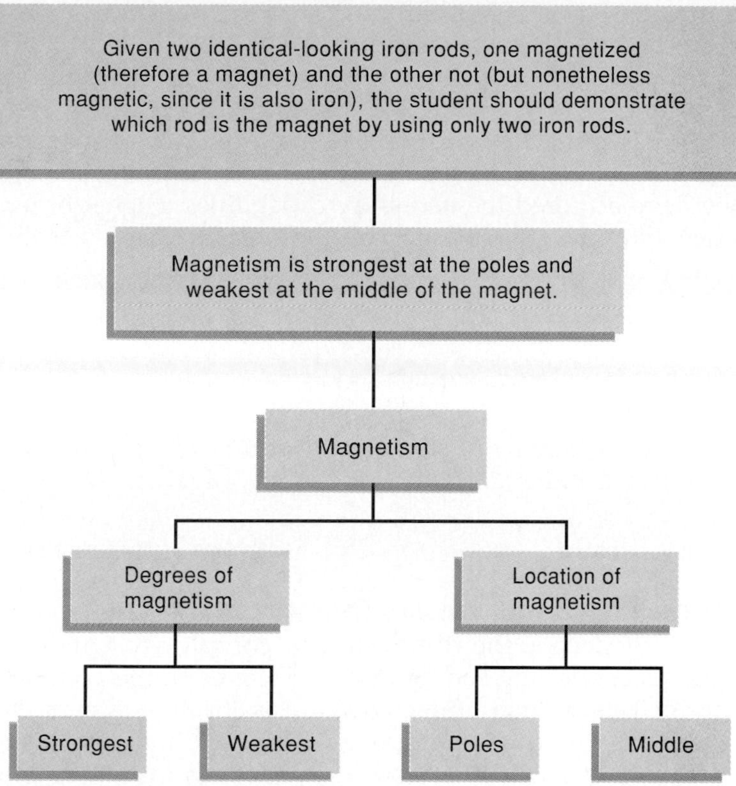

Figure 6.1 An Example of a Task Analysis in Science. Source: Trojcak, 1977.

CAUTIONS ABOUT USING TASK ANALYSIS

Not all learning theorists believe that the foregoing approach to developing a task analysis can guide instruction in a systematic and hierarchical fashion in all subject areas. Instructional objectives in areas that are less structured, such as literature and social studies, do not lend themselves as easily to a highly structured and sequential approach to learning. Another issue revolves around the belief that learning is more likely to occur when instruction is global, or holistic, rather than reductionistic (i.e., broken down into small parts). This latter issue is an important distinction between many behavioral (Chapter 2) and cognitive (Chapter 3) approaches to instruction. There are other approaches to task analysis (e.g., Klausmeier, 1976; Merrill, 1983; Reigeluth & Stein, 1983) and sequencing of instruction (Patten, Chao, & Reigeluth, 1986) that the interested reader may want to investigate.

Taxonomy of Educational Objectives. A classification system developed by Bloom that divides objectives into two domains: cognitive and affective.

cognitive domain. A part of Bloom's *Taxonomy of Educational Objectives*, consisting of knowledge, comprehension, application, analysis, synthesis, and evaluation.

affective domain. A part of Bloom's *Taxonomy of Educational Objectives* consisting of recieving, responding, valuing, organizing, and characterizing by a value.

psychomotor domain. Objectives involving physical ability.

R. M. Gagné (1977, 1985) has contributed a great deal to the theory and research on task analysis. He arranges types of learning in a hierarchy of relationships based on the assumption that the higher levels of learning depend on the lower levels of learning. Each type of learning is distinguished from the others primarily by the conditions required for the specific learning.

Gagné stresses the importance of developing a task analysis *before* beginning instruction. This prepares students for learning something new after they have acquired the necessary capabilities. Higher-order skills or capabilities, like problem solving, are more easily learned if the student has a foundation of lower, or subordinate, capabilities.

? What is the difference between the organization of the cognitive and affective domains of the Taxonomy of Educational Objectives?

A TAXONOMY OF EDUCATIONAL OBJECTIVES. The second dimension of academic content is the dimension of complexity. One of the most helpful guides in selecting and defining objectives on this continuum is the **Taxonomy of Educational Objectives**, a classification system devised by Bloom that comprises two handbooks. The handbook on the **cognitive domain** (Bloom et al., 1956) classifies objectives involving intellectual tasks; the handbook on the **affective domain** (Krathwohl, Bloom, & Masia, 1964) classifies objectives involving attitudes, values, and interests. Each taxonomy organizes objectives into a hierarchical framework of behaviors that are more complex or internalized than the previous category (see Tables 6.2 and 6.3).

In the cognitive domain, the categories are arranged along a continuum from simple to more complex: knowledge, comprehension, application, analysis, synthesis, and evaluation. In the affective domain, the continuum is based on the degree of internalization that each behavior exhibits. That is, the classification begins with an attitude or value from the level of awareness, proceeding to the point at which it guides or directs a person's actions: receiving, responding, valuing, organizing, and characterizing a value or value complex.

Harrow (1972) has developed a separate taxonomy for the **psychomotor domain**. It is arranged from the simplest level of observable movements to the most complex. There are six levels in the taxonomy:

1. *Reflex movements*. Actions that occur in response to some stimulus without conscious awareness (e.g., blinking and stretching).
2. *Basic fundamental movements*. Basic movements developed from a combination of reflex movements (e.g., walking and jumping).

CLASSROOM

Application

USING THE TAXONOMY OF EDUCATIONAL OBJECTIVES

Tables 6.2 and 6.3 include brief definitions of each of the major categories in the cognitive and affective domains, examples of instructional objectives, and behavioral terms (action verbs) for writing objectives at various levels of the domains. (A more detailed treatment of the various categories and their subcategories appears in the taxonomy handbooks with illustrative examples and test questions.)

TABLE 6.2 MAJOR CATEGORIES IN THE COGNITIVE DOMAIN OF THE TAXONOMY OF EDUCATIONAL OBJECTIVES

Categories	Illustrative Behavioral Terms
1. *Knowledge:* The ability to recall previously learned information. Knowledge typically involves the memorization of facts and is considered to represent the lowest level of objectives in the taxonomy. *Example:* Recalling the rhyming patterns of standard sonnet forms.	*list, define, identify, recall, name, recognize*
2. *Comprehension:* The ability to understand the meaning of learned information. *Example:* Interpreting the meaning of a sonnet.	*predict, interpret, explain, summarize, estimate, evaluate*
3. *Application:* The ability to use learned information in a novel situation. *Example:* Identifying the components of a given limerick.	*demonstrate, explain, solve, calculate, identify, infer, use, apply*
4. *Analysis:* The ability to separate material into its component parts for the purpose of understanding its organizational structure. *Example:* Discriminating between the styles of two poets.	*distinguish, discriminate, categorize, outline, identify, separate*
5. *Synthesis:* The ability to combine component parts into a new structure. *Example:* Composing a poem.	*create, design, organize, derive, formulate, compose, write*
6. *Evaluation:* The ability to judge the value of material according to specified criteria. *Example:* Critiquing a poem.	*criticize, examine, judge, compare, contrast, conclude, critique*

Source: Bloom et al., 1956.

continued

TABLE 6.3 MAJOR CATEGORIES IN THE AFFECTIVE DOMAIN OF THE TAXONOMY OF EDUCATIONAL OBJECTIVES

Categories	Illustrative Behavioral Terms
1. *Receiving:* An awareness of the importance of learning combined with a willingness to concentrate on learning activities. *Example:* Observing that some people live in poverty.	*listen, ask, concentrate, observe, follow, attend, demonstrate*
2. *Responding:* A willingness to participate actively in a given activity and derive satisfaction from this participation. *Example:* Volunteering to donate an old toy to a charitable organization.	*volunteer, comply, perform, answer, participate, assist, help*
3. *Valuing:* The perception that an object, phenomenon, or behavior has worth. Valuing also implies a commitment to an idea or position. *Example:* Working on a food line.	*appreciate, differentiate, justify, select, share, value, invite, work*
4. *Organization:* The process of integrating different values, reconciling these differences, and formulating an internally consistent value system. *Example:* Integrating personal beliefs to develop one's own value system.	*compare, combine, organize, defend, explain, synthesize, integrate, recognize*
5. *Characterization by a Value or Value Complex:* The possession of a value system that governs a personal behavior. *Example:* Acting in ways consistent with one's own value system.	*act, display, perform, influence, practice, demonstrate*

Source: Krathwohl et al., 1964.

An English teacher who wants to write an objective at the evaluation level of the cognitive domain can review illustrative behavioral terms (Table 6.2) for writing instructional objectives (e.g., "critique,

3. *Perceptual abilities*. The translation of visual stimuli into appropriate movements (e.g., following verbal instruction and jumping rope).
4. *Physical abilities*. Basic body movements and abilities that are important in the development of more highly skilled movements. These movements incorporate the following characteristics: endurance, strength, flexibility, and agility (e.g., weight lifting and basic ballet exercises).
5. *Skilled movements*. Complex body movements indicating a degree of proficiency (e.g., performing a dance or making a jump shot in basketball).

compare, conclude"). Using this information, the teacher might write the following as a performance objective:

> After reading *Profiles in Courage*, the student will compare the political behavior of one individual in the book with one of his or her own U.S. senators.

An elementary school teacher deplores students' intragroup hostility, wants the students to be more cooperative, and would like to include this behavior in the list of instructional objectives. In Table 6.3, which summarizes the affective domain, the teacher notices the verb *help* from the behavioral terms column at the responding level of the taxonomy and writes the following instructional objective:

> After discussing the importance of cooperation in the classroom, the student will help peers having homework problems.

Notice that some behavioral terms are used at several levels of the taxonomy (Table 6.2). The term *identifies*, for example, can be used as follows (Gronlund, 1991):

- *Knowledge*: Identifies the correct definition of a term.
- *Application*: Identifies proper grammar usage.
- *Analysis*: Identifies the parts of a sentence (p. 30).

The use of a particular action verb does not necessarily place the objective at a particular level of the taxonomy, although many terms are more directly relevant to one category than another. Examples are *criticize* (evaluation) and *solve* (application).

One of the important uses of the taxonomy is to make you aware that it is possible to write objectives for and measure more complex skills than the recall of basic facts.

6. *Nondiscursive communication*. Complex movements that communicate feelings, needs, or interests to another individual (e.g., facial expressions and choreographed dance movements).

The following are examples of psychomotor objectives:

Using correct body movements, physical education students will swim the breast stroke for 50 yards.

Without the use of a diagram, the student will correctly assemble the biology lab equipment to demonstrate osmosis.

lesson plan. A detailed outline of the objectives, content, procedures, and evaluation of a single instructional period.

unit plan. A detailed outline for a series of interrelated lesson plans on a particular topic of study.

PLANNING FOR INSTRUCTION

? How do a unit and a daily lesson plan relate to each other?

Now you are ready to apply your knowledge of objectives to planning for instruction. Teacher planning serves a number of important functions, including reducing anxiety, helping to organize time, and, most important, providing a framework for instruction and evaluation. Researchers have found that teachers' plans influence the content of instruction, the sequence of topics (Clark & Elmore, 1981; Smith & Sendelbach, 1979), and the time teachers allocate to subject matter areas. Studies of reading teachers have found that their early decisions about testing, grouping, materials, and management strongly influence the nature of their instruction (Buike, 1980; Stern & Shavelson, 1981).

During the school year teachers are engaged in various types of planning—yearly, term, unit, daily. In this chapter, we focus on unit and daily lesson planning. A daily **lesson plan** is a detailed outline of the objectives, content, procedures, and evaluation of a single instructional period. A **unit plan** is a detailed outline for a series of interrelated lesson plans on a particular topic of study lasting from two to four weeks. A good unit plan organizes the individual lesson plans into a meaningful experience (Jacobsen et al., 1989).

There is evidence that unit planning is perceived as more important than daily lesson planning (Clark & Yinger, 1979). Unit planning provides a broad framework for the activities in which the teacher and students will be involved over a long period. Jacobsen et al. (1989) describe how unit planning can lead to more effective lesson planning. Unit planning begins with the selection of a unit topic. This topic may come from the school district's curriculum guide for your subject area, or from the chapter topics in the textbook. Unit topics for different subject areas might include:

Science	**Social Studies**
Electricity	World War II
Solar Energy	The American Justice System
Scientific Inquiry	Cultural Pluralism
Astronomy	Maps

Consider the overall goal of the unit. One way to accomplish this task is to summarize the major outcomes that you hope to accomplish in a summary statement that describes the content to be covered and what students will do with this content. Examples of such a statement are:

> The goal of the unit on maps is to provide students with the skills necessary to read maps for functional use. Students will be able to interpret a map key, determine direction with a compass, and compute distance using a scale of miles. Last, students will become acquainted with varied types of maps from which to derive special information.

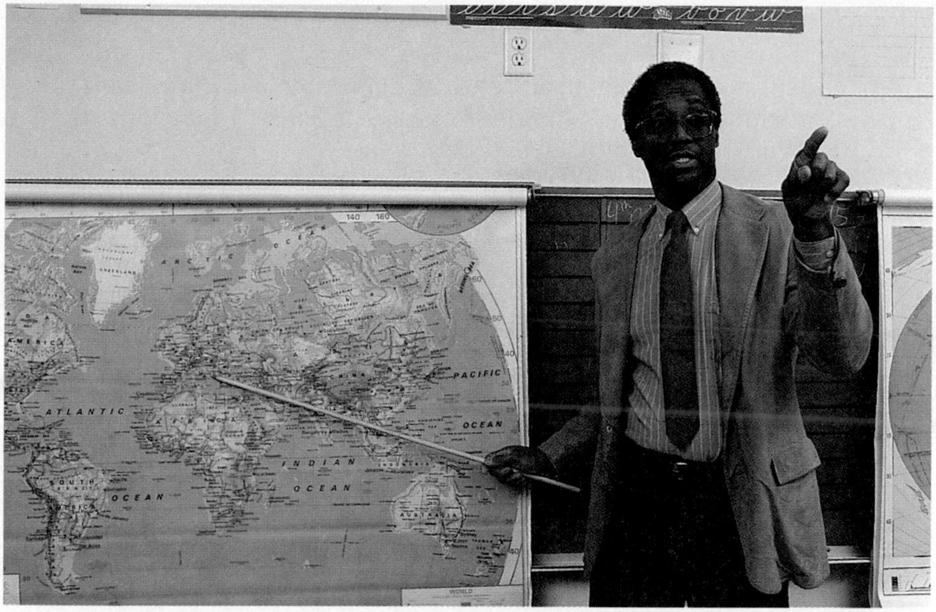

Lecturing is but one of many different methods of instruction available to a teacher. Can you think of some different ways a teacher could teach a geography lesson?

> The goal of the unit on the newspaper is for students to learn the significance of the free press from its inception to present-day production. Through integration of the content areas, students will report for many of the paper's departments and contribute to the construction of a complete newspaper.

Having completed the goal statement for the unit, you are now ready to outline the major concepts, or ideas, in the unit. Outlining will help you to organize the content to be taught for proper sequencing of instruction and writing objectives. The outline also can be used to help students to understand the purpose of studying the unit. In addition, as daily lessons are presented, you can review the outline to help students understand the relationship of a particular lesson to previous and future lessons. Figure 6.2 shows two examples of outlining the content of a unit. The first outlines a unit on maps; the second outlines a unit on the newspaper and is based on a more ambitious unit that attempts to integrate a number of content areas.

Using the outline as a planning guide, you are now ready to consider specific objectives for the unit. The task at this point of the planning process is to translate content topics into more specific objectives. Experienced teachers find that it is wise to limit a lesson to one, or at most two, important objectives and avoid the temptation of trying to teach too much in a short period. The danger of trying to accomplish too much is that you may end up accomplishing much less than you originally expected. The outline also will help you to decide how you will sequence your instruction. Some objectives that can be developed for the unit on maps follow:

- Students will identify the use of each part of a map by matching the term to its appropriate description.
- Using a compass, students will label the north, south, east, and west points on a map.

- Using a scale of miles, students will compute distances between points on a map.
- Students will translate written instructions consisting of key places, approximate distances, and compass readings to map directions to discover an unknown destination.

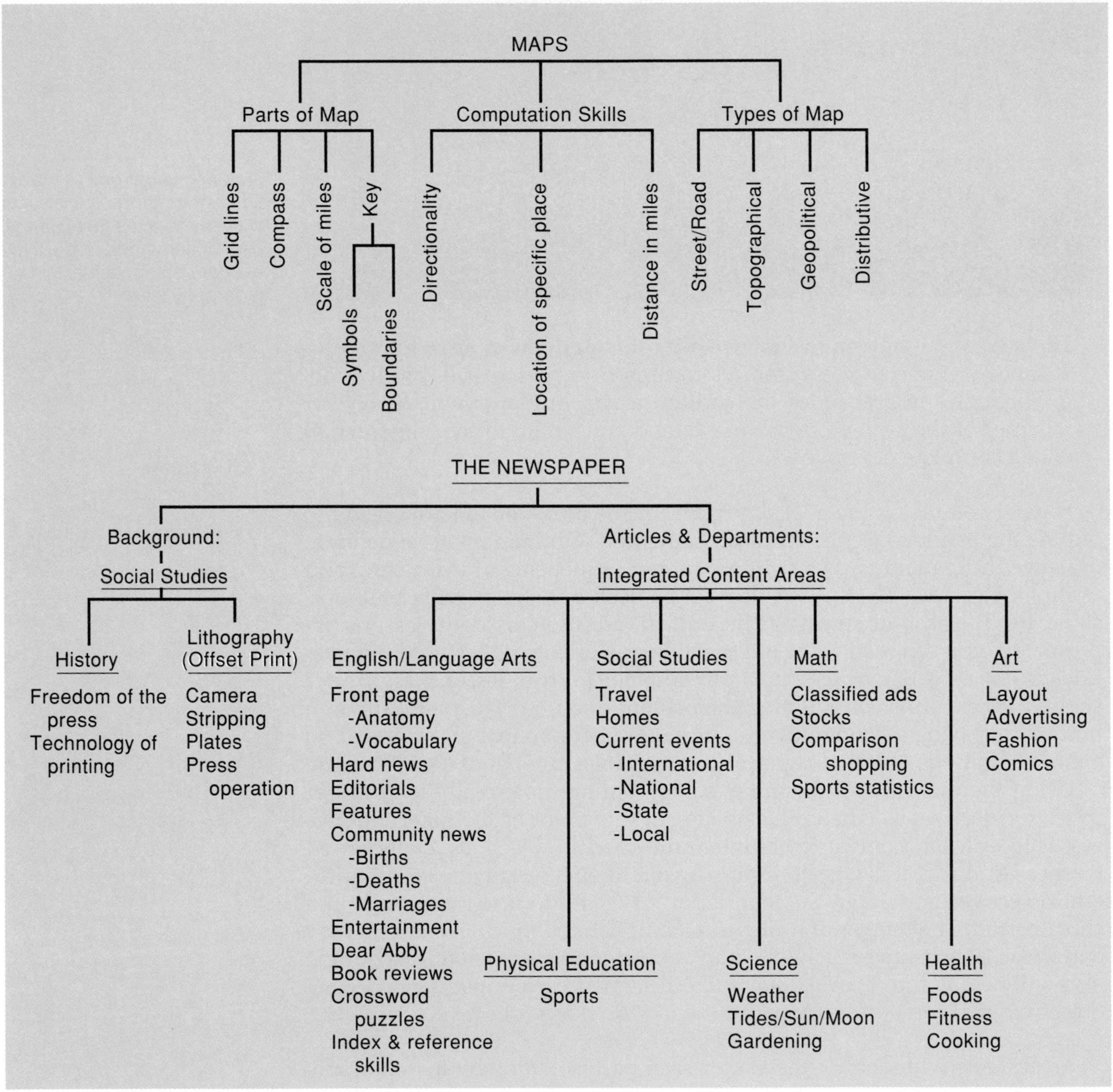

Figure 6.2 Examples of Unit Outlines. Source: Developed by Linda Organ.

The following are some objectives that can be established for the unit on the newspaper:

- Students will write the outline of a "hard news" article using the "inverted pyramid" format.
- Students will collect the background notes on a "hard news" report by answering the five "W" questions: Who? What? Where? When? Why?
- Students will analyze the point of view of a writer by comparing "hard news" reports of three classmates who witnessed the same incident.
- Students will judge the amount of fact and opinion found in "hard news" reports by selecting and reading an article and underlining fact in blue and opinion in red.

Did you recognize how different levels of the Taxonomy of Educational Objectives were used in developing the objectives from the unit outlines?

Although your supervising teacher may require you to use a particular lesson plan format once you begin student teaching, it is important that you realize that there is no one best way to plan lessons. You need to experiment with different formats and determine the one or two that you feel most comfortable using.

Homework

? What factors should a teacher or school consider in developing guidelines for a homework policy?

The public's attitudes toward homework during the past century have shifted considerably along a positive-negative continuum. Earlier in the twentieth century, memorization was stressed and homework was seen as a way to discipline a child's mind. In the 1940s, the importance of problem solving was stressed in schools, with a de-emphasis on learning through drill. Homework was considered less important than developing student initiative and positive attitudes toward learning. This trend was reversed in the late 1950s after the Soviets launched the Sputnik satellite and Americans became concerned that their educational system was not preparing students for the demands of a technological society. As a result, more rigorous courses were instituted in the curriculum and homework was seen as an important way to acquire greater knowledge. By the mid-1960s, the pendulum swung again. Homework was considered an indicator of excessive pressure on students to achieve, and educators began questioning the value of homework. Today attitudes toward homework have shifted again toward the positive side of the continuum. The public is concerned with students' declining achievement scores (National Commission on Excellence in Education, 1983) and believes that more homework should be assigned (Cooper, 1989).

CLASSROOM Application

ESTABLISHING HOMEWORK POLICY GUIDELINES

For Districts

Homework is a cost-effective instructional technique. It can have positive effects on achievement and character development and can serve as a vital link between school and family.

Homework should have different purposes at different grades. For younger students it should foster positive attitudes, habits, and character traits. For older students, it should facilitate knowledge acquisition in specific topics.

Homework should be required at all grade levels, but a mixture of mandatory and voluntary homework is most beneficial.

For Schools

The frequency and duration of homework assignments should be further specified to reflect local school and community circumstances.

In schools where different subjects are taught by different teachers, teachers should know:

1. What days of the week are available to them for assignments
2. How much daily homework time should be spent on their subject

Recently I heard two parents comparing notes regarding the schools their children were attending. One of the parents was boasting about the amount of homework his child was assigned each night. His reasoning went as follows: The amount of homework assigned is an indicator of the rigor of the school's academic program, which, in turn, will lead to higher academic achievement for his child. Based on your own experiences, what do you think about the parent's reasoning? How much time do you think children and adolescents should spend doing homework? Should young children do any homework at all?

Cooper (1989) completed a comprehensive review of the research on homework. What follows is a summary of his findings and his recommendations for establishing a homework policy:

Administrators should:

1. Communicate the district and school homework policy to parents
2. Monitor the implementation of the policy
3. Coordinate the scheduling of homework among different subjects, if needed

Teachers should state clearly:

1. How the assignment is related to the topic under study
2. The purpose of the assignment
3. How the assignment might best be carried out
4. What the student needs to do to demonstrate that the assignment has been completed

For Teachers

All students in a class will be responsible for the same assignments, with only rare exceptions.

Homework will include mandatory assignments. Failure to turn in mandatory assignments will necessitate remedial activities.

Homework will also include voluntary assignments meant to meet the needs of individual students or groups of students.

All homework assignments will *not* be formally evaluated. They will be used to locate problems in student progress and to individualize instruction.

Topics will appear in assignments before and after they are covered in class, not just on the day they are discussed.

Homework will not be used to teach complex skills. It will generally focus on simple skills and material or on the integration of skills already possessed by the student.

Parents will rarely be asked to play a formal instructional role in homework. Instead, they should be asked to create a home environment that facilitates students' self-study.

These guidelines are taken from Cooper, 1989, pp. 190–191.

- Homework does have positive effects on achievement. However, the impact of homework is related to students' grade level. Homework has a strong effect on the achievement of high school students, about average for junior high students, and little or no effect for upper-level elementary school students. There were no studies investigating the impact of homework for the earliest grades.
- Homework appears to have a greater effect on learning simple tasks than on learning complex tasks.
- There are no consistent positive effects associated with the individualization of homework assignments.
- The effects of homework tend to be similar for different types of students.

Teachers should consider the purpose of homework before deciding how much and what type of work to assign.

- Since research results are mixed on parents' participation in homework, no conclusions can be reached at this time concerning the advisability of directly involving parents in their child's homework assignments.

Cooper points out that one should not conclude that for older students, the more homework, the better! For example, junior high students who spent more than 10 hours a week on homework had slightly *lower* achievement scores than students spending 5 to 10 hours on homework. Thus it seems that 1 to 2 hours a night might be the optimal amount of homework for junior high students. For high school students, homework did not have any effect until somewhere between 1 and 5 hours were completed and had an increasingly positive effect through 10 hours a week. We don't know, at this time, the peak level at which homework for high school students would have no additional benefit.

Cooper stresses that homework can serve many purposes. In the early grades, it should develop positive attitudes and study habits needed to excel in school; short and simple assignments are sufficient. Teachers should neither assign homework to young children with the expectation that it will enhance achievement nor expect students to teach themselves complex skills at home. In the upper grades, teachers often use homework to develop interest in a topic; more challenging assignments requiring higher-level thinking skills might best meet this purpose.

Finally, Cooper (1989) finds no evidence that any particular type of grading or evaluative comments on homework assignments has an impact on achievement: "Intermittent grading and comments are no less effective than providing continuous feedback" (p. 183). In fact, he suggests that when the teacher uses homework to develop positive attitudes toward the subject matter, grading should be kept to a minimum.

Learn about the homework policy at your school. If teachers are given some responsibility in establishing their own policy, think carefully about the purpose and goals you wish to achieve by assigning homework.

DEBATE FORUM

Does Reducing Class Size Affect Achievement?

Argument: One of the major difficulties facing teachers is the number of students in their classes. Teachers would be more effective if class sizes were reduced.

Counterargument: No research has yet proved that small class ratios always lead to increased achievement (Cooper, 1989; Slavin, 1989). When increased achievement has been linked to small class sizes, the achievement effects are small.

Response: The main reason that reduction in class size does not improve student achievement is that teachers' behaviors don't change with the size of the class. That is, teachers teach a class with a large number of students in the same basic way that they teach a class with a small number of students. What has not been carefully researched to date is whether major changes in teacher behavior (e.g., individual tutoring) would have a stronger affect on achievement (Slavin, 1989).

Response: Reduction of class size can have other benefits. Smith and Glass (1980) found that in smaller classes, teachers' morale and attitude toward students were more positive, and satisfaction with their own teaching was greater. The researchers also found that students in smaller classes had more positive attitudes about their teacher, school, and themselves.

Response: Considering the current economic climate, it is unlikely that funds will be available to reduce class size even if researchers could show more dramatic impact on students. Therefore, we need to explore other methods for improving the quality of instruction.

What do you think? Could educational technology be used to provide greater individualized instruction? Do you have other ideas for improving classroom instruction if smaller class sizes can't be achieved?

direct instruction. An instructional method that emphasizes the mastery of basic skills.

DEVELOPING A LESSON PLAN

After stating the instructional objective of the lesson, a basic lesson plan typically begins by identifying the content of the lesson in outline form and the instructional procedures. Whereas the content section of the lesson plan identifies what is to be taught, the instructional procedures section outlines how it will be taught. Another component is a checklist of all the materials and aids the teacher needs to teach the lesson (e.g., handouts, books, and charts). It is distressing to be in the middle of a lesson and find that you do not have important handouts or other resource material to complete the lesson. Finally, the last section of a lesson plan usually includes the evaluation procedures that describe how the teacher will assess student performance. That is, did the students master the stated objective of the lesson? Keep in mind that not all lessons require that the students demonstrate attainment of the objective on a test on the exact day that instruction is provided. The teacher may want to combine several objectives before testing students. Orlich et al. (1985) provide some good questions for teachers to consider during this stage: "Were the objectives realistic and appropriate? Did the instructional methods work? For what learners and [to] what degree? What components of the lesson succeeded? What aspects need to be improved?" (p. 144). The answers to these questions can help the teacher to improve instruction and future planning. Planning for the evaluation of the lesson should become a part of any lesson plan.

Following are three different lesson plan formats based on learning principles discussed in the previous chapters: direct instruction, discovery or inquiry learning, and cooperative learning.

Direct Instruction

During the late 1970s and early 1980s, a number of large-scale investigations found that students taught with a structured curriculum with direct or active involvement by the teacher learned more than students taught with more individualized, or discovery learning, methods. These studies were conducted at the elementary and junior high school level and focused on instruction in basic academic areas such as reading, mathematics, and English (Rosenshine, 1983).

This instruction has been called **direct instruction**, *explicit instruction*, or *active teaching*, depending on the individual researcher. This type of instruction appears to be most successful in highly structured academic areas where there is a specific body of knowledge to learn, and less relevant in more subjective areas such as identifying the moral positions of world leaders, analyzing literature, or discussing political views of senatorial candidates. In these areas, instructional objectives are less clear, the material is less structured, and the skills or knowledge do not follow in any particular order.

Rosenshine (1986) has identified the following six major teaching functions that aid the learning of explicit, well-structured content:

- *Review.* Each day, start the lesson by correcting the previous night's homework and reviewing what students have recently been taught.
- *Presentation of new material.* Tell students the goals of today's lesson. Then present new information a little at a time, modeling procedures, giving clear examples, and checking often to make sure students understand.
- *Guided practice.* Allow students to practice using the new information under the teacher's direction; ask many questions that give students abundant opportunities to correctly repeat or explain the procedure or concept that has just been taught. Student participation should be active until all students are able to respond.
- *Feedback and corrections.* During guided practice, give students a great deal of feedback. When students answer incorrectly, reteach the lesson if necessary. When students answer correctly, explain why the answer was right. It is important that feedback be immediate and thorough.
- *Independent practice.* Next, allow students to practice using the information on their own. The teacher should be available to give short answers to students' questions, and students should be permitted to help each other.
- *Weekly and monthly reviews.* At the beginning of each week, the teacher should review the previous week's lesson and at the end of the month review what students have learned during the last four weeks. It is important that students not be allowed to forget past lessons once they have moved on to new material. (p. 68)

There are several applications of direct instruction in the literature. Good, Grouws, and Ebmeier (1983) developed the *Missouri Mathematics Program*, in which teachers were trained to use effective teaching behaviors (similar to the steps identified by Rosenshine) in mathematics instruction. They found that the teachers implemented many of these behaviors in the classroom and taught differently from teachers who did not receive the training. For example, the trained teachers conducted more reviews and checked homework and student seatwork more frequently. The result was that the test scores in mathematics for the students in classes with the trained teachers were higher than for the students in classrooms with teachers who had not received any special training.

Good, Grouws, and Ebmeier prefer the term *active teaching* to *direct instruction* or *explicit teaching*, because they believe that the term identifies a wider range of teaching behaviors than is specified by the other two terms. In active teaching, students can learn independently or through direction by the teacher. Most important, instruction can become less direct as students become more mature and the instructional goals become less concerned with basic skills. Rosenshine (1986) has pointed out that direct forms of instruction can be modified to suit different students. For example, slower students need less presentation but more review and practice. Faster students benefit from more presentation and need less review and practice.

CLASSROOM Application

DEVELOPING A LESSON PLAN USING DIRECT INSTRUCTION

The following teaching processes and example of a lesson plan that uses a form of direct instruction were developed by Hunter (1982):

1. Anticipatory set
2. Instruction or providing information (which includes modeling and checking for understanding)
3. Guided practice
4. Closure (or checking for performance)
5. Independent practice

Sometimes you will use all five of these teaching processes in sequence, but it is important to notice that these processes may not be *taught* in every lesson. Instead, they should be *considered* in every lesson. Wolfe (1984) developed a training manual for teachers in which she discussed each step in detail. Figure 6.3 shows a lesson plan on maps that Linda Organ developed from the Hunter model.

ANTICIPATORY SET

The key question is: How do you get the students' minds ready to learn? The anticipatory set has five possible functions:

1. It can serve to focus the learner's attention on the lesson (e.g., the teacher conducts a laboratory experiment as the students enter the classroom).
2. It can relate previous learning to the present learning (e.g., the teacher asks, "Do you remember last week when we discussed different parts of a short story? Today we're going to analyze a short story and locate those parts").
3. It can diagnose the students' skills as they relate to the lesson (e.g., "Write down three things you learned from yesterday's lesson on immigration").
4. It can let the students know what the objective is (e.g., "By the end of the period today, you're going to be able to determine the distance between two points on a map").
5. It can provide reasons why the lesson is important (e.g., "In a few weeks you're going to write a term paper. Today you're

going to learn how to locate references in the library, one important skill for writing a term paper").

Very seldom will you include all five possible functions of an anticipatory set. You need to consider before you begin a lesson which function or functions you want to include. Your decision will be based on the difficulty of the content to be taught, the student's readiness level, and/or how motivated you feel the students are for the lesson.

INSTRUCTION

This step includes the learning activities to be experienced by the students in order to accomplish the objective and the manner in which you provide information or help students to achieve skills. You must consider two points in providing this information: (1) determine the basic information and organize it, and (2) present the basic information in its simplest and clearest form.

It is helpful for students to see examples of what the new learning looks like. This procedure is called *modeling*, a process by which a person learns from observing the behavior of another person (Chapter 2). During the modeling phase of a lesson, the teacher (or a student who can perform the task correctly) models or demonstrates the skills or process for the student. A verbal description often should accompany the model. A good example is a mathematics teacher who "talks through" each step of a problem as he solves it on the chalkboard.

While you are teaching, you need to check for the students' understanding of the new skill or concept so that you can correct errors in their thinking by using a different example, providing another model, and so forth. Posing a question to the entire group and then getting responses from students of varying ability levels can be a useful approach.

The three strategies (input, modeling, and checking for understanding) are generally used throughout a lesson in a cyclical fashion. This is especially true if the objective requires considerable new information.

GUIDED PRACTICE

After the initial instruction, it is important that you monitor the students' initial practice to make certain they understand the material before turning them loose to practice. You should not simply ask, "Are there any questions?" or "Does everyone understand?" These questions are generally ineffective because students are usually uncomfortable admitting to the whole class that they do not under-

continued

stand something. In addition, students often *think* they understand, but when asked to demonstrate, they are unable to show their knowledge.

TITLE OF LESSON: USING THE SCALE OF MILES **DATE** ________

1. BEHAVIORAL OBJECTIVES	2. ANTICIPATORY SET (FOCUS)	3. PROCEDURE FOR LESSON	4. CHECK FOR UNDERSTANDING
What will the learner be able to do when you are finished? Students will: compute distances between points on a map using the scale of miles.	**How will you focus the learner's attention?** Someday you will receive your license to drive a car. While driving, you're liable to become lost. If you are able to use the scale of miles on a map, you will know how far away you are from your destination.	**What will you do?** Provide information: a. locate key on map b. interpret scale of miles (inches = miles) c. demonstrate use of ruler to determine inches d. demonstrate computation of inches times miles Model: a. use of ruler b. multiplication	**How will you know if you're presenting clearly?** a. Students will use individual maps and rulers to follow along with the teacher as she models examples. b. Students will volunteer answers to each step in the teacher's sample problems.

5. GUIDED PRACTICE (ACTIVITY)	6. CLOSURE (FINAL CHECK FOR UNDERSTANDING)	7. INDEPENDENT PRACTICE (ASSIGNMENT)	8. COMMENTS ABOUT HOW THE LESSON WENT
How will the learner practice with you there? a. give a map to each student b. break class into small groups of 4 to 5 students. c. have groups use the scale of miles to calculate real distances between points on the map. d. after, groups explain answers to each other.	**How will you know if each student has reached the objective?** Each student will use the scale of miles on a map to determine the total distance in miles of a journey through eight towns.	**What will the learner do for additional practice to develop speed and fluency?** a. Every student will create an imaginary country, a map, a scale of miles, and 2 trips for his fellow students to calculate in miles. b. Each student will calculate 10 trips designed by classmates.	

Figure 6.3 An Example of a Lesson Plan Using a Form of Direct Instruction.
Source: Wolfe, 1984.

The key to guided practice is to obtain *overt* responses from students. Have them work a problem, show how something is done, or tell you the steps of an equation. Overt responses let you know where your students are and what they are thinking so that you can correct any problems immediately and move on.

CLOSURE

At some point during the lesson, you must decide if the students can meet the objectives of the lesson. Closure is a final check for understanding or performance, when you can determine the status of each student's progress toward the achievement of the instructional objectives. Closure is *not* a summary of the lesson; you do not tell the students what they have learned. Rather, it is a time when the students demonstrate to you what they have learned. Closure answers three questions regarding the achievement of the objective: Which students have reached the objective and are ready to move on and practice independently? Is more guided practice, or reteaching, necessary for some students? Should the lesson strategy be altered, or should the teacher move on to another activity?

You achieve closure in a lesson in several ways: question and answer, discussion, explanation by students regarding what they learned, and paper-and-pencil activities.

INDEPENDENT PRACTICE

The last step in planning and teaching an effective lesson is called *independent practice*. After students have demonstrated that they can perform the new skills or use the new knowledge, they are ready to practice alone or with minimal supervision.

At the beginning of this Classroom Application, I mentioned that you should consider each step in every lesson but that you do not have to follow each step in every lesson. For example, if a lesson is a continuation of some class activity, it may not be necessary for you to include an anticipatory set because the students may already understand the objective and be motivated. In another situation, you might be expecting the students to discover the concept on their own with minimal guidance. In such an instance you would not present the material. Guided practice may be omitted in a class discussion in history on equal rights. If you want the students to apply what they learned during the discussion, however, you may give them an assignment on a topic that will fulfill the purpose of guided practice. You also may want to omit closure because more guided practice is necessary or because closure is not desired (as in a music appreciation lesson). Finally, independent practice may be omitted in a lesson if the students have not demonstrated a readiness to practice alone.

discovery learning. The learning of new information largely as a result of the learner's own efforts.

inquiry learning. Students learn strategies to manipulate and process information, test hypotheses, and apply their conclusions to new content or situations.

Hunter (1982) developed a direct instruction model that was evaluated over a four-year period. Students involved in the program during the four years increased their reading and mathematics achievement test scores during the first three years, but their scores declined during the last year of the program. The investigators raised a number of questions about maintaining the positive outcomes of the program after supervision from the trainers was withdrawn (Stallings & Krasavage, 1986; Stallings et al., 1986). More recently, a large-scale investigation of Hunter's model in South Carolina (Mandeville & Rivers, 1988/1989) indicated that the program failed to improve student achievement. Hunter's (1986; 1988/1989) response to the critics in both programs was that poor implementation was a factor in limiting the outcomes of the program.

Discovery Learning

The essential criterion for **discovery learning** is that the learner organize into final form the material to be learned. The discovery of the relevant concept or abstraction occurs during the student's involvement in a learning activity. This procedure differs from *expository teaching* (sometimes referred to as *didactic teaching*), in which the teacher explains to students all the information they must learn.

Bruner (1961) believes that discovery learning helps students take responsibility for their own learning, emphasizes high-level thinking, focuses on intrinsic rather than extrinsic motivation, and helps students remember important information.

Some educators use the term **inquiry learning** interchangeably with *discovery learning*, and others make a distinction between the terms. Both terms can be viewed on a continuum based on the amount of structure provided in the lesson. Although it is possible to provide no structure and have students discover all information totally on their own, most school programs use a form of *guided discovery*, or *guided inquiry learning*, whereby the teacher plays a role in the planning and facilitation of learning.

One distinction often made between discovery and inquiry learning is as follows: In discovery learning, the students are provided with data; with questioning by the teacher, they are expected to discover the particular principle or abstraction identified in the goal of the lesson. In inquiry learning, the goal is for students to develop strategies to manipulate and process information. Students identify problems, generate hypotheses, test the hypotheses in terms of the data, and apply their conclusions to new content or situations. The purpose of this type of instruction is to teach students process (thinking) skills that can be applied to new situations. Carin and Sund (1985) state: "Inquiry focuses upon *how* students process data (processes) rather than *what* they process (product)" (p. 102).

In many situations discovery and inquiry learning involve the same problem-solving skills. Thus I am more concerned that you be able to use an inductive method of instruction (i.e., reasoning from the particular to the general) than that you attempt to make discriminations between various forms of discovery and inquiry learning.

This method is not as effective as direct instruction in teaching basic skills (Slavin, Karweit, & Madden, 1989). Discovery learning techniques are most useful when students have the necessary skills and motivation to succeed. Although I would not suggest that discovery learning be used on a regular basis as the primary method of instruction, it can be used as a supplementary procedure to teach problem-solving skills, stimulate curiosity, and encourage more self-directed learning.

CLASSROOM Application

DEVELOPING A LESSON PLAN USING DISCOVERY LEARNING

The teaching methods used for discovery and inquiry learning vary greatly, depending upon the particular program developed and the content area taught. Planning for discovery and inquiry learning is an important aspect of the process. If you think all one has to do is tell students to discover something and sit back and wait for the results, you are going to be disappointed. Discovery and inquiry methods often take more time to plan than expository teaching methods.

In discovery learning, you must carefully plan the questions that should be asked in order to help students to attain the principle or abstraction being taught, order the examples in the lesson, and be sure that the reference materials and/or equipment are readily available. Otherwise, a good deal of time will be wasted.

Figure 6.4 presents a detailed example of a lesson plan for a guided discovery lesson in science. The entries on the left side of the lesson serve as a guide for planning.

There are many different forms of inquiry learning. I suggest that you use the following steps in developing your own lesson plans and make modifications as you learn more about the strategy:

1. Identify and define the problem.
2. Formulate hypotheses.
3. Collect data.
4. Analyze data and form conclusions.

In planning, you can identify a problem in the particular content area you teach or capitalize on situations arising spontaneously in the class or in current events. As in discovery learning, you need to arrange opportunities for data collection and make needed resources available. In helping the students to develop hypotheses, provide a focusing event to capture their attention. For example, in science you

continued

can set up a perplexing experiment, or in social studies you can focus on a national or international issue such as the use of atomic energy. After the students have had time to investigate the problem, you should encourage them to offer ideas about solutions. This will help students to redefine their hypotheses or develop new hypotheses. Next, the students should collect data to test their hypotheses. Depending on the complexity of the problem, time both in and out of class can be used for the activity. The final phase of inquiry learning is analysis of data, a process that involves examining hypotheses in terms of the information obtained. The students need to decide whether their hypotheses can be confirmed or whether they have to be changed or modified as a result of the available data. Finally, the

What Is the Law of the Pendulum?

What Are Students to Discover?

Students are to discover that a weight attached to a string will swing rhythmically back and forth when given a push.

The frequency of the swinging motion depends on the length of the string, not on the amount of weight attached or on the original push. (Teachers: Students should arrive at this conclusion on their own with your guidance. Do not "short circuit" the learning by telling students the rule of the pendulum and then asking them to verify the fact, as is the case in so many hands-on experiences.)

Teacher Tips

If students do not know what a pendulum is, the teacher should demonstrate how to construct one and safely use it. Teachers may also want to introduce the term *frequency* as the number of swings in a given unit of time (minute).

Necessary Materials (per Pair of Students)

Pendulum support
(such as a ring stand)
String
Scissors
Weights (nuts, heavy washers, fishing sinkers, etc.)

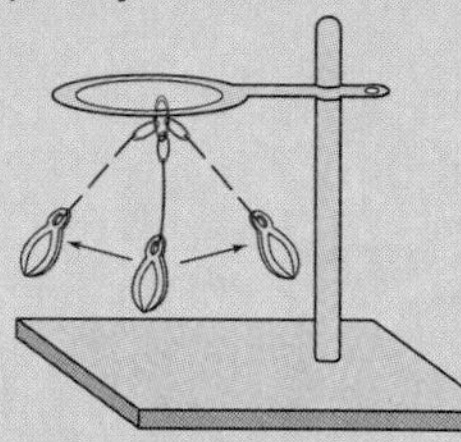

Procedure

With the discovery teaching technique, it is important not to give too much direction, or the activity becomes a cookbook lesson. It is more effective to give the students challenges to guide their exploration. In this case, teachers should ask the students to make pendulums with various lengths of string with different weights and observe the resulting behavior. Some students will probably decide to time the swings, but for some groups, this suggestion might be made by the teacher after watching the students at work. Students may also be challenged to make side-by-side pendulums in order to compare the effects of certain variables.

Challenges to Students

1. Given the materials provided, try to determine the relationship between string length, weight, and frequency.
2. Try to make a pendulum with a frequency of 15 swings per minute.
3. Try to make two pendulums with the same frequency with two different string lengths.

Figure 6.4 Lesson Plan for Discovery Learning. Source: This lesson plan was developed by William McComas at the University of Southern California.

major outcome of the lesson should be the conclusions reached by the students as a result of the inquiry process (Jacobsen et al., 1989).

SOCIAL INQUIRY: A CLASSROOM EXAMPLE

The following teaching example illustrates the use of social inquiry in a high school classroom. The four basic steps in the process are identified in parentheses.

Miss West began the lesson by stating, "The influx of immigrants into Monterey Park, California, means that only approximately twenty-three percent of the people speak English as a native language. A walk through the streets of the Monterey Park business district illustrates the variety of languages spoken in the city. Does this situation present a problem to residents and visitors of Monterey Park?" [*Identify and Define Problem*]

Mary responded, "Well, if the business signs aren't in English, how will English-speaking people know what is sold in the store?"

Bill added, "You just don't go into stores if you can't figure out what is being offered. Besides, it doesn't sound like there are many English-speaking people in Monterey Park."

"What if there were a fire or another emergency? How would the firefighters know which business to go to?" asked Joe.

Celia asked, "Do the businesses have their street numbers on the shops?"

Miss West asked, "Why is that important, Celia?"

Celia responded, "Well, at least a common style for displaying an address would help if you need to locate a particular business or office."

"You said there are a variety of languages spoken in the city. How do people conduct business? Just because only twenty-three percent speak English as a native language doesn't mean that other people don't know English," replied Bob.

"Do you want to explore that some more, Bob? What are you getting at?" asked Miss West.

Bob continued, "I was just thinking what would happen if I went into a bank in Monterey Park and nobody understood me. What would I do?"

Miss West commented, "Let's stop and reflect a moment. What are the issues involved here?"

"Isn't the main issue whether or not English should be required to conduct business in Monterey Park?" Betty asked.

"Miss West, you asked us whether or not the variety of languages spoken in Monterey Park was a problem to residents and visitors. I don't think it is a problem unless the residents of Monterey Park see it as a problem," responded Marty.

Miss West asked, "How many agree with Marty?"

continued

[Agreement is expressed by the students.]

Miss West continued, "Could we suggest alternative hypotheses to focus on the problem? Marty, why don't you try?"

Marty [after some thought] commented, "Some residents of Monterey Park may believe that English should be the required language of the city."

Shelly quickly added, "Yes, and some residents may believe that they have a right to speak whatever language they want to."

"Well done," Miss West replied. "Okay, now let's see what is involved in the two positions."

Marty answered, "If you believe that English should be required, then you probably believe that Congress should pass a law that English is the only language to be used in this country." [*Formulate Hypotheses*]

Terry responded, "On the other hand, if you don't want it required, then you believe that the Constitution protects your right to speak whatever language you want." [*Formulate Hypotheses*]

Miss West requested, "How many agree that the question has to do with constitutional rights?" [The students appear to agree.] "Is there another issue here? Are values involved?" (The students nod their heads.)

Bella asked, "Miss West, doesn't one of the values revolve around the need for people to maintain their own cultural identity?"

Miss West replied, "You may be right, Bella. Why don't we now see if we can identify the implications involved in the two positions?"

She wrote the two positions on the chalkboard and guided the students to explore the underlying assumptions and implications of the positions. When this task was completed, she told the students that she would provide them with some current newspaper articles about the language rift in Monterey Park and that they should also use their government text to gather facts to support their position. Miss West then divided the class into four teams. Two groups took the position that English should be required, and two groups took the opposite position. The students began work to gather facts and evidence to support their hypotheses. While the students worked in their groups, Miss West listened to them as they discussed the issues. Sometimes she asked the students questions in their groups to clarify specific points of view. On one occasion, she suggested that a group read the Bill of Rights. [*Collect Data*]

The students continued to work at the task as a homework assignment, and on the following day each team reported its findings. Because there is no solution to the problem, each team's conclusion was presented in the form of a statement about the issues, values, and probable consequences concerning the two different actions that could be taken. [*Analyze Data and Form Conclusions*]

This example was developed by Johanna Lemlech at the University of Southern California.

CLASSROOM Application

DEVELOPING A LESSON PLAN USING COOPERATIVE LEARNING

This lesson plan involves four instructional periods and is for a ninth-grade English class that is reading short stories: Four students of different ability levels are assigned to each group. The lesson has two objectives:

- The students will identify the literary elements in a short story.
- The students will apply the literary elements to analyze a short story.

DECISIONS PRIOR TO TEACHING

Materials

1. Student-prepared flash cards with literary terms (one set per student)
2. Teacher-prepared test on literary terms (one test per student)

continued

Cooperative Learning

In Chapter 4, I discussed different types of cooperative learning situations as well as factors that need to be considered when formulating groups and preparing students to work cooperatively. I have found Slavin (1990) and Johnson, Johnson, and Holubec (1987) useful references for developing lesson plans for cooperative learning. It is important to mention that your first attempt with cooperative learning may not be as successful as you would like. It takes time to prepare students to work cooperatively and for you to feel comfortable with this instructional method. You will learn in Chapter 9 that students from certain cultural groups prefer to work cooperatively rather than competitively. Cooperative learning can be an effective approach to dealing with the diversity of students in your classroom.

The cooperative lesson in the Classroom Application above is only one of many different ways you can organize the lesson. As you read the lesson plan, devise at least two different modifications that can be made in it.

3. Short story analysis form (one form per group)
4. Short story analysis form in four separate parts (one part to each group
5. Literature books (one per student)
6. Job description cards (four cards per group)

Student Roles in Group

When preparing for the test on literary terms, the group divides into partners and alternates roles to quiz each other. Next, when the group analyzes the short story, each student has a separate set of literary terms to apply and becomes the group expert. Finally, when the group assembles the finished analysis form, each member is assigned a role:

Recorder: Reads the answers of the group members and transcribes the answers for the group.
Summarizer: Summarizes the material the group writes and puts the information in final form for presentation.
Editor: Makes sure all group members complete their assignment, sees that the final analysis form is completed as required, and makes any corrections in spelling and punctuation.
Researcher: Investigates the short story to settle any differences of opinion in the group on literary terms or on the correct answers for the short story analysis form. This student also acts as a liaison between the group and the teacher when assistance is needed either for content or cooperative skills.

Summary

HOW SPECIFIC SHOULD EDUCATIONAL OBJECTIVES BE?

1. Educators disagree about what students should learn in school.
2. Instructional goals come from many sources: the student, society, and academic discipline.
3. Learning goals are expressed in terms of educational objectives that are written at different levels of specificity.
4. An explicit instructional or behavioral objective is a precise statement of what a student will be able to do as a result of instruction.
5. There are several ways to write behavioral objectives. One approach includes a *behavioral term* that expresses the type of task required of the

THE LESSON

Before the cooperative learning experience begins, the teacher discusses the following literary terms: *plot, setting, exposition, climax, resolution, theme, character, symbol, figurative language,* and *point of view.*

Day 1. Students are divided into study partners to review the literary terms on flash cards. A test is administered at the end of the period, with passing set at 80 percent. If the group meets the criterion, members receive the short story analysis form (comprising the 10 literary terms) and story assignment. If the group does not meet the criterion, members spend the rest of the period studying the literary terms and repeat the test the next day. At the end of the period, all groups receive the short story assignment to read for homework.

Day 2. The first 10 minutes of the period are used for retesting. Each member of the group is responsible for two or three terms. Members take their short story analysis form and meet with students of other groups who have the same terms to analyze. Each member of the group is given a special job: recorder, summarizer, researcher, or editor.

Day 3. Students return to their original groups and analyze the short story according to their assigned literary terms. At the end of the period, each group will have analyzed the short story using all literary terms. The purpose of this class session is to begin preparing for an examination on the analysis of the short story.

Day 4. Students take a multiple-choice test on the analysis of the short story. Grades are assigned according to the composite scores of the group members.

This lesson plan was developed by Lucinda Boswell.

student; the *situation*, or *condition*, under which the behavior is to be performed; and the *criterion*, or *level of performance*, that will be used to evaluate the success of the performance or product. Another approach uses only the behavioral term.

THE VALUE OF INSTRUCTIONAL OBJECTIVES

6. Not all educators agree on the need to state goals explicitly before instruction.
7. There is some concern that explicit objectives may dehumanize the educational process and force teachers to emphasize experiences that are easiest to measure.
8. Knowledge of objectives can help the teacher to plan appropriate instructional procedures and methods.

DEVELOPING OBJECTIVES FOR INSTRUCTION

9. Academic content can be assessed by the type of learning, the degree of difficulty, and the level of complexity.
10. Teacher-made tests help the teacher to determine the students' present knowledge. The Taxonomy of Educational Objectives helps to identify objectives at different levels of complexity.
11. A teacher needs to consider adaptations for individual students in planning lessons.

PLANNING FOR INSTRUCTION

12. Teachers' plans influence their classroom behavior.
13. In planning lessons, teachers should consider the major goals of the instructional program at the school, the content of the course, and the students' present knowledge.
14. A good unit plan can organize daily lesson plans.
15. There is no one best way to plan lessons.
16. An evaluation component is an important part of any lesson plan.
17. A teacher needs to carefully consider the amount of homework assigned. In some situations, too much homework can have a negative impact on both academic achievement and attitude toward learning.
18. It is not necessary to grade all homework assignments.
19. The reduction of class size doesn't necessarily lead to higher academic achievement.

DEVELOPING A LESSON PLAN

20. Direct instruction tends to be most successful in highly structured subjects in which there is a specific body of knowledge to learn.
21. Although there are various applications of direct instruction in education, the following teaching functions are included in most programs: review, presentation of new material, guided practice, feedback and corrections, independent practice, and weekly and monthly reviews. The amount of time or emphasis on each function can vary, depending on the characteristics of the students.
22. Students tend to learn more and reach objectives in basic skills when taught with a structured curriculum with direct or active involvement by the teacher.
23. Discovery learning can be used occasionally to change the format of classroom instruction, motivate students, and focus on higher-level thinking skills.
24. Cooperative learning is effective in achieving both cognitive and affective objectives.

Reflecting on Planning for Instruction

1. Evaluate the Six Most Recent Goals of American Education

In 1990, President George Bush and the governors of each state met to formulate the following six goals for American education to achieve by the beginning of the twenty-first century (Ysseldyke, Algozzine, & Thurlow, 1992):

- All children in America will start school ready to learn.
- The percentage of students graduating from high school will increase to at least 90 percent.
- Students will leave grades four, eight, and twelve having demonstrated competency in challenging subject matter, including English, mathematics, science, history, or geography; and every school in America will ensure that all students learn to use their minds well so they may be prepared for responsible citizenship, further learning, and productive employment in our modern economy.
- U.S. students will be first in the world in science and mathematics achievement.
- Every adult American will be literate and will possess the knowledge and skills necessary to compete in a global economy and exercise the rights and responsibilities of citizenship.
- Every school in America will be free of drugs and violence and offer a disciplined environment conducive to learning. (p. 42)

How would you evaluate these goals? Do you think they are attainable? What changes or modifications would you make to the six goals?

2. Justify Your Own Subject Matter

Suppose a student asked you on the first day of class, "Why do I have to take this course?" Generate a list of reasons to support the existence of your subject area in the school curriculum.

3. Interview Teachers Regarding Their Use of Objectives

Interview teachers and ask them whether they use instructional objectives and to what degree of specificity. What reasons do they give for and against developing explicit objectives?

4. Write Behavioral Objectives

Select a topic in your teaching field and write an objective for each level of the Taxonomy of Educational Objectives in both the cognitive and affective domains.

Cognitive	**Affective**
• Knowledge	• Receiving
• Comprehension	• Responding
• Application	• Valuing
• Analysis	• Organization
• Synthesis	• Characterization by a value
• Evaluation	

5. Complete a Task Analysis

In this activity you will have a chance to apply what you have learned in developing a task analysis for a small instructional unit. The activity involves the following basic steps: choosing a task, specifying the entry behavior (skills a student has already mastered before instruction), defining the prerequisite skills (all skills and behaviors that must be mastered prior to attaining the terminal objective), and determining the order in which the skills must be taught. Choose a task in your field of specialization that is relatively small and simple. Your instructor may want to approve part one of the activity before allowing you to proceed to part two.

Part One: Task Analysis Activity

a. What is the task you are going to analyze?
b. What is the makeup of the student population to whom you would teach the task? Identify the grade level, age, and possible background of the students.
c. Specify the task as a behavioral objective.
d. What are the entry behaviors for this task?

Part Two: Task Analysis Activity

a. What are the prerequisite skills?
b. What are the relationships between the prerequisite skills?
c. Diagram your task analysis using the format shown in Figure 6.1.

6. Develop a Lesson Plan

Use any of the lesson plan formats discussed in the chapter, or use one given to you by your instructor, to develop a lesson plan on a topic in your teaching specialty.

Key Terms

behavioral objectives, p. 241
expressive objectives, p. 246
Taxonomy of Educational Objectives, p. 252
cognitive domain, p. 252
affective domain, p. 252
psychomotor domain, p. 252
lesson plan, p. 256
unit plan, p. 256
direct instruction, p. 264
discovery learning, p. 270
inquiry learning, p. 270

Suggestions for Further Reading

The following books provide an excellent discussion of planning for instruction as well as different methods of teaching:

Borich, G. D. (1988). *Effective teaching methods*. Columbus, OH: Merrill.

Cangelosi, J. S. (1992). *Systematic teaching strategies*. White Plains, NY: Longman.

Davis, G. A., & Thomas, M. A. (1989). *Effective schools and effective teachers*. Needham Heights, MA: Allyn & Bacon.

Dick, W., & Reiser, R. A. (1989). *Planning effective instruction*. Englewood Cliffs, NJ: Prentice-Hall.

Jacobsen, D., Eggen, P., & Kauchak, D. (1989). *Methods for teaching: A skills approach* (3rd ed.). Columbus, OH: Merrill.

Joyce, R., Weil, M., & Showers, B. (1992). *Models of teaching* (4th ed.). Needham Heights, MA: Allyn & Bacon.

Kauchak, D. P., & Eggen, P. D. (1989). *Learning and teaching: Research-based methods*. Needham Heights, MA: Allyn & Bacon.

Orlich, D. C., Harder, R. J., Callahan, R. C., Kravas, C. H., Kauchak, D. P., Pendergrass, R. A., & Keogh, A. J. (1985). *Teaching strategies: A guide to better instruction* (2nd ed.). Lexington, MA: Heath.

Excellent sources for writing instructional objectives:

Gronlund, N. E. (1991). *How to write and use instructional objectives* (4th ed.). New York: Macmillan.

Mager, R. F. (1978). *Preparing instructional objectives*. Belmont, CA: Fearon.

A position paper by one of the leading critics of behavioral objectives:

Eisner, E. W. (1967). Educational objectives: Help or hindrance? *School Review, 75*, 250–260.

References on different teaching methodologies:

Carin, A. A., & Sund, R. B. (1989). *Teaching science through discovery* (6th ed.). Columbus, OH: Merrill. An excellent source for examples on discovery learning lessons.

Good, T. L., Grouws, D., & Ebmeier, H. (1983). *Active mathematics teaching*. White Plains, NY: Longman. A description of a successful inservice training program using a structured method of teaching.

Rosenshine, B. V. (1986). Synthesis of research on explicit teaching. *Educational Leadership*, 43, 60–69. A good review of literature on the effectiveness of structured (explicit) teaching.

See Suggestions for Further Reading in Chapter 4 for information on using cooperative learning.

Chapter 7

Classroom Management and Discipline

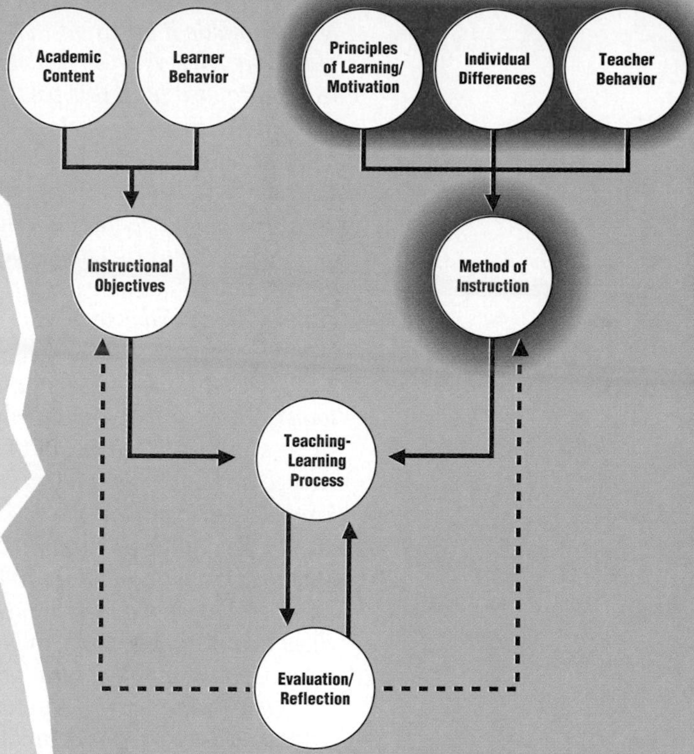

OBJECTIVES

After mastering the material in this chapter you will be able to:

- Establish a management system for a classroom.
- Use teacher behaviors that lead to greater student involvement in tasks.
- Use behavioral techniques to modify behavior.
- Teach students appropriate social skills.
- Use I-messages and active listening responses to improve communication.
- Conduct classroom meetings.

Orientation

classroom management. Teacher behaviors and activities that encourage learning in the classroom.

discipline. The degree to which students behave appropriately, are involved in classroom activities, and are task oriented.

Since the first day of class, Ruth Alba knew that Monica was going to be difficult to work with. Of the 30 students that she had in her fifth-grade class that semester, Monica made it apparent that she was going to demand special attention. What follows is Mrs. Alba's recollections of that first day with Monica and how she learned to deal with this particular student:

"On the first day of class, I give my students a writing assignment, asking them to tell me which subjects they like the best and least in school, and to explain their choices. Monica's response was direct and to the point: 'I hate all my classes, and I really hate math. I am no good at math, and I hate it.'

"It took about two weeks before I began to understand what may have been going on and was able to start focusing upon what could be done to improve this child's self-confidence in my class. The turning point occurred when I gave the students their first test.

"I was still handing the test out to the students when I heard Monica say, quite loudly, 'Mrs. Alba, I need help!' I told her to wait for a moment, until I had passed the exams out to the rest of the class, and then I would help her. No sooner had I turned around when I heard Monica sighing deeply, and then she began to rap her knuckles furiously on the desk top.

"I talked with a few of my colleagues, and we agreed that Monica's behavior stemmed from an inability to persist in the face of what she considered frustrating tasks. I requested a meeting with Monica and her parents, at which time I told them about my plan to help her persist on tasks requiring problem solving. It was based upon giving Monica 'points' for certain behaviors in the classroom.

"I decided to reward Monica with points if she could show a sincere attempt to solve at least a few math problems by herself, and extra points for each correct answer. If she attempted to solve these problems, she would be allowed to ask for help, but only by raising her hand and waiting. This behavior would also be rewarded in the form of points. If I was unavailable to help at that moment, she would be allowed to draw at her desk.

"Coupled with the tangible rewards, which Monica could accumulate through cooperative behavior, it was equally important that both her parents and I give Monica expressions of praise for her efforts. By the end of the school year, Monica was no longer requiring the use of points in order to work on her math problems. It seemed that just letting her know that I was proud of her was enough."

Classroom management and **discipline** are important components of effective teaching. In fact, these areas consistently rank at or near the top of the list of teacher concerns. *Classroom management*, a broader term than discipline, refers to the teacher behaviors and activities that encourage learning in the classroom. The term *discipline* is used to indicate the degree to which students behave appropriately, are involved in classroom activities, and are task oriented (Emmer, 1987). Thus, one aspect of classroom management is discipline; other aspects of management are related to instructional organization, teacher behavior, and classroom organizational patterns (e.g., how the teacher structures the classroom in terms of individualistic, competitive, and cooperative learning activities) (Jacobsen, Eggen, & Kauchak, 1989).

Classroom management provides a good example of the influence of many variables in the teaching-learning process. Well-organized and well-managed classrooms provide students with more opportunities to learn. However, the teacher behaviors that lead to well-organized and well-managed classrooms are *not* authoritarian or harsh. Successful teachers tend to be businesslike, yet they develop a warm and accepting classroom climate. I mention this because sometimes beginning teachers believe that the only way to manage a classroom effectively is to be dogmatic or authoritarian.

One of the most important objectives for this chapter is for you to develop your own goals for student behavior. What is the purpose of classroom management and discipline? Simply to keep students quiet or under control so you can teach? To help students develop self-control so they can regulate their own behavior? In the chapter on cognitive psychology, we learned how to promote a classroom environment that encourages a mastery goal orientation. Researchers are just beginning to consider the type of classroom management system that develops greater self-regulation of students' social behavior.

McCaslin and Good (1992) are concerned that the classroom management system be aligned with the instructional system. They warn educators about the danger of "a curriculum that urges problem solving and critical thinking and a management system that requires compliance and narrow obedience" (p. 12). They further point out that it is as important to teach students to manage and control their own social behavior as it is to manage and control cognition.

Some teachers are disappointed when they find it difficult to model a respected teacher's management style. While you can learn a great deal from observing good teachers, you need to realize that you have to find a style that is comfortable for you. The advantage of observational experiences and student teaching is that one has the opportunity to practice and evaluate different management styles.

The research on motivation has some important implications for teachers as they consider different management styles. For example, management style can influence continuing motivation or whether students are more likely to develop a mastery goal orientation. If the teacher's primary goal is to keep students quiet, he may use control techniques that get the job done but have negative consequences on students' attitudes toward learning.

In Chapter 4, I discussed teacher efficacy and expectations and their impact on student behavior and achievement. Teachers who have high expectations for student achievement expect their students to master the curriculum, and they allocate most of their classroom time to the attainment of academic objectives. In contrast, if teachers do not believe that their students can learn the material in a course, the classroom focus will have less emphasis on mastery of academic material. If students perceive that little academic work is expected from them, the consequent behavior (e.g., talking, daydreaming, getting out of one's seat) can lead to considerable discipline problems. Therefore, teachers need to assess how their behavior influences student responses in the classroom.

It is important to realize that there are many different reasons for discipline problems. Teachers must be able to analyze situations and determine what steps need to be taken to solve problems that interfere with classroom instruction. Keep in mind that the problem is not always the students; teachers may also aggravate the situation through inconsistent management techniques, inappropriate reinforcement, poor instruction, overreliance on punishment, inappropriate expectations for students, insensitivity to students' legitimate concerns, and/or unwillingness to try new strategies to solve teaching problems (Kauffman, Pullen, & Akers, 1986).

The extensive research on classroom management indicates that the key to successful management is not in what teachers do *after* misbehavior but what they do to *avoid* misbehavior and *prevent* it from occurring in the first place (Brophy & Evertson, 1976; Kounin, 1970). The differences between successful and unsuccessful classroom managers are related to the planning and preparation for instruction and to the techniques of group management used by the successful teachers to prevent inattention and boredom.

This chapter is organized in two major sections: developing a management plan to prevent problems and dealing with problems once they occur.

- *Developing a management plan and implementing effective instructional strategies.* This is the time before and at the beginning of school when you make your most important decisions about how the class will be organized and run. The main purpose here is to reduce the probability of problems occurring in the first place. Classroom rules are established and the students soon determine whether or not you mean what you say. Your instructional organization and teaching strategies play an important role in increasing learning and minimizing disruptions that interfere with learning. For example, many discipline problems occur when students don't understand the assignment, don't know what to do when they finish their work, have to wait for long periods of time for direction, and are not supervised carefully during seatwork. Researchers have found a positive relationship between effective managers and effective instructors (Brophy, 1979; Emmer, Evertson, & Anderson, 1980; Evertson & Emmer, 1982a). Because good management leads to an increase in the time that students can spend on academic activities, the students will cover more work and generally perform better on academic tasks.
- *Dealing with management problems.* This is the time when you have developed rules and implemented basic classroom instructional procedures, but still experience problems. Various intervention strategies need to be used with the entire class or with particular students to maintain learning in the classroom.

As you read this chapter you will see how behavioral, cognitive, and humanistic theories of learning and motivation can be applied to classroom management.

DEVELOPING A MANAGEMENT PLAN

Evertson and Emmer (1982a) recommend three major phases in the development of an effective management system: planning before the year begins, managing during the first few weeks, and developing important behaviors needed to implement and maintain the system for the year.

Planning Before the Year Begins

THE PHYSICAL ENVIRONMENT. Arranging the physical environment of the classroom is a good starting point for classroom management. Some important questions include: How are the desks to be arranged? Where should my desk be located? Where are the pencil sharpener and the water fountain, and how does their location affect the students in the class? Where will I meet reading groups? Where can students work cooperatively?

Remember that you and your students will be working in the classroom environment for long periods of time. Your task is to provide the best environment to permit orderly movement, reduce distractions, and make the best use of available space. Evertson et al. (1989) recommend four keys to good room arrangement:

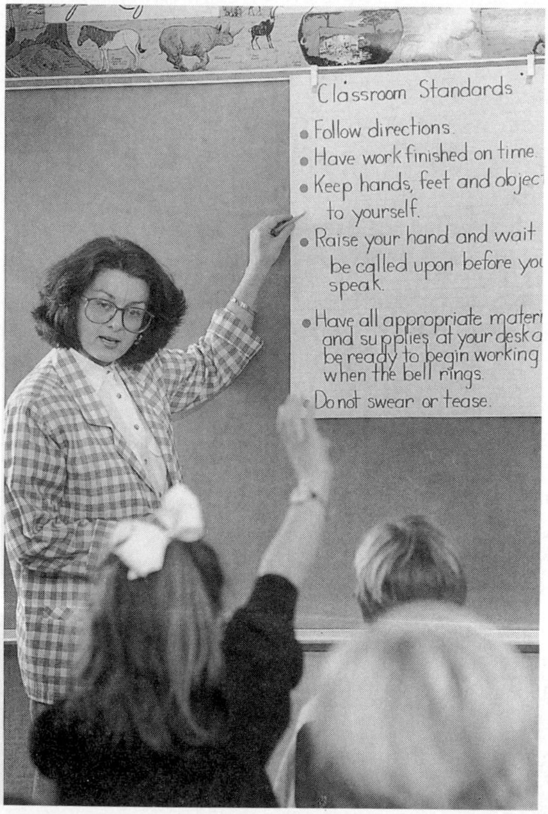

Establishing classroom rules during the first few weeks of school and teaching students to follow them can lead to fewer discipline problems during the school year.

- Keep high traffic areas free of congestion.
- Be sure students can be easily seen by the teacher.
- Keep frequently used teaching materials and student supplies readily accessible.
- Be certain students can easily see instructional presentations and displays. (pp. 4–5)

Once the classroom environment is arranged, you can shift your attention to other aspects of classroom management.

The planning phase for establishing guidelines for appropriate student behavior consists of three steps: (1) determining expected student behaviors, (2) translating expectations into procedures and rules, and (3) identifying consequences.

STEP 1: DETERMINING EXPECTED STUDENT BEHAVIORS. The important aspect of this step is to determine how you want to run your classroom. You must be thinking about expectations *before* you enter the classroom. Take notes of effective classroom procedures that you observe in other classrooms and during your student teaching experiences so that you will be in a better position to make these decisions.

Keep in mind that rules need to be established for the diversity of activities found in the classroom (e.g., seatwork, small-group discussions, whole-class instruction, and independent projects). These situations call for different student behaviors. For example, knowing that they are expected to listen quietly while the teacher presents information does not guide students to the appropriate behaviors for small-group discussions. You must also consider the optimal use of available space, traffic patterns, equipment storage, and routine procedures such as handing in papers.

STEP 2: TRANSLATING EXPECTATIONS INTO PROCEDURES AND RULES. After you have identified your expectations, you must translate them into specific procedures and rules. Following are some basic rules that you can modify for different grade levels (Mayer et al., 1983):

- Raise your hand before asking questions.
- Listen carefully to teachers' instructions.
- Follow directions.
- Cooperate with your classmates.
- Work on assigned tasks.
- Complete assignments on time.
- Treat others as you would like to be treated.
- Bring books, pencil, and paper.
- Be in your seat before the tardy bell rings.
- Keep your hands, feet, and objects to yourself. (p. 23)

Keep the rules simple and concise so that there is no misunderstanding about what you expect.

STEP 3: IDENTIFYING CONSEQUENCES. The purpose of this step is to discuss with students the consequences of following or neglecting classroom rules and procedures. You learned in Chapter 2 that behavior followed by positive consequences is likely to be repeated. It is important that you reinforce students for behaving appropriately. In addition, various incentive systems can be used, such as awarding "happy faces," certificates, and honors for elementary school children and free time and special privileges for secondary students.

You also need to determine what you are going to do, without being punitive or authoritarian, when rules are violated. Some commonly used penalties include detention, demerits, and withholding of privileges. The key is to develop an effective reinforcement system for appropriate behavior so that punishment can be limited.

Activities at the Beginning of the School Year

? Although I understand that I must first formulate my rules, what else can I do to increase my success during the first week of school?

The beginning of the school year is important because the teacher formulates the basic system of rules and procedures, and students develop expectations about their behavior in the class. Evertson and Emmer (1982b) suggest the following procedures for the first few weeks of school:

- Set aside some time during the first day or first class meeting for a discussion of rules.
- Teach classroom procedures as systematically as any other learning objective.
- Teach procedures as they are needed by students to help them deal with specific aspects of the classroom routine.
- Involve children in easy tasks and promote a high rate of success for the first few days of school.
- Use only those activities and formats that have a whole-group focus or that require simple procedures, at least for the first several days.
- Don't assume students know how to perform a procedure after one trial. In other words, the fact that you explain something once does not mean that the students understand what you want them to do, or if they understand what you said, that they can do it. Ask the students to perform the task or procedures.

Several investigations indicate that the first few weeks of the school year are important in determining how the students in the classroom will interact with one another and with the teacher for the rest of the year. Emmer, Evertson, and Anderson (1980) studied third-grade teachers from the beginning of school to the end of the year. They identified teachers who had comparable classes at the beginning of the year but differed in their management effectiveness during the year. Table 7.1 summarizes the mean (arithmetic average) behavioral ratings for the more effective and less effective managers in the group on a number of important instructional behaviors.

TABLE 7.1 RATINGS OF BEHAVIORS FOR MORE EFFECTIVE AND LESS EFFECTIVE MANAGERS

	Mean	
Variable	**More Effective Managers**	**Less Effective Managers**
Variety of rewards	4.3	3.1
Signals appropriate behavior	5.4	3.8
Eye contact	6.1	4.9
States desired attitudes	5.5	3.9
Describes objectives clearly	5.1	3.1
Materials are ready	6.2	4.4
Clear directions	5.2	3.8
Clear presentation	5.8	4.1
High degree of student success	5.5	3.9
Content related to student interest	5.2	3.6
Teacher listening skills	5.4	3.8
Teacher expression of feelings	5.0	3.2

Note: The scales range from 1 to 7, where 1 represents little or no evidence of the rated characteristics or behavior; 7 indicates relatively high amounts or frequent occurrences.
Source: Adapted from Emmer, Evertson, and Anderson, 1980.

The researchers found differences between more effective and less effective managers beginning on the first day of school. The more effective teachers were well prepared for students, had name tags, explained some basic rules, and had activities for the students to keep them occupied when the teachers were distracted by administrative tasks. The less effective managers started the first day in a less organized fashion, with no clear rules or name tags for students, and the students wasted a great deal of time waiting for directions.

More effective managers did not take any previous knowledge for granted. They began the year by establishing rules and procedures and actually taught "mini-lessons" on these rules and routines. They explained, posted, and discussed the rationale for each rule (e.g., "If I am trying to help someone and you interrupt me, it will take me longer to help the student," or "If everyone talked at once, I wouldn't be able to hear anyone"). More effective managers also drilled students on the rules and routines and monitored the extent to which they followed them. In some cases, the teachers themselves modeled proper behaviors or asked certain students to demonstrate them (e.g., cleaning up one's desk before leaving the room, or placing equipment in its proper place). Less effective managers also had rules, but their rules often were vague (e.g., "Be in the right place at the right time") and were introduced casually without discussion.

More effective managers also dealt with problems immediately by not ignoring deviations from classroom rules and procedures. They assumed that students would complete assignments, and they held the students accountable for work. Most important, students learned what to do when they finished assignments, and they moved directly to the next activity. The less effective managers were poor monitors of their classes, allowed inappropriate behavior to occur, and failed to admonish students who were not following the rules and procedures.

The more effective managers gave clearer directions and had better instructional procedures to organize their time, deal with transitions from one activity to another, and provide feedback to students. Less effective managers had more disorganized classrooms, in which students did not work on academic material for long periods, were often confused about their directions, and didn't know what to do after they completed assignments.

Finally, the more effective managers appeared to have a better understanding of student needs and concerns than did the less effective managers. As a result, they were more likely to know when to modify instructional activities, planned better, and used more interesting material.

A second investigation was conducted at the junior high level in seventh- and eighth-grade mathematics and English classes (Evertson & Emmer, 1982a). Most of the characteristics differentiating more effective from less effective managers at the elementary school level were similar for their counterparts at the junior high school level. However, the junior high teachers did not have to spend as much time explaining rules and routines. It was important for the junior high teachers to develop expectations and procedures about academic work (e.g., monitoring completion of assignments and keeping track of student progress).

Maintaining an Effective Management System throughout the Year

> **?** What's the key to maintaining a successful management system throughout the year?

As soon as you have established your rules and procedures, it is important that you carefully *monitor* student behavior to determine whether the rules and procedures are being followed. The purpose of this monitoring is to detect inappropriate behavior before it becomes a major problem and to clarify any misunderstanding students may have about what you expect. Many teachers have to practice their monitoring skills to become effective. This means that as you work with a small group of students, you need to look up occasionally and scan the classroom or move around the room to check students' work.

Monitoring early in the year is especially important to determine whether the amount and difficulty of homework and other assignments are appropriate to the ability levels of the students in the class. If certain students are having difficulty, you can decide whether changes in instructional approaches are needed.

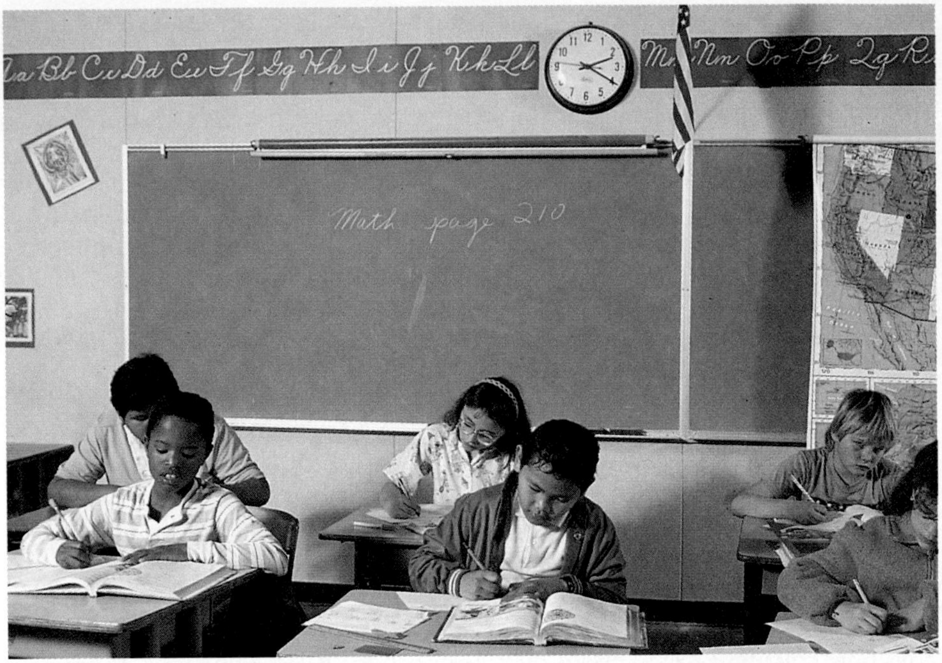

It takes careful planning, teaching rules, and monitoring student behavior to develop the type of classroom environment that is conducive to learning.

Another aspect of maintaining a good management system is *managing inappropriate behavior.* You may do an excellent job of presenting the rules and procedures, but if inappropriate behavior is not called to the attention of students, you can expect trouble. For example, once students begin missing assignments, they are likely to develop a pattern of behavior that is difficult to change for the remainder of the year.

Evertson and Emmer (1982b) report that effective managers in their study used direct and simple methods to deal with failure to follow rules. They made clear requests regarding the behavior they expected and avoided overreaction and emotionality, using the following procedures:

- Ask the student to stop the inappropriate behavior. The teacher maintains contact with the child until the appropriate behavior is correctly performed.
- Make eye-contact with the student until appropriate behavior returns. This is suitable when the teacher is certain the student knows what the correct procedure is.
- Restate or remind the student of the correct rule or procedure.
- Ask the student to identify the correct procedure. Give feedback if the student does not understand it.
- Impose the consequence or penalty of the rule or procedure violation. Usually, the consequence for violating a procedure is simply to perform the procedure until it is correctly done. When the student understands the procedure and is not complying in order to receive attention or for other inappropriate reasons, the teacher can use a mild penalty, such as withholding a privilege.

- Change the activity. Frequently, off-task behavior occurs when students are engaged too long in repetitive, boring tasks or in aimless recitations. Injecting variety in seatwork, refocusing discussion, or changing the activity to one requiring another type of student response is appropriate when off-task behavior spreads widely throughout a class. (p. 27)

assertive discipline. A method of classroom management developed by Canter that emphasizes the rights of teachers to teach and the rights of students to learn.

The final aspect of Evertson and Emmer's approach to formulating an effective management system is *developing student accountability.* This phase involves several important behaviors:

- *Clarity of work assignments*, covering such details as completeness, due dates, and procedures for makeup work
- *Communicating assignments* so that every student knows exactly what to do and how assignments will be graded
- *Monitoring student work* during class by moving around the room and systematically checking each student's progress
- *Checking work* to provide feedback for assignments
- *Giving feedback to students* by returning assignments as soon as possible, meeting with them to review progress, and/or allowing them to keep a record of their own work in each grading period

The primary purpose of accountability is to communicate to students that you really mean what you say and that you are implementing the procedures you established on the first day of class. It does not take students long to determine inconsistency between what a teacher says and does. Think of some of your own instructors who began the first day of class discussing how the course would be taught and what was expected of the students. Did the instructors follow through? How did students respond? Sharing some of these experiences with other students in your class would be helpful in understanding the importance of establishing accountability.

Assertive Discipline

? How does assertive discipline differ from Evertson and Emmer's recommendations for classroom management?

One of the most popular and controversial methods of classroom management is **assertive discipline.** Thousands of teachers are trained in this method throughout the country each year. Assertive discipline, developed by Canter (1976), emphasizes teachers' rights to an orderly classroom and identifies procedures that they can take to ensure these rights. Assertive discipline encourages teachers to expect students to behave appropriately;

DEBATE FORUM

How Effective Is Assertive Discipline?

Argument: After reviewing the research on assertive discipline, Curwin and Mendler (1989) stated:

> We see assertive discipline as little more than an attractive, well-marketed behavior modification program in which one person (teacher or administrator) has all the power to define the rules while offering group and individual rewards for compliance and administering punishments through public disclosure. There is no systematic means by which students are allowed any input into the process. Nowhere are they viewed as capable critical thinkers or decision makers. . . . [Canter's] program implicitly sees students as the cause of all problems, so there are no demands on anybody else in the system to change. (p. 83)

to use an assertive response style—for example, "Don't answer questions unless you raise your hand and I call on you," rather than "You are constantly answering questions without raising your hand" (nonassertive style) or "Learn the rules or you're going out of here" (hostile response style); to set limits (i.e., tell students what behaviors you want and need from them); and to follow through on limits (i.e., tell students the positive consequences of appropriate behavior and the negative consequences of failure to comply).

Assertive discipline is a more "take charge" approach than recommended by Evertson and Emmer (1982b). Canter (1976) suggests the following for the beginning of the school year:

- Decide on behaviors you want from students, together with the positive and negative consequences.
- Take your list to the principal for approval and support.
- At the first meeting with new students, discuss the behavior, consequences, and methods to follow through you intend to use. Keep the list of behaviors (rules) to six or less.
- Stress that no student will be allowed to break the rules. Tell the students exactly what will happen each time a rule is broken (e.g., first offense, name written on blackboard and warning issued; sec-

In addition, Render, Padilla, and Frank (1989a, 1989b) have presented critical reviews of assertive discipline emphasizing that the research does not support the claim by Canter that it will greatly reduce discipline.

Counterargument: Teachers have a right to function in a orderly classroom. If they take the steps recommended by assertive discipline they can develop such a classroom. Many teachers report that assertive discipline does work despite what the research says (McCormack, 1989)!

What do you think? This issue forces teachers to consider where they stand on the continuum between obedience to authority and teaching personal responsibility (Curwin & Mendler, 1988). Is there a middle ground? Is it essential first to establish obedience and respect before one can teach personal responsibility? Or is student input in establishing rules a necessary step in teaching personal responsibility? In Chapter 5 you read about values clarification. Here's an excellent opportunity to clarify your own values! If you are interested in this issue, you may want to read the references in this section to further explore the issue.

ond, check placed by name and 10-minute removal from lesson; third, second check by name and 15-minute removal from lesson; fourth, third check by name and teacher calls parents; fifth, fourth check and student meets with the principal).
- Ask the students to write the behaviors and consequences on a sheet of paper, take the plan home, have their parents read and sign it, and return it the next day.
- Emphasize repeatedly that these rules will help the class toward its responsibility of learning and behaving acceptably.
- Ask students to repeat orally what is expected and what will happen for compliance and for violations.
- Prepare a short letter concerning the plan to go home to parents, indicating your need for their support and your pleasure in collaborating with them toward the benefit of their child.
- Implement the assertive discipline plan immediately. (pp. 136–139)

Canter believes that reinforcement or positive consequences are important aspects of developing a management plan and favors the use of such consequences as personal attention from the teacher, positive notes to parents, special awards and privileges, and material (e.g., stickers and tickets to special events) and group rewards (e.g., class parties).

with-it-ness. A teacher's ability to communicate to students that he or she knows what is happening in the classroom

KEY INSTRUCTIONAL STRATEGIES

? What type of instructional behaviors lead to effective classroom management?

In the orientation to this chapter, I pointed out that the differences between successful and unsuccessful classroom managers are related to the planning and preparation for instruction and to the techniques of group management used by the successful teachers to prevent inattention and boredom.

The major instructional behaviors used by effective classroom managers that were identified by Kounin (1970) and supported by research by Brophy and Evertson (1976) and Anderson, Evertson, and Brophy (1979) include the following.

With-it-ness

With-it-ness refers to teachers' ability to communicate, by their actual behavior, that they know what the students are doing. Students often refer to these teachers as "having eyes in the back of their head." The *with-it* teachers were quick in reacting to possible problems in the classroom, whereas the less successful managers often made mistakes that led to disruptions. Examples include waiting too long to respond to misbehavior, thereby causing a minor problem to turn into a major one; blaming the

Can you recall past teachers who had different levels of with-it-ness? How did their behavior influence classroom management?

wrong individuals for misbehavior; and overreacting by shouting or screaming, when the situation called for a lesser response. The major advantage of with-it-ness is the ability to respond to potential problems before they become serious. When students realize that the teacher knows what is going on, they are less likely to become involved in unproductive classroom behavior.

overlapping. The ability of a teacher to do two or more things at once.

signal continuity. The ability of a teacher to move lessons along at a brisk pace and to alert students to what they should attend to.

Overlapping

Overlapping refers to teachers' ability to deal with two matters at the same time and to make transitions between different kinds of activity smoothly without having to stop and break the pace of classroom activities. A good example of overlapping occurs when two students are talking to each other while the teacher is presenting a lesson. Rather than call attention to the students, the teacher walks slowly toward them while continuing the presentation. The students would most likely stop talking, and the teacher would continue the lesson uninterrupted. Think of examples of situations in which overlapping did *not* take place because the teachers you observed handled the matter inappropriately.

Signal Continuity and Momentum in Lessons

Lessons of successful teachers proceed smoothly and at a good pace. In addition, they waste little time moving from one activity to another, and students are given a *signal* as to what they should attend to. The lessons of unsuccessful teachers lack cohesiveness and **signal continuity**. Kounin found that student inattentiveness and misbehavior often were linked to discontinuity in a lesson, which in turn was linked to inadequate teacher preparation. Classroom discipline problems increased when the teachers began to wander for no apparent reason, repeat and review material that was understood, pause to think about their next move, prepare materials, or interrupt the lesson to deal with other concerns that could have been postponed (e.g., writing a note to the principal or reminding a student to complete a chore in the middle of an algebra lesson).

Variety and Challenge in Seatwork

Kounin also found that students' involvement in seatwork was related to the challenge and variety that the work provided. They became bored with busywork. The implication is that if students are expected to work diligently at independent work for long periods, the work should be at an appropriate level of difficulty and provide interest and variety. However, take some caution in applying this information. The research indicates that learning is increased when students experience a high level of success in completing tasks (e.g., 80–90 percent). The teacher must balance the degree of challenge with the probability of success, because variety and challenge with *low* levels of success will lead to less learning.

In summary, teachers who produce substantial achievement gains in their students tend to behave in the following ways (Brophy & Evertson, 1976):

- They prevent most potential problems from occurring.
- They move activities along at a good pace without confusion or loss of focus.
- They provide seatwork that is at the right level of difficulty for students and is interesting enough to hold their attention.
- They monitor the entire class continuously and can do two or more things simultaneously without having to break the flow of classroom events.

TOWARD SELF-REGULATION OF CLASSROOM BEHAVIOR

In Chapter 3, I emphasized the importance of developing self-regulated learners and discussed how various learning strategies (see Table 3.1) could be used by students to help them become more successful. It might be useful at this time to consider how self-management might be applied to students' social behavior. First, students could be more involved in the development of classroom rules. Second, more time could be allotted to asking students to reflect on the reasons that certain rules are needed as well as reasons for their misbehavior. Third, students could be given opportunity to consider how they could plan, monitor, and regulate their own behavior in the future. The Classroom Application on improving social skills later in the chapter (page 312) is helpful toward this end. Fourth, as the year begins the teacher could ask students to review the classroom rules and recommend needed modifications.

McCaslin and Good (1992) state that students interpret classroom events differently. Therefore, any management system must be modified for different students. For example, some students need more signaling or alerting that they are not attending to the task. Also, if the teacher assumes all the responsibility for management (e.g., does the alerting and maintains the accountability), the students will not learn self-regulation and self-control.

INSTRUCTIONAL ORGANIZATION

Well-managed classrooms facilitate more learning and higher rates of student achievement than do poorly managed classrooms. One of the major reasons for this finding is that more effective managers are better users of instructional time.

Use of Time

allocated time. The time that a teacher designates for a particular learning task.

> Why is the use of time an important component of an effective management system?

How does the use of classroom time relate to learning? In a typical elementary school classroom, the daily activities can be divided into three major parts: academic activities (e.g., reading, mathematics, and social studies), nonacademic activities (e.g., music, art, storytime, sharing), and noninstructional activities (e.g., transitions, class business). The Beginning Teacher Evaluation Study (BTES) reported that at the fifth-grade level, the average amount of time spent in academic, nonacademic, and noninstructional activities was 60 percent, 23 percent, and 17 percent, respectively (Rosenshine, 1980). Individual teachers vary greatly in the time used for different activities and subjects, and as a result, students in some classes have much more opportunity to learn subject matter than do others.

Educators are interested in many different aspects of time—the length of the school year, the number of days a student attends school in a given year, or even the length of the school day. Researchers have identified that the more time a student spends actually engaged in an academic task, the higher the student's achievement (Fisher & Berliner, 1985).

Four types of instructional time need to be differentiated (see Figure 7.1). **Allocated time** is the time that a teacher designates for a particular

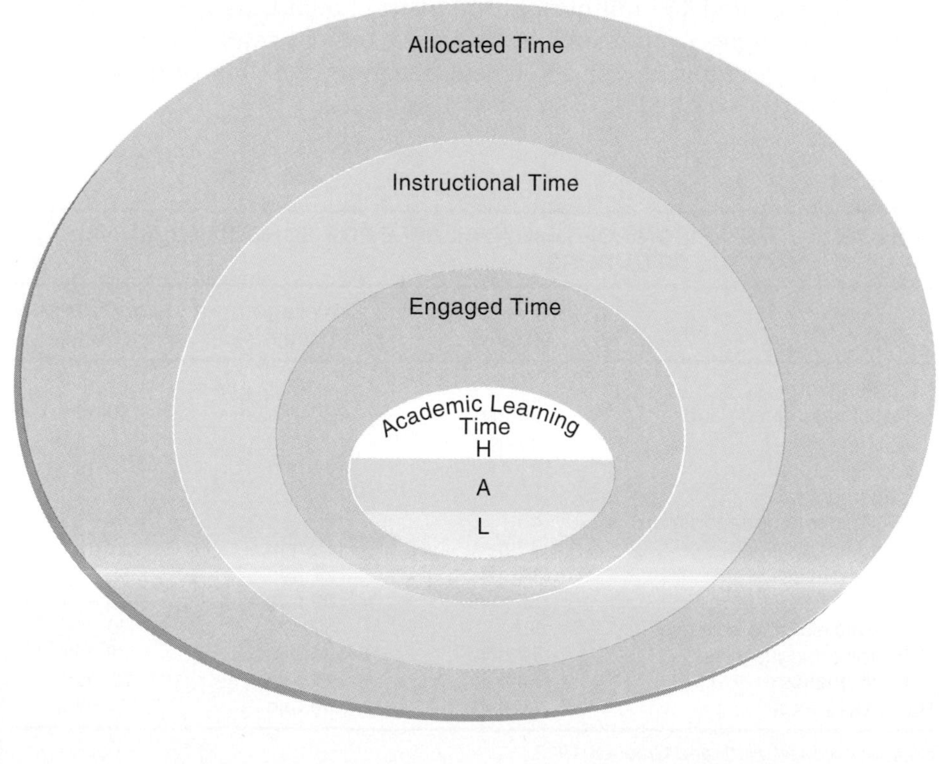

Figure 7.1 Different Levels of Time in Instruction.

instructional time. The amount of time left for instruction after routine management and administrative tasks are completed.

engaged time. The time students are actively paying attention or learning.

academic learning time (ALT). The amount of time a student spends on academic tasks while performing at a high rate of success.

learning task. In an elementary school classroom a teacher may allocate an hour for reading. In junior high or high school, teachers have less control over the allocation of time because most of the instruction is determined by fixed periods of time. **Instructional time** is the amount of time left for teaching after routine management and administrative tasks are completed (e.g., taking attendance, making announcements, and dealing with classroom behavioral problems). **Engaged time** (also called time-on-task), a subset of instruction time, refers to the time students are actually involved in the task. Finally, a student can be successful at different rates—high (H), average (A), and low (L). Thus **academic learning time (ALT)**, a subset of engaged time, is the amount of time a student spends on academic tasks while performing at a high rate of success. For some students, this time is minimal compared with the allocated time for instruction. Researchers have determined that the more a measure relates to the quality of a student's classroom time, such as engaged time or academic learning time, the more the measure is related to achievement. The amount of time scheduled for instruction is not as crucial as how well the students are engaged in the particular lesson and their rate of success; students can be engaged in instruction, but if they are not learning the material, then obviously the engagement will have little impact on their achievement.

Table 7.2 depicts three hypothetical elementary school classrooms in terms of the use of time. The averages were obtained from data reported in a number of investigations (Caldwell, Huitt, & Graeber, 1982). Look at the average situation, in which the length of the school day is about five hours. The total allocated time for basic skills is 165 minutes a day. Sixty percent (99 of the allocated 165 minutes) of the instructional time is spent actively working, or engaged, in a subject area (engagement rate). The percentage of academic learning time is 50 percent, meaning that half of the engaged time is spent at a high level of success.

TABLE 7.2 COMPARISONS OF TIME AVAILABLE FOR SCHOOLING ACROSS VARIOUS SITUATIONS

	Low Average (Daily)	Average (Daily)	High Average (Daily)
Allocated time			
Reading/language arts	90 min.	120 min.	150 min.
Mathematics	30 min.	45 min.	60 min.
Basic skills total	120 min.	165 min.	210 min.
Engagement rate			
(% Student engaged time)	45	60	75
Reading/language arts	41 min.	72 min.	113 min.
Mathematics	14 min.	27 min.	45 min.
Basic skills total	55 min.	99 min.	158 min.
Academic learning time (%)	30	50	70
Reading/language arts	12 min.	36 min.	79 min.
Mathematics	4 min.	14 min.	32 min.
Basic skills total	16 min.	50 min.	111 min.

Source: Caldwell, Hutt, and Graeber, 1982.

The school day is 4½ hours and 5½ hours, respectively, for the low-average and high-average classrooms. Compare the differences in time use. What is striking about the data is that the daily average for academic learning time ranges from a low average of 16 minutes a day to a high average of 111 minutes a day. This means that the students in the high-average class spend twice as much academic learning time as in the average class and almost seven times as much as in the low-average class. Furthermore, because these data were generated for average situations, there are classrooms in which the daily academic learning time for basic skills is *less* than 16 minutes a day! Also notice that the time spent on mathematics is considerably less than the time spent on reading and language arts. You can begin to understand why engaged time and academic learning time are related to school achievement. If students are working at a high success rate in mathematics for *4 minutes or less* a day, how can they possibly cover the content of the course during the year?

It is important for teachers to evaluate the amount of time allocated to different subject areas to ensure that all content areas receive the recommended instructional time during the year. In addition, improvements should be made in the use of time. I am not saying that students must be kept busy every single minute during the day. Time spent in transition from one activity to the next, daydreaming, socializing, working on special assignments, and experiences out of the classroom are a normal part of classroom life. But if these activities take up too much time, they can interfere with learning. Consider for a moment that an improvement of engaged time of 10 minutes a day translates into 50 minutes a week, and 1,500 minutes a year (based on a 150-day school year). Much of this improvement can be made by more effective management procedures such as starting class on time and avoiding early finishes, developing routines to handle classroom procedures and interruptions, and minimizing time spent on discipline.

Seatwork

? How can seatwork be more productive?

One aspect of school that most students remember is the hours spent doing seatwork at one's desk. At times, the work was interesting and useful, but sometimes it was redundant and boring. In fact, very often you probably didn't even know why you were doing the work.

In order to deal with the individual differences in the classroom, teachers work with small groups of students while giving independent seatwork to the remaining students in the class. In some classes students spend up to 70 percent of their time doing independent work (Fisher et al., 1978). If students do not use this time effectively, they will waste a large amount of the instructional time available to them. In addition, confusion during seatwork can disrupt the class and limit the effectiveness of the teacher who is working with other students in the classroom.

Data from the Beginning Teacher Evaluation Study (BTES) indicated that students are less likely to be on-task doing seatwork than when they are working with their teacher. In mathematics, increased seatwork was negatively related to engagement, which means that the more time spent doing seatwork, the less students were engaged in their work. Recommendations from this study were that teachers should keep seatwork time as low as possible and increase students' substantive interaction with the teacher or aide during seatwork (e.g., by having students ask them more questions about their seatwork) (Rosenshine, 1980).

Anderson et al. (1984) have investigated student behavior during seatwork assignments and gathered important information on how students think about what is occurring in the classroom and how teachers affect students' learning in the classroom. Low achievers often did not have the skills to complete their assignments independently. As a result, they developed strategies to complete their assignments that did not contribute to their knowledge of the subject matter. Students obtained "correct" answers without practicing the skill or concept that was the basis of the lesson. The students' behavior was similar to behavior observed by Holt (1982)—children often perceive the main purpose of school as getting daily tasks done, or at least out of the way, with a minimum of effort and unpleasantness. Whether they learn something during this process appears to be a secondary concern of these students.

Anderson et al. (1984) found differences in the way high achievers and low achievers approached seatwork. The high achievers expected the work to make sense to them and asked questions when they did not understand something, or they developed useful strategies for solving the problems themselves. The low achievers, however, were more likely to develop strategies to merely complete the assignment and did not ask questions

It is important for teachers to monitor students' seatwork.

CLASSROOM Application

IMPROVING INSTRUCTIONAL ORGANIZATION

Effective classroom management can lead to greater student learning. The paragraphs that follow contain suggestions for making seatwork more effective and are adapted from Anderson et al. (1984).

SELECTING SEATWORK ASSIGNMENTS

Select content that is at the correct level of difficulty, and diagnose the assignments to determine possible problems that students may have in completing the work. In this way you will be able to point out strategies before the students begin and are more likely to determine the nature of the problems during the completion of the assignment.

PRESENTING SEATWORK ASSIGNMENTS

Remind the students before they start the assignment why they are doing it (e.g., "This will help you prepare for adding fractions") and the strategy that they should use to solve the task. You may even "think aloud" while solving one or two problems on the board to demonstrate them.

MONITORING ASSIGNMENTS

Circulate around the room to see how students are doing before beginning a lesson with another group. If you note a pattern of errors,

continued

when they failed to understand. The researchers suggested that low achievers were so used to classroom learning not making sense to them that they thought that not understanding something was "business as usual." The following (Anderson et al., 1984) are two examples of ineffective seatwork strategy:

> Randy could not read some of the words on the board assignment. Even when he did read some, he tried to decide on a word to go in the blank as soon as he came to the blank in the sentence, even if it was the second or third word. That is, he did not read the entire sentence to provide a context for the choice. When he did not figure out the answer

you can give a quick explanation, change the assignment, or ask the students to wait until you can give them more attention. Second, occasionally ask the students to explain how they obtained certain answers (both correct and incorrect). This forces the students to think about the strategies they use to solve problems and demonstrates to the students that obtaining right answers is not the only goal of education. Third, establish a system through which students can receive help when they have problems. Some teachers set up a buddy system so that students can help one another; other teachers use a system whereby students with a problem place a "help card" at their desk and wait for help from the teacher.

EVALUATING SEATWORK

Develop routines for checking seatwork. Some teachers check it immediately after it is completed, and others check it the next day. The important point is that if you expect students to take seatwork seriously, you must provide feedback. If not, strategies for completing seatwork without real understanding will surely increase.

I have heard many students ask: "Why should I spend a lot of time on this assignment? The teacher never corrects it, anyway!" One of the problems that I faced as a beginning math teacher was spending hours correcting papers, only to see the students throw them in the wastebasket without even looking at them. I mentioned this situation to an experienced teacher, who suggested that the next day I walk around the class and ask the students to explain why the problems were marked wrong. After continuing this monitoring for a few days, I noticed that the students began analyzing their papers in preparation for my visit to their desks. This advice went a long way in making my first year of teaching more effective.

Table 7.3 includes a list of teacher behaviors related to instructional organization that can improve a teacher's use of time and make seatwork more effective. You can use this list to help you plan for instruction and evaluate your performance.

immediately, he asked another child for the answer. In this manner, he often received most of the answers from others and completed his assignment without learning to read the new vocabulary words (ostensibly the purpose of the task). (p. 18)

Beth, unable to read enough of the Weekly Reader articles to answer the questions, simply copied the questions and wrote answers that seemed

TABLE 7.3 INSTRUCTIONAL ORGANIZATION

	Competencies
	Allocated Time
1.1	Maximizes time in instruction by continually scheduling students in direct instruction (e.g., interacts with 70 percent or more of the students per hour).
1.2	Minimizes time in noninstructional activities (e.g., spends 80 percent or more of the class time in instructional activities).
1.3	Keeps transition time between lessons short (e.g., no more than 3 minutes between change of students and activity; no more than 30 seconds when a change of activity only).
1.4	Establishes procedures for lessons that signal a clear beginning and end.
1.5	Gains all students' attention at the beginning of the lesson, and maintains student attention during lesson at 90 percent level.
1.6	Prepares students for transitions in advance by stating behavioral expectations and informing students that lesson is drawing to a close.
	Engaged Time
2.1	Maintains students' attention during seatwork at 80 percent levels or higher.
2.2	Monitors seatwork students continuously through eye scanning.
2.3	Circulates among seatwork students between lessons to assist students and to monitor progress.
2.4	Maintains seatwork accuracy at 90 percent level or higher.
2.5	Tells rationale for seatwork, and communicates the importance of the assignment.
2.6	Provides active forms of seatwork practice clearly related to academic goals.
2.7	Sets seatwork and assignment standards (neatness, accuracy, due dates).
2.8	Uses tutoring (e.g., peer, volunteers, aides) and other specialized instructional technology to increase opportunity for active academic responding during seatwork.
2.9	Establishes procedures for early finishers, students who are stalled, and those seeking help.
2.10	Schedules time to review seatwork.
2.11	Requires that students correct work and make up missed or unfinished work.
2.12	Gives informative feedback to students in making written or verbal corrections.

Source: Englert, 1984.

logical to her, without consulting the articles. In the one instance when she did look, she searched for a number word to answer "How many legs does a grasshopper have?" She came to the phrase "five eyes" in the article and copied the number five. (p. 19)

Do you have any favorite seatwork strategies you can recall from your school days?

token economy. Reinforcing students by supplying tokens that can later be exchanged for some reinforcement.

response cost. The removal of previously earned tokens or points in a token economy intervention program.

DEALING WITH MANAGEMENT PROBLEMS

You can choose from a number of approaches to classroom management, each of which views the role of the teacher in a different manner and reflects different beliefs about students. The behavioral approach is based on the assumption that children's behavior is a product of their reinforcement history. The teacher's role is to establish rules and procedures, communicate them to students, and implement rewards and punishment according to how well students comply with the rules. The humanistic approach is based on the notion that students, in general, want to behave appropriately, but sometimes they don't understand the causes or consequences of misbehavior. The teacher's role is to develop a strong, trusting relationship and encourage good communication in the classroom so that students can learn to solve problems more effectively. Finally, an approach that is based on both behavioral and humanistic notions (what Glickman & Wolfgang, 1979, call the *interactionist* approach) holds that a student is influenced by both personal and environmental factors. The teacher's role is to help students understand their own behavior and its consequences. This position is intermediate to the behavioral and humanistic positions in that it stresses the importance of students' rational decision making while creating an important role for the teacher in *collaboratively* establishing rules and confronting students when they deviate from them (Jacobsen, Eggen, & Kauchak, 1989).

Behavioral Approaches to Classroom Management: Arranging Consequences That Increase Behavior

TOKEN ECONOMY. Many students can't function successfully in the classroom if they must wait for an extended period of time for reinforcement. In addition, for many students, social reinforcers (e.g., a smile or the statement "good work") alone are not sufficient to maintain proper classroom behavior. In these cases, the use of a **token economy** has proved to be a good method of behavior change intervention (Walker & Shea, 1988).

Tokens can be points, stars, stickers, or other objects that usually are valueless to students. Their value becomes apparent when they are exchanged for a variety of rewards such as free time, a magazine to read, the chance to be first in line for lunch, a candy bar, and so forth. This system allows teachers to provide immediate reinforcement for appropriate behavior and is especially useful when teachers are attempting to provide reinforcers to many students at once. Some teachers use an additional component called **response cost,** a system in which tokens are removed for specific inappropriate behaviors.

The following is an example of a token economy, introduced in an elementary classroom, that increased the number of completed assignments (McLaughlin & Malaby, 1972): The teacher used points as tokens and gave each student a special form to record the points; the form included the various behaviors that earned points. The behaviors were typed on the left side of the page with enough squares after each item so that students could record their earned points for each assignment and for their social behavior.

Nineteen different behaviors were identified. They included assignment completion, appropriate noon hour behavior, listening, studying, writing neatly, and so forth. In addition, a response cost component was used, in which failing to complete work, chewing gum, eating candy, and cheating resulted in losing points.

The teacher had a meeting with the students to develop a list of activities that they enjoyed. From this list, they ranked the different activities in terms of their preference. Twelve activities were listed on a bulletin board, with the price of each listed alongside. These activities included playing with classroom pets, sharpening pencils, writing on the board, playing games, and so on.

During the first token economy condition, the students earned points each day of the week, and these were exchanged each Friday. This procedure was changed later to a variable number of school days. On the day before the exchanging of points for activities, the teacher collected all the point charts, and a student in the room summed the points for other students. The students' totals for academic and social behavior were compared with the teacher's records to ensure accurate self-monitoring of points earned and lost. A student who failed to self-record enough points was given the missing points. If a student recorded more points than earned, then the student lost the opportunity to exchange points for that week.

Walker and Shea (1988) recommend the following guidelines to be applied when establishing a token economy for the classroom:

- Identify the desired classroom behaviors.
- Discuss these behaviors (in positive terms) with the students and explain exactly how the program will operate.
- Post the rules and review them often. Begin by including just a few basic rules. You can use more complex regulations after the system is operating smoothly.
- Select an appropriate token. (One of the easiest methods is to give each student a card numbered 1 to 100 or strips of colored paper.) Beware of the problem in using objects such as marbles that can be distracting if they are dropped on the floor.
- Establish reinforcers for which tokens can be exchanged.
- Develop a reward menu and post it in the classroom (e.g., reading a magazine for 15 minutes is worth 20 points, getting free time for 10 minutes is worth 15 points).
- Implement the token economy program.
- Provide immediate reinforcement for proper behavior. Many systems don't succeed because teachers fail to dispense the tokens at the appropriate time.
- Gradually change from a continuous to a variable schedule of reinforcement.

- Provide time for the students to exchange tokens for rewards.
- Revise the reward menu frequently so that the students do not get bored with the same activities or privileges.

CONTINGENCY CONTRACTING. In Chapter 2, I discussed Premack's (1959) principle that a high-probability response can be used to reinforce a low-probability response. Parents often use Premack's principle effectively: "Eat your vegetables and you can have dessert," or "Clean your

Figure 7.2 Formats Used in Contracting.
Source: Kaplan, Kohfeldt, & Sturla, 1974.

room and you can use the car to drive to the beach." Teachers have found that **contingency contracting** is another way to systematize and individualize the use of reinforcement in responding to a student's interests, needs, and abilities. *Contracting* is a procedure whereby the contingencies for reinforcement are placed into a verbal or written statement. Although the wording can differ for various students, all contracts contain some form of the basic "If . . . , then . . . " statement (Alberto & Troutman, 1990). Figure 7.2 illustrates a sample contract.

contingency contracting. A document in which a teacher and a student agree that when the student satisfactorily behaves in some specified way, he or she will be able to engage in a stated amount of some privilege.

group contingency. A rule that specifies exactly how a consequence is applied to a group.

In developing contracts with students, remember to involve the student in developing the contract, including the reinforcers; make the contract clear, and fair for both the student and the teacher (i.e., the reinforcement should be in proportion to the amount of behavior required); make the contract emphasize and reinforce accomplishments rather than obedience; and, finally, reinforce the desired behavior after it occurs (Homme et al., 1979).

GROUP-BASED CONTINGENCIES. A **group contingency** is a standard of behavior that specifies how a consequence is applied to a group. For example, it is often easier for teachers to establish a group contingency program when they have trouble instructing the class because of continuous noise rather than attempt to change the behavior of each student separately. Another factor is that when many students are misbehaving at the same time, it is often difficult to monitor each student to determine who is engaging in the misbehavior and who should receive reinforcement for appropriate behavior. In applying a group contingency, the teacher might identify an activity as a reinforcer if the noise level is reduced. If the noise level increases, the whole class would miss the activity.

Group contingencies are most appropriate when peer reinforcement is a factor in maintaining misbehavior, such as laughing at funny noises or engaging in pranks to defy the teacher for the benefit of other students. These attention-based behavior problems often are reinforced by other students in the class. Once the attention stops, the problems stop (Jenson, Sloane, & Young, 1988).

One variation of group contingencies is the "good behavior game" (Barrish, Saunders, & Wolf, 1969), in which the teacher divides the class into two teams and each team receives marks on the chalkboard each time one of its members exhibits misbehavior (e.g., talked out or got out of her seat, or moved his desk without permission). *Both* teams are winners if they receive five or fewer marks on the board over a specified period of time. If one team has more than five marks and the other team has fewer, the team with the fewer marks is the winner. In this situation, both teams can win or lose, or one team can win and the other lose.

The use of peer influence in maintaining discipline in the classroom can have powerful effects. Therefore, you should use caution to avoid negative side effects such as students threatening their teammates to "shape them up." Another caution is the possibility that one student might find it reinforcing to sabotage the team's efforts by misbehaving (Barrish et al., 1969). In this situation, the student should be removed from the team and placed in a one-person team.

Name ______________________________ Date ____________

Subject ______________________________

Was prepared for class	yes	no	NA	
Used class time well	yes	no	NA	Homework assignment
Participated in class	yes	no	NA	
Handed in homework	yes	no	NA	

Homework grade	F	D	C	B	A	NA	
Test grade	F	D	C	B	A	NA	Teacher's Initials ______

Comments

Figure 7.3 Sample School-Home Note.
Source: Kelley and Carper, 1988.

How can I involve parents in modifying their children's behavior?

HOME-BASED CONTINGENCIES. Another effective behavior-change program is to allow the student's behavior in the classroom to earn reinforcers provided by the parents at home. The student is reinforced for school performance but receives the reward at home. The teacher needs to meet with the student's parents and discuss the nature of the misbehavior and establish the guidelines for the programs. Parent-teacher cooperation often can make a program more consistent and lead to greater effectiveness. In addition, parents often can provide a greater variety of reinforcers than teachers have at their disposal in the classroom (Kelley & Carper, 1988).

While teaching junior high school mathematics, I worked with the parents of a student who never completed any homework assignments. We met and agreed upon a program whereby I would notify them each day if their child completed her homework. They agreed to purchase a ticket to a concert she wanted to attend if she handed in 90 percent of the assignments during the month.

If parents are to help the teacher reinforce appropriate academic behaviors, parents must be provided with sufficient information concerning their children's behavior so that effective consequences can be delivered at home (Kelley & Carper, 1988). One way to provide such information is through school-home notes (see Figure 7.3). Many parents never hear from a teacher unless their children have a problem. Many principals encourage teachers to call one or two parents a week or send them a note telling them the *good* behavior their children or adolescents have displayed. If you develop a positive relationship with parents, it is easier to work with them when problems develop.

? How are different learning principles used in teaching social skills?

SOCIAL SKILLS TRAINING. Many students behave inappropriately in the classroom because they lack the appropriate social skills. Social skills can be described as being either *task related* or *person related*. The former include such behaviors as attending, displaying task persistence, and complying with teacher requests; and the latter include helping and sharing, greeting others, and moderating one's aggressive behavior (Hops & Cobb, 1973). There is evidence that poor social behavior in school can adversely affect students' academic achievement and later psychological adjustment (Gresham, 1988b).

A number of strategies for training students in social skills have been developed. They are designed to teach students better interpersonal behavior and skills for functioning more successfully in the classroom. The strategies use a variety of techniques derived from behavioral psychology, many of which have already been discussed in previous chapters in this book. The following strategies are most often used in training in social skills:

- Having students *model* such exemplary behavior of others as self-control, sharing, and cooperation
- Giving students the opportunity to practice, or *role-play*, appropriate behaviors
- Using *positive reinforcement* to teach new social skills and/or to maintain the frequency of previously acquired skills
- Using *cognitive behavior modification* such as self-instructional training to emphasize the development of specific thinking skills (self-statements) to guide one's behavior in social situations

Another cognitive technique teaches students to recognize problem situations and to stop and think before acting. In essence, students are taught to interrupt their habitual nonproductive, or self-defeating, thought patterns and instead engage in more positive and productive thought processes that will guide them through problem situations (Bash & Camp, 1980) (e.g., "What is the problem?" "What is my plan?" "Am I using my plan?" and "How did I do?").

Keep a few ideas in mind before beginning training in social skills in the classroom. First, select for training only the social skills that are considered significant in the students' natural environment. This will help to ensure that the new behavior will be appreciated by others (especially parents) and, thus, reinforced. Second, make sure you select a training method that matches the students' level of functioning or ability. For example, don't require very young children to engage in detailed self-statements regarding their social behavior. Finally, when you teach a student a new skill, such as waiting for a turn, you want the student to be able to behave

CLASSROOM Application

IMPROVING STUDENTS' SOCIAL SKILLS

The five steps in the skill-streaming program for improving social behavior are as follows (McGinnis et al., 1984):

1. Modeling
2. Role-playing
3. Performance feedback
4. Practice
5. Reinforcement

As an example, let's see how each of these steps is used to teach the skill "Dealing with Your Anger."

MODELING

The first step in teaching students how to deal with anger is to model this skill for them. To do this, you must first task-analyze the skill into specific behavioral steps. For example, try the following steps:

1. Stop and count to 10.
2. Think about your choices: I can tell the person why I'm angry, I can walk away, or I can try to relax.
3. Act out your best choice.

Then demonstrate each of these steps as it would be performed in a real-life situation. As you model, verbalize the skill steps. Verbalizing aids learning and helps to increase the effectiveness of the modeling display by demonstrating the cognitive process underlying the skill.

It is sometimes helpful to model more than one example of the skill so that the students can see how it is used in different situations. You might, for example, model controlling anger with a teacher, a parent, and a peer. It is also helpful to use more than one model and to select models who are like the student in important ways (same age, sex, socioeconomic status, etc.).

ROLE-PLAYING

After you have modeled the skill steps, the students should practice the demonstrated behaviors. This is best accomplished by having the students role-play a situation relevant to the use of the skill. For example, they could role-play controlling anger if they lose a game or get hit with a ball. To add realism to the role-play, students can choose role-playing partners who closely resemble someone they have previously encountered in anger-provoking situations.

While they are role-playing, encourage the students to verbalize the skill steps. This aids in controlling impulsivity and in organizing skill steps in sequence.

To facilitate generalization of the new skill, have the students role-play various situations (e.g., getting angry in class, out on the playground, and at home), and with a variety of different partners (e.g., other peers, teachers, the bus driver).

FEEDBACK

When the students have finished role-playing, it is important that you give them feedback about their performance. Feedback should be quite specific, focusing first on the accuracy of the performance (Were all the steps enacted, or were some omitted?) and then on the quality of the performance (Were the students enthusiastic? Was their body language appropriate for their roles?). If a student skipped a step or otherwise performed poorly, show what to do by reteaching or prompting. Always follow your negative comments by constructive suggestions on how to improve.

Be sure to praise or otherwise reinforce students following a good performance. This engenders feelings of success in the students and gives them confidence to perform the skill in a real situation. However, try to avoid giving reinforcement if the students significantly depart from their prescribed roles. McGinnis et al. (1984) suggest that in these instances a poor performance can be praised as "a good try," and then corrective feedback, reteaching, or direct guidance can be given so that the students know how to perform the skill successfully.

PRACTICE

Once the students know how to perform a new skill successfully, they should have opportunities to practice the skill in other settings. You can accomplish this in a variety of ways. For example, the teacher can enlist the services of an informed collaborator (someone outside the training setting) who is willing to practice with the students. A fellow teacher or an older student could be a good choice. Practicing with

continued

other people helps the children hone their skills and aids in the generalization of new behaviors.

Social skills learned in school can also be practiced at home. McGinnis, Sauerbry, and Nichols (1985) suggest the use of "homework" assignments that require students to select particular skills for home practice. Practice results, which are recorded by the students on a homework sheet, are later evaluated by students and teacher.

Another technique for practicing skills comes from the work of McGinnis et al. (1984). This technique, called "Red Flag," involves testing students on skill use in "set-up" situations. For example, for the skill of dealing with anger, students may be told that they will be provoked by the teacher sometime during the day (the exact time is not given). When this happens, the students should try to remember to respond appropriately. When the teacher has provoked the students and they have responded, the teacher calls, "Red Flag." The students' responses are then mutually evaluated by student and teacher.

Regardless of how a student practices, it is important to keep in mind that practice makes perfect only if the student practices correctly. Incorrect responses are difficult to remediate once they become part of a student's behavioral repertoire, and thus one cannot overemphasize the need to carefully monitor each step in the acquisition of a new behavior.

REINFORCEMENT

Reinforcement, the final component in the social skills training program of McGinnis et al. (1984), helps in maintaining and generalizing newly trained skills. Once a skill such as dealing with anger is learned, encourage the students to use it whenever appropriate. One way to do this, at least initially, is to reward the students each time the skill is performed. Rewards can be either tangible (such as prizes, food, or privileges) or of a social nature (e.g., praise, positive attention, smiles). The type of reward should depend on the age of the students, their level of maturity, and so on. As the students become more proficient in using the skills, reinforcement can be "thinned" or reduced to a level that is comparable to its occurrence in the natural environment.

A primary goal in training is to get the students eventually to reinforce themselves for appropriate behavior. Self-reinforcement can be encouraged by teaching students to make positive self-statements and to reward themselves for a job well done. It is important, however, that the students learn to evaluate their behavior accurately so that they do not reward themselves for poor or inappropriate responses.

appropriately in a variety of settings (e.g., classroom, playground, and home) and with various people (e.g., teachers, peers, and parents). As a result, plan for the practice of the skill in several situations and with various people to ensure generalization of the trained skill. This issue is a major concern in all programs of behavior modification.

The classroom application beginning on page 312 involves a five-step social skills training program developed by McGinnis et al. (1984) for elementary school children, called *skill-streaming.* A similar program is available for adolescents (Goldstein et al., 1980).

Behavioral Approaches to Classroom Management: Arranging Consequences That Decrease Behavior

In Chapter 2 you learned about extinction as a method for decreasing behavior. It is based on the principle that if a reinforcer is removed, the probability of recurrence of the behavior is decreased. Other methods of decreasing and eliminating behavior are reinforcement of incompatible behavior, stimulus control techniques, and punishment (including the use of time-out).

REINFORCING INCOMPATIBLE BEHAVIORS. The key to changing undesirable behavior is the successful strengthening of desirable behavior that will compete with and eventually replace undesirable patterns of behavior. Reinforcing a student for cooperating with the teacher is incompatible with sitting passively; working at one's desk is incompatible with wandering around the room. Gardner (1974) states:

> It is easy to punish inappropriate behavior as it occurs; it is more difficult to identify and to provide systematic reinforcement for appropriate competing modes of responding. The major question should be "what should the child be doing at the time he is behaving inappropriately?" Once this is established and demonstrated to the child, such behaviors or reasonable alternatives can more easily be strengthened through reinforcement. (p. 136)

Becker et al. (1967) demonstrated that selective reinforcement of desired behaviors can replace a variety of undesirable ones. A group of children attending elementary school exhibited a high degree of undesirable behaviors—pulling hair, ignoring the teacher's requests, fighting, and walking around the room. After explaining the classroom rules to the children, the teacher ignored the inappropriate behavior but praised any behavior that enhanced learning. In a short time the social reinforcement for appropriate behavior led to a significant reduction in the behaviors that were incompatible with effective classroom learning.

CHANGING THE STIMULUS ENVIRONMENT. Some behavior can be controlled by changing the stimulus condition that influences the behavior.

If a student is distracted by the noise outside the classroom, shutting the window may alleviate the distraction. If a difficult task is frustrating to a student, the teacher may want to replace the task with a less difficult one.

Instead of changing the stimulus conditions influencing inappropriate behavior, the teacher may find it helpful to present cues that inhibit problem behaviors. When two students are not working, the teacher may sit down by the students or walk by them.

Last, the teacher can prompt desired behavior that competes with problem behavior. The student who finishes work and gets into mischief can be asked to help pass out some material to the rest of the class.

Each of these procedures can prevent the occurrence of inappropriate behavior and provide the teacher with an opportunity to prompt desirable behaviors that can be reinforced.

? What are the advantages and disadvantages in the use of punishment?

USING PUNISHMENT. The last procedure used to weaken behavior is punishment. There are two basic forms of punishment: the presentation of a distressing stimulus (being yelled at, ridiculed, or threatened) and the withdrawal of a positive reinforcer (taking away a magazine or preventing a child from playing with peers).

Most of us have witnessed teachers who spend considerable time yelling at students but rarely get students to maintain appropriate behaviors for very long. You might wonder why some teachers continue to nag, yell, and scream. One reason is that they have probably been reinforced for this behavior! Let's look at how this might work in getting students to stay in their seats. When the teacher sees a student out of his seat, she begins the tirade: "Get back in your seat. How many times . . . blah . . . blah . . . blah . . . !" The student returns to his seat; the teacher has been reinforced. This behavior sequence leads to an increase in yelling and a decrease in ignoring out-of-seat behavior. Soon the process recommences. The teacher often feels bad about yelling so much but learns that yelling suppresses behavior—albeit only for a while (Poteet, 1973).

Psychologists have found that punishment does not eliminate behavior; it merely suppresses it (Cooper, Heron, & Heward, 1987). Clarizio (1980) points out that "punishment simply serves notice to stop inappropriate behaviors. It does not indicate to the student what behaviors are appropriate in the situation" (p. 133). He believes that positive reinforcement should be used with punishment so that desirable behavior can be developed to replace the unacceptable behavior. Earlier in the chapter you read about how important it is to teach students appropriate behavior beginning the first day of school.

Sometimes a teacher's behavior instills undesirable behavior in students, unbeknownst to the teacher. In an interesting study, Madsen et al. (1968) found that the more frequently teachers asked young children to sit down after getting out of their seats at inappropriate times, the more fre-

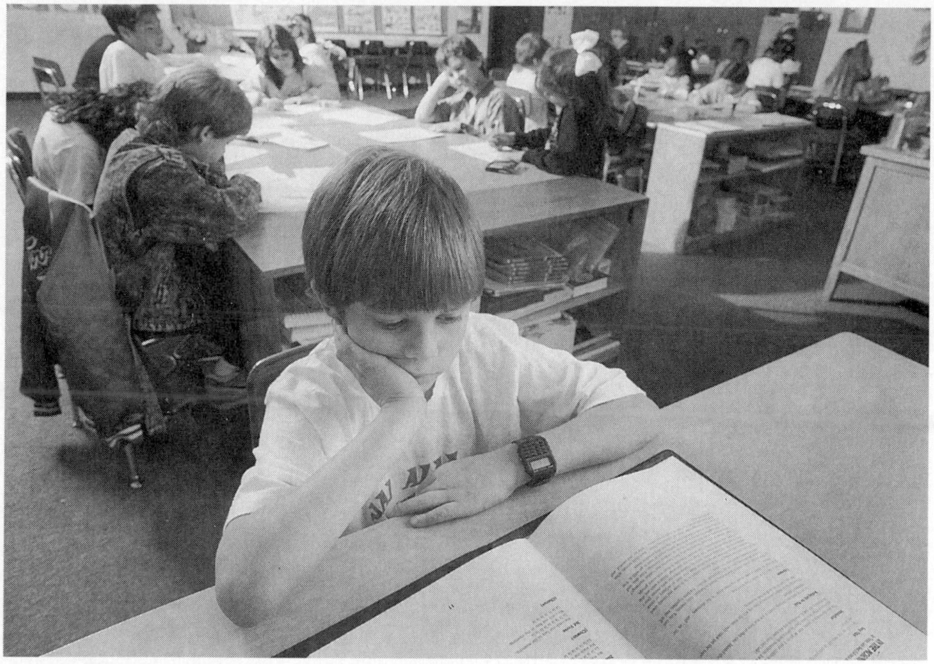

Placing a student who doesn't follow classroom rules in time-out can be an effective method of behavior modification.

quently they stood up. It appeared that although the teachers intended their remarks as only mild reprimands, their social attention was reinforcing to the students. The undesired behavior increased rather than decreased.

There is evidence to suggest that punishment administered immediately upon the child's initiation of inappropriate behavior is more effective than deferred punishment (Walters, Parke, & Cane, 1965). Once the child has completed the misbehavior, self-reward or peer reward maintains the behavior and to some extent counteracts the inhibiting effects of punishment. In other words, the child has already accomplished what was intended! As a child, you may have heard a baby-sitter say something like, "Just wait until your parents come home!" This threat probably didn't change your behavior much while the baby-sitter was there, but you probably did learn one thing—to avoid your parents' return.

The teacher should be aware of some other effects of punishment. First, the person undergoing constant punishment learns to avoid situations. The student may not want to attend class, or, if physical escape is impossible, may psychologically escape by not listening in class. Second, punishment can produce fear or anxiety so that the teacher, the classroom, or educational materials can become aversive (negative) stimuli because of their association with unpleasant consequences. The anxiety response occurs through the process of classical conditioning. Last, punishment does not direct the student to alternative behavior.

Time-out. Many teachers prefer the withdrawal of a positive reinforcer, used under the proper conditions, as a more effective use of punishment. One technique in this category is *time-out,* a procedure that temporarily removes the student from a reinforcing situation and places him or her in a location where the reinforcement is minimal or unlikely to occur. This procedure is used in assertive discipline when two or more checks are placed by a student's name on the chalkboard.

Three types of time-out procedures can be used in the classroom (Lewellen, 1980). *Observational time-out* is a procedure in which students are removed from a reinforcing situation by being placed on the outer perimeter of the activity, are asked to place their heads down on their desks, and/or have all materials taken from them. Sometimes they are asked to observe the appropriate behaviors of the rest of the students in class. *Exclusion* is a procedure in which the students are not allowed to observe the activities of the group and are placed in a location in the room where there is little interest, such as behind a cabinet or bookcase. Finally, *seclusion* is a procedure whereby the students leave the classroom and go to a special "time-out room."

Sometimes teachers use time-out ineffectively because the experience actually ends up as reinforcing rather than nonreinforcing to the student. I can remember a situation in high school in which the teacher placed a student behind a large bookcase in the back of the classroom. As the teacher presented his lesson, the student kept peeking from behind the bookcase and making funny faces. The rest of the students in the class started laughing and no longer attended to their work. A good time was had by all! Unfortunately, the student was reinforced (by receiving attention from his classmates) for his inappropriate behavior.

There are some important guidelines to use for time-out procedures. First, check to see whether your school has policies regarding the use of time-out and follow the policies in developing your own procedures. The courts have reviewed time-out procedures and have emphasized that "exclusion should be from privileges and not from substantive rights" (Wherry, 1983, p. 49). This means a teacher cannot bar a student from access to water or the bathroom. Second, use the procedure only for changing behaviors that are clearly intolerable. Third, make sure the time-out area is safe and easily supervised. Fourth, identify the behaviors that will result in time-out and determine how long the time-out period will be. (Many teachers use a timer so they don't forget about the student.) Fifth, when the misbehavior occurs, calmly identify it and tell the student to go to time-out for a designated number of minutes. Don't make any other comments, and ignore pleas of how the behavior will never happen again. In some cases, you may have to escort the student to the time-out area.

Criticisms of Behavioral Approaches

Cote (1973) has raised a number of issues regarding the use of behavior modification techniques in the schools. First, he questions how a teacher can reconcile the objective—the development of creative, free, and open individuals—with a program that controls and manipulates behavior. Behavior modification can create, maintain, or eliminate almost any behavior. However, in the process students lose control over their own behavior. It is the teacher who has the control, and it can be misused! Second, behavior modification is used when students' motivation and achievement are low or when classroom behavior is inappropriate. But are the students telling us something about themselves, the teacher, or the classroom environment when they behave in ways that call for the use of behavior modification? Perhaps we should spend more time attempting to diagnose the problem than quickly deciding that the students' behavior must be changed to fit the environment. Cote states:

> The child may be acting more like an accurate weather vane than a troublesome pupil. He may be telling us that something is radically wrong with the way we are trying to educate him .... Is it moral to use a system of control to adjust a child to a learning environment that his behavior tells us does not work? Should we change the environment instead of changing the child? (p. 278)

Behavior modification was never intended to force students to adapt to a boring or dull classroom environment. A danger is that it may take the pressure off the teacher to develop a more stimulating environment and an improved teacher-student relationship.

In response to the critics of behavior modification, its proponents are sensitive about any criticisms concerning the blocking of students' creativity or creating a mechanistic or dull environment. For example, Givner and Graubard (1974) respond that creativity can come about only when the foundation has been laid. That is, students cannot be creative if they do not have the basic skills with which to be creative. If they are given these skills and the ability to interact with individuals in their environment, students can create new ideas and behaviors. Nolan (1974) identifies four strengths of behavior modification:

1. It extends the system of rewards to those who rarely, if ever, receive them.
2. It removes the punitive aspects from the educational process.
3. It systematizes what we have always done so that we do it more effectively.
4. It demands better teaching by forcing the teacher to analyze carefully the learning behavior of each student. (p. 337)

You have been presented with the major arguments on both sides of the issue. What are your beliefs about behavior modification? Would you use it? Why or why not? If so, under what circumstances would you use behavior modification?

In closing this section, I must emphasize that behavioral procedures can have powerful effects on student behavior. Attention must be given to ethical and legal issues involved in any procedure you use (Corrao & Melton, 1988; Jenson, Sloane, & Young, 1988). Don't hesitate to ask your principal or school psychologist for help in initiating a behavioral change program.

DEBATE FORUM

Is There an Alternative to Reinforcement and Punishment?

Argument: One of the most successful and widely used methods of behavior change is applied behavior analysis. Parents and teachers who learn how to use reinforcement and punishment appropriately can train children to act appropriately.

Counterargument: Dreikurs and Stoltz (1964) argue in *Children: The Challenge* that reinforcement and punishment simply encourage children to believe that their worth depends upon the opinions of others. Instead, parents should spend more time encouraging children to take responsibility for their own behavior. For example, when a student receives a good grade on a report card and asks: "Are my grades okay?" parents should respond: "Yes, you must be proud of your hard work," or "I knew you could do it!" In other words, parents should encourage children by valuing and accepting them *as they are* so they learn to judge the quality of their own behavior.

Dreikurs and Stoltz recommend that parents communicate to children that they have the ability to take care of many of their problems. They suggest that parents use natural and logical consequences in dealing with children's misbehavior. *Natural consequences* occur when children learn from the natural order of the physical world—for example, that not eating is followed by hunger. *Logical consequences* occur when children learn from the reality of the social order—for example,

Parents often seek help from teachers regarding effective methods for disciplining their children.

children who do not get up on time may be late to school and have to make up work (Dinkmeyer & McKay, 1976).

A mother tired of picking up clothes to wash says to her son: "I only wash clothes that are in the hamper." The next time the son frantically asks about his favorite shirt, his mother doesn't get upset. She simply reminds him that she would be pleased to wash his shirt if it were in the hamper (logical consequence).

I know a parent who spent a night typing a term paper for a high school senior because of her fear that he might get a poor grade and not get into the college of his choice. This parent continually took responsibility for the student's procrastination and poor study habits. Dreikurs and Stolz would say that if the parent allowed the adolescent to fail when he didn't take the proper steps to complete his assignments, he would learn that the responsibility for passing or failing was his and not his mother's. The same suggestion would be given to parents who feel stressed because they have to wake up their daughter every day so she will get to work on time.

Many parents have participated in workshops in *Systematic Training for Effective Parenting* (Dinkmeyer & McKay, 1976), which teaches parents how to use natural and logical consequences. Research evidence indicates that this approach can be successfully implemented by parents and can lead to a change of behavior (Dembo, Sweitzer, & Lauritzen, 1985).

What do you think? What do you think of the use of natural and logical consequences for dealing with children and adolescents' behavior? What behavior management approaches did your parents use? What approaches will you or do you use with your own children?

active listening. A type of communication in which teachers summarize and paraphrase what students have said.

A Humanistic Approach—Teacher Effectiveness Training (T.E.T.)

Thomas Gordon (1974) has used Carl Rogers's ideas concerning human relationships in developing Teacher Effectiveness Training (T.E.T.), a method of interaction that seeks to enhance the teacher-student relationship through the development of effective communication skills. T.E.T. provides a model for establishing open and honest communication in the classroom and for resolving teacher-student conflicts in a way that is mutually beneficial and democratic.

? How can I become a better listener?

ACTIVE LISTENING. A primary goal of T.E.T. is to improve the quality of communication between teachers and students. One way this can be done, says Gordon, is for teachers to practice **active listening** with their students. This requires the teacher to summarize or paraphrase what the student has said so that the student feels understood and encouraged to communicate more honestly and directly. According to Gordon, active listening helps students to express feelings, solve problems, and develop trust in the teacher.

The following examples from Gordon's book *T.E.T.: Teacher Effectiveness Training* (1974) demonstrate how active listening is done:

1. STUDENT: Sally tore up my drawing. (*Sobs*)
   TEACHER: You're disappointed at losing your drawing and angry at Sally for tearing it up.
   STUDENT: Yeah. Now I'll have to do it over!
2. STUDENT: Richard always cheats. I'm not going to play with him anymore.
   TEACHER: You hate the way Richard treats you so much that you're going to quit playing with him.
   STUDENT: Yes, I'll play with Tommy and David instead.
3. STUDENT: This school sure isn't as good as my last one. The kids there were friendly.
   TEACHER: You feel pretty left-out here.
   STUDENT: I sure do. (p. 70)

As you can see from these examples, the teacher reflects back the meaning of the student's message in a clear and objective way. The teacher focuses on the student's feelings and avoids giving advice. This helps to confirm and validate the student's feelings, as well as to set the stage for problem solving by getting the student to talk it out.

Gordon believes that active listening is effective because it avoids the blocks that interfere with or stop the two-way process of communication.

Teachers who develop good listening skills often find that students want to share their concerns with them.

Such blocks include ordering, threatening, moralizing, lecturing, judging, labeling, sympathizing, questioning, being sarcastic, and the like. According to Gordon, such blocks often lead to negative student reactions (resentment, defensiveness, anger, etc.), which can impair teacher-student communication and result in classroom management problems.

I-messages. Gordon's strategy for changing student behavior, in which a teacher describes the problem behavior, the concrete effect the behavior is having on the teacher, and the way the behavior makes the teacher feel.

PROBLEM SOLVING. In addition to the goal of improving communication, T.E.T. attempts to help teachers solve classroom problems more effectively. Basic to T.E.T.'s problem-solving approach is the idea of problem ownership. Problems can be owned by either the teacher or the student. According to Gordon, the concept of ownership is important because it helps to determine how problems will be solved. For a student-owned problem, the approach is to use active listening; and for a teacher-owned problem, the approach is to use "**I-messages**" and/or the "no-lose" method of conflict resolution.

Before we consider each of these approaches, let's take a closer look at what Gordon means by problem ownership.

WHO OWNS THE PROBLEM? Gordon (1974) describes the difference between student-owned and teacher-owned problems in terms of tangible and concrete effects. When the problem has a real, direct, and undesirable effect on the teacher, it is the teacher's problem; when the problem has a real, direct, and undesirable effect on the student, it is the student's problem.

Gordon says that teachers can distinguish their problems from those of their students by asking themselves such questions as, "Am I being interfered with, damaged, hurt, or impaired by the student's behavior in some way? Or am I feeling unaccepting merely because I'd like the student to act differently, not have a problem, feel the way I think the student should?" If the teacher answers yes to the first question, the problem belongs to the teacher. If the answer is yes to the second question, the problem belongs to the student.

Brophy and Rohrkemper (1981) investigated the ways in which elementary teachers viewed 12 problem behaviors such as underachievement, hostility, defiance, hyperactivity, rejection by peers, and shyness and withdrawal. The researchers classified the problems according to Gordon's perspective:

- Teacher-owned problems: The students' behavior interferes with the teacher's needs or plans (e.g., defiance).
- Student-owned problems: The students' needs or plans are frustrated by individuals other than the teacher (e.g., rejection by peers).
- Shared problems: The students' behavior does not directly affect the teacher but has an impact on general classroom management and control (e.g., hyperactivity).

The researchers found that teachers who perceived students as presenting teacher-owned problems viewed the students as acting intentionally and, as a result, blamed the students for their misbehavior. The students demonstrating student-owned problems, in contrast, were viewed as victims of circumstances beyond their control. Teachers were pessimistic about their ability to deal with students who presented teacher-owned problems. As a result, they made no major attempts to modify the students' behavior. They were, however, more motivated to modify the behavior of students who were seen as having student-owned problems.

WHAT TEACHERS CAN DO TO HELP STUDENTS WITH PROBLEMS. Gordon (1974) suggests a number of strategies for helping students who have problems. The most basic is simply to listen. Gordon states that saying nothing is actually a form of communication "Silence—'passive listening'—is a powerful nonverbal message that can make a student feel genuinely accepted and encourage him to share more and more with you" (p. 61). In conjunction with passive listening, Gordon also suggests using "acknowledgment responses"—nonverbal and verbal cues that signal to the student that you are truly attentive. Smiling, nodding, saying "Uh-huh," or "Oh," or "I see" are examples of responses that tell the student that you are really attuned to what he or she is saying.

On occasions when students are reluctant, shy, or hesitant to speak, teachers can use another strategy that Gordon calls "door openers" or "reopeners." These are messages that take the form of nonevaluative questions and statements that are intended to encourage students to talk more openly and honestly about their concerns and feelings. Some examples include: "What you're saying sounds serious, tell me more," "Why don't we talk a while?" "You seem upset," or "What you say is interesting. I'd like to hear more about it."

WHAT TEACHERS CAN DO TO HELP THEMSELVES. When problems belong to the teacher—that is, when student behaviors are interfering with the teacher's needs—a strategy called "I-messages" can be used. Gordon describes I-messages as statements made by the teacher to the student that clearly describe the student's troublesome behavior and how it is negatively affecting the teacher. Gordon states that I-messages are effective because they have a high probability of changing the student's undesirable behavior, are only minimally negative, and do not impair the teacher-student relationship. I-messages place the responsibility for the student's behavior with the student. I-messages tell students that their behavior is having a direct, adverse effect on the teacher. Gordon claims that when students realize that their behavior is causing the teacher a genuine problem, they will be motivated to change.

Effective I-messages have three components:

1. A nonblaming, nonjudgmental description of the student's behavior;
2. A description of the tangible, or concrete, effect the behavior is having on the teacher; and
3. A description of how this behavior is making the teacher feel.

Each of these components can be seen in the following example of an effective I-message: "When you leave the room without my permission, I have to waste a lot of time looking for you, and this makes me feel frustrated and angry."

As you can see, this I-message has clearly described the student's behavior (leaving the room without permission), its effect on the teacher (wastes her time), and how it makes the teacher feel (frustrated and angry). Because this type of message focuses on the teacher's feelings, it is far less likely to generate negative student responses, like anger or resentment, than would a *you-message*: "You are always leaving the room without my permission. When will you grow up?" Unlike the I-message, the you-message is almost always interpreted by students as an evaluation of how bad they are. Gordon maintains that you-messages have a detrimental effect on the student's self-esteem, make students feel inferior and inadequate, and often carry the hidden message, "There's something wrong with you, or you wouldn't be causing me this problem!" I-messages, on the other hand, are noncritical statements about the effects of the student's behavior on the teacher. The negative impact of the you-message is thus avoided, and students are more likely to feel motivated to be considerate and helpful.

RESOLVING CONFLICT. There are times when it is not possible to solve classroom problems by using such strategies as active listening or I-messages. Such times usually occur when teachers and students interfere with the fulfillment of each other's needs. In these situations, *both* teachers and students are said to own the problem. For example:

TEACHER: Tom, you're late for class again! Each time this happens I have to repeat the instructions for the day's activities for you personally. I'm getting tired of having to do that.

STUDENT: Well, it's not my fault. I have morning basketball practice, and the coach keeps us until the last minute.

It is apparent from this dialogue that the needs of the teacher and student are in conflict. When conflicts occur in the classroom, they are usually resolved, according to Gordon, by one of two power-based methods. In Method I, the teacher uses power and authority to override the student's needs; the teacher wins and the student loses. In Method II, the teacher defers to the student's needs, with the student winning and the teacher losing. Here are examples of each method applied to the conflict just described.

Method I: Teacher wins, student loses

TEACHER: Tom, you're late for class again! I've had it. Either you get here on time, or you're out of the class. And that's final!

Method II: Student wins, teacher loses

TEACHER: Tom, I sure wish you would get here on time. It makes it easier for me when I don't have to repeat everything you've missed.

STUDENT: With basketball practice, I just can't. If you keep hassling me, I'll drop your class.

TEACHER: Okay, okay. Don't get so upset. Just try to get here on time.

Note that in each case power is used to resolve the conflict and that one of the parties is forced to give in to the other. This generates feelings of anger and resentment in the loser, and, in the case of the student, precludes the development of self-control and personal problem-solving skills.

As an alternative to these win-lose methods of conflict resolution, Gordon offers Method III, a no-lose approach in which teacher and student cooperatively achieve a solution to their problem without the use of power or threat. Method III is based on a scientific model of problem solving and includes the following steps:

1. Defining the problem
2. Generating possible solutions
3. Evaluating the solutions
4. Deciding which solution is best
5. Determining how to implement the decision
6. Assessing how well the solution solved the problem

Earlier we saw how Tom's problem of arriving late to class was "resolved" by Methods I and II. Let's now see how this same problem is handled with Method III.

TEACHER: Tom, when you get to class late, I have to waste a lot of time repeating instructions for you, and this makes me feel frustrated and upset. [*I-message*]

STUDENT: It's not my fault, Mr. Smith. I have morning basketball practice, and the coach won't let us go until the last minute.

TEACHER: I understand. You feel that you have to stay until the last minute so you won't get into trouble with the coach. [*Active listening*]

STUDENT: Yeah, that's it.

TEACHER: Maybe it would help if I talked to him.

STUDENT: No, it won't help. Other kids have tried. If you're gonna play basketball, you've got to stay for the whole practice period. I think your class is important, but I can't cross the coach.

TEACHER: Well, we do have a problem. I need you to get here on time. There's no doubt about that. Got any ideas about how we might figure out a way to make us both happy?

STUDENT: Well, maybe what I could do is have Gabriel write out the instructions for me, and when I come in I could look them over quietly. That way, I'd know what was going on, and I wouldn't have to bother anybody.

TEACHER: Sounds good to me. I'll make sure that Gabriel has time to write the instructions down if he's willing.

STUDENT: Thanks, Mr. Smith.

Reality Therapy (RT). A counseling approach by Glasser based on the principle that human problems arise when the primary needs of love and worth go unfulfilled.

It is apparent that in Method III cooperation and not power was the basis of resolving the problem. Neither the teacher nor the student lost, and no resentment was generated, as in Methods I and II. Other advantages of Method III, as noted by Gordon, are that it increases student motivation to carry out solutions; it enhances feelings of mutual respect, caring, and trust; and, because students are a part of the problem-solving process, it fosters greater student responsibility and maturity .

An Interactionist Approach—Glasser's Reality Therapy

William Glasser, a psychiatrist, has developed a model of classroom management that stresses social interdependence and the meeting of needs in a socially responsible and realistic way. His model is based on **Reality Therapy (RT)**, a counseling approach that evolved from his work with delinquent adolescents. The basic principle of RT is that human problems arise when the primary needs of love and worth go unfulfilled. This need deficiency results in disruptive behaviors that tend to alienate individuals from the reality of the world around them. The primary goal of RT is to help individuals meet their needs within the context of the real world in ways that are responsible and sensitive to the needs of others (Glasser, 1965).

REALITY THERAPY IN THE CLASSROOM. Following are some strategies from RT for communicating with students and assisting them in meeting individual goals.

Agreeing on Rules. Rules are an essential part of Glasser's system. The rules need to be reasonable, enforceable, and either cooperatively developed or at least agreed to. The rules for behaving should be characterized by small, manageable steps and goals that can be easily attained. A student who has mutually agreed to rules and then chooses to misbehave also has chosen to receive a consequence.

Focusing on Current Behavior. Glasser (1972) has observed that "people often avoid facing their present behavior by emphasizing how they feel rather than what they are doing" (p. 114). It is important, therefore, that teachers help students to focus their attention on behavior. Although feelings are important, in problematical situations it is behavior that must be changed.

Commitment. Once plans are developed, the students need to make a firm commitment to carrying them out. This commitment can be either oral or written. If written, it should include a list of specific actions or behaviors to be performed. In this way, the students' progress in carrying out the plan can be more clearly evaluated.

Using Directive Statements. When a child misbehaves, the teacher confronts the student with directive statements such as, "Susan, if you are going to talk, you must raise your hand." The teacher needs to tell the student to stop the wrong behavior and to act correctly and responsibly.

Accepting No Excuses. No excuses are accepted by the teacher for a student's failure to abide by the plan. In accepting excuses, the teacher weakens the student's commitment to the plan and gives the student a way out. When failure does occur, the student should be encouraged to try again. If necessary, small modifications to the plan can be made, but only if they do not compromise the overall goal of improving the student's behavior.

Evaluating Behavior. Students are more motivated to improve when they understand the effects of their self-defeating and irresponsible behavior on others. In this regard, the teacher can help students to accept responsibility for their actions by getting the students to examine their behavior and its effect on others in the classroom.

Providing Consequences. A student needs to have logical consequences follow his or her behavior, whether that behavior is positive or negative. The student is encouraged to determine what those privileges or negative results should be. A student who continues to misbehave or refuses to work out the problem should be isolated within the room (see discussion of time-out earlier in the chapter).

No Punishment. In Reality Therapy, punishment is seen as reinforcing feelings of failure and should be avoided. It is more valuable to let students experience the natural consequence of their failure than to punish them for it. With repeated failure, it may be necessary to re-examine the plan; it may be beyond the ability of the students to fulfill its requirement.

Glasser's Control Theory

? How does Glasser's approach to discipline differ from assertive discipline?

More recently, Glasser (1985) has developed a new therapeutic approach with implications for school discipline that is called *control theory.* Control theory suggests that students will follow rules and work hard in school to the extent that their needs to belong, to be free, to gain power, and to have fun are satisfied. Glasser's emphasis now appears to be more on the schools meeting student needs than on helping students deal with the conditions that they encounter in school (Charles, 1989). These needs can be satisfied through such activities as classroom discussions, school-supervised work opportunities in the community, student-directed learning, and cooperative learning in academic areas. Glasser believes that when control theory is practiced in school, externally imposed behavioral programs of discipline will no longer be necessary; students will be motivated to control themselves.

Glasser's (1990) newer views on discipline have been influenced by his work in secondary schools. He maintains that "no more than half of our secondary school students are willing to make an effort to learn, and therefore cannot be taught" (p. 3) and, despite the best efforts of teachers, "we have gone as far as we can go with the traditional structure of our secondary schools" (p. 6).

Recently, Glasser (1990) has used control theory to describe a new management system to make schools more successful. He describes the typical school administration as "boss management"—an adversarial relationship between teachers and students occurring when the teacher attempts to use coercion to make students work harder. The result is that "the child learns less and resists more; the teacher coerces more and teaches less" (p. 431). Glasser would like administrators and teachers to adopt "lead management" methods that are noncoercive and that are based on the assumption that motivation comes from within ourselves (a major premise of humanistic psychology). In order to become harder working, Glasser suggests, students need to believe that there is value in what they are being asked to do, they need to be encouraged to set their own standards for quality, and they need to be given more encouragement to succeed.

Charles (1989) doesn't see Glasser's recent work as inconsistent with his early work on Reality Therapy. Glasser would have teachers attempt to develop classroom rules, procedures, and instructional methods sensitive to student needs. This approach would help a large percentage of students succeed in school, but there would still be some behavioral problems. Glasser's earlier suggestions for dealing with misbehavior would be used as an intervention strategy for controlling and improving student behavior.

As you can see, Glasser's humanistic approach to classroom management and instruction is in sharp contrast to assertive discipline. He would encourage teachers to organize the classroom to meet students' needs rather than teachers' needs! Is this a realistic approach? Do you agree with his position that few students are doing high-quality work in their regular academic classes? Do teachers need to re-evaluate the ways they attempt to motivate students? What's your position on this issue?

CLASSROOM Application

CONDUCTING CLASSROOM MEETINGS

The application of Reality Therapy to problems of classroom management centers on creating an atmosphere of mutual caring and involvement among students and teachers. When students feel connected to what is going on in the classroom, they are more likely to engage in responsible behavior and to develop feelings of importance and self-worth. One of the ways in which teachers can make students feel more involved is to conduct classroom meetings. Glasser (1969) defines these sessions as "meetings in which the teacher leads a whole class in a non-judgmental discussion about what is important and relevant to them" (p. 122). Table 7.4 identifies three types of classroom meetings.

TABLE 7.4 TYPES OF CLASSROOM MEETINGS

Meeting	Purpose	Leading Questions
Social-problem solving	Helps students solve individual and group problems of the class and school	"How are we going to share time on the classroom computer?" "How can we help Bill and John stop fighting?"
Open-ended	Stimulates student thinking on questions related to their lives or to the classroom curriculum	"What does it feel like to be blind?" "What is friendship?"
Educational-diagnostic	Helps the teacher evaluate student understanding of school curriculum or the effectiveness of their own teaching strategies	"What is the Constitution?" "How did you like working in groups?"

Source: Glasser, 1969.

To conduct a classroom meeting, Glasser (1969) recommends the following strategies:

- Sit in a circle.
- Keep it short—for primary grade children about 10 to 30 minutes, and for upper grade children 30 to 45 minutes.
- Meet regularly—every day or, at least, every other day.
- Begin with open-ended meetings, because these are the easiest to conduct and the best for acquainting students with the concept of class meetings.
- Introduce a topic or problem, or ask students to identify a subject of interest to them.
- Encourage a free exchange of ideas by telling students that there are no right or wrong answers. The purpose of the meeting is to allow all students to express their opinions, feelings, and ideas in a nonthreatening environment.
- Be *nonjudgmental* in reactions to the students in the group. Your primary role is to guide the discussion, keeping students on track and encouraging everyone to participate.
- Any topic is open for discussion. The discussion should always be directed toward solving the problem in a positive way, avoiding punishment or fault finding.
- Focus students' attention on the present problem. Students' dwelling on the past is unprofitable and wastes time.
- Paraphrase or summarize periodically. This helps students to feel that they are being listened to, and it keeps the discussion focused on the topic or problem at hand.
- Don't expect to solve problems in a single class meeting. Some problems are quite complex, especially those that affect large groups of students, and may require several meetings before a satisfactory solution is achieved. Also, it may be necessary to hold further meetings if the solution chosen fails to work.

Glasser notes that classroom meetings can provide an effective format for resolving problems of the individual student or the whole class and for getting students to participate cooperatively in group activities. Holding meetings on a regular basis, he says, encourages students to become more involved with one another, their teacher, and their school. Moreover, responding in a group helps students to gain self-confidence by giving them the opportunity to express their ideas and opinions in front of others.

See Palomares and Ball (1974) and Fearn and McCabe (1975) for further information about conducting group discussions with students.

Summary

DEVELOPING A MANAGEMENT PLAN

1. Effective classroom managers also tend to be effective instructors.
2. The key to classroom management is the ability to prevent misbehavior from occurring.
3. Effective classroom managers prevent problems from occurring by using the following behaviors: with-it-ness, overlapping, signal continuity and momentum in lessons, and variety and challenge in seatwork. They teach students appropriate behavior based on specific rules taught the first weeks of school and hold students accountable for following the rules and procedures by carefully monitoring their behavior.
4. Assertive discipline is a "take-charge" approach to discipline that emphasizes the importance of teacher rights to an orderly classroom.
5. An important issue in establishing a management system is the procedure for teaching students to abide by the rules established by the teacher and teaching personal responsibility.

INSTRUCTIONAL ORGANIZATION

6. In general, the more time a student spends actually engaged in an academic task, the higher the student's achievement.
7. Classrooms vary in the extent to which students are engaged in instruction.
8. Teachers can influence students' engagement in instruction by the way they organize and manage the classroom.
9. In general, the more time students spend doing seatwork, the less they are engaged in instruction. The fact that teachers cannot easily monitor seatwork contributes to this outcome.
10. High and low achievers approach seatwork differently. High achievers expect the work to make sense to them, ask questions, and are more likely to benefit from their seatwork. Low achievers are more likely to develop strategies to complete their assignments and are less likely to ask questions when they do not understand something.

DEALING WITH MANAGEMENT PROBLEMS

11. Behavioral approaches to classroom management emphasize the establishment of rules and the implementation of rewards and punishment according to how well students comply with the rules.

12. Behavioral techniques used to increase appropriate behavior include token economy, contingency contracting, group-based contingencies, home-based contingencies, and social skills training. Behavioral techniques used to decrease behavior include reinforcing incompatible behavior, changing the stimulus environment, and time-out.
13. Some educators question the use of behavioral techniques on ethical grounds, whereas others defend their use because such procedures provide students with greater opportunities to succeed in the classroom.
14. Gordon believes that active listening and the use of I-messages can improve teacher-student communication.
15. Glasser states that when students feel more connected to what is going on in the classroom, they are more likely to engage in responsible behavior and develop feelings of importance and self-worth. He recommends that teachers conduct classroom meetings on a regular basis as a means of accomplishing this goal.

Reflecting on Classroom Management and Discipline

1. Think about the Discipline Problems of Past Teachers

All of us have been in classes in which teachers had problems managing and disciplining students. Identify specific problems some of your past teachers had and describe what steps could have been taken to improve their management skills.

2. Debate the Use of Reinforcement Systems

Is the use of systematic reinforcement and token economies a form of bribery? Select one of the following statements that comes closest to your point of view, and defend the reasons you support the statement:

a. Students should not be "paid off" for something that they should do naturally. The problem with society today is that individuals are not developing self-initiative because they expect someone to give them something for acting responsibly.
b. Bribery is an incentive for someone to participate in illegal or immoral behavior. Reinforcement in school is used to encourage positive, not negative, behavior. Also, bribery offers an incentive at the time that

students are not performing, to get them to perform. Reinforcement programs specify the rules for earning tokens and obtaining privileges *before* the program starts. Thus, reinforcement is not bribery (Jenson, Sloane, & Young, 1988).

3. Observe a Teacher's Management Skills

Make arrangements to visit a class to observe a teacher's instructional organization and management skills. Use the organizational skills given in Table 7.3 to rate the teacher's degree of effectiveness on a scale of 1 (very effective) to 10 (very ineffective). Are students engaged in academic instruction? How is teacher behavior related to the students' engagement rates? What are the teacher's strengths and weaknesses? Write a brief description of the teacher's behavior and discuss why you rated the teacher as you did.

4. Teach a Social Skill

Using the information on teaching social skills in this chapter, describe how you would train a student in one of the following social skills:

a. Waiting your turn
b. Making friends
c. Asking for help
d. Interviewing for a part-time job

5. Experiment with Behavior Modification

If you have the opportunity to work with students on an individual or group basis, you might try to use behavior modification. Review the principles of learning and basic techniques covered in Chapter 2 before you begin. First, state operationally the behavior to be changed. Next, obtain an operant level of this behavior. Then write a procedure for changing the behavior. Try out your plan, and maintain records of the reinforced behavior to keep track of whether or not strength or frequency of response has increased. Evaluate the effectiveness of your behavior modification program. Use the following checklist as a step-by-step plan:

- Description of behavior to be changed
- Operant level of behavior (use a graph to chart behavior over a period of time)
- Procedure used to change behavior
- What happened when you tried out procedure (plot behavior on the graph used in the second step)
- Evaluation of behavior modification program

Key terms

classroom management, p. 284
discipline, p. 284
assertive discipline, p. 293
with-it-ness, p. 296
overlapping, p. 297
signal continuity, p. 297
allocated time, p. 299
instructional time, p. 300
engaged time, p. 300
academic learning time (ALT), p. 300
token economy, p. 306
response cost, p. 306
contingency contracting, p. 309
group contingency, p. 309
active listening, p. 321
I-messages, p. 323
Reality Therapy (RT), p. 327

Suggestions for Further Reading

Cangelosi, J. S. (1988). *Classroom management strategies.* White Plains, NY: Longman. Includes numerous classroom experiences to illustrate how problems can be resolved.

Charles, C. M. (1992). *Building classroom discipline: From models to practice* (4th ed.). White Plains, NY: Longman. A good review of the different approaches to discipline.

Duke, D. L., & Meckel, A. (1984). *Teacher's guide to classroom management.* New York: Random House. Provides helpful ideas for handling behavior problems.

Fisher, C. W., & Berliner, D. C. (Eds.). (1985). *Perspectives on instructional time.* White Plains, NY: Longman. Reviews the research on time and learning.

Johns, F. A., MacNaughton, R. H., & Karabinus, N. G. (1989). *School discipline guidebook: Theory into practice.* Needham Heights, MA: Allyn & Bacon. Some good practical advice for teachers.

The following two books provide a comprehensive discussion of preparing a management program for the classroom:

Emmer, E. T., et al. (1989). *Classroom management for secondary teachers* (2nd ed.). Englewood Cliffs, NJ: Prentice-Hall.

Evertson, C. M., Emmer, E. T., Clements, B. S., Sanford, J. P., & Worshem, M. E. (1989). *Classroom management for elementary teachers* (2nd ed.). Englewood Cliffs, NJ: Prentice-Hall.

To read more about the approaches discussed in this chapter:

Canter, L. (1976). *Assertive discipline: A take-charge approach for today's educator.* Seal Beach, CA: Canter and Associates.

Glasser, W. G. (1965). *Reality Therapy: A new approach to psychiatry.* New York: Harper & Row.

Glasser, W. G. (1969). *Schools without failure.* New York: Harper & Row.

Glasser, W. G. (1985). *Control theory.* New York: Harper & Row.

Gordon, T. (1974). *T.E.T.: Teacher Effectiveness Training*. White Plains, NY: Longman.

Martin, G., & Pear, J. (1988). *Behavior modification: What it is and how to do it* (3rd ed.). Englewood Cliffs, NJ: Prentice-Hall.

Walker, J. E., & Shea, T. (1988). *Behavior management: A practical approach for educators* (4th ed.). Columbus, OH: Merrill.

Part 3 Synthesis

You have seen in this part of the book that good planning is an important aspect of both instruction and classroom management. The type of instructional task given to students (e.g., reading a story versus writing a story) influences how students think about themselves as learners and how much effort they put into academic work. In addition, the task influences how students interact with others and behave in the classroom (Doyle, 1983). The relationship between planning, instruction, and management helps explain the finding I first mentioned in the orientation section of Chapter 7: Effective classroom managers tend to be effective instructors.

A number of different approaches to preventing and dealing with management problems were discussed. An important decision that you must make is how much responsibility you want to give students in the planning and operation of your management system.

The following exercise is included to help you review the content in the last two chapters:

> Select a student in your class with whom to work as a team to complete the following assignment: (a) write an instructional objective, (b) plan a lesson using *two* of the following methodologies—direct instruction, cooperative learning, and discovery learning—for the same objective, and (c) discuss how the methodologies differ in teaching the objective.
>
> Describe your own management system for the class. Suppose that as you teach your lessons, a number of misbehaviors occur. Describe how you would handle each of the following misbehaviors consistent with your management system:
>
> a. Fighting with another student
> b. Showing disrespect for another student
> c. Annoying another student after his or her own work is completed
> d. Failing to do any classwork

Part four

Development and Individual Differences

One of the most important variables influencing the effectiveness of instruction is individual differences. The variety of student abilities; developmental, language, and cultural differences; interests; and attitudes found within any classroom leads to a wide variety of results. Some students will enjoy more success in school and experience more favorable teacher and peer interaction than other students will.

Teaching would be much easier (but less interesting) if all students were alike. Instructional decisions would be greatly reduced. Lesson plans would not have to be modified, teachers would not have to consider alternative instructional procedures, and teacher-student interaction would probably be more uniform. However, the reality of teaching is that student differences present one of the greatest challenges to teachers.

Think back to your own elementary and secondary school days. These types of students were probably acquaintances of yours:

the student who was always the first to answer the instructor's question; the student who infuriated the teacher by asking different or unusual questions; the student from a different cultural background who had difficulty learning; the student whose primary language was not English; the student who always panicked during exam time; the student who always sat in the back of the classroom, rarely said anything, and had an implicit "contract" with the teacher stating: "You don't bother me and I won't bother you." Try to recall additional types of students who had varying success in school. Try to pinpoint the characteristics that appeared to help or hinder them in the classroom.

From the teacher's perspective, it is important to understand what student characteristics should be considered in planning and implementing instruction. Chapter 8 deals with intelligence and cognitive development; Chapter 9 with cognition, culture, and language; Chapter 10 with personal and social factors influencing learning. Finally, Chapter 11 discusses exceptional children, who often differ in both cognitive and social attributes. As you read the next four chapters, identify the individual differences that would influence the types of instructional decisions you might make in the classroom.

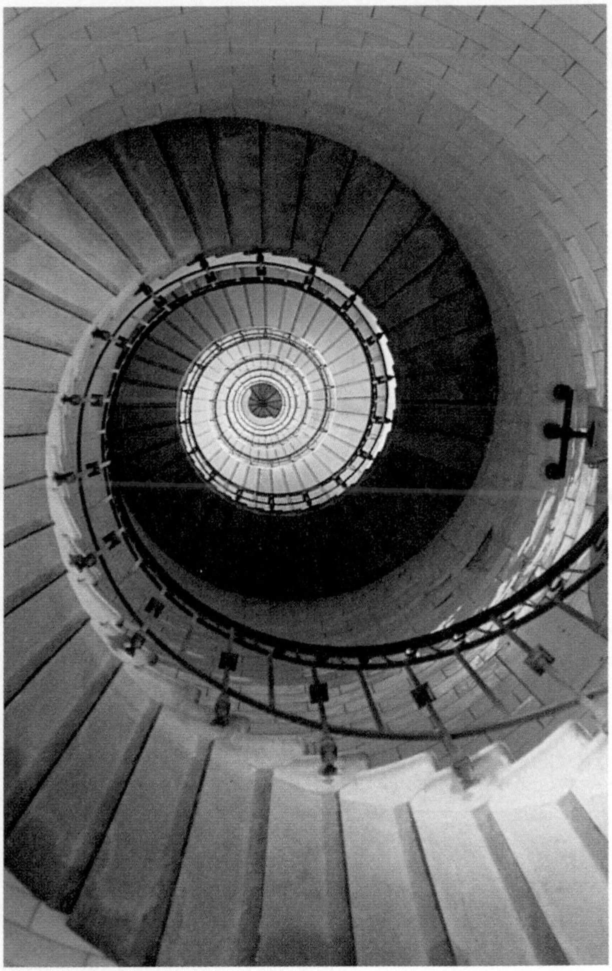

Chapter 8

Intelligence and Cognitive Development

The Psychometric Perspective

The Composition of Intelligence
Individual Intelligence Tests
Uses of Intelligence Tests
Some Misconceptions about Intelligence Tests
Intelligence Test Bias and Fairness
Educational Interventions to Increase Intelligence and Academic Performance

The Piagetian Perspective

The Process of Cognitive Development
Piaget's Developmental Stages
Criticisms of Piaget's Theory

Implications of Piaget's Theory for Education

Teaching Strategy
Curriculum

The Information-Processing Perspective

Neo-Piagetians;
Information Processing and Human Abilities

Debate Forum: Are People Left-Brained and Right-Brained?

The Sociocultural Perspective

Vygotsky's Sociocultural Approach to Cognitive Development

Classroom Application: Using Reciprocal Teaching

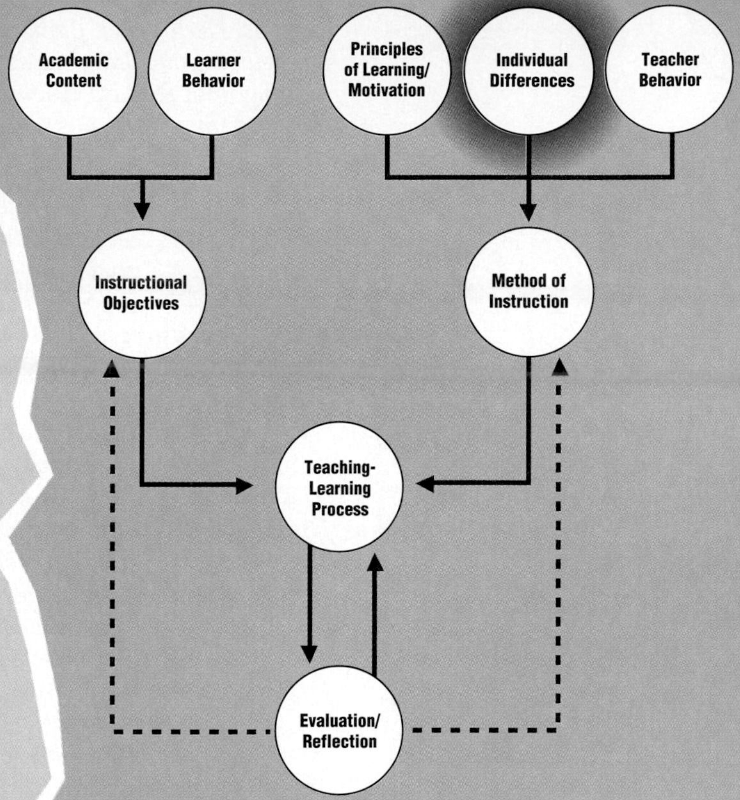

OBJECTIVES

After mastering the material in this chapter you will be able to:

- Identify the psychometric, Piagetian, information-processing, and sociocultural approaches to intelligence.
- Explain how the theory of intelligence a person adopts can influence intervention strategies designed to enhance cognitive development and academic achievement.

Orientation

Melinda was one of the most popular students in the fourth grade. She could hold the other students entranced telling them stories about ghosts, princesses, and dragons. Her teacher, Barbara Jones, knew that Melinda was bright, but was confused about something she saw in her file. This confusion led Barbara to request a meeting with Richard Palomino, the school psychologist. Here is an account of their meeting:

Barbara: *Dr. Palomino, I was looking at Melinda Abernathy's file yesterday, and I noticed that her intelligence test results show that she's below average. I'm a bit confused about this, Doctor. Her grades are good, and she's very creative. I thought the tests were supposed to be pretty accurate.*

Dr. Palomino: *It would be nice if we could give one test that would tell us everything about a child's ability and aptitude. Unfortunately, Barbara, there isn't any such test. There are different types of what we would call "IQ" tests, and all of them are subject to some error.*

Barbara: *If they're not reliable, what are we supposed to use them for?*

Dr. Palomino: *I think the main idea to keep in mind is that one test can't give you the whole picture about a child and her abilities. If I were a medical doctor and gave you only one test before making a diagnosis, would you feel comfortable?*

Barbara: *Of course not! I'd want more tests done.*

Dr. Palomino: *It's pretty much the same with intelligence tests. They give us a measurement in only one area of that child's life, but you need to rely upon other "tests" to get the whole picture.*

Barbara: *What kinds of tests?*

Dr. Palomino: *Well, one of the most important sources of information about a student would be the teacher. Look at what happened with Melinda. You had formed your own professional conclusion about her abilities, and found this conclusion didn't agree with the "official one," right?*

Barbara: *Right.*

Dr. Palomino: *Well, which one is correct? Which "test" correctly identifies Melinda?*

Barbara: *I would like to think that I'm right on this one. I mean, I know that little girl pretty well, and I know she's capable of doing very well in school. She may have to work a little harder than some of the kids, but she always gets the job done. What would happen if another teacher saw her file before they even had her in class? They might think that she's not capable, even before they gave her the chance to prove she was.*

Dr. Palomino: *That's why we need to rely on more than one assessment of a child before we reach any definite conclusion. You're right, Barbara, if a teacher based her assessment of a student on only one test, the child would be at a disadvantage. But when you can use different ways to assess that child's abilities, and understand that children have different types of abilities that may not be measured by the "tests," then these students have a real advantage.*

The study of intelligence—its general nature and measurement—is one of the most emotional issues in educational psychology. Probably no other area is more discussed and less understood by educators. In this chapter, we will explore four major perspectives of intelligence and cognition: psychometric, Piagetian, information-processing, and sociocultural.

Briefly, the **psychometric** perspective attempts to understand intelligence by identifying the factors or mental structures (e.g., reasoning ability, spatial ability, and verbal ability) that are responsible for individual differences on intelligence tests. The Piagetian perspective focuses on qualitative developmental changes in children's thinking by identifying how children think and reason differently from adults. The focus in this approach is on the development of intellectual processes that are common to all children rather than on individual differences. The **information-processing** perspective looks at the specific processes that underlie intelligent behavior. Information-processing psychologists ask the following questions: What are the underlying aspects of thinking in specific areas? How do individuals with superior ability differ from individuals who are less competent in the area? Do they change with age? Do people differ in their skill in using different abilities? Finally, the sociocultural perspective considers how mental abilities develop from social experience.

The four perspectives should be considered complementary rather than mutually exclusive, since they deal with different but overlapping aspects of intelligence (Laboratory of Comparative Human Cognition, 1982; Wagner & Sternberg, 1984). In general, the psychometric perspective assesses *what* we know (the product). Although the specific approaches are different, the Piagetian and information-processing perspectives emphasize *how* we think (the process). The sociocultural perspective emphasizes both *how* and *why* individuals may think differently. Each perspective has different implications for designing intervention strategies for cognitive development and academic success. I will integrate the perspectives discussed in this chapter with the discussion of culturally different students in the succeeding chapter.

psychometric. An approach to the study of intelligence that uses statistical procedures to identify the factors or mental structures responsible for individual differences on tests.

information processing. The study of specific thinking processes that underlie intelligent behavior or *cognition.*

intelligence. The capacity or set of capacities that allows an individual to learn, to solve problems, and/or to interact successfully with his or her environment.

THE PSYCHOMETRIC PERSPECTIVE

The Composition of Intelligence

? Is intelligence a unitary trait or a composite of traits?

Introductory textbooks usually provide a definition of the concept under discussion to clarify any misconceptions regarding its meaning. An intelligent definition of **intelligence** would probably compose a booklet. The definition of intelligence varies with each psychologist's philosophy. In general, intelligence is viewed as the capacity or set of capacities that allows any individual to learn, to solve problems, and/or to interact successfully with the environment. For the most part, theories of intelligence have been viewed from one of two perspectives. The first suggests that one general factor accounts for most of our mental ability. In 1927, Spearman was one of the first psychologists to propose that intelligence involves a high degree of general ability. He hypothesized an intellect composed of a general factor (*g*) underlying all mental functions and a multitude of specific factors (*s*) related to a given task or situation.

According to Spearman's theory, people differ in the degree of the general factor as well as in the quality of the specific factors involved in a given task, so that a person could be relatively "more intelligent" than another person because of a superior *g* but less capable in a given area (for example, science) because of deficient or inferior *s* factors in that area. However, since *g* represents a form of mental ability included in all mental operations, a person who is grossly lacking in general intelligence would probably not be gifted in a specific field.

Teachers are often surprised that various intelligence tests ask different questions and wonder how students who take these tests can be compared. Psychologists who support Spearman's theory would explain to them that it does not matter what particular combination of mental tests or performances any given test calls for, because they all tap the same general factor.

Any reading and arithmetic test will result in an overlap of the general abilities common to both tests. The *g* factor in both reading and arithmetic tests is vocabulary and word meaning. The measure of intelligence in this case is general ability, although specific abilities that are not common to both tests (that is, computational skills and reading speed) also enter into play.

The second basic psychometric approach to intelligence, one that has received more attention in recent years, is the study of specific abilities, especially as they relate to success in various subject areas. Thorndike (1927), unlike Spearman, believed that intelligence was the sum of specific abilities. He identified intelligence as (1) *abstract ability*—the ability to deal with ideas and symbols, (2) *mechanical ability*—the ability to deal with mechanisms and tasks involving sensory-motor activities, and (3) *social ability*—the ability to deal effectively with people.

Thurstone (1938) also disagreed with Spearman after his battery of 56 tests produced no common intelligence factor. Thurstone concluded that there was no general factor; he conceived of intelligence as a number of *primary mental abilities*. His research indicated that mental ability could be grouped into seven factors and that intelligence could be measured by sampling individual performance in seven areas: number, word fluency, verb meaning, associative memory, reasoning, space, and perceptual speed.

GUILFORD'S STRUCTURE OF THE INTELLECT. One of the most extensive multifactor theories of intelligence was presented by Guilford (1959, 1988), who developed the Structure of Intellect (SOI) model that identified 180 different abilities. He hypothesized that human intellect is composed of a three-dimensional system of numerous intellectual abilities classified on the basis of (1) the material or *contents* processed (visual, auditory, symbolic, semantic, and behavioral), (2) the processes or *operations* performed with the material (**convergent thinking** and **divergent thinking**, evaluation, memory retention, memory recording, and cognition), and (3) the forms or *products* of the processed information (units, classes, relations, systems, transformations, and implications).

Theoretically, 180 different factors, or abilities, can be generated from the model (5 contents × 6 operations × 6 products), because any operation can be performed on any content and can result in any product. This model implies that an individual's intelligence cannot be adequately assessed by means of a single score.

Guilford (1959) was among the first psychologists to suggest that intelligence and **creativity** were not synonymous. In his discussion of the human processes or operations, he distinguished between convergent thinking and divergent thinking. Convergent thinking produces a well-determined answer to a routine problem, whereas divergent thinking generates new ideas and solutions to problems that have more than one correct answer.

Convergent thinking would produce the answer "16" to the question "What is the square of 4?" Divergent thought production might entail finding unusual uses for a knife. In theory, the latter form of thinking is associated with creativity. Some students are better at divergent tasks than convergent tasks and vice versa, while some students are strong in both types of thinking.

Guilford identified four characteristics of divergent thinking:

Fluency—coming up with a large quantity of ideas, words, and ways of expressing things
Flexibility—thinking up a variety of ideas and new ways of dealing with situations
Originality—thinking of uncommon, clever, and novel ideas and images
Elaboration—packing detail into the response

An important issue for the teacher is whether classroom activities provide opportunities to develop both convergent and divergent thinking skills. Students with excellent divergent thinking abilities often have difficulties in a classroom where the instructor emphasizes primarily convergent-thinking activities. In addition, divergent thinkers may be viewed by the teacher as troublemakers or difficult students because they approach learning tasks differently than other students.

convergent thinking. A term used by Guilford to describe thinking in which an individual produces a single response to a specific question or problem.

divergent thinking. A term used by Guilford to describe thinking wherein an individual produces multiple responses or solutions to a single question or problem.

creativity. The capacity of individuals to produce novel or original answers or products.

Individual Intelligence Tests

? How is intelligence measured?

The first intelligence test was developed in the early 1900s by Alfred Binet, a French psychologist, who was commissioned by the Ministry of Public Instruction in Paris to identify retarded children who could not benefit

mental age. A concept used in intelligence testing as a basis for determining the level of an individual's mental functioning.

intelligence quotient (IQ). A term originally defined as an individual's mental age divided by his or her chronological age.

from a traditional French education. The target of this investigation was the establishment of special schools for children who needed help.

Binet had no particular theory of intelligence but had been working on a series of tests that appeared to be reasonable samples of children's behavior and that distinguished abilities at different age levels. He found that at each age level, some children performed better than others. The children who performed the best on these tests were also rated by their teachers as "bright." Conversely, children who performed poorly on the tests were rated by their teachers as poorer students.

Binet based his tests on the comparison of a particular child with the child's age group. A child who was above average in intelligence could answer more questions than the average child in the age group. If the child answered about the same number of questions as the average child in the group, the child was considered average in intelligence. The child whose performance was below average for the age group was considered below average in intelligence.

Binet established the use of the term **mental age** as a basis for determining the level of a given child's mental functioning. A child of 8 years who could answer questions that the average 10-year-old child could answer would have a mental age of 10 years.

There were many translations of Binet's test in this country. Lewis Terman created one in 1916 at Stanford University that became widely used. His test, known as the Stanford-Binet, is still used today in revised form. Terman defined intelligence as the ability to think in abstract terms, and this definition served as the basis for establishing test items.

The popular term **intelligence quotient (IQ)** was first used by the psychologist William Stern, who proposed that a child's mental age should be divided by his or her chronological age, the most important factor being the relationship, or ratio, of the two numbers. Therefore, IQ = Mental Age (MA) ÷ Chronological Age (CA) × 100 (to remove the decimal).

Stern believed that the IQ would be relatively stable throughout an individual's life. For example, a child of 6 years (CA) with a mental age of 8 years has an IQ that equals 133 (8 ÷ 6 × 100). Stern theorized that at age 12 the child's mental age would be 16 and the IQ would still equal 133.

Later research on the growth of intelligence did not support this linear relationship, and psychometrists (measurement specialists) disregarded the IQ formula in determining mental ability (we still use the term *IQ* to indicate intelligence, or a score on an intelligence test). Presently, the meaning of a student's score on an intelligence test is determined by how much the score deviates from the average score of other individuals of the same chronological age. (This score is discussed in more detail in Chapter 13.)

Other reasons for disregarding the use of the IQ ratio have to do with mental age, which loses its meaning for adults. For example, describing a 25-year-old as having the mental ability of a 30-year-old didn't make much sense. Also, the IQ ratio cannot be used to compare results on different tests.

Most intelligence tests are constructed to have an average score of 100. Approximately two-thirds of a random sample of people score between 85 and 115; about 2 percent score above 130 and below 70. The most widely used **individual intelligence tests** are the Revised Stanford-Binet and the Wechsler Intelligence Scale for Children—Third Edition (WISC-III). These tests are administered to a single student at a time by a trained examiner, usually a school psychologist.

individual intelligence test. An intelligence test administered to one individual at a time by a trained specialist.

The WISC-III includes 10 subtests divided into two groups—*verbal* and *performance*. Each type of question in each subtest goes from very easy to very difficult. Unlike the Binet, which has separate tests for children of different age groups, the WISC-III uses the same questions for all school-age children. The following is a list of the subtests, with examples similar to actual items on the subtests (Bee, 1989):

Verbal Tests

General information. "How many eyes have you?"
General comprehension. "What is the thing to do when you scrape your knee?"
Arithmetic. "James had ten marbles and he bought four more. How many marbles did he have altogether?"
Similarities. "In what way are a pear and an orange alike?"
Vocabulary. "What is an emerald?"

Performance Tests

Picture completion. The child is shown pictures of familiar objects in which a part has been left out. He has to identify the missing part, such as a tooth missing from a comb.
Picture arrangement. Pictures like the frames of a comic strip are laid out in the wrong order in front of the child. The child has to figure out the right order to make a story.
Block design. Sets of special blocks (red, white, or half red, half white on the different sides) are given to the child. Using these blocks, she has to copy designs. The first problems involve only four blocks; harder problems include nine blocks.
Object assembly. Large pictures of familiar objects like a horse or a face have been cut up into pieces—rather like jigsaw puzzles, but in bigger pieces. The child has to put them together in the correct configuration as rapidly as possible.
Coding. A series of abstract symbols like balls and stars or curved lines are shown in pairs. The child must learn which symbols go together, because he is given several rows of boxes that show only one of each pair, and he must fill in the paired symbol in each box as quickly as possible. (p. 191)

The WISC-III provides three separate IQs: verbal, performance, and total. More can be said about the persons at the extremes of the distribution than those in the middle. Although there are other factors involved in the classification, students with IQ scores above 130 are frequently identified as gifted, and those with scores below 70 are classified as mentally retarded. (See Chapter 11 for further discussion.)

Uses of Intelligence Tests

Individually administered intelligence tests are most frequently used for making decisions about educational placement, since intelligence test scores generally are good predictors of academic achievement (Sattler, 1988). For example, if students are having difficulty in class, they may be given an IQ test (as one indicator) to determine whether they may have some specific learning problems or may be retarded. On the other end of the spectrum, an IQ test may help identify gifted students. There are also intelligence tests for young children to help predict whether they will be able to handle kindergarten work.

Gronlund (1985a) cautions those making educational decisions that intelligence test scores are less dependable for the following types of students:

- Those whose home environment does not provide the opportunity to learn the types of task included in the test
- Those who are little motivated by school tasks
- Those who are weak in reading skills or have a language handicap
- Those who have a poor emotional adjustment (p. 308)

Some Misconceptions about Intelligence Tests

? Can intelligence tests measure innate ability?

You, among many others, may be confused about what intelligence tests measure. They do *not* measure "innate" or "natural" ability to learn new behavior. In fact, no test can measure innate ability to learn! An intelligence test measures present ability—specifically, the behavior required by the test at the time the test is given. Since the environment interacts with heredity at the time of conception, it is impossible to determine the exact contributions of each.

Many psychologists question whether a child's intelligence test score is even an accurate reflection of learning ability. The argument is that children's performances on an intelligence test are based on the faulty assumption that equivalent chronological age implies equivalent learning opportunities. An intelligence test compares what a child has learned over some period of time to what his or her peers have learned. However, not all children of the same chronological age have had an equal opportunity to learn the material tested by an intelligence test. Because of this inequity, psychologists argue that the teacher who concludes that a student with a low intelligence test score simply lacks the capacity to learn is making a serious error in interpreting the meaning of the test score.

Some people mistakenly believe that once an individual's IQ is determined, the score doesn't change. Research has determined that intelligence tests given to infants do not correlate well with their scores when they become children or adolescents (Kopp & McCall, 1982). In fact, there are even fluctuations in IQs throughout childhood and adolescence.

Another mistaken belief is that intelligence tests measure all educators need to know about human abilities. Earlier I mentioned some of the abilities identified by Guilford that are not emphasized in school. Later in this chapter we will discuss the work of Robert Sternberg (1988) and Howard Gardner (1983), who are concerned about the limitations of traditional intelligence tests. Intelligence test scores, in general, correlate fairly high with academic achievement in school and can be used to predict scholastic success. However, the skills measured by intelligence tests are limited to a narrow range of human abilities.

Intelligence Test Bias and Fairness

? Are intelligence tests fair to all students?

The issues of bias and fairness regarding intelligence tests have been debated for years. Fairness is a philosophical issue and most often relates to how tests are used (or misused); test bias is concerned with the controversy over the items contained on the tests and whether they provide a true measure of ability within the socioeconomic or ethnic group tested. Test experts often disagree about both issues.

White students tend to score higher than African American students, and middle-class students tend to score higher than lower-class students (Jensen, 1980). Critics argue that the poor performance on IQ tests by some African American students stems from bias in the test items and administration. Let's review the arguments and responses by the proponents of IQ testing (Fogel & Melson, 1988).

IQ tests require verbal responses, and since some African American students do not speak Standard English, they may be reluctant to respond freely in front of white adults. Also, since many African American students are criticized for their language skills, they may feel unmotivated or discouraged when they take a test. These conditions can lead to poor test performance. On the other hand, advocates of intelligence tests counter that African American children's performance is not influenced by whether the examiner is white or African American, and in some situations, African American children score higher when the examiner is white (Sattler & Gwynne, 1982). Second, the proponents indicate that African American children tend to score lower on performance rather than verbal items (where language bias would be most evident) (Reynolds & Jensen, 1983).

Others argue that there may be bias in the test items themselves. African American and Latino children may perform less well on items that are more familiar to white children. Jensen (1980) has pointed out, however, that when the most culturally specific items are removed from tests, racial differences in test results still exist. In addition, he reports that when white and African American students are compared on the most culturally biased items, African American students do not respond more poorly.

The responses to the critics of IQ tests do not "close the book" on further criticism, for there may be more subtle sources of bias that have yet to be uncovered (Fogel & Melson, 1988). More recently, other racial differences in IQ performance have been found. Japanese children now frequently score higher on IQ tests than whites do (Lynn, 1982), and in many areas of the country, certain Asian Americans are the top students in their school and are gaining admission to major universities in record numbers. Could their performance be due to the emphasis their parents put on the importance of school, the amount of time spent studying, and their own motivation to succeed?

Another major concern is that some teachers use intelligence test scores, consciously or unconsciously, to label children as poor or bright students. A teacher who has noticed that a student has a low intelligence test score may hold a low expectation for the student's classroom performance and may be less likely to provide remedial instruction. The teacher may even act in ways that contribute to the fulfillment of the expectation, such as calling on the student less often.

A final concern is that intelligence tests are often a basis for discriminatory practices in school, especially in the placement of poor and minority students in special classes for mentally retarded or slow students. Mercer (1971) studied the distribution of ethnic group members in special education classes in the public schools of Riverside, California. Although the ethnic group distribution of children in the classes tested by psychologists closely approximated the ethnic group distribution of the entire school population, a disproportionate number of Latino and African American children had intelligence test scores below 80. In addition, more Latinos than whites were recommended for and finally placed in classes for the mentally retarded. Mercer argued that neither genetic factors nor environmental deficiencies could account for the large percentage of low test scores among minorities. However, children from low socioeconomic status (SES) groups or from ethnic minorities are more vulnerable to being labeled mentally retarded because clinical measures (primarily intelligence tests) are interpreted from a culture-based perspective. Federal legislation now provides guidelines for identifying students needing special education (see Chapter 11). The purpose of these regulations is to reduce the probability of unfair testing procedures and improper placement of students in special education classes.

The controversy over the benefits of IQ testing has reached the courts. In a widely publicized case, a lawsuit was initiated in the state of California because of the overrepresentation of African Americans in classes for the mentally retarded. The plaintiff charged that the intelligence test was a biased assessment of the students' abilities. The judge ruled in *Larry P. v. Riles* (1979) that school officials in California could not use an intelligence test for identification of African American educable mentally retarded children. After the U.S. Court of Appeals for the Ninth Circuit upheld, by a 2–1 margin, the judge's ruling, the California State Department of Education issued a directive to prohibit all individually administered intelligence tests for use in the assessment of African American children referred for any special education placement.

In two other court cases, judges ruled that intelligence testing was not discriminatory against African American children. In *PASE v. Hannon* (1980), a judge in Chicago stated that he could find little evidence that intelligence tests were biased. The judge found only eight test items on the WISC-R (which was the test version preceding the WISC-III) and one item on the Stanford-Binet to be biased against African American children. He also noted that the judge in *Larry P. v. Riles* failed to analyze the items on the intelligence tests. Finally, in *Georgia Conferences of NAACP v. Georgia* (1985), both the trial court and the Court of Appeals rejected the claims that intelligence tests were discriminatory.

It is obvious that the issue of bias in mental testing is not resolved. Some jurists have noted that the courts may not be the most appropriate place to resolve complex issues concerning the fairness of tests in educational decision making (Sattler, 1988).

Can the issue of bias in testing be solved by developing "culture-free" tests? There have been a number of attempts to develop a "culture-free" test (e.g., Davis-Eells Games) or at least a "culture-fair" test (e.g., Culture Fair Intelligence Tests). These measures are nonverbal tests that use pictures and diagrams common to many cultures. Unfortunately, these tests have not been successful because, first, lower socioeconomic status and some minority students score lower than white, middle-class students; and, second, the tests fail to predict scholastic achievement as well as do other intelligence tests (Jensen, 1980).

Educational Interventions to Increase Intelligence and Academic Performance

? Is intelligence fixed, or can it be changed?

One of the important educational implications of the psychometric perspective is to develop intervention programs aimed at improving intellectual skills related to school success as indicated by scores on achievement tests. Since the mid-1960s considerable federal funding has been used to establish preschool programs (for example, Head Start, which services students from age 3 to school entry), summer programs, special educational equipment, tutoring, trips, and other extracurricular activities for children from poverty-stricken and low socioeconomic areas.

Much of this funding has come from Title I of the Elementary and Secondary Education Act of 1965. Since 1981 the funds have come from federal legislation called Chapter 1. Much of the support for special funding was and continues to be based on the belief that children reared in poverty areas are not motivated to learn in school and are deprived of the stimuli that affect intellectual and cognitive development. General sensory deprivation results from lack of sufficient auditory and visual stimulation, and poor verbal skills stem from arrested language development in children's speech at home.

The goal of these special programs is to compensate for the inadequacies of deprived children through a planned enrichment program of various sensory experiences and language skills. Thus, *culturally deprived* and *compensatory education* became widely used terminology in educational circles. Numerous books and journal articles were written in the 1960s and 1970s on the problem of and possible solutions for educating "disadvantaged" children. Today, educators are more likely to use the term *culturally different* than *culturally deprived*.

The proponents of compensatory education believed that improved environmental conditions could influence children's intellectual and academic development, and they attempted to equalize individual differences that existed before the children started school. In fact, Hunt (1961), a crusader for early childhood programs, argued that "with a sound scientific educational psychology of early experience, it might become possible to raise the level of intelligence . . . by thirty points" (p. 267).

The research on Head Start has been mixed. One problem is that there is no standard Head Start program; the term is a label for many different types of programs using a variety of instructional methods—some of which have been more successful than others. In general, for the programs that had significant impact on children's intellectual and academic performance, the gains were lost by the time the students were in the primary grades (Haskins, 1989; McKey et al., 1985). However, there is evidence that children benefit in other ways by attending preschool programs. Lazar and his colleagues (1982) found that students who had participated in preschool programs were less likely to be assigned to special education classes, were less likely to be retained in school, and had more positive attitudes toward achievement. Another investigation of students at age 19 showed that students who attended basic skills–oriented preschool programs were more likely to finish high school, had a lower rate of delinquency, and were earning more money (Barnett, 1985).

In 1967 a program called Project Follow Through was established to service children in kindergarten through the third grade and to build upon Head Start programs. Unfortunately, budget cuts kept this program small and resulted primarily in demonstration projects throughout the country to determine what programs worked best. In one investigation, Becker and Gersten (1982) studied Project Follow Through students in grades 4 and 5. They found that the Follow Through students scored significantly higher in reading, spelling, and math than students who were not involved in the program. However, when they compared the achievement scores of the Follow Through students with a national sample of students, they found that the Follow Through students' achievement scores steadily declined from the third grade (when they left the program) to the sixth grade.

In both the Head Start and Follow Through programs, students' IQ and/or achievement gains diminished once they left the program. Bjorklund (1989) sees the implications of this finding as follows:

> Intelligence is not something that once you "get" you necessarily keep. Intelligence, as measured by IQ tests, is a reflection of a person's intel-

lectual functioning at a given time. Once established, intelligence (or any other complex behavior, for that matter) must be maintained. If the environmental supports responsible for establishing competence are removed, one should not be surprised that intelligence suffers. (p. 246)

heritability. The extent to which differences in a trait are attributed to inheritance.

? Is intelligence determined by environment or heredity?

A CRITIC OF COMPENSATORY EDUCATION PROGRAMS. In 1969 a highly controversial article was written by Arthur R. Jensen entitled, "How Much Can We Boost IQ and Scholastic Achievement?" In this article, Jensen concluded that the main reason compensatory education programs have failed is that they concentrated on environmental experiences as the determining factor in intellectual development. He presented data to support the position that about 80 percent of variations in IQ occur because of genetic differences, with environmental factors contributing to only a small portion of the differences among individuals.

Jensen raised an old controversy in psychology: **heritability**—the extent to which differences in a trait (such as intelligence) are attributed to inheritance. Psychologists refer to heritability in terms of a percentage that can range from 0 (none of the differences in the trait are related to inheritance) to 1 (100 percent of the differences in a trait are attributed to inheritance). The present estimate of the heritability of intelligence is .50, meaning that, on the average, 50 percent of the differences in intelligence test scores in a population of people can be attributed to inheritance (Bjorklund, 1989). The relationships among people increase as genetic similarity increases. For example, the intelligence correlations of identical twins (i.e., they come from the same zygote or egg) reared together is .86; reared apart, .72; whereas the correlations of fraternal twins reared together is .60; siblings reared together, .47; reared apart, .27 (Bouchard & McCue, 1981).

Although there is evidence that inheritance plays an important role in determining intelligence, there also is evidence that environmental factors similarly play an important role. For example, there are adoption studies demonstrating that when children from impoverished environments are reared in more affluent environments, the children's IQ scores are 10 or 15 points higher than those of their birth mothers (Scarr & Kidd, 1983; Skodak & Skeels, 1945). Also, the Transracial Adoption Study of Scarr and Weinberg (1976, 1983) reported that when African American children born of parents from low-income environments were adopted by white, upper-middle-class parents, the average IQ of the adopted children was 20 points higher than the average IQ of a comparable group of children reared in the local African American community.

Current evaluation studies have failed to change Jensen's opinions regarding the success of preschool educational programs. In a more recent article, Jensen (1985) points out that preschool programs have had success in such areas as involving parents in school and improving children's self-esteem and their attitudes toward school, but he continues to question the impact of preschool programs on intelligence and academic achievement. He believes that more research needs to be done to learn how compensatory education influences children's *thinking processes* (or information processing). In the past, the research focus has been on children's deficiency in *knowledge*, which involved the erroneous belief that intelligence is identified with the content of the test items found in intelligence tests—that is, if a child learns the material tested, the child will become more intelligent. Jensen believes that intelligence is related to thinking processes, not the amount of acquired knowledge.

THE PIAGETIAN PERSPECTIVE

Through analysis of the processes involved in the organization of knowledge, the Swiss psychologist Jean Piaget (1895–1980) developed a theory of how a child's thinking process gradually shifts from concrete to abstract intellectual functioning. Piaget is considered a developmental psychologist because of his study of the developmental stages, or age-level changes, that determine what children can learn at various ages. The unique aspect of Piaget's theory is that it separates and identifies stages of intellectual, or cognitive, development. The child's stage of development sets limits on learning and influences the type of learning that can take place.

Piaget worked at Binet's laboratory in Paris testing children for the development of the first intelligence tests. He became interested in how children of various ages passed or failed certain sections of the tests. By asking certain probing questions about their reasons for making certain responses, he was better able to understand their thinking. This experience laid the foundation for his major contribution to psychology—a theory of cognitive development.

Piaget is one of the few psychologists who present a comprehensive theory of the development of intelligence, or the thought process. His theory is different from the psychometric perspective discussed earlier in the chapter. The first part of the following discussion deals with the development of the stages in the thinking process; the second part derives the instructional and learning implications of the theory.

The Process of Cognitive Development

From the Piagetian perspective, mental growth means the acquisition of new mental abilities not previously present. Intellectual growth is not a quantitative process, but a qualitative process in which there are significant differences between the thinking of children and adolescents, as well as between preschool and school-age children (Elkind, 1974).

Biologists are hard-pressed to explain how structures evolve so that organisms can adapt to their environment. Piaget has explored this same problem in regard to human adaptation and has researched a theory of intellectual or cognitive development based on the premise that intellectual structures—organizational properties of thought—are formed in the individual during interaction with the environment. The emerging structures enable the individual to cope better with the increasing demands of the environment.

Piaget uses the term *scheme*[1] almost interchangeably with *structure*. A scheme is a repeatable behavior pattern. Initially, scheme relates to inborn reflexes such as the "sucking scheme"; during adolescence schemes are mental, as in the "scheme of classification," "scheme of probability," and "operational schemes," or "operations" for short. The acquisition of a scheme implies that there has been a change in the child's intellectual development.

An important aspect of functioning is **adaptation**. All organisms are born with a tendency to adapt to their environment. The ways in which adaptation takes place differ from organism to organism. Adaptation may be considered in terms of two complementary processes—**assimilation** and **accommodation**. Assimilation refers to the process by which an individual uses an existing structure or ability to deal with some problem in the environment. Accommodation is a process by which the individual must change in response to environmental demands. This adaptation necessitates a modification, or rearrangement, of the individual's existing mental structures.

The following example illustrates the relationship between assimilation and accommodation. A child who has learned to open cabinets by pulling on them will have to develop a new sequence of hand movements in order to open a cabinet with a handle that must be turned. The child will have to accommodate to the environment. However, once this new response has been learned, the child will be able to recall the sequence of behaviors when opening this particular type of cabinet door. The child will have assimilated the new experience. In review, if an individual has an existing behavior pattern for interacting with the environment, this behavior is assimilated. If the individual does not have an appropriate set of behaviors to deal with a situation, the pattern of response must change to allow accommodation to the environment.

To Piaget, adaptation is a balance of assimilation and accommodation. If, in the process of assimilation, the individual cannot adapt to the environment, a state of **disequilibrium** exists. Accommodation is the result of this disequilibrium, and either the individual's present structures are altered or new ones emerge. Intellectual growth is a continual process of equilibrium-disequilibrium states. However, when equilibrium is restored, the individual is at a higher intellectual level than before (Sullivan, 1967).

Adaptation can also be applied to classroom learning. Cognitive progress depends partly on accommodation for development. The student must enter an area of the unknown in order to learn. We cannot study only what we already know—we cannot rely on assimilation. In a situation in which your existing cognitive processes are not used, accommodation, but no assimilation, occurs. In courses that present you with nothing new, you have probably overassimilated; in courses that you don't grasp, you have overaccommodated. Neither situation will facilitate your cognitive growth.

adaptation. Changes in an organism in response to environmental demands.

assimilation. Piaget's term for the process of making sense of experiences and perceptions by fitting them into previously established cognitive structures.

accommodation. Piaget's term for the modification or reorganization of existing cognitive structures to deal with environmental demands.

disequilibrium. Piaget's term for the state when, in the process of assimilation, the individual cannot adapt to the environment.

[1] I am using the terminology suggested by Ginsburg and Opper (1988), who state that Piaget's French term *scheme* is usually translated as *schema* (plural: schemata). They suggest that because Piaget has used the French word *schema* for another purpose, the retention of the French word *scheme* in English is preferable.

equilibration. A motivation principle in Piaget's theory that identifies humans as active and exploratory in attempting to impose order and meaningfulness on experiences.

sensorimotor stage. Piaget's first stage of intellectual development, in which the child moves from the reflexive activities of reaching, grasping, and sucking to more highly organized forms of activity.

In summary, there are three aspects of intellectual growth: structure, content, and function. As the child develops, structure and content change but functions remain the same. The organization and adaptation functions create a series of stages, each possessing particular psychological structures that determine the child's thinking ability. Intelligence for Piaget, then, is the sum of available structures an individual has available at a particular point in development.

Piaget's Developmental Stages

A question often asked about Piaget's stages is, "What causes an individual to move from one stage to another?" Piaget (1964) identifies four factors that influence this transition.

1. *Maturation*. The development of the central nervous system, brain, motor coordination, and other physical manifestations of growth influence cognitive development. Until the child's motor coordination is developed to a certain extent, walking cannot occur, and if the child is limited in exploring the environment, not much will be learned about it. Although maturation is an important factor in intellectual development, it does not sufficiently explain it. If it did, teachers would play a very minor role in influencing intellectual development.
2. *Physical experience*. The child's interaction with the physical environment can increase the rate of development because observation and manipulation of objects aid the emergence of more complex thinking.
3. *Social transmission*. This marks the influence of language, formal instruction, and reading, as well as social interaction with peers and adults. These experiences also influence cognitive development.
4. **Equilibration**, or self-regulation. This factor incorporates the ability to re-establish equilibrium states during periods of disequilibrium. It is a process by which the individual attains higher levels of cognitive functioning through a step-by-step assimilation and accommodation.

Piaget's stages are presented in Table 8.1. Note that these age ranges are only approximations. You may encounter slightly different classifications in other readings, especially for middle childhood. All children proceed through each stage, but at different rates. Thus it is possible for a 6-year-old child to be at the concrete operations stage or an 8-year-old child still to be at the preoperational stage in thinking. However, the *sequence* of development is the same for all children; each successive stage is built in a hierarchical fashion on the preceding stage. Structures belonging to earlier stages become integrated and incorporated as part of the stages that follow.

SENSORIMOTOR STAGE (0–2 YEARS). **Sensorimotor** thought occupies approximately the first two years of life, when infants experience the environment primarily through their senses and motor activity. The

TABLE 8.1 PIAGET'S STAGES OF COGNITIVE DEVELOPMENT

Stage	Approximate Age	Characteristics
Sensorimotor	0–2 years	Begins to make use of imitation, memory, and thought. Begins to recognize that objects do not cease to exist when they are hidden. Moves from single reflex actions to purposeful activity.
Preoperational	2–7 years	Gradual language development and ability to think in symbolic form. Able to think operations through logically in one direction. Thought and language both egocentric.
Concrete operational	7–11 years	Able to solve concrete problems in logical fashion. Understands laws of conservation and is able to classify and seriate. Reversibility attained.
Formal operational	11–15 years	Able to solve abstract problems in logical fashion. Thinking becomes more scientific. Solves complex verbal and hypothetical problems.

Source: Wadsworth, 1989.

object permanence. Piaget's term for children's understanding that objects continue to exist apart from the children's perception of them.

infant begins life with innate reflexes, schemes that are modified and combined with other schemes to form more complex behavior. By the end of this stage, babies begin to acquire a primitive symbol system (such as language) to think about and represent events in their lives.

During this time, the infant has no conception of **object permanence**. When an object is hidden from view, the infant fails to look for it. As infants continue to experience the environment, toward the end of the sensorimotor period they behave as though they realize that a hidden object still exists and begin looking for it after they have seen it hidden. Other primitive concepts not present at birth—space, time, causality—develop and become incorporated into the child's behavior patterns.

Our interest in the school-age child prompts us to move on to the remaining stages in Piaget's theory, on which we shall spend more time.

? What are the limitations of children's thinking at the preoperational stage?

PREOPERATIONAL STAGE (2-7 YEARS). Although the child makes rapid cognitive growth during the first two years of life, abilities are limited to objects that can be seen in the environment. The child's "thinking" acts on objects that can be perceived directly. However, toward the end of the second year, the child begins using symbols to represent various aspects of the environment. For example, the child can use the word *ball* to represent a real ball when it is not in immediate view. This

preoperational stage. The second stage in Piaget's theory of cognitive development, in which the lack of logical operations forces children to make decision based on their perceptions.

reversibility. In Piaget's theory, the process of performing an action and then restoring the original condition.

symbolic ability adds a new dimension to the child's thinking ability (Ginsburg & Opper, 1988).

A great deal of Piaget's research on childhood concerns understanding the nature of a class—a set of objects that are united by some relationship, such as girls, dogs, balls, or red circles. The ability to add classes together, multiply classes, and break down classes into subclasses is necessary for conceptual thinking. The child at this period has a difficult time with such classification tasks and is capable of formulating only primitive concepts that are referred to by Piaget as "preconcepts."

Phillips (1969) has summarized some of the limitations of **preoperational** thought under six headings.

1. *Concreteness*. Preoperational children are capable of manipulating symbols and, when compared with the children in the sensorimotor period, are rather abstract in their thinking. Nevertheless, when compared with an adolescent or adult, the preoperational child is still oriented toward the concrete.
2. *Irreversibility*. **Reversibility** is the ability to return to the point of origin, to do and undo, to go in one direction and compensate for it in another direction. Every mathematical or logical operation is reversible: 4 + 8 = 12, and 12 − 8 = 4; all boys + all girls = all children, and all children − all girls = all boys. The preoperational child does not have the ability to deal with problems that necessitate reversible thinking.

To understand that the amount of liquid does not change when it is poured into different size beakers, the child must consider both the length and width of the beakers at the same time. According to Piaget, volume conservation is not usually present until the concrete operations stage.

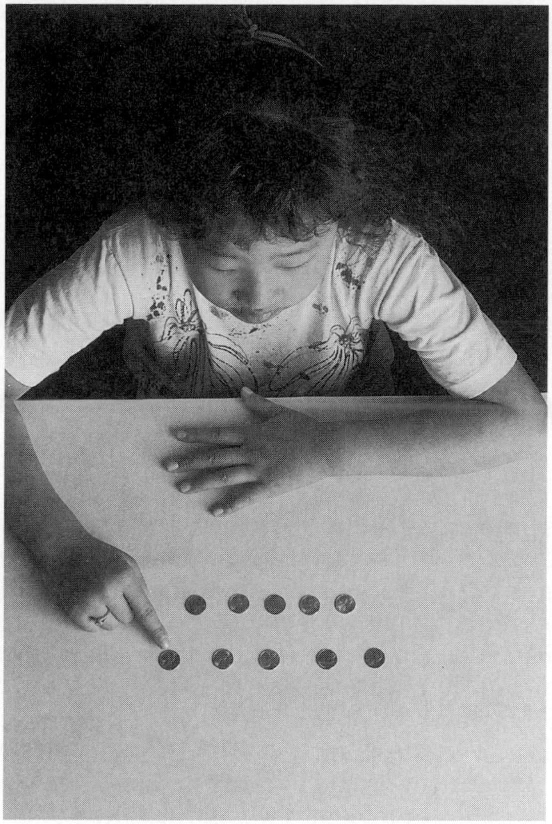

Around the age of 6 or 7 the child learns to conserve numbers. Even though the child sees one row lengthened without any change in the number of pennies, she declares that both rows are equivalent.

Phillips (1969) illustrates this limitation from one of his own observations. He asked a 4-year-old boy, "Do you have a brother?"

"Yes."
"What's his name?"
"Jim."
"Does Jim have a brother?"
"No." (p. 61)

conservation. A Piagetian term for the realization that certain properties of an object remain the same regardless of changes in its other properties.

Conservation experiments further illustrate the lack of reversible thought. The idea that the amount or quantity of a matter stays the same regardless of any changes in shape or position is incomprehensible to the child. For example, a child observes two small glasses, A and B, identical in size and shape and filled with an equal amount of water, and, in turn, observes as the water from glass A is emptied into another glass, C, which is taller and narrower. The child tends to conclude that the quantity of water has changed. Glass C contains more water than glass A because "it is higher," even though the child readily admits that no water has been added or removed.

In another example, a child presented with two rows of pennies states that the rows contain the same number of pennies. If one row is elongated without any change in the number of pennies, the child usually declares that the rows are no longer equivalent.

decenter. The ability to take into consideration two or more details or dimensions at the same time.

egocentrism. Piaget's term for describing children in the preoperational stage, who have difficulty in assuming the point of view of others.

transductive reasoning. Piaget's term to describe thought in the preoperational stage when the child moves from the particular to the particular without touching on the general.

Finally, two clay balls of equal size are shown to the child, and the child agrees that they are the same size. Then one of the balls is rolled into a sausage shape and the child is asked the same question. The usual response is that the sausage-shaped ball is larger.

Conservation does not take place at the same time in all subject areas. Children usually grasp conservation of numbers (age 5–6) before conservation of substance, or mass (age 7–8), and weight (age 9–10), followed last by conservation of volume (age 11–12).

3. *Centering*. Children tend to focus on only one dimension or detail of an event and neglect other important aspects. In the water-level problem demonstrating irreversible thinking, one reason for the difficulty is that the child focuses on length—the taller glass—and forgets about width. The preoperational child cannot **decenter**, or focus back and forth between details, and reasoning is necessarily distorted.
4. *Egocentrism*. Many of Piaget's readers have misunderstood the term **egocentrism** (sometimes called *perspective taking*). It is not used in a derogatory sense to describe personality; it simply means that the child has difficulty taking another person's point of view. Egocentrism enters the arena of language and communication. Watch any group of preschool children playing together, and you will hear egocentric speech. You may hear children repeating words merely for the pleasure of pronouncing them or talking "toward" each other without really expecting the others to listen or reply.
5. *States versus Transformations*. The preoperational child focuses on the static aspect of an event rather than on the transformations from one state to another. In the water-level problem, the child is intent on the height of the water, not on the act of pouring. In the conservation-of-substance problem with the clay balls, the child retains the image of the shape of the clay and ignores the transformations—the change from the round to the sausage shape. In one experiment (Flavell, 1963), the child is asked to "depict the successive movements of a bar which falls from a vertical, upright position to a horizontal one" (p. 158). Although the solution of this problem is obvious to the adolescent, the preoperational child fails to draw the intermediate positions of the bar.
6. *Transductive Reasoning*. Deduction is reasoning from the general to the specific. Assuming that all children are good, if we see a child, we deduce that the child is good. Induction proceeds in the opposite direction, establishing generalizations from specific instances: If we meet a large number of good children, we can conclude that they are all good.

   According to Piaget, the preoperational child's thinking is somewhere in between, moving from the particular to the particular without touching on the general. The child sees some relationship between particular instances when there is none. Piaget calls this **transductive reasoning**. The child who walks through the forest, not knowing whether a succession of turtles is appearing or whether the same turtle is reappearing time and time again, is thinking transductively. This is an example of the preconcept I discussed earlier.

Piaget (1952) reported an example of transductive thinking: When his daughter failed to take a nap one afternoon, she said to him, "I haven't had my nap, so it isn't afternoon" (p. 232). It is very common for children at this age to see relationships between particular instances, such that if *A* causes *B*, then *B* causes A.

concrete operations stage. The third of Piaget's four major stages, characterized by children's ability to think logically, but only about concrete problems and objects.

How is thinking more advanced at the concrete operations stage?

CONCRETE OPERATIONS STAGE (7–11 YEARS). The **concrete operations stage** marks the beginning of operational thought. That is, the child acquires logical thought processes (operations) that can be applied to concrete problems. When faced with a discrepancy between thought and perception, as in the conservation problems, the child in the concrete operations period opts for logical decisions instead of the perceptual decisions a child in the preoperational period makes.

The following mathematical symbols are examples of operations: = (equal), + (combining), – (separating). Each of these operations has its counterpart in logic; for example, + is equivalent to *and*, – is equivalent to *except* (Phillips, 1969). Piaget uses the structure of logic as a model for explaining the qualitative differences in children's thinking ability during both the concrete and formal operations periods.

The operations of this period are tied to personal experience. They are concrete but not formal operations. The child is still unable to deal with abstract material such as hypotheses and verbal propositions. The following are an important set of concrete operations:

The manipulation of concrete objects can provide an important foundation for higher-level thinking.

combinativity. An operation in which two or more classes are combined into a larger group.

associativity. An operation wherein several classes can be combined in any order to produce the same results.

identity. An operation involving recognition that physical substances retain their volume or quantity, even when moved or reorganized, as long as nothing is added or taken away.

serializing. The process of ordering objects in terms of one or more properties.

- **Combinativity**, or classification, is an operation by which two or more classes are combined into a larger group: all boys + all girls = all children. Relationships such as $A > B$ and $B > C$ can be combined into a new relationship, $A > C$. For the first time, the child can form a variety of class relationships and understands that some classes can be included in other classes.
- *Reversibility* is the major criterion for operational thought in Piaget's system. It implies that every logical or mathematical operation can be canceled by an opposite operation. All children – all girls = all boys; or 7 + 3 = 10 and 10 – 7 = 3.
- **Associativity** is an operation by which several classes can be combined in any order (1 + 3) + 5 = 1 + (3 + 5). In reasoning, this operation allows a child to arrive at answers in many different ways.
- **Identity** is an operation in which there exists a null element that, when combined with any element or class, produces no change: 10 + 0 = 10. Also, a quantity can be nullified by combining it with its opposite: 10 – 10 = 0; or, if I walk 3 miles east and 3 miles west, I end up where I started.

Children at the concrete operations stage are not "brighter" than preschool children, they have simply acquired certain abilities (operations) for solving problems that they could not solve correctly before. Concrete operational thinking is stable, compared with the highly impressionistic and static thinking of the preoperational period.

Concrete operational children can bring these operations to bear on such problems as class relationships. If you ask preschoolers if there are more girls or more children in the room, they may respond that there are more boys than girls, for young children have difficulty dealing with classes and subclasses at the same time. They cannot conceive that it is possible to belong to two classes at the same time (e.g., boys and children). However, 6- or 7-year-old children will have no difficulty with this problem. They are capable of deducing the following: boys + girls = children (combinativity), since children – boys = girls (reversibility); thus, children ≠ boys (Elkind, 1968).

Using these same operations, children develop an awareness of the principles of conservation. The child can focus on both length and width (decentration) and can recognize that pouring water into different-size beakers does not change the amount of water because the amount of water is the same as in the beginning (identity and reversibility).

The child in this period can now rank in order a series of objects, such as wooden dolls or sticks, according to their size. Piaget refers to this operation as **serializing**. However, the child can do this only as long as the problem is presented concretely; it is not until adolescence that such a problem can be solved mentally using verbal propositions.

Language also changes at this time. The child becomes less egocentric and more sociocentric in communication. The child now makes an attempt to understand other people and communicate feelings and ideas to adults and peers. Thought processes also become less egocentric, and the child can now take another's point of view.

FORMAL OPERATIONS STAGE (11 YEARS AND ABOVE). At approximately 11 years of age, a new operations period emerges in which the older child can use concrete operations to form more complex operations. Flavell (1963) discusses some characteristics of **formal** operational thought. First, the adolescent uses **hypothetico-deductive reasoning**. Many alternative hypotheses in dealing with a problem can be formulated, and data can be checked against each of the hypotheses to make an appropriate decision. Children in the concrete operations stage also can reason deductively, but their thinking is limited to events and objects with which they are familiar. The adolescent's major advance during this stage is that it is now no longer necessary to think in terms of objects or concrete events; he or she now has the ability to think *abstractly*.

Second, this period is marked by **propositional reasoning**. The adolescent is not limited to concrete objects or events in reasoning but can deal with statements or propositions that describe these concrete data. The adolescent can even deal with contrary-to-fact propositions. If you ask a child in one of the other developmental stages to pretend to be the president of the United States and then ask the child a question about a hypothetical situation he or she might encounter as president, the child is likely to say, "But I'm not the president of the United States." The adolescent has no trouble accepting contrary-to-fact propositions, and reasoning from them (Elkind, 1968).

Last, the adolescent can consider many possible solutions to a problem, by isolating individual factors and possible combinations of factors that may figure in the solution.

formal operations stage. Piaget's final stage of cognitive development, characterized by children's increasing ability to employ logical thought processes.

hypothetico-deductive reasoning. The ability to formulate many alternative hypotheses in dealing with a problem and to check data against each of the hypotheses to make an appropriate decision.

propositional reasoning. The ability to deal with statements or propositions that describe concrete data.

imaginary audience. The belief that other people are preoccupied with one's appearance and behavior.

personal fable. The belief in one's immortal and unique existence.

? How does adolescent egocentrism explain certain aspects of social behavior?

ADOLESCENT EGOCENTRISM. Egocentrism was discussed in Piaget's preoperational stage of development. It is defined as the inability to distinguish between one's own point of view and that of another person. During adolescence the ability to think about one's own thinking and to think abstractly frees the individual from the egocentrism of childhood. However, according to Elkind (1967), new types of egocentric thinking emerge—the **imaginary audience** and the **personal fable.**

The imaginary audience is the belief that other people are preoccupied with the adolescent's appearance and behavior. For example, when my daughters were in their early teens and were getting dressed to go out, they would try on numerous outfits before they settled on one. I couldn't believe all the time they took to select an outfit. Elkind would say that they were concerned about the "audience" that (they believed) was focused on them once they entered the dance or party. In other words, adolescents often think that they are always on stage and often become self-conscious about their behavior and dress. This audience is actually "imaginary" because, in most circumstances, others are not preoccupied with the adolescent. Elkind (1978) also has suggested that vandalism may involve the same principle: "The vandal is angry and wants to ensure that his or her audience will be angry too. In committing vandalism, the young person has the imagined audience in mind . . . " (p. 130).

The personal fable is the belief that the normal laws of nature that apply to other people don't apply to the adolescent. It results from adolescents' belief in their immortal and unique existence. The following are some typical comments by adolescents that represent this thinking: "Mom, you don't know what it is to be in love!" or "Other people may become addicted to drugs, but not me!" Elkind believes that the personal fable may account for the risk-taking behavior exhibited by many adolescents.

Criticisms of Piaget's Theory

Although Piaget's theory made important contributions to the understanding of cognitive development, there are a number of criticisms of his theory. In particular, Piaget's notion of structurally distinct stages is questioned. His critics argue that Piaget underestimated the intellectual abilities of the preschool child and overestimated the formal operations thinking of adolescents and adults. The clinical method that Piaget used to interview children may have contributed to this situation. Some researchers have found, for example, that children's performance on conservation tasks is influenced by the types of questions that are asked of them. Gelman and Gallistel (1978) have found that children as young as 2½ years already understand certain number principles even though they cannot correctly perform Piaget's conservation task. Also, researchers have shown that conservation can be accelerated by a variety of training procedures (e.g., Field, 1987). Under some conditions, children much younger than 11 have displayed formal operations reasoning (Hawkins et al., 1984; Slater & Kingston, 1981).

A large portion of the adult population may never go beyond concrete thinking (Schwebel, 1975). Research has shown that Piaget may have overestimated the ability of adolescents and adults to use formal operations thinking. For example, Kuhn et al. (1977) administered a battery of formal operations tasks to 265 adolescents and adults. They found that only about 30 percent of adults could be classified in the formal operations stage.

Although Piaget describes in detail the quality of children's thinking at various developmental stages, he fails to explain in the same detail how these changes in structure come about. Why does the child move from the preoperational to the concrete operational stage? Piaget's explanation is that when children acquire the necessary schemes, or intellectual structures, they move to the next stage. This explanation involves circular reasoning: "Children don't conserve because they are in the preoperational stage, and we know they are in the preoperational stage because they don't conserve."

The sequencing from one stage to another may be only an artifact of the evaluation procedure Piaget used. Given the way in which children's knowledge is assessed, it would be difficult for them to demonstrate any other pattern of cognitive development than that which is found (Brainerd, 1978). The issue is whether the sequence of stages depends upon some innate maturational blueprint or whether the stage sequence can be explained by other means (Gross, 1985). Learning theorists argue that higher-order skills require prerequisite knowledge that can be *learned*. Therefore, the educator does not have to rely on the development of schemata but instead needs to *teach* the necessary prerequisite skills to the child.

In general, many psychologists believe that the stages of cognitive development are not as clear-cut as Piaget has proposed and that new research is needed to explain some of the discrepancies found in his theory (Bjorklund, 1989). Psychologists who are making modifications in Piaget's theory are called neo-Piagetians and are discussed under information processing.

I don't believe that Piaget's theory has been discredited by recent research. He was not totally correct about the characteristics of the stages of development but appears to have been on target concerning the notion of a sequence in cognitive development and in the identification of qualitative changes in children's thinking between preschool and adolescence. In general, he has made considerable contributions to understanding children's cognitive development.

IMPLICATIONS OF PIAGET'S THEORY FOR EDUCATION

? What instructional processes would a Piagetian emphasize in the classroom?

Two major aspects of Piaget's theory have influenced educators. One is that children are active thinkers who construct their own understanding of the events in the world around them. This notion implies that the school curricula should involve students as active participants in the learning process rather than treat them as absorbing knowledge by passively listening to teachers. The development of open classrooms (Chapter 5), in which students work on projects in different learning centers, is one attempt to apply Piagetian concepts. Another teaching strategy consistent with Piaget's theory of cognitive development is discovery learning (Chapter 6), in which students acquire concepts on their own rather than through explanation by the teacher.

The second major Piagetian contribution to educational theory is that knowledge is constructed by systems of "logico-mathematical operations" (e.g., reversibility and associativity) that develop through a series of stages. Piaget's delineation of the relationship between a child's level of conceptual development and the complexity of the subject matter implies that teachers should heed what and how they teach. Piagetians maintain that the ideal learning situation arises from the match between the complexity of the subject matter and the child's level of conceptual development. A teacher who uses the best textbooks available and develops the most interesting and stimulating lesson plans can still fail to reach a majority of students who do not have the necessary structures (operations) to enable them to "understand" the presented material. This means that the classroom teacher should (1) assess a child's level of cognitive development and (2) determine the type of abilities the child needs to understand the subject matter.

Teaching Strategy

A teaching strategy developed from Piaget's theory is to "confront the child with the illogical nature of his point of view" (Siegel, 1969, p. 473). During the discussion of the assimilation-accommodation process, I mentioned that when assimilation fails, the child is in a state of disequilibrium and must begin to accommodate in order to adapt to the environment. You create disequilibrium in a child when you ask questions about some illogical statement the child has made. The child's attempts to reconcile this disequilibrium create new plateaus in cognitive development. The confrontation strategy implies that a student's incorrect answers should receive as much teacher attention as do correct answers.

In reacting to this same confrontation, the child advances from egocentric to sociocentric thought. Children have difficulty conceiving of a point of view different from their own. When they locate other individuals standing at different vantage points, the discovery plays an important role in modifying their point of view (Ginsburg & Opper, 1988).

Confrontation takes many forms, including questions, demonstrations, and/or environmental manipulations. Duckworth (1964) quotes Piaget:

> Good pedagogy must involve presenting the child with situations in which he himself experiments, in the broadest sense of that term—trying things out to see what happens, manipulating things, manipulating symbols, posing questions and seeking his own answers, reconciling what he finds one time with what he finds at another, comparing his findings with those of other children. (p. 2)

The preceding statement also emphasizes the active role that children play in the learning process. The Piagetian type of classroom de-emphasizes the transmission of knowledge through the lecture-discussion method and encourages the teacher to act more as a catalyst in situations in which children do their own learning.

Piaget was constantly asked (particularly during his travels in the United States) whether educators can speed up the transition between stages by teaching the operations or structures, such as reversibility, necessary for logical thinking. His statement (quoted in Duckworth, 1964) makes his position on the matter clear:

> The question comes up whether to teach the structure, or to present the child with situations where he is active and creates the structures himself. The goal in education is not to increase the amount of knowledge, but to create the possibilities for a child to invent and discover. When we teach too fast, we keep the child from inventing and discovering himself. . . . Teaching means creating situations where structures can be discovered; it does not mean transmitting structures which may be assimilated at nothing other than a verbal level. (p. 3)

Curriculum

Some educators suggest that Piaget's observations can aid teachers in the structure and sequencing of subject matter in the curriculum. Elkind (1980) identified problems that can occur when students are asked to deal with subject matter requiring formal operations. Consider a student attempting to understand $(a + b)^2 = a^2 + 2ab + b^2$. The student understands the equation for two numbers, say, for 4 and 5, but cannot understand that the equation holds for all numbers. In other words, the student believes that the letters stand for specific numbers rather than standing for all numbers.

Another problem involves interpreting literature. Reading good literature is an important goal in English, but requiring students in the concrete stage to describe what a poet had in mind when a certain poem was written or why an author approached a story in a particular way is likely to lead to failure. These questions ask a student to hypothesize about intentions—a difficult task for a student in the concrete operations stage. Elkind believes it is difficult enough for young people to deal with complex plots and metaphorical language without dealing with another person's intentions. He believes that a teacher must understand that there are different levels of understanding in literature.

Last, Elkind points out that the formal operations stage is necessary for understanding experimental science. He states that students are introduced to experimental science too early, since it presupposes an understanding of quantification along one or more dimensions, propositional logic, and the ability to analyze reality and to distinguish between reality and appearance (e.g., to recognize that two liquids of the same color can have different compositions). In sum, experimentation presupposes a level of thinking that many young students simply do not possess. Elkind believes that more appropriate scientific activities for students in the concrete operations stage are classifying and describing.

THE INFORMATION-PROCESSING PERSPECTIVE

One attempt to provide an alternative perspective to explaining children's cognitive abilities is *information-processing theory*. In this approach, the human mind is viewed as a type of computer that processes various types of information. This theory, of which there are different kinds, attempts to explain "how information is taken into the organism, interpreted, represented, transformed, and acted upon" (Gross, 1985, p. 19).

In studies of children's thinking, there are at least two branches to the information-processing approach. One group of researchers believe that children's thinking develops in stages, but suggest different structures and processes from those proposed by Piaget (see Sternberg, 1987a, for a review of these neo-Piagetian theories). These psychologists integrate the Piagetian perspective with the information-processing perspective. Another group of researchers investigate basic information-processing strategies to learn more about the processes that are the basis of human abilities or intelligent behavior. Many of these information-processing psychologists use the mental structures identified by the psychometric perspective to study the specific mental processes that constitute intelligent behavior.

Neo-Piagetians

? How have neo-Piagetian theorists modified Piaget's theory?

Fischer (1980; Fischer & Pipp, 1984) has suggested a modification of Piaget's developmental stages into 10 levels. He places greater emphasis on the role of the environment than Piaget did in explaining cognitive development. Fischer believes that children develop *skills* that are specific to particular objects and tasks. Thus he would not find it unusual for a child to be at one level on one task, and at a higher level on another task.

Another neo-Piagetian researcher, Pascual-Leone (1970, 1989), believes that the development of memory capacity is the major reason that children demonstrate different thinking at different ages. He finds that younger children are much more limited in the amount of information they can deal with at any one time than are older children or adults. For example, if one can think about only two or three things at once, rather than six or seven, this limitation will influence one's thinking and problem-solving ability. As capacity increases with increasing age, the child can deal with more information, and cognitive growth can occur. More specifically, Pascual-Leone found that the developmental transition from the preoperational to the concrete operational stage requires an increase of one information chunk in the child's memory. Until the child's mental capacity increases by that one unit, the change in developmental stage will not occur. Thus mental space (M-space) and its growth are an alternative approach to explaining cognitive development.

Case (Case & Griffin, 1989) also uses the notion of mental space in formulating his own theory of cognitive development, but emphasizes that working memory is not the only constraint on the quality of children's thinking. Although he proposes four stages, and three substages within each stage, the difference between his and Piaget's theory is that he does not assume that each new stage involves totally new types or forms of thinking; he assumes only that each stage requires more complex levels or integrations of the same basic processes. Case hypothesizes that children actively process and transform information by the use of a central conceptual structure, an internal network of concepts and conceptual relations that permit children to problem-solve and develop new structures for dealing with more complex situations. Case's notion of structures is different from Piaget's use of the term in that Case's structures are potentially teachable and are domain specific (i.e., related to specific tasks or subject matter).

Case points out that the rate at which children progress through his developmental sequence can vary from one domain (or area) to the next. This development is influenced by the child's experience exploring and solving problems in the domain. Thus, if a child conducts basic scientific experiments at home, reads books on science, and/or asks questions about scientific phenomenon, he or she is going to be a more advanced thinker in science than another child who has not had such experiences.

Information Processing and Human Abilities

? How do information-processing theorists approach the study of intelligence?

I have pointed out that psychometric theorists attempt to understand intelligence in terms of factors, or mental structures, and show how individuals differ on these factors. Sternberg (1987b), a proponent of the information-processing approach, criticizes the psychometricians by pointing out that

> when one says that a person is better on a reasoning test because he or she has a higher score on a reasoning factor, it does not seem to go much beyond saying that the score is higher because it is higher. So what we ask is: What are the underlying mental processes that contribute to individual differences in intelligence? (p. 194)

Let's use an example from intelligence testing to understand better the information-processing approach. Inductive reasoning ability is a factor or structure that is measured in almost all intelligence tests and has been shown to be a good indicator of general intelligence. Induction is the establishment of general rules or ideas from sets of specific instances or examples. Inductive reasoning tasks have similar characteristics. The learner is presented with a set of stimuli and asked to infer the pattern or rule for the task. One of the most common tasks is the verbal analogy, such as: BOY is to GIRL as FATHER is to (a. WORKER, b. MOTHER, c. MAN, d. BROTHER).

The information-processing psychologists would begin with the following question: "What are the basic psychological processes involved in solving inductive reasoning problems?" In solving verbal analogies, the person must first *encode*, or think about, the different terms in the analogy, identify each, and decide the attributes that may be relevant to a solution. Next, the person *infers* the relationship between the two terms (BOY and GIRL); *maps* or connects the higher-order relationship that links the first half of the analogy with the second half (the boy half with the father half); *applies* the relationship inferred between the first two terms (BOY and GIRL) to create the best completion to the analogy (MOTHER); *justifies* the answer option as preferable to the others, even if it is not the ideal response; and, finally, responds with the answer that seems best (Sternberg, 1988). This process is an example of *task analysis*, which we discussed in Chapter 6.

Once these processes have been defined, researchers would attempt to propose a theory as to how these processes are performed and executed, the sequence of the processes, the length of time needed to solve each item, and which items were more difficult. Finally, they would attempt to determine how individuals differ in the speed and accuracy of executing separate mental processes. When information-processing psychologists are finished, they expect to have a good understanding of inductive reasoning and hope to develop training programs to improve this human ability.

Let's look at another example. Mathematical ability is another human structure, or factor measured on intelligence tests. The psychometrician would identify mathematical ability as the ability to score well on tests of mathematics problems. In contrast, the information-processing approach would attempt to identify the mathematical components (e.g., skills, knowledge, mental operations) that are necessary to solve problems.

Consider the cognitive processes and knowledge required to solve simple word problems such as: "John has a nickel. Pete has 3 more cents than John. How many cents does Pete have?" Table 8.2 identifies two major parts—*problem representation* (changing a problem from words into an internal representation) and *problem solution* (applying mathematical knowledge to the internal representation to arrive at an answer). Five types of knowledge are used in solving such a problem (Mayer, 1985b):

1. *Linguistic knowledge* refers to knowledge about the English language, such as how to parse a sentence into parts of speech, or what various words mean.
2. *Factual knowledge* refers to knowledge about the world, such as units of measure.
3. *Schema knowledge* refers to knowledge of problems types, such as the difference between word problems and motion problems.
4. *Strategic knowledge* refers to knowledge of how to develop and monitor a solution plan.
5. *Algorithmic knowledge* refers to a procedure for carrying out a planned operation, such as how to compute a long division. (p. 131)

TABLE 8.2 TYPES OF KNOWLEDGE REQUIRED IN PROBLEM SOLVING

Sample problem: John has a nickel. Pete has 3 more cents than John. How many cents does Pete have?

Step	Knowledge	Examples from Sample Problem
Problem representation		
Translation	Linguistic	"Pete has 3 more cents than John" means "P = J + 3"
	Factual	A nickel equals 5 cents.
Integration	Schema	This is a "comparison" problem, consisting of two subsets and a superset.
Problem solution		
Planning	Strategic	The goal is to add 3 plus 5.
Execution	Algorithmic	Counting-on procedure.

Source: Mayer, 1985b.

The mathematical ability of students to solve algebraic word problems can be analyzed according to their translation, integration, planning, and execution abilities and related knowledge. Since students often demonstrate different patterns of strengths and weaknesses with respect to these abilities, the instructor can provide different training for individual students to improve their mathematical ability to solve these types of problems.

DEBATE FORUM

Are People Left-Brained and Right-Brained?

The human brain is divided into two hemispheres. Although the halves look alike and work together, they appear to function differently. The right side of the brain has been identified as more intuitive, while the left side is more logical. The left side appears to focus on such domains as speech, abstraction, logic, and reading; the right side focuses on innovation, creativity, intuition, and spatial relationships.

Argument: Secondary schools tend to ignore activities supported-by the right side of the brain. The typical high school curriculum emphasizes sequenced, verbal, numerical, and analytical skills—all left-brain functions. The right-brain—more difficult to work with—is less valued because it supports activities that do not lend themselves to tests or grades. The adolescent who functions better in a nonverbal, intuitive, nonsequential manner may have difficulty attaining success in school. Claims about the benefits of stimulating right-brain functions are made in conferences, workshops, and self-help books such as *The Right Brain* (Blakeslee, 1980) and *Drawing on the Right Side of the Brain* (Edwards, 1979).

continued

? How does Sternberg attempt to offer a new approach to the study of intelligence?

STERNBERG'S TRIARCHIC THEORY OF INTELLIGENCE. Sternberg (1988) believes that human intelligence is a dynamic process that is used in all aspects of our lives—at work, at social gatherings, at home, and at school. He suggests that we are constantly attempting to make sense of and solve problems to function successfully in our environment. Unfortunately, present intelligence tests measure only a small part of "mental self-management skills." To understand intelligence fully, we need to go beyond the current tests and see how intelligence operates in our everyday lives. The type of intelligence needed to succeed in school only partly determines success in out-of-school situations.

Sternberg (1985, 1988) proposes that individuals are governed by three aspects of intelligence—*componential, experiential,* and *contextual*—that are exercised in different domains. Componential intelligence identifies the

Counterargument: Sharp distinctions between the functioning of the two halves of the brain cannot be made, because the two halves work together (Levy, 1982). Although one hemisphere may be more differentially aroused than the other, it is simply wrong to state that students learn with only one side of the brain. The appreciation of literature, for example, depends on learning the meaning of words and sentences as well as responding to the rhythms of language, imagining and feeling scenes and moods, and empathizing with characters. This totality of experience cannot be accomplished by either side of the brain but depends on integrated activity; and it is difficult to say which side of the brain contributes to which activity.

Response: Harris (1985) criticizes educators for misunderstanding and, in many cases, simply ignoring basic neuropsychological literature: "If educators are unsatisfied with the educational *curriculum*, they ought to present the case for change on its *own* merits, and not seek to win scientific respectability for their arguments by cloaking them in neuropsychological jargon" (p. 267). After reviewing the literature on hemisphericity, Hellige (1990) made even stronger conclusions:

> Although the concept of hemisphericity has a certain simplistic elegance and intuitive appeal, there is no scientific foundation for the idea that individuals rely on only one hemisphere for thinking. Several neuroscientists have suggested that the concept of hemisphericity be viewed with skepticism or abandoned altogether. (p. 76)

mental components involved in analytical thinking (e.g., planning, organizing, remembering facts, and applying them to new situations). This component includes what is normally measured on IQ or achievement tests. Experiential intelligence refers to how individuals face new situations in which intuition, insight, and creativity are brought to bear. Contextual intelligence is the environment in which intelligence functions (e.g., the classroom, home, work). Some individuals call this component "social intelligence" or "street smarts." Sternberg believes that there are various ways of being intelligent, or smart. In the best situation, an individual uses basic thinking or analytical skills, applies them to experience, and uses the resulting ability to adapt to and shape his or her environment.

Some individuals may have a good deal of ability in all three components; others may have strength in only one or two of the three components. Sternberg is concerned that present intelligence tests measure only the componential component. However, in the real world, experiential and contextual intelligence may be more in demand than the kind of intelligence emphasized in school (Bee, 1989).

Hellige doesn't deny that individuals may have different ways of thinking. He simply states that there is no evidence that individuals can be trained to think differently by modifying or expanding different space in the brain used for thinking.

Response: Levy (1983) believes that some important implications for education may eventually arise from brain research. She suggests that "the *gateway* into whole-brain learning may differ for different children, *not* that one hemisphere or the other should be the object of education" (p. 70). Kaufman and Kaufman (1983) developed the Kaufman Assessment Battery for Children (K-ABC), based on the controversial brain research of Das, Kirby, and Jarman (1975). Their instrument measures intelligence through two different types of information processing—sequential (or successive) and simultaneous (or holistic). Sequential processing places stimuli into sequences to solve a problem, whereas simultaneous processing synthesizes separate elements into spatial groupings. The K-ABC has been criticized on theoretical and methodological grounds (Sattler, 1988), but it represents an attempt to improve on standard intelligence tests by incorporating brain research.

What do you think? Have you read any literature in this field? Does knowledge of the functions of both sides of the brain have any implications for understanding student learning styles? Does the vast explosion of neuroresearch in the last five years hold possible keys to understanding how we process information?

On the basis of his theory, Sternberg is currently working on a new type of intelligence test—the Sternberg Multidimensional Abilities Test—that will measure intelligence in a much broader way than current tests. In his 1986 book, *Intelligence Applied,* he discusses how people can be trained to be more intelligent. Earlier approaches to intelligence have made few contributions in this area. Only time will tell if Sternberg's approach is more successful.

GARDNER'S THEORY OF MULTIPLE INTELLIGENCES. Gardner (1983) was not pleased with the narrow emphasis in school on verbal and logical-mathematical thinking. He believed that many other forms of thinking were prominent both within and outside the school. As a result, he proposed the existence of multiple intelligences (see Table 8.3), but departed from the traditional psychometric approach where intelligence test items are developed by their ability to predict who will succeed in school.

There are two components to this approach to intelligence: individuals and societies. Individuals develop competences in different domains. Each competency is independent from the others in terms of how and when it develops. Societies play a role in shaping and defining the competences

TABLE 8.3 GARDNER'S SEVEN INTELLIGENCES

Intelligence	End-States	Core Components
Logical-mathematical	Scientist Mathematician	Sensitivity to, and capacity to discern, logical or numerical patterns; ability to handle long chains of reasoning.
Linguistic	Poet Journalist	Sensitivity to the sounds, rhythms, and meanings of words; sensitivity to the different functions of language.
Musical	Composer Violinist	Abilities to produce and appreciate rhythm pitch, and timbre; appreciation of the forms of musical expressiveness.
Spatial	Navigator Sculptor	Capacities to perceive the visual-spatial world accurately and to perform transformations to one's initial perceptions.
Bodily-kinesthetic	Dancer Athlete	Abilities to control one's body movements and to handle objects skillfully.
Interpersonal	Therapist Salesman	Capacities to discern and respond appropriately to the moods, temperaments, motivations, and desires of other people.
Intrapersonal	Person with detailed, accurate self-knowledge	Access to one's own feelings and the ability to discriminate among them and draw upon them to guide behavior; knowledge of one's own strengths, weaknesses, desires, and intelligences.

Source: Gardner and Hatch, 1989.

through its value system and providing opportunities for them to develop. In turn, the competences allow the individual to adapt to society (Davidson, 1990).

Gardner and Hatch (1989) are currently developing assessment instruments to measure the different types of intelligences. These instruments take considerable time to develop since they are not short test items but require performance in specific domains that are culturally valued activities. For example, students are required to write dialogue for a play, draw, play an instrument or dance at a recital, or debate a current social topic. Gardner's assessments to date indicate that the intelligence measures are independent of one another (i.e., no one intelligence accounts for the others), and students demonstrate different profiles or patterns of strengths and weaknesses.

Research on this theory is in its infancy; it is too early to determine whether or not it will be confirmed. In the meantime, the theory has encouraged some educators to develop curriculum materials in aspects of the school program that have been neglected (e.g., creative writing, visual arts, and music) and encouraged the field-testing of new instruments to measure aptitudes in different areas. Preliminary analysis of these assessments has led Gardner and Hatch (1989) to conclude: "Our programs with both older and younger children confirm that a consideration of a broader range of talents brings to the fore individuals who previously had been considered unexceptional or even at risk for school failure" (p. 7). Continued progress in this area could have important implications for new

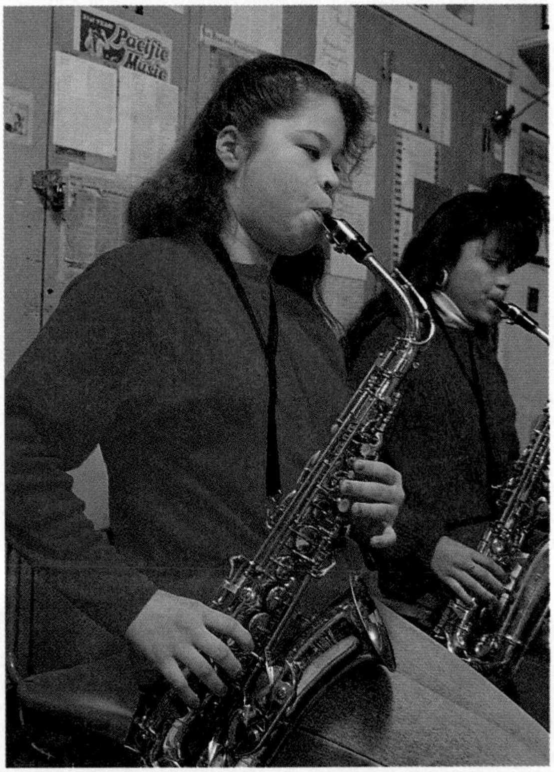

Many educators believe that there are different types of intelligences that should be recognized in school.

educational programs that recognize a wide variety of talent and cognitive processes among the student population.

Gardner's approach doesn't fit clearly into any of the four perspectives. His theory and research bridges both the information-processing and sociocultural perspectives in that he

- considers both the individual and his or her environment as important determinants of intelligence
- like Sternberg, takes a broad view of intelligence and believes that intellectual performance should be developed as well as assessed

THE SOCIOCULTURAL PERSPECTIVE

The sociocultural approach to intelligence and cognitive development is somewhat more loosely defined than the perspectives we have already examined. While the psychometric, Piagetian, and information-processing perspectives are firmly rooted within the field of psychology, the sociocultural perspective develops from several disciplines—anthropology, sociology, and psychology. You may see other terminology used to identify this perspective, such as ecocultural framework (Laboratory of Comparative Human Cognition, 1981), social transmission (McKeough, 1991), or the sociohistorical approach (Vygotsky, 1978). The factor that best distinguishes a sociocultural perspective from the others is that all learning and cognitive development is viewed as a social activity that can be understood only within a given cultural setting. Cognition is seen as something that takes place in all cultures and in all settings, but the forms it takes may vary depending upon the survival needs of the group. What is considered intelligent behavior in one setting may not be viewed as intelligent in another, as it may not have the same survival value.

Vygotsky's Sociocultural Approach to Cognitive Development

? According to Vygotsky, what role does social interaction have on cognitive development?

One of the leading proponents of the sociocultural perspective was Lev Vygotsky (1896–1934), a Soviet psychologist whose ideas are just beginning to be applied widely in the Western world. Three major themes, described below, characterize his writing (Wertsch, 1991).

Cultural, historical, and institutional factors reflect and shape an individual's mental processes. If we want to understand an individual's thinking, we have to understand where it came from. Thus, a Vygotskian question would be: What is it that makes me as an American in the late twentieth-century different from a nineteenth-century Russian aristocrat, or a fourteenth-century English peasant? Or, more relevant for today's classroom: What shapes the thinking of a sixth-grade refugee student from Cambodia or a recent immigrant from Mexico or Japan?

Higher mental function in the individual has its origins in social activity. That is to say, we can't understand a child's development simply by focusing on his or her individual behavior. We must also study the social world in which that individual life has developed. Learning takes place first on an interpsychological (social) level and only later on an intrapsychological (person) level. Children do things with the help of others around them long before they can do things on their own. The child who does not remember where she left an item often reconstructs memory with an adult, who asks questions that help to locate the object. The dialogue for a first-grade child who can't find her book might proceed as follows:

zone of proximal development. Vygotsky's description for the difference between an individual's current level of development and his or her potential level of development.

CHILD: Have you seen my book?
MOTHER: No, when did you last see the book?
CHILD: I had it in school.
MOTHER: Did you bring it home with you?
CHILD: I don't know.
MOTHER: Where did you put your things when you came home from school?

Quickly the child goes into the family room and finds her book next to her coat. This example points to the social nature of memory—neither the child nor the adult would be able to recall where the object was on his or her own (Wertsch, 1991). As the child develops, she acquires the metacognitive ability to ask herself the same questions initiated by her mother. Vygotsky believes that a child's thinking abilities develop from similar dialogues in the home, community, and school. I will point out later how this notion underlies one of his most widely known ideas—the **zone of proximal development**.

Language is an important mediator between learning and development. Language develops initially because of a child's need to communicate with people in the environment. During the child's development, language is converted to internal speech as it becomes an internal process and organizes the child's thoughts. Tharp and Gallimore (1988) provide the following explanation of this phenomenon:

> Language appears to be like Mercury, the messenger who carries content from the interpsychological plane to the intrapsychological plane, a messenger with unique gifts for translation from one plane to the other. What is spoken *to* a child is later said *by* the child to the self, and later is abbreviated and transformed into the silent speech of the child's thought. (p. 44)

Remember the discussion of cognitive behavior modification in Chapter 2 in which self-talk was used to guide one's reading comprehension and reduce the tendency to act impulsively. Self-talk interventions are examples of how speech is used to guide behavior.

How do Piaget and Vygotsky differ on the relation between development and learning?

ZONE OF PROXIMAL DEVELOPMENT. Piaget believes that development precedes learning, whereas Vygotsky believes that learning precedes development. According to Piaget, an individual's developmental stage determines the quality of thinking, and instruction above this level would not produce learning. Vygotsky (1978) believes that developmental processes lag behind the learning processes. He points out that children can often complete tasks with the help of peers or teachers that they could not accomplish working independently. The abilities that children can demonstrate when given assistance are not yet developed; they are in the process of becoming internalized. The zone of proximal development (often referred to as the ZPD) is the difference between an individual's current level of development and his or her potential level of development.

Vygotsky (1978) points out that mental tests measure children's current level of development, or what they can do on their own. However, with some questioning or prodding, children often can demonstrate considerably more ability. In fact, what children can do with the assistance of others may be more indicative of their true abilities than what they can do

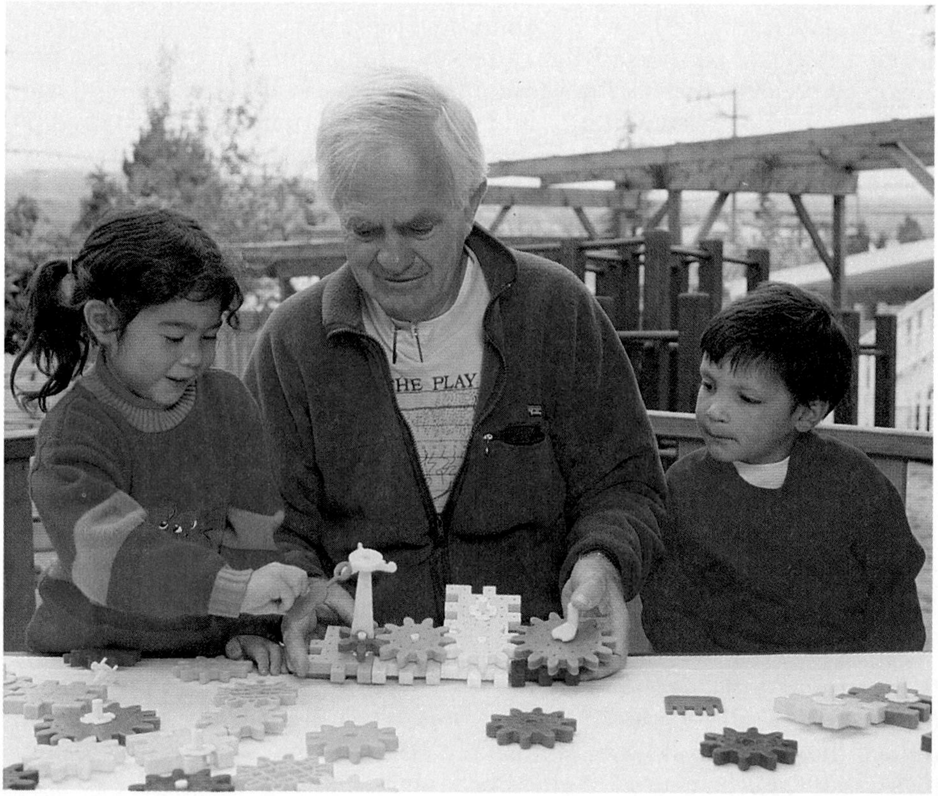

Providing assistance to learners can help them move through the zone of proximal development.

alone. Vygotsky argues that we cannot really understand children's development unless we consider *both* their actual development and their potential developmental level. The following is the basis of his argument:

scaffolding. Support for learning and problem solving.

> Suppose I investigated two children upon entrance into school, both of whom are ten years old chronologically and eight years old in terms of mental development. Can I say that they are the same age mentally? Of course. What does this mean? It means that they can independently deal with tasks up to the degree of difficulty that has been standardized for the eight-year-old level. If I stop at this point, people would imagine that the subsequent course of mental development and of school learning for these children will be the same, because it depends on their intellect. Of course, there may be other factors, for example, if one child was sick for half a year while the other was never absent from school; but generally speaking, the fate of these children should be the same. *Now imagine that I do not terminate my study at this point, but only begin it.* These children seem to be capable of handling problems up to an eight-year-old's level, but not beyond that. Suppose that I show them different ways of dealing with the problem. Different experimenters might employ different modes of demonstration in different cases: some might run through an entire demonstration and ask the children to repeat it, others might initiate the solution and ask the child to finish it, or offer leading questions. In short, in some way or another I propose that the children solve the problem with my assistance. Under these circumstances, it turns out that the first child can deal with problems up to a twelve-year-old's level, the second up to a nine-year-old's. Now, are these children mentally the same? (pp. 85–86, italics added)

Since Vygotsky believed that higher-level thinking develops best in social contexts, he encouraged learning situations in which teachers, parents, and more capable peers interact directly with students who are at lower levels of thinking. The significant people in their environment can help guide their thinking by providing hints as to how they should proceed when they cannot manage on their own. More specifically, the expert can describe what needs to be done, taking the student through the problem, while demonstrating appropriate strategies. Also, the expert can reduce some of the demands of the task by taking responsibility for some parts while allowing the student to concentrate on other parts. In this way, students can learn even though they can't solve the whole problem on their own. They employ those skills that they have acquired and with help begin to internalize other relevant skills and knowledge. Over time, the students assume more responsibility for completing the task (Day, Cordon, & Kerwin, 1989).

Wood, Bruner, and Ross (1976) described the tutoring process in terms of providing a scaffold that helps a student solve a problem or perform a task that he or she couldn't do alone. This **scaffolding** allows the adult initially to control elements of a task that are beyond the learner's ability, thus allowing the learner to concentrate upon and complete those elements of the task that are within his or her ability level.

reciprocal teaching. Interactive dialogue between teacher and students in which they take turns being the teacher.

CLASSROOM Application

USING RECIPROCAL TEACHING

Palincsar and Brown (1986) have applied the notion of scaffolded instruction to improve reading comprehension. They developed an instructional routine called **reciprocal teaching**. In this effective method, students and teachers talk to each other about the meaning of text and take turns implementing various strategies during dialogues structured by the teacher to incorporate the following:

- *Summarizing*—Identifying and paraphrasing the main ideas in the text
- *Question Generating*—Self-questioning about the type of information that is generally tapped on tests of comprehension
- *Clarifying*—Discerning when there has been a breakdown in comprehension and taking the necessary action to restore meaning (e.g., reading ahead, rereading, asking for assistance)
- *Predicting*—Hypothesizing what the structure and content of the text suggest will be presented next (Palincsar, 1986, p. 119)

Introduce reciprocal teaching by discussing the many reasons that text may be difficult to comprehend, and explain the importance of strategic approaches to reading and studying. Present your students with a general description of the procedure. At first, lead the dialogue, modeling the specific strategies. As your students assume responsibility for leading the dialogue, they practice the strategies within a familiar and meaningful context, and as they become increasingly knowledgeable in understanding the material, you can gradually provide less support and become less involved in the dialogue.

The following is a partial transcript from a lesson conducted with first graders who have listened to a paragraph about aquanauts. Student 1 begins facilitating (Palincsar & Brown, 1986):

STUDENT 1: [*Question*] My question is, what does the aquanaut need when he goes under water?
STUDENT 2: A watch.
STUDENT 3: Flippers.
STUDENT 4: A belt.
STUDENT 1: Those are all good answers.
TEACHER: [*Question*] Nice job! I have a question too. Why does the aquanaut wear a belt, what is so special about it?
STUDENT 3: It's a heavy belt and keeps him from floating up to the top again.
STUDENT 1: [*Summary*] For my summary now. . . . This paragraph was about what the aquanauts need to take when they go under the water.
STUDENT 5: And also about why they need those things.
STUDENT 3: [*Clarify*] I think we need to clarify "gear."
STUDENT 6: That's the special things they need.
TEACHER: Another word for gear in this story might be equipment, the equipment that makes it easier for the aquanauts to do their job.
STUDENT 1: I don't think I have a prediction to make.
TEACHER: [*Prediction*] Well, in the story they tell us that there are "many strange and wonderful creatures" that the aquanauts see as they do their work. My prediction is that they will describe some of these creatures. What are some of the strange creatures that you already know about that live in the ocean?
STUDENT 6: Octopuses.
STUDENT 3: Whales?
STUDENT 5: Sharks!
TEACHER: Let's listen and find out! Who will be our teacher? (pp. 771–772)

Summary

THE PSYCHOMETRIC PERSPECTIVE

1. The psychometric approach to intelligence attempts to identify the content and structure of mental abilities.
2. Intelligence is defined as a single or multifactor trait.
3. Guilford's multifactor theory of intelligence lists 180 characteristics or capacities that contribute to intelligence.
4. Binet developed the first intelligence test and based it on the concept of mental age.
5. Individual intelligence tests are primarily used to make placement decisions.
6. The Stanford-Binet and Wechsler are two individually administered intelligence tests.
7. Teachers must not be hasty in interpreting intelligence scores of students who have not had an opportunity to learn tasks included in the test, are unmotivated, have poor reading skills, or are not well adjusted emotionally.
8. Some common *misconceptions* of intelligence tests are that they measure "innate" or "natural" abilities, are an exact indicator of all learning abilities, and provide unchangeable scores.
9. White students tend to score higher than African American and other minority students, and students from high socioeconomic backgrounds score higher on intelligence tests than do students from low socioeconomic backgrounds.
10. Intelligence tests are criticized for emphasizing verbal ability over other types of mental ability.
11. Educators as well as the courts disagree whether intelligence tests provide biased scores for minority students.
12. Teachers and schools may use low intelligence test scores as a basis for discriminatory practices in school.
13. Intelligence tests may not adequately measure the academic potential of minority-group children.
14. Attempts at developing culture-free intelligence tests have not been successful.
15. Preschool programs were established to increase the intellectual development and academic performance of children from impoverished backgrounds. Although there are many personal and social benefits to these programs, research has shown that academic and cognitive gains diminish once students leave these programs.
16. Jensen questions the ability of preschool programs to accomplish their objectives because of their focus on academic knowledge or skills rather than thinking processes.

THE PIAGETIAN PERSPECTIVE

17. According to Piaget, children proceed through four distinct stages of cognitive development.
18. The imaginary audience and personal fable can be used to explain certain aspects of adolescents' social behavior when they enter formal operations thinking.
19. Critics of Piaget question the validity of distinct stages of development, believe that he overestimated the ability of adolescents and adults to move into formal operations thinking, and challenge his methodology.
20. Information-processing theorists studying cognitive development believe that children can be taught problem solving at an earlier age than Piaget's theory would predict. They also tend to disagree with Piaget's notion that each stage of development involves a totally new form of thinking.
21. Piaget's theory can be used as a guide in the structuring and sequencing of subject matter in the curriculum.
22. Teachers should be conscious of the cognitive-developmental level of their students.
23. Teachers should analyze tasks in the curriculum to determine the level of reasoning required for the successful solution of each task.
24. Teachers should use concrete learning experiences whenever possible and not move into abstract levels of thinking too quickly.

THE INFORMATION-PROCESSING PERSPECTIVE

25. Because of its emphasis upon the processes and strategies individuals use in intelligent behavior, the information-processing approach has been particularly useful in suggesting directions for training intelligent performance.
26. There is little evidence to support major distinctions between the functioning of the two parts of the brain because the two parts work together.
27. Sternberg's triarchic theory of intelligence focuses on three different aspects of intelligence exercised in different domains. The implication of this theory is that current intelligence tests tap only a small part of intelligent behavior.
28. Gardner's theory of multiple intelligences is based on the interaction between individuals and societies.

THE SOCIOCULTURAL PERSPECTIVE

29. The sociocultural perspective views cognitive development in terms of one's culture and social interaction.
30. Piaget believes that development precedes learning, whereas Vygotsky believes that learning precedes development.

31. Vygotsky believes that educators should consider *two* levels of development—an individual's current level and potential level.
32. Vygotsky believes that current intelligence testing may not predict future academic attainment because it doesn't consider what a person can attain with help.
33. Reciprocal teaching is an example of how a teacher can use Vygotsky's notion of the zone of proximal development in learning.

Reflecting on Intelligence and Cognitive Development

1. Compare and Evaluate the Psychometric, Piagetian, and Information-Processing Perspectives of Intelligence

Suppose a psychologist representing each of these perspectives is asked to train a student to solve analogy problems in the form A: B :: C: (D1,D2). Compare and contrast how a psychometric, Piagetian, and information-processing psychologist would approach the task (see Wagner & Sternberg, 1984, for an explanation).

2. Analyze a Piagetian Quotation

> The goal in education is not to increase the amount of knowledge, but to create the possibilities for a child to invent and discover. When we teach too fast, we keep the child from inventing and discovering himself. . . . Teaching means creating situations where structures can be discovered; it does not mean transmitting structures which may be assimilated at nothing other than a verbal level. (Piaget, 1964, p. 3)

What does Piaget mean by teaching too fast? Can you relate this statement to your own learning?

3. Assess a Child's Level of Cognitive Development

In Piaget and Szeminska (1952, p. 165), Piaget places 20 beads (18 brown and 2 white) in a box, the child acknowledging that they are all made of wood. Piaget asks the following question: "In this box, which are there more of, wooden beads or brown beads?" (All the beads are visible.) The child replies that there are more brown beads,"since there were only two white ones." Piaget then asks the child, "Are all the brown ones made of wood?" The child responds, "Yes." Piaget questions further, "If I take away all the wooden beads and put them in a second box, will there be any beads left in the first box?" The child replies, "No, because they are all made of wood." The child is then asked, "If the brown ones are taken away, will there be any beads left?" The child responds, "Yes, the white ones."

In which period is the child? What operation(s) is Piaget testing? Why does the child respond as described?

4. Try a Piagetian Experiment

Conservation of Quantity

Material: A ball of clay.

Presentation: Give the child a ball of clay and ask the child to make another exactly like it—just as big and just as heavy.

Activity: After the child has done the activity, retain one of the balls as a standard of comparison. Change the other one by stretching it into a sausage, flattening it into a cake, or cutting it into smaller pieces. Ask if the amount of clay, its weight, and its volume have changed or remained invariant (conserved) as a result of the transformation. "Do the two pieces of clay have the same amount of clay?"

Justification: "How do you know?"

5. Apply Vygotsky in the Classroom

Vygotsky believed that higher mental functioning occurs on two levels—the interpsychological (social) before the intrapsychological (personal). If a teacher accepted this perspective, how could he or she encourage this development?

Key Terms

psychometric, p. 343
information processing, p. 343
intelligence, p. 343
convergent thinking, p. 345
divergent thinking, p. 345
creativity, p. 345
mental age, p. 346
intelligence quotient (IQ), p. 346
individual intelligence test, p. 347
heritability, p. 353
adaptation, p. 355
assimilation, p. 355
accommodation, p. 355
disequilibrium, p. 355
equilibration, p. 356
sensorimotor stage, p. 357
object permanence, p. 357
preoperational stage, p. 358
reversibility, p. 358
conservation, p. 359
decenter, p. 360
egocentrism, p. 360
transductive reasoning, p. 360
concrete operations stage, p. 361
combinativity, p. 362
associativity, p. 362
identity, p. 362
serializing, p. 362
formal operations stage, p. 363

hypothetico-deductive reasoning, P. 363
propositional reasoning, p. 363
imaginary audience, p. 363
personal fable, p. 363
zone of proximal development, p. 377
scaffolding, p. 379

Suggestions for Further Reading

Bjorklund, D. F. (1989). *Children's thinking: Developmental function and individual differences*. Pacific Grove, CA: Brooks/Cole. A review of the theories and research of intellectual and cognitive development.

Gardner, H. (1983). *Frames of mind: The theory of multiple intelligences.* New York: Basic Books. Gardner identifies his seven forms of intelligences and describes how he identified them.

Sattler, J. M. (1988). *Assessment of children* (3rd ed.). San Diego: Sattler. A comprehensive assessment of intelligence tests currently in use.

Wagner, R., & Sternberg, R. J. (1984). Alternative conceptions of intelligence and their implications for education. *Review of Educational Research, 54,* 179–223. Compares three major views of intelligence: the psychometric, the Piagetian, and the information processing.

Wertsch, J. V. (1991). The problem of meaning in a sociocultural approach to mind. In E. McKeough (Ed.), *Toward the practice of theory-based instruction.* Hillsdale, NJ: Erlbaum. An excellent discussion of Vygotsky's approach to intelligence.

Select any of the following for more detailed study of Piaget:

Flavell, J. H. (1985). *Cognitive development* (2nd ed.). Englewood Cliffs, NJ: Prentice-Hall.

Ginsburg, H. P., & Opper, S. (1988). *Piaget's theory of intellectual development* (3rd ed.). Englewood Cliffs, NJ: Prentice-Hall.

Labinowicz, E. (1980). *The Piaget primer.* Menlo Park, CA: Addison-Wesley. Uses illustrations to explain children's responses to different tasks.

Phillips, J. L., Jr. (1975). *The origins of intellect: Piaget's theory* (2nd ed.). San Francisco: Freeman.

Wadsworth, B. (1978). *Piaget for the classroom teacher*. White Plains, NY: Longman. Good discussion of how Piaget's theory relates to teaching reading, mathematics, science, and social studies. Part III deals with cognitive-developmental assessment.

Wadsworth, B. (1989). *Piaget's theory of cognitive and affective development* (4th ed.). White Plains, NY: Longman.

Wolman, B. B. (Ed.). (1985). *Handbook of intelligence: Theories, measurements, and applications*. New York: Wiley. Includes chapters on various approaches to intelligence.

To learn more about Sternberg's work:

Sternberg, R. J. (1985). *Beyond IQ: A triarchic theory of human intelligence.* Cambridge: Cambridge University Press.

Sternberg, R. J. (1986). *Intelligence applied: Understanding and increasing your intellectual skills*. San Diego: Harcourt Brace Jovanovich.
Sternberg, R. J. (1988). *The triarchic mind: A new theory of human intelligence*. New York: Viking.

Chapter 9

Cognition, Culture, and Language

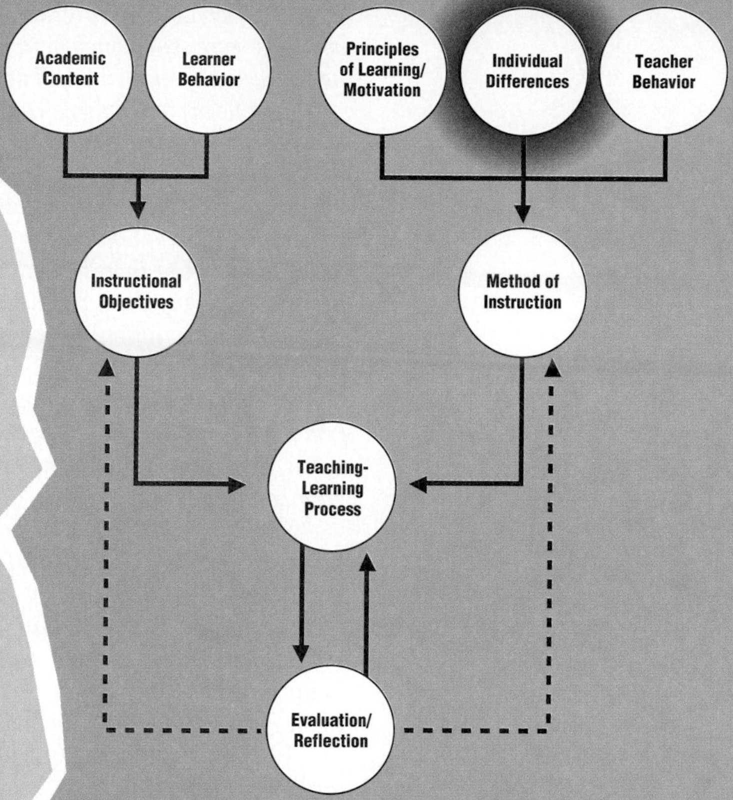

OBJECTIVES

After mastering the material in this chapter you will be able to:

- Describe different explanations for the low achievement of some culturally different students.
- Provide effective instruction for culturally different students.
- Develop multicultural educational experiences.
- Enhance the language development of students.

Orientation

culture. The ways in which a group of people think, feel, and react in order to solve problems of living in their environment.

Sophal had overcome a lifetime of challenges in his 16 years. He and his mother had spent five of those years in a refugee camp in northern Thailand, and had recently been able to emigrate to the United States. His father and two older brothers were still somewhere in his native Kampuchea, although there had never been any official word about them.

When he arrived in this country, Sophal had promised his mother that he would take care of her, and she would never have to worry about material needs again. At the tender age of 16, he already knew the importance of having an education as a vehicle to the fulfillment of that promise.

Unfortunately, Sophal's first couple of years in American schools proved to be more challenging than he had expected. He knew that nothing could ever be so difficult as escaping from the Khmer Rouge, but he began to wonder if he could ever escape from the difficulties he encountered in the school he attended. Sophal explains some of his frustrations:

"When I first arrived from Thailand, I knew that I would need to learn to become like an American, so that I could make a life in America for my mother. I never really understood how hard 'becoming like an American' would be, until I entered school.

"At first, I didn't speak any English, so I was put into an English as a Second Language (ESL) class, where I was able to learn the language. I did very well in those classes, and my teacher recommended me for the regular classes. My hopes were very high for eventually getting into a major university, and I knew I had to take advanced classes, so I requested that I be placed in Honors classes. I didn't know how hard it would be to understand, but I was determined that I could do it. I had overcome bigger problems in my life, and this wasn't going to stop me.

"The major obstacle I faced in my classes was understanding the teachers. They all liked to lecture in class, and I constantly had to refer to my dictionary. I never would have thought of asking them to speak more slowly, or to repeat something, because that would be rude.

"Outside of the classroom, however, the major difficulty for me was being able to fit in with other students. There were only eight Cambodian students in my school, and in the beginning I didn't really want to associate with them. I wanted to be like all of the American kids, but that was almost impossible because I had a very strong accent, and I was very unfamiliar with American customs. Sometimes, the most difficult thing was having other students laugh at me when I spoke, or make comments behind my back when I walked down the hallway, comments about the way I dressed or about the type of food I eat, or any number of things they didn't like about me.

"That was over three years ago, and I am finally a senior. I have been accepted at the university that was my first choice, and I have been offered a scholarship. I plan to study medicine, and I know, now, that I will be able to fulfill my promise to my mother. Nothing can stop me from reaching that goal!"

In this chapter we will explore the role of cognition (thinking), **culture,** and language in learning. We focus on these variables not only because they represent critical aspects of *all* learning, but also because many teachers will find themselves working with students whose backgrounds and experiences differ from their own.

A number of variables in the teaching-learning model are relevant to our discussion of culturally different students. Teacher behavior plays an important role in dealing with student diversity in the classroom. Teachers often have different attitudes toward the academic potential and future success of students from different races and cultural groups, sometimes holding more negative attitudes about minority-group students than about white, middle-class students (Nieto, 1992). In addition, studies have shown that they give more praise and attention to white students than to students from culturally different groups (Baron, Tom, & Cooper, 1985). You have already learned how teacher expectations and organization of the classroom can influence student motivation. You will benefit most from this chapter if you explore your own beliefs and experiences with individuals who differ from your own cultural and ethnic heritage.

Linguists have found that student motivation, anxiety, and perceptions of ability are important personal variables that can influence second language acquisition. Brown (1987) states: "Understanding how human beings feel and respond and believe and value is an exceedingly important aspect of a theory of second language acquisition" (p. 101). Information acquired from the chapter on humanistic education will be useful as you interact with the diversity of students found in most classrooms.

Evaluation is another variable in the teaching-learning model. In the previous chapter, we explored issues about the mental testing of children from diverse cultures. Since teachers use a variety of formal and informal procedures to evaluate student progress, attention must be given to cultural factors that might influence students' response to assessment devices. Be especially careful judging the responses of children whose primary language is not English.

In this chapter we will integrate the discussion of culture and cognition with knowledge you have acquired in the previous chapter. For example, I will examine how the four perspectives on intelligence address cultural differences.

In Chapter 3 you learned about individual differences in thinking and remembering. More recently, some researchers have argued that cognition cannot be understood if it is divorced from its social context. Culture plays a large role in how we think and the linguistic processes we use to communicate with one another. Many definitions have been offered for culture. Some focus only on the tools and symbols used by a group of people; others focus only on observed behavior or customs. A cognitive perspective considers aspects that are not directly observable. Casanova (1987) states that culture is the "sum total of ways in which a group of people think, feel, and react in order to solve problems of living in their environment" (pp. 372–373).

An understanding of the role of culture and language in cognition is more important than ever for educators, as the children entering our schools come from more diverse cultural backgrounds, and increasing numbers come from homes where English is not spoken. In California, one out of six children entering public school in the fall of 1989 did not speak English.

sociolinguistics. The study of language in its social context.

multicultural education. An educational reform process whose major goal is to change educational institutions so that all students have an equal chance to achieve academically in school.

Educators are challenged to provide effective methods of instruction to *all* students. Since culture is largely transmitted through language, teachers must also be concerned with **sociolinguistics**—the study of language in its social context. Linguistic rules of the classroom may differ from students' linguistic behavior at home. As a result, teachers need to be sensitive to these differences and not underestimate the academic abilities of students who display linguistic behavior that differs from their own cultural norms.

We also need to understand the impact of language and culture on cognition because many ethnic minority students are *not* experiencing success in schools today. Much of a student's success in school depends on making the transition from the home or community culture to the school culture (Casanova, 1987). In this chapter, we will examine the explanations that have been given for the higher rates of school failure among some minority populations. We will also take a look at some strategies and programs that have been proven effective in reversing these trends.

Finally, there is more concern today about **multicultural education** and about what education should look like in a pluralistic society. Many educators think that society and its institutions (e.g., the school) should change to assist immigrants' adaptation to a new culture and should accommodate the diverse cultural ways of nonimmigrant minorities as well. The purpose of changing the structure of educational institutions is to allow all students—regardless of their gender, social class, or racial, ethnic, and cultural background—the opportunity to achieve success in school (Banks, 1989). An objective of this chapter is to provide you with the knowledge and competencies to help you achieve this goal.

THE CHANGING FACE OF AMERICA

Neil Diamond sings: "Everywhere around the world, they're coming to America." This lyric appropriately describes the influx of immigrant students into American public schools. This migration presents a major challenge for teachers as they attempt to educate large numbers of language minority students. The number of legal immigrants, refugees, and undocumented immigrants entering the United States between 1981 and 1990 is estimated to be the largest migration in history. The result is that we now have the most ethnically and culturally diverse society in the history of the United States.

Kellogg (1988) presents demographic information about the new immigrants. They come primarily from Asia (34 percent), Latin America (34 percent), and Europe (16 percent) (Muller & Espenshade, 1985) and have concentrated in California (28 percent), New York (16 percent), Texas (9 percent), Florida (8 percent), Illinois (6 percent), New Jersey (4 percent), Massachusetts (3 percent), Pennsylvania (2 percent), Michigan (2 percent), Ohio (1 percent), and in the remaining 40 states (21 percent). Fifty percent of the undocumented immigrants are estimated to be in California.

One of the characteristics of today's migration is its youth. Approximately 60 percent are between the ages of 16 and 44, with the median age of many Southeast Asian immigrants between 13 and 21 (Muller &

Espenshade, 1985). The implication of their young age is that the immigrants are coming to America at their prime working and childbearing years. This new immigration is predicted to change the population demographics as follows: By the year 2020, whites will comprise 70 percent of the U.S. population. By the year 2050, this percentage will have dropped to 60 percent. The African American population will increase slightly, to about 16 percent of the total population. The Latino population will more than double (from 6.4 percent to 15 percent), and Asians will climb from 1.6 percent of the total population to as much as 10 percent (Bouvier & Agresta, 1987). Figure 9.1 presents the projected proportions of the population 0–17 years old by race/ethnicity between 1982 and 2020.

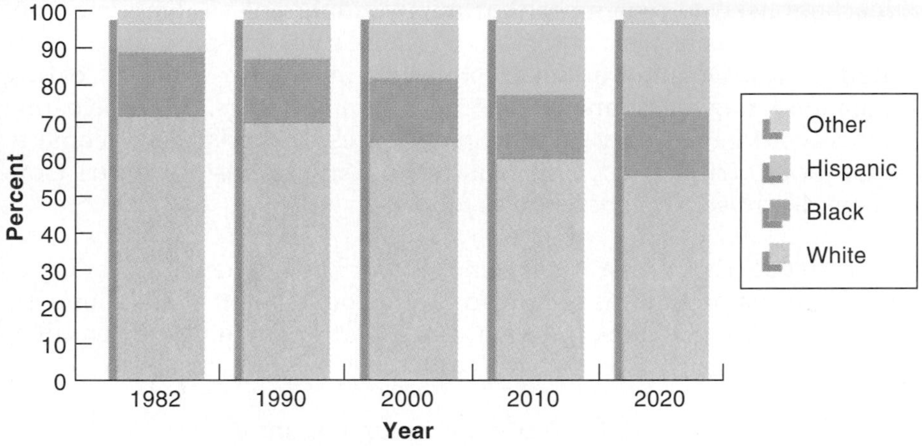

Figure 9.1 Projections of the 0–17 Population by Race/Ethnicity, U.S. Total, 1982–2020. Source: Pallas, Natriello, and McDill, 1989.

CHALLENGE FOR THE SCHOOLS

The current migration brings a variety of backgrounds, languages, and cultures—many of which are new to the United States. The immigrant students bring to the public schools unique life experiences, different skills, and a new set of challenges for teachers. The language roots of many of the new immigrants are not similar to English, their religions may not stem from the Judeo-Christian heritage, and their parents may have a value system different from that of the mainstream American society (Kellogg, 1988). This immigrant population joins with second- and third-generation ethnic minority students whose cultural values, while perhaps more closely aligned with mainstream values, still differ in important ways that are not always recognized by the schools.

You may be concerned about the legal implications of educating undocumented immigrants. The U.S. Supreme Court ruled in 1982, in *Plyler v. Doe*, that the state has an obligation to educate the children of undocumented immigrants. Thus there are no legal grounds to deny an education to any group of immigrant children. At the same time, teachers may need to be aware that families' concern over their legal status may inhibit their involvement in school.

The diversity of students in public schools presents challenges to teachers, who must learn about their culture, help them acquire English, and deal with their emotional needs. Olsen (1988) illustrates this challenge by the following incident:

> In a San Francisco elementary school, a teacher plays hangman with her students to enliven a spelling lesson. As the class eagerly shouts out letters, one child bursts into tears. A Cambodian immigrant recently arrived from a Thai refugee camp, the child speaks little English. Another child is found who can interpret, and the hysterical child finally manages to communicate that she had witnessed the hanging of her father in Cambodia. (p. 211)

Teachers need to remember that many immigrant students may not understand what are basic classroom or school rules and procedures in the United States. Opening a locker, standing in line for lunch or eating strange food, moving to another room when a bell rings, or participating in schoolyard games may be new experiences. Many students come to school alone, frightened, and frustrated. An eighth-grade girl from Vietnam described her experience as follows:

> I felt so out of place that I felt sick. I didn't know where to sit or eat or where the bathroom was or how to eat the food. I felt that all around me activities were going on, but I was not a part of anything. (Olsen, 1988, p. 214)

Can you imagine how difficult it is for an immigrant high school student who has no or limited English to prepare for a test or participate in other academic activities he or she doesn't understand, while at the same time attempting to cope with the stressors of the migration experience?

CULTURE AND INTELLIGENCE

? How do different theories of intelligence account for cultural experiences?

The Psychometric Perspective

The psychometric perspective focuses on cognitive differences as measurable activities of mental processes. Psychometricians (i.e., test specialists) have developed a large battery of tests to measure innumerable processes and to categorize people in different ways, but have generally paid only minimal attention to cultural differences. Often, psychometric tests that are based on one population are used to explain differences in another. Intelligence tests are a classic example of this phenomenon.

Some educators recognize that there are problems with using any one task to assess the performance of any group of students, even with students who share a common cultural background. The problem arises not in *noting* differences in performance but in interpreting them. Are the differences due to experience, motivation, background knowledge, task, anxiety, and/or cultural norms? How generalizable are the results?

In multicultural situations, these problems are compounded. Cross-cultural psychologists point out that we cannot always assume that people from different cultures *understand the tasks* in the same way; the concepts involved may mean very different things to different groups. The processes viewed as the "right" or the "wrong" way to approach a task may also vary from culture to culture. Miller-Jones (1989) gives examples of responses to the Stanford-Binet Intelligence Scale: "sticks," "nails," and "walls" are considered incorrect answers to the question "What is a *house* made of?" while "wood," "boards," "bricks," "cement," "stucco," "shingles," "stone," "lumber," "blocks," and "rocks" are considered correct. Miller-Jones questions the intellectual distinction that can be made between acceptable and unacceptable responses. He notes that the arbitrary nature of the scoring is especially problematic when tests are used with culturally different students.

The Piagetian Perspective

Piaget assumed that there are universal processes of cognitive development that are "culture-free." Cultural differences, when considered by developmentalists like Piaget, are usually seen as variations in the *rates* at which people pass through development stages, rather than as qualitative differences in the stages themselves.

Research in several cultures on the attainment of Piaget's mental operations has not clearly supported his universalist position. While there is some evidence that individuals in most cultures demonstrate cognitive operations indicated by Piaget's early stages (i.e., preoperational and concrete operational thinking), there is great variation in their attainment of formal operations thinking. Both the type of reasoning and the measures used to assess them appear to be influenced by cultural experiences (Miller-Jones, 1989).

The Information-processing Perspective

The information-processing perspective contends that the processes associated with intelligence can be identified. Historically, this perspective did not emphasize cultural differences as a major factor influencing thinking. More recently, however, attention to the role of cultural differences in thinking can be seen in both neo-Piagetian approaches (e.g., Case, 1985), which attempt to use information processing to modify Piaget's theory, and in Sternberg's (1985) triarchic theory of intelligence. Sternberg includes a contextual component that attempts to relate the internal world of the individual to his or her environment. He argues that a critical aspect of intelligence is how individuals either adapt to or attempt to shape the environment in which they find themselves, stating that because of the major differences in socialization processes in various cultures, "intelligence is not the same for everyone" (Sternberg & Suben, 1986, p. 213).

The Sociocultural Perspective

This perspective by its very nature, of course, places prime focus on the role of society and culture in learning. Cultural differences in achievement, testing, and performance are seen as the product of particular social environments and the interaction of cultural forces. Developmental factors may be considered within this perspective, but the universality of developmental processes is questioned, as well as the validity of psychometric tests when used with nonmainstream populations. The following statement summarizes the sociocultural perspective regarding intelligence:

> A clear implication of this line of reasoning is that *intelligence* will be different across cultures (and across contexts within cultures) insofar as there are differences in the kinds of problems that different cultural milieus pose their initiates. *In this sense,* we must adopt the position of cultural relativists . . . that no universal notion of a single, general ability, called intelligence, can be abstracted from the behavior of people whose experiences in the world have systematically been different from birth in response to different life predicaments handed down to them. . . . (Laboratory of Comparative Human Cognition, 1982, p. 710)

In summary, most traditional theories of intelligence failed to consider the importance of the individual's social context in evaluating behavior. However, with the exception of the psychometric perspective, more recent approaches tend to define intelligence as an interaction between the individual and his or her environment. The view of many of these newer approaches is that the social context—the home, testing situation, school, work, and so forth—does more than facilitate intelligent behavior; it also defines it. As a result, more attention is now placed on developing measures of intelligence that are more comprehensive and more accurately assess the abilities of students from diverse cultural settings (Davidson, 1990).

DIFFERENTIAL EDUCATIONAL PERFORMANCE

Many ethnic minority students are not faring well in our schools. Educators need to examine their own beliefs about *why* this is so. It may help to compare those beliefs with the explanations that have been offered by social science researchers. Many people operate with implicit theories about minorities that involve stereotypes and assumptions that may not be grounded in reality. You need to be aware of the dangers of forming stereotypes about particular groups and understand how their own actions can play a role in ensuring the success or failure of individual students.

The facts about ethnic underachievement are clear: In California in 1980, only 69 percent of African Americans over the age of 24, 66 percent of Native Americans, and 44 percent of Latinos had graduated from high school, compared with 77 percent of Anglo Americans (Sue & Padilla, 1986). Asians in the same age group, on the other hand, were almost as likely as Anglos to have a high school degree (76 percent). The figures are more extreme at the college level. More recent demographic data indicate little change in the differential performance of students from different ethnic groups (Tomás Rivera Center, 1991). Similar figures can be found on other measures: drop-out rates, grade retention rates, grade point average, and scores on standardized tests. Something is very wrong for many culturally different students in the United States.

The causes for this underachievement have been hotly debated. Take a minute to think about your own beliefs and compare them with the following explanations provided by social scientists. What evidence exists to support your own perspective? Think about what implications follow from your own beliefs. How may your beliefs influence your classroom behavior?

Deficit Explanations

Deficit explanations assume that students who perform poorly in school do so because they are inferior to other students in some way. They may be less intelligent, less motivated, or have specific learning problems. The assumption in deficit models is that something is wrong in the individual rather than in the classroom environment. When deficit explanations are offered for the underachievement of ethnic minority students, they may take several forms: genetic inferiority, cultural deficits, or language problems.

Genetic inferiority is probably the oldest explanation; it was used as justification for the enslavement of Africans in the 1800s and to devalue certain ethnic groups at different times throughout history. For example, in 1854 the California Supreme Court ruled that the Chinese were incapable of intellectual development due to their racial inferiority and thus should not be allowed to testify against whites in court (Kitano, 1980). With this example, we can see how stereotyped assumptions change over time; many people now think of Chinese people as exceptionally talented for academic work. Jensen's (1969, 1980) research on intelligence has often been used to support arguments for the inferiority of African Americans. It is important to note that while explanations of genetic inferiority for particular races or ethnic groups have changed over time, and are currently viewed with disfavor by most researchers, they have not been abandoned. We still find examples of racism in our society. However, the particular group or characteristic that is viewed as "inferior" *does* seem to change over time.

Cultural deficit models are more subtle approaches to viewing particular groups as inferior. These see nothing inherently inferior in individuals from different groups but see problems in the socialization practices of some cultures. The cultural practices of particular ethnic groups are seen as resulting in children being culturally "deprived," "underprivileged," or "deviant." The focus here is on things that are wrong, maladaptive, or in need of being fixed within a culture; these weaknesses are sometimes used as a way of "blaming the victims," while the strengths and competencies of the group are often overlooked.

Anthropologists take issue with any claim of cultural inferiority or superiority for a particular group. They argue that every culture adapts to the environment in which it finds itself and takes on the characteristics that it needs to survive.

Explanations of *linguistic deficits* have been discounted by linguists in much the same way that anthropologists discount models of cultural deviance. Linguists deny the assumption implicit in the linguistic deficit perspective that entire communities of people can be characterized as "semi-lingual" or lacking language. Such charges have been levied against speakers of Black English, and against Latinos and Puerto Ricans who may use English and Spanish in the same sentence. Linguists have demonstrated that Standard English is not superior to Black or Latin English in form or function; each is rule based, grammatically complex, and internally consistent. The difference, of course, is that Standard English is the language of the schools, and other forms of English are often not recognized or understood.

It is important to note that proponents of deficit models may not always use the word *deficit* because of the negative connotations of the term. It is not always readily apparent when a person is operating with such a perspective. Also, some social scientists have used the term *modern racism* to describe more subtle approaches to racism used today. It is not uncommon for writers and speakers to use certain "code words" to express their discontent with certain individuals or groups. For example, the term *immigrant* can be used to express one's discontent with individuals from a particular ethnic or cultural group. Can you identify other forms of "modern racism"?

> **?** How can teachers misinterpret the behaviors of culturally different students?

LOW EXPECTATIONS FOR SUCCESS. A teacher's error in estimating a student's or a cultural group's academic potential can lead to low expectations for success. In one investigation, Deyhle (1987) studied tests and test-taking behaviors among Navajo students in a Bureau of Indian Affairs day school and white students in a large western city. Unlike the teachers of the white students, the teachers of Navajo children were angry that their students didn't seem to care about low grades. Of particular concern was the fact that the students threw away their test papers after receiving them. The teachers concluded that the academic failure of the Navajo students was caused by a culture that didn't value academic achievement.

After visiting classrooms and interviewing both the white and Navajo students, Deyhle found that the two groups of students viewed the results of the tests very differently. The white students saw the tests as directly related to their learning, while the Navajo students did not. Within the Navajo culture, it generally is not considered appropriate to display one's knowledge in public competition. Both groups valued learning, but they did not measure or demonstrate it in the same way.

When teachers have low expectations for students' success, a very real danger exists that the expectations may become self-fulfilling prophecies, as teachers may unknowingly change their behaviors and interact in qualitatively different ways with different groups of students. This teacher expectancy effect may not go unnoticed by students, who may adjust their own levels of aspiration to match their teachers' beliefs. Nieto (1992) cites several studies that indicate that teachers' expectations may be mediated by previously held stereotypes, such that how students are treated may depend on an interaction between teachers' beliefs about students' abilities and their attitudes toward the students' culture, ethnicity, or class.

Difference Explanations

Proponents of difference explanations argue that some ethnic minorities do not do well in school because of a cultural mismatch or incompatibility between their home and school culture. Thus, where deficit models point to things that are wrong, lacking, or inferior in a particular culture (which invariably involves value judgments as to what is considered superior), difference models argue that ethnic minorities merely *differ* from the dominant culture. Skills that work well in one culture may not serve that group's members equally well in another. This position tacitly acknowledges that the culture of school is much more consonant with white, middle-class, Anglo-American cultural values, which may help explain why some children do better in school than others.

Advocates of this view point to the difficulties that minority students have in adjusting to a classroom with different social and linguistic interaction patterns. The argument is that these differences can lead to cultural conflicts that interfere with minority children's abilities to perform well in school.

Although the difference explanation is more comprehensive than the cultural or genetic deficit theories, and doesn't include any implicit racist overtones, it is still not an adequate explanation for the differential academic performance of students (Nieto, 1992). The difference explanation is not able to explain why some ethnic minorities seem to do well in school despite large cultural differences, or why some groups do well in one environment but not in another. Ogbu (1992), a longtime critic of the "difference explanation," states:

> There is evidence from comparative research suggesting that differences in school learning and performance among minorities are not due merely to cultural and language differences. Some minority groups do well in school even though they do not share the language and cultural backgrounds of the dominant group that are reflected in the curriculum, instructional style, and other practices in the schools. Such minorities

Nonstandard English. An English dialect that deviates from the standard pronunciation, vocabulary, and grammar.

may initially experience problems due to the cultural and language differences, but the problems do not persist. (p. 7)

For example, Gibson (1987) found that although Punjabi students in Northern California are very culturally different from their peers, they have been very successful in school. This achievement is attained in spite of several handicaps: Their parents are primarily farm laborers and factory workers who often are illiterate and speak little or no English, and they have faced considerable discrimination. Also, the parents rarely visited their children's school. However, their parents urged their children to spend considerable time on their homework and consider schoolwork a job. Another example to consider is the fact that Korean immigrants to the United States typically do well in school, while Koreans from the same socioeconomic sector who immigrate to Japan are less likely to experience academic success (DeVos & Lee, 1981) .

Research by anthropologists and linguists indicates that differences are not deficits. Examples in countries throughout the world could be used to illustrate that minority students do not fail in school simply because of cultural/language differences (see Taylor & Hegarty, 1985; Gibson, 1991).

? Can students be successful in school if they don't speak Standard English?

SOCIOLINGUISTICS. Misunderstanding of cultural differences can lead teachers to misjudge their students' language abilities. When students and teachers differ in their use of language forms, teachers are more likely to consider their own language the proper form of expression. The most obvious differences in the use of language are those indicated by dialects, which are noticeable in the communication of individuals in different regions of the country (Casanova, 1987).

One of the most widely discussed language patterns is called Black English, or **Nonstandard English,** a dialect that differs from Standard English in pronunciation, vocabulary, and grammar. Some educators believe that Nonstandard English is a defective form of Standard English and that it is detrimental to learning. As a result, these educators urge teachers to instruct students in Standard English and to avoid any recognition of Nonstandard English. Linguists such as Labov (1970) and Gee (1990), however, who have spent years studying the language patterns of African American youths, have clearly demonstrated the grammatical and syntactical complexity of this discourse form. Labov points out that early childhood education programs such as Head Start, which were designed to overcome lower- and middle-class language differences, may have aggravated the African American students' learning difficulties in school.

Labov does not say that children using Nonstandard English do not need to develop additional verbal skills, some of which are characteristic of middle-class verbal behavior: precision in spelling, manipulation of abstract symbols, the ability to define words explicitly, and a broad vocabulary. He would argue, however, that teachers need to recognize and respect nonstandard forms while at the same time helping students to acquire standard forms that they will be expected to use in mainstream society (as well as in future academic work). If teachers are not familiar with dialect differences in pronunciation and grammar, communication problems may result in the classroom. For example, Nonstandard English distinguishes between a continuing state and a temporary condition: "He working" corresponds to "He is working right now," whereas "He be working" means "He usually works" or "He has a steady job" (Labov, 1969). Another characteristic of the nonstandard language is the tendency to omit what linguists call the *medial r,* which the listener interprets as a "lost" syllable. The pronunciation of *sto'y* (*story*) and *ma'y* (*marry*) can lead to misunderstandings as to meaning (Adler, 1979). Labov (1974) questions whether all middle-class verbal habits are functional and desirable in school:

> Before we impose middle-class verbal style upon children from other cultural groups, we should find out how much of it is useful for the main work of analyzing and generalizing, and how much is merely stylistic or even dysfunctional. In high school and college, middle-class children spontaneously complicate their syntax to the point that instructors despair of getting them to make their language simpler and clearer. (p. 160)

Labov's basic point of view is that the school faced with cultural differences should change its orientation. Rather than seek ways to modify students' behavior, educators should consider how the school can accommodate its instructional program to students' strengths. In terms of language instruction, teachers could use Nonstandard English as a springboard for teaching Standard English instead of criticizing students for speaking and writing "incorrectly." This means that instead of insisting that speakers of Nonstandard English follow phonetic rules in reading Standard English materials, teachers would permit children to read standard materials in their own dialect, and focus on students' comprehension of the material rather than on aspects of form. Many teachers are reluctant to follow this advice because they fear that children will not learn Standard English. Linguists arguing for this approach point out that speaking and understanding have been shown to be separate aspects of language development. Children can understand written or spoken Standard English without producing standard pronunciations and grammatical forms in their own speech (Jackson, Robinson, & Dale, 1977).

While the dialectical differences of Black English have been well documented, much less work has examined dialect differences among other ethnic minorities, or the ways in which English language acquisition may vary across immigrant populations. The important point for teachers to keep in mind when working with students who do not seem to speak "proper English" is that the student may be employing a dialect that operates with different rules for both grammar and discourse patterns. While teachers may work to develop Standard English for classroom work, they should be careful not to assume that the way the child speaks is wrong or in need of being "fixed."

CLASSROOM INTERACTION. The linguistic processes in a classroom may differ from the oral discourse experienced by students from different cultural backgrounds (Ainsworth, 1984). An example of this linguistic conflict is described by Philips (1983), who studied how children's lack of responsiveness in the classroom influenced their academic achievement.

Teachers at the Warm Springs Indian Reservation in central Oregon noted that the Native American children would not talk in front of the class and participated less and less in verbal interaction as they proceeded through school. Philips points out that teachers use classroom recitation to allow students to learn from their own public mistakes; the Native American children were not familiar with this approach to learning. The children's home learning involves watching an adult perform a task or skill and practicing it alone, unsupervised. When the children are successful, they perform the skill in front of the adult who taught it. Only when the task or skill is fully developed is it demonstrated publicly. The use of speech in the learning process from instruction to evaluation plays a minor role, because verbal instruction is confined to corrections or answering questions.

This process provides some insight into the Native American children's reluctance to speak in front of their peers. The assumption by the teacher that students learn more effectively by making mistakes in front of others is inconsistent with the children's background. The Native American children have no opportunity to observe others performing successfully before they attempt a task or skill, and they don't have the freedom to determine whether they know enough to demonstrate their knowledge because the

Educators can learn a great deal about culturally diverse students by better understanding how they learn in their homes and communities.

teacher determines when they must respond. Finally, competence is demonstrated verbally in the classroom rather than nonverbally.

Philips found that the children's classroom participation increased when the teacher interacted privately with individual students and when students worked together in small groups. Many teachers eventually changed their methods to include the participation structures that increased the children's oral discourse. However, Philips questions the desirability of complete accommodation to the children's learning preferences, because such change may not prepare the children to succeed in later grades, when they would be with white children. She suggests that the children gradually be taught the traditional classroom discussion procedures so that they would be able to cope effectively in other classroom environments.

cognitive style. The consistent way in which an individual responds to a wide range of perceptual tasks.

NONVERBAL INTERACTION. Misunderstanding of cultural differences can influence the quality of teacher-student interaction (Hall & Hall, 1987). If you have taken courses in anthropology or read such classic books as *The Silent Language* (Hall, 1959) or *The Hidden Dimension* (Hall, 1966), you are already aware of important cultural differences in social interaction, time, space, and materials. Hall (1969) has also written about cultural differences in listening behavior, a topic of particular interest to teachers. He argues that a series of responses governing the use of the eyes, the hands, the orientation and position of the body, and the tone of voice exists in African American culture. Many of these characteristics are frequently misread by whites. Hall notes an informal rule in African American culture: "If you are in the room with another person or in a context where he has ready access to you, there are times when there is no need to go through the motions of showing him you are listening because that is automatically implied" (p. 380). This behavior causes some difficulty when African Americans and whites interact. Whites expect some visible or audible sign that one is listening, but African Americans, according to Hall, have no such expectation. So when a polite African American child casts his eyes downward as a sign of respect, instead of looking straight at his teacher, he might hear his teacher angrily state, "Johnny, look at me when I talk to you!"

Many other nonverbal cultural distinctions may affect classroom behavior and interaction. For example, for some Asian groups, crossed fingers are not a sign of good luck; they are considered an obscene gesture. Folded arms or tightly crossed legs indicate that the individual is not interested in communication. Calling a person by gesturing with an index finger is an insult, since such a motion would be applied only to animals (Divoky, 1988).

COGNITIVE/LEARNING STYLES. **Cognitive style** refers to the consistent ways in which individuals respond to a wide range of perceptual and intellectual tasks. Considerable work by educators and psychologists has gone into examining individual differences in style. Messick (1976) identified more than 20 dimensions of cognitive style that have derived, for the most part, from the research in laboratory investigations studying cognitive differences in humans.

DEBATE FORUM

Does Matching Learning Style with Instruction Lead to an Increase in Achievement?

aptitude by treatment interaction (ATI). Research that focuses on how different aptitudes matched with different instructional methods affect learning.

learning style. Individual differences that influence learning in classroom situations.

Argument: Rita and Kenneth Dunn (1972, 1987) have developed the Learning Style Inventory to identify student learning styles so that teachers can group students on that basis and develop special learning environments for them. The Dunns' research supports greater classroom learning when teachers match instruction and students' learning styles.

Counterargument: Cohen et al. (1989), in a review of the research on instruction, indicate that achievement gains are greater when teachers match *objectives*, instruction, and testing than when attempts are made to match *learning style* and instruction. Their conclusion is supported by other research (Cronbach & Snow, 1977; Kampwirth & Bates, 1980). In addition, some scholars criticize the Dunns' research on methodological grounds (Curry, 1990; Snider, 1990). In any case, Doyle and Rutherford (1984) note the problems inherent in trying to match learning styles with instruction, including deciding which of the many styles represented in a classroom are important, measuring the styles, and making decisions about how to apply the sometimes hundreds of learning style/instructional strategy combinations generated by current instruments.

Cronbach and Snow (1977) report the most extensive research literature on **aptitude by treatment interaction (ATI),** which includes studies of how aptitude interacts with instructional methods to affect student learning. The major conclusion of the review was that high-ability students learn best when they are free to impose their own

Educational reseachers became interested in the implications of cognitive-style research for adapting instruction for different types of students. In some cases they have used cognitive-style instruments in educational settings. They also have developed special instruments for use by teachers. As a result, the term **learning style** is used to identify this new orientation. Although the definitions of learning style differ, most definitions focus on individual differences that influence *learning in classroom situations.*

Some of the work that has been done on individual differences in cognitive or learning style has also been examined as *cultural* differences. One of the most widely investigated forms of cognitive style is the **field-**

structure on educational tasks, while low-ability students appear to learn best when the instructor imposes the structure. Student preferences reflect a different reality, however. Clark (1982) reports that students often say they enjoy most those methods from which they learn the *least*, perhaps because they underestimate the amount of effort needed for success. That is, low-ability students prefer more permissive methods of instruction (e.g., independent study or small-group activities) because they can maintain a low profile that makes their failure less visible. However, these students need more direction and attention to achieve success in academic tasks. High-ability students, on the other hand, like structured methods (e.g., lecture-recitation sessions), which they believe will help them learn more efficiently. However, the research indicates that students with high ability actually learn more from permissive methods, which allow them more independence in using their abilities.

Although this research is limited to structured and permissive environments and to students with high and low ability, it does suggest that a teacher should consider whether it is always advantageous to match student preferences and instructional environment—not only because the preferences may not lead to improved academic achievement but because students simply may benefit from certain instructional approaches whether they like them or not.

There doesn't appear to be much support for matching cognitive or learning styles with instruction. However, no one can argue with the fact that teachers need to be more sensitive to the individual differences of students in the classroom and may be more successful if they try different teaching methods with different students. However, teachers must be aware of the danger of incorrectly categorizing any group of students according to a specific learning style.

What do you think? Would you have been more successful in school if teachers had asked you how you thought you learned best? If they had paid more attention to how you actually learned? How can teachers be more sensitive to student differences in their classrooms?

field-independent. A cognitive style in which the individual is capable of overcoming the effects of distracting elements when attempting to differentiate relevant aspects of a particular situation.

field-dependent. A cognitive style in which the individual operates in a global manner and is distracted by, or sensitive to, background elements.

independent/field-dependent dimension. This dimension is a measure of the extent to which individuals are able to overcome effects of distracting background elements (the field) when they attempt to differentiate the relevant aspects of a particular situation. The more independent the person is of distracting elements, the more analytical, or field-independent, that person is. The more dependent on or incapable of ignoring the distracting elements an individual is, the more global, or field-dependent, that person is. For example, an individual who has difficulty reading a diagram to assemble a bicycle or barbecue set may be field-dependent.

Reviewing the research in this area, Witkin et al. (1977) pointed out the characteristic orientation of individuals classified as field-dependent and field-independent. Field-dependent persons are particularly attentive to the social field and will look to others in defining their own attitudes and beliefs. They reflect a considerable degree of social sensitivity. In contrast, field-independent persons show greater interest in the more impersonal, abstract aspects of various stimuli.

These two types of individuals interact differently with the environment. Field-dependent persons are drawn to people, favor occupations such as teaching that require involvement with others, and prefer academic areas, such as the social sciences, that are more people oriented. Field-independent persons prefer occupations such as astronomy and engineering, in which there is less emphasis on interpersonal interaction. They also favor school subjects, such as mathematics and the physical sciences, that stress the impersonal and abstract. Field-dependent persons are better at learning and remembering social material, and field-independent persons are better at learning and remembering impersonal material.

Cultural differences have been claimed in the area of cooperative/competitive orientation, with Latino and African American students considered to be more cooperative and affiliative than white students in their interpersonal relations (Slavin, 1983). Some researchers claim this is because these groups are field-dependent in their cognitive style. Yet while these groups may tend to have a more cooperative orientation than whites in the classroom, other causal factors could be at work. For example, Delgado-Gaitan and Trueba (1985) observed Latino children interacting in four different classroom participation structures and found copying to be a legitimate learning tool that built on students' home patterns of collective task engagement. In addition, family size, birth order, parental practices, and classroom structure have all been suggested as possible factors leading to a cooperative orientation (Kagan, 1984). Also, the cooperativeness of Latino students appears to lessen with successive generations (Knight & Kagan, 1977). This may be due to their acculturation to American societal norms.

The field-independent/field-dependent dimension has been criticized on methodological and conceptual grounds (Tiedemann, 1989). The bipolar nature of this dimension simplifies the complex nature of human learning and opens the door to broad generalizations and oversimplifications about cultural groups, such that *all* Latinos are seen as field-dependent. A possible discriminatory teaching technique resulting from such a conclusion would be seldom allowing Latino students solo performances in plays or leadership activities (Nieto, 1992).

Because most classrooms still emphasize competitive, field-independent tasks, these cultural differences are posited as one factor in ethnic students' underachievement in school. Children who have more of a cooperative, field-dependent orientation may benefit from working in a classroom that engages in cooperative learning, where helping other students is seen as a form of learning rather than "cheating." At the same time, it should be recognized that *all* children may benefit from cooperative learning activities, even those students who come to school with a more competitive orientation.

Voluntary versus Involuntary Minority Explanation

? Why do some minority groups do well in school while others face academic difficulties?

An alternative to the difference explanation for underachievement—that is, conflict between home and school— is based on the reasons for *why* or *how* a minority group came to the United States. Ogbu (1987, 1992) explains why some minority groups have been very successful in school whereas others have not been. He differentiates between minority groups termed *involuntary* or *castelike* (e.g., certain Latinos, African Americans, and Native Americans), who were incorporated into U.S. society against their will (through slavery, conquest, colonization, or forced labor) and who tend to do poorly in school; and minority groups termed *voluntary* or *immigrant* (e.g., certain Asian Americans) who come to the United States by their own choice because they want to better themselves economically or want greater political freedom. These minorities tend to do well in school.

Ogbu (1992) believes that involuntary minorities experience difficulties in school partly because of the relationship between their cultures and the dominant white (American) culture. That is, they have more difficulty crossing cultural/language boundaries in school than voluntary minorities with similar cultural/language differences. Gibson (1987) has made the same point. She states that involuntary minorities often equate school learning with the loss of their own cultural and ethnic identities, while voluntary groups view school learning and acquisition of the majority culture as an additional set of skills to use when appropriate. Therefore, some minority groups see school learning and acculturation as leading to assimilation, whereas other minority groups view school learning and acculturation in a broader perspective, in which new knowledge is incorporated into their own culture, transforming but not replacing it.

Ogbu's (1992) analysis of the behavior of involuntary minorities shows that they differ significantly from the voluntary minorities. He points out that the involuntary minorities interpret culture and language as indicators of the identity that should be maintained, not as barriers to be overcome. School learning is viewed as "the learning of the cultural and language frames of reference of their 'enemy' or 'oppressors'. . . . They fear that by learning the White cultural frame of reference, they will cease to act like minorities and lose their identity as minorities and their sense of community and self-worth"(p. 10). Members of these minority groups point to the fact that even if individuals learn the culture and language, they seldom are accepted by the mainstream culture and given equal opportunities to advance economically.

Another important point Ogbu makes is that there are social pressures discouraging involuntary minority students from behaving and acting in ways that enhance their school achievement (e.g , completing homework assignments, studying for examinations, asking questions in class). Peers often consider such behavior as "acting white" or being a "schoolboy," and as a result, often criticize or isolate peers making good grades. While parents of voluntary minorities encourage school attendance and good grades, parents of involuntary minorities do not communicate the importance of education to their children. This behavior leads to less interest and involvement in formal education.

As teachers, we need to become aware of the various strategies students use to try to attain academic success without losing their cultural identities (Ogbu, 1992). A counselor expressed one strategy this way: "Do your Black thing [in the community] but know the White man thing [at school]" (p. 11). Another common strategy is *camouflage* (i.e., disguising true academic attitudes and behaviors). One approach is becoming the class clown, demonstrating lack of interest in school but studying in secret. The good grade that such students attain can be attributed to their "natural smartness," not to their effort or school behaviors. Can you think of other ways that students camouflage their behavior?

The following are some suggestions for helping minority children learn (Ogbu, 1992):

- Recognize that involuntary minority children come to school with cultural and language frames of reference that are not only different from but oppositional to those of the mainstream and school.
- Study the histories and cultural adaptations of involuntary minorities in order to understand the bases and nature of the groups' cultural and language frames of reference as well as the children's sense of social identity.
- Develop counseling programs to help students learn to separate attitudes and behaviors that enhance school success from those that lead to losing one's cultural identity.
- Help increase students' adoption of the strategy of "accommodation without assimilation" or "playing the classroom game."

What do you think of Ogbu's explanation of the differential success of minority groups? He has been criticized for failing to account for the large variations that exist within ethnic groups. Do you think that he generalizes too much? Is his analysis useful to you as a parent or teacher?

Contextual Interaction Explanations

Contextual interaction explanations developed in response to the limitations of the deficit and differences perspectives in explaining why certain students had difficulty learning in school. Both deficit and difference models tend, for the most part, to be "single cause" analyses—either the individual *or* the culture *or* language differences *or* the classroom is the root cause of student failure. Where deficit models look at the inadequacy of particular cultural traits, and difference models redefine those traits to be merely "different," the contextual interaction approach argues that all traits develop in specific *contexts* or environments, and the interaction of many factors—societal and school—must be examined if we are to understand why some students achieve in school and others fail. School factors include such elements as instructional practices, language proficiency, self-image, motivation, teacher competencies, and expectations. Societal factors include such elements as the mass media, family, community, and socioeconomic status. This perspective also allows for cultural change as groups come into contact with each other; the cultural traits are not fixed or static. The proponents of this approach argue that improvements must be addressed at many different levels if success is to be ensured for all students (Cortes, 1986; Sue & Padilla, 1986).

A limitation of the early contextual interaction explanations is that they are insufficiently elaborated; the ways in which different factors may interact with each other is not well understood. In addition, the nature of the model is such that it does not provide any easy solutions for educators. Individual cases must be examined from a variety of situations, considering multiple factors within a given environment.

More recently, Tharp and Gallimore (1988) have presented a contextualist view of development and learning that focuses on changing schools and classroom instruction to improve learning for *all* students. This approach is an extension of Vygotsky's (1978) concepts of learning, especially the *zone of proximal development*. I will begin discussing the work of Tharp and Gallimore and other psychologists who emphasize the contextual approach in the next section.

IMPLICATIONS FOR INSTRUCTION IN THE CULTURALLY DIVERSE CLASSROOM

Only recently has explicit attention been given to the role of culture in learning and cognition. Two different points of view have dominated instructional improvement for culturally different students (Goldenberg & Gallimore, 1989):

- Instructional programs should be adapted to the particular characteristics of different groups (the *cultural compatibility hypothesis*).
- Instructional programs should employ general and universal principles of learning and instruction that are relevant for all students (*the universalistic hypothesis*).

In the first part of this book I introduced teaching-learning practices that are to some degree effective with all students. These practices include direct instruction, cooperative learning, and the use of learning strategies. I will begin this section by providing an example of the cultural compatibility approach and show that it does not have to be inconsistent with the universal approach.

wait-time. The period of time that a teacher waits for a student to respond to a question.

Developing Culturally Compatible Classrooms

? How can a teacher make modifications in the classroom to help culturally different students?

Evidence suggests that when schools and classrooms are changed to adapt to the students' cultural background and experiences, students' academic achievement increases. An example of the impact of classroom modifications for instruction is the Kamehameha Early Education Program (KEEP), designed to develop a culturally compatible language arts program for Hawaiian children in the primary grades. Tharp (1989) explains how the KEEP program modified four areas to make the classroom more compatible with the Hawaiian culture: *social organization, sociolinguistics, cognition,* and *motivation.*

SOCIAL ORGANIZATION. Teachers had difficulty maintaining the attention of Hawaiian students in the traditional classroom structure, in which students are asked to work independently. Since the Hawaiian students begin learning social responsibility by taking care of their siblings, they are used to collaboration, cooperation, and assisting others rather than working individually and competitively. As a result, the directors of the KEEP program designed an instructional situation in which almost all the instruction is in small groups (four to five students of both sexes) emphasizing peer interaction. Students move to different learning centers located throughout the classroom every 20 to 25 minutes (see discussion of open classrooms in Chapter 5). They work together at these centers on different language activities.

SOCIOLINGUISTICS. Instead of focusing on phonics, a process of teaching reading by identifying letters and the sounds represented by them (an analytic approach), the KEEP program focuses on whole-story discussions and general themes (a holistic approach). The students begin by reading small segments of each story silently, after which they discuss the meaning of the events in the story and relate them to their own lives. At the end, they put the smaller parts together and discuss the overall meaning of the story. Word identification skills are not taught separately but are always presented in the context of sentences, emphasizing meaning over the sounds of letters (Vogt, Jordan, & Tharp, 1987).

COGNITION. An important linguistic process in the classroom is **wait-time,** or pauses in interaction. One type of wait-time is the amount of time given the student to answer questions; another is the amount of time following a student response that the teacher waits before making another response (Rowe, 1974). It appears that students from different cultures have different preferences for the way they respond.

White and Tharp (1988) report that Hawaiian children have a negative wait-time; they tend to talk as the teacher is responding. Although this behavior would be considered a rude interruption by some observers, in the Hawaiian culture it demonstrates involvement and concern. If a

Teachers need to encourage mutual acceptance and respect among students from diverse backgrounds.

teacher attempts to curtail the behavior, the classroom participation of the students would be inhibited. In the KEEP program, researchers developed an instructional format whereby each day the students meet in a small group with the teacher for a 20-minute discussion of some text. The "one person at a time" rule of interaction was dropped to allow students to participate in interaction characterized by "rapid-fire response, liveliness, mutual participation, interruptions, overlapping volunteered speech, and joint narration" (Tharp, 1989, p. 352). Researchers have found that this type of communication pattern leads to higher academic achievement than lessons taught in a more traditional manner (Au & Mason, 1981).

MOTIVATION. Finally, researchers found that many of the competitive techniques used to motivate students were not effective with the Hawaiian students. The students were more involved in academic tasks when teachers used school-based praise and incentives rather than individual praise and incentives. The KEEP project trains teachers to be both warm and firm. To be accepted in one's peer group, Hawaiian children must show warmth and also prove toughness. Teachers are evaluated by their students using the same criteria (D'Amato, 1986).

Goldenberg and Gallimore (1989) point out that many of the practices implemented by the KEEP program are consistent with universally effective teaching/learning practices:

- active, direct teaching of reading comprehension
- peer-group/cooperative learning
- frequent assessment of student progress
- well-run and organized classroom
- appropriate balance among word-recognition, skills, and comprehension instruction
- positive classroom management strategies
- teacher consultants who model, coach, give feedback, assistance, etc. (p. 47)

assisted performance. Instructional procedures where the teacher provides certain structure so that students can learn even if they can't complete all aspects of the task by themselves.

They suggest that teachers working with a culturally diverse student population should begin their instructional planning by considering universal principles of effective teaching and learning. The next step would be to consider modifications consistent with cultural and individual variations. For example, cooperative learning was used effectively in the KEEP program in Hawaii. When the program was tried with Navajo students in Arizona, the teachers and researchers had to make certain changes to promote student participation and smooth classroom functioning. In the Hawaiian program, the best group functioning included mixed-sex and mixed-ability groups of four or five students. However, the teachers found that the Navajo students responded best to smaller, same-sex groups of more equal ability. The important point is that children in two different cultures benefited from cooperative learning, as the universal principle would predict. Yet specific modifications had to be made in the instructional procedure for "local" variations.

? What type of student-teacher interaction can improve classroom instruction?

Beyond KEEP. Tharp and his colleagues initially developed the KEEP program (1970–1983) to demonstrate how classrooms could be made more culturally compatible. More recently, Tharp and Gallimore (1988) have taken the core concepts in KEEP and expanded Vygotsky's ideas about the importance of the interaction between the individual and his or her social world to recommend changes in classroom instruction.

They believe that teachers must modify the "recitation script" where the teacher usually is at the center of attention instructing students in a large group. The rules of communication that dominate include a pattern of question-and-answer sessions, in which the teacher asks a question, obtains a response from a student, and then reacts to that response. Spontaneous speech on the part of students is generally discouraged.

Goodlad's (1984) study of schools indicated that, on the average, only 7 of 150 minutes of the school day is used by teachers to respond to students' work. He reports:

> A great deal of what goes on in the classroom is like painting-by-numbers—filling in the colors called for by numbers on the page. . . .[Teachers] ask specific questions calling essentially for students to fill in the blanks: "What is the capital city of Canada?" "What are the principle exports of Japan?" Students rarely turn things around by asking the questions. Nor do teachers often give students a chance to romp with an open-ended question such as "What are your views on the quality of television?" (p. 108)

ASSISTED PERFORMANCE. Tharp and Gallimore (1988) argue for another kind of teaching defined as **assisted performance.** The example of reciprocal teaching (Chapter 8) to improve reading comprehension is an

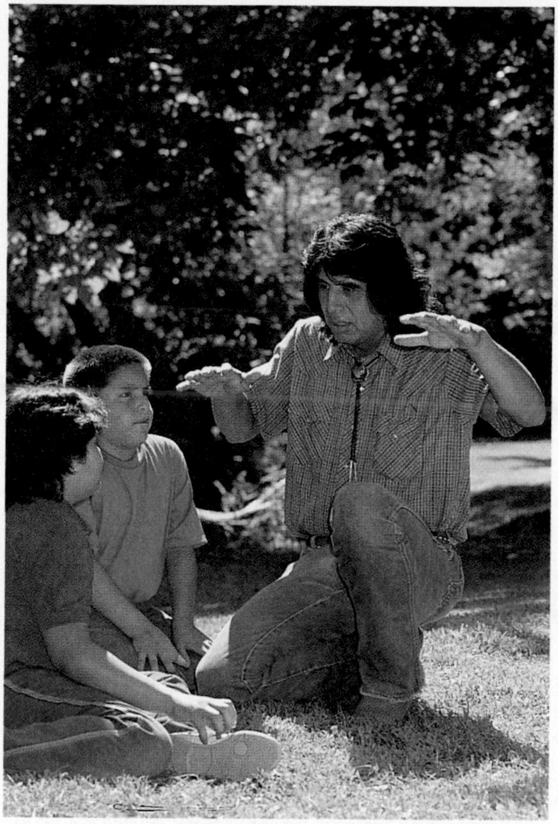

What types of instructional assistance have you found useful in your learning? Do you think that some students have difficulty in school because of the incompatibility between home and school learning?

example of assisted performance. The description of how Native American children learn by observing adult models in their community (Philips, 1983), discussed earlier in this chapter, is another example.

An effective use of assisted performance is the dialogue or *instructional conversation*. Tharp and Gallimore (1988) provide the following example of a teacher and children reading and discussing a story, "Freddie Finds a Frog." Freddie shows his Frog to Mr. Mays, who says that he might just take the frog fishing. None of the children understands the double meaning of the statement. Note how, in the following dialogue, the teacher assists the children by asking a series of questions to organize their knowledge from the text and their own experiences into a coherent understanding of Mr. Mays's joke:

TEACHER: What did Mr. Mays say he would do with the frog?
LON: He would take . . .
MELE: . . . water, 'um fishing?
TEACHER: Do frogs like to go fishing?
GROUP: Noooo. [When the teacher repeats the question, one child says "yes," and several say "no"]
TEACHER: Why don't they like to go fishing?
[The children give several opinions] Frogs don't like water, don't like flies, don't like fish.
BILL: They use for da bait.

TEACHER: If you use it for bait, what do you have to do to the frog? [The children give several opinions, including one exclamation of disgust]
ALICE: Put it on a hook (p. 20)

The teacher assists the students by providing a structure, and the students supply the information for the discussion. Without the teacher, the students would not understand the story. They understood what Mr. Mays meant by reviewing different possible explanations, until they reached the one conclusion—frog as bait—that satisfied the logic of the story.

Children with assisted performance eventually learn to internalize the strategy so that they query themselves as to the possible meaning of situations and events they encounter in and outside of the classroom. However, until such internalization occurs, children's performance must be assisted. Tharp and Gallimore (1988) state: "The *principles* of good teaching are not

CLASSROOM Application

EFFECTIVE INSTRUCTIONAL PRACTICES FOR CULTURALLY DIVERSE STUDENTS

Eugene García (1992), in a report from the National Center for Research on Cultural Diversity and Second Language Learning in Santa Cruz, California, summarizes the findings from research on effective instructional practices used with linguistically and culturally diverse students in four different areas of the United States. The studies summarized in the report focused on schools where ethnic and language minority students experienced *success* in school such that their academic achievement measured at or above national averages. You will note that the findings are consistent with Tharp and Gallimore's (1988) work. García reports that while there was considerable variation in the curricular design across sites, several key elements were apparent:

1. *High levels of communication:* Communication between teachers and students and among students was higher than in most classrooms. Classrooms were often "noisy" due to an emphasis on collaborative group projects and learning centers. The teacher typically circulated around the room assisting small groups on their projects and activities.

different for school than for home and community. When true teaching is found in schools, it observes the same principles that good teaching exhibits in informal settings" (p. 27). This type of assistance can and should be used in all subject areas, not just reading comprehension.

Many strategies other than instructional conversations can be classified under assisted performance. For example, modeling is an effective way to guide students through a cognitive task, such as when a teacher talks aloud to describe the steps taken to solve a mathematics problem. Other techniques include using reinforcement to communicate to students that appropriate behavior was displayed; providing feedback on tasks with specific standards; using prompting questions to encourage students to think more about the topic (e.g., "How did you reach this conclusion?" "Is there another possible solution?"; and task structuring such as showing students how to use task analysis to separate a large task into smaller ones (Tharp & Gallimore, 1991).

2. *Thematic, integrated curriculum:* Instruction was largely organized around thematic units that were selected by the students in consultation with the teacher. The teachers organized the instruction so that students would reach the grade-level objects while at the same time becoming "experts" on topics and issues that interested them.
3. *Collaborative learning:* Students worked actively together in all or most activities. Cooperation between students was emphasized. The student-student interactions allowed a space where considerable high-level cognitive thinking occurred on a regular basis.
4. *Language and literacy:* More instruction in the native language of the students occurred in the early grades, but even in the upper grades students were allowed to respond in the language of their choice. Students initially wrote in their native language, but made the transition to English on their own, without outside pressure. Their English writing ability, when it emerged, was equal to or greater than their native language writing ability.
5. *Perceptions:* Teachers had high expectations for all their students; they strongly supported them and rejected any hint that their students were intellectually "disadvantaged." The teachers saw themselves as innovators in instructional practices and were very committed to ensuring success for their students. Teachers collaborated with other teachers in support networks and maintained open communication with their students' families.

funds of knowledge. The essential cultural practices and bodies of knowledge that households use to survive, to get ahead, or to thrive.

Building on Families' Funds of Knowledge

? How can teachers involve low-income and language-minority parents in classroom instruction?

The education literature is filled with articles emphasizing the importance of involving parents in the education of their children. The history of public education indicates that middle-class parents have always been more involved in schools than low-income or language-minority parents. Lareau (1990) believes that children and families from different socioeconomic levels have access to different resources for interacting with schools. For example, middle-class parents often have certain advantages over low-income or language-minority parents: They have experienced more schooling than low-income parents and better understand the curriculum; they can hire tutors when their children need help; they may feel more comfortable interacting with teachers; they can hire baby-sitters when they need to attend school meetings.

Although both middle- and low-income parents want their children to succeed in school, low-income parents often don't actively intervene in schools because they depend on teachers to make the right decisions concerning their children. The strategy used by low-income parents has not been successful, while the strategy of middle-class parents of actively participating in their children's education has lead to academic success (Mehan, 1991).

Recently, Moll (1992) described a study that utilized a sociocultural approach to instruction influenced by Vygotsky's (1978) ideas of how cultural experiences and social practices mediate thinking. This study has important implications for parental involvement in schools, since he describes how knowledge of children's communities can be used to improve instruction.

Moll and his colleagues developed the **funds of knowledge** that students from a small Latino community in the Southwest use in their everyday lives. This knowledge is largely acquired through work and daily life experiences. The networks through which this knowledge is shared are built out of social interactions between extended family and community members.

Teachers and researchers worked together to talk and meet with the members of the local school community, in order to understand what kinds of skill and expertise exist in the community, and to see how that knowledge is shared or exchanged. While these funds of knowledge exist in different forms in all communities, they are especially important in recent immigrant/ethnic minority settings, where people often rely on the informal exchange of resources in order to survive. The knowledge that such groups possess, however, often goes unrecognized by mainstream culture and is only rarely acknowledged within formal institutions of learning. Many teachers have little idea about the wide range of knowl-

Parents are children's first teachers and can play an important role in classroom instruction.

edge that can be tapped within a few blocks of the school, because traditional approaches to education do not allow for such exploration.

The researchers assessed parents' knowledge and competencies from the jobs they held as well as their stated interests and competencies. The knowledge and competencies included agriculture and mining (e.g., ranching, animal husbandry, timbering, and minerals), economics (e.g., building codes, accounting, and sales), household management (e.g., budgets, child care, and cooking), material and scientific knowledge (e.g., carpentry, roofing, and design and architecture), medicine (e.g., first aid procedures, anatomy, and midwifery), and religion (e.g., baptisms, Bible studies, and moral knowledge and ethics).

Moll provides an example of how a sixth-grade teacher integrated home and school knowledge around an academic unit of instruction. She chose to develop her instructional unit on construction and building. After discussing the unit with her students, she encouraged them to visit the library and start locating information on the topic in both Spanish and English. In addition, he brought various books into the classroom on the topic. Students also built model houses for homework and wrote brief essays describing their research or their construction methods. Next, the teacher invited parents who had expertise in construction to the classroom to provide additional information to the students. The students were surprised that the teacher would want to invite their parents *as experts*, especially since many of them lacked formal education. She was especially interested in having them describe their use of construction instruments and tools and their use of mathematics in their work. The visits were so successful that she invited a total of 20 different community people during the semester to contribute knowledge to other lessons she developed.

CLASSROOM Application

IMPROVING MULTICULTURAL EDUCATION

What is the first thing that comes into your mind when I mention multicultural education? Some people first think of units about ethnic holidays or multicultural food festivals. These activities are how some teachers "do" multicultural education, failing to realize that it is not an event but a process that should encompass all aspects of instruction and social interaction throughout the school year. Nieto (1992) views multicultural education as a process that challenges and rejects all forms of discrimination in schools and society and accepts differences among students and families. She argues that it should permeate the curriculum and instructional strategies used in schools and the interaction among teachers, students, and parents. Last, multicultural education should further the democratic principles of social justice.

The following discussion of multicultural education is based on Sonia Nieto's (1992) book, *Affirming Diversity*. Suggestions for specific activities are quoted from Chapter 12 (pp. 284–300) of her book.

MAKING DIFFERENCES AND SIMILARITIES AN EXPLICIT PART OF THE CURRICULUM

It is never too early to begin teaching students about human differences and similarities. Teachers can use students' comments about skin color, physical characteristics, handicaps, or gender as a basis for developing lessons to promote positive attitudes about people. Also,

A focus on families' funds of knowledge can serve many purposes:

- It helps to counter the notion that certain ethnic or low-socioeconomic communities possess few usable skills.
- It shows how knowledge that the community possesses can become a focal point of students' academic work.
- It can improve student learning and motivation by making classroom learning relevant to their life experiences.
- It can enhance parent involvement in schools by communicating that they can play an important role in the educational experiences of their children.

class projects can focus on the similarities and differences of children and adolescents living in different parts of the world.

- Focus on your specific curriculum. How can you make similarities and differences an explicit part of your curriculum? If you are a subject matter specialist, list the topics that you will be teaching in the next month. If you are an elementary or preschool teacher, list the themes or topics you will be teaching. How can you make them more explicitly multicultural and antisexist? Write down specific ideas, along with resources to help you accomplish this task.
- Think about the resources you have in your school and your classroom. Develop an environment that is physically multicultural. Write down as many concrete ideas as you can think of or actually draw the floor plan of your classroom, indicating where and how resources that are multicultural might best be used.

MAKING RACISM AND DISCRIMINATION AN EXPLICIT PART OF THE CURRICULUM

Focusing on similarities and differences alone will not automatically make racism and discrimination disappear in the classroom. There are times when specific issues and behavior must be addressed even if this leads to uncomfortable topics of conversation. A good place to begin is to use some of the name-calling by students in school to confront racism and discrimination.

- Stereotypes of racial and cultural groups, women, social classes, and disabled people, among others, are all around us. Develop some ways to make these an explicit part of the curriculum. Locate appropriate materials and describe how you would have students go about countering the stereotypes they see.

continued

- How might you use stories in the news to bring up issues of racism and other forms of discrimination? Develop a number of activities, related to your subject area and grade level, that focus on current news in which stereotyping, racism, or exclusion can be found.

EXPANDING THE CURRICULUM

Teachers can help students analyze events by expanding the typical coverage in textbooks. For example, when studying the Revolutionary War, students can examine events from the perspective of African Americans, Native Americans, women, and others not covered in the textbook. Also, teachers can develop a multicultural library in their classrooms to which students can bring in stories, poems, and other materials to share with classmates.

- Look at the next unit you plan to teach. Think of some ways in which you can make it more inclusive, while taking care not to make it scattered and irrelevant. Develop a number of activities that are more reflective of the backgrounds of the students in your class, school, and community.
- How can you develop an oral history in your class based on the subject you are studying? Plan a unit that uses the talents and experiences of people in the community as a basis for the curriculum. Develop lessons in which you teach your students the specifics of identifying subjects, interviewing, transcribing, and developing a final product. Think of how you can integrate this project into the rest of your curriculum.

RESPECTING AND AFFIRMING CULTURAL DIFFERENCES

Visit the homes of the children in your community. Take your class on these home visits, or simply take a walk through the neighborhood. Have students keep journals of their interaction with students from another community. Help your students to examine their experiences and to reconsider certain assumptions they may have made about other groups.

- Ask your students to talk about their culture from time to time. Even young students can do so, although in a more limited way than older ones. The point of this activity is to help make students' cultures visible in the school.

- Encourage students to share their culture with others. Artifacts from home, cultural traditions that they celebrate, books and stories, and important people in their lives can all be brought into the school to help make the curriculum more inclusive.

USING LANGUAGE DIVERSITY AS A RESOURCE

The languages that students speak in the classroom can be an important resource for expanding students' linguistic knowledge and for communicating that language diversity is valued in the classroom. Unfortunately, in many schools, speaking a different language is seen as a deficit rather than an asset on which further learning can be built.

- Think about students in your classes who speak a language other than English. Ask them to teach you and the other students some words in the language. Use these words in the classroom context. Write them up and put them on bulletin boards or use them in homework or project assignments.
- Ask students to bring in poems, stories, legends, or songs in their native language. They might want to teach these to their classmates. Have them available (in written form or on tape) for other students to read or listen to.

Before we leave multicultural education, we should relate it to Ogbu's (1992) perspective about the important distinctions between minority groups. He doesn't believe multicultural education, *by itself,* is an adequate strategy for improving the learning for all minority children. Ogbu believes that much of multicultural education tends to focus on changes in teacher behavior and attitudes. As a result, he would like more focus on minority students' own responsibility for their academic success: "School success depends not only on what schools and teachers do but also on what students do" (p. 6). Although many proponents of multicultural education would agree with his perspective, it is still important to consider that promoting cross-cultural understanding and reducing prejudice is extremely important, but it may not be a sufficient condition for successfully educating all students. What is your perspective on this issue?

bilingual education. Classroom instruction in two languages.

LANGUAGE ISSUES

The face of America is changing. Because increasing numbers of students entering school in the United States do not speak English as their primary language, an important issue for teachers is what language is best suited to instructing students and how best to promote academic growth as well as English language acquisition. Teachers may find themselves working in a classroom with students who speak a variety of languages in their homes. For example, administrators in the Los Angeles Unified School District report that they have students from over 80 different language backgrounds.

There are already over 30 million individuals living in the United States whose primary language is not English (Hakuta & Garcia, 1989). Figure 9.2 shows estimated or projected figures for the years 1982 to 2020 for the number of children speaking a primary language other than English. This increase will present a great challenge to educators to increase the effectiveness of all language programs.

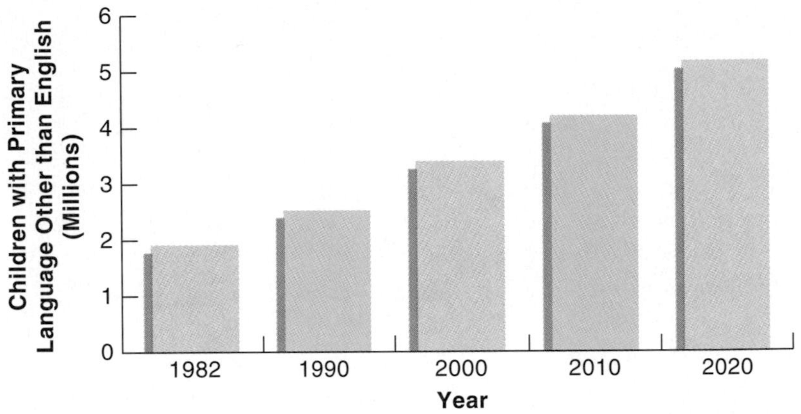

Figure 9.2 Projected Number of Children with a Primary Language Other Than English, U.S. Total, 1982–2020.
Source: Pallas, Natriello, and McDill, 1989.

Let us return once again to the work of Tharp and Gallimore (1988). They believe that one reason for students' problems in learning a language in a classroom setting is that they have little opportunity to practice (again, because of teacher-dominated recitation). Students need more opportunity for extended meaningful conversations on history, science, mathematics, and other school subjects. The following sections will provide more information about developing students' language competencies.

Bilingual Education

? What are the issues involved in developing bilingual rather than English-only programs?

A major debate among educators is how best to teach non-English-speaking students: Should they be taught in their primary language? Should they be encouraged to speak English? Should they receive **bilingual education** (i.e., instruction in both English and their primary language)?

One of the early approaches to language diversity was the "sink-or-swim" method. Children were put into English classes and expected to succeed in school. In some cases, children were punished if they were found speaking Spanish in the classroom or on the playground. Can you imagine being placed in a classroom in Mexico, Germany, or France and being expected to compete with the other students in the class without being able to speak the dominant language? How do you think you would describe your predicament—unpleasant, frustrating, traumatic? How do you think your teachers would judge your ability? How would you feel about yourself and your culture? The chances are that such an experience would not be positive if you were left on your own to learn the language without any support system. Would you stay in school? Spanish-speaking students have faced this problem for decades. Cummins (1981) believes that schools have contributed directly to the problems that minority students have in school by undermining their cultural identity, diminishing the value of their primary language, and providing them with English material that makes little sense to them.

Some educators are opposed to bilingual education because they believe students would learn English more rapidly if they spent more time exposed to the language (Rossel & Ross, 1986). Other educators have concerns regarding the role of minority groups in society: fear that cultural groups would retain their primary language and not assimilate into American culture; belief in the unwillingness of immigrants to speak the English language; and belief that allowing individuals to speak their native language in school would interfere with their learning English (a phenomenon called the *interference theory*) or cause confusion in their thinking (Cardenás, 1986). The first two reasons are emotional issues that cannot be logically refuted. Some countries function very well when citizens and other residents speak more than one language. The United States is among the few countries in the world in which students are not proficient in more than one language upon graduation from high school (National Commission on Excellence in Education, 1983). As for the third issue, there is no evidence that bilingualism interferes with performance or thinking in either language. In fact, bilingual education increases achievement in areas other than the language studied (Hakuta, 1986).

One of the problems of conducting research in this area is that both the programs and the language proficiency of teachers vary widely. For example, many bilingual programs are implemented with only the classroom aide speaking Spanish. Therefore, it is easy to find bilingual programs that have little impact on students. Troike (1978) and Willig (1985) found that when programs were well organized and had proficient teachers, bilingual instruction was more effective than English-only instruction in developing English academic skills. Other research (e.g., Carter & Chatfied, 1986; Krashen & Biber, 1988) has identified specific instructional procedures that produce bilingual students who succeed in school.

More recently, a longitudinal study commissioned by the U.S. Department of Education (Ramirez et al., 1990) compared the effectiveness of two kinds of programs for language minority students—structured English immersion and late-exit transitional bilingual education—with the most typical form of bilingual education in operation in the schools—early-exit transitional bilingual education. Structured English immersion classes are classes composed entirely of limited-English-speaking students, taught by a bilingual instructor. Students in these classes can speak in their home language and be understood by their teacher, but they are taught entirely in English. The early-exit programs are programs where the home language is used as the medium of instruction for a limited time each day for a total of two to three years. By third grade, most students work entirely in English. Late-exit programs, on the other hand, have students doing most work in their native language and gradually increasing the amount of English work over many years.

The "Ramirez Report," as it has come to be known, is an important study because of the scope of the project (data on 2,300 Spanish-speaking children in more than 500 classrooms were collected over a four-year period). The study found that students in the English immersion and early-exit bilingual programs achieved at the same level in mathematics, English language skills, and English reading. Students in the late-exit program had the greatest growth in these same areas. Cziko (1992) notes: "The impressive growth rates shown by students in late-exit bilingual programs suggest that giving the native language a much more important role than is typically done in traditional bilingual education programs may enable these at-risk students to achieve at levels comparable to those of majority students" (p. 12).

How does bilingual education benefit students? How is it that the students who were in the program that used the *most* Spanish, over the longest period of time, showed the greatest gain in *English*? Cummins (1981) posits a common proficiency dimension that underlies the development of academic skills in both languages. This means that either language can promote the development of a basic proficiency in both languages. As students learn English, they continue to develop their cognitive skills by receiving instruction in content areas in their primary language. As a result, limited English skills do not impede the intellectual or academic progress of the students, as would occur in an all-English program. What the students learn in the native language transfers readily to English after they acquire English. Furthermore, the students are less likely to feel alienated in school and are more likely to develop a positive self-concept.

Many states have mandated bilingual education. In 1971 Massachusetts was the first state to legislate bilingual education. That state required that a program be instituted whenever 20 or more students of the same language background were present in the same school. In addition, the law stipulated a three-year period for preparing students for a monolingual English classroom. California requires a bilingual program whenever there are 10 or more students of the same language in the same grade and school. At present, the states vary as to the requirements of establishing bilingual programs and the types of programs developed.

Language Acquisition

Teachers of students whose first language is not English will want to have some understanding of the processes by which language is acquired. Are the processes involved in first and second language acquisition similar or different? For a long time, linguists believed that different theories were needed to explain first and second language acquisition. Today, many linguists support the view that there are sufficient similarities between first and second language acquisition to support a common theory on how language is acquired (e.g., Ellis, 1986; Krashen, 1982).

Humans are truly remarkable in their ability to acquire language. The average child learns most of the sounds of his or her first language before the age of 3 and uses most of its grammatical patterns before the age of 5 or 6 (Gleason, 1985). Some linguists believe that humans are born with a language acquisition device, which allows them to derive different grammatical structures from the speech of adults (Chomsky, 1965). This innate structure provides the ability to comprehend and produce sentences that were never heard before. Thus a child can take a sentence such as "I like to walk" and can generate. "I like walking," "I like to take walks," and so forth.

> **?** How does Krashen's approach to language acquisition differ from traditional approaches?

KRASHEN'S i + 1 CONCEPT. One of the major approaches to second language acquisition is the interactional approach—an approach that emphasizes interesting and relevant subject matter in low-anxiety classroom environments. One such program, called the *natural approach*, is proposed by Stephen Krashen (Krashen, 1982; Krashen & Terrell, 1983). The following discussion of Krashen's approach follows the explanation by Richard-Amato (1988) in *Making It Happen: Interaction in the Second Language Classroom.*

Krashen distinguishes between two different linguistic systems: *learning* and *acquisition*. He views learning as something that occurs through conscious study of formal aspects of language. Language information that is learned (i.e., the formal rules of the language) is used in speech production only if it is relatively simple, if the speaker is concerned with form, *and* if the speaker has time to apply the information in speech. Acquisition, on the other hand, operates as a subconscious process when people are intent on communicating and not worried about form or rules. According to Krashen, one acquires the rules of language best not by studying them but by exposure to the language over time.

Krashen believes that the teacher does not have to focus on formal instruction in the target language. Instead, he or she should provide optimal input that is comprehensible, interesting, and/or relevant, not grammatically sequenced, and in sufficient quality. The teacher's input must approximate the student's "i + 1." It must be comprehensible in that it is near the student's actual level of development (i), but then it must stretch beyond that to include concepts and structures that the student has not yet acquired (i + 1). Krashen's "i + 1" concept is conceptually similar to the Vygotskian notion of the zone of proximal development. People learn best in social interactions when they are operating at a level of difficulty just a little bit beyond the level they could operate on independently.

motherese. A language used by caretakers involving the simplification of speech by using short, slow, and repetitive phrases.

Think for a moment how a child learns a primary language. Parents use a simplified form of communication called **motherese.** They don't worry about grammar or correct form; their primary concern is to communicate with their child. Why shouldn't the classroom use a similar model? If the language teacher treated "errors" as evidence that the language was being acquired, the learner might be more willing to take risks of being wrong and might be more uninhibited in developing competency in the language (Ellis, 1985). Observe the instruction in the following dialogue:

STUDENT: I throw it—box. [He points to a box on the floor.]
TEACHER: You threw the box.
STUDENT: No, I threw *in* the box.
TEACHER: What did you throw in the box?
STUDENT: My. . . I paint. . .
TEACHER: Your painting?
STUDENT: Painting?
TEACHER: You know. . . painting. [The teacher makes painting movements on an imaginary paper.]
STUDENT: Yes, painting.
TEACHER: You threw your painting in the box.
STUDENT: Yes, I threw my painting in box. (Richard-Amato, 1988, p. 40)

Krashen would say that the teacher is speaking near the student's i + 1. The vocabulary is simple, repetition is frequent, and the focus is on meaning, not form. Notice how the teacher produced changes in the child's speech (e.g., *throw* became *threw*) without teaching grammar.

What about all the errors students make in learning a language? Doesn't the teacher need to correct students? Although Krashen believes there is a role for error correction in language acquisition, he doesn't believe error correction is an important factor in learning a language. Sutherland (1979) provides support for Krashen's position in stating that both accuracy and fluency can't be achieved in the early stages of learning a language. Sutherland contends that students develop very little proficiency in a language when teachers emphasize accuracy over fluency. He believes that many language teachers mistakenly feel that if they don't correct their students' mistakes, they will never accurately learn the language.

Krashen also minimizes the role of output (what the learner says) in the acquisition process. He believes that comprehension precedes production. "We acquire spoken fluency *not* by practicing talking but by understanding input by listening and reading" (Krashen, 1982, p. 59). The implication for the teacher is that there is a "silent period" during which children acquire a great deal of understanding in a language but can't achieve an equal amount of production. Thus, the teacher can't always judge a student's progress in a language by what he or she says in class.

Although Krashen's approach to language acquisition has been well received by teachers, there have been some criticisms of his theory and instructional approach (see Ellis, 1986; Higgs & Clifford, 1982; McLaughlin, 1978). One concern is based on the role of grammar in learning a language. If little or no attention is paid to grammatical inaccuracies through corrective feedback early in the language acquisition process, students may not be able to advance to higher levels of proficiency. What do you think about Krashen's approach? What type of experiences did you have learning a language? What changes in language instruction would you recommend?

CLASSROOM Application

IMPROVING CHILDREN'S LANGUAGE

You can play an important role in helping students to develop their language skills. Following are some recommendations for classroom practices (adapted and quoted from Jackson, Robinson, & Dale, 1977, pp. 5–6):

1. "*Give young children ample opportunities to play and talk with one another and with adults.*" Although children talk a great deal among themselves, they sometimes are less verbal near adults. Teachers should ask questions about situations that interest children rather than always appearing to ask questions to "test" their knowledge. Also, when teachers show more interest in *what* children say than *how* they say it, children are more likely to talk in the future.
2. "*Create situations in which children want and need to formulate and elaborate their messages. When they have difficulty with this task, help them by asking probing questions ('What else did it look like?' 'What did you do then?') and by providing examples of good messages.*" Much of what a young child says can be understood only if the listener knows the present or past events leading up to the current situation, because the speaker omits much of the information needed by the listener. For example, a preschooler may go to the teacher and state: "I want the big one!" Young children fail to communicate clearly because they often don't understand what the listener needs to know or how to relay the information. Therefore, learning to use language effectively requires an understanding of the needs of the listener. An important classroom strategy is to give children opportunities to play the role of both speaker and listener. Several communication games can be designed to meet this objective. For example, two children might sit at a table with a screen blocking their view of each other. One child is given objects with which to make a design that must be described to the other child, who then attempts to draw the design. The children can take turns being speaker and listener (Bartlett, 1972).

continued

3. *"Provide children with extended exposure to the meaning of words such as* more, on, before, *and so on in a variety of contexts. In your own use of these words, check to make sure that the children understand the meanings you intend."* Certain vocabulary words such as *more, less than,* and *under* deal with relationships that are useful in many learning situations. These words, or the concepts they express, are difficult to learn because they convey ideas that require children to attend to the unchanging feature or relationship that must be separated from the specific situation in which the word is used. Teachers need to be careful in assuming that children understand a word merely because they use it correctly in one situation.
4. *"Provide examples of good English in your own speech, but resist the impulse to nag children about their grammar."* Teachers often become frustrated in attempting to change children's grammar or pronunciation. Research investigations have indicated that correcting students' errors in language usage does not lead to immediate changes in behavior (Dulay, Burt, & Krashen, 1982). Sometimes children will modify their grammar simply by listening to an adult model the correct usage. However, the child must be ready to imitate or to accommodate the change. In many situations, it may take weeks or months before a child will make the change. Providing opportunities for children to hear correct adult speech is a good way to improve the use of grammar. However, expecting children to use grammar or pronunciation too far from their own level will lead to disappointment.
5. *"In teaching reading to all children, but particularly to children who speak Nonstandard English, begin by emphasizing comprehension rather than Standard English phonetics [pronunciation]. Adapt phonics lessons in spelling and reading to the pronunciation used by children in class."* Emphasis on Standard English phonetic reading may lead to anxiety and frustration for both teacher and student. If the purpose of reading instruction is to enable students to comprehend messages, then overemphasis on pronunciation is not the best approach. This approach assumes, of course, that the student's pronunciation can be understood.
6. *"Don't assume that children from disadvantaged backgrounds are 'nonverbal' or that they lack the verbal skills necessary for thinking."* Adler (1979) points out the problems with the following reasoning: "Language is inferior; therefore, thought is inferior" (p. 76). There is little evidence that any one dialect or language enables an individual to reason more successfully. Therefore, beliefs that lead to negative attitudes and behavior toward students' language can have a detrimental effect on classroom interaction.

Summary

CHALLENGE FOR THE SCHOOLS

1. Recent increases in immigration to the United States have led to one of the most ethnically and culturally diverse societies in history.
2. All states are mandated by law to educate undocumented immigrants.

CULTURE AND INTELLIGENCE

3. Some theories of intelligence consider the importance of an individual's culture and social context in determining ability.
4. Deficit explanations of underachievement assume that some students are inferior to others in certain ways.
5. Many problems can arise when teachers do not understand cultural differences. They may underestimate students' academic potential, believe that their language is inferior, or misinterpret their classroom behavior.

DIFFERENTIAL EDUCATIONAL PERFORMANCE

6. The reasons for certain minority groups coming to the United States, and the economic and political conditions existing at the time they arrive, may be factors influencing the level of their motivation and achievement.
7. Teachers should not assume that students from any one ethnic group have a specific cognitive or learning style.
8. There is little support for matching cognitive or learning styles with certain types of instruction.

IMPLICATIONS FOR INSTRUCTION

9. Recent approaches to improving instruction for culturally different students emphasize the importance of studying the social interactions of teaching and learning. Many educators argue that teaching in school should follow the same principles that good teaching exhibits in informal settings.
10. Cognition, classroom organization, sociolinguistics, and motivation are factors that need to be considered in developing culturally compatible classrooms.
11. There is a common ground in which both universalistic and culturally compatible teaching and learning practices can be used for improving instruction for culturally different students.
12. Culture, cognition, and language are interrelated variables.
13. Teachers should attempt to modify the traditional classroom "recitation script" by using more forms of assisted instruction like instructional conversations.
14. All parents have knowledge and skills that can be used in the classroom.
15. Multicultural education should be considered a process, not an event.
16. The discussion of similarities and differences as well as racism and discrimination should be an explicit part of the school curriculum.

LANGUAGE ISSUES

17. There is no evidence that bilingual education interferes with language proficiency or thinking in either language.
18. Krashen believes that the key to language acquisition is comprehensible input rather than formal instruction in the rules of the language.
19. Optimal input must be near the learner's actual level of development, but it must stretch beyond that to include concepts and structures that the learner has not yet acquired.
20. According to Krashen, the grammar of a language is learned best by speaking the language and hearing the appropriate form rather than by studying rules.
21. Some linguists believe that students develop very little proficiency in the early stages of language acquisition when the teacher emphasizes accuracy over fluency.
22. Krashen minimizes the importance of output (what the learner says) in the acquisition process because of his emphasis on comprehension.
23. Some linguists criticize Krashen's de-emphasis on the importance of formal instruction of the rules of a language.
24. There is no evidence that any dialect or language is inferior to another.

Reflecting on Cognition, Culture, and Language

1. Critique Different Models for Understanding Pluralism

Three different models for understanding pluralism or the lack of it are these (Nieto, 1992, p. 282):

- *Anglo-conformity*—All newcomers need to conform to the dominant European American, middle-class, and English-speaking model.
- *"Melting pot"*—All newcomers "melt" to form an amalgam that becomes American.
- *"Salad bowl"*—All newcomers maintain their languages and cultures while combining with others to form a "salad," which is our uniquely U.S. society.

In three groups, take one of the above and argue that it represents the dominant ideology in U.S. society. Give concrete examples. Afterward, in a large group, decide if one of these ideologies is really the most apparent and successful. Give reasons for your conclusions.

How would you critique each of these ideologies? What are the advantages and disadvantages of each?

2. Debate the Value of Bilingualism

In recent years, some political figures have lobbied for a constitutional amendment that would make English the country's single official language.

Governor Richard Lamm of Colorado was quoted by *Time* magazine in the August 25, 1986, issue as stating: "We should be color blind but not linguistically deaf. . . . We should be a rainbow but not a cacophony. . . . We should welcome different people but not different languages."

What is your position on bilingualism and bilingual education? Is bilingualism a barrier to a unified nation? Does it allow immigrants to avoid learning English and form self-perpetuating ghettos? Is bilingualism a positive factor in American society? Does our country benefit from the diversity of languages spoken in various cultures?

3. Debate the Best Approach to Cultural Literacy

With the increasing diversity of the student population in U.S. schools, some educators are concerned that students are not becoming literate in the American culture. Hirsch, in *Cultural Literacy* (1987), lists 500 things every American adult should know; more recently, in *A First Dictionary of Cultural Literacy* (1989), he lists 2,000 things he thinks grade school students should know.

What do you think it means to be culturally literate? Do we need a common body of information to ease the assimilation of culturally diverse individuals? Is Hirsch's approach to cultural literacy useful or is it dangerous? Will it reinforce the beliefs among minority students that certain people don't belong or that aspects of their culture are not worthy of consideration? (See the December/January 1988 issue of *Educational Leadership* for articles by Hirsch and his critics.)

4. Evaluate the Benefit of Culturally Congruent Classrooms

Zeuli and Floden (1987) raise a number of issues for teachers as they consider how best to educate culturally different students: Is cultural congruence the solution to the inequities of schooling? How does a teacher determine which classroom practices obstruct the learning of culturally different students? Are all cultural differences significant enough to warrant changes in instruction? Do students sometimes benefit from instruction that forces them to deal with content from perspectives that are unfamiliar to them? Think about these issues and discuss your views with other students in your class.

Key Terms

culture, p. 390
sociolinguistics, p. 392
multicultural education, p. 392
Nonstandard English, p. 400
cognitive style, p. 403
aptitude by treatment interaction (ATI), p. 404
learning style, p. 404
field-independent, p. 405
field-dependent, p. 405
wait-time, p. 410
assisted performance, p. 412
funds of knowledge, p. 416
bilingual education, p. 422
motherese, p. 426

Suggestions for Further Reading

The following references provide a good discussion of issues in cognitive and learning styles:

Matching teaching and learning styles. (1984, Winter). [Special issue]. *Theory into Practice, 23.*

October 1990 issue of *Educational Leadership, 48.*

The following references focus on language differences and bilingual education:

Adler, S. (Ed.). (1985). *Cultural language differences: Their educational and clinical-professional implications.* Springfield, IL: Thomas.

Alatis, J. E., & Staczek, J. J. (Eds.). (1985). *Perspectives on bilingualism and bilingual education.* Washington, DC: Georgetown University Press.

Ambert, A. N., & Melendez, S. E. (1985). *Bilingual education: A sourcebook.* New York: Garland.

Richard-Amato, P. A. (1988). *Making it happen: Interaction in the second language classroom. From theory to practice.* White Plains, NY: Longman.

The following journal articles and books are helpful in understanding the culturally different student:

Dealing with diversity: At risk students. (1989, February). [Special issue]. *Educational Leadership, 23.* Contains excellent research reviews and descriptions of successful programs.

Moll, L. C. (Ed.). (1990). *Vygotsky and education.* Cambridge, England: Cambridge University Press. The reader can find excellent examples of how Vygotsky's ideas are being applied to teaching and learning.

November 1988 issue of *Phi Delta Kappan, 70.* A special section on educating immigrant children.

Spindler, G. (Ed.). (1982). *Doing the ethnography of schooling.* New York: Holt, Rinehart & Winston. Provides examples of field studies done by anthropologists on educational issues.

Tharp, R. G., & Gallimore, R. (1988). *Rousing minds to life: Teaching, learning, and schooling in social context.* New York: Cambridge University Press. The authors use Vygotsky's ideas for recommending changes in the nature of teaching and learning in schools.

Trueba, H. T. (1987). *Success or failure? Learning and the language minority student.* Cambridge, MA: Newbury House.

For information on multicultural education:

Banks, J. A. (1988). *Multiethnic education: Theory and practice* (2nd ed.). Boston: Allyn & Bacon. Identifies actions that educators can take to develop programs related to ethnic and cultural diversity.

Banks, J. A., & Banks, C. A. (Eds.). (1989). *Multicultural education: Issues and perspectives.* Boston: Allyn & Bacon. The book describes how race, social class, gender, exceptionality, language, and religion must be considered in teaching.

Nieto, S. (1992). *Affirming diversity: The sociopolitical context of multicultural education*. White Plains, NY: Longman. The author provides a comprehensive framework for analyzing the multiple causes of school failure for students from certain ethnic and cultural groups.

Chapter 10

Personal and Social Development

Erikson's Theory of Personal and Social Development
Basic Trust versus Mistrust
Autonomy versus Shame and Doubt
Initiative versus Guilt
Industry versus Inferiority
Identity versus Identity Confusion
Intimacy versus Isolation
Generativity versus Stagnation
Ego Integrity versus Despair
Gender Differences in Identity

Implications for Instruction: Erikson's Theory

Gender Differences
The Development of Sex-Role Stereotyping
Androgyny
Gender Differences in Cognitive Abilities
Psychosocial Gender Differences
The School's Response to Gender Differences

Debate Forum: Do Teachers Favor Male Students?

Classroom Application: Reducing Sex-Role Stereotyping

Self-Concept

Debate Forum: Do Minority Students Have Low Self-Concepts?

Self-Concept and Achievement
Physical Growth and Development
School Experiences
The Effects of Working on Adolescent Development

Socialization and the Family
Parenting Practices

Debate Forum: What Is the Purpose of Sex Education?

Child Abuse and Neglect
Student Stress
Suicide
Maternal Employment
Divorce
Latchkey Children

Television as a Socialization Agent

Classroom Application: Helping Parents Monitor Their Children's Television Viewing

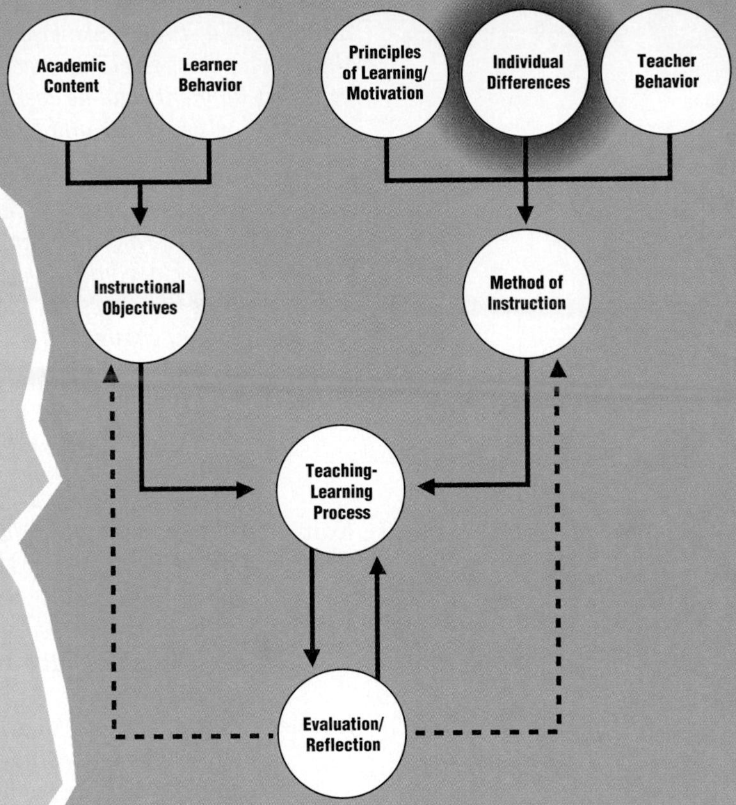

OBJECTIVES

After mastering the material in this chapter you will be able to:

- Use Erikson's theory of personal and social development to explain students' identity formation.
- Reduce sex-role stereotyping in the classroom.
- Explain how different child-rearing practices influence students' behavior.
- Identify child abuse and neglect.
- Identify warning signs for possible suicide.
- Interact with students facing family transitions.
- Provide guidelines to parents who want to monitor their children's television viewing.

Orientation

As a first-year teacher at Hamilton High, Jack Parmenter was given three freshman classes to teach. He knew that it was going to be a challenge, but he never anticipated a student like Jason Brownley. Over the course of the school year, with the assistance of a veteran teacher, Joanne Walton, Jack learned more about adolescent development than he ever had in his education classes. What follows is a conversation between Jack and Joanne dealing with Jason Brownley:

Jack: *Joanne, I've got this kid in class, Jason, who is driving me nuts!*

Joanne: *What's he doing, Jack?*

Jack: *Well, at the beginning of the year, he was this really nice, clean-cut little guy. He would always answer questions in class discussions, and got an A at the semester. Then, right after he came back from spring break, he totally changed.*

Joanne: *In what ways?*

Jack: *His appearance, for starters. When he came back from break, he was wearing boots almost to his knees, flannel shirts, and torn jeans. Remember, this is a kid who used to wear sweaters and dress shoes to school, then all of a sudden he's wearing this stuff.*

Joanne: *What else changed, Jack?*

Jack: *His attitude changed along with the clothes. This kid started to confront me in class, almost challenging me in front of the other students. I'd call on him, and he'd say something smart, like "I don't know" or "Call on somebody else." It's driving me crazy, Joanne. What do you think is happening?*

Joanne: *Jack, I think we have a case of growing up here. I don't know Jason, but I've seen a lot of students go through the same changes, almost as quickly. They're trying to find out where they feel comfortable, with this style of clothes and hair, or that. It's like they are one person one day and a completely different person the next. Right?*

Jack: *You got it!*

Joanne: *The attitude usually is intended to win the respect of the other kids in class. If they can see Jason as the tough guy, especially the other boys, they will "respect" him more. You said he is "little," right?*

Jack: *He's a short kid, and on the skinny side.*

Joanne: *Sounds like Jason is trying to feel like one of the "guys," to keep from being put down by the bullies. The main thing to remember, Jack, is that you can't let this identity crisis be an excuse for him to be rude or disrespectful.*

Jack: *What can I do?*

Joanne: *Make sure that Jason understands that you are not going to tolerate his disrespect, especially in front of the other students. It may be a good idea to take him into the hallway to discuss things with him. He will consider it a "win" if he can "ambush" you in front of the class. Talk to him without the other students present. It should help. Not only does he want to get along with the other kids, but he also needs to get along with you, and he knows it. Most kids finally figure out how to do both.*

In Chapters 8 and 9 we focused primarily on cognitive factors influencing learning. In Chapter 9 attention shifted to the relation between culture and learning. You learned how social factors can shape a student's academic adjustment and performance in school.

In this chapter we will discuss a number of personal and social factors that are likely to influence students' interaction with teachers and influence their involvement in academic tasks. These characteristics will influence your decision making in determining how you can best facilitate learning. We begin with a discussion of Erikson's theory of psychosocial development, which provides a framework for how personal identity or self-concept develops through experiences in the home, school, and community.

You learned in Chapter 4 (Motivation and Learning) about the importance of a student's perception of ability. This self-perception greatly influences the student's selection of academic tasks, persistence, and willingness to try different learning strategies to succeed. In this chapter you will learn more about students' self-concepts and why teachers have difficulty trying to change students' perceptions of themselves.

Gender is an important individual difference factor. Consider how different cultural groups may think about the roles of males and females. Remember that some cultural groups have traditional patterns of expectations for males and females that may be contrary to what you might teach in class. Also, parents of different cultural groups have different goals of parenting and child rearing. In some families, children are not to question their parents' authority. Parents from immigrant groups often have difficulty raising their children when they exhibit behavior that is accepted by the dominant cultural group but considered inappropriate by the standards of the immigrant group. How does the teacher mediate problems between parent and child under such circumstances?

Although teachers don't have control over many of the developmental factors influencing their students' classroom behavior, they must deal with the outcomes of family socialization. One factor influencing the teacher's role is the major changes in family functioning during the last few decades. Many of these changes have weakened and modified the traditional position and function of parents.

Economic developments have caused both mothers and fathers to join the labor force, keeping them away from their homes and children for much of the day. This condition, in many cases, has lead to children being unsupervised before and after school. Many adolescents work during the school year, an additional burden on them. Occupational opportunities have caused married children to move away from their parents to face child rearing without the support of an extended family. In addition, divorce and various patterns of custodial arrangements are no longer considered atypical family transitions.

As you read this chapter I would like you to consider how the family, school, and peers influence the personal and social development of children and adolescents. Think about how family transitions may require greater attention to the adjustment of certain students, how you may need to reorganize your time to schedule parent conferences, how you may need to communicate with both custodial and noncustodial parents, and how you can make recommendations to parents who indicate that they need to improve their child-rearing skills.

psychosocial crises. Erikson's psychological tasks, or dilemmas, which have their roots in the demands of society and which individuals experience over the course of their lives.

Finally, think about possible organizational and instructional decisions that you might make using your knowledge of students' cognitive, personality, and social differences.

ERIKSON'S THEORY OF PERSONAL AND SOCIAL DEVELOPMENT

Erik Erikson (1963, 1968) has delineated eight major **psychosocial crises**, or dilemmas, that have their roots in the demands of society and that individuals experience over the course of life. Each crisis represents an important turning point in which major psychological issues are faced and resolved on a continuum from a positive (desirable) pole to a negative (undesirable) pole. The resolution of each crisis adds a new dimension to one's identity. Table 10.1 summarizes each of these crises.

A central theme in Erikson's theory is that the way individuals resolve developmental dilemmas in one stage will influence the resolution of developmental dilemmas in other stages. As a result, our past experiences influence the way we resolve our present developmental crises.

The fact that developmental crises are resolved on a *continuum* means that the resolutions are not necessarily all positive or all negative. A variety of possible developmental outcomes emerges as individuals interact with significant others in their environment. Each of the crises identified by Erikson is discussed in the following section.

? How do parents influence identity development?

Basic Trust versus Mistrust

A sense of trust develops in an infant through the social care and comfort provided by the primary care giver. The infant, who has experienced the warmth and protection of the uterus, faces the reality of discomfort and hunger immediately on contact with the outer world. To develop a sense of trust, the infant requires a feeling of physical comfort and a minimum of fear and uncertainty. Erikson emphasizes the underlying emotional and attitudinal themes that motivate the parent handling and caring for the infant, rather than any particular method of care. Once this feeling of trust is established, it generalizes to new experiences. However, if the infant does not receive the necessary physical warmth and care, a sense of mistrust develops that leads to apprehension or fear in novel situations.

Autonomy versus Shame and Doubt

During this stage, society makes demands on the child to do things alone. For example, parents make their first major demands on the child when they require that toilet training be accomplished. The manner in which this

TABLE 10.1 ERIKSON'S EIGHT STAGES OF THE HUMAN LIFE CYCLE

Stage	Age	Central Conflict	Primary Implications for Optimal Development
1	Infancy	Trust versus mistrust	Developing general security, optimism, and trust in others (based on consistent experiences involving satisfaction of basic needs)
2	Toddlerhood	Autonomy versus shame and doubt	Developing a sense of autonomy and confident self-reliance, taking setbacks in stride (based on consistent experiences involving encouragement and limit setting without rejection or blame)
3	Early childhood	Initiative versus guilt	Developing initiative in exploring and manipulating the environment (based on consistent experiences of tolerance, encouragement, and reinforcement)
4	Middle childhood	Industry versus inferiority	Enjoyment and mastery of the developmental tasks of childhood, in and out of school (based on consistent experiences of success and recognition of progress)
5	Adolescence	Identity versus identity confusion	Achievement of a stable and satisfying sense of identity and direction (based on consistent personal experiences involving success and satisfaction combined with social acceptance and recognition)
6	Young adulthood	Intimacy versus isolation	Development of the ability to maintain intimate personal relationships (based on personal openness and confidence complemented by consistently rewarding experiences with intimate others)
7	Adulthood	Generativity versus stagnation	Satisfaction of personal and familial needs supplemented by development of interest in the welfare of others and of the world in general (based on achievement of a secure and rewarding personal life and a freedom from pressures which limit one to self-preoccupation)
8	Aging	Ego integrity versus despair	Recognizing and adjusting to aging and the prospect of death with a sense of satisfaction about the past and readiness about the future (based on consistent success in prior stages which provides a real basis for satisfaction in having led a full and good life and for accepting death without morbid fears or feelings of failure)

Source: Good and Brophy, 1990.

psychosocial moratorium. A period of delay granted by society to someone not ready to meet obligations.

crisis is handled influences whether children feel that they are effective and able to control their environment (autonomy) or are ineffective and controlled by others (shame or doubt). The parent-child relationship again is important in the resolution of this crisis. Warm and accepting parents are likely to structure the environment so that children can experience success and a sense of autonomy, whereas hostile and overly controlling parents can promote a sense of doubt. Toilet training is important because the process often involves emotional overtones. The child who has difficulty in this task and is criticized by his or her parents does not separate the difficulties and incompetence of the toilet training situation from other life experiences. The lack of success in toilet training can cause the child to develop a sense of shame and doubt regarding his or her competency.

Initiative versus Guilt

During this period, children gain greater freedom in exploring their environment and often attempt tasks of which parents do not approve. When children master these new tasks, they feel a sense of self-responsibility, establishing a sense of purpose. As a result, they are likely to attempt to meet new challenges in the future. Guilt occurs when the initiation of these acts or tasks either exceeds the limits of their capabilities or is constantly held in check by parents who want their children to curtail their initiative. A difficult aspect of child rearing is to determine how much freedom and protection children should be given as they develop their competence.

Industry versus Inferiority

The major theme of this period reflects the determination of children to master whatever they are doing. Erikson believes that many individuals' later attitudes toward work and work habits can be traced back to the degree of a successful sense of industry fostered during this phase. In acquiring a sense of industry, children must feel competent in what they are doing while accepting their limitations. A sense of inferiority is caused when the child is not ready for the challenges of school and/or is unable to measure up to the expectations of parents, teachers, or friends.

Identity versus Identity Confusion

The critical issue that adolescents must resolve is the question "Who am I?" Children enter adolescence in a diffuse state. They are not sure of their attitudes, beliefs, and values. During this period, they experience various situations, meet many people, experiment with various identities, and begin to integrate their previous and present identities into a meaningful sense of self. On the negative side, they have a sense of confusion about their identity or role in society. Some adolescents become delinquents—choosing an identity that is the opposite of what society expects—because they would rather have a negative identity than remain a nonentity.

Erikson points out that adolescents are provided with a **psychosocial moratorium**, a period of delay that is granted to someone who is not ready

Friends play an important role in helping adolescents develop an identity.

to meet obligations. A psychosocial moratorium is a permissiveness on the part of society that allows young people to try different identities and to fail or have difficulties but that protects them from many of the consequences of their actions. It may be a time of adventure, academic study, troublesome pranks, wandering, or social action. For example, youths who tell their parents that they plan to quit their job because it's boring or because they simply don't want to work anymore expect that their parents will provide shelter and other support until they find another job. Middle-class youths generally have more protection from the demands of society than lower-class youths. The differences in the way some courts treat juvenile offenders from various socioeconomic backgrounds provide further evidence of the differential impact of society's psychosocial moratorium.

? What factors account for different patterns of identity development?

MARCIA'S IDENTITY STATUSES. Marcia (1980) has provided more information about the development of identity by distinguishing four different patterns and common issues that adolescents experience during the psychosocial crises of identity versus identity confusion. According to Marcia, the criteria for the attainment of a mature identity are based on two factors: *crisis* and *commitment*. "Crisis refers to times during adolescence when the individual seems to be actively involved in choosing among alternative occupations and beliefs. Commitment refers to the degree of personal investment the individual expresses in an occupation or belief" (Marcia, 1967, p. 119). The following is a brief discussion of the four identity statuses (see Figure 10.1).

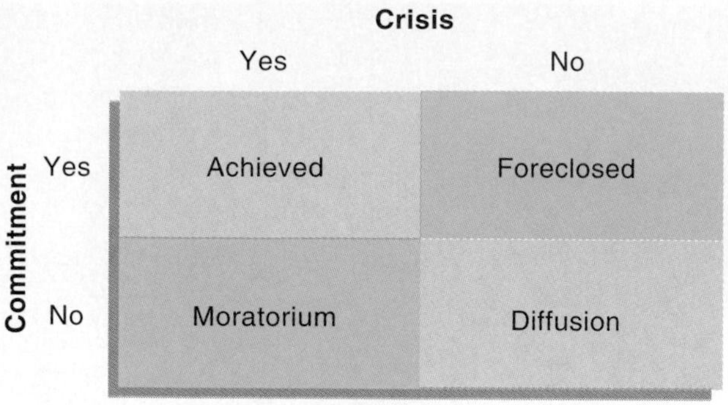

Figure 10.1 Criteria for Marcia's Identity Status.
Source: Marcia, 1980.

identity diffusion. The adolescent has not made any firm commitments to any ideology, occupation, or interpersonal relationship.

identity moratorium. The adolescent considers alternative choices, experiences different roles, but has made no final decision regarding his or her identity.

identify foreclosure. The adolescent selects a convenient set of beliefs and goals without carefully considering the alternatives.

identity achievement. The adolescent has a strong sense of commitment to life choices after careful consideration of options.

Adolescents begin in a state of **identity diffusion** (or confusion)—a situation in which the individual has not made any firm commitments to any ideology, occupation, or interpersonal relationship and is not currently thinking about such commitments (no crisis, no commitment).

As adolescents develop and have greater interpersonal, work, and educational experiences, they may begin to reflect on the kinds of long-term commitments that could be made. This status is called **identity moratorium**—a situation in which alternative choices are considered and different roles are experienced, but final decisions are deferred during a period of uncertainty (crisis, no commitment).

Sometimes the uncertainty of thinking about one's future can produce a great deal of anxiety, especially when one doesn't have the answers to the questions from parents and friends about future careers and educational options. For this reason, some adolescents choose to remain in a state of identity diffusion, during which they stop thinking about choices and commitments, or opt for **identity foreclosure.** In this status condition, the individual selects some convenient set of beliefs or goals without carefully considering the alternatives. The best example of this status is the high school student whose mother is a doctor or lawyer and who answers the typical question, "What do you want to study in college?" by stating "prelaw" or "pre-med" when he really hasn't considered the implications of the career in detail. Such a response gets people to stop asking further questions about life goals and is satisfying to the individual (for the time being) because he can stop worrying about what course of study to pursue (no crisis, commitment).

Additional experiences help clarify attitudes, values, and self-evaluations, so that the adolescent resolves the identity crises and settles on the relatively stable commitments that constitute **identity achievement.**

These four identity statuses may be perceived as a developmental transition, but one stage is not a prerequisite for another, as in Erikson's eight stages. Only the moratorium status appears to be necessary for identity achievement, since one can't develop a mature identity without considering alternative options. Waterman (1982) has identified possible patterns in identity formation. For example, one model may be diffusion to moratorium or identity achievement; another model may begin with foreclosure, moving to moratorium and then toward identity achievement. The latter model often occurs when individuals find out in college that they really don't have the interest or aptitude for a particular goal. Still another model may be identity diffusion to moratorium to identity achievement to identity diffusion. In this situation, the individual may lose a sense of purpose as a result of some life experiences and fail to seek new commitments.

Intimacy versus Isolation

The development of a sense of intimacy results in an integration in the form of sexual union and close friendship. According to Erikson, an individual cannot develop a fully intimate relationship until he or she has established a clear identity. (Erikson has focused on the identity development of males, saying little about females—a shortcoming of his theory.) In other words, individuals must know who they are before they can develop a shared identity with another person. The negative polarity is a sense of isolation that is characterized as self-absorption. Because of a fear of losing oneself in the identity of another, some individuals are incapable of developing a strong intimate relationship.

Individuals who trust others, feel a sense of autonomy, are willing to take initiatives, and have a good sense of their abilities and beliefs are more likely to maintain intimate relationships. Individuals who show a mistrust of others and who fear making decisions or taking the initiative in new situations are often less willing to establish intimate relationships.

Generativity versus Stagnation

A sense of generativity involves a sense of responsibility to parents and the community for the improvement of oneself and society. Parenting and teaching the young in order to improve the quality of life for the next generation is an important responsibility for an adult. These activities reflect a sense of productivity and creativity. On the negative polarity is the adult who cannot find any meaning or purpose in life and who has little interest in self-improvement or making contributions to society.

Ego Integrity versus Despair

Successful resolution of this crisis leads to feelings of accomplishment and fulfillment of one's life cycle. Adults with ego integrity can look back on their lives and feel that they were worthwhile. Unsuccessful resolution leads to feelings of despair, incompleteness, and an unfulfilled life.

Gender Differences in Identity

> **?** Are there any differences in the identity development of males and females?

A criticism of Erikson's theory is that his description of identity development may not accurately describe the development of women. For example, there is evidence that females tend to focus on interpersonal aspects of identity formation, whereas males focus on intrapersonal aspects. As a result, late adolescent females are more likely to learn about themselves through the individuals with whom they have good relationships, whereas late adolescent males are more likely to develop an identity on the basis of skills and competencies they develop rather than on interpersonal relations (Marcia, 1980). The result of different paths toward identity development may cause researchers using criteria for assessing the identity of males to conclude erroneously that some women may lag in their development.

Erikson also has suggested that women have a different developmental trend than men in the achievement of identity. While he indicates that men move from identity to intimacy, he thinks that for women, identity and intimacy are interrelated. For a woman following a *traditional* role, identity comes from marriage because her identity is closely tied to the man she marries. Many feminists are critical of Erikson's perspective of the process of women's identity, arguing that the demands of modern society make such an alternative route of identity achievement (i.e., waiting for marriage to develop an identity) unsatisfactory. With the necessity for women to work, increased divorce, and single living, women can no longer delay their identity development until they become wives and mothers. Instead, like men, they must develop the knowledge, competencies, and values necessary to attain unique identities (Fuhrmann, 1986).

Schiedel and Marcia (1985) suggest that either women reach a ceiling on identity development before men do, or women follow a different developmental pattern, with one group achieving an initial identity before age 20 and the other forming a self-constructed identity after fulfilling the socially prescribed roles of wife and mother. In this developmental pattern, the task of identity formation appears to begin in adolescence for women as it does for men. For some women (notably those who will follow nontraditional lifestyles of continuous employment), late adolescence is expected to be the optimal time of life for resolution of the identity versus identity confusion crisis. For other women, the task of defining a personal sense of identity may wait, not as Erikson supposed, for the arrival of a mate and children, but for the partial departure of children (in school), which allows the time for these women to identify and pursue identity commitments of their own choosing.

IMPLICATIONS FOR INSTRUCTION: ERIKSON'S THEORY

A good way to understand any developmental theory is to attempt to apply it to your own development. How do you think you resolved the major psychosocial crises in your life? What effect did your parents, teachers, and peers have on your early development? Did your parents encourage autonomy and initiative? Were you successful in your early schooling? Did you develop a sense of industry? A positive identity? Can you evaluate your own identity development according to Marcia's stages?

Erikson provides some good advice if you are currently involved in a relationship. He believes that a truly intimate relationship depends on a shared identity. This type of identity occurs when each partner develops a strong self-identity rather than one partner losing his or her identity in the relationship. The implication for enhancing a relationship or marriage is for both partners to develop their own abilities and interests to the maximum.

Erikson's stage theory can help teachers to understand the types of conflict students face in the developmental periods. Students in the early grades are resolving the crises of initiative versus guilt and industry versus inferiority. They need support as they attempt new tasks and meet new challenges.

Elkind (1986) believes that the development of a sense of initiative is more likely to occur when adults allow children to become more self-directed in choosing their own learning activities. For example, the danger of directing young children to read before they are ready may cause them to "become dependent on adult direction and not to trust [their] own initiative" (p. 635).

Erikson's theory helps the teacher to understand why young adolescents may have personality or social adjustment problems in school if their psychosocial crises have been resolved toward the negative polarities—mistrust, shame, guilt, and/or inferiority. Teachers and parents must be concerned with healthy adjustment throughout the developmental stages.

A teacher can help to establish a classroom climate in which failure is seen as a natural part of the learning process and where it is appropriate to be understanding and helpful to others. In junior and senior high school, where students are attempting to develop a sense of identity, teachers should understand that students need numerous opportunities to experience various situations and to evaluate their behavior, attitudes, and beliefs. It is important to provide opportunities for students to talk with teachers about educational and career concerns. In addition, teachers can often use certain course assignments such as diaries, position papers on controversial issues, and field experiences in the community to help students to learn more about themselves.

Finally, teachers need to help female students achieve the knowledge and skills necessary to help them develop realistic occupational goals while they make decisions concerning the nature of their spousal and maternal roles (Fuhrmann, 1986). I shall now discuss gender differences to help you understand how the school contributes to the socialization of males and females.

GENDER DIFFERENCES

The Development of Sex-Role Stereotyping

> **?** How do socialization experiences influence different behavior for males and females?

Most psychologists and sociologists view gender differences in terms of role training and social expectations. For example, despite the fact that developmental psychologists report few differences in the behavior of infant girls and boys, parents soon begin to interact with them differently. As children grow, mothers talk more to female toddlers and encourage them to stay near them when they play. Boys are allowed to explore and wander farther away from their mothers' grasp, and they demonstrate more aggression than girls. When a little boy falls, he is told to get up and "try it again," whereas a little girl is picked up and cuddled. It is clear that passivity and dependency training for most girls begins very early in their lives (Brooks-Gunn & Matthews, 1979).

As children grow, they learn what is "appropriate" male and female behavior from family, teachers, peers, television, and books. This learning often emphasizes that the female-male relationship is not equal and that each sex has certain gender-related roles.

One of the classic studies on the socialization of females to lower their achievement goals is Komarovsky's *Women in the Modern World* (1953), which contains reports by college women describing advice not to set their sights too high and not to reveal their intellectual abilities or goals to potential boyfriends until they anticipate a favorable reaction. We must wonder about the number of outstanding women who have been talked out of high educational and occupational achievement, by themselves or by others.

In a more recent book, *The Cinderella Complex,* concerning the socialization of women, Dowling (1981) writes that women have not entirely freed themselves from some of the traditional aspects of sex-role stereotyping in society. She believes that women are still being socialized to feel that they are not successful unless they have someone to take care of them. This form of psychological dependence is a major factor preventing women

Seeing this photo in a textbook in the 1950s or 1960s might cause some reaction. Today, most individuals view cooking as a nonstereotyped activity.

from achieving according to their potential. Dowling states that the need to be taken care of formerly began at age 16 or 17, when females relinquished their desire to go to college and opted for early marriage. Today the desire to be "saved" begins after college, when the initial sense of freedom subsides and anxiety begins to arise.

androgyny. A condition that comprises both male and female traits.

Dowling traces the socialization pattern of males and females and points out that "girls . . . are trained *into* dependency, while boys are trained out of it" (p. 105). This trend begins in infancy and continues throughout the girl's family life and school career. If you have a brother or sister or know a family of male and female siblings, think about incidents in which parents treated them differently. For example, are the two siblings receiving equal encouragement for independence? Are they protected by the parents in the same or different ways? Are they both encouraged to experience various activities and value systems to help establish an identity? Would they receive similar reactions if they told their parents they were leaving home? Finally, do you think the Cinderella complex applies to women from all cultural and ethnic groups?

Androgyny

For a long time psychologists viewed certain traits as either masculine or feminine. For example, aggression, independence, competitiveness, and adventurousness were traits attributed to males, whereas sensitivity, gentleness, dependence, and submission were traits attributed to females. More recently, the concept that masculinity and femininity possess dual sets of traits has been stressed (Bem, 1974; Spence & Helmreich, 1978).

Bem (1974) has developed an instrument, the Bem Sex-Role Inventory, that classifies individuals into four categories. One category consists primarily of males who are high in traits that are considered masculine and low in traits that are regarded as feminine. A second category consists primarily of females who are high in feminine traits and low in masculine traits. A third category consists of individuals who are low in both masculine and feminine traits. The fourth category consists of individuals who are high in both masculine and feminine characteristics. Bem identifies individuals in this last category as *androgynous*.

Androgyny means, literally, "man-woman" and comes from the Greek *andro* (male) and *gyn* (female). The term describes individuals who are able to choose the most appropriate response to a given situation. For example, androgynous individuals can be either assertive or tender or perhaps a combination of the two qualities, depending on which is the appropriate response to the situation facing them. Androgynous women and men are high in *both* independence and nurturance (Bem, 1974, 1975).

More recently, Bem (1981, 1984) has developed the Gender-Schema Theory to describe how individuals differ in the ways they use culturally based definitions for appropriate female and male behaviors as guides for evaluating behavior. She believes that some children view the world through "gender-colored glasses" because they learn to process information in terms of a schema—a network of associations that organizes and guides individuals' perception. This schema imposes meaning on incoming stimuli and influences decisions and judgments, as well as the acquisition of knowledge and content. The gender schema also influences certain aspects of one's self-concept (Liben & Signorella, 1987).

Gender Differences in Cognitive Abilities

In 1974, Maccoby and Jacklin completed a comprehensive review of gender differences and determined that females excelled at verbal tasks and males at mathematics and visual-spatial tasks. After 20 years, it appears that there are now few differences in cognitive abilities between males and females (Linn & Hyde, 1989). One exception is that males continue to score higher on the Scholastic Aptitude Test's (SAT, as of March 1994 called the Scholastic Assessment Test) quantitative (mathematics) section. An explanation given for this difference is the fact that the test requires students to solve verbal problems quickly, and males may have some advantage in quantitative speed tests, especially when some of the items are learned from gender-type activities (e.g., questions derived from sports activities).

In 1990 the New York State Board of Regents decided to stop using the SAT scores as a basis for determining college scholarships given by the state of New York when it became known that girls received only 28 percent of the awards while males received 72 percent. What is interesting is that whereas there is a large gap in the SAT math scores of males and females, the state of New York found no gender differences in statewide math tests given at the ninth-, tenth-, and eleventh-grade levels. In the first year that the scholarships were based on grades, girls for the first time won a majority of the scholarships, 51.3 percent (Verhovek, 1990).

?

What factors account for the differences in male and female achievement in mathematics?

MATHEMATICS ACHIEVEMENT. Gender differences in mathematics achievement are small and continue to decline (American Association of University Women [AAUW], 1992). Although various arguments have been made for the genetic basis for male-female differences in math performance (e.g., Geschwind & Galaburda, 1985), a number of researchers have challenged this perspective (see Eccles & Jacobs, 1986, and Lips, 1988, for critical reviews of the genetic explanation). The major argument is that social, not biological, factors are responsible for sex inequality related to the learning, valuing, and career implementation of mathematics. Boys take more higher mathematics courses, have more confidence in their ability to learn math, and perceive math as a more useful subject than do girls. In addition, there is evidence that counselors, parents, and teachers do not provide the same amount of support for females that they do for males in studying and valuing math. Last, there is evidence that math is perceived by females as a male domain since the main users of math in careers are males. Thus, if females believe that the study of mathematics is inappropriate for them, they will feel anxious about succeeding in the area.

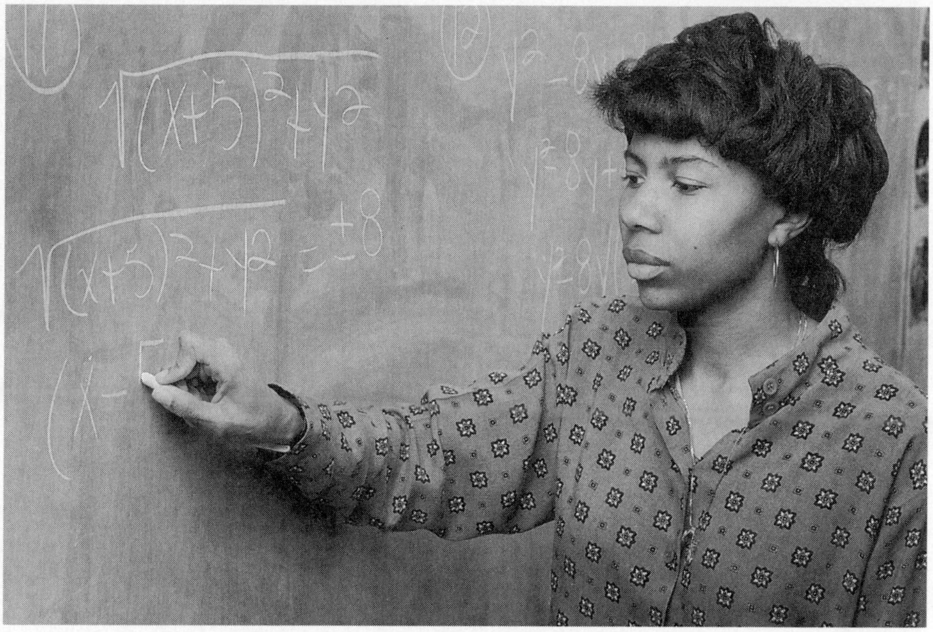

Both males and females who receive encouragement and good instruction in mathematics can be highly successful.

Fennema (1983) reported on a special school program, Multiplying Options and Subtracting Bias, that attempts to encourage more female involvement in mathematics. The investigators developed four workshops that focus on stereotyping of mathematics as a male domain and other social factors limiting female involvement in mathematics. Students, teachers, and counselors participated in the program. The evaluation indicated that the program influenced female students' attitudes toward mathematics, decreased mathematics stereotypes, and influenced their willingness to take more courses in the subject.

? What can teachers do to increase the motivation and achievement of females in mathematics?

Eccles (1991) has reviewed the research on math and science teachers who were successful in encouraging girls to continue their studies and reported the following characteristics in their teaching:

- Effective teachers are more likely to use cooperative or individualized learning strategies than to rely solely on public drill and seat work.
- Effective teachers are less likely to use competitive motivational strategies than non-effective teachers.
- They use more hands-on learning opportunities.
- They use practical problems with the possibility for creative solution, e.g., build a bridge, and allow students to work in teams in solving these problems.

- They engage in a great deal of active career and educational guidance in the classroom, stressing the importance and the usefulness of math and science for students in other courses and for their future employment opportunities.
- They insist on full class participation; no one is allowed to "drop out" and no one is allowed to dominate class discussion or laboratory equipment. (p. 6)

These teaching practices make sense when you think about how gender roles influence behavior especially during the adolescent years—girls often associate math as a masculine activity, prefer not to compete with boys in this area, and doubt their ability in math. Therefore, by changing the instructional environment, it is possible to increase girls' interest and motivation to achieve in mathematics (Eccles, 1991).

READING ACHIEVEMENT. As in mathematics, gender differences in reading also appear to be declining. However, performance on different reading tests may depend on the type of reading exercise. For example, on the National Assessment of Educational Progress (NAEP), boys achieved as well as girls on the expository passages but performed lower than girls on the literary passages. The results are consistent with the finding that boys tend to read more nonfiction than girls, and girls read more fiction than boys (AAUW, 1992).

Psychosocial Gender Differences

Only two major differences emerge from the research in psychosocial variables—aggression and expectancy for success. Males tend to demonstrate more aggression than females, but the differences are larger for children than adults (Linn & Hyde, 1989). In regard to expectancy for success, females as compared to males tend to enter learning situations with lower expectations of success and with a lack of self-confidence in their ability to achieve. The research in gender differences in causal attributions indicates that males are more likely to attribute success to ability and failure to a lack of effort, while females are more likely to attribute success to luck or effort and failure to a lack of ability. The consequence of these perceptions is that males are more likely to develop a sense of mastery and control over their fate, experience greater self-confidence, and persist longer on difficult academic tasks (Sadker, Sadker, & Klein, 1991).

A number of investigators (e.g., Dweck & Goetz, 1978; Simpson & Erickson, 1983) have explored classroom dynamics as a possible explanation for gender differences in causal attributions. Since males receive more attention of all kinds in classrooms (including being called on more often), the interaction serves to boost their confidence and self-esteem. Also, the difference in teacher interaction with males and females may communicate that males are the more valued students (Sadker, Sadker, & Klein, 1991).

In summary, although researchers do not have all the answers as to the causes of gender differences, present evidence indicates that nothing in the intellectual or social-emotional makeup of either sex imposes limits on what members of that sex may hope to become or achieve. However, societal expectations can impose limits on achievement and vocational success. Parents and teachers need to make decisions based on the characteristics of a particular child rather than on sex-role stereotypes.

The School's Response to Gender Differences

? How can teacher expectation and interaction with males and females influence their motivation and achievement?

Many educators believe that the combination of courses, materials, and student-teacher interaction makes the majority of female students passive, shy, and dependent but provides male students with learning experiences that help them become self-assured, competitive, and independent. Marland (1983) views the school as a "sexist amplifier" because many conscious and unconscious decisions made by teachers magnify, or amplify, sex differences (e.g., the selection of learning material, subject content, division of tasks in the class, and different interaction with males and with females). Marland states: "Not only do schools treat boys and girls differently, but they actually make girls and boys more different than would normally happen" (p. 2).

Content analyses of textbooks used in various subject areas reveal that females sometimes are portrayed in stereotyped ways (see Gollnick, Sadker, & Sadker, 1982; Klein, 1985). Here is how researchers have found males and females portrayed in reading texts (Gollnick, Sadker, & Sadker, 1982, p. 65):

Males	**Females**
ingenious	dependent
creative	passive
brave	incompetent
persevering	fearful
achieving	victims
adventurous	docile
curious	concerned with domesticities
autonomous	objects of scorn and ridicule
athletic	aimless
self-respecting	concerned about physical appearance
problem solver	spiritless

Although conditions improved during the 1980s and 1990s as a result of the development of guidelines by local and state textbook adoption committees who review new textbooks, many books still used in the schools reflect stereotyping.

One of the major developments leading to more sex equity in the schools has been the passage of Title IX of the 1972 Education Amendments:

> No person shall, on the basis of sex, be excluded from participation in, be denied the benefits of, or be subjected to discrimination under any education program or activity receiving federal financial assistance.

This law makes it illegal to treat students differently or separately on the basis of sex. The regulations cover such areas as course offerings, counseling services, extracurricular activities, athletic programs, facilities, and financial assistance.

DEBATE FORUM

Do Teachers Favor Male Students?

Argument: The research over the last 20 years indicates that both male and female teachers provide more attention to male than female students from preschool through high school. In preschool, males receive more instructional time, hugs, and teacher attention (Greenberg, 1985). Males in elementary and secondary schools are called on more frequently and receive more praise, acceptance, remediation, and criticism than female students (Sadker & Sadker, 1986).

Counterargument: Classroom interaction differences are more a result of student effects on teachers than teacher effects on students. Because males are more salient and active in the classroom, they are more likely to receive teacher attention to all types of behavior. The fact that teachers interact more with males does not necessarily suggest bias on the part of the teacher. The fact is that boys are more forceful in gaining their teachers' attention (Brophy, 1985b).

Response: It doesn't matter *why* the situation occurs; it is the responsibility of teachers to understand how their classroom behavior can influence the achievement of different students. For example, Sadker and Sadker (1986) report that in both elementary and secondary schools, boys are eight times as likely as girls to call out answers in class. They also found that teachers responded differently to call-outs from males and females. Teachers tended to accept call-outs from males but remediated the behavior of girls and advised them to raise their hands when they called out answers. Sadker and Sadker suggest that one reason boys may score higher than girls on tests like the SAT is that boys receive more attention in the classroom. In content areas like science and math, where inquiry and questioning are important conditions of learning, lower rates of initiation and general interaction during instruction place females at a disadvantage.

What do you think? Did your teachers provide different attention to males and females in class? How did your math and science teachers interact with males and females? How did your teachers' treatment influence student motivation?

CLASSROOM

Application

REDUCING SEX-ROLE STEREOTYPING

Sex-role stereotyping in the classroom is often referred to as the "hidden curriculum." Teachers are often unaware of how their own expectations and behaviors contribute to sex-role stereotypes and the development of different academic abilities and behaviors between male and female students (Serbin, 1983). Eccles and Blumenfeld (1985) point out that although teachers may not be the major source of sex-role stereotypes, they do not play an active role in changing them or providing boys and girls with the types of information that might lead them to change their sex-stereotyped beliefs. As a result, teachers passively reinforce the sex-typed academic and career decisions made by their students that contribute to the differences in the levels of educational attainment achieved by males and females.

The following are some guidelines for taking a more active role in developing a sex-equitable classroom environment (adapted and heads quoted from Shapiro, Kramer, & Hunerberg, 1981, pp. 8–15):

HELP CHILDREN BECOME MORE AWARE OF SEX-ROLE STEREOTYPING AND OF THE VARIETY OF FORCES THAT INFLUENCE ATTITUDES, THINKING, AND BEHAVIOR

Teachers often hear comments like, "You can't expect girls to do that," "I don't want to sit with the boys," "Only girls do that." Respond immediately to these types of statement by replying, "Who said girls or boys can't do that?" or, "In this class, people sit together." Sometimes using comments from students as a basis of discussion can be effective. This provides an opportunity for boys and girls in the class to point out examples of males or females accomplishing tasks that are considered stereotypical by some individuals.

You can also discuss how individuals develop ideas about appropriate male and female behaviors. Give assignments in which children analyze television programs and commercials, books, and magazines for sex-role stereotypes.

Another area that can be explored in the classroom is children's attitudes and feelings about members of the opposite sex. "I hate those boys; they always mess up our game" and "Girls are so emotional" are examples of comments often heard in school or at home. Activities or discussions are not likely to change attitudes overnight, but in time, students learn that many of their criticisms apply to people in general, rather than specifically to males or females.

continued

CHANGE SCHOOL PRACTICES THAT CONTRIBUTE TO THE SEPARATION AND STEREOTYPING OF CHILDREN BY GENDER

Teachers often do not realize that certain school rules, procedures, or casual remarks contribute to expectations regarding sex-role behavior. The following are some practices that need to be *eliminated:*

- Establishing classroom seating arrangements and lines by sex
- Using techniques that needlessly emphasize sex in managing groups of children (e.g., "Boys, be quiet," or "The girls can go first because . . .")
- Assigning classroom or school jobs on the basis of sex (e.g., boys are assigned to moving equipment and girls are given clerical chores to complete)
- Perpetuating stereotyping while talking or disciplining students (e.g., "How pretty you look today," "Boys should be more polite with girls," or "Girls don't behave like that!")
- Allowing students to self-select facilities, materials, and people with whom they work and play (girls may choose to cook while boys choose woodworking projects)
- Using sexist terms when referring to girls or women (e.g., *darling, doll, cutie, sweetie*)
- Creating needless competition between the sexes (e.g., "Who will finish their work first—the boys or girls?" or, "The girls do their homework so neatly")
- Requesting parental cooperation focused on the mother and assuming, sometimes erroneously, that fathers and mothers perform stereotypical jobs inside and outside the home (e.g., "Please invite your mothers to attend our show," "Please ask your mother to bake a cake for our party," "We need a class mother to go on a trip with us")

For each of these practices, suggest some nonsexist alternatives.

HELP CHILDREN SEE THAT SEX-ROLE DEFINITIONS CHANGE WITH TIME AND VARY IN DIFFERENT CULTURES

Another important way to demonstrate that sex roles are not inherited or unchanging is for children to learn how sex roles vary in different cultures as well as how roles have changed in our own culture. Children can ask their mothers or fathers about sex-role behavior when they were growing up and discuss present conditions in their families and communities.

Lessons can be developed to study the responsibilities that men and women have in different cultures. For example, in many agricultural communities in the United States, both men and women work in the fields, but in China field work is largely women's work. In the United States, doctors are primarily men (although the percentage of women in medical schools is increasing), whereas in Russia there are more women than men physicians.

HELP CHILDREN UNDERSTAND THAT THERE IS A DIFFERENCE BETWEEN SEX ROLES, GENDER IDENTITY, AND SEXUAL PREFERENCE

When children begin learning about roles for women and men, they may fear that the modification of the roles assigned to a gender will affect their gender identity or sexual behavior. The important point that must be taught is that human feelings or characteristics neither belong uniquely to one gender nor influence one's sexual preference. For example, women can be assertive or men can be sensitive without its having any impact on their "femaleness" or "maleness." Be sensitive to the fact that students from some cultural groups experience clearly defined sex-role behaviors in their home and community.

Let children see pictures of men taking care of children and pictures of women engaging in nonstereotypical occupations. I once saw a teacher bring in a picture of a football player who knitted for relaxation. The students were quite surprised by this.

ENCOURAGE CHILDREN TO LEARN TO WORK AND PLAY TOGETHER AND EXPERIENCE A VARIETY OF ROLES WITHIN A GROUP

Provide opportunities for males and females to work together in completing assignments, to learn to help each other, and to enjoy activities together. Unless you plan for such activities, they are unlikely to occur. Current research indicates that sex segregation among children may have social consequences that persist into adulthood (Lockheed & Klein, 1985). The sex segregation that typically occurs at the elementary school level may not simply represent a "harmless" developmental stage (Serbin, 1983) but may provide the foundation for further interaction patterns. Boys dominate the interaction patterns when working in mixed-sex, problem-solving groups in elementary school, and men dominate the interaction and decision making in mixed-sex groups (Lockheed & Hall, 1976). It appears that stereotyped expectations regarding the relative abilities of males and females begin in childhood. Furthermore, Webb and Kenderski (1985) reported differential behavior in high-achieving, mixed-sex groups in which males have higher attainment than females. They found that males were more likely to help males when they requested help, but males did not reciprocate when females asked for help.

By allowing the sexes to segregate and not cooperate with each other, the teacher may communicate acceptance of sex segregation and its consequences. Increase the opportunity for cross-sex interaction by using cooperative cross-sex learning and discussion groups, reinforcing cross-sex play, and making use of seating and team assignments that place males and females in close proximity. When students work in groups, assign different roles (e.g., leader, recorder) to students in each group, so that all students experience roles of different responsibility and status (Lockheed & Klein, 1985).

self-concept. The total organization of the perceptions individuals have of themselves.

self-esteem. The value individuals place on their behavior.

SELF-CONCEPT

Self-concept, our ideas or perceptions about ourselves, is a very important factor affecting behavior (Combs & Avila, 1985). Educators have become increasingly aware of the impact that an individual's self-concept and **self-esteem** have on classroom behavior and achievement.[1] Students' problems in school may have their sole source in the lack of a positive self-concept.

A number of investigations have provided important data to help explain the characteristics of the self-concept (Marsh, Byrne, & Shavelson, 1988; Marsh & Shavelson, 1985; Shavelson, Hubner, & Stanton, 1976).

- Self-concept is *organized*. Individuals collect a great deal of information on which to base their perceptions of themselves. To arrive at a general picture of the self, the individual organizes the information into fewer and fewer broad categories.
- Self-concept is *multifaceted*; we should not regard it as a single entity. Individuals categorize self-perceptions into such areas as social acceptance, physical attractiveness, athletic ability, and academic ability. Students who have low self-concepts of their academic abilities could have high self-concepts in physical ability or peer relationships. Also, students have distinct self-concepts in a variety of specific school subjects (Marsh, 1992). One should always identify the specific *type* of self-concept when referring to any given student.
- The multifaceted structure of self-concept may be *hierarchical* on a dimension of generality. A representation of the organized, multifaceted, hierarchical nature of self-concept is shown in Figure 10.2.

[1] Many psychologists believe that the self has two aspects—self-description and self-evaluation—and therefore distinguish between *self-concept* and *self-esteem*. Self-concept is the total organization of the perceptions an individual has of the self. Self-esteem is the value or judgments the individual places on self and behavior. However, other psychologists fail to make the distinction and refer to *self-concept* as a global term that includes personal judgment. For this reason, *self-concept* and *self-esteem* have been used interchangeably in psychological literature.

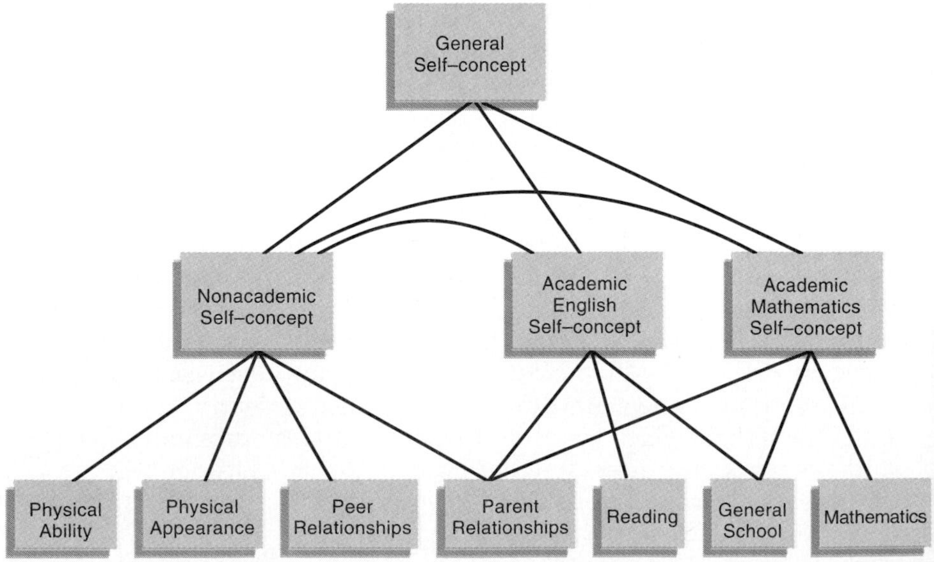

Figure 10.2 A Hierarchical Organization of Self-Concept. Source: Adapted from Marsh and Shavelson, 1985.

- Self-concept is *stable.* Notice, however, that as one descends the self-concept hierarchy, self-concept depends increasingly on specific situations and thus becomes less stable. This fact is supported by Ludwig and Maehr (1967), who found that success and failure in an athletic task changed subjects' self-concept of specific physical ability but did not change their general self-concept.

Why do most attempts to change students' self-concepts fail?

Schools have developed many special programs to improve students' self-concepts but have failed to demonstrate any change. Two of the major problems are the weak intervention programs and the poor relationship between the intended goals of the intervention and the specific dimensions of self-concept being evaluated. To improve the possibility of producing effective interventions, we must first establish the specific type of self-concept to be changed, develop activities and experiences related to the dimension of self-concept selected, and, finally, measure the specific dimension (Marsh, 1990).

Intervention programs that improve performance or skill in a particular area may not improve self-concept in the same area. For example, Marsh and Pear (1988) compared the impact of a cooperative and competitive physical fitness program on self-concept of physical ability. They found that in the competitive program, physical fitness improved but self-concept of physical ability decreased. In the cooperative program, both physical fitness and self-concept of physical ability were enhanced. The researchers attributed the results to the differences in the participants' frames of reference in both programs (i.e., competition affected perceptions of self differently from cooperation).

- The self-concept hierarchy is *developmental.* As children mature, they develop concepts and categories for organizing events and situations. By the time they reach school, they have acquired a good deal of information about themselves from others and begin to act like the type of person they conceive themselves to be. Their initial school experiences often reinforce these beliefs. During the preadolescent years, self-concept becomes increasingly differentiated with increasing age. Also, during preadolescence and early adolescence, self-concept declines with age (Marsh, 1990). Students "learn" to regard themselves positively or negatively as they assimilate their experiences with significant people in their life—parents, peers, and teachers.
- Self-concept is *evaluative.* Not only do individuals form a description of themselves in a particular situation, but they also form evaluations of themselves in the situation. Some students see themselves as successful achievers, but others believe they are inadequate and inferior

to their classmates. Frame of reference can be an important factor in how an individual evaluates his or her self (Marsh, 1990).

In an extensive investigation of the antecedents of self-esteem among 1,700 fifth- and sixth-grade children, Coopersmith (1967) found that persons with positive self-esteem viewed themselves along the following general lines:

> I consider myself a valuable and important person, and am at least as good as others of my age and training. I am regarded as someone worthy of respect and consideration. . . . I'm able to exert an influence upon people and events, partly because my views are sought and respected and partly because I'm able and willing to present and defend those views. I have a pretty definite idea of what I think is right . . . and have a fairly good understanding of the kind of person I am. I enjoy new and challenging tasks and don't get upset when things don't go well right off the bat. (p. 47)

DEBATE FORUM

Do Minority Students Have Low Self-Concepts?

Argument: Minority students have poor self-concepts. In fact, many of the Head Start and other early childhood education programs still focus on improving self-concepts of children of color.

Counterargument: Research evidence indicates that, although the academic performances of African American and Latino students are lower on the average than those of whites, these students often exhibit high self-ratings of self-perceived ability (Franco, 1983; Hare, 1985). In fact, when socioeconomic level is controlled, African American students exhibit *higher* self-perceptions of ability than do whites (R. Clark, 1983).

Covington (1992) offers some possible explanations for this finding. First, he suggests that for many minority students, positive feelings about themselves have little to do with their school performance. Instead, these students find recognition in peer acceptance, nurturance, and cooperation (Hare, 1985). In addition, they tend to view ability differently than whites. In some African American communities, for example, ability is measured in a broader, more practical, everyday context than in the academic orientation in which being bright is related to getting good grades. Ability is more related to effective coping and survival skills in their community than in the classroom. Second, minority students sometimes reject the competitive aspects of academics by withdrawing from active classroom

At the same time, a similar monologue by an individual with negative self-esteem might proceed as follows:

> I don't think I'm a very important or likeable person, and I don't see much reason for anyone else to like me. I can't do many of the things I'd like to do or do them the way I think they should be done. I'm not sure of my ideas and abilities, and there's a good likelihood that other people's ideas and work are better than my own. Other people don't pay much attention to me and given what I know about myself, I can't say I blame them. I don't like new or unusual occurrences and prefer sticking to known and safe ground. . . . I don't have much control over what happens to me and I expect that things will get worse rather than better. (p. 47)

The characterization of a person with moderate self-esteem falls between these two descriptions and is less precise in its evaluation of competence and expectations.

participation. Steele (1988) refers to this self-distancing process as "disidentification"—a process in which individuals devalue experiences in their life that negatively affect their self-perceptions.

Recently, Steele (1992) expanded his notion of "disidentification" in explaining the underachievement of African Americans from elementary school to college, especially those who have excellent academic credentials. He provides an example of a young African American student who enters college to be a doctor. She begins college by being offered academic support services indicating that she is "at risk" and is introduced to a social atmosphere where she is separate from whites. Her experiences with professors and other students often make her feel that she has to justify her intellectual ability. Steele writes:

> In reaction to some modest setback, she withdraws, hiding her troubles from instructors, counselors, even other students. Quickly, I believe a psychic defense takes over. She *disidentifies* with achievement; she changes her self-conception, her outlook and values, so that achievement is no longer so important to her self-esteem. She may continue to feel pressure to stay in school—from her parents, even from the potential advantages of a college degree. But now she is psychologically insulated from her academic life, like a disinterested visitor. Cool, unperturbed. But, like a pain-killing drug, disidentification undoes her future as it relieves her vulnerability. (p. 74)

What do you think? Does any part of this issue relate to any of your own experiences? What special educational challenges do students from different cultural backgrounds face?

self-fulfilling prophecy. A phenomenon in which the teacher's attitude may help produce the "expected" behavior in students.

Self-Concept and Achievement

? Which comes first—positive self-concept or high achievement?

The relationship between self-concept and achievement has been discussed extensively in the psychological literature. One could argue that doing well in school is likely to enhance the student's positive self-concept. On the other hand, it also can be argued that students who develop positive self-concepts feel better about themselves and their ability, and as a result they do better academically. It is difficult to resolve this issue because there is evidence to support both positions. Although it is difficult to determine which comes first, high achievement or high self-concept, it is likely that a positive change in one facilitates a positive change in the other (Hamachek, 1985).

Students' self-concept can be an important aspect in understanding how young people deal with academic tasks. Many students are caught in a vicious circle. They believe they can't perform well in a certain activity and they avoid it. Because they avoid it, they fail to get practice in the activity and don't perform well when they are asked to respond in class. The negative experiences caused by the inability to respond correctly only reinforce their initial belief about their inability. This dynamic process is called the **self-fulfilling prophecy**. Adults as well as children are victims of the beliefs they hold about themselves. My main point is that a negative self-image can be self-perpetuating, and over time it can have a negative effect on academic achievement.

Have you ever considered the consequences of attending a high school with high academic standards and ranking toward the middle of the class, or attending a less demanding school and ranking near the top? Marsh (1989; Marsh & Parker, 1984) has investigated the impact of what he calls "the big-fish-little-pond effect" on academic self-concept. He finds that equally able students have lower academic self-concepts in high-ability schools than in low-ability schools. This result is attributed to social comparison processes with a reference group that is perceived to be more able or less able than oneself. This research presents a dilemma for parents who are dissatisfied with public schools and want to send their children to high-achieving private schools: The private school environment is likely to challenge students to excel. However, the early formation of a self-image as a poor student may be more detrimental than attendance at a mediocre school. Can you relate this research to your experiences in high school?

Two factors especially mold various dimensions of students' self-concepts: physical growth and development and school experiences. The next two sections focus on these topics.

Physical Growth and Development

There is a strong correlation between self-image and body image for both boys and girls. In our society, having an acceptable body build is an important factor in evaluating ourselves. Most of us are well aware of adolescents' concern over their changing bodies. There is evidence that boys and girls in elementary school also are well aware of different body builds and often have negative reactions to their own physique (Lerner & Gillert, 1969; Staffieri, 1967).

anorexia nervosa. An eating disorder in which individuals starve themselves to maintain a slim figure.

THE IMPACT OF OTHERS. Self-concept is influenced by the reaction of others concerning physical appearance and body size, as well as by activities in which success is contingent on body size and/or physical skills. For example, the awkward child or adolescent who does not possess the athletic agility that is highly valued by the child's peers will not be accepted with open arms when the time comes to select team members. Do you know what it feels like always to be selected *last* for team competition? In addition to awkwardness or lack of ability, physical features—height, weight, complexion, or general body proportions—are very much related to feelings about one's self.

Children and adolescents of both sexes are influenced by mass media stereotypes of the beautiful body. Television, movies, and magazines such as *Playboy, Playgirl, Esquire,* and *Mademoiselle* reinforce unrealistic notions about body build with which individuals compare themselves. Jourard and Secord (1955) found that the ideal height and weight for college women were 5 feet 5 inches, 120 pounds, with bust, waist, and hip measurements of 35, 24, and 35 inches, respectively. The more a woman's dimensions deviated from this ideal, the more she disliked her physique. During different historical periods in our society, certain aspects of the ideal body build have changed. Since the 1980s considerable attention has been given to the illness **anorexia nervosa**, in which adolescent girls (and sometimes boys) often starve themselves to maintain a slim figure. In studies of men's perceptions of satisfactory body builds, men consistently rate

Sometimes students have more important concerns than listening to the teacher.

puberty. The biological changes that lead to reproductive maturity.

the wide-shouldered, narrow-hipped, athletic type of body build over the obese or thin body build (Brodsky, 1954).

RATE OF DEVELOPMENT. Another area of growth that can affect the self-concept is one's rate of development (i.e., early versus late maturation). The emergence of **puberty**, the biological changes that lead to reproductive maturity, has important psychological and social implications for the adolescent. Early-maturing males have been found to be more relaxed, less dependent, more self-confident, and attractive to both adults and peers than late-maturing males (Jones & Bayley, 1950; Mussen & Jones, 1957).

? What types of experiences do early-maturing males have that influence a positive self-esteem?

First, because females mature approximately two years earlier than the average male, the early-maturing males are more likely to begin dating and developing social relationships with girls in junior high school and high school, whereas their late-maturing peers do not develop these social skills until late in their high school career. As a result, the early-maturing males develop important social skills that give them a sense of confidence when interacting with people, particularly members of the opposite sex. Second, because early-maturing males tend to be bigger and stronger than late-maturing males, they are more likely to gain prestige from participating in athletics, a major source of pride for males. Third, again because of their size, early-maturing males are more likely to be given more responsibility by parents and teachers, at an earlier age, which adds to their confidence and positive self-image.

For females, the research is more ambiguous and confusing (Jones & Mussen, 1958). The advantages to females of early or late maturation are not always clear-cut. Many of the same advantages of early maturation accrue to girls in the same way as they do to boys. However, it can have some disadvantages such as lack of popularity and greater internal turbulence, because early-maturing girls feel and often look different from their peers. For girls, lacking the support of a peer group also going through puberty can be difficult. In an investigation, Tobin-Richards, Boxer, and Petersen (1983) reported that boys who matured earlier perceived themselves more positively than boys who were either on time (in relation to their peers) or late in their development. However, girls who were in mid-development or who perceived themselves to be on time in their physical maturation felt more attractive and more positive about their bodies than the girls who were early or late developers. The researchers also found that the late maturers felt more positive about themselves than the early maturers. The differential effects of early or late maturation for girls in various investigations may depend on different value systems and attitudes among peer groups in different communities.

School Experiences

The teacher sometimes can exert considerable influence on the direction of a child's self-concept by establishing a positive learning environment and by communicating effectively with students in the classroom. An important point to remember is that a student's concept of ability develops mainly from performance on classroom tasks, and the teacher can enhance the self-concept of ability by helping students to select learning objectives according to their abilities.

Another important factor in school experience that can have a strong effect on self-esteem is the school setting. Blyth, Simmons, and Bush (1978) found that for girls the discontinuity of moving from the sixth grade to the seventh grade in a new school can have a negative effect on self-esteem. In contrast, girls who stayed in the same school from kindergarten through the eighth grade showed no negative effects. In another investigation, Simmons, Rosenberg, and Rosenberg (1973) reported that 12-year-old girls in the seventh grade were more likely to demonstrate negative self-images than 12-year-olds in the sixth grade who were in elementary school. The researchers found no differences in self-images between 11- and 12-year-olds in the sixth grade or between 12- and 13-year-olds in the seventh grade. The key factor leading to a negative self-image for girls was being in a traditional junior high school at the time of puberty. Boys do not appear to be as affected by the transition from one type of school environment to another.

? Why do girls experience more stress than boys when they make the transition to a new school during puberty?

Simmons et al. (1979) believe the differences between pubertal boys and girls may be understood by exploring their value systems at this developmental period. Girls value sociability and appearance because these traits determine popularity. Therefore, girls rely more on the opinions of others to determine their self-esteem and position in their peer group. When girls move to a new school, they are faced with an entirely new reference group, in which the peers who are evaluating them are less well known. If a girl is engaged in dating during the change in schools, she is even more vulnerable to developing a negative self-image.

The impact of school transition is different for boys, who rely more on physical or athletic competence and less on "looks" as a factor in their total evaluation of themselves. In addition, the nature of the change in body image is different for the sexes. Girls develop a figure, which makes them different from the way they were in elementary school. Boys become taller and more muscular and athletic-looking, a less dramatic change, which is more in line with their existing values concerning athletics and body strength. Thus boys are more likely to view the changes as an improvement in their own appearance, whereas girls are less sure whether their particular figure will be viewed by others in a positive manner (Simmons et al., 1979).

While Simmons and her colleagues have argued that the *timing* of the transition to junior high school results in more disruption to the individual than would occur if the school change were made later in adolescence, Eccles and Midgley (1989) point out that the *nature* of the transition should be considered. They believe that it is the developmental mismatch between young adolescents and the traditional junior high school environment that causes the decrease in students' motivation and achievement-oriented beliefs about themselves. If the junior high school environment were supportive and less competitive, the change could have a positive impact on how adolescents view themselves.

Eccles and Midgley's analysis of the research is as follows: The junior high school student experiences more teacher control, competition and social comparison, and whole-class instruction, less personal contact with the teacher, and fewer opportunities for student decision making and self-management than does the elementary school student. At the same time, adolescents are more self-conscious and concerned about comparing themselves to others and desire more freedom in decision making. The consequence in this mismatch is an increased focus on ability assessments and anxiety over one's relative ability and performance levels, and a decreased sense of personal control. This situation causes many adolescents to have lower self-esteem and negative attitudes toward school and learning.

Are you convinced that more attention needs to be given to how the school environment meets the developmental needs of students? Perhaps encouraging dating behavior and developing activities that model the high school is not the best course for students in early adolescence. Does society push young adolescents to exhibit "grown-up" behavior too early? Think back to your own junior high school days. We can now laugh at certain awkward social experiences, but they were not funny when they occurred. Can you think of ways in which parents and teachers can be more supportive during this difficult developmental period? Did you attend a middle school (grades 6–8)? If so, was there less pressure to grow up?

The Effects of Working on Adolescent Development

? Do adolescents benefit from working during the school year?

Thousands of American adolescents work at jobs outside of school. Some of the reasons given for why adolescents should work include: it teaches responsibility, it provides opportunities to learn about adult roles, it increases the opportunity to gain employment after school, and it provides the opportunity to learn new skills.

In a comprehensive study of middle-class white adolescents who held their first job in the 10th and 11th grade, however, Greenberger and Steinberg (1986) found that working during school had more negative than positive impact on adolescents. They found

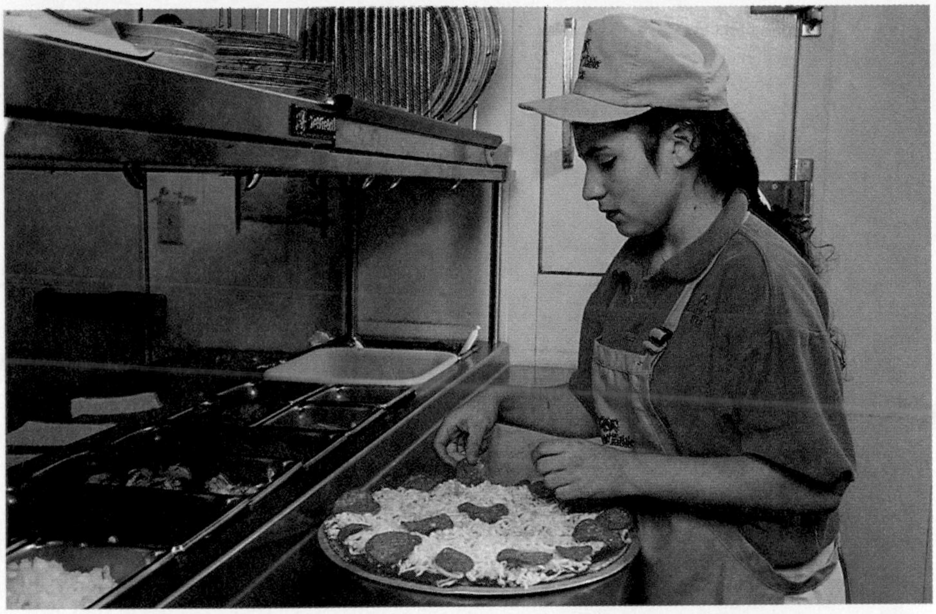

Adolescents' grades and school participation may be negatively affected by working more than 20 hours a week.

- a decline in school grades of nearly one full letter grade for students who worked more than 20 hours per week as compared to those who worked fewer than 10 hours per week
- diminished involvement in school activities
- no enhancement in the development of social responsibility
- higher incidence of alcohol and other drug use
- higher rates of "occupational deviance" (within eight months of their first job, two-thirds of the students had done something on the job that they knew was illegal or unethical)

On the positive side, there was some indication of gains in practical knowledge, for example, consumer affairs and personal finance. However, this knowledge was gained by students after a few hours of work and no more knowledge was gained with additional hours of work. Also, some evidence suggested that working facilitated the development of personal responsibility, particularly among girls.

When Greenberger and Steinberg observed what the adolescents were doing in their jobs, they found that over one-third of the students had jobs in the food service industry that provided little opportunity to apply their academic knowledge. The average worker spent only 7 percent of his or her time in activities involving reading, writing, or arithmetic computation and received little supervision. Basically, they spent their time doing highly routinized jobs with little supervision, little cognitive challenge, and little autonomy.

In a follow-up investigation, Steinberg and Dornbusch (1991) studied over 4,000 students using a socioeconomically and ethnically diverse sample of students with a variety of work histories and found similar results. They substantiated most of the findings of their earlier study and emphasized that the most important issue regarding work is *how much*, not *whether*, a student works.

authoritarian parenting style. A method of child rearing in which parents attempt to control their children's behavior and attitudes to conform to strict rules of conduct.

permissive parenting style. A method of child rearing in which parents make few demands on their children.

authoritative parenting style. A method of child rearing in which parents direct their children's activities by establishing firm rules and standards but are willing to discuss the reasons for their rules.

I believe there are two important implications from this research:

- Students must be made to realize the detrimental effects of working 20 hours per week or more during the school year.
- You, as teacher or parent, need to explore what adolescents plan to get out of work in addition to financial remuneration. If they don't receive supervision and are given little opportunity to apply any knowledge they acquire in school, they shouldn't have high expectations for gaining worthwhile information or insight that will benefit them in the future.

Did you work during high school? What were some of the positive and negative outcomes from your work experience?

SOCIALIZATION AND THE FAMILY

Parenting Practices

? How do parents' child-rearing styles influence their children's social behavior?

A number of researchers have shown that parents' child-rearing practices influence children's behavior. Erikson's theory of identity formation provides some insight into child-rearing practices as they pertain to important psychosocial crises at different developmental periods. In particular, providing a sense of trust, allowing children to explore their environment, and encouraging them to try new situations while providing support if they fail are important parenting behaviors in developing children's identity. Coopersmith (1967) found three child-rearing conditions to be related to a high self-esteem: parental acceptance of children, parental enforcement of clearly defined behavioral limits and rules, and parental respect for the freedom of their children's actions within the established limits.

Baumrind (1966, 1967, 1971) demonstrated how different parenting styles influence the social/personality development of children. She studied the impact of child-rearing practices by observing the social behavior of preschool children age 3 and 4. She then observed and interviewed the parents of the children and identified three categories of parenting styles—the **authoritarian**, the **permissive**, and the **authoritative**—and described typical behavior patterns of the children raised according to each style.

Authoritarian parents attempt to control their children's behavior and attitudes to conform to strict rules of conduct. These parents value obedience and favor punitive measures when their children attempt to behave contrary to their parents' expectations. They don't like to discuss standards with their children; they are more detached, more controlling, and less warm than other parents; their children are more discontented, withdrawn, and distrustful.

Permissive parents make few demands on their children, allowing them to regulate their own behavior. They hardly ever punish their children for misbehavior, make few demands for responsibility at home, and avoid the exercise of control; their children are the least self-reliant, explorative, and self-controlled.

Authoritative parents try to direct their children's activities by establishing firm rules and standards but are willing to discuss the reasons behind their regulations. They don't threaten their children, are loving, consistent, and respectful of their children's independent decisions; their children are the most self-reliant, self-controlled, explorative, and contented.

Although there are many different explanations for antisocial behavior, Patterson, DeBaryshe, and Ramsey (1989) have constructed a developmental model (see Figure 10.3) that emphasizes the role of faulty child-rearing methods as the basis for later antisocial behavior. Research indicates that the families of antisocial children use harsh and inconsistent discipline, have little positive interaction with their children, and don't adequately monitor and supervise their activities (Loeber & Dishion, 1983; McCord, McCord, & Howard, 1963). These parents are not consistent in the use of rewards for appropriate behavior and punishment for deviant behavior. Of particular concern is that they allow their children to be aggressive with other members of the family. The result of this early family experience is that the children learn to control their environment through coercive means and fail to learn appropriate social behaviors. When they go to school, their difficulty in conforming to classroom regulations leads to difficulties with teachers and peers, and ultimately to poor academic achievement. Finally, at early adolescence, the children's antisocial behavior and peer rejection motivate them to seek out a deviant peer group with which to identify. Many of these individuals become adolescent delinquents and adult offenders.

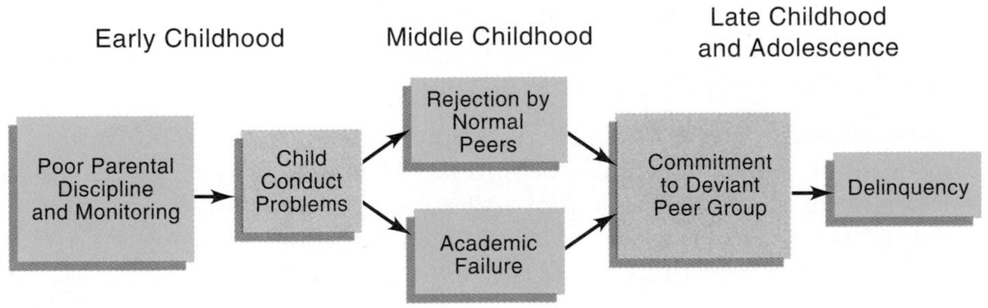

Figure 10.3 Developmental Progression for Antisocial Behavior. Source: Patterson, DeBaryshe, and Ramsey, 1989.

IMPLICATIONS FOR TEACHING. Many schools provide parent education courses or information about where parents in the community can obtain help. One problem is that parents who need the most help often don't contact schools or social agencies for assistance. Since there is evidence that successful interventions occur at the preadolescent stage (Kazdin, 1987), it is important for teachers and mental health professionals to identify children who exhibit antisocial behavior at an early age. In addition to parent training, there are interventions that include teaching children academic and social skills.

A number of books and programs are available for parents who want guidance in child rearing. Some of the more popular books include *P.E.T.: Parent Effectiveness Training* (Gordon, 1975); *Children: The Challenge*

(Dreikurs & Soltz, 1964); *Systematic Training for Effective Parenting* (Dinkmeyer & McKay, 1976); and *Living with Children* (Patterson & Guillion, 1971). These books can be useful to the teacher who may be asked questions by parents regarding specific approaches to dealing with child-rearing problems. Readers interested in an evaluation of some of the major parent education programs will find Dembo, Sweitzer, and Lauritzen's (1985) review helpful. Last, many of the methods discussed in Chapter 7 regarding classroom management also are applied to child-rearing techniques.

DEBATE FORUM

What Is the Purpose of Sex Education?

Sex education in America's schools is a relatively recent phenomenon. Only since the early 1970s has the topic of sexuality been added to the curriculum of a large percentage of the schools in the United States. And we can easily understand why: Over 1 million women under age 20—and approximately 31,000 under age 16—become pregnant each year (Henshaw et al., 1989). Roughly half of these pregnancies end in abortion. By December 1989, almost 2,500 cases of AIDS among adolescents had been reported to the Centers for Disease Control (Kerr, 1990).

Argument: A major goal in most sex education programs is to reduce teenage pregnancy, AIDS, and venereal diseases. Therefore, we need to provide programs in the schools that emphasize abstinence as the only truly safe form of sex.

Counterargument: Sex education in the schools should be precisely that—*education.* Students should be taught how to minimize risk through the use of condoms and other contraceptives, and they should be taught the facts about pregnancy, sexually transmitted disease, and other potential consequences of intimacy.

Response: Research on sex education programs provides little support for the notion that improved information on sexuality changes adolescent behavior (Kirby, 1989; Miller et al., 1992).

What do you think? Sex education, and AIDS education in particular, evokes intense, passionately held opinions and fears from parents, for many of whom such topics as homosexuality, drug use, and condoms are extremely difficult to address (Kirp & Epstein, 1989). What are your beliefs about the purposes and goals of sex education? What do you think needs to be done to make sex education more effective? Who should be responsible for sex education—families, schools, or both?

Child Abuse and Neglect

In Section 3 of the Child Abuse Prevention and Treatment Act (P.L. 93-247), *child abuse* and *neglect* are defined as "the physical or mental injury, sexual abuse, negligent treatment, or maltreatment of a child under the age of eighteen by a person who is responsible for the child's welfare under circumstances which indicate that the child's health or welfare is harmed or threatened thereby."

According to the National Center for Child Abuse and Neglect, approximately 1 million children are abused or neglected each year. More than 2,000 children die each year because of abuse or neglect by their adult caretakers. Many individuals incorrectly believe that child abusers come from some particular type of background. The fact is that child abusers come from all religious, ethnic, occupational, and socioeconomic groups. Furthermore, many child abusers were themselves abused as children.

> What type of parent is likely to abuse his or her child?

McNeese and Hebeler (1977) have stressed that prerequisites to an incident of abuse are "a *child* who is difficult to manage (or is merely considered difficult by parents), a *parent* or *family* that has the potential to abuse, and a *stressful event* that precipitates the abuse" (pp. 5–6). Infants who are born with low birthweight, congenital malformations, and other developmental deviations and handicapped children often are vulnerable to abuse because they may not live up to their parents' expectations or may be difficult to rear (Morgan, 1987). Researchers have found that certain family and/or personal problems of mothers and fathers can be an important determinant in child abuse. For example, stress, isolation, poor information about child care procedures or unrealistic expectations concerning child development (e.g., expecting a child to be toilet trained by the first birthday), serious marital problems, unemployment, and crises involving separation or divorce can all be possible factors that cause an adult to abuse or neglect a child (Gelardo & Sanford, 1987).

Implications for Teaching. Teachers are in an excellent position to identify signs of abuse and neglect, provided they know what to look for (Cartwright, Cartwright, & Ward, 1984). Teachers should be alert to the symptoms described in Table 10.2.

It is not always easy to determine clear-cut cases of abuse or neglect. For example, a child who is consistently tired or sleepy in class may have some illness. However, every state requires that suspected child abuse be reported. For example, in California, teachers and other professionals who have contact with children are required by law to report child abuse immediately by telephone to a child protection agency and send a written report within 36 hours of learning about an incident. Failure to comply with this law is a misdemeanor punishable by six months in jail and/or a $500 fine. The reporting teacher is not required to provide proof of the abuse. The agency that receives the report has that responsibility.

TABLE 10.2 SYMPTOMS OF ABUSE AND NEGLECT

Symptoms of Abuse	Symptoms of Neglect
Evidence of repeated injury	Clothing inappropriate for weather
New injuries before previous ones have healed	Torn, tattered, unwashed clothing
Frequent complaints of abdominal pain	Poor skin hygiene
Evidence of bruises	Rejection by other children because of offensive body odor
Bruises of different ages	Need for glasses, dental work, hearing aid, or other health services
Welts	Lack of proper nourishment
Wounds, cuts, or punctures	Consistent tiredness or sleepiness in class
Scalding liquid burns, especially those with well-defined parameters	Consistent very early school arrival
Caustic burns	Frequent absenteeism or chronic tardiness
Frostbite	Tendency to hang around school after dismissal
Cigarette burns on the back of the neck, head, or extremities.	

Source: Adapted from Kline, 1977.

Many school districts have formal procedures to report cases of child abuse and neglect. It is important that you ask about the procedures and regulations regarding the reporting of child abuse in your school district. All states now provide immunity for those who report suspected cases of child abuse in good faith.

IMPLICATIONS FOR TEACHING: CHILD SEXUAL ABUSE. Recently, the mass media have paid a great deal of attention to the sexual abuse of children. Many schools have developed special educational programs for young children emphasizing primary prevention (keeping the abuse from occurring in the first place) and detection (encouraging disclosure of past and present abuse so that children can receive intervention and protection). Research in this area is insufficient to determine whether these prevention programs are effective (Reppucci & Haugaard, 1989).

An important concern is the possibility of teachers and other school personnel being falsely accused of improper behavior. As a result, teachers need to avoid situations in which their interaction with children could be questioned. The following are some do's and don'ts (adapted from Morgan, 1987, pp. 97–98):

- Never give a child a ride in your car, even in an emergency.
- Never take children on field trips away from the school unless at least two parents are present.
- Never go into a bathroom alone with children.
- Never touch children, except on the shoulder to lead them to their seats or wherever it is you want them to be.
- Never hug, kiss, or pat a child on the bottom, and do not allow students to give you extended hugs or allow them to kiss you.
- Never let students into your home.
- Always document for your file any false accusations a child makes, such as: "You are mean to me. You hate me."

- Always take a child immediately to the school nurse if he or she acquires an injury, whether self-inflicted or accidental.

In reading this list, you might conclude that educators may be overreacting to isolated incidents. Unfortunately, present circumstances require greater awareness on the teacher's part to prevent false accusations regarding professional conduct.

Student Stress

Some of us can tolerate more stress than others and react differently to stressful situations. In fact, there is some indication that an individual's personality may influence the ways in which he or she responds to stress factors. Friedman and Rosenman (1974) identified Type A and Type B behavior in the way individuals respond to their environment. Individuals with Type A behavior tend to be aggressive and ambitious and to have a sense of time urgency in their quest to excel. Individuals with Type B behavior also may be aggressive or ambitious, but they are more easygoing and relaxed in their quest for excellence. Friedman and Rosenmann believe that Type A individuals are more likely to have heart attacks and other physical ailments.

Some psychologists believe that many children are currently being reared in an environment that fosters Type A behavior. David Elkind (1988) has described the socialization factors that cause stress in children in his book *The Hurried Child: Growing Up Too Fast Too Soon*. According to Elkind, the "hurried child" is often forced to assume adultlike behaviors before being prepared to do so. We dress our children like adults, allow them to view sex and violence in the media, make unreasonable demands on them to attain goals beyond their ability, and expect them to deal with changes in the family such as divorce and single parenthood without any difficulty. Elkind states that pediatricians report a greater incidence of chronic psychosomatic complaints such as headaches, allergic reactions, stomach-aches, and even ulcers in today's children than in the past.

The scale (Table 10.3) reported by Elkind (1988) provides an estimate of the impact of various stressful changes in a child's life. He estimates that for a given year, if a child scores below 150, the child is about average with respect to stress load. If the child's score is between 150 and 300, the child has better than an average chance of demonstrating some symptoms of stress. If the child's score is above 300, there is a strong possibility that some changes in health and/or behavior will be observed. These numbers should be used only as guidelines, because a child may show symptoms of stress with a much lower score.

IMPLICATIONS FOR TEACHING. As you talk to children, be cognizant of the stressors in their lives. Such information may provide you with insights as to why certain students may not be performing up to standards.

An important factor for teachers to consider is that children do not deal with stress as well as adults do. In many ways, society permits more acceptable outlets for adults than it does for children. For example, a teacher can be angry with a student, but it is inappropriate for a student to display anger toward a teacher; adults can walk away from a stressful situation, but children often do not have this option at home or in the classroom; adults can daydream or become involved with some other activity to reduce the effects of stress, but children are expected to maintain their attention on school-related tasks; adults can get a prescription drug for "nerves" from a physician, but it is inappropriate for children to deal with stress in the same manner (Youngs, 1985).

TABLE 10.3 ASSESSMENT OF STUDENT STRESS

	Points	Child's Score
Parent dies	100	
Parents divorce	73	
Parents separate	65	
Parent travels as part of job	63	
Close family member dies	63	
Personal illness or injury	53	
Parent remarries	50	
Parent fired from job	47	
Parents reconcile	45	
Mother goes to work	45	
Change in health of a family member	44	
Mother becomes pregnant	40	
School difficulties	39	
Birth of a sibling	39	
School readjustment (new teacher or class)	39	
Change in family's financial condition	38	
Injury or illness of a close friend	37	
Starts a new (or changes an) extracurricular activity (music lessons, Brownies, and so forth)	36	
Change in number of fights with siblings	35	
Threatened by violence at school	31	
Theft of personal possessions	30	
Changes responsibilities at home	29	
Older brother or sister leaves home	29	
Trouble with grandparents	29	
Outstanding personal achievement	28	
Move to another city	26	
Move to another part of town	26	
Receives or loses a pet	25	
Changes personal habits	24	
Trouble with teacher	24	
Change in hours with baby-sitter or at day-care center	20	
Move to a new house	20	
Changes to a new school	20	
Changes play habits	19	
Vacations with family	19	
Changes friends	18	
Attends summer camp	17	
Changes sleeping habits	16	
Change in number of family get-togethers	15	
Changes eating habits	15	
Changes amount of TV viewing	13	
Birthday party	12	
Punished for not "telling the truth"	11	

Source: Elkind, 1988.

CONTROLLING STRESS THROUGH RELAXATION. Psychologists have developed programs to help children understand and become aware of stressors in their lives as well as to help them manage their stress (see Humphrey & Humphrey, 1985; Youngs, 1985). One of the most common strategies for reducing stress is to alleviate its symptoms. In this regard, relaxation techniques have been successful in dealing with many psychosomatic illnesses such as migraine headaches. For example, controlling one's breathing is an effective way to relax. Many experts in stress reduction teach individuals breathing exercises that involve a long, slow exhalation. Your diaphragm expands and tenses when you take in air and relaxes when you let the air out. Thus one way to relax is to increase the time you spend exhaling. This process is called *diaphragmatic breathing.* Certain measures of anxiety can be lowered as a result of using relaxation procedures (Johnson & Spielberger, 1968; Keat, 1972). The following is a simple exercise to teach individuals to relax (Youngs, 1985). Experience the following technique by asking a friend to read each step as you attempt it:

1. Get comfortable. Move your arms and legs around to make your muscles loose.
2. Close your eyes.
3. Take a deep breath in and count slowly one . . . two . . . three . . . four . . . five . . . six.
4. Let the air out very slowly, counting one . . . two . . . three . . . four . . . five . . . six.
5. Repeat the above, but this time place your hands on your stomach and feel it filling up with air (pushing out) when you breathe.
6. Breathe in deeply one . . . two . . . three . . . four.
7. Let the air out slowly one . . . two . . . three . . . four . . . five . . . six . . . (feel your stomach pull back in).
8. Repeat this a few more times.
9. Open your eyes.
10. Now how do you feel? (p. 117)

Don't get too relaxed. You have more material to cover in this chapter!

Suicide

Sometimes student stress reaches a point that it can't be alleviated simply by rest or relaxation. A concern of parents, educators, and mental health practitioners is the increasing rate of suicide among adolescents, caused, in part, by the stressors in their lives. The number of adolescents who commit suicide has increased 300 percent since the 1960s (National Center for Health Statistics, 1985). Many adolescents have maladaptive coping strategies to handle their problems. Instead of dealing directly with problems, they seek methods that temporarily give them relief (e.g., experiment with alcohol and other drugs or engage in other risk-taking behaviors). The result, however, is that these behaviors do not resolve the problems that they face (Frymier, 1988).

The problems that suicide victims face usually are common to most adolescents (failing grades, difficulties with peers, tension at home, and so forth). What makes the situation different is that the accumulation of stress is so great that they come to believe that suicide is the only solution open to them. There are, however, some stressors that can be particularly dangerous. For example, a history of physical and sexual abuse is associated with a higher rate of self-destructive behaviors (Frymier, 1988).

IMPLICATIONS FOR TEACHING. Schools are preparing materials and programs dealing with this issue for students and their parents. In addition, many teachers participate in staff development workshops on suicide and are trained to present workshops for students. The student-centered programs usually focus on teaching the warning signs of an impending suicide, promoting listening skills on the part of the students, and stressing how to get professional help for suicidal peers. The five warning signs identified by the American Association of Suicidology are

> (a) a suicide threat or other statement indicating a desire or intention to die, (b) a previous suicide attempt, (c) depression, (d) marked changes in behavior, including eating and sleeping patterns, acting out, hyperactivity, substance abuse, or high risk taking behavior, and (e) making final arrangements or saying good-bye to possessions and/or individuals. (Davis, Wilson, & Sandoval, 1988, p. 560)

Other types of programs available for adolescents include peer counseling in schools, mental health consultation by school psychologists and other professionals, screening to identify students at risk, and special programs to provide information on life skills, with a focus on helping young people cope with the stressors in their lives.

There are some steps that teachers can take if they suspect that a student may engage in self-destructive behavior. Your first step is to find out if there are specific procedures established by your school district. If there are no specific guidelines, consider the following (Frymier, 1988):

- Tell the principal, guidance counselor, and/or school psychologist about your concern.
- With one of these individuals, confront the student to discuss what is causing him or her to consider suicide.
- Alert the student's family and with the principal or mental health professional meet with them to discuss your concerns.
- Monitor the student's behavior.

The process for dealing with students who need special attention differs from school to school. Sometimes a principal will prefer that the school psychologist handle the situation without direct involvement with the classroom teacher. In other situations, the teacher may work together with the school psychologist. Don't ever try to handle the problem alone. Get the help of professionals in your school for advice on how to proceed.

Maternal Employment

> **?** What factors determine whether maternal employment has beneficial or harmful effects on children?

With the increasing number of single-parent families and dual-career parents, more mothers are working today than ever before. It is estimated that 71 percent of mothers with school-age children from two-parent families are presently working outside the home (Hoffman, 1989).

Hoffman (1989) has reviewed the research on the effects of maternal employment in two-parent families and has found the following:

- Children of employed mothers have fewer gender stereotypes.
- Employed mothers teach their children to be more independent than nonemployed mothers do.
- Employment has the potential to increase a mother's sense of contentment if she likes her job, has adequate support from her husband for working, and is satisfied with the quality of child care.
- Few differences are found in parent-child interaction between employed and nonemployed mothers. Although employed mothers spend less time with their children during the week, they often compensate by spending more time with them on weekends.

Thus, in general, if a mother receives the necessary support while working, there do not appear to be any detrimental effects for either the mother or child.

Divorce

> **?** How can divorce impact students of different developmental ages?

At one time relatives and friends were shocked to hear about a divorce. Today divorce is no longer considered atypical, but instead is viewed as a normal process of family change (Ahrons & Rodgers, 1987). Some 40 to 50 percent of all schoolchildren will experience their parents' divorce and will spend an average of five years raised by single parents before a parent remarries (Glick & Lin, 1986).

Although there is more acceptance of divorce in society, the negative impact on children has not changed. In general, parent conflict is associated with adjustment problems among children—especially boys, who react less well to divorce than girls. This is not to say that all children from divorced families are maladjusted. In some cases, a supportive one-parent household is more beneficial for children than a two-parent household with conflict (Hetherington & Anderson, 1988).

How will a specific child or adolescent respond to parental separation and divorce? Such factors as the age of the child at the time of separation, the child's personality, the degree of parental conflict, the economic position of the child's residential family, and the quality of the child's relationship with his or her residential parent are all factors to be considered. It is not the simple event of divorce itself that produces the negative impact but the subsequent events—the inconsistent parenting, conflict between parents, economic hardships on the family—that have the greatest effect on the child's development and adjustment (Emery, 1988).

There is a no "good time" for a divorce, since it affects children at all ages. In some cases, delayed responses are observed many years after the event. At one time it was believed that adolescents handled marital transition better than younger children. However, Wallerstein, Corbin, and Lewis (1988) reported data from the 10-year follow-up of the California Children of Divorce Study indicating that contrary to earlier findings, older children appear to suffer the most from divorce. They found that large numbers of young men and women had personal problems, and one-third of the women were very concerned about commitment and were fearful of being betrayed.

Wallerstein and Kelly (1980) provided information on some common responses to divorce related to the developmental level of the child. Preschool children were likely to regress in the area of recent achievement such as toilet training, dressing, and going to school. They feared routine separation, had trouble sleeping, became concerned with abandonment, and were irritable and demanding. Some preschool children blamed themselves for the divorce.

Children between 5 and 8 years of age cried a great deal and were preoccupied with feelings of rejection. Boys, in particular, missed their father and expressed anger at their mother for causing him to leave. The school performance of these children declined.

Children between 9 and 12 were angry, particularly at the parent they saw as causing the divorce, and tended to align with one parent against the other—most frequently with the mother against the father. They grieved, were anxious and lonely, and some also had academic problems.

Adolescents, who were already experiencing their own developmental difficulties, acquired additional problems with the separation. They became anxious as they realized their parents were not perfect, were concerned with their own futures and with the possibility of their own sexual and marital failure. Finally, they tended to disengage from their families and sought support from peers and other significant adults.

IMPLICATIONS FOR TEACHING. The teacher should be prepared for the possibility of adjustment problems following parental separation, especially if custodial changes are involved. The tendency for diminished parenting following a divorce (Hetherington, Cox, & Cox, 1982; Wallerstein & Kelly, 1980) can lead to less parental discipline and more independence given to the child. The result can influence the student's classroom behavior and academic achievement.

Hamner and Turner (1985) developed the following guidelines for teachers (based on Black, 1979, and Hammond, 1981):

- Talk with the child, encouraging expression of feelings, and be a willing and receptive listener.
- Recognize emotions and accept them.
- Deal openly in class with a variety of family situations. Avoid referring only to nuclear families. Be sensitive to language used. Avoid stereotyping terms such as "broken homes."
- Do not expect children from one-parent homes to fail; children live up to expectations.
- Make information on divorce available to children and their parents.
- Establish communication with both parents, if possible.
- Learn about custodial and other arrangements for the children.
- When possible, place young children without fathers in classrooms with male teachers. (p. 179)

latchkey children. Children or adolescents who are without supervision for long periods of time before or after school.

Latchkey Children

One serious problem resulting from the increase in dual-career and single-parent families is the growing number of children and adolescents caring for themselves after school. Estimates of **latchkey children** range from 2 million to 6 million. The term *latchkey* originated in the eighteenth century and denoted the implement used to lift the door latch to gain entry into one's house.

Many families cannot afford to pay for child care before or after school; even if they can, they often can't arrange for suitable care. A 1987 Harris poll reported that teachers considered the lack of adequate child care the number one problem in schools, surpassing drug use, truancy, and discipline.

Although not all latchkey children are maladjusted or do poorly in school, there is evidence that as parental supervision declines, the possibility of psychological and behavioral problems increases. For example, latchkey children report more fear and anxiety, have more academic and social problems, and are more susceptible to peer pressure to commit antisocial acts than children who are supervised after school (Long & Long, 1989). Richardson et al. (1989) found that eighth graders who took care of themselves for 11 or more hours a week were at twice the risk of substance use—alcohol, tobacco, and marijuana—as those who did not take care of themselves at all. This relationship held for all levels of socioeconomic status, gender, ethnicity, extracurricular activities, or sources of social influence (e.g., whether the parents smoked or drank). The significance of this investigation is that it demonstrated that the likelihood of becoming a substance abuser is not limited to children of any one type of family.

IMPLICATIONS FOR TEACHING. Schools and communities are making attempts to help children and their families deal with the problem. Some communities have organized hot lines where children can speak to adults about their fears or concerns. *The Handbook for Latchkey Children and Their Working Parents* (Long & Long, 1983) should be recommended to parents who need advice about reducing the dangers of unsupervised care. One of the most important steps parents can take is to establish a contact person, a parent or some other adult, for the child to call once he or she comes home. Other advice in this book is to provide the child with structured activities to complete while alone in the house.

Teachers can also play an important role by listening to students' concerns and providing information about personal safety. In addition, advising parents how to monitor students' homework and television viewing can be helpful in ensuring normal academic progress.

TELEVISION AS A SOCIALIZATION AGENT

Television has both positive and negative influences on children. It teaches academic and cognitive skills and social behaviors, and targets children as a market for advertising toys, cereals, and other foods (Huston, Watkins, & Kunkel, 1989). Steinberg (1985) reported that the average television set is on more than 7 hours a day. In fact, the average high school graduate will have watched up to 20,000 hours of TV (much more time than in the classroom) (Kaye, 1979). Have you thought about what life would be like without TV? Can you imagine family members having to talk to one another rather than watch TV? In some homes, family members each have their own TV and often watch the same program by themselves. There have been many investigations of television's effects on young people (see Liebert & Sprafkin, 1988, for a comprehensive review of these studies). The research to date indicates that TV violence is *a* cause of aggressiveness and that parents need to monitor their children's viewing behavior. Also, young children do not understand the purpose of advertising and are, therefore, especially vulnerable to its appeals. Finally, there is a great deal of stereotyping of minorities, women, and the elderly. On the positive side, programs can teach important academic skills (e.g., "Sesame Street") and

Parents often ask teachers about guidelines regarding television viewing.

important **prosocial behaviors** (e.g., "Mister Rogers' Neighborhood"), such as generosity, helping, cooperation, and self-control (Hearold, 1986).

Can you identify some of the social behaviors or attitudes you developed from watching television? Did your parents place any restrictions on your viewing? The following Classroom Application can serve as a guide for your discussions with parents as they consider how they should deal with their children's television viewing.

prosocial behavior. The demonstration of positive social behavior such as helping, sharing, and cooperating.

CLASSROOM Application

HELPING PARENTS MONITOR THEIR CHILDREN'S TELEVISION VIEWING

KNOW WHAT YOUR CHILDREN WATCH AND WHEN

A log of how much time is spent in front of the tube will often speak for itself about whether TV is playing too large a role in their lives.

Be alert to the content of the program as well as the commercials. Notice ways in which viewing affects your children's behavior. Do they become transfixed after watching for a while? Or does viewing make them tense and lead to fighting? What effects does it have on family communication when you all watch together?

How are ethnic groups, sex roles, age groups presented? How are conflicts resolved?

CHOOSE WHAT TO WATCH

Don't leave watching to chance—you wouldn't put a refrigerator in your children's rooms and allow them to eat what they wanted on the chance they would eventually meet their nutritional requirements. Learn to turn off the set when your choice is over.

SET LIMITS

Talking over a set of guidelines with family members, agreeing upon them, and sticking to them is effective in establishing a new routine for viewing TV. For example, your family may choose to ban TV dur-

continued

ing dinner, to allow viewing only after other responsibilities (homework, chores) have been done, or to allow each family member to have a choice of selecting a program each week.

Help children choose activities to do when the TV is off (read a book, draw a picture, play a game).

WHENEVER POSSIBLE, VIEW WITH CHILDREN

When watching with young children, point out what is real and what is fantasy.

When values presented on TV conflict with your family values, say so! When values agree, say so too!

- Discuss the differences between fantasy and reality.
- Discuss conflict situations and how problems could be solved without violence.
- Discuss situations involving cooperation and note behaviors your child might imitate.
- Point out characters who represent a variety of ethnic groups.
- Point out men/women who represent a variety of occupations.
- Discuss food advertisements in terms of what is healthy and nutritious.
- Discuss toy advertisements in terms of play potential, safety, and age appropriateness.

USE THE TIME IN FRONT OF TV TO BENEFIT THE CHILD

Television can be a rich source of vocabulary development. Explain new words to children.

Television can expand a child's horizons. Talk about other places in the world, other cultures, new experiences.

Television programs can stimulate reading of related material, if the child is encouraged.

Television can stimulate discussions on sensitive topics by older children—such as drugs, rape, teenage pregnancy—and thus may provide the opportunity for parents to discuss such topics.

Quoted from Berns, 1989, p.296.

Summary

ERIKSON'S THEORY OF PERSONAL AND SOCIAL DEVELOPMENT

1. Erikson has identified eight major psychosocial crises that individuals experience over a life span.
2. Teachers can play an important role in helping students to develop a sense of initiative and industry.
3. Marcia has identified four different identity statuses during adolescence—diffusion, moratorium, achievement, and foreclosure.

GENDER DIFFERENCES

4. There is little evidence to support any argument for innate differences between genders in the cognitive and social areas; socialization experiences appear to account for most differences in performance among males and females.
5. During the last 20 years, gender differences in cognitive abilities have narrowed to the point that only negligible differences exist.
6. Classroom practices can contribute to sex-role stereotyping.

SELF-CONCEPT

7. Individuals' self-concepts embody the ideas they have about themselves and the value they place on their behavior.
8. The self-concept is organized, multifaceted, hierarchical, stable, developmental, and evaluative.
9. It is incorrect to assume that minority students have poor self-concepts.
10. It is more useful to refer to specific types of self-concept than to general self-concept.
11. Special programs designed to change self-concept generally have not been successful.
12. Students with negative beliefs and feelings about themselves are likely to be underachievers or failures in school.
13. The transition from elementary to junior high school can be particularly stressful for some females.
14. The rate of physical development can influence students' self-concepts of physical appearance.
15. Working 20 hours or more per week during the school year can have negative consequences for adolescents.

SOCIALIZATION AND THE FAMILY

16. A description of parenting styles includes the authoritarian, permissive, and authoritative parent.
17. Parenting styles influence different social/personality development of children.
18. Educators and parents have different beliefs about the purpose and goals of sex education.

19. Teachers have a legal responsibility to report suspected cases of child abuse.
20. Teachers should avoid situations in which they can be falsely accused of unprofessional conduct.
21. Stress can have a detrimental effect on an individual's health.
22. Teachers should be alert to the warning signs of an impending suicide.
23. In general, there is no evidence that maternal employment has any detrimental effect on children, assuming the mother wants to work and receives the necessary support while working.
24. Divorce takes its toll on all children and may have delayed effects on adolescents.
25. Children's adjustment to divorce depends on such factors as age at the time of divorce, personality, degree of parental conflict, the family's economic situation, and relationship with custodial parent.
26. Boys generally have a more difficult time adjusting to divorce than girls do.
27. Latchkey children tend to be at a higher risk for substance abuse, report more fear and anxiety, and have more academic and social problems than children who are supervised after school.

Reflecting on Personal and Social Development

1. Analyze Your Own Identity Development

Review Erikson's theory of identity development and Marcia's research on identity statuses. Analyze your own identity development and discuss how useful Erikson's and Marcia's writing are in understanding your own development.

2. Debate Gender Differences in Behavior

Read some books and articles on sex-role behavior. Decide which of the following positions (Gall & Ward, 1974) is closest to your point of view on sex-linked differences in behavior and defend your position:

a. Everyone, whether male or female, should have an opportunity to develop full intellectual potential. Teachers and others should strive to eliminate traditional sex-role stereotypes, because these biases influence what is learned by boys and girls, and thus prevent them from reaching their full potential.
b. Many differences in the behavior of boys and girls are desirable. They should not be eliminated even if it means some individuals will not achieve their full potential. For example, achievement of a woman's full intellectual potential may not be desirable if it, in turn, necessitates the loss of her sensitivity to others. (p. 263)

3. Analyze Texts for Sex Stereotyping

A number of studies have uncovered sex stereotyping between the covers of books used in public schools. For example, the authors often depict boys as ingenious, creative, brave, and adventurous—and depict girls as lonely, frightened, and poorly motivated.

Examine at random three books used at the elementary level in a local school or in the curriculum materials section of your college library. Ask a class member of the opposite sex to examine the same books and record the titles and grade levels of the books. Indicate the number of times males and females are the central characters and put a tally mark next to the words listed below that you feel reflect the behavior of characters portrayed in the texts. Include some direct quotes or situations that illustrate sex stereotyping (Biehler, 1974).

Males		Females
	Number of main characters	
	Adventurous	
	Ambitious	
	Creative	
	Dependent	
	Engaged in home chores	
	Engaged in important, exciting work	
	Helpless	
	Self-confident	

What conclusions do you draw from your analysis?

4. Learn about Child-rearing Methods

Read one of the following books on child rearing: *P.E.T.: Parent Effectiveness Training* (Gordon, 1975); *Children: The Challenge* (Dreikurs & Soltz, 1964); *Systematic Training for Effective Parenting* (Dinkmeyer & McKay, 1976); or *Living with Children* (Patterson & Guillion, 1971). Summarize the major ideas in the book and report how they can be helpful to parents.

Key Terms

psychosocial crises, p. 438
psychosocial moratorium, p. 440
identity diffusion, p. 442
identity moratorium, p. 442
identity foreclosure, p. 442
identity achievement, p. 442
androgyny, p. 447
self-concept, p. 456
self-esteem, p. 456
self-fulfilling prophecy, p. 460
anorexia nervosa, p. 461
puberty, p. 462
authoritarian parenting style, p. 466
permissive parenting style, p. 466
authoritative parenting style, p. 466
latchkey children, p. 477
prosocial behavior, p. 479

Suggestions for Further Reading

Adams, G. R., Gullotta, T. P., & Montemayor, R. (Eds.). (1992). *Adolescent identity formation.* Newbury Park, CA: Sage. A book of readings analyzing research issues in identity formation.

Emery, R. E. (1988). *Marriage, divorce, and children's adjustment* (Vol. 14). Newbury Park, CA: Sage. A helpful review of literature on family transition.

Grusec, J. E., & Lytton, H. (1988). *Social development: History, theory, and research.* New York: Springer-Verlag. Provides excellent discussions of family socialization, prosocial behavior, and divorce.

Hamner, T. J., & Turner, P. H. (1991). *Parenting in contemporary society* (2nd ed.). Englewood Cliffs, NJ: Prentice-Hall. A comprehensive review of parenting techniques, family variations, and support systems for parents.

The following books focus on the role of self-concept in school achievement:

Beane, J. A., & Lipka, R. P. (1986). *Self-concept, self-esteem, and the curriculum.* New York: Teachers College Press. Shows how curriculum planning can lead to improved self-perceptions.

Canfield, J., & Wells, H. C. (1976). *100 ways to enhance self-concept in the classroom.* Englewood Cliffs, NJ: Prentice-Hall.

Hamachek, D. E. (1978). *Encounters with the self* (2nd ed.). New York: Holt, Rinehart & Winston. Discusses the many factors influencing an individual's self-concept.

For more information on the treatment of male and female students in school:

American Association of University Women. (1992). *How schools shortchange girls.* Washington, DC: AAUW. This reference is a comprehensive report on the major research findings on girls and education.

Sadker, M., & Sadker, D. (1986). Sexism in the classroom: From grade school to graduate school. *Phi Delta Kappan,* 67, 512–515. Reviews classroom research on teacher interaction with males and females.

Shapiro, J., Kramer, S., & Hunerberg, C. (1981). *Equal their chances: Children's activities for non-sexist learning.* Englewood Cliffs, NJ: Prentice-Hall. A good reference for making changes in the treatment of male and female students.

The following references deal with student stress:

Blom, G. E., Cheney, B., & Snoddy, J. E. (1986). *Stress in childhood: An intervention model for teachers and other professionals.* New York: Teachers College Press. Provides an intervention model that can be applied in school.

Humphrey, J. H., & Humphrey, J. N. (1981). *Reducing stress in children through creative relaxation.* Springfield, IL: Thomas.

Humphrey, J. H., & Humphrey, J. N. (1985). *Controlling stress in children.* Springfield, IL: Thomas.

Kuczen, B. (1982). *Childhood stress: Don't let your child be a victim.* New York: Delacorte Press.

The following work is on child abuse:

Brassard, M. R., Germain, R., & Hart, S. N. (Eds.). (1987). *Psychological maltreatment of children and youth.* New York: Pergamon Press. Focuses on various forms of physical and psychological mistreatment of children.

Chapter 11

Exceptional Children

Exceptional Children—An Overview

Labeling: Pro and Con

Categories in Special Education

Mental Retardation

Learning Disabilities

Behavior Disorders

Hearing Impairment

Visual Impairment

Communication Disorders

Physical and Health Impairment

Gifted and Talented

Legal Rights of Exceptional Children and Their Parents

Public Law 94-142

Individualized Education Program (IEP)

Debate Forum: Is the Regular Classroom the Best Place to Remediate Most Academic Deficiencies?

Public Law 99-457

Classroom Application: Preparing an Individualized Education Program (IEP)

Public Law 101-476

Parents of Exceptional Children

Implications for Instruction: The Challenge to the Regular Classroom Teacher

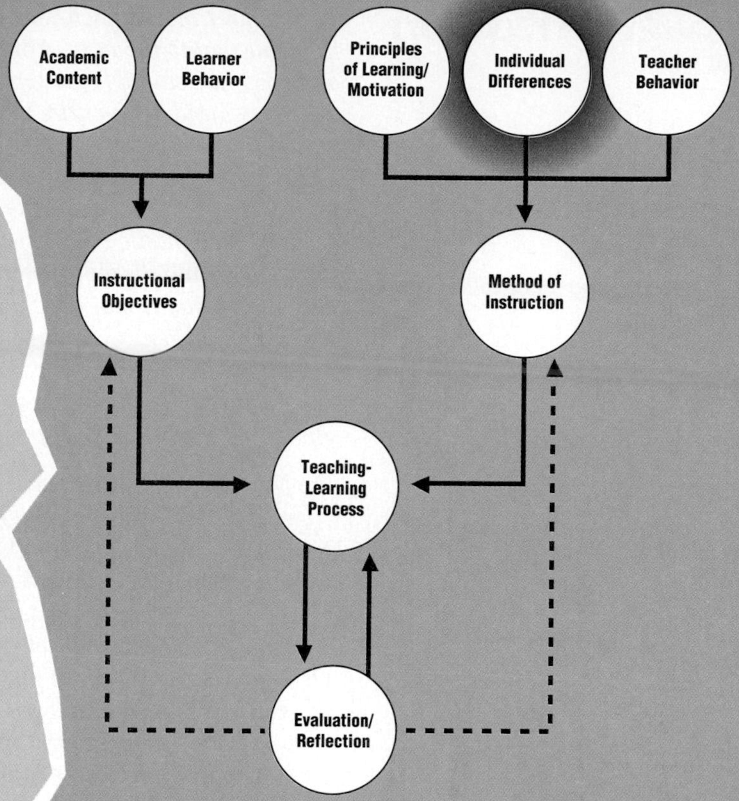

OBJECTIVES

After mastering the material in this chapter you will be able to:

- Identify students who may need special education assistance.
- Identify the legal requirements and issues in special education.
- Identify the teacher's role in referral, assessment, and placement procedures.
- Implement intervention strategies that can help exceptional students succeed in the regular classroom.

Orientation

Christie is a shy, withdrawn 9-year-old who is repeating the third grade. Her parents decided to retain her based on a recommendation from her previous teacher. Throughout the year, Christie had been unable to remember what she had learned from one day to the next. Although she was able to sound the first couple of letters, and knew the sounds of letters in isolation, this young girl was unable to reproduce the sound of an entire word. She also was having a great deal of difficulty with writing her name.

Because Christie was attending a private elementary school last year, there was no reading specialist available. When her parents inquired about having Christie assessed by a public school specialist, her teacher replied that she "had seen this type of learning disability many times. I know what to do." She suggested, for Christie's benefit, that the child be retained another year to let her catch up with the other children.

Fortunately, Christie's parents inquired independently and were able to make an appointment with a school psychologist in their school district. Here is a brief glimpse of the initial conversation between Christie and Dr. Morgan:

Dr. Morgan: *Hi, Christie. Your mom and dad have told me about some of the problems you have been having with reading. Why don't you tell me how it feels when you try to read.*

Christie: *Well, I want to read things, like the other kids, but I forget how to put all the sounds together. If I look at each one alone, it's pretty easy, but when I try to put them all together, it's hard.*

Dr. Morgan: *You mean putting all the sounds of the letters together?*

Christie: *Uh-huh. I try to remember how they go, but after I get the first one, I forget the rest.*

Dr. Morgan: *How does it make you feel when you can't get the sound out?*

Christie: *I get really mad at myself, and then I begin to think I'm dumb. If the other kids can do it, why can't I? I don't want to be in a different class than my friends, but now I have to be with the little kids.*

Dr. Morgan: *Christie, I think I know what the problem is, but I'm going to have to give you some tests that may help me to better understand your problem, okay?*

Christie: *Will they hurt?*

Dr. Morgan: *Oh, no, they're not those kind. These are really easy tests to see what's making it so hard for you to remember letters and sounds. Is it okay with you if I give you a few of these tests?*

Christie: *Sure. Does this mean I don't have to stay in third grade again next year?*

Dr. Morgan: *Let's see what the tests show, and then we can talk to your parents, okay?*

Christie: *Okay.*

A sizable group of students possess individual differences that require special types of education. At one time, classroom teachers had little to do with children with disabilities because they were rarely included in the regular classroom. Instead, they were educated, if at all, by special education teachers in self-contained classrooms or residential schools separated from their nonhandicapped or nonexceptional peers.

A federal law passed in 1975, the **Education for All Handicapped Children Act (P.L. 94-142)** mandated many changes in the education of exceptional students. These changes require that such students have the right to due process, protection against discriminatory testing in diagnosis, individualized program plans, and placement in an educational setting that is the least restrictive environment.

One of the requirements of P.L. 94-142 is that an **individualized education program (IEP)** be written by a committee for each student who is receiving special education services. The IEP is a system of accountability that requires specific learning objectives. As the student's teacher you will be one person on this committee. You will need to learn how to write specific objectives, translate them into effective teaching strategies, and evaluate their outcomes.

The concept of **least restrictive educational environment** has especially important implications for the classroom teacher because it implies that children with disabilities should be educated with their nonhandicapped peers in regular settings whenever possible. As a result, it is not uncommon to observe a student who is mentally retarded, learning disabled, or visually impaired in a regular classroom for all or part of the day. It is now essential for all teachers to acquire knowledge about exceptional children.

Three terms—**exceptional**, **disabled**, and **handicapped**—are widely used by educators to identify children who need special educational services. *Exceptional* refers to any student whose performance significantly departs from the average or typical student, either below or above, to such an extent that special education is needed. As a result, the exceptional student includes both the intellectually gifted and the severely retarded. *Disability* (or impairment) is a particular condition that limits a student's functioning in certain tasks (e.g., visual, motor, or auditory). *Handicap* refers to the difficulties that an individual who is disabled faces because of possible limitations encountered in the interaction with the environment. *Handicapped* is a more restrictive term than *exceptional* and does not include the intellectually gifted (Heward & Orlansky, 1992).

A disabled person may be handicapped in one situation but not in another. For example, a person in a wheelchair is not handicapped when participating in a debate tournament but is handicapped when encountering a flight of stairs that must be ascended.

Educators use the following classification for exceptional students:

1. Mental retardation
2. Learning disabilities
3. Behavior disorders (emotional disturbances)
4. Communication (speech and language) disorders
5. Hearing impairments
6. Visual impairments
7. Physical and other health impairments
8. Severe and multiple handicaps
9. Gifted and talented

The purpose of special education is to develop educational programs to help exceptional children to achieve the greatest possible self-sufficiency

Education for All Handicapped Children Act (P.L. 94-142). A federal law that mandates specific educational procedures and rights for children with disabilities.

individualized education program (IEP). A document that details a yearly instructional plan for a child with a disability.

least restrictive educational environment. The educational setting most like the regular classroom in which an individual can succeed.

exceptional. A term describing children whose performance deviates from the norm to the extent that special education is needed.

disabled. A term describing children with physical problems that limit their ability to perform certain tasks.

handicapped. A term describing children who have a physical disability or behavioral characteristic so severe that they require special help to profit from instruction.

and academic success—goals that are appropriate for all students (Heward & Orlansky, 1992).

The discussion of self-concept in the previous chapter has important implications for exceptional students. Recent research indicates that students with learning problems do not have a low general self-concept; they appear to have a lower *academic* self-concept than their nonhandicapped peers. There also is evidence to indicate that these students believe that they don't have the ability to achieve and have low expectations for future achievement (Chapman, 1989). Since students with learning problems have the potential to succeed, teachers need to be especially sensitive to negative perceptions by these students as they attempt to help them succeed. The discussion of maladaptive self-perceptions in Chapter 4, (Motivation) is especially relevant to some exceptional students.

Knowledge of teacher behavior and classroom management, discussed in Chapter 7, will be helpful for organizing the classroom and for managing and interacting with students. As you will learn in this chapter, the teacher's attitudes regarding exceptional children in regular classrooms can play an important role in successful mainstreaming. Therefore, you need to explore your attitudes and beliefs about special education and exceptional children because your beliefs and expectations often determine the way students are treated and how much they will learn.

Finally, exceptional students probably are subjected to more testing than average students are. Information derived from various assessments can help the classroom teacher to develop the most appropriate instructional program for the student. Therefore, because the classroom teacher has to make important decisions regarding instructional strategies, you need to understand what the diagnostic instruments indicate so that you can teach more effectively.

Before reading this chapter, you should be aware of a number of points:

- Books and journal articles are available for all categories of special education. This chapter does not attempt to provide all the information you will need to know about a particular student, but it will provide you with a good foundation on which to build your knowledge concerning exceptional children.
- Although areas in special education are discussed separately for clarity, many children have multiple handicaps and must be dealt with accordingly.
- Exceptional children represent a heterogeneous group. For example, even though two children may be identified as mentally retarded, they will differ as much as two of their nonhandicapped peers. Students with a similar handicap have individual personalities, interests, and educational needs.
- The limitations resulting from a handicap can be lessened by positive interaction and assistance from teachers and peers. As a teacher, you can greatly influence the quality of your students' educational and social experiences. Don't underestimate your impact!

Think about your past and present experiences with children with disabilities. Were these experiences positive? Have you been in situations that you found uncomfortable? Why? How do you feel about teaching exceptional children?

EXCEPTIONAL CHILDREN—AN OVERVIEW

It is difficult to determine exactly how many children with disabilities there are among the estimated 40 million students enrolled in U.S. public schools (preschool through grade 12). The *Fourteenth Annual Report to Congress on the Implementation of the Education of the Handicapped Act* (U.S. Department of Education, 1992) presents data on the percentage and number of students *enrolled* in special education in 1990 to 1991 (see Table 11.1). Of the 4,367,630 served in various school programs, the largest number were classified as learning disabled (49.1 percent), followed by speech or language impaired (22.7 percent).

TABLE 11.1 NUMBER OF CHILDREN AGES 6–21 WITH DISABILITIES

Disability	Percentage Enrolled in Special Education	Number Enrolled in Special Education
Learning Disabilities	49.1	2,144,377
Speech or Language Impairments	22.7	990,186
Mental Retardation	12.7	552,658
Behavior Disordered	9.0	392,559
Multiple Disabilities	2.2	97,625
Hearing Impairments	1.4	59,312
Orthopedic Impairments	1.1	49,393
Other Health Impairments	1.3	56,312
Visual Impairments	0.5	23,686
Deaf-blindness	0.0	1,522
All conditions	100.0	4,367,630

Source: U.S. Department of Education, 1992.

The report, however, contains no estimates of the total number of children with disabilities in the United States. Educators and government officials often debate whether all or nearly all handicapped students are being served by special education programs. Recent data indicate that the number of students identified as learning disabled has increased every academic year since 1976–1977, when the federal government first required states to count their special education students in order to receive federal financial assistance. Some educators believe this steady increase is caused by inaccurate assessment that leads to overplacement, whereas others believe that students with handicaps other than learning disabilities are being placed in the wrong category. For example, a decreasing number of children are being identified as mentally retarded, a fact that may be related to the increase in the identification of learning disabled children (*Education of the Handicapped,* 1986). On the other hand, many special educators believe that social influences since the 1970s, such as the breakup of the family unit and the use of drugs by parents, may contribute to the *actual* increase in learning disabilities found in children.

One of the major debates in special education involves the pros and cons of using categories, or labels, to distinguish one type, or group, of students from another. Some educators argue that a system of classification is needed in order to provide special education services to meet the students' unique needs in the classroom, to educate teachers and give them the necessary skills to maximize the achievement of students with various handicapping conditions, and to document the prevalence of specific disabilities to guarantee continued funding for special educational programs. For example, the federal government has spent as much as $1 billion a year for special education. Unless categories are established to determine who should get these funds, there could be a decrease in the support for special education. Other educators believe that the labels are not helpful in providing educational services for students and, in fact, may be detrimental for some.

Labeling: Pro and Con

? What are the advantages and disadvantages of special education labels?

Heward and Orlansky (1992) provide a comprehensive list of the arguments raised for and against the classification of exceptional children. As you read about different types of exceptional children, think about whether the benefits of labeling outweigh the disadvantages.

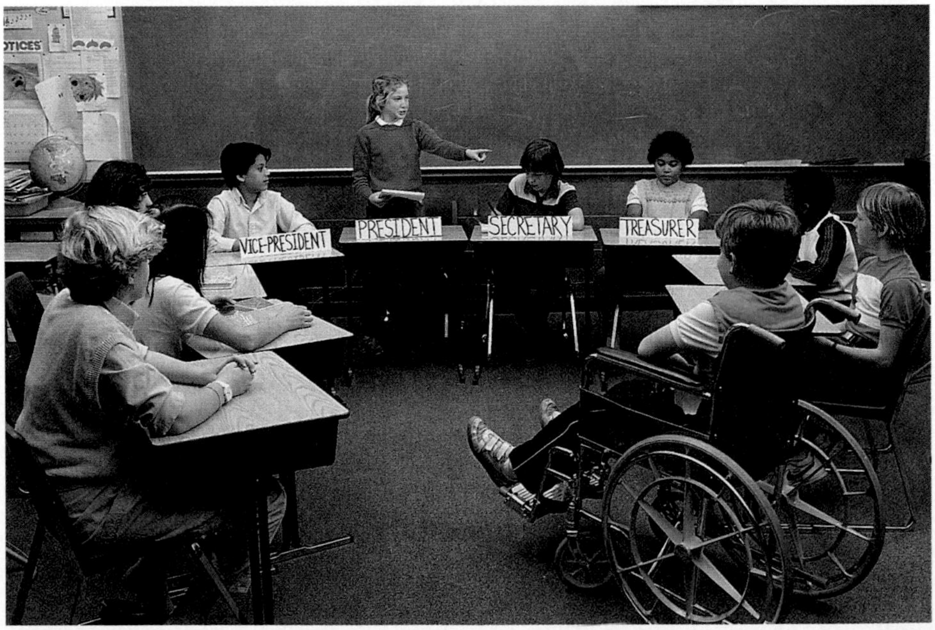

Many children with disabilities are able to function successfully in the classroom.

Possible Benefits of Labeling

1. Categories can relate diagnosis to specific treatment.
2. Labeling may lead to a "protective" response, in which nonlabeled children accept certain behaviors of their handicapped peers more fully than they would accept those same behaviors in "normal" children.
3. Labeling helps professionals to communicate with one another and to classify and assess research findings.
4. Funding of special education programs is often based on specific categories of exceptionality.
5. Labels allow special interest groups to promote specific programs and spur legislative action.
6. Labeling helps make the special needs of exceptional children more visible in the public.

Possible Disadvantages of Labeling

1. Labels usually focus on a child's negative aspects, causing others to think about the child only in terms of inadequacies or defects.
2. Labels may cause others to react to and hold expectations for a child based on the label, resulting in a self-fulfilling prophecy [see Chapter 10].
3. Labels that describe a child's performance deficit often mistakenly acquire the role of explanatory constructs (e.g., "Sherry acts that way because she is emotionally disturbed").
4. Labels tend to suggest that learning problems are primarily the result of something wrong within the child, thereby reducing the systematic examination of instructional variables as the cause of performance deficits.
5. A labeled child may develop a poor self-concept.
6. Labels may lead peers to reject or ridicule the labeled child.
7. Special education labels have a certain permanence; once labeled "retarded" or "learning disabled," a child has difficulty ever again achieving the status of being "just another kid."
8. Labels often provide a basis for keeping children out of the regular classroom.
9. A disproportionate number of children from minority culture groups have been inaccurately labeled "handicapped," especially as educable mentally retarded.
10. The classification of exceptional children requires the expenditure of a great amount of professional and student time that could better be spent in planning and delivering instruction. (pp. 13–14)

CATEGORIES IN SPECIAL EDUCATION

Each of the various categories of exceptional children includes a definition, methods of classification, characteristics and etiology (causes) of the handicap, and some suggestions for the regular classroom teacher for helping the student. As you read this section, keep in mind that in some categories

mental retardation. A significantly subaverage general intellectual function existing concurrently with deficits in adaptive behavior and manifested during the development period.

identification and diagnosis are not always clear-cut (especially in the areas of mental retardation, learning disability, and behavior disorders) and that each category of exceptionality is not necessarily independent. For example, the child with a hearing impairment may also exhibit a learning disability and/or a behavior disorder, making it difficult to sort out a specific causality and making it necessary to employ a wide variety of intervention strategies. Thus, appropriately educating exceptional students is a process built on determining each individual child's needs, rather than on providing the "correct" label and following a prescribed intervention.

Mental Retardation

DEFINITION/CLASSIFICATION. The American Association of Mental Deficiency (AAMD) defines **mental retardation** as follows (Grossman, 1983):

> Mental retardation refers to significantly subaverage general intellectual functioning resulting in or associated with concurrent impairment in adaptive behavior, and manifested during the developmental period. (p. 11)

This definition includes two important characteristics—*below average intellectual functioning* and *deficits in adaptive behavior* (i.e., how one deals with the demands of one's environment). Both criteria must be met for a child to be classified mentally retarded. This definition attempts to protect individuals from improper diagnosis and labeling.

? Why is an IQ score alone insufficient to label a student mentally retarded?

In the past, many children (especially from minority groups) were identified as retarded inside the school but were functioning very effectively outside the school (i.e., the students were not deficient in adaptive behavior skills) (Landesman & Ramey, 1989). This condition led the President's Committee on Mental Retardation to entitle its 1970 report *The Six Hour Retarded Child.* Many individuals, such as sociologist Jane Mercer (1973), believe that it is the individual's social system that determines whether the person is considered retarded. Remember the discussion in Chapter 8 regarding the large number of African American and Latino students that Mercer found in special education classes in Riverside, California. Many educators don't realize that "mental retardation is an arbitrarily defined diagnostic category [and the] actual practices used to identify children with mental retardation vary dramatically across states and school districts" (Landesman & Ramsey, 1989, p. 409).

The research by Mercer and others has focused more attention on cultural diversity in special education. According to Kamp and Chinn (1982), about one-third of the entire population of special education students in the United States consists of students from diverse cultural groups. Educators have a responsibility to ensure that culturally diverse students receive a fair assessment of their ability and that instruction be sensitive to their cultural background.

educable mentally retarded (EMR). A label for mildly retarded children.

The words *significantly subaverage general intellectual functioning* in the AAMD's definition usually refer to performance on an individually administered standardized test of intelligence. This level of functioning is generally defined as an IQ of 70 or below. However, this upper limit is intended only as a guideline and can be raised according to the type of test used or if a psychologist determines that an individual's deficits in living in the environment are caused by impaired intellectual functioning. The AAMD distinguishes the severity of retardation as mild, moderate, severe, or profound. Mildly retarded children and adolescents are sometimes referred to by educators as **educable mentally retarded (EMR).** The majority of students who are mentally retarded are identified in the mild category and can become independent and learn to read, write, and use basic mathematics.

An important aspect of the mental retardation definition is that it recognizes the influence of adaptive behavior. A person may score low on an intelligence test but have adequate adaptive ability. These behaviors are age- and situation-specific (e.g., eating, toilet use, money handling, shopping skills, and language development). Many adaptive behavior scales have been developed. Two commonly used scales are the AAMD Adaptive Behavior Scale and the Vineland Social Maturity Scale. Mercer (Mercer & Lewis, 1978) has developed a comprehensive system designed to evaluate the current level of functioning and the potential of children from various cultures. The System of Multi-Cultural Pluralistic Assessment (SOMPA) is especially useful in identifying the learning potential of students who may not have had the opportunities to learn the skills measured by individual tests of intelligence. The SOMPA includes a measure of intelligence, but its interpretation is based on the students' cultural background.

CAUSES. In most cases of mild retardation, the causes are unknown. However, psychologists believe that the combination of poor social and cultural environment early in a person's life may lead to retarded development. Psychologists are particularly interested in studying the impact of diet and certain prenatal influences such as drugs, alcohol, and smoking on fetal abnormalities and intellectual development.

There are many known causes of moderate, severe, and profound retardation. The AAMD has identified the following categories: infections and intoxications; trauma and physical agents (such as accidents before, during, and after birth); metabolism and nutrition; and gross postnatal brain disease (such as tumors). An example of an infection that can cause retardation is rubella, or German measles. When contracted by a woman during the first three months of pregnancy, it may cause visual impairments, hearing impairments, mental retardation, and/or other birth defects in her child. Additional categories include prenatal influence (such as hydrocephalus, a condition involving an enlarged head caused by accumulated

learning disabilities. A wide variety of disorders causing learning problems that cannot be attributed to emotional difficulties, retardation, or sensory impairment.

cerebrospinal fluid); chromosomal abnormality (such as Down syndrome[1]), and gestational disorders (such as premature birth) (Heward & Orlansky, 1992).

The most common characteristics that you may notice with students classified as having varying degrees of mental retardation are social and academic learning problems. They need more practice and experience than others of the same age to retain information previously learned, to generalize or transfer recently learned skills to new situations, to learn language, and to develop self-care skills and peer interactions. They often display immature and inappropriate classroom behavior and often are subjected to teasing and isolation by their nonhandicapped peers. You must be aware that because of the history of failure that many of these children experience, they tend to become overly dependent upon others to tell them what to do or may develop a general reluctance to engage in new learning situations. As with other handicaps, mental retardation may co-occur with any number of additional handicaps, such as hearing, visual, or motor deficits.

IMPLICATIONS FOR TEACHING. Hallahan and Kauffman (1988) provide a number of suggestions for the regular teacher who may have students with mental retardation in the classroom:

1. Separate learning tasks into small steps, sequence them in the proper order, and teach one skill at a time [remember the discussion of task analysis in Chapter 6].
2. Use drill and repetition.
3. Ask the students to rehearse orally what they learn. This procedure will help their memory.
4. Use different motivational strategies. Novelty in presenting lessons is a good strategy, but too much change can be confusing to students who are mentally retarded because they need a sense of structure and familiarity.
5. Use consistent reinforcement, especially in the development of learning skills (e.g., working independently and completing assignments).
6. Assess the students' progress on a regular basis so that changes in objectives and/or instruction can be made.
7. Provide continuous and immediate feedback for all learning activities.

Learning Disabilities

What are the special problems in identifying students with learning disabilities?

DEFINITION/CLASSIFICATION. There is much controversy in the area of **learning disabilities** about the identification of its population, primarily

[1] *Down syndrome* is a condition resulting from a chromosomal abnormality characterized by such physical signs as slanted-appearing eyes, flattened features, shortness, and a tendency toward obesity.

because the term *learning disability* is not a unitary concept and does not represent a homogeneous population. The Education for All Handicapped Children Act (P.L. 94–142) includes the following definition:

> "Specific learning disability" means a disorder in one or more of the basic psychological processes involved in understanding or in using language, spoken or written, which may manifest itself in an imperfect ability to listen, think, speak, read, write, spell, or to do mathematical calculations. The term includes such conditions as perceptual handicaps, brain injury, minimal brain dysfunction, dyslexia, and developmental aphasia.[2] The term does not include children who have learning problems which are primarily the result of visual, hearing, or motor handicaps, of mental retardation, or of environmental, cultural, or economic disadvantages. (United States Office of Education, 1977, p. 65083)

The criteria for classification to receive special education services under this category vary from state to state. Most states and school districts require that three criteria be met (Heward & Orlansky, 1992, p. 134):

- A discrepancy between the child's potential and actual achievement
- An exculsion criterion
- The need for special education services

The *discrepancy criterion* attempts to protect against misidentifying students as having a specific learning disability. For example, if a student has a minor or temporary problem in learning a mathematical concept, the child should not be labeled as having a learning disability. However, if the student consistently functions significantly below the expected level of achievement and his or her academic potential is at least average, he or she may have a learning disability. The *exculsion criterion* limits the label *learning disability* to those students whose learning problems are not explained by other diagnostic categories (e.g., mental retardation or visual impairment) or by a social and/or environmental deprivation causing a lack of opportunity to learn. The *special education criterion* indicates that the students show specific learning problems in spite of normal educational efforts and therefore require special educational services to help them become successful learners.

Even with these criteria there is confusion. For example, what constitutes a discrepancy between intellectual potential and academic achievement—one year or two years or more below grade level? Is a one-year discrepancy at the third grade the same as at the eighth grade? What about preschoolers or first graders who have learning problems but the comparison of intelligence and achievement tests indicates that the students are only slightly below expected achievement levels? Based on this criterion, they would not receive special services until they "qualify" by falling further behind their classmates (Chalfant, 1989).

The literature identifies many characteristics of students with learning disabilities. Tarver and Hallahan (1976) list the 10 most often cited traits:

[2] *Dyslexia* is an impairment of the ability to read. *Aphasia* is the loss or impairment of the ability to understand or formulate language and is caused by neurological damage.

1. Hyperactivity
2. Perceptual-motor impairments
3. Emotional lability (ups and down, moodiness)
4. General coordination deficits
5. Attentional disorders (distractibility)
6. Impulsivity
7. Memory and thinking disorders
8. Specific academic problems
9. Speech and hearing disorders
10. Equivocal neurological signs (e.g., abnormal brain wave patterns that are difficult to explain or interpret) (p. 13)

A student *may be* identified as having a learning disability if the student exhibits one or more of the foregoing characteristics; not all characteristics would be present within one student. The key determiner is whether or not he or she meets the specific criteria designated by the state or local school district. Table 11.2 identifies specific classroom behaviors that the teacher should be concerned about. Again, it is important to note that if a child possesses any of the identified characteristics but is achieving normally in school, the child would not be considered learning disabled.

TABLE 11.2 WAYS TO RECOGNIZE A LEARNING DISABLED STUDENT

Classroom Behavior	***Spelling***
Moves constantly	Uses incorrect order of letters in words
Has difficulty beginning or completing tasks	Has difficulty associating correct sound with appropriate letter
Is often tardy or absent	Reverses letters and words (mirror image)
Is generally quiet or withdrawn	
Has difficulty with peer relationships	***Writing***
Is disorganized	Cannot stay on line
Is easily distracted	Has difficulty copying from board or other source
Displays inconsistencies in behavior	Uses poor written expression for age
Seems to misunderstand oral directions	Is slow in completing written work
Academic Symptoms ***Reading***	Uses cursive writing and printing in same assignment
Loses place, repeats words	
Does not read fluently	***Verbal***
Confuses similar words and letters	Hesitates often when speaking
Uses fingers to follow along	Has poor verbal expression for age
Does not read willingly	
Arithmetic	***Motor***
Has difficulty associating number with symbol	Displays poor coordination
Cannot remember math facts	Has problems of balance
Confuses columns and spacing	Confuses right and left
Has difficulty with story problems	Lacks rhythm in movement
Fails to comprehend math concepts	Has poor muscle strength

Source: Summers, 1977.

CAUSES. The suspected causes of learning disabilities fall into three major categories: minimal brain damage, biochemical imbalance, and environmental factors (Heward & Orlansky, 1992). Some specialists (particularly in the medical profession) believe that learning disabled children suffer from some form of brain injury. Because the injury is not extensive enough to cause serious intellectual impairment (i.e., mental retardation), the term **minimal brain damage** is used in discussing learning disabled children. Special educators do not like this label because it is misleading. First, the problems faced by many students with learning disabilities are far from small. Second, the label conveys little hope for improved learning through effective intervention strategies. Finally, there is a lack of clear evidence to support brain damage as a cause for all learning disabilities. Research studies have identified children with brain damage who are not learning disabled and learning disabled children who do not display clinical (medical) evidence of brain damage (Coles, 1978; Nichols & Chen, 1981).

minimal brain damage. A term used by some specialists, who subscribe to the controversial belief that learning disabled children suffer from some form of brain injury.

Some specialists claim that biochemical disturbances within children lead to learning disabilities. Feingold (1975a, 1975b) has received a good deal of publicity regarding his claims that hyperactivity and learning problems are caused by artificial colorings and flavorings in many of the foods children eat. He claims that placing hyperactive children on special diets will bring about a change in behavior. In a similar vein, Cott (1972) hypothesized that learning disability can be caused by a vitamin deficiency. Many physicians supporting this contention began megavitamin therapy with learning disabled children. This therapy involves massive daily doses of certain vitamins to overcome the suspected deficiencies. Research investigations on food additives (Kavale & Forness, 1983) and vitamin deficiency (Kershner, Hawks, & Grekin, 1977) have failed to show that such specific corrective actions improve the performance of learning disabled children.

Another group of specialists believe that the quality of instruction and the student's emotional and motivational state greatly influence academic performance (e.g., Engelmann, 1977; Lovitt, 1978). These researchers think that the best way to help students with learning disabilities is to focus on the specific deficiencies in reading, math, or language that are causing the academic problems.

IMPLICATIONS FOR TEACHING. There are several approaches to planning educational programs for learning disabled students. A complete discussion of these techniques is beyond the scope of this book. For the most part, these approaches are related to the specialist's belief in the causes of the disability and the student's specific problem. For example, educators who believe that the learning problem is caused by dysfunctional psychological processes would provide training in these areas. Thus a student believed to have reading problems because of difficulties in visual perception would receive training in visual perception rather than in reading techniques (see Lerner, 1984, for a discussion of these methods). Don't confuse perceptual problems with visual acuity problems, which will be discussed later in this chapter. A child may have 20/20 vision but have

Special equipment is available to help students improve their listening skills.

difficulty in organizing and interpreting visual stimuli. Likewise, a child may have normal hearing (acuity) but still have a problem with interpreting or discriminating sounds (auditory perception).

Today, many educators are taking a more direct approach in working with students with learning disabilities. That is to say, rather than training psychological processes that are linked to learning, they emphasize techniques that are directly related to learning subject matter. Behavioral psychologists focus on breaking subject matter into small steps and carefully teaching the knowledge prerequisite for learning. Cognitive psychologists emphasize techniques based on information processing. This approach stresses learning strategies to teach students "how to learn." One example of such a program for secondary learning disabled students is the Learning Strategies Curriculum (Schumaker et al., 1983; Schumaker, Deshler, & Ellis, 1986). It emphasizes strategies for acquiring information from written material, techniques for remembering information, and methods for improving written expression.

Current research indicates that techniques that stress careful instruction in the academic areas and the information-processing approaches tend to be more successful than the earlier indirect approaches that attempted to train students in the dysfunctional process interfering with learning (Lloyd, 1988). These new programs offer considerable assistance for helping students with learning disabilities become successful learners.

The classroom teacher needs to keep in mind a number of special considerations when working with learning disabled students (Hallahan & Kauffman, 1988):

1. Set reasonable goals. Because some students may have a relatively high IQ, you may assume they can do more than they are actually

capable of doing. Since students with learning disabilities often find it difficult to tolerate failure, find opportunities for them to experience success.
2. Provide clear instructions for the students and assume that your directions may not be understood. Be aware that students with learning disabilities often look as if they understand what is being said, when in fact they are confused.
3. Make special physical arrangements for the highly distractible and hyperactive student (e.g., place the student's desk in a corner or use walls to form a "cubicle"). (The teacher must be sure to communicate to the student and parents that these procedures are not punitive.) Also, to reduce overstimulation, remove extraneous materials from the student's desk so that the student can concentrate on the immediate task.
4. Be prepared for emotional outbursts by learning disabled students; set guidelines for appropriate classroom behavior and help the students to work toward them.

behavior disordered. A category in special education for students exhibiting serious and persistent inappropriate behaviors that result in social conflict and/or personal unhappiness that affects school performance.

Behavior Disorders

DEFINITION/CLASSIFICATION. Many labels are used as general terms for emotional and behavior problems (e.g., *emotionally disturbed, behavior disorders, socially maladjusted, emotionally handicapped, psychologically disordered*).

Seriously emotionally disturbed was the term used when P.L. 94–142 was passed. However, many special educators prefer the term **behavior disordered** because it focuses attention on the most obvious problem of these children—disordered behavior (Hallahan & Kauffman, 1988). Although there are many definitions and classification procedures to identify these individuals, P.L. 94–142 uses the following:

> (i) The term means a condition exhibiting one or more of the following characteristics over a long period of time and to a marked extent, which adversely affects educational performance:
> (A) An inability to learn which cannot be explained by intellectual, sensory, and health factors;
> (B) An inability to build or maintain satisfactory relationships with peers and teachers;
> (C) Inappropriate types of behavior or feelings under normal circumstances;
> (D) A general pervasive mood of unhappiness or depression;
> (E) A tendency to develop physical symptoms or fears associated with personal or school problems. (*Federal Register*, August 23, 1977, p. 42478)

Behavior displayed by behavior-disordered students is characterized by *excesses* and *deficits* (Whelan & Gallagher, 1972). Behavior excesses are outcomes that are exhibited to a great extent (e.g., too many fights or tantrums). Deficits are behaviors that are exhibited very infrequently or not at all (e.g., few social contacts or homework assignments not completed). The problem in diagnosis is that it is not always easy to determine when a behavior is excessive or when there is a deficit in behavior.

Many teachers are most concerned with behavioral excesses. However, lack of interest, laziness, daydreaming, and general passivity can be more serious problems. It is important for the teacher not to neglect the polite, shy student who never says anything in class or appears withdrawn. That student may need help.

Students with behavior disorders are usually identified first by the classroom teacher, followed by direct classroom observation of the behavior by a school psychologist. Personality tests are used frequently in the diagnosis and classification process. After reviewing research on the role of teacher tolerance in identifying children as behaviorally disordered, Whelan (1981) stated that "emotional disturbance is a function of the perceiver . . . what is disturbance to one teacher may not be to another" (pp. 4–5).

You may be interested in some other data regarding the prevalence of behavior disorders in school. First, more boys than girls are labeled as behavior disordered. Second, more low-socioeconomic and minority-group students are classified as behavior disordered. Third, most behavior-disordered students have academic problems (note that part [A] of the behavior disorders definition could also apply to a student with learning disabilities) (Smith, Wood, & Grimes, 1988).

CAUSES. Although it is often difficult to identify the specific causes of behavioral disorders, four general areas have been identified (Smith & Luckasson, 1992):

- *biology* (e.g., children born with fetal alcohol syndrome (FAS) exhibit emotional problems resulting from brain damage caused by mothers drinking alcohol during pregnancy)
- *school* (e.g., improper classroom environment where aggression, frustration, and/or withdrawal are common responses to the teacher or peers)
- *society* (e.g., extreme poverty, disrupted families, and violent communities can lead to or aggravate behavioral disorders)
- *family* (e.g., unhealthy interactions among family members can create disorders and/or aggravate existing problems)

IMPLICATIONS FOR TEACHING. Many educational strategies for behavior-disordered children have been developed. Nelson and Rutherford (1988) and Carpenter and Apter (1988) provide a detailed explanation of these procedures. Most schools use a variety of approaches such as behavior modification, individual and group counseling, and humanistic school climates for students who have difficulty functioning in traditional educational settings.

Hallahan and Kauffman (1988) provide helpful information for regular classroom teachers who have behavior-disordered students:

hearing impaired. Having a hearing loss significant enough to require special education or training.

1. Ask the special education teacher for advice concerning behavior management and teaching techniques.
2. Let the students know from the beginning that you expect a reasonable standard of conduct to be maintained in the classroom.
3. Communicate your expectations to the students clearly and firmly.
4. Provide consistent and appropriate consequences for behavior. Reward desirable behavior immediately and ignore or, if necessary, use mild punishment for inappropriate behavior.
5. Develop realistic expectations concerning the students' academic goals. Tasks should be challenging but within the students' capacity. Modify objectives if the work is too difficult.
6. Empathize with the students and understand how negative aspects of their social environment (e.g., abuse or criticisms at home or in school) may contribute to the inappropriate behavior. Attempt to improve the quality of their interaction with parents, teachers, and peers.

Hearing Impairment

DEFINITION/CLASSIFICATION. Hearing-impaired children are in two major categories—the deaf and the partially hearing (or hard-of-hearing). The categories are defined as follows (Report of the Ad Hoc Committee to Define Deafness and Hard-of-Hearing, 1975):

> A *deaf* person is one whose hearing disability precludes successful processing of linguistic information through audition, with or without a hearing aid. A *hard-of-hearing* person is one who, generally with the use of a hearing aid, has residual hearing sufficient to enable successful processing of linguistic information through audition. (p. 509)

Sound is measured in units that identify its intensity and frequency. The decibel (db), a unit for measuring the loudness or perceived intensity of sound, is used as a means of classifying the degree of functional hearing. The classification is based on the degree of hearing loss in five categories, from mild to total, and is done by an audiologist, a specialist in the identification and measurement of hearing disorders. The frequency, or pitch, of sounds is assessed in cycles per second, or hertz units. Many hearing loses are only in the pitch range for certain speech sounds. For example, a student whose hearing loss is more serious in the higher frequencies will have difficulty in discriminating the /s/ sound (Heward & Orlansky, 1992).

CAUSES. The major causes of hearing impairment in childhood stem from rubella, meningitis (a viral infection that can destroy the sensitive acoustic apparatus of the inner ear), prematurity and complications of pregnancy, and heredity. Moores (1987) estimates that 30 percent of the school-age population have deaf relatives.

Hearing impairments hinder the development of language and communication ability because individuals learn language through hearing, interpreting, and imitating it. If an individual receives inadequate auditory feedback when making sounds and is unable to hear an adult model adequately, communication problems are likely to develop. The age of onset of the hearing impairment is one of the most important factors in determining the child's language development.

Because language plays such an important role in school learning, one can understand why hearing-impaired children frequently have academic problems. In particular, their reading achievement may be below grade level.

? Is a student's intelligence affected by a hearing impairment?

For a long time, many individuals believed incorrectly that children with hearing impairments, especially those identified as deaf, were also intellectually deficient. The thinking processes of deaf children are similar to those of hearing children, although their verbal intelligence test scores are generally lower than their performance (nonverbal) test scores (Moores, 1987). Unless a hearing-impaired child has other disabilities, as with brain damage, there is no causal relationship between deafness and intelligence. However, a child may not reach full potential unless effective communication training is given.

Language deficiencies can also influence the hearing-impaired child's personality and social development because these factors are greatly dependent upon the communication process. Social interaction, by definition, comprises the communication of ideas between individuals. The hearing-impaired child may respond inappropriately in play situations because of lack of understanding of the rules of games or others'

With appropriate instruction, hearing-impaired students can be successful learners.

intentions. Furth (1973) believes that the greatest disability facing the hearing-impaired individual is not the hearing disability but the failure of parents, professionals, and people in general to understand and accept the person with the disability. Through the use of a total communication method involving a combination of speech therapy, speechreading (also called *lipreading*), and sign languages, hearing-impaired children can function more effectively today than ever before (Hallahan & Kauffman, 1991).

IMPLICATIONS FOR TEACHING. The teacher needs to be alert to possible hearing problems in the classroom. It is not unusual for a child with a mild hearing loss to remain undiagnosed throughout elementary school. The child learns to compensate for the hearing loss so that parents and teachers are unaware of the problems. What is even more distressing is that the children themselves are often unaware of their hearing loss and, as a result, become frustrated and anxious learners as they attempt to adjust to the social and educational demands of the classroom. These children are often inappropriately labeled as slow learners, unmotivated, shy, or lazy.

The following are some of the situations in which the regular classroom teacher should recognize possible symptoms of auditory impairment:

- A child misses school frequently because of earaches or sinus congestion; these illnesses can be a source of temporary or permanent hearing loss.
- A child suffers from allergies and develops head congestion severe enough to bring about reduced hearing acuity for a short time.
- A child appears inattentive or seems to be daydreaming and may not hear the teacher's directions.
- A child is reluctant to participate in class activities; the child may be fearful of failing because of inability to understand.
- A child has problems speaking or understanding language.
- A child demonstrates unusual behavior in response to oral directions.

A teacher should notice specific behaviors indicative of hearing problems, such as cupping the hands behind the ears when attempting to listen or turning one side of the head toward the speaker to favor the better ear.

With enactment of P.L. 94-142, it is not uncommon for the regular classroom teacher to have hard-of-hearing children in class. The following are some suggestions for helping these students succeed (Hallahan & Kauffman, 1988):

1. Allow the students the freedom to move their chairs around the room so that they can position themselves to take advantage of visual and auditory cues.
2. Keep to a minimum all auditory and visual distractors such as noises from the hall, other rooms, and outside. These distractions are also a problem for students with hearing aids because all noises are amplified for them.
3. Optimize the students' opportunities to speechread by maintaining a distance of about 6 feet between yourself and the students. Face the students when talking to them.

visual impairment. A difficulty in clearly distinguishing forms or discriminating details by sight at a specified distance.

4. Facilitate speechreading by speaking naturally. Some individuals have a tendency to exaggerate movements of the mouth when speaking to hearing-impaired children. These children are trained to read lips that form words naturally, so any deviation from normal speech patterns may confuse them rather than help them.
5. Be aware that some hearing-impaired students withdraw from class discussions because they do not hear everything that is said or may be self-conscious about their imperfect speech. Involve them in groups in which they can get support from other students. Ask questions that require only short answers to build their confidence.
6. Be aware that some hearing-impaired students have learned coping skills that help them look as if they understand what is going on when in fact they do not. Many of these skills involve imitating their peers (e.g., raising their hands when other students in the class do or laughing when their classmates laugh). Call by name each student before they speak to alert the hearing-impaired student as to who is about to talk.
7. Encourage the students to ask questions.
8. Make every effort to use visual aids (e.g., overhead projector or chalkboard). Providing hearing-impaired students with a written outline of what will be covered in a lecture or asking a classmate to take notes using carbon paper (the copy to be given to the hearing-impaired) can be helpful to the students.

Visual Impairment

DEFINITION/CLASSIFICATION. There are both legal and educational definitions of **visual impairment.** The legal concept is defined by visual acuity—that is, the ability to discriminate details at a specific distance. The term *20/20* means that at a distance of 20 feet the normal seeing eye should be able to discriminate objects or letters of a certain size. A person with 20/30 or 20/40 vision has a minor visual problem. As the bottom number of the fraction increases, visual acuity decreases. A person whose visual acuity is 20/200 or less in the better eye after correction is legally blind. Persons may also be considered legally blind if their field of vision is extremely restricted.

When looking ahead, a normal eye is able to see objects within a range of approximately 180 degrees. An individual who has extremely restricted vision, 20 degrees or less, is considered legally blind even though the visual acuity in the small area may be good (Heward & Orlansky, 1992).

According to the legal classification system, partially sighted individuals "have visual acuity falling between 20/70 and 20/200 in the better eye with correction" (Hallahan & Kauffman, 1991, p. 304). The educational definition of visual impairment considers the extent to which a student's visual impairment influences learning and the need for special equipment and materials. Educators distinguish between blind and partially sighted, or low vision, students. Blind students are almost totally without sight and can learn to read Braille, using the tactile sense in their fingertips to feel the raised dots of the Braille alphabet. Partially sighted students are able to see the visual print even though they need to use magnifying devices or books with large print.

The federal regulations for P.L. 94–142 define *visually handicapped* for school purposes in such a way that functional vision is primary: "Visually handicapped means a visual impairment which even, with correction, adversely affects a child's educational performance. The term includes both partially seeing and blind children" (U.S. Office of Education, 1977, p. 42479). Educators have determined that functional visual efficiency—the way in which children use their vision—is more important than visual acuity alone in determining the educational needs of the children.

CAUSES. The most common visual problems are the result of errors of refraction. That is, the structure and/or malfunctions in the eye prevent the light rays from focusing correctly, causing myopia (nearsightedness), hyperopia (farsightedness), and astigmatism (blurred vision). These conditions can generally be corrected with glasses or contact lenses. More serious problems are a result of glaucoma (caused by excessive pressure in the eyeball) and cataracts (caused by a clouding of the lens of the eye), which result in blurred vision, and diabetic retinopathy (caused by interference in the blood supply to the retina). There are many other causes for visual problems. Many problems are due to hereditary factors.

Early identification of visual problems is important because students can benefit from specialized intervention as soon as they begin school. Most schools provide services for testing visual acuity. More thorough visual examinations can be conducted by an ophthalmologist (a licensed medical doctor who specializes in the diagnosis and treatment of eye disorders) or an optometrist (a licensed specialist in vision who is trained to examine eyes and enhance vision by nonsurgical means such as glasses and contact lenses).

IMPLICATIONS FOR TEACHING. As a teacher, you must be alert to possible visual disabilities in children. The following are symptoms to watch for (National Society to Prevent Blindness, 1977):

Behavior

- Rubs eyes excessively
- Shuts or covers one eye, tilts head, or thrusts head forward
- Has difficulty in reading or in other work requiring close use of the eyes
- Blinks more than usual or is irritable when doing close work
- Holds books close to eyes
- Is unable to see distant things clearly
- Squints eyelids together or frowns

Appearance

- Crossed eyes
- Red-rimmed, encrusted, or swollen eyelids
- Inflamed or watery eyes
- Recurring sties

Complaints

- Eyes itch, burn, or feel scratchy
- Cannot see well
- Dizziness, headaches, or nausea following close eye work
- Blurred or double vision

There are a number of ways a teacher can help visually impaired students in the classroom. Harley (1973) points out that seeing is affected by factors such as brightness, size of image, contrast, time, and distance. Brightness, or proper illumination, is necessary for students to be able to function successfully in visual tasks. Some students function better with a decrease in normal lighting. Proper seating in the classroom can prevent glare that may be present near the windows. The size of printed symbols is very important to students with visual impairment. Books with large print can be obtained from many publishers. In addition, optical aids for magnification are useful to many visually impaired children. The amount of contrast between an object and its background also affects visual acuity. Nolan (1961) stated that black on white or white on black provides the best contrast for partially seeing students. Time is another important factor in visual acuity. Some students need frequent periods of eye rest, and with their limited field of vision, partially seeing students often proceed at a slower rate. As a result, the teacher should provide the necessary time for these students to complete academic tasks. Last, distance is a factor that should be considered when organizing student seating patterns and presentations of lessons. Visually impaired students should be moved closer to the front of the room and chalkboard or seated so that they can see more effectively.

Hallahan and Kauffman (1988) make some additional suggestions for helping visually impaired students in the classroom:

1. Require the students to care for their own materials in order to foster a sense of independence.
2. Assign sighted students in the class to act as a guide as long as the visually impaired students do not become too dependent upon them.
3. Treat the students the same as their sighted peers; the same expectations should be maintained for all students.
4. Encourage interpersonal interaction between blind students and their sighted peers.
5. Encourage the students to participate in as many activities as possible. Alternative activities should be arranged if it is impossible for them to join in with the rest of the class.
6. Give the students the same kinds of special tasks or responsibilities that are given to other students in the class.

Communication Disorders

DEFINITION/CLASSIFICATION. According to Van Riper (1978), a person has a communication problem when that person's speech differs from

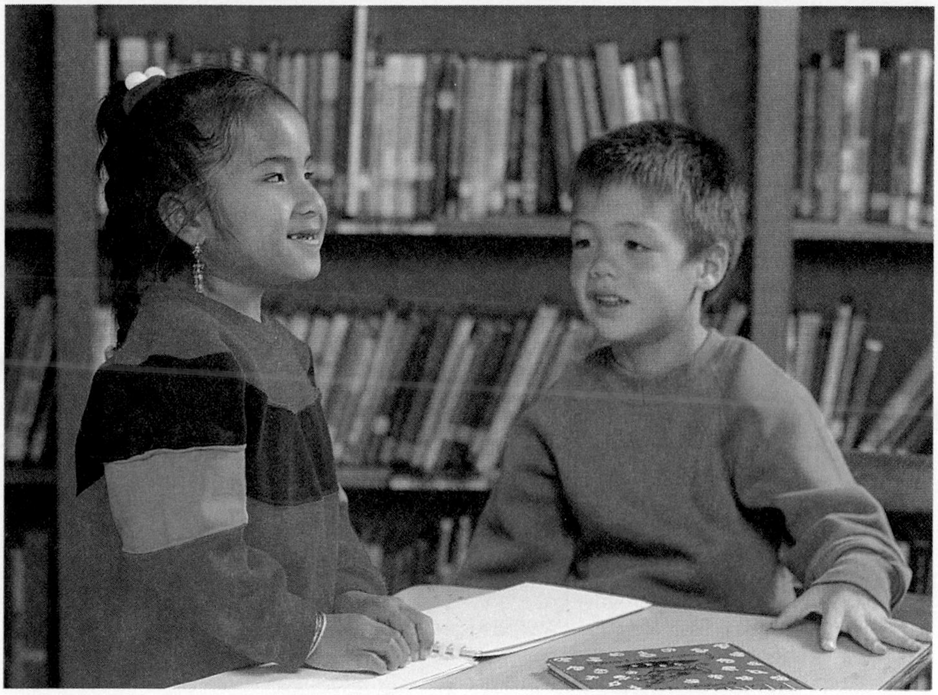

Individualized instructional assistance can help children with disabilities attain educational objectives.

the speech of others to the extent that it calls attention to itself, interferes with the intended message, or causes the speaker or listener to be distressed. The term *speech impaired,* as defined under P.L. 94–142, describes someone with "a communication disorder, such as stuttering, impaired articulation, a language impairment, or a voice impairment which adversely affects a child's educational performance" (*Federal Register,* August, 23, 1977, p. 42479). The speech and language problems referred to in the federal definition can be summarized as problems of articulation, voice, fluency, and language disorders.

speech disorder. Problems associated with production of the oral symbols of language.

language disorder. Difficulties with the linguistic code or rules and conventions for linking symbols and symbol sequences.

Speech disorder and **language disorder** are related, but they are not the same thing. Cartwright, Cartwright, and Ward (1984) state: "Speech problems are those associated with the production of the oral symbols of language, whereas language problems are difficulties with the linguistic code or rules and conventions for linking the symbols and symbol sequences" (p. 115). The Speech and Language Checklist in Table 11.3 serves as a useful guide for helping the classroom teacher to identify students who may need speech or language services. The diagnosis of speech and language disorders is a complex process that requires extensive training. It is conducted by a speech pathologist, a clinician who applies medical and behavioral science to the correction of speech and language disabilities.

CAUSES. The inability to articulate speech sounds correctly can be caused by biological factors (e.g., brain damage, damage to the nerves controlling the muscles used in speech, or gross abnormalities of the oral structures, such as a cleft palate). Other possible conditions contributing to communication disorders are environmental factors—primarily the quality of parent-child communication, emotional disturbances, and hearing loss.

TABLE 11.3 SPEECH AND LANGUAGE CHECKLIST

Communication
Talks very little to adults and/or peers Uses poor eye contact Avoids situations in which communication is imperative
Articulation
Omits sounds in words (e.g., says ouside/outside; tar/star) Distorts sounds in words (e.g., sounds are not precisely on target) Substitutes one sound for another in words (e.g., wed/red; motha/mother; thit/sit; dod/dog) Sounds are unintelligible because of multiple articulation errors
Language
Uses poor sentence structure or has multiple grammatical errors Appears to have limited vocabulary Has difficulty explaining what is intended Frequently gives inappropriate responses Unable to understand the meaning of words, gestures, and/or expressions Unable to understand or follow directions, and asks for frequent repetitions Unable to comprehend or sequence word problems or information presented orally Easily distracted by ambient noises
Fluency
Repeats or prolongs the first sound or syllable of words Repeats whole words or phrases Has difficulty getting some words started (i.e., sound appears blocked) Gets upset when speaking is difficult Frequently looks away while talking Pauses a long time before responding even when the answer is known
Voice
Has constant hoarse or husky voice Sounds unusually high or low in pitch for age and sex Has excessively loud or soft voice Has a nasal-sounding voice most of the time
Hearing
Uses little or no speech Appears shy or withdrawn in a group setting Relies heavily on visual clues (watches speakers' lips, watches and follows movements of others) Asks to have information repeated Lacks clear or distinct speech

Source: Developed by Bernice Sedlik, speech pathologist.

IMPLICATIONS FOR TEACHING. As a teacher, you should be aware of the potential negative consequences in interpersonal relations and the possible development of a poor self-concept by speech-impaired students. For example, the student who stutters is usually subjected to extensive criticism and demands for better speech production.

The following teaching practices can help students with communication disorders in the classroom (Hocevar & Arnold, 1979):

1. Provide a model of acceptance for the students to follow. Show by actions that a communication disorder makes no difference with respect to friendship, academic status, or any other relationship in school.
2. Encourage the students with speech impairments to talk about activities they are involved in outside the school.
3. Children with communication disorders may need to hear a word, expression, sound, or concept used appropriately many times before they will be able or willing to use it.
4. Give the students opportunities to speak without interruption or pressure. Don't finish sentences for the students or add words.
5. Ask the students open-ended rather than yes-no questions. If you get no response, repeat the question or statement, using natural gestures.
6. Listen to what students have to say, and listen attentively with active interest. Do not look away from the students. (p. 175)

Physical and Health Impairment

DEFINITION/CLASSIFICATION. This category of exceptionality involves a broad range of disabilities, including functional (e.g., hand use or mobility), medical, or additional handicaps associated with emotional, social, or educational needs. The guidelines for P.L. 94–142 define *orthopedic impairments* as those having

> a severe orthopedic impairment which adversely affects a child's educational performance. The term includes impairment caused by congenital anomaly (e.g., clubfoot, absence of some member, etc.), impairments caused by disease (e.g., poliomyelitis, bone tuberculosis, etc.), and impairments from other causes (e.g., cerebral palsy, amputations, and fractures or burns which cause contractures. (*Federal Register*, August 23, 1977, p. 42478)

Also identified are those students with *health impairments*, who may exhibit

> limited strength, vitality, or alertness, due to chronic or acute health problems such as a heart condition, tuberculosis, rheumatic fever, nephritis, asthma, sickle cell anemia, hemophilia, epilepsy, lead poisoning, leukemia, or diabetes, which adversely affect a child's educational performance. (*Federal Register*, August 23, 1977, p. 42478)

TABLE 11.4 COMMON PHYSICAL HEALTH DISORDERS OF CHILDHOOD

Name	Diagnostic Description	Important Characteristics
Cerebral palsy	A crippling condition of the neuromuscular system; disorder of movement and posture; central characteristic is neurological motor dysfunction caused by brain damage (birth injury, congenital defect, infection); not a clear-cut syndrome but includes children with a variety of symptoms, such as muscle weakness or involuntary muscle movements.	Brain damage involved in CP may also affect IQ but not inevitably; however, a greater proportion of CP children are mentally retarded than is the case with general population; since condition involves brain damage, it cannot be cured, but physical therapy and surgery can improve function.
Epilepsy	A condition of the neuromuscular system involving recurring attacks of loss of consciousness, convulsive movements, or disturbances of feeling and behavior; also known as *seizure* or *convulsive disorder*; caused by as yet undetermined brain damage.	Focus of treatment is the control of seizures; many effective anticonvulsant medications are now available; although many mentally retarded individuals suffer from seizures, the seizures themselves do not seem to cause mental retardation.
Spina bifida	A congenital defect of the spinal column; in its more severe forms, paralysis of lower limbs is virtually inevitable without surgical intervention; condition is evident at birth; most severe form is termed *myelomeningocele.*	Children are susceptible to hydrocephalus; if not surgically corrected, it can cause mental retardation and related behavior problems.
Muscular dystrophy	A degeneration of the muscles; disease is progressive and grows worse with age.	These children typically require a wheelchair in the normal course of the disease; cognitive abilities are not affected.
Limb deficiencies	Caused by genetic birth defects, amputations due to disease, or accidents.	Mechanical limbs (prosthetic devices) can frequently be fitted, but considerable training in use of limb as well as supportive attitudes are necessary.
Cystic fibrosis	Symptoms include generalized dysfunction of the exocrine glands, very high salt cocentrations in sweat, and chronic pulmonary dysfunction with repeated episodes of pneumonia (with severe bouts of coughing); most lethal hereditary disorder of children in U.S.; specific cause unknown; no known cure, and illness is inevitably fatal; many patients, however, survive into adolescence and young adulthood.	These youngsters are encouraged to lead active lives, and no physical restrictions are placed on behavior; cognitive development is normal and they typically remain in regular school placement; extensive therapeutic regimen is required in the home; patients frequently feel emotionally inhibited due to mucous excretions, chronic coughing, and breathing difficulty.
Leukemia	A group of diseases characterized by sudden increases of white blood cells in the bone marrow and peripheral blood; most common form of childhood cancer; in the late 1970s, the disease was considered fatal; recent advances in chemotherapy have made it possible to expect cure or at least long-term leukemia-free survival.	Many children can be treated with medication on an outpatient basis; others require surgery, radiation therapy, or bone marrow transplantation; fear of death is frequent concern of child and family, even in remission, and an atmosphere of normalcy should be stressed, with emphasis on positive aspects of living.

(*continued*)

TABLE 11.4 (*Continued*)

Name	Diagnostic Description	Important Characteristics
Asthma	Causes unclear; involves both psychological and somatic factors; often described as *psychophysiologic* illness; characterized by difficulty in breathing due to narrowing of airways; involves severe and life-threatening attacks of wheezing; may cause death because of inability to breathe.	Sometimes described as the "vulnerable child syndrome"; breathing attacks are frightening and parents may tend to overprotect the child; drug therapy can be very effective in preventing attacks and aerosol (fine mist spray) can be helpful in controlling attack.
Diabetes	Characterized by an inability to store sugar in the blood because of dysfunction of the pancreas; symptoms include loss of weight, frequent urination, and excessive thirstiness; treatment involves diet management and insulin therapy as needed.	With proper management, diabetes can be brought under control; risks involve diabetic coma (excess of sugar in blood causing nausea, abdominal pain, labored breathing) and insulin reaction (lack of sugar causing hunger, sweating, tremors, drowsiness).
Spinal cord injury	Accidents are the most common cause of injury. The extent of disability is determined by where the damage occurred. Paralysis and loss of sensation occur below the location of the injury.	Students with major injuries require wheelchairs for mobility; those with quadriplegia may also have difficulty breathing and lack bowel and bladder control.
Sickle cell anemia	A hereditary blood disorder found more commonly in the African American population; red blood cells distorted and don't circulate properly; results in severe pain to abdomen, arms, and legs.	Many orthopedic problems may result that affect full participation in certain physical activities; frequent absences from school can impact academic achievement.

Source: Adapted from Suran and Rizzo, 1979.

CAUSES. Table 11.4 presents identifying information regarding the major categories of physical disabilities and health impairments.

IMPLICATIONS FOR TEACHING. Many students with physical health disorders are not placed in special education classes; they remain in regular classrooms. The teacher working with these students must remember that they are frequently absent from school for long periods, sometimes need special medication, and raise many concerns for their peers. As a result, the children's social and emotional development, especially their self-esteem, can be influenced by the health problem. The teacher needs to plan carefully both the academic and social aspects of classroom activities to ensure maximum participation.

These are number of recommendations for the regular teacher who may have students with physical and health handicaps in the classroom (Glass, Christiansen, & Christiansen, 1982):

1. Review student records at the beginning of the year, noting which students have unusual health problems. If you will have a student with a health problem, develop an understanding of the problem by

gifted and talented. A category in special education that defines individuals who give evidence of high-performance capability in certain areas.

reading and by consulting the school nurse. Since some conditions require modifications in the classroom environment and/or instructional procedures, you should make preparations for the students before the start of school. Consulting previous teachers of the students to find out about successful procedures also is helpful.

2. Many students with physical and health impairments suffer from excessive pity or overprotection. Other such students are excluded from class activities or are rejected by their peers. It is important that you treat these students as worthwhile, competent students who have interests and needs like any other students. As a result, never expect them to do less than they are capable of. Develop reasonable objectives and expect them to be attained.
3. Spend time helping the class develop realistic attitudes about physical and health impairments and ways of interacting with their handicapped peers.
4. Because of fatigue, students who are handicapped or health impaired may not be able to participate in all class activities or finish certain assignments on time. Provide suggestions for parents for home tutoring, and provide opportunities if possible for rest during the school day for students who tire easily.
5. If a student is hospitalized during the school year, it is helpful to communicate with the hospital's teachers or to send work home for the student to complete if possible. The goal should be to continue to support the student's contact with the school and to prevent the child from falling too far behind, while at the same time not making demands that cannot be attained because of the student's health condition.
6. Make the student feel welcome on return to school from an illness, and allow sufficient time for makeup work.

Gifted and Talented

DEFINITION/CLASSIFICATION. Although P.L. 94–142 does not specifically apply to the **gifted and talented,** these exceptional children also need special educational services to reach their potential. The classification covers a wide range of abilities and traits and is defined by the Gifted and Talented Children's Act of 1978, Section 902:

> Gifted and talented children means children, and whenever applicable, youth, who are identified at the preschool, elementary, or secondary level as possessing demonstrated or potential abilities that give evidence of high performance capability in areas such as intellectual, creative, specific academics, or leadership abilities, or in the performing and visual arts, and who by reason thereof require services or activities not ordinarily provided by the school.

The definition of the term and the identification of gifted and talented children, like other areas of exceptionality, have been characterized by controversy stemming from the following questions:

1. What are the different ways in which these children excel in such areas as intelligence, creativity, and special talents?
2. How should one measure the areas of students' expertise—with standardized tests, teacher judgments, past performances, and so on?
3. To what degree must a child excel to be considered gifted or talented?
4. Who should compose the comparison group?

As you might expect from the possible answers to these questions, giftedness can be identified in many ways. The 1987 *State of the States Gifted and Talented Education Report* (Council of State Directors, 1987) showed that each state has its own procedures for identifying and establishing special services for these children. At the time this report was published, 22 states did not mandate programs for the gifted and talented. However, those states that do have programs are providing greater financial support for them than they provided in the past.

There is still considerable confusion over who should be labeled as gifted and talented. In one publication, 17 different conceptions of giftedness were identified (Sternberg & Davidson, 1986)! Many school districts use multiple criteria for identifying students, such as achievement test scores, intelligence test scores, teacher nominations, parent nominations, student interviews, grades, classroom performance, and creativity. The problem regarding diverse definitions is that often the definition used in identifying students is not consistent with the instruments used to select students or with the type of program provided for students. For example, many definitions incorporate statements about the levels of motivation, creativity, and/or leadership, yet use an individual intelligence test as the sole indicator to select students. The inconsistency between the definition and type of program occurs when students are selected because of their high intelligence but are then placed in gifted programs that emphasize independent work or special talent that is not necessarily related to high intelligence. It is important to realize that just because students are labeled as gifted or talented does not mean that they will be placed in a program suited to their unique abilities and needs (Hoge, 1988; Sosniak, 1987).

INTELLIGENCE AS AN INDICATOR OF GIFTEDNESS. The traditional definition of *giftedness* is based on general intelligence in that a student with an intelligence test score of 130 or above would be selected for special education in most schools. Terman and Oden's (1925, 1954) study of highly gifted children (those with a score over 140) is still considered to be one of the classic works in the field. An important aspect of their study was that in addition to high academic achievement, gifted children's physical and social development was found to be above average when compared with that of their normal peers. Furthermore, contrary to popular notion, gifted children become gifted adults. They do not burn themselves out. Also, children identified as gifted according to intelligence test scores tend to score above average on tests of special ability (Gallagher, 1975).

CREATIVITY AS AN INDICATOR OF GIFTEDNESS. In Chapter 8, I discussed the difference between convergent and divergent thinking, pointing out that the latter is associated with creativity. It is important that you understand the distinction between intellectual giftedness and creativity. The results from a number of studies (Getzels & Jackson, 1962; Wallach & Kogan, 1965) indicate that although persons above average in intelligence are more likely to be creative, this does not mean that above average or highly intelligent persons are necessarily creative. In fact, Torrance (1962) states that "if we were to identify children as gifted simply on the basis of intelligence tests, we would eliminate from consideration approximately 70 percent of the most creative" (p. 5).

Students with high grades in school may or may not be creative. Many noncreative, highly intelligent individuals perform very well in school or on the job but never generate any original ideas. There are also students who do poorly in school and demonstrate little motivation but have a high degree of creative talent.

During the 1960s, a number of issues regarding the traditional means of identifying the gifted were raised. Some educators became concerned that many gifted children were going unidentified, especially those from various cultural groups, because of the biased nature of intelligence tests. As a result, many states placed more emphasis in their selection process on teacher and parent nomination and on work samples (particularly in talent areas such as the visual and performing arts), in addition to intelligence and achievement tests. Furthermore, many psychologists and educators believed that high intelligence was not the only trait needed for outstanding accomplishments in society.

SPECIAL TALENTS AS AN INDICATOR OF GIFTEDNESS. Although *giftedness* and *talent* are often used interchangeably, *talent* usually refers to specialized ability in such areas as art, music, drama, science, mathematics, and leadership. Although psychomotor ability is not mentioned in the federal definition of giftedness, it was identified as an area of giftedness as defined in a U.S. Office of Education report to the Congress (Marland, 1972). Table 11.5 identifies characteristics of children with special talents.

AN INTEGRATIVE PERSPECTIVE. Renzulli (1982) has suggested a multiple-criterion definition of giftedness that includes high ability (including high intelligence), high creativity, and high task commitment (a high level of motivation and the ability to see a project through to its conclusion). He believes that all three characteristics are necessary for truly gifted performance in any field. Using this definition, a student who has an average intelligence test score but is talented in areas not measured by an intelligence test would be included in gifted programs. On the other hand, the definition excludes children who have high intelligence test scores but are not exceptionally creative or committed to a field of interest (Berdine & Blackhurst, 1985).

PROGRAMS FOR GIFTED AND TALENTED STUDENTS. Two of the most common programs for gifted and talented students include *enrichment* and *acceleration* (Heward & Orlansky, 1992). Enrichment experiences are those

TABLE 11.5 CHARACTERISTICS OF CHILDREN WITH SPECIAL TALENTS

Talent Area	Abilities	Personality Attributes
Mathematics	Ability to manipulate symbolic material more effectively and more rapidly than classmates	Highly independent Enjoy theoretical and investigative pursuits Talented girls less conforming than general population
Science	Ability to see relationships among ideas, events, and objects Elegance in explanation: the ability to formulate the simplest hypothesis that can account for the observed facts	Highly independent "Loners" Prefer intellectually rather than socially challenging situations Reject group pressures Methodical, precise, exact Avid readers
Language arts	Capability of manipulating abstract concepts, but sometimes inferior to the high general achiever in working with mathematical material Imagination and originality	Highly independent Social and esthetic values (girls) Theoretical and political values (boys) Avid readers
Leadership	Ability to effect positive and productive change Good decision-making ability Proficiency in some area, such as athletics or academics Ability to communicate	Empathic Sensitive Charismatic—can transform the group through their enthusiasm and energy Superior communication skills
Psychomotor ability	Gross motor strength, agility, flexibility, coordination, and speed Excellence in athletics, gymnastics, or dance Fine motor control, deftness, precision, flexibility, and speed Excellence in crafts—jewelry making, model building, mechanics, working with electronic equipment, etc. Ability to use complicated equipment with little or no training	Enjoy and seem to need considerable exercise Competitive Interested in mechanics, electronics, or crafts Have hobbies such as model building, origami, pottery
Visual or performing arts	Ability to disregard traditional methods in favor of their own original ones Resourcefulness in use of materials Ability to express their feelings through an art form Attention to detail in their own and others' artwork	Self-confident Competitive Prefer working alone Sensitive to their environment Gain satisfaction through their feelings artistically Responsive to music, sculpture

Source: Pendarvis, in Berdine and Blackhurst, 1985.

that allow each student to investigate topics of interest in depth. Some of these activities are completed in the regular classroom, whereas others are experienced in special classes, field trips, camps, and hobby clubs. Acceleration programs provide a child with learning experiences that are usually given to older children. It means speeding up the usual presentation of content—early admission to school, grade skipping, concurrent enrollment in both high school and college, advanced placement tests, and early admission to college.

Were you or any of your friends identified as gifted? What did you think of the educational program? Did it help you develop your potential or was it a waste of time? Do you think gifted and talented students should be educated separately? What are some of the possible consequences of such action?

IMPLICATIONS FOR TEACHING. The following are teaching practices that can help gifted and talented students in the classroom (Glass, Christiansen, & Christiansen, 1982; Hallahan & Kauffman, 1988):

1. Periodically review the characteristics of students in your class to determine whether certain students show particular ability, creativity, and task commitment. Give special concern to culturally diverse students who may be gifted or talented but who are not achieving at a high level. Refer students who show indications of giftedness to the school psychologist for testing and observation.
2. Analyze your instructional program for gifted students. It is common for gifted children to become bored with the school routine because the work is not challenging. Teach the students independent research skills. Because many gifted and talented children are self-motivated, they are able to work independently for long periods. Develop specific goals and objectives for the students that provide an organized program of instruction.
3. Use instructional methods and procedures that encourage students to be creative and to explore their environment. These activities will benefit all the students in the class.
4. Be a good model. If you accept intellectual and personal differences, the students in your class are likely to imitate your behavior. If you show excitement about exploring new areas of knowledge, so will your students.

LEGAL RIGHTS OF EXCEPTIONAL CHILDREN AND THEIR PARENTS

During the 1960s and 1970s, questions about the rights of students were raised in such areas as hair length, corporal punishment, discipline, and confidentiality of records. The student rights movement also influenced the schools' treatment of exceptional children. This movement began in many states by litigation that prevented the exclusion of exceptional children from certain educational programs and that instituted due process in deciding how and where a child was to be educated.

To understand the significance of the right to due process, you must understand the way many children with disabilities were treated in the past. At one time, a school administrator or school psychologist could decide without any consultation with others whether a handicapped child could attend school and where in school the child was placed. These decisions were often made with little or no supporting data, on no legal basis, and with no parental involvement. This same person could exclude a child from school if the person believed that the child could not benefit from a public education or did not meet arbitrarily designated ability and behavior standards. Stated simply, one person could decide the educational destiny of a child or adolescent.

Children with handicaps faced many problems in obtaining an appropriate education. First, they often remained in special programs throughout their educational careers. This was especially true of students classified as mildly mentally retarded. The tendency was to consider special education placements as permanent assignments rather than short-term options designed to help the individual prepare for return to the regular class.

Second, a disproportionate number of minority children were assigned to special education classes without consideration of the cultural and educational backgrounds contributing to their academic and intellectual deficiencies. As a result, many children were inappropriately placed in special classes.

In general, there were few protective safeguards to ensure the application of due process for the handicapped. Schools often labeled children, subjected them to psychological assessments by an individual, and placed them in educational programs without appropriate supporting data and often without parental consent.

Public Law 94-142

> ? What legal rights do parents have in the identification, assessment, and educational placement of an exceptional child?

In 1975 a major federal law pertaining to children with disabilities, the Education for All Handicapped Children Act (P.L. 94–142), was passed. This law has had a major impact on special education. The key aspects of the law are as follows:

1. A free, appropriate public education is mandated for all children with disabilities.
2. School systems must protect the rights of children with disabilities and their parents.
3. The placement of children with disabilities must be in the least restrictive educational environment (i.e., children with disabilities

must be educated with nonhandicapped children to the maximum extent possible).
4. An individualized education program (IEP) must be developed and implemented for every child with disabilities.
5. Parents of children with disabilities must be involved in the decision-making process affecting the education of their child.

FREE AND APPROPRIATE EDUCATION. This provision mandates that all special education needs and related services must be provided to students and parents by schools without cost. The term *appropriate* addresses the issue of *quality* of education and is in part guaranteed by other provisions of the law, such as the annually reviewed IEP, parental participation in decision-making processes, and due process. *Appropriate* has thus far been interpreted by the courts to imply an adequate, not necessarily optimum, program.

DUE PROCESS. P.L. 94–142 attempts to protect against abuses such as permanent placement in special education programs, improper diagnosis, disproportionate placement of minority children in special education classrooms, and low-level educational services. The law does this by requiring the following (adapted from Meyen, 1988):

1. All school records must be open to parents.
2. Assessment of children considered for special education programs must be "nondiscriminatory." This means that children must be tested in their native language, using multiple criteria for decision making. The child cannot be placed in a special education program on the basis of the results of a single test.
3. Parents may obtain evaluations of their children from specialists outside the school.
4. A child advocate must be appointed if the parents or guardian of the child are not known or available. The child advocate cannot be an employee of the school district.
5. Parents must receive written notice in the parents' native language whenever the school proposes a change in the identification, evaluation, or educational placement of their child.
6. Parents must be given the opportunity to present complaints on any matter pertaining to the identification, evaluation, or educational placement of their child. The school must provide parents with information on the specific procedures they should follow to voice their complaints.
7. If parents are not satisfied with the educational program provided by the school, they can request a due process hearing. Guidelines for these hearings are specified in the law.

LEAST RESTRICTIVE EDUCATIONAL ENVIRONMENT. The requirement for placement in the *least restrictive educational environment* attempts to reverse traditional procedures for dealing with children with disabilities. Historically, children with disabilities were referred out of the regular classroom for special services. The law now states that to the maximum extent appropriate, children with disabilities are to be educated with children who are not handicapped. Removal of the student from the regular class for part or all of the day should occur only when the nature or severity of the handicap is such that education in the regular class with supplementary aids and services cannot be achieved satisfactorily. This aspect of the law is often called **mainstreaming.** The emphasis has shifted to the regular classroom as the preferred instructional base for all children. The law does not state that all children with disabilities must be placed in regular classrooms, but it puts the burden of proof on the schools when placement is other than the regular classroom. A child's IEP must show cause if and when the child is moved from a least restrictive educational environment.

mainstreaming. The return to the regular classroom, for all or part of the school day, of exceptional children previously educated in self-contained, special classrooms.

Hallahan and Kauffman (1988) point out that in studies of the effectiveness of mainstreaming, *temporal integration* (i.e., the amount of time spent in a regular classroom) and *physical placement* have been the focus of research, often to the exclusion of what goes on in that physical setting. This makes the literature evaluating the efficacy of different programs somewhat suspect and difficult to compare, offering no clear-cut answers.

Mainstreaming considers the continuum of educational options available to the child with disabilities. The purpose of mainstreaming is to match more effectively the characteristics and needs of the child and the type of educational environment in which the child is placed, while at the same time attempting to maximize interaction with children who are not disabled. Merely including a child with disabilities in a regular classroom will not eliminate the child's problems. For example, the research on mildly retarded students indicates that their social acceptance does not necessarily improve by placing them in regular classrooms. In fact, placing children with and without disabilities together can actually result in lower acceptance for the children with disabilities (Strain & Kerr, 1981). However, when teachers structure their classrooms to help these students exhibit more appropriate classroom behavior and individualize instruction, acceptance can be improved and achievement can increase (Madden & Slavin, 1983).

Table 11.6 illustrates the continuum of educational alternatives for children with disabilities, from least restrictive environment (regular classroom) to most restrictive environment (residential facility and homebound/hospital environment). Notice that educators have two options—regular class and resource room—before considering full-time placement in a special class or school. The regular classroom teacher for these children may have the assistance of a consultant or itinerant teacher (e.g., a speech therapist, who may work with the child individually and offer curriculum materials and/or other instructional support for the classroom teacher), resource teacher, or special day teacher. Children who attend special classes on a full-time basis still have some interaction with their nonhandicapped peers—at lunch and recess—if their class is in the same facility as a regular education program. Although more restrictive than the regular class, the special class is less restrictive than placement in a special school or residential institution.

TABLE 11.6 PERCENTAGE OF ALL STUDENTS WITH DISABILITIES AGE 3–21 SERVED IN SIX EDUCATIONAL PLACEMENTS: SCHOOL YEAR 1989–1990.

Level 6	*Homebound/hospital environment* includes students placed in and receiving special education in hosptial or homebound programs. (0.7%)
Level 5	*Residential facility* includes students who receive education in a public or private residential facility, at public expense, for greater than 50 percent of the school day. (0.9%)
Level 4	*Separate school facility* includes students who receive special education and related services in separate day schools for students with disabilities for greater than 50 percent of the school day. (5.2%)
Level 3	*Separate class* includes students who receive special education and related services outside the regular classroom for more than 60 percent of the school day. Students may be placed in self-contained special classes with part-time instruction in regular classes, or placed in self-contained classes full-time on a regular school campus. (25.2%)
Level 2	*Resource room* includes students who receive special education and related services outside the regular classroom for 21 percent to 60 percent of the school day. This may include students placed in resource rooms with part-time instruction in a regular class. (35.5%)
Level 1	*Regular class* includes students who receive a majority of their education in a regular classroom and receive special education and related services outside the regular classroom for less than 21 percent of the school day. It includes children placed in a regular class and receiving special education within the regular class as well as children placed in a regular class and receiving special education outside the regular class. (32.5%)

Source: U.S. Department of Education, 1992.

resource room. A special education classroom to which students come from regular classes to receive academic help to remediate their particular learning problems.

A common educational service for mildly handicapped students is Level 2, the **resource room,** a special classroom within a school in which a special education teacher provides services for exceptional children. Depending upon the needs of the student, instruction can be from 30 to 60 minutes two to five times a week, or as much as half of the school day. The teacher assesses the needs of the students and works with them individually or in small groups to remediate the identified deficiencies. The resource teacher works closely with the regular classroom teacher.

Individualized Education Program (IEP)

? What is the teacher's role in the development of an IEP?

The IEP is a written educational program agreed upon by parents and specialists at a meeting at which each handicapped child's educational needs are discussed. It is important to note that an IEP must be written for each child rather than for a class or group of children. A number of steps must be taken before an IEP is written. First, a teacher must initiate a *referral* for

DEBATE FORUM

Is the Regular Classroom the Best Place to Remediate Most Academic Deficiencies?

Even with the least restrictive environment stipulation in the law, many educators and researchers still argue that special education is too separate from general education. Today some advocate what has been called the **regular education initiative**, an alternative to special education. The goal is to restructure the regular classroom to be more responsive to students with special needs, benefiting not only handicapped students but also economically disadvantaged, non-English-speaking, gifted, and other special needs students.

regular education initiative. An attempt to restructure special education so that the regular classroom would serve as the primary setting for special education services.

Argument. The regular classroom is the best place to remediate academic deficiencies; educating students in separate "pull-out" programs (e.g., resource room instruction) results in substantial reduction in classroom instruction (often because of the lack of coordination between resource and regular classroom teachers); and the procedures for classifying students for special education are flawed. Research demonstrates that the same instructional methods that produce achievement gains are appropriate for all groups of students. Thus, why not focus on effective instruction in a heterogeneous environment rather than segregate students into separate groups (Wang, Reynolds, & Walberg, 1988).

Counterargument: Today's general education teachers are not well prepared to meet the special needs of students with handicaps, and as a result the plan would lead to a less-than-adequate education for special needs students. Also, changes in the present program can be made to improve it without overhauling the total system of instruction.

What do you think? Would most exceptional children benefit from receiving all instruction in the regular classroom? Do you have some concerns about this plan?

a student who is having difficulties in the classroom. This referral may go to the principal or to the special education teacher (sometimes called the *resource specialist teacher*). Second, a team of professionals identified by various names (e.g., *local review committee* or *student study team*) is established to *review the request for referral and conduct a preliminary screening* to determine whether there is enough evidence to accept or reject the referral (i.e., whether the problem appears serious enough for special education services). The team reviews the student's school records and meets with the referring teacher and other school personnel who may know the student. If the team accepts the referral, it requests parental permission for a comprehensive assessment to analyze the problem in depth. Third, the *comprehensive assessment* is usually completed by a school psychologist, special education teacher, and other specialists when particular expertise is needed (e.g., an audiologist or speech therapist). The assessment includes both achievement tests and special diagnostic tests to attempt to pinpoint the student's particular learning problems. Finally, when the comprehensive assessment is completed, the evaluation team (1) determines whether the student is eligible for special education and then (2) makes a decision as to the best type of placement for the student (keeping in mind the least restrictive environment provision in the law). The team may decide that the regular classroom teacher can work with the student without additional special education services. If it does determine that special education services are needed, the team will *prepare an IEP* for the student. The parents or guardian must sign the IEP to indicate agreement with the placement and type of educational program. If the parents disagree with the conclusions of the assessment team, they may appeal the decisions through the guidelines established by the school district. Each student's IEP must be re-evaluated yearly. Although school districts use various formats, most IEPs include a statement of the following:

- The child's present educational level or performance.
- The annual goals, including short-term objectives.
- The anticipated duration of the specific educational services, appropriate objective criteria, evaluation procedures, and schedules for determining, on at least an annual basis, whether instructional objectives are being met.

The law requires that at least four individuals be involved: the parents or guardian, the child's teacher, a representative of the local educational agency who is qualified to provide or supervise special education (usually a principal or director of special education or a representative), and, whenever appropriate, the child. In many situations, additional teachers who interact with the child and certain specialists (e.g., speech therapists, nurses, physicians, and psychologists) are also present at the meeting. The parents may invite an additional person familiar with their child to the meeting.

Public Law 99-457

In 1986 an amendment to P.L. 94-142 was passed. The law, P.L. 99-457 (Part H), Services for Infants and Toddlers with Handicapping Conditions, provides funding for eligible children from birth to age 2 who need early intervention services because of a developmental delay or who have a diagnosed condition that could result in developmental delay. This

CLASSROOM Application

PREPARING AN INDIVIDUALIZED EDUCATION PROGRAM (IEP)

The following represents the development of an actual IEP. The names and some minor data have been changed to maintain the confidentiality of the family involved. Notice the following steps: referral, review of the request for referral, comprehensive assessment, preparation of the IEP, and placement. Remember that the procedures may differ somewhat from one school district to another. In addition, because prevailing learning problems and student characteristics differ greatly, there is no such thing as a typical IEP.

REFERRAL

Frank Davis, a fourth-grade teacher at Wilson Elementary School, was concerned about one of his students, Billy Fields, who was having difficulty with math and language arts. Billy read below grade level and had difficulty completing follow-up work. Mr. Davis moved Billy's seat to the front of the room to alleviate any hearing difficulty he might have when instructions were given to the entire class, to facilitate any copying from the chalkboard, and to observe his behavior more closely. In addition, he worked individually with Billy as time permitted. Unfortunately, none of these remediations seemed to help.

Mr. Davis decided to review Billy's school records to see if any other teacher had noted similar problems. He learned that retention had been recommended in the first grade but was refused by the parent, and that the second- and third-grade teachers had noted that Billy was deficient in many basic academic skills and needed a great deal of attention.

Mr. Davis decided to discuss the problem with Lori Gordon, the resource specialist teacher at the school. He expressed his concern that Billy was beginning to fall behind in all subjects. Mrs. Gordon suggested that he complete the school's formal referral form with all the information he could address and attach work samples and anecdotal observations he had made to identify the problem. In addition, Mrs. Gordon agreed to observe Billy's classroom behavior.

continued

REVIEW OF THE REQUEST FOR REFERRAL

Billy was observed during three basic periods—physical education, math, and spelling. In physical education, Mrs. Gordon noted that Billy was the third person chosen for a position on a team. His physical coordination and gross motor skills were excellent. Therefore, there was no reason to refer him to the adaptive physical education teacher (an individual trained to assess and work with children with physical and motor handicaps). In a conversation with Mrs. Gordon during his wait for a turn at bat, Billy exhibited clear articulation, normal vocabulary, and good sentence formation for a fourth-grade student. As a result, Mrs. Gordon did not believe that there was any reason to refer him to the speech and language consultant for evaluation. Observations during math indicated that Billy was having left-right sequencing problems. He was adding three-column figures of three digits and reversing numerals when regrouping (e.g., the first column of numbers totaled 24; Billy wrote 2 and carried the 4, instead of writing 4 and carrying the 2). During spelling he had good recall for basic reading words but did not get one word correct that involved simple phonic rules for long vowel sounds (e.g., *grat* instead of *great* and *trid* instead of *tried*).

After these observations Mrs. Gordon met with Mr. Davis to discuss her findings. She took his referral form, the formal request for assessment, and presented it at the team assessment meeting, which is held every other week at her school. Attending this meeting are the principal, school psychologist, Mrs. Gordon, and teachers who had referred children for various problems since the last meeting. The committee members discussed Billy's problem and decided that a formal assessment was necessary to determine whether Billy had a specific disability and was in need of special education services. They reached this decision on the basis of Mr. Davis's attempts to remediate the problem on his own, the observational reports by Mrs. Gordon, the indication by previous teachers that Billy needed special attention, and the fact that Billy was dropping further behind his classmates in all academic areas.

Billy's mother was contacted by Mrs. Gordon to request a conference to discuss Billy's academic problems and the recommendation by the evaluation team. Mrs. Fields stated at the conference that she was extremely worried about his learning problems. She believed that his problems were originally caused by emotional stress at age 6, when she and Billy's father were divorced. She regretted that she had not allowed Billy to be retained in the first grade, as recommended by the school. After her rights were explained, Billy's mother signed the permission form allowing for the assessment of her son. A copy of these rights accompanied her copy of the signed assessment. She was told that she would be notified as soon as the testing was completed and that a school assessment team meeting for the IEP would be held.

PUPIL NAME *Billy Fields* B/D __/__/__ Date of Meeting __/__/__ **Page 2 of 3**

G. ANNUAL GOALS AND SHORT TERM OBJECTIVES (Use of a number/code system for writing of goals/objectives must first be approved by the Division of Special Education and, if approved, explanatory material shall be attached to the IEP for parent and service provider.)

Goals/Responsible Personnel	Short Term Objectives	Evaluation Criteria For Objectives
1. ☐ Instruc Area *Math* ☐ DIS Area Goal: *To add and subtract to the thousands with re-grouping in correct right-left sequence to the 80% level 1.* Responsible Personal: *Resource Specialist Teacher* Beginning Date: __/__ Ending Date: __/__ If RSP ☑ or DIS ☐ indicate frequency and total minutes per week: *4 x 150 min 200 min per week*	a. *Billy will use correct right-left sequence in addition and subtraction. He will begin with two columns of numbers and progress to five columns re-grouping accurately at the 80% level 2.* b. *He will recite the multiplication tables 1-10.*	Objectives: a *6 mos*, b *1 year* (expected date of achievement) Observation: a ☑ b ☑ Informal Assess.: a ☑ b ☑ Formal Test: a ☐ b ☐ Other *selected work samples*: a ☑ b ☑ Date achieved: _/_ _/_ Not achieved: a ☐ b ☐ Comment
2. ☐ Instruc Area *Reading* ☐ DIS Area Goal: *To read and write from dictation all short CVC and long CVCV vowel silent "e" words at 80% level[1].* Responsible Personal: *Resource Specialist Teacher* Beginning Date: __/__ Ending Date: __/__ If RSP ☑ or DIS ☐ indicate frequency and total minutes per week: *4 x 150 min 200 min per week*	a. *Billy will use basic phonic reading rules beginning with short vowel words combined with consonant digraphs and consonant blends by writing from diction at the 80% level[2].* b. *He will learn all silent "e" long vowel words combined with consonant digraphs and consonant blends by writing them from dictation at the 80% level.*	Objectives: a *6 mos*, b *1 year* (expected date of achievement) Observation: a ☑ b ☑ Informal Assess.: a ☑ b ☑ Formal Test: a ☐ b ☐ Other *selected work samples*: a ☑ b ☑ Date achieved: _/_ _/_ Not achieved: a ☐ b ☐ Comment
3. ☐ Instruc Area *Reading Comprehension* ☐ DIS Area Goal: *To read paragraphs and correctly respond to questions at 80% level.* Responsible Personal: *Classroom Teacher* Beginning Date: __/__ Ending Date: __/__ If RSP ☐ or DIS ☐ indicate frequency and total minutes per week:	a. *Billy will read short paragraphs and identify who, what, when, where, and why questions.* b. *He will read more than one paragraph and properly respond to the comprehension questions following the passage at the 80% level.*	Objectives: a *6 mos*, b *1 year* (expected date of achievement) Observation: a ☑ b ☑ Informal Assess.: a ☑ b ☑ Formal Test: a ☐ b ☐ Other: a ☐ b ☐ Date achieved: _/_ _/_ Not achieved: a ☐ b ☐ Comment
4. ☐ Instruc Area ☐ DIS Area Goal: Responsible Personal: Beginning Date: __/__ Ending Date: __/__ If RSP ☐ or DIS ☐ indicate frequency and total minutes per week:	a. b.	Objectives: a, b Expected date of achievement Observation: a ☐ b ☐ Informal Assess.: a ☐ b ☐ Formal Test: a ☐ b ☐ Other: a ☐ b ☐ Date achieved: _/_ _/_ Not achieved: a ☐ b ☐ Comment

STUDENT FILE

Figure 11.1 Individualized Education Program. Source: Los Angeles Unified School District, Division of Special Education, 1981.

[1] CVC refers to consonant-vowel-consonant words (e.g., *hat, hit, hot*): CVCV, to consonant-vowel-consonant-vowel words (e.g., *hate, cape, tape*).
[2] Consonant digraphs are "*sh, wh, th*" sounds. Consonant blends are "*bl, dr, cr*" sounds.

continued

COMPREHENSIVE ASSESSMENT

The individual battery of tests given to Billy were divided into two sections: an intelligence test given by the school psychologist (the Wechsler Intelligence Scale for Children—Third Edition (WISC-III)* and achievement tests in the content areas given by Mrs. Gordon (see Chapter 12 for a discussion of intelligence and achievement tests). The school psychologist reported the following:

> He is presently functioning within the average range of intellectual abilities, but there is a significant discrepancy between his high average verbal skills and his average performance skills. He has difficulty with tasks requiring part-whole relationship and flexibility for new material and information. Billy is performing significantly below his ability level in language and mathematics. As a result, it appears that he would benefit from a more individualized instructional program to remediate those areas. It is recommended that he participate in a special education program for part of the school day.

Mrs. Gordon used both the Peabody Individual Achievement Test (PIAT) and the Basic Achievement Skills Individual Screener (BASIS). Although both tests are achievement tests, they differ in the procedures of testing. The PIAT uses a visual selection process in which the student need only point to one of four responses to each of the examiner's questions in math, reading recognition and comprehension, and spelling. No written work is necessary for scoring. The BASIS requires written work in math, spelling, and written composition (from the third grade up). This test was selected because Mrs. Gordon believed that Billy's written work in math and spelling would best document her observations regarding reversals in math sequencing and poor spelling and writing patterns.

*The WISC-III is an intelligence test that measures ability in verbal and nonverbal, or performance, areas such as visual-spatial competency.

condition can be in cognitive, physical, psychosocial, language, or speech development. The purposes of the law are:

1. To enhance the development of handicapped infants and toddlers and to minimize their potential for developmental delay.
2. To reduce the educational costs to our society . . . by minimizing the need for special education and related services after handicapped infants and toddlers reach school age.
3. To minimize the likelihood of institutionalization of handicapped individuals and maximize the potential for independent living in society.

PREPARATION OF THE IEP/PLACEMENT

When the assessment report was completed, the school assessment team meeting was scheduled for the formal IEP meeting. Present at this meeting were the school psychologist, Mrs. Gordon representing special education, a teacher (Mr. Davis), the principal, and the parent (Mrs. Fields). All of the findings were explained to Mrs. Fields. The school psychologist explained that Billy had high average skills but was not achieving close to his potential academic ability. Mrs. Gordon explained that her observations and assessments were in agreement with those of the school psychologist and further explained some of the particular problems she had observed in the classroom and documented on the BASIS. The committee discussed Billy's social and emotional behavior and answered numerous questions that Mrs. Fields had about the special education services at the school. Mrs. Fields and the committee agreed that Billy should be placed in the resource program for two periods a day (at least two hours), where he would receive special instruction related to his particular needs. The rest of the day he would receive instruction in his regular classroom, with Mr. Davis working closely with Mrs. Gordon to provide academic activities that would further Billy's academic progress. Mrs. Fields was satisfied with the established program and signed the IEP. A copy of the educational objectives for the IEP is shown in Figure 11.1. Notice that it was signed for the duration of one academic year, with goals of 6 and 12 months. Mrs. Fields received a copy of this sheet along with a summary and interpretation of Billy's test scores, and a copy of the signature sheet signed by all the participants.

Mrs. Fields was told that she would be called for regular conferences and could at any time call the resource teacher if she had any questions. At the end of the 12-month period there would be another assessment to review Billy's progress. Another IEP meeting would be held, and a decision would be made to determine whether full remediation had been achieved or whether a new IEP with new goals should be written (again with parental consent) if additional special education was required.

4. To enhance the capacity of families to meet the special needs of their infants and toddlers with handicaps. (paragraph 671a)

The legislation allows each state to define "developmental delay" as it sees fit. In addition, the law recognizes that it is often difficult to diagnose accurately the precise handicapping condition at such a young age. As a result, the law allows the states to serve "at risk" children—that is, medically at risk, or environmentally at risk, or both (Gallagher, 1989).

Among infants and toddlers considered to be at risk are those who have been exposed to street drugs (e.g., cocaine, PCP, crack) in utero or who were born drug addicted, low-birth-weight infants, and babies born with the HIV infection that causes AIDS. It is too early to determine what, and if any, educational disabilities will become manifest in these children in a predictable way. Regardless of the etiology (cause) of their condition, these children, whether or not they are labeled as exceptional children, as well as regular education children who may be experiencing temporary disruptions in their lives, will be a part of your classroom. It is up to you to be sensitive to and recognize their special needs.

One of the major purposes of the legislation is to help families deal with infants and toddlers who have special problems. For this reason, the individualized family service plan (IFSP) requires the participation of a parent or guardian in the development and review of the program. The IFSP identifies the child's development, the family's ability to deal with the situation and its needs, and the intervention services that will be provided to help the family deal with its needs.

Public Law 101-476

In 1990, P.L. 94-142 was amended by Congress again. The new law (P.L. 101-476) retained all the provisions of P.L. 94-142 but made the following additions (Lewis, 1990):

- All references to "handicapped children" were replaced with "children with disabilities."
- Two new categories (autism[3] and traumatic brain injury) were added to the definition of "children with disabilities."
- Schools must now provide transition services to students with disabilities. Transition services are activities that help a student move from school to postschool activities (e.g., job, vocational training, college, independent living).
- IEPs must now identify the needed transition services for students beginning no later than age 16 and annually thereafter.
- Rehabilitation counseling and social work services were added to the services that students can receive.

This new modification in the law allows more students to be included for special services and broadens the services they can receive. The changes are especially sensitive to the needs of adolescents and young adults.

PARENTS OF EXCEPTIONAL CHILDREN

The importance of involving parents in their children's educational program cannot be overemphasized. In particular, parents of exceptional children can play an important role in helping to teach their children with disabilities and in being active in the assessment and decision-making process regarding their children. Remember that P.L. 94-142 requires parents' involvement in developing an instructional plan for their child.

[3] A severe behavior disorder usually characterized by extreme withdrawal and lack of language and communication skills. Self-abuse and aggressive behavior are also common in autistic children.

Unfortunately, parents tend to be rather passive in the IEP meetings (Gilliam & Coleman, 1981) and often don't know (or don't feel qualified to comment upon) how their children are functioning in school (Abramson et al., 1983). To fulfill their roles adequately, it is important that parents acquire the knowledge and skills to do so. The schools must provide the necessary parent education.

Research has indicated that when parents are involved in their children's education, the children do better in school (Bailey & Worley, 1984; Bronfenbrenner, 1974; Zigler & Valentine, 1979). In addition, although P.L. 94-142 applies to all families, parents who are more involved in the school or are more articulate in expressing their point of view often are more successful in obtaining the services they want. Many school districts and private educational consultants offer special seminars on the rights of parents and the IEP procedure to equalize the impact of politics in the process.

> What special challenges do parents face in raising their exceptional child?

As a teacher, you need to be sensitive to the pressures on a parent of an exceptional student. Remember that parents face extra responsibilities when raising children with disabilities. They may feel overwhelmed, anxious, or stressed (Peterson & Cooper, 1989) and often have more marital and family conflict (Moroney, 1981). Some parents adjust well to learning about their child's handicap, but other parents have a difficult time accepting the realization of their child's problem. As a result, you will meet various types of parents. At one extreme you will find parents who are very supportive of your instructional program; at the opposite extreme you will find parents who question almost everything you do and are less supportive. In general, parents will be cooperative with you in helping their child or adolescent receive a good education.

Teacher-parent conferences are an important source of information for both you and the parent. After all, the parent has a great deal of information that can be useful in the classroom. In addition, you can provide assessment of the child's progress and make recommendations for parental involvement at home. In Chapter 13, I provide detailed information for conducting parent-teacher conferences that will help you in dealing with all parents.

IMPLICATIONS FOR INSTRUCTION: THE CHALLENGE TO THE REGULAR CLASSROOM TEACHER

> How can a regular classroom teacher improve the quality of a special education program?

Teachers play important roles in the identification, diagnosis, referral, and instruction of exceptional students and are important members of the assessment team. First, they must be able to identify students who can be considered at risk for academic failure. Teachers have a role in screening students to identify possible handicapping conditions. Second, they must learn to use informal and formal assessment methods to obtain precise information about students' academic skill (i.e., they must develop the ability to diagnose). Third, they must decide when a student should be referred to a school psychologist, speech therapist, or other professionals for more intensive evaluation. Fourth, they must contribute to the assessment team's deliberation concerning the type of educational services the diagnosed student needs (Moran, 1978). Finally, the teacher must implement the specialized program in the classroom.

When you are concerned about a child's progress, the first avenue that must be investigated is always physical. It may seem too obvious to mention, but a child who, for example, is experiencing reading difficulties needs to have his or her vision checked. Visual acuity deficits are common, and even children who already wear corrective lenses should have a vision screening. All too often the obvious or simple causes are overlooked.

It is important to realize that not every student who demonstrates some disability will fall under the guidelines of P.L. 94-142 and receive an evaluation by an assessment team. A student may have low achievement in an academic area, but because the gap between the student's scholastic aptitude and actual achievement is not large enough (e.g., an eighth-grade student with normal intelligence functioning at the seventh-grade level in

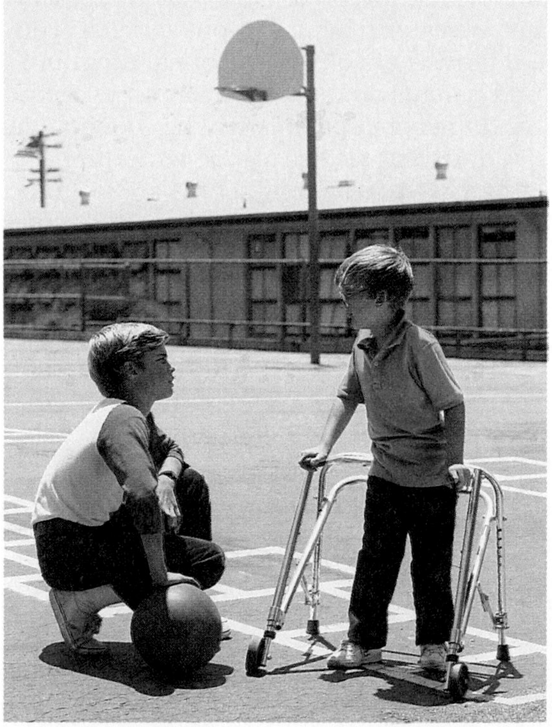

When a teacher establishes a climate in the classroom that differences are not necessarily deficits, children tend to be more tolerant of individual differences.

mathematics), he or she generally will not qualify for special education services. This means that the responsibility for developing an appropriate educational program for low achievers often rests entirely with the classroom teacher. Assistance from other professionals is usually limited to consultation on methods and materials.

When students do qualify for special services and remain in the regular classroom for part or all of the day, it is the responsibility of the teacher to implement the classroom program as specified in the student's individualized education plan. Research on regular teacher attitudes toward mainstreaming shows that many teachers are not positively disposed toward having children with disabilities in their classrooms and feel unprepared to teach them effectively (Madden & Slavin, 1983; Semmel, Gottlieb, & Robinson, 1979). Some teachers view mainstreamed students with academic handicaps as an additional burden placed on them. Teachers appear to be most concerned about (1) their own ability to provide an instructional program according to the needs of students with disabilities and (2) the social acceptance of students with disabilities by their peers. Fortunately, teachers are now receiving more training in exceptional education in both preservice and inservice education. In addition, more books and materials are available as resource information for teaching exceptional children. As a result of these efforts, many educators expect that regular teachers will develop greater confidence and expertise in teaching exceptional children.

Madden and Slavin (1983) identified a number of teaching methods that have been successful in improving children with disabilities' social acceptance and/or academic achievement in the regular classroom. Problems of social rejection of mainstreamed students can be remedied by providing *social skills training* (i.e., training students in the social skills necessary for forming friendships). Examples of social skills that can be taught are learning to recognize that one interrupts at the pause or at the lowering of the voice, learning how to deal with conflict and anger, learning how to interpret the nuances of facial expressions and body postures, and learning to use polite words (Gresham, 1984, 1988a, 1988b). Another type of intervention used for improving both social acceptance and academic achievement is *cooperative learning,* in which handicapped and nonhandicapped students work in teams on academic and class projects. Finally, *individualized instruction* is a widely used method for accommodating the needs of low-achieving and handicapped students. For example, Wang (1980) has developed the Adaptive Learning Environments Model (ALEM), which takes into consideration the fact that students learn in different ways and at different rates. The program provides several types of instruction for a variety of student differences. You will learn to use successful teaching practices. What is most interesting is that these same practices have proven to be successful with regular students as well as with exceptional children (Larrivee, 1985).

In summary, laws can be passed to protect the rights of students. However, the quality of the implementation of educational programs ultimately determines the benefits of these programs. The teacher's attitudes and skills play a major role in determining the success of mainstreaming.

The major theme of this chapter is that teachers will have to make adjustments in their methods when dealing with exceptional children. Such children cannot be placed in a regular class and be expected to learn by the same methods every other child is using. The reason these children have been identified as being exceptional is that they cannot profit from *only* the normal methods of instruction. Another important implication is that teachers need to be concerned with the children's personal and social development as well as their academic progress.

Summary

LABELING

1. Educators debate the pros and cons of labeling exceptional children.

MENTAL RETARDATION

2. Children must score below 70 on an intelligence test *and* have deficits in adaptive behavior before they can be labeled as mentally retarded.
3. Educable mentally retarded (EMR) students are often "retarded" only in school. In addition to functioning well outside school, they can generally master very basic academic skills.

LEARNING DISABILITIES

4. There is no one universal definition of *learning disabilities*.
5. Using direct instructional approaches rather than training psychological processes appears to be more successful for helping students with learning disabilities.

BEHAVIOR DISORDERS

6. Behavior displayed by children with behavior disorders is characterized by excesses and deficits.
7. Teachers' tolerance of classroom behavior is an important factor in their identification of behaviorally disordered students.
8. More male, low-SES, and minority-group students are classified as behavior disordered than are females and middle-SES students.

HEARING IMPAIRMENT

9. Hearing-impaired children usually have language and communication problems.
10. There is no causal relationship between deafness and intelligence.
11. Teachers need to recognize signs of possible auditory and visual impairment.

VISUAL IMPAIRMENT

12. There are both legal and educational definitions of visual impairment.

13. The visually impaired child is affected by such factors as brightness, size of image, contrast, time, and distance.

COMMUNICATION DISORDERS

14. The teacher should be aware of potential negative interpersonal relations and poor self-concept of speech-impaired children.
15. Speech and language disorders are related but are not the same disability.

PHYSICAL AND HEALTH IMPAIRMENT

16. Students with physical and health impairments are frequently absent from school for long periods of time; special arrangements often need to be made for private tutoring and other academic assistance to complete missed assignments.
17. Children with physical and health impairments may need special equipment and other modifications for learning in a regular classroom.

GIFTED AND TALENTED

18. Gifted and talented students possess a wide range of abilities and traits.
19. Although persons above average in intelligence are more likely to be creative, persons of average or high intelligence are not necessarily creative.

LEGAL RIGHTS OF EXCEPTIONAL CHILDREN AND THEIR PARENTS

20. The Education for All Handicapped Children Act (P.L. 94-142) provides for a free, appropriate public education for all children with disabilities, the right to due process, protection against discriminatory testing in diagnosis, individualized education programs (IEPs), and placement in an educational setting that is the least restrictive environment.
21. Teachers play an important role in the development of an IEP in terms of referral, assessment, placement, and instruction.
22. Mainstreaming is a term used to describe programs that educate children with disabilities, whenever possible, with their nonhandicapped peers.
23. Some educators believe that special education should be implemented within the regular school program, whereas others believe that general education teachers are not trained sufficiently to meet the needs of exceptional students.
24. The pull-out or resource approach to special education has not had positive effects on student achievement.
25. Public Law 99-457, an amendment to P.L. 94-142, provides funding for eligible children from birth to age 2. The purpose of this funding is to furnish early intervention services because of a developmental delay or for a diagnosed condition that could result in a developmental delay; P.L. 101-476 includes more students under P.L. 94-142 and provides more services during postschool activities.

PARENTS AND TEACHERS OF EXCEPTIONAL CHILDREN

26. Parents need to be more involved in the education of their exceptional children.
27. Teachers need to be sensitive to the child-rearing pressures on parents of children with disabilities.
28. Teacher attitude toward mainstreaming is an important factor in determining the success of a student's placement.
29. Training in social skills, cooperative learning, and individualized instrution are important methods of educating exceptional children.
30. The regular class teacher should meet with the special education teacher to determine specific strengths, weaknesses, and needs of exceptional children.

Reflecting on Exceptional Children

1. Educate Exceptional Children

Give a brief report to the class on how a teacher can help an exceptional child learn more effectively in a regular classroom. Select material for this report from books on exceptionality listed in the Suggestions for Further Reading section of this chapter or from the following journals:

Exceptional Children
Journal of Special Education
American Journal of Mental Deficiency
Mental Retardation
Journal of Learning Disabilities
Behavioral Disorders
Behavior Therapy
Journal of Speech and Hearing Disorders
The Volta Review (about hearing problems)
Journal of Visual Impairment and Blindness
Education of the Visually Handicapped
Journal of Rehabilitation
The Gifted Child Quarterly
Journal of Creative Behavior

2. Observe an Exceptional Child in the Classroom

Identify an exceptional student to observe in a special education class or in a regular classroom. After observing the student's behavior, ask the teacher to discuss attitudes and perceptions about the student's academic progress. Briefly report on your observation and discussion with the teacher. Include in your report the specific behavior you observed, any problems the student had in the classroom, how the teacher attempted to help the student, and recommendations for educating the student more effectively in the classroom.

3. Interview a Handicapped Adult

Interview a handicapped adult and ask about personal educational experiences. What were the most pleasant and unpleasant experiences? How did teachers react toward the individual? What recommendations does the person have for helping students with the same handicap?

4. Report on a Current Issue in Special Education

Identify a current issue in special education from your reading in journals and textbooks (e.g., instructional approaches, labeling, legal rights of the handicapped, and mainstreaming). Write a report about your research on the issue and include the following (Test, Heward, & Orlansky, 1980):

1. Define the issue.
2. Describe the various viewpoints covering the issue; compare and contrast these viewpoints.
3. Discuss your personal reactions to the issues.

5. Teach Students about Exceptional Children

Develop a lesson plan that could be taught when a handicapped student joins a class. Assume that the students have never had a handicapped student in class. Select the grade or subject area related to your teaching specialization. Use the reference material in the Suggestions for Further Reading section of this chapter. What are the advantages and disadvantages of special education labels?

Key Terms

Education for All Handicapped Children Act (P.L. 94-142), p. 489
individualized education program (IEP), p. 489
least restrictive educational environment, p. 489
exceptional, p. 489
disabled, p. 489
handicapped, p. 489
mental retardation, p. 494
educable mentally retarded (EMR), p. 495
learning disabilities, p. 496
minimal brain damage, p. 499
behavior disordered, p. 501
hearing impaired, p. 503
visual impairment, p. 506
speech disorder, p. 509
language disorder, p. 509
gifted and talented, p. 514
mainstreaming, p. 521
resource room, p. 522
regular education initiative, p. 523

Suggestions for Further Reading

The following books are good basic references for special education:

Bauer, A. M., & Shea, T. M. (1989). *Teaching exceptional students in your classroom.* Needham Heights, MA: Allyn & Bacon.

Cartwright, G. P., Cartwright, C. A., & Ward, M. E. (1989). *Educating special learners* (3rd ed.). Belmont, CA: Wadsworth.

Gearheart, B. R., & Gearheart, C. (1989). *Learning disabilities: Educational strategies* (5th ed.). Columbus, OH: Merrill. Contains a good chapter on programs for adolescents and adults.

Gearheart, B. R., Weishahn, M., & Gearheart, C. J. (1988). *The exceptional student in the regular classroom* (4th ed.). Columbus, OH: Merrill.

Hallahan, D. P., & Kauffman, J. M. (1991). *Exceptional children: Introduction to special education* (5th ed.). Englewood Cliffs, NJ: Prentice-Hall.

Heward, W. L., & Orlansky, M. D. (1992). *Exceptional children: An introductory survey of special education* (4th ed.). Columbus, OH: Merrill.

Kerr, M. M., Nelson, C. M., & Lambert, D. L. (1987). *Helping adolescents with learning and behavior problems*. Columbus, OH: Merrill.

Kirk, S. A., & Gallagher, J. J. (1989). *Introduction to special education* (6th ed.). Boston: Houghton Mifflin.

Long, D. (1978). *Johnny's such a bright boy. What a shame he's retarded: In support of mainstreaming in public schools*. Boston: Houghton Mifflin. An experienced teacher writes about the effects of labeling.

Wang, M. C., Reynolds, M. C., & Walberg, H. J. (Eds.). (1987). *Handbook of special education. Vol. 1: Learner characteristics and adaptive education.* New York: Pergamon Press. Has chapters on research on learning characteristics of handicapped students, differential programming in serving handicapped students, and noncategorical programming for mildly handicapped students.

Wang, M. C., Reynolds, M. C., & Walberg, H. J. (Eds.). (1988). *Handbook of special education. Vol. 2: Mildly handicapped conditions*. New York: Pergamon Press. Includes chapters on research on mild mental retardation, behavioral disorders, and learning disability.

Ysseldyke, J. E., Algozzine, B., & Thurlow, M. L. (1992). *Critical issues in special education* (2nd ed.). Boston: Houghton Mifflin. A comprehensive book on all the major issues in special education.

The following books are helpful references for the regular class teacher working with exceptional children:

D'Zamko, M. E., & Hedges, W. (1985). *Helping exceptional students succeed in the regular classroom.* West Nyack, NY: Parker.

Kroth, R. L., & Otteni, H. (1985). *Communicating with parents of exceptional children: Improving parent-teacher relationships* (2nd ed.). Denver: Love.

Moran, M. R. (1978). *Assessment of the exceptional learner in the regular classroom.* Denver: Love.

Schulz, J. B., & Turnbull, A. P. (1984). *Mainstreaming handicapped students: A guide for classroom teachers* (2nd ed.). Boston: Allyn & Bacon.

Shea, T. M., & Bauer, A. M. (1991). *Parents and teachers of exceptional students: A handbook for involvement* (2nd ed.). Boston: Allyn & Bacon.

Turnbull, A. P., Strickland, B. B., & Brantley, J. B. (1982). *Developing and implementing individualized education programs.* Columbus, OH: Merrill.

Wood, J. W. (Ed.). (1989). *Mainstreaming: A practical approach for teachers.* Columbus, OH: Merrill.

Part 4 synthesis

The following is a list of developmental and individual differences discussed primarily in the preceding four chapters and a list of instructional procedures you learned about in the first part of the book:

Development and Individual Differences

cognitive abilities
cognitive development
cultural experiences
disabilities
ethnicity
family and other socialization experiences
gender differences
language development
motivational differences
physical development
self-concept
social development

Instructional Procedures

applied behavioral analysis
computer-assisted instruction
cooperative learning
direct instruction
discovery learning
higher-level thinking skills
instructional objectives
learning strategies
mastery learning
modeling
moral education
open education
Personalized System of Instruction
programmed instruction
task analysis
values clarification

An important aspect of good decision making is to use instructional methods and make necessary adaptations that are appropriate to the students in your classroom. These adaptations may involve such factors as the delivery of instruction (i.e., the method used to teach an objective), who teaches the student (i.e., peer, teacher, or aide), the instructional setting (i.e., size of group, seating arrangement, etc.), the type of homework assignments, and procedures used to motivate students to achieve.

The following are brief descriptions of instructional situations that teachers have faced in attempting to teach different students. For each situation, consider all possible developmental and individual difference factors that might be considered, explain why the factors are important, and recommend and defend an instructional approach you would use with each student.

1. Mr. Hanson's eighth-grade history class is probably the most diverse of all of the classes at the Middle School. Not only are there an equal number of boys and girls, but it is virtually impossible to point to one specific ethnic group as dominant. When Mr. Hanson gave his students a "pretest" at the beginning of the year to assess their incoming ability levels, he found that there was a wide range of abilities, further adding to the diversity of the group. He had students who were barely able to read at grade level, as well as those who were reading at the high school level.

   Mariah had recently transferred to the Middle School from another state, and it was into Mr. Hanson's history class that she was placed. Her previous academic work had been very poor at the other school, and her parents were hoping that the change would have a positive effect upon her academic performance. When asked about her low marks in previous classes, Mariah would respond with such comments as "I'm just a failure" or "I'm dumb." Ironically, Mariah had been very involved with the sports program at her other school, excelling in volleyball and basketball, in which she received numerous trophies as an "Outstanding Player." When she was questioned by her teacher as to why she seemed to excel outside of the classroom, but did poorly in class, she would make it clear that she had confidence in her abilities at those sports, and that she enjoyed being part of a team.

   Another interesting bit of history about Mariah was that she had been a member of the "Explorer Scouts" for the past year, and that she was a leader of her troop. She had reached the highest level that a scout could achieve and had accomplished this in record time.

   After meeting with Mariah and her parents, Mr. Hanson decided that his immediate goal for this young lady was to have her get at least a B on her semester project, which was 25 percent of the overall grade. Students would be required to choose something in their everyday environment that has made a significant contribution to our culture. They were to research its history, explain how it works, and provide a defense of its contribution.

2. Tim Gilbert had taught career education for a number of years, until he was informed that his department's budget was being cut. As a result, Tim was for the first time in 15 years going to be required to teach two ninth-grade mathematics courses. For the past five years, Tim had been in charge of the career center, and he was concerned that his absence from the classroom might have a negative effect

on his new classes. In his capacity as the career education director, he was able to work at his own pace, primarily being responsible for advising students about postsecondary opportunities, either in continuing their education or in the workplace, a position made more important by the fact that he worked with inner-city kids.

Now, very abruptly, Tim found himself confronted with two classes full of students who were going to be required to learn a great deal of material, and he was scared to death. "It's been years since I taught in a classroom," he thought. "How do I start?" When he asked the department chairman, Bob Jones, for assistance, Bob's response was: "The main thing to keep in mind, Tim, is that there is a very specific body of information that these students need to learn by the end of the year, in order to move to the next level. Adopt a teaching strategy that will help to ensure that all of your kids are able to make that transition next year." Armed with this bit of advice, Tim set out to develop a strategy for accomplishing that goal.

3. It had been Jack Hawkin's experience that most seniors who took his required economics class were extremely uncomfortable for the first few weeks of class but eventually began to settle in and actually enjoy the course. Unfortunately, he did have that occasional student, like Maria, who was obviously uncomfortable almost halfway through the semester.

Maria was a Latina girl who had arrived in the United States less than four years ago. She had excelled throughout her four years at the high school, receiving numerous awards for her work in both math and science. Those classes in which she was not able to maintain her high level of academic performance were primarily those that required a facility with the English language. Maria had taken U.S. History with a teacher who liked to lecture quite often, and she had received her lowest grade to date, a C. According to Maria, when she asked the teacher what she could do to improve her class standing, his response was a curt "Take better notes." He did, however, allow the students to work in groups throughout the year, and he did hold class discussions once or twice a week on current topics, but these activities never appealed to Maria. She enjoyed being able to work independently, at her own pace, which she knew was a bit slower than most of her fellow students. She liked to take her time and be certain that she understood the material she was required to learn.

Maria found herself considerably uncomfortable with Jack's economics class, at least at this point in the school year. Although he tried not to emphasize lecturing in his classes, he knew that he did have a tendency to lecture too much and that his pace was rather quick. He also favored putting students into groups, a strategy that he knew made Maria uncomfortable.

His main objective for the remainder of the semester was to assist the students in developing an understanding of how the business cycle works. They were to translate this understanding into a report that would be presented, in written form, as their final examination. It was to be Maria's final opportunity to raise her current grade to an appropriate level, and he was concerned about how he might assist her in this project.

4. This was Dan Cleveland's first year teaching automotive repair. He had spent the last eight years working for a large car dealership as their head mechanic, while he worked on his degree and teaching credential. He knew that he would enjoy working with youngsters, teaching them how to take a car apart and put it back together, make minor repairs on their own cars, and eventually gain the skills to find work for themselves in the automotive industry. He enjoyed the idea of giving all types of students, male or female, able bodied or disabled, the opportunity to learn a marketable skill and to help enhance their self-esteem. What he found, the first week of class, was that accomplishing these goals was going to be more of a challenge than he ever imagined.

   Dan had started that first class session with a lecture about how a car works. He thought that the lesson was going well, until a young lady in the back of the room asked, "Hey, Mr. Cleveland, when are we gonna work on some cars? We already know this stuff." At that point, Dan realized that he was going to have to use another strategy in communicating with these eager youngsters. Most of these students were kids who found traditional classrooms to be, in their words, "boring." Sitting down at their desks and listening to a lecture about their first love, cars, was going to be impossible.

   After a conference with the head of the vocational education department, Dan decided to focus upon the goal of having each student able to assemble a dismantled engine as their final project for the first semester. Students were to be judged upon knowledge of individual parts of the engine, how quickly they were able to assemble the unit, and how effective they had been in their assembly, as evidenced by the engine actually starting and continuing to run.

5. The Vietnam War is usually the period of U.S. History with which high school students are most familiar. They have read about it, seen videos and feature films that seek to interpret causes and effects, and heard stories from relatives about U.S. involvement in that conflict. Jane Watson wanted her students not only to understand, at a deeper level, what the causes and effects of the war were, but to be able to actually experience some of the emotions with which key individuals in that war had to grapple: the feelings of the grunt in the field who was ordered to burn down an entire village because of a suspected collaboration with the Viet Cong; the

anxiety of the president as he struggled with a decision to send more young men into a situation that would mean, for many, the end of their lives, and for all, the end of their innocence.

Jane knew that there were differing opinions about U.S. involvement in Vietnam. During a discussion the previous week, Jane had discovered just how deeply and passionately their opinions ran regarding this situation. Some students were zealously in favor of an all-out victory, and their only regret was that the United States "wimped out." On the other hand, other students were equally passionate in their position, regretting that the United States had ever become involved in such an effort and decrying the "stupidity" of the president in ordering American troops into Vietnam. In the middle of this debate stood students like Tim Nguyen, who had his own opinion, based not upon secondhand accounts by historians or film directors but upon the experiences of his parents during the war.

Jane intended to develop an awareness in her students of how behaviors and actions, both at the personal level and at the national level, are based upon the emotional experiences of the actors in such situations. Her goal was to have her students experience some of these same emotions in the safety of the classroom.

Part five

Assessment and Evaluation

The evaluation of student performance is an important responsibility of both school and teacher. The public is so concerned about the quality of education today that statewide testing results by school and by grade are published in local newspapers in many communities, and the public uses scores to determine how successful each school has been in educating students. Although scores are important, assessment and evaluation involve much more than giving achievement tests to determine competency in different subject areas. Teachers use a variety of assessment procedures, both informal and formal, to make instructional decisions on a daily basis.

Throughout the next two chapters the terms *test, assessment,* and *evaluation* will be used repeatedly. A *test* is a measure containing a series of questions, each of which has a certain correct answer. *Assessment* (sometimes called measurement) is a broader concept because educators and psychologists can assess characteristics in ways other than by testing (e.g., using observation, interviews, and rating scales). Assessment involves all the processes and procedures used to make decisions about students' progress. Finally, *evaluation* is the process of obtaining information to form judgments so that educational decisions can be made. Evaluation is the most comprehensive of the three terms and always includes value judgments regarding the desirability of the data collected.

Teachers need to consider how classroom evaluation practices influence students (Crooks, 1988). For example, the cognitive level of teacher questions or test items influences the student's level of thinking and methods of studying. Do you study the same for an instructor who focuses on memory level information as compared with the instructor who requires you to analyze and synthesize information? Have you considered how different evaluation procedures motivate students differently? Think about these issues as you read the next two chapters.

Chapter 12

Classroom Assessment

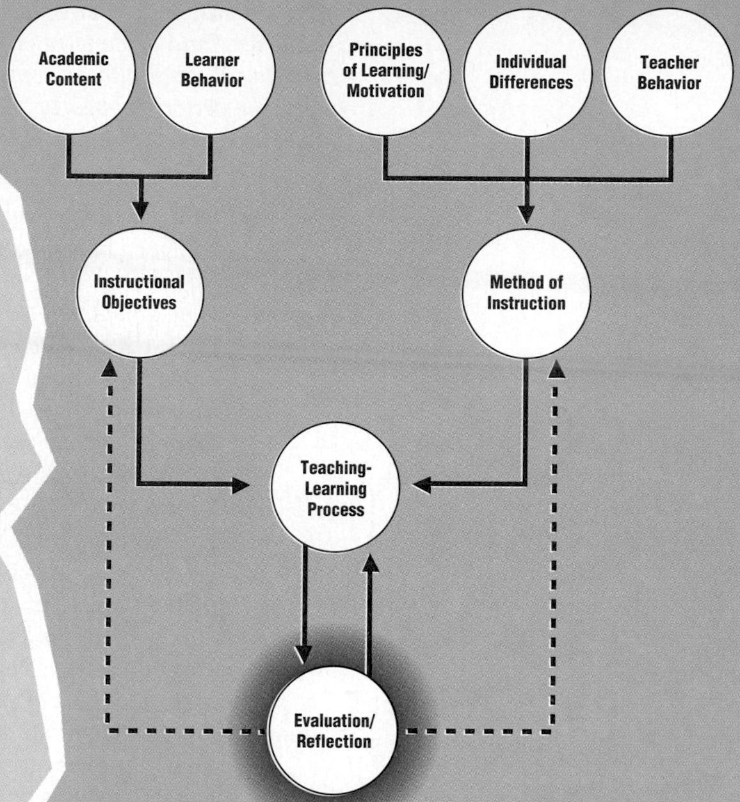

OBJECTIVES

After you master the material in this chapter you will be able to:

- Explain why teachers need assessment skills.
- Identify the characteristics of good evaluation measures.
- Evaluate standardized tests.
- Teach test-taking skills.
- Write test questions.
- Measure affective outcomes.

Orientation

Rudy Mahoney had been teaching U.S. History for about five years before he encountered Paul Warshawsky. Paul was one of those students who cause teachers to re-evaluate their entire teaching practice, from individual style to assessment strategies. Paul demonstrated consistent strengths in class, always contributing to class discussions, always completing assignments on time. But just as consistently, he performed poorly on exams. Rudy decided to talk with a senior teacher in his department, Jolinda Robinson, about his dilemma.

Rudy: *Jolie, I've got a problem with this kid, Paul Warshawsky. He's a great kid, but I have to give him a D on his report card when he should be getting at least a B—maybe even an A.*

Jolinda: *How do you know he should be getting a B?*

Rudy: *Well, I've watched him for the last semester. In class he is always the first to answer questions, and he can think through anything I toss out. I mean, if the questions require higher-level skills, I can always count on Paul. I know the kid is bright, but when it comes to the tests, he either fails or barely pulls out a D.*

Jolinda: *How do you figure out your kids' report card grades, Rudy?*

Rudy: *I average the tests. I don't grade homework, just check it. So I really have nothing else to go on except the tests. I test every three weeks, and then give a review final.*

Jolinda: *Do you make up the tests yourself?*

Rudy: *I don't like to use the tests that come with the book, so I use them as a base, but I sort of customize each one for that particular class.*

Jolinda: *Are you sure that your tests measure what it is you want your students to learn in your class?*

Rudy: *What do you mean?*

Jolinda: *I mean your tests measure one kind of knowledge—probably primarily dates and places—but Paul's showing you a different kind of knowledge in his classroom participation. Maybe you need to take that into consideration. Let me give you an analogy: If you went to a doctor with a variety of symptoms, and all she did was take your temperature, would you be satisfied with her diagnosis?*

Rudy: *Of course not.*

Jolinda: *So all I'm saying is, teaching is sort of like being a doctor, in that you have to constantly assess where each student is academically relative to where he or she is going. If you use only one measure to make that assessment, it's probably not going to give you as adequate a result as if you used a variety of measures.*

Rudy: *So, you're saying I should add in grades for class participation?*

Jolinda: *I'm just saying that there are lots of ways of assessing student progress. And putting together a package that you're comfortable with, and looking at the combined results, would give you a much more comprehensive picture than the one you're getting now.*

Rudy: *And in a case like Paul's, where the kid is clearly learning a big part of what I want him to learn, he has the opportunity to get a grade that reflects that learning.*

Jolinda: *Right. And then you move to the next piece—figuring out instructional strategies that will help him learn the dates and places, too!*

Why do you need to know about **assessment?** Teachers are constantly faced with the need to make decisions based on **evaluation.** In the simplest terms, you need to know what your students understand in order to know where to begin teaching; you need to know if they are learning what you want them to learn; and, you need to know what they have learned in order to give them appropriate grades. Table 12.1 provides a quick rundown of some of the instructional decisions you'll have to make and the evaluation strategies you might use to make them. This table is not meant to provide an all-inclusive list; rather, the questions cover a broad range of

assessment. The processes and procedures used to make decisions about students' progress.

evaluation. The process of obtaining information to form judgments so that educational decisions can be made.

TABLE 12.1 INSTRUCTIONAL DECISIONS AND EVALUATION STRATEGIES

Instructional Decision	Evaluation Strategies
How realistic are my teaching plans for this particular group of students?	Scholastic aptitude tests Past records of achievement
Should students be grouped for more effective learning	Aptitude and achievement scores Past records
To what extent are students ready for the next learning experience?	Readiness tests Pretests of needed skills Past records
To what extent are the pupils attaining the course's minimum essentials?	Mastery tests Observation Portfolios Projects
To what extent are pupils progressing beyond minimum essentials?	Periodic quizzes General achievement tests Observation Portfolios Projects
At what point would a review be most helpful?	Periodic quizzes Observation Portfolios
What type of learning difficulties are the pupils encountering?	Diagnostic tests Observation Pupil conferences Portfolios Pupil self-evaluation
Which pupils should be referred for counseling, special classes, or remedial programs?	Scholastic aptitude tests Achievement tests Diagnostic tests Observation
Which school mark should be assigned to each pupil?	Review of all evaluation data
How effective was my teaching?	Achievement tests Pupil ratings Supervisors' ratings Portfolios

Source: Adapted from Gronlund, 1985a, p. 4.

performance assessment. Measurement activities that ask students to demonstrate skills similar to those required in real-life settings.

portfolio. A file or folder containing a variety of information that documents a student's experiences and accomplishments.

concerns that you will need to address during the instructional process and the assessment strategies illustrate some of the options available to you. Keep in mind that there is no right way to evaluate students. Also, remember that the questions in Table 12.1 do not necessarily occur in the order in which they are listed, but are interrelated in the teaching-learning process.

Right now, educators are raising important questions about the limitations of current measurement and evaluation procedures. These questions focus on the facts that

- much assessment is based on factual information rather than thinking skills, and
- much assessment has little to do with actual skills that students will need outside the classroom. Students in "real life" will rarely have to diagram sentences, fill in blanks for missing pieces of mathematical formulas, match dates with events, or complete analogies.

Educators today are debating the value of **performance assessment** (also called authentic assessment), which uses strategies for assessment based on individual accomplishments geared to real-life circumstances. Students keep journals and **portfolios**, for example, which teachers evaluate periodically. Baker and Linn (1992) report an assessment strategy in which students read speeches from the Lincoln-Douglas debates and then write essays demonstrating their understanding of the issues and facts presented in them. Think about your own experiences with tests. How relevant have most of these tests been to actual skills you need outside the classroom?

The new trends in assessment are based on the following developments about teaching and learning (Herman, Aschbacher, & Winters, 1992):

- Cognitive learning theories have influenced instruction such that more emphasis is placed on complex thinking skills. In the past, behavioral learning theories dominated educators' thinking about instruction. As you recall from Chapter 2, behaviorists view learning as the acquisition of knowledge in small steps, that is, learning basic skills in a carefully arranged sequence. As a result, the assessment strategy of the past tended to focus on the evaluation of basic rather than complex knowledge.
- Cognitive learning theories also emphasize the reflective and self-regulated aspects of the learner. Thus, more attention is now given to how students interpret and use knowledge to solve complex problems. It is difficult to measure such skills with multiple-choice tests.
- More attention is given to multiple intelligences (for example, Gardner and Sternberg) that emphasize the existence of a variety of human talents and abilities. New assessment measures need to be developed to evaluate these characteristics.
- Recent studies indicate the integration of learning and motivation. In Chapters 3 and 4 you learned that a person may acquire knowledge but may not be motivated to use it. Today, in the area of writing,

researchers are demonstrating the value of involving learners in the thoughtful consideration of what constitutes good work and then having them evaluate their own products (Burnham, 1986). This ongoing reflection appears to help them understand and internalize high standards.

- We have learned a good deal about the role of the social context in influencing cognitive abilities (see Chapter 4 on cooperative learning and Chapter 9 on sociocultural factors in learning). We now need to develop assessment measures to identify learning outcomes in collaborative settings.

standardized test. A test commercially prepared by measurement experts who have carefully studied all test items used in a large number of schools.

You are fortunate. You are coming into the classroom with an extremely wide range of assessment strategies and instruments available to you, from informal observation, portfolios, and journals to an extraordinary variety of **standardized tests** and measures. Many publishing companies now provide computerized test banks where you can choose your own test items for each chapter in a textbook. In this chapter, I will explore the basic components and issues, so that you can feel confident you are making appropriate and effective instructional decisions about your students.

At the center of the assessment process, of course, are your students. When students hear the term *evaluation* or *assessment*, they usually think "test" and "grade." By the time students reach college, they will have taken literally hundreds of tests, some welcomed but most feared. Can you remember how you felt as a child, waiting for your teacher to return a test or a homework assignment? What about the sleepless night before an important examination in college, or waiting for the postcard reporting your final grade?

Students usually do not understand the purposes of testing and evaluation. Take the time to explain the purpose of assessment activities, so your students can better understand the need for them—and how you will use the information. Also, consider how your policies and procedures regarding assessment and evaluation may influence students' achievement, motivation, and classroom behavior.

In the remainder of the chapter, I will examine the terminology associated with testing, determine what makes a good assessment instrument, and assess the strengths and weaknesses of the instruments available to you. I also will spend some time discussing the controversies about performance assessment and standardized tests, describe strategies for helping your students become efficient test takers, and provide guidance for creating your own assessment instruments.

THE USE OF EVALUATION IN CLASSROOM INSTRUCTION

In Chapter 1, I suggested that teachers are involved in evaluation throughout the teaching-learning process. The examples of instructional decisions identified in the preceding section illustrate this involvement: Teachers

Teachers evaluate student progress so that they can make more effective instructional decisions.

placement evaluation. A process of determining performance at the beginning of instruction to decide where a student should begin in the instructional sequence.

must make some decisions before beginning instruction (e.g., How realistic are my teaching plans for this particular group of pupils?); during instruction (e.g., To what extent are the pupils progressing beyond the minimum essentials?); after instruction (e.g., Which school mark should be assigned to each pupil?).

Airasian and Madaus (1972) developed a classification system for describing evaluation procedures for various instructional purposes that helps to organize the types of questions that concern teachers in planning, implementing, and evaluating the outcomes of instruction. The system includes four functions of evaluation—*placement* (to determine student performance at the beginning of instruction), *formative* (to monitor learning progress during instruction), *diagnostic* (to diagnose learning difficulties during instruction), and *summative* (to evaluate achievement at the end of instruction). I first introduced formative and summative evaluation in Chapter 2 when describing mastery learning. Gronlund (1985) provides a summary of each type of evaluation.

Placement Evaluation

Placement evaluation is concerned with the student's entry behavior before the beginning of instruction. A number of important questions need to be answered at this stage of instruction: Does the student have the needed knowledge and skills to begin instruction? Has the student already mastered the objectives of the particular lesson or unit? Does the student's ability, attitude, or interest indicate that he or she would benefit from a particular method of instruction? To answer these questions, teachers use a variety of instruments such as readiness tests, aptitude tests, pretests on course objectives, and observational techniques. In summary, placement evaluation concerns relate to placing students in the proper position in the instructional sequence and providing the most beneficial method of instruction for each student.

Formative Evaluation

Formative evaluation is used to provide ongoing feedback to the teacher and student regarding success and failure during instruction. This feedback is helpful in deciding whether changes in subsequent learning experiences are needed and in determining specific learning errors that need correction. Formative evaluation depends on the development of specific tests to measure the particular aspect of instruction that is covered. For example, if you spend two weeks covering World War I in a history class, you may want to determine students' knowledge after the first week in order to decide what should be reviewed and how the second week of instruction should be approached. In this case, you'll need a specially designed test on the material in the first week to provide the information. Observational methods, in addition to paper-and-pencil tests, and review of homework assignments also are useful in monitoring student progress.

formative evaluation. The measurement of student achievement before or during instruction.

diagnostic evaluation. Tests and observational techniques designed to assess the skills and abilities that are important in learning a particular subject.

summative evaluation. The measurement of student achievement at the end of an instructional unit.

Diagnostic Evaluation

Diagnostic evaluation is used when formative evaluation does not answer all the questions regarding problems students have with certain instructional objectives. For example, why is it that Manuel cannot divide by two digits? Why does Sarah confuse certain letters in reading? Diagnostic evaluation searches for the underlying causes of learning problems in order to formulate a specific plan for remedial action. It involves special diagnostic instruments as well as observational techniques.

Summative Evaluation

Summative evaluation generally comes at the end of instruction to determine how well students have attained the instructional objectives, to provide information to grade students, and/or to evaluate teacher effectiveness. This type of evaluation usually includes achievement tests, rating scales, and evaluations of student products. Some educators believe that teachers overemphasize this category of evaluation while neglecting the other three categories in improving student achievement. It is important to remember that giving students grades is only a small part of the assessment and evaluation process.

JUDGING STUDENT LEARNING: NORM-REFERENCED AND CRITERION-REFERENCED ASSESSMENT

? How do norm-referenced and criterion-referenced assessment differ?

In evaluating achievement, you can interpret student learning in one or both of two ways: (1) in terms of performance relative to a group, or (2) in

norm-referenced assessment. A rating based on an individual's performance when compared with the performance of others on the same test.

criterion-referenced assessment. A testing procedure in which an individual's performance is based on whether specific objectives have been achieved.

terms of performance relative to a behavioral criterion of proficiency. The first method is called **norm-referenced assessment;** the second, **criterion-referenced assessment.**

Norm-referenced assessment is the most common method of testing used by teachers and thus receives the most attention in this book. Students' scores on most tests reflect their performance as compared with that of their classmates. Giving students grades based on students' ranking in class, such as "grading on the curve" in college classrooms, is an example of norm-referenced assessment.

In recent years, *criterion-referenced assessment* has become more widely used. With this method, the performance of a student is measured in terms of the learning outcomes or objectives of the course. The statement "Lisa did better than 80 percent of the students on a test of biological terminology" (although she may have answered only 60 percent of the questions correctly) is a norm-referenced assessment. In criterion-referenced assessment, we might say that Lisa correctly answered 80 percent of the items on a test of biological terminology. Thus, *80 percent* means something quite different in the two situations.

In *criterion-referenced assessment,* the teacher concentrates on a limited number of specific objectives. Explicit instructional objectives are necessary because each test item must correspond to a particular objective or criterion. The following objectives and corresponding test items reflect this relationship:

Objective	**Sample Test Item**
A. Discriminates between +, −, =, ×	A. Draw a circle around the sign that means "to add": + − = ×
B. Names the instrument used for measuring each weather unit.	B. The instrument used to measure the amount of precipitation in a city is called a (an) ____________.

In criterion-referenced assessment, the teacher is primarily concerned with how many items in a set of specific objectives a particular student has mastered. In norm-referenced assessment, the test items are written to reflect the objectives and content in a more diffuse manner and result in a large spread of scores, which is necessary to rank students reliably in order of achievement. Criterion-referenced assessment does not aim for a wide range of scores because the purpose is to have all students master the objectives. You may want to review the discussion of writing objectives (Chapter 6) before you read on.

The actual construction of norm-referenced and criterion-referenced tests is similar, using both essay and objective items. The difference lies in the purpose of the tests.

Criterion-referenced testing tends to be used more in mastery learning programs (discussed in Chapter 2) when the instructional intent is to raise almost all students to a specified level of achievement. Presently, classroom instruction uses this testing to greatest advantage when the learning outcomes are cumulative and progressively more complex, as in mathematics, reading, and foreign languages, and when minimum levels of mastery can be established. When the subject matter is not cumulative, when the student does not need to reach some specified level of competency, and when tests measure success in comparative steps, norm-referenced testing is preferred.

validity. The appropriateness of the interpretation of a test score with regard to a particular use.

reliability. The extent to which a test is consistent in measuring what it is supposed to measure.

CHARACTERISTICS OF A GOOD TEST

? Why are both validity and reliability necessary in evaluating tests?

A good test measures what it is intended to measure and does so in a way that achieves consistent results over time. Anyone can develop an instrument and state that it serves a specific function or purpose. For example, we often find pamphlets in drugstores describing how for a small fee individuals can determine their personality profiles by completing a brief questionnaire. In most cases, these questionnaires cannot accurately measure personality or any other trait. Fortunately, evaluation specialists have developed specific criteria for judging the quality of various assessment instruments. Test specialists are expected to provide detailed information concerning these criteria. Two of the most important criteria for evaluating instruments are **validity** and **reliability**. Each criterion is discussed in terms of norm-referenced assessment.

Validity

Test validity refers to the appropriateness of the interpretation of the test scores with regard to a particular use. For example, if a test is to be used to measure reading comprehension, it should measure reading comprehension. It should not measure other irrelevant factors unassociated with comprehension. The more a test can be shown to accomplish this goal, the more valid is the test.

It is important to realize three things about validity:

1. Validity refers to the *appropriate use of test scores* and not to the test itself. A test may measure knowledge in reading validly, but if the score is used to support a claim that an individual is gifted, then it is invalid.
2. Validity is a *matter of degree,* rather than an all-or-nothing proposition. Tests are not absolutely valid or invalid, but rather more or less valid for the purpose for which they are intended.
3. Validity is *specific to a particular use.* No test serves all purposes equally well. A test may have high validity for measuring mathematical reasoning, but low validity for measuring computational skills (Gronlund, 1985).

In the past, validity was separated into three types—content, criterion related, and construct. However, the most recent revision of the *Standards*

content validity. The ability of a test to sample adequately a specific universe of content.

criterion-related validity. The extent to which scores on a test are in agreement with or predict some given criterion measure.

construct validity. The degree to which a test measures specific psychological traits or constructs.

for Educational and Psychological Testing (1985) takes the position that validity is *unitary* and that each of what used to be considered separate types of validity should be thought of as approaches to establishing validity. Messick (1981) points out that this change was made because the notion of separate types of validity gives the impression that the types are equal and that any one type could be used by test developers to establish validity.

? How is content validity related to the objectives of a course?

Content validity aims for an adequate sampling of a specified universe of content. To the teacher constructing a test, this means that the test should include test items that sufficiently represent the instructional objectives of the unit and the subject matter. After analyzing the test questions in their courses, students often remark that some material was not even tested on the examination. Such tests may have low content validity. Later in this chapter, I will identify some guidelines to help you ensure content validity when constructing your own tests.

Criterion-related validity is concerned with two questions: How well does the test judge present ability? How well does the test judge future ability? Let us take two examples of tests: A typing test determines an applicant's ability as a secretary; the Scholastic Assessment Test (SAT) predicts a student's future academic performance in college. In the first example, we want to estimate present ability, and we obtain the relationship between the test score and present performance at the same time. A high correlation in this case would suggest that the typing test is a good indicator of typing skills on the job. This type of criterion-related validity is often called *concurrent validity*. In the second example, we are interested in prediction, and we extend the criterion related to the test scores over a period of time (usually a student's grade-point average during the first semester in college). This type of criterion-related validity is called *predictive validity.* Time is the variable in the two types of criterion-related validity. The typical procedure for reporting criterion-related validity is by the use of a *validity coefficient*, which reveals the correlation, or relationship, between the test and the criterion. Although the criterion could be another test, it usually is some other type of performance indicator.

The third approach to validity is **construct validity**. Psychologists develop tests to measure traits and abilities such as intelligence, anxiety, creativity, and social adjustment. These traits are also called *constructs.* The tests determine the "amount" of the trait or construct a person possesses.

Although a test may exhibit more than one approach to validity, some tests are constructed with one major source of validity in mind. Content validity is an earmark of teacher-made tests and standardized achievement tests. Criterion-related validity is the main factor in the scholastic aptitude tests used to predict school or college success. Construct validity justifies the use of a test for measuring specific psychological traits or abilities.

Reliability

> **?** Why are different types of reliability used in measurement?

test-retest reliability. A type of reliability measure obtained by administering the same test a second time, after a short interval, and correlating the two sets of scores.

equivalent forms reliability. Two tests having nearly the same level of difficulty.

split-half reliability. A measure of reliability obtained by correlating the odd and even items on a test.

Reliability refers to the *consistency* of test scores or other evaluation results from one measure to another. The methods available for determining reliability are evidence of the recognition that there are different types of consistency. Two important kinds of reliability are consistency over time and consistency over different forms of an evaluation instrument.

CONSISTENCY OVER TIME. Consistency over time is often referred to as **test-retest reliability**. In this procedure, individuals take the same test at two different times, and the results of the tests are compared by using a correlation coefficient (see appendix to Chapter 1). If the results are stable—students who score high on the first administration score high on the second administration, and low achievers score low both times—this consistency will be indicated by a high positive correlation.

CONSISTENCY OVER EQUIVALENT TESTS. Consistency over different but **equivalent forms** of the *same* test is determined by administering these forms to the same students in close succession and then correlating the resulting scores. The correlation coefficient so obtained provides a measure of equivalence indicating the degree to which the two forms of the test measure the same aspects of student behavior. A high correlation coefficient would indicate that either test could be used to measure students' knowledge of the material. A low correlation coefficient would indicate that the two forms of the test *do not* measure the same material or that they differ in the degree of difficulty. This type of reliability is important when using different forms of a test to measure the growth of students over a period. For example, students can be given form *A* of an achievement test in September and form *B* at the end of the year. If a history teacher has many sections of the same class, the teacher may want to use two forms of the same test. However, unless the two tests cover the same material with a similar level of difficulty, the procedure will be unfair to some students. The teacher should evaluate the equivalent form reliability of the tests before using them.

INTERNAL CONSISTENCY. A third type of reliability is called **split-half,** a measure of the internal consistency of the test. It is similar to the equivalent forms method. In the split-half method the two equivalent forms are contained in the same test. Thus, instead of two different tests, only one test is administered. Suppose a teacher has a 100-item multiple-choice test. After the test is completed, he divides the test into two 50-item tests and gives each student a score on the odd items and another score on the even items. The assumption is that students should score about the same on the odd and even items of the test.

IMPLICATIONS FOR TEACHING. In general, teachers can improve the reliability of their tests in three ways:

- Include items that discriminate among students, so that almost no one gets all the items correct or incorrect (reliability is higher when the items are of medium difficulty because the scores are spread out over a greater range).
- Use objective scoring procedures.
- Include a sufficient number of test items. In general, a longer test is more reliable than a shorter one. This is why test specialists recommend that multiple-choice tests include at least 35 to 40 items.

In thinking about reliability and validity, remember that a test can be reliable without being valid, but a valid test must be reliable. For example, your instructor could give a spelling test for the final examination in this course. The instructor could show that the test produces relatively consistent scores on test-retest reliability. However, does the test measure knowledge of educational psychology? Is the test valid? Obviously not! If you can determine that a test has a high degree of validity, then you can be assured of a reasonable level of reliability.

We are now ready to explore the types of measurement instruments—both formal and informal—used by teachers in making placement, formative, diagnostic, and summative evaluations. Remember, no matter what the function or purpose of the instrument being used, the goal is to select or develop the most valid and reliable instrument possible.

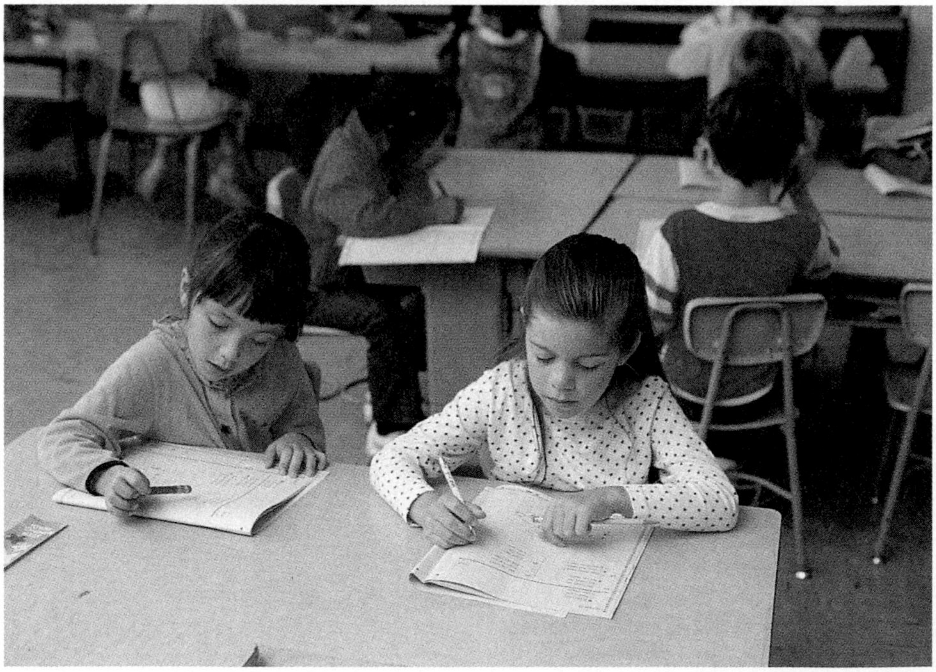

Children begin taking standardized achievement tests in the first grade.

STANDARDIZED TESTS

norms. Test results from a sample of students similar to those who will take the test.

Can you remember during your elementary or secondary education when you were told that you were going to be given a special test? The test may have been given in a large auditorium with many other students. The test booklets were sealed and you were told not to open them until you were told to do so. You knew from the way the proctor spoke that the test was different from other tests you experienced.

The tests you took are called standardized tests and include the following characteristics:

- They are commercially constructed by measurement experts who have carefully prepared and studied all test items.
- They measure various aspects of human behavior under uniform procedures.
- They include a fixed set of questions with the same directions, timing, constraints, and scoring procedures.

? Why is it important for educators to learn about test norms before selecting an achievement test?

Test publishers provide a reference, or norm, group of students who have already taken the test so that teachers can compare their students' performances with those of other students in the state or nation. Thus test **norms** provide a standard for comparing an individual's relative level of performance on a specific test. Test norms usually are provided in tables in the test manual.

Norms are established as part of the standardization process by administering the test to representative groups of students for whom the test was constructed. For example, if a test is designed to measure the arithmetic achievement of seventh and eighth graders, the test specialists would obtain scores of representative seventh and eighth graders from many regions and schools throughout the country. The size and sampling procedures for selecting schools and students differ from one test to another. As a result, the educational committee responsible for selecting tests in a school district must evaluate the appropriateness of the norm or comparison group provided by the test publishers before selecting a test. In some situations, a test may have a norm group (e.g., students in urban areas) with which it would be inappropriate to compare the performance of students in another group (e.g., students in a rural school). Most test publishers who distribute achievement tests nationally undertake large-scale norming procedures that involve representative groups from all geographical regions of the country and from schools of different sizes and cultural and ethnic composition.

aptitude test. A test used to predict how well a student will learn unfamiliar material.

achievement test. A test that measures how much a student has learned in a subject area.

? What is the difference between an aptitude test and an achievement test?

The two types of standardized tests most used in school evaluation programs are the **aptitude test** and the **achievement test.** An aptitude test attempts to predict a student's potential for success in learning. The individual intelligence tests and group scholastic aptitude tests are the most widely used aptitude tests. They are useful in comparing a students' actual achievement, in the form of school grades, with their potential achievement. The results of an aptitude test often indicate that a student has the potential to attain a higher achievement level than is presently being achieved. Aptitude tests are often used in placement evaluation.

An achievement test measures how much of the academic content a student has learned in a particular grade level or course. Various forms of achievement tests are used in placement evaluation (to determine whether students have the needed knowledge to begin instruction), in diagnostic evaluation (to determine the underlying causes of learning problems), and in summative evaluation (to determine how well students have attained the instructional objectives). A school district can evaluate its instructional program by comparing students' achievement test results with those of other students in the state or nation. For example, if the students in a particular high school score consistently lower than the norm in mathematics, the school district should evaluate its curriculum and instructional methods.

The SAT examination that is required as part of the admission procedure for most colleges involves both aptitude and achievement testing. The aptitude section provides a verbal and quantitative score and is used to predict students' academic success during their freshman year. The SAT also offers numerous achievement tests in different academic areas to determine how much *knowledge* students have acquired in each area. How predictive were your own SAT scores? According to the norms, the higher a student scores over 1000 (total verbal and quantitative scores), the more successful he or she will be during the first year of college. Keep in mind that the SAT tests don't measure motivation, study habits, and other personal characteristics that also influence academic achievement.

Since schools often judge their success based on their students' scores on standardized achievement tests, principals want their teachers to prepare their students for the tests by teaching the appropriate curriculum. For a long time, standardized tests were considered *the* measure of academic achievement. Today, they are more likely to be considered *one* type of measure. A recent national study by Madaus (1992) has raised some concern that the tests may be forcing teachers to teach "low-level" facts and skills that are measured by the tests rather than higher-level thinking skills. Some educators argue that these tests are necessary to maintain standards; others argue that the tests have a negative influence on what is taught in schools. The material in Chapters 12 and 13 will help you analyze different achievement tests, administer them appropriately, and discuss your students' test results with their parents.

Other standardized tests used to a lesser extent in school are interest, attitude, and personality inventories. Guidance counselors use interest inventories to help them in vocational counseling. Attitude and personality inventories identify factors that may influence study habits, motivation, and adjustment in school, and they can be helpful in furthering teachers' and counselors' understanding of their students.

Because most of the standardized tests used in school are aptitude and achievement tests, this chapter focuses on them. If you are interested in learning more about other types of tests, see the list of suggested readings at the end of this chapter for basic textbooks on measurement and evaluation that include discussions on a wide variety of standardized tests.

APTITUDE TESTS

In Chapter 8, I introduced individual intelligence tests as one method of assessing aptitude. Most of the aptitude testing in schools is done on a group basis. *Scholastic aptitude tests*, like achievement tests, are usually administered to a large number of students at one time by persons with relatively little training in test administration. These aptitude tests attempt to predict school success. The names of group tests often cause confusion over what they measure; do not make a decision to use a test on its name alone, for it may turn out to measure something entirely different from what you intended.

The use of group tests above the first two to three grades requires that the students be able to read the questions and the choice of responses and indicate their responses on a special answer sheet. School officials need to make decisions about the appropriateness of the test format, types of test items, and their level of difficulty for various ages and grade levels.

Some group aptitude tests provide a single score similar to that of the Stanford-Binet, whereas others provide two or more scores based on separate types of mental ability. Examples of single-score tests are the Henmon-Nelson Tests of Mental Ability (grades 3–12) and the Otis-Lennon Mental Ability Test (grades K–12). Tests which include both verbal and performance or quantitative scores are the Cognitive Abilities Test (CAT) (grades K–12) and the Kuhlman-Anderson Measure of Academic Potential (grades K–12).

Although group tests are economical and easy to administer, they have some disadvantages. First, the uninterested and unmotivated student may score lower on a group test than on an individually administered test because there is no individual examiner to focus specifically on that student's responses. Second, group tests rely heavily on paper-and-pencil items and emphasize speed, verbal ability, and reading comprehension to a much greater extent than do individual tests. Last, the scoring is completely objective and allows no room for judgment of test-taking behavior. It is not uncommon for a teacher to ask for the administration of

teacher-made test. An *achievement test* constructed by classroom teachers to measure the specific goals or objectives of particular courses.

an individual intelligence test when information about a student appears to be inconsistent with the group test result.

ACHIEVEMENT TESTS

The measurement of educational achievement is an important part of developing effective educational programs because not all methods and procedures are uniformly successful. As a result, students, teachers, parents, and school officials need to know how successful their efforts have been, so that decisions can be made regarding which practices to continue and which to change. Two types of achievement tests provide information about student progress—*standardized* and **teacher-made tests.**

Standardized achievement tests are constructed by test publishers for wide distribution in schools throughout the country. As a result, the content coverage must be broad enough to include the basic content taught in many schools. As mentioned earlier, scores are interpreted with reference to how well a given student achieved in comparison with a state or national sample of students at the same age or grade level. Teacher-made achievement tests are constructed by the classroom teacher, or sometimes by several teachers, to measure the specific curriculum of a particular course in a particular school. Scores are interpreted with reference to a student's classmates. I first focus on standardized achievement tests and discuss teacher-made tests later in the chapter.

Standardized Achievement Tests

The standardized achievement test can be classified by content area and function (Brown, 1983). Some achievement tests measure knowledge of arithmetic; others, history, physics, and other school subjects. Many achievement tests are batteries, measuring many content areas rather than only one. The teacher can then compare test scores on the separate subtests to determine the relative strengths and weaknesses of students in the areas covered by the test.

Elementary school achievement tests focus on the basic skills taught in school: reading, language, mathematics, and study skills. Some tests also include measures of achievement in social studies and science. High school curricula vary more than do elementary school curricula, and, as a result, it is more difficult to develop achievement test batteries that have high content validity in all high schools. Therefore, in addition to using test batteries, high school teachers can select separate tests from specific content-oriented tests to measure achievement in English, social studies, science, or mathematics. Another approach is to use tests that measure general educational development and do not depend on any particular courses for their questions. One such test battery is the Sequential Tests of Educational Progress (STEP II). The unique aspect of this test is that it emphasizes application, interpretation, and evaluation of academic content to a greater extent than do tests that measure basic skills. Because the questions are not derived from specific course content, this test provides a fairer measure of achievement for students with different educational experiences.

School districts need to select achievement tests with care. First, although the tests have similar titles, they often differ in how much emphasis they place on the various skills measured. For example, the specific arithmetic skills tested on two achievement tests may differ. One might emphasize computational skills and the other, problem-solving abilities. Second, standardized achievement tests measure only a portion of the knowledge and skills taught in school, so be sure to choose the most appropriate test for your school's curriculum.

You can locate information about most standardized tests from *Tests in Print* (Mitchell, 1983) and *Mental Measurements Yearbooks* (Mitchell, 1985). The latter provides reviews of tests by measurement experts. You can order specimen sets of the examinations that appear in the above sources from test publishers. These sets include a copy of the actual examination booklet and test manuals that evaluate the validity and reliability of the test. Check the test items against the course content in the areas to be tested to determine whether the test adequately measures the objectives of the school.

The following are some achievement test batteries commonly used in schools:

- California Achievement Tests (grades K–12)
- Iowa Tests of Basic Skills (grades K–9)
- Comprehensive Tests of Basic Skills (grades K–12)
- Metropolitan Achievement Tests (grades K–12)
- SRA Achievement Series (grades K–12)
- Stanford Achievement Tests (grades 1–12)

A number of special types of achievement test are particularly useful in making placement and diagnostic evaluations. These instruments include the diagnostic, readiness, and individual achievement tests.

DIAGNOSTIC TESTS. A special type of achievement test used in schools is the diagnostic test, which is designed to assess those skills and abilities that are important in learning a particular subject, usually reading or mathematics. The Durrell Analysis of Reading Difficulty, for example, covers student performance in silent and oral reading, listening, comprehension, word analysis, phonetics, pronunciation, writing, and spelling. The teacher can recommend remedial instruction to overcome the learning problems identified by the test.

There are two important differences between a diagnostic test and a general achievement test. First, the diagnostic test analyzes knowledge in a single subject area in depth, whereas the general achievement test collects information on the distribution of knowledge across many subject areas. Second, the diagnostic test includes a larger proportion of items that are relatively easy to answer, the better to assess below-average performance, whereas the achievement test includes a wider range of items from very easy to very difficult, the better to assess a greater ability span for different grade levels.

READINESS TESTS. Sometimes teachers need to know whether students are ready for certain learning tasks. Reading readiness tests are most commonly used in elementary school, but other types of tests are also used. The reading readiness tests are used to determine whether the student has the necessary knowledge and skills to begin reading. They measure such skills as visual discrimination (identifying similarities and differences in words, letters, pictures), auditory discrimination (identifying similarities and differences in spoken words and sounds), and verbal comprehension. Other readiness tests measure basic concepts and skills that are important for school success. One example is the Boehm Test of Basic Concepts, which measures whether the student has learned concepts (e.g., biggest, nearest, several) needed to understand oral communication (Gronlund, 1985a).

INDIVIDUAL ACHIEVEMENT TESTS. Individual achievement tests are used to identify students who may have learning disabilities. Individual achievement tests are more likely to determine the cause of a student's difficulty because the examiner can observe the student's attention, motivation, understanding of directions, and other factors that cannot be identified on a group achievement test. In the assessment of the learning problem discussed in the development of the IEP in Chapter 11 (p. 528), the Basic Achievement Skills Individual Screener (BASIS), an individual achievement test, was used by the special education teacher to understand the nature of Billy Fields's problem. Other widely used individual achievement tests include the following:

- Peabody Individual Achievement Test (grades 1–12)
- Key Math Diagnostic Arithmetic Test (K–adult)
- Woodcock Reading Mastery Tests (K–grade 12)

Special Achievement Testing Programs

A number of large-scale testing programs have important implications for judging both student and teacher competence. As you read about these testing programs, identify your position as to the usefulness of the programs in terms of improving the quality of instruction in schools.

NATIONAL ASSESSMENT OF EDUCATIONAL PROGRESS. The National Assessment of Educational Progress is a nationwide testing program designed to report to the public and educational policymakers the educational achievement of children and young adults in the United States. This testing program involves approximately 1,500 schools representing the diversity of the school population. Student names are not identified on the tests, and no reports are available for school districts or for states. The purpose of the program is not to measure individuals or schools but to report the level of achievement attained by various groups and the nature of changes in achievement over time.

Student achievement is monitored in the following areas: reading and literature, writing, mathematics, science, social studies and citizenship, art, music, and career and occupational development. Each area is assessed every four to eight years through representative sampling of students at ages 9, 13, and 17, and of young adults from 26 to 35 years of age. The results of the testing are reported separately by test item. National results are reported for each age group by religion, sex, race, size and type of community, and level of parent education.

minimum competency testing. A testing program designed to evaluate the mastery of specified academic knowledge before granting promotion.

Data from this testing program are useful in addressing such questions as: What is the current level of academic achievement? What percentage of students can perform certain arithmetic computations? Does the assessment indicate that student performance is increasing or decreasing compared with previous assessments in the area(s)? How do rural and urban youth perform in relation to the rest of the nation? What are the differences among various groups over time? For example, have females increased their mathematical ability since the previous assessment?

? What are the strengths and weaknesses of minimum competency testing?

MINIMUM COMPETENCY TESTING FOR STUDENTS. Public schools have been criticized because of declining test scores and because students are often passed each year to the next grade without regard to their level of academic achievement. Such a promotion policy results in many students graduating from high school unable to read and deficient in the basic skills necessary for survival in society.

To rectify this problem, many states have passed laws to mandate the establishment of **minimum competency testing** for elementary and secondary school students (see Jaeger, 1989, for a comprehensive review of the issues involved in minimum competency testing). The minimum standards are determined by local school districts, or they are established on a statewide basis. The standards are measured by tests given at various grade levels, and the tests must be passed by the time the student expects to graduate. Early testing allows students who fail one or more parts of the tests to receive remedial instruction designed to help them pass the tests before the completion of the twelfth grade. A student who continues to fail the tests is usually given a "certificate of attendance" rather than a diploma.

Each state has its own regulations and procedures to determine how the testing program should operate. Some states focus primarily on basic skills in reading, writing, and arithmetic. Other states incorporate a combination of basic academic skills with "survival skills" such as consumer knowledge, oral communication, and governmental processes. In addition, the setting of standards, the grade levels assessed, and the types of testing instrument used vary widely among the states. You should find out if your state has a minimum competency testing program and how the program operates.

Included in the many issues concerning minimum competency testing programs that need to be resolved are the definition of competencies, the specification of minimal competency, and the testing of minimum competence (Haney & Madaus, 1978). Not everyone agrees on the identification of "life skills," "essential skills," or "survival skills" that should be required in education. Are the "essential skills" for a baker, a lawyer, and a salesperson the same? Perhaps skills taught in preparation for passing a test will be of little value later on. Furthermore, not everyone agrees on the appropriate cutoff levels for minimum competency. Haney and Madaus state: "In practice, the setting of minimum scores seems to be the result of compromise between judgments of what minimums seem plausible to expect and judgments about what proportions of failure seem politically tolerable" (p. 468). Larkins (1981) is more critical: "Improving the percentage of high school seniors who can pass a sixth-grade standardized reading test is not likely to halt the flight of parents who seek quality education in the form of a strong college preparatory program" (p. 136).

Testing for minimal competency raises many additional issues, among them: Are the tests measuring what students have been taught? This is an especially important concern in states requiring one test for all students in the state. In Florida, a court order prohibited the use of the mandatory literacy test (as it is called) before it was to go into effect in 1979. The test was challenged by a suit brought by a group of parents whose children failed the test. In *Debra P. v. Turlington*, a federal judge ruled that there must be a sufficient amount of time between the time the test is announced and the date when diplomas are actually denied in order to allow students the opportunity to take remedial courses. An appeals court upheld the ruling and issued an additional requirement that the state must show that the test is related to what is taught in the school curriculum (content validity). In 1983, the court was satisfied that Florida had met all the conditions and allowed it to deny diplomas to students who did not pass the test (Brown, 1983).

Other issues that are still being resolved by the states are the following: What type of remedial instruction is most appropriate for students failing the tests? How can fairness to minority group members and handicapped students be ensured? How do we know what the testing program itself is contributing to student learning?

Not all educators believe that minimum competency tests are the panacea for improving school achievement. Larkins (1981) raises a number of concerns about minimum competency programs:

- The standards often are set very low. When improvement is noted, it is difficult to determine whether it has been caused by increased knowledge or instructors teaching to the test.
- The testing programs do not address the problems with education. Larkins believes that the focus on rote learning and the overemphasis on ditto sheets to keep students busy at their desks are problems that are not being addressed.
- There is a danger that teachers will emphasize basic skills at the expense of the higher levels of learning because the higher levels are not emphasized on tests. In fact, Madaus (1981) presents evidence that the decline in Scholastic Aptitude Test (SAT) scores reflects a decline in higher-level cognitive skills, not in basic skills.

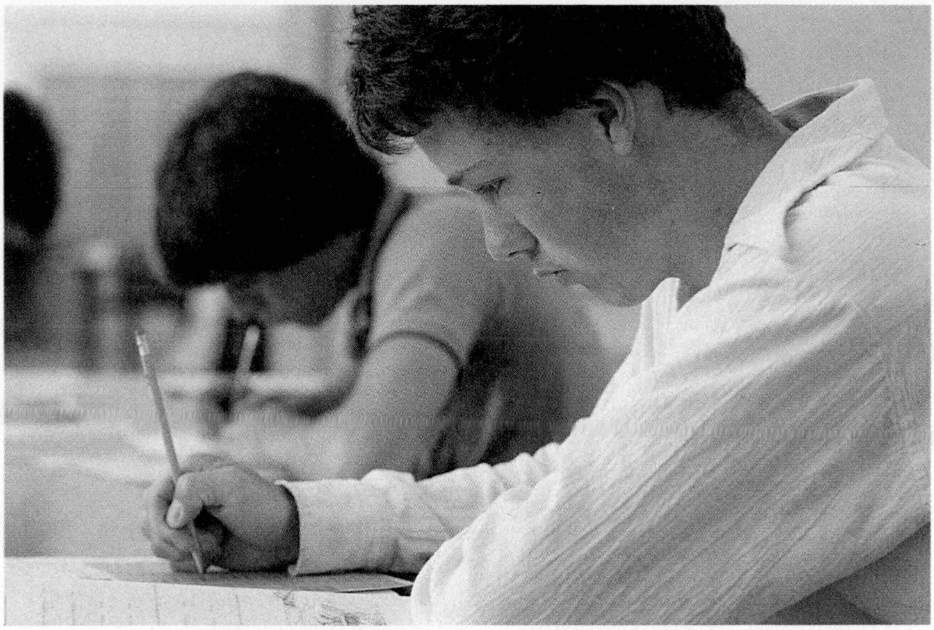

There is considerable debate as to the extent that coaching can improve students' test scores. What test strategies have you used in the past?

test-wiseness training. A program to teach students general test-taking skills.

- Minimum competency tests will drive from school students who need to be there. If students are not promoted and are placed in grades where the disparity in ages between children becomes too great, the students who are not promoted will drop out of school rather than remain for continual remediation.

Despite the controversy, it appears that minimum competency testing for students is here to stay. In the past few years, a number of different variations have emerged. For example, some states have taken a "no-pass, no-play" approach to extracurricular activities, where a student must maintain a C average to compete in any school activity. In some locations, an F grade in any subject, even though a student might have a C or better average, disqualifies a student from participating in extracurricular activities. Do you think these policies serve to motivate students to improve their academic performance? What do you see as the pros and cons?

PREPARING STUDENTS FOR TESTS

One of the major controversies in the area of testing is the effect on test scores of coaching in test-taking skills, or **test-wiseness training.** Test wiseness is defined (Millman, Bishop, & Ebel, 1965) as "a set of cognitive skills that one may employ on a myriad of tests regardless of the nature of the tests or subject content" (p. 707). Test-wiseness training teaches students general test-taking skills regarding time management, techniques to avoid errors, and guessing strategies—information that is independent of any particular content preparation.

DEBATE FORUM

Should Teachers Be Required to Pass Minimum Competency Tests?

Argument: Standards for entering and graduating from accredited teacher education programs are too low, and state certification and school selection processes are inadequate. As a result, teachers enter the profession having neither gained nor demonstrated teaching competency and knowledge of basic academic skills (Hathaway, 1980). Therefore, we need to require minimum competency or literacy tests for prospective teachers in such areas as reading, writing, language, and mathematics as a requirement for certification—and virtually every state has now legislated this requirement (Rudner, 1988). After all, if attorneys, real estate agents, and barbers have to take tests to obtain a license, why should teachers not be required to do the same? Most important, proponents believe that the testing will lead to the improvement of education as a profession.

Counterargument: Competency testing will not improve the quality of teaching. The time for assurances of competencies should be at the end of the teacher education program—not at the beginning or middle of a teaching career.

Competency tests are not valid. Such tests generally measure not classroom teaching ability but basic academic skills—which don't

coaching. A program of test preparation to increase scores on specific tests.

The term **coaching** as it relates to test preparation refers to training to increase scores on specific tests. Classes that prepare students for the Scholastic Achievement Tests (SAT) are involved in coaching to improve test scores. Although test-wiseness training and coaching have a different focus, there is some overlap of their goals. For example, certain general test-taking skills are taught in preparation for specific tests like the SAT. In addition, specific content areas can be introduced in test-wiseness training programs.

? Can students improve their test scores by attending special classes to prep for a test?

Although there is evidence that certain types of coaching can increase test scores (see Bond, 1989; Messick, 1982; Messick & Jungeblut, 1981), a number of questions remain: How much coaching? What kinds of coaching? How much improvement? Because programs vary greatly, it is important

predict on-the-job success. In those few states whose tests include some measure of actual teaching ability, no data suggest that the tests effectively predict teacher performance.

And the test standards are not high enough. A good test performance on basic skills provides no assurances that a teacher is proficient in teaching advanced mathematics or English classes.

Response: Competency testing is not the whole answer to improving the quality of education, but it represents *part* of the solution. The rest lies in attracting more competent individuals to the profession, in screening prospective teachers better, in providing more effective teacher education, and in instituting effective staff development programs in schools (Hathaway, 1980).

Newer competency tests focus more on actual classroom performance and often include such items as videotapes of lessons; portfolios including a written overview of three to five weeks of instruction, resources used in lessons, copies of handouts to students, samples of student work; and exercises evaluating the teacher's ability to solve classroom problems. Some educators believe that improved teacher assessment will lead to national standards for the teaching profession (Haertel, 1991b).

What do you think? Do you think that tests will lead to improved education? What other ways of assessing teacher performance might be valid? Would national standards for teachers upgrade the profession?

to evaluate the particular programs before reaching any conclusions about their effectiveness. Researchers have learned that the greatest change in test scores comes with more intensive training programs in terms of the number of sessions and the degree to which the programs focus on broad cognitive skills (Bangert-Drowns, Kulik, & Kulik, 1983; Messick & Jungeblut, 1981). Also, certain types of test are more responsive to coaching than are others. For example, coaching is more likely to raise test scores on the mathematics section of the SAT than on the verbal section. Finally, is the improvement worth the effort, time, and money? Students do benefit slightly from coaching, particularly if they are not familiar with the testing procedures. However, there are few students who, as a result of their coaching experience alone, score high enough to get accepted into a program of study.

The results of investigations into training in test-taking skills, or test wiseness, are similar. The training can produce a small but significant effect on academic achievement, and the longer the program, the greater the effect. Programs lasting from five to seven weeks yield greater gains (Samson, 1985; Sarnacki, 1979).

CLASSROOM Application

TEACHING TEST-TAKING SKILLS

What follows are general guidelines for teaching test-taking skills. The guidelines include anxiety reduction and an attributional focus on effort rather than on ability (Chapter 4). More advanced principles covering deductive reasoning strategies and procedures for recognizing and making use of any consistent idiosyncrasies of the test constructor (e.g., the correct option is consistently longer than the incorrect options) can be found in Millman, Bishop, and Ebel (1965) and Sarnacki (1979).

You may want to include additional information depending on the grade level and subject specialty. For example, provide practice in certain computational problems in math, demonstrate how to identify main ideas in a reading comprehension passage, and give tips for using correct grammar in sentences. After students take tests, you can ask for recommendations from them that can be added to the guidelines for improving test-taking skills. Such a discussion can be useful in focusing on specific student concerns.

Positive Motivation: Doing Your Best

1. All I ask is that you do your best. I will be really pleased if you try to do your best.
2. Before we begin, remember to listen carefully to me, be quiet, take a deep breath, and feel relaxed.

Positive Motivation: Expectancy Reassurance

1. Some tests have some very hard problems. Don't worry if you can't do some problems.

NEW DEVELOPMENTS IN TESTING

You have learned that standardized tests serve many different functions in education. Because of the importance of these tests, they tend to influence both the nature of the curriculum and the instruction that goes on in the schools. This influence should not be surprising since administrators, teachers, and parents want students to do well on the tests, which suppos-

2. If you work hard but don't finish a test, don't worry about it! The most important thing to me is that you try hard and do as well as you can. I know you'll do a good job if you try!

Use Your Time Carefully

1. Always know how much *time* you have for the test.
2. During the test, *do not* watch the clock, but check it every once in a while so that you will know how much time is left.
3. When you begin the test
   a. Answer the questions you know first.
   b. Do not spend too much time on hard questions. Try not to get upset when you cannot answer a hard question.
   c. Skip hard questions and go back to them at the end of the test.
4. When you have answered all the questions, go back and check your work.
5. Do not leave any questions blank.

Answer Every Question

1. If you do *not* know the answer to a question, read the question again.
2. Read each of the answers.
3. Mark the best answer only after you have read all the answers.
4. If you cannot figure out the answer to a question, *guess.*
5. Be sure you mark *one answer for each question. Do not leave a question blank.*

When Should You Change an Answer?

1. When you make a mistake.
2. When you think another answer is better. A few minutes after you start taking a test, you sometimes get into the swing of the test and see things in the questions that you did not notice at first. After you finish the test and start going back over the questions, if a different answer seems better, you should *change your answer.*

The two "Positive Motivation" lists are adapted from Hill & Wigfield, 1984, p. 123; the other three lists are adapted from Urman, 1982, pp. 111–115.

edly indicate that students are "learning" the prescribed curriculum. As a result, schools tend to align their curriculum and instruction to the tests.

An issue that is now being raised is whether the influence of traditional tests on the curriculum and instruction best serves the individuals who are being educated. The concerns by many educators are that not all information about students can be converted into a single score, the tests do not measure all the important abilities and skills in an educational program, and the tests focus too much on factual information.

The Importance of Measuring Higher-Level Thinking and Learning Strategies

In Chapter 3 you were introduced to cognitive psychology and its role in improving teaching and learning. Both teachers and students would clearly benefit from tests that would provide information about students' use of cognitive strategies, metacognition, and affective thought processes such as motivation and anxiety. Unfortunately, traditional standardized aptitude and achievement tests were not designed to measure these types of cognitive processes that researchers are now finding relevant to instruction. This means that new types of measurement instruments need to be developed.

In the past, aptitude tests were used to predict a student's academic performance and even place a student in a certain track or ability group in school. Herman (1991) points out:

> What we used to think of as aptitude may well be more malleable than once thought. Research on metacognition and learning strategies suggests that we can teach students to learn, and that what the uninitiated once thought of as basic ability is actually trainable. (p. 155)

As we learn more about how to measure cognitive processes, our instruction may improve to the extent that we are able to educate a larger proportion of our population more effectively.

Some progress has been made toward the development of new types of tests. For example, the Learning and Study Strategies Inventory (LASSI) (Weinstein & Palmer, 1990) and the Motivated Strategies for Learning Questionnaire (MSLQ) (Pintrich et al., 1991) are designed to measure high school and college students' use of learning and studying strategies. The MSLQ measures the learning strategies discussed in Chapters 3 and 4 (see Table 4.3).

Another criticism is that current tests place too much emphasis on factual knowledge. One can argue that multiple-choice questions can be developed to measure thinking for analysis, synthesis, and evaluation. However, other dimensions of higher-level thinking need to be evaluated. For example, we need to know more about the knowledge and level of understanding that a student brings to a mathematics or science course. We know that students have misconceptions about science that influence their learning of scientific theory and concepts. Learning more about how a student thinks about scientific phenomena could be extremely useful in planning for instruction and evaluating the success of a curriculum.

TEACHER-MADE TESTS

? How do standardized tests differ from teacher-made tests?

Although standardized tests play an important role in measurement and evaluation in education, most tests used in school are developed by classroom teachers. Standardized tests seldom fit the specific content and objectives of a given course. If you want to measure student learning at the end of a unit on the Civil War, for instance, you will have to construct your own test.

Standardized tests are useful for determining how local achievement compares with national norms; the teacher-made test is useful for measuring individual classroom instruction. Table 12.2 presents the comparative advantages of teacher-made and standardized tests of achievement.

Teacher-made achievement tests are usually divided into two categories:

1. *Objective tests,* which are highly structured and limit the type of response a student can make. The answer key designates a response as either correct or incorrect. These tests include multiple-choice, completion, matching, and true-false items.
2. *Subjective, or essay, tests,* which allow students to impose their own organization on the material and present it in their own words. In scoring an essay test, the teacher must make qualitative decisions about how close a student's answer is to the model answer.

There are no definite rules for using an objective or subjective test other than the considerations of what the teacher wants to measure and the

TABLE 12.2 COMPARISONS BETWEEN TEACHER-MADE AND STANDARDIZED ACHIEVEMENT TESTS

Characteristic	Teacher-Made Achievement Tests	Standardized Achievement Tests
Directions for administration and scoring	Usually no uniform directions specified	Specific instructions standardize administration and scoring procedures
Sampling of content	Both content and sampling are determined by classroom teacher	Content determined by curriculum and subject matter experts; involves extensive investigations of existing syllabi, textbooks, and programs; sampling of content done systematically
Construction	May be hurried and haphazard; often no test blueprints, item tryouts, item analysis or revision; quality of test may be quite poor	Uses meticulous construction procedures that include constructing objectives and test quality blueprints, employing item tryouts, item anlaysis, and item revisions
Norms	Only local classroom norms are available	In addition to local norms, standardized tests typically make available national, school district, and school building norms
Purposes and uses	Best suited for measuring particular objectives set by teacher and for intraclass comparisons	Best suited for measuring broader curriculum objectives and for interclass, school, and national comparisons.

Source: Mehrens and Lehmann, 1984.

available time for the task. Many teachers use combinations of the two types of test, since each has its merits and limitations. A comparison of essay and objective tests appears in Table 12.3. The research over the past five decades indicates that if the cognitive level of test questions is similar, telling students that the test will comprise objective or essay questions has no effect on their achievement (Crooks, 1988). Thus students who believe that the type of test question is an important factor in their performance need to be told that their studying behavior is a far more critical factor affecting their performance.

Taking time to plan a test pays dividends in a more reliable and valid measurement instrument. Too often, teachers compose tests at the last

TABLE 12.3 COMPARISONS BETWEEN ESSAY AND OBJECTIVE TESTS

	Essay	Objective
Abilities Measured	Requires the student to express himself in his own words, using information from his own background and knowledge.	Requires the student to select correct answers from given options, or to supply an answer limited to one word or phrase.
	Can tap high levels of reasoning such as required in inference, organization of ideas, comparison, and contrast.	Can also tap high levels of reasoning such as required in inference, organization of ideas, comparison, and contrast.
	Does not measure purely factual information efficiently.	Measures knowledge of facts efficiently.
Scope	Covers only a limited field of knowledge in any one test. Essay questions take so long to answer that relatively few can be answered in a given period of time. Also, the student who is especially fluent can often avoid discussing points of which he is unsure.	Covers a broad field of knowledge in one test. Since objective questions may be answered quickly, one test may contain many questions. A broad coverage helps provide reliable measurement.
Incentive to Pupils	Encourages pupils to learn how to organize their own ideas and express them effectively.	Encourages pupils to build up a broad background of knowledge and abilities.
Ease of Preparation	Requires writing only a few questions for a test. Tasks must be clearly defined, general enough to offer some leeway, specific enough to set limits.	Requires writing many questions for a test. Wording must avoid ambiguities and "giveaways." Distractors should embody most likely misconceptions.
Scoring	Usually very time-consuming to score. Permits teachers to comment directly on the reasoning processes of individual pupils. However, an answer may be scored differently by different teachers or by the same teacher at different times.	Can be scored quickly. Answer generally scored only right or wrong, but scoring is very accurate and consistent.

Source: Educational Testing Service, 1973.

minute without giving careful consideration even to the purpose of the examination. Ms. Smith, an American History teacher, announces on Monday a test for Wednesday. After school she skims through the textbook and her lecture notes for information for the examination. She writes test items until satisfied that she has a sufficient number for the test.

table of specifications. A two-way chart that relates desired learning outcomes of course content.

Ms. Smith's strategy raises a number of questions. First, does she know what learning outcomes she is measuring? If she spent most of the class time on the *analysis* of political parties' influence on foreign policy, her examination should emphasize this learning outcome and not the *recall* of factual material about the parties. Second, did she adequately cover the content of the entire unit? Perhaps she completed her test items before reaching the last chapter in the book and failed to include any questions from an important section of the material. The first question asks the teacher to think about the cognitive level of the test item. The second question shows concern for adequate coverage of the material. Taken together, the answers to these questions evaluate the content validity of the measuring instrument.

Think about the tests you have taken during your school experience. Can you identify situations in which important lecture information or required readings were not even included in the examination? What about the level of questions? Have you taken examinations that asked for an almost total regurgitation of factual material? Make a list of some characteristics of teacher-made tests that have irritated you at some time during your academic career. Maybe your instructor would like to see your list!

PLANNING THE TEST

Before beginning to write any test items, the teacher should perform three tasks. These steps can alleviate many problems in the nature and scope of the examination.

Step 1. Identify the learning outcomes to be measured by the test. Here is where instructional objectives and the *Taxonomy of Educational Objectives* (Bloom et al., 1956) come in handy. If you have written your objectives before instruction, you should have little difficulty in completing this planning phase. If you had no specified objectives for the unit, this initial step will require more time and effort.

Step 2. Outline the subject matter to be measured by the test to ensure that you identify all important content.

Step 3. Prepare a test plan or **table of specifications**. A table of specifications is a two-dimensional table on which the learning outcomes are listed along one axis and the subject matter topics along the other axis. The intersecting cells in the table allow the teacher to fill in the proportion of test items devoted to each learning outcome and each subject matter topic. An example of a table of specifications for a short unit on test construction is given in Table 12.4.

Table 12.4 A TEST PLAN FOR A UNIT ON TEST CONSTRUCTION

	Topics		
Learning Outcomes	***Characteristics of a Good Test***	***Planning a Test***	***Writing Test Items***
Evaluation			
Synthesis			
Analysis			
Application			
Comprehension			
Knowledge			

CLASSROOM Application

WRITING OBJECTIVE TEST QUESTIONS

The following guidelines demonstrate the physical makeup of the most common kinds of test items, show you how to write your own questions, give examples of good and bad items, and provide the pros and cons of their use.

MULTIPLE-CHOICE ITEMS

Format

The multiple-choice item contains a *stem,* which identifies a problem situation, and several *alternatives,* or *options,* which provide possible solutions to the problem. The alternatives include a correct answer and several plausible wrong answers, or distractors. The stem may be stated as a direct question or as an incomplete statement. The student's task is to select the correct (or best) response from the list of alternatives. The following are examples of multiple-choice items with the two types of stem:

As the teacher writes a test item, he or she makes a tally in the corresponding cell in the table. This procedure directs the teacher's attention to the assessment of instructional outcomes other than those at the knowledge level and ensures that test items are drawn from the different topics or readings in the unit. By examining the table, the teacher can easily determine whether the items adequately measure the nature of the instruction as well as the emphasis or weight given to each learning outcome and topic.

Regardless of the type of test items written for an examination, the following general guidelines for writing tests are always applicable (Chase, 1974):

- Avoid replication of the textbook in writing test items.
- Begin writing items well in advance of the test, and allow time for test revision.
- Avoid trick items and procedures.
- Make sure the directions are clear.

The last two guidelines are especially important. Some teachers forget that the purpose of examinations is to assess students and not to outwit them.

Question Variety

Stem: What is the most important type of validity in teacher-made tests?

Responses:
A. predictive
B. content
C. construct
D. concurrent

Incomplete Statement Variety

Stem: The arithmetic average is the same as the

Responses:
A. median
B. mode
C. mean
D. variance

Some items are more easily written in one format than in the other. The question format is generally easier to write and encourages the item writer to pose a clear problem, but it often results in a longer stem.

Most multiple-choice items offer four or five choices to reduce the student's chances of obtaining a correct response by guessing. There is no reason for all items on the test to include the same number of alternatives; some items generate more plausible distractors than others.

The quality of a multiple-choice item is a combination of the clarity

continued

of the stem and the skill with which the various alternatives are written. Here are some suggestions for writing multiple-choice items:

1. The stem should be clear and concise, and present only a single problem. Irrelevant detail should be left out.
   Poor: There are many important characteristics of standardized tests. The purpose of norms is to. . .
   Better: The purpose of norms is to. . .

2. Make all alternative responses grammatically consistent with the stem and parallel in form.
   Poor: The type of validity of major concern in teacher-made tests is
      1. predictive and concurrent.
      2. content.
      3. construct and content.
      4. predictive and construct.
   Better: The type of validity of major concern in teacher-made tests is
      1. predictive.
      2. content.
      3. concurrent.
      4. construct.

3. Avoid making the correct response consistently longer or shorter than the others.
   Poor: The purpose of aptitude tests in school is to
      1. predict a student's potential for success in learning.
      2. measure achievement.
      3. measure motivation.
      4. evaluate learning.
   Better: The purpose of aptitude tests in school is to
      1. predict a student's potential for success in learning.
      2. measure knowledge in different subject areas.
      3. measure a student's motivation.
      4. evaluate the validity of teacher-made tests.

4. When possible, avoid repeating words in the alternative when they can be placed in the stem.
   Poor: A percentile score
      1. indicates the percentage of students scoring above the average.
      2. indicates the percentage of students scoring below the average.
      3. indicates the percentage of scores equal to or lower than a given score.
      4. indicates the percentage of items answered correctly on a test of basic skills.

Better: A percentile score indicates the percentage of
1. students scoring above the average.
2. complex items on the test.
3. students who scored at or below a given score.
4. correct items divided by the total items on the test.

5. Underline or italicize negative wording whenever it is used in the stem of an item.
   Poor: Which of the following is not a type of teacher-made test?
   Better: Which of the following is *not* a type of teacher-made test?
6. Avoid overuse of the alternatives "all of the above" and "none of the above."
7. Vary the position of the correct answer in a random manner.
8. Be sure each item is independent of the other items in the test.

Pros and Cons

The multiple-choice item has many merits:

- It can measure objectives from the entry knowledge level to the most complex level.
- The teacher can sample a great deal of information in a relatively short time.
- Scoring is completely objective; the correct answer is not open to interpretation.
- The four or five choices reduce the possibility of obtaining a correct answer through guessing.

The main problems with multiple-choice items are the difficulty of writing test items, the overemphasis on lower cognitive skills by some teachers, and student complaints that there is often more than one defensible "correct" answer. You can remedy the latter two problems by writing items carefully.

Students commonly believe that they should stick with their first answers on multiple-choice tests. However, research studies find that students who change their responses raise their scores (Lynch & Smith, 1972; Reiling & Taylor, 1972). One explanation for this finding is that students taking examinations are aided by information from other test items as they go along, so careful reconsideration can result in a correct response.

Lynch and Smith (1972) think that when students go over a corrected examination, they are more concerned with why they got a question wrong than with why they got certain questions right. They are more likely to notice right-to-wrong changes and conclude that changing responses lowers test scores. Thus many students do not change responses. A good rule to follow if you understand a question better or recall additional information is: Change your answer!

continued

MATCHING ITEMS

Format

The matching item is a modification of the multiple-choice form. A series of stems appears in one column and the responses in another. The student must select the option that is correctly associated with the stem. The following is an example of such an item:

In the left-hand column are terms associated with different psychologists and educators. For each term, choose a name from the right-hand column, and place the letter identifying it on the line preceding the number of the term.

____ 1. self-actualization	a)	Binet
____ 2. mastery learning	b)	Bloom
____ 3. operant conditioning	c)	Bruner
____ 4. assimilation	d)	Maslow
____ 5. discovery learning	e)	Piaget
	f)	Skinner

These are some suggestions for constructing matching test items:

1. Include only homogeneous material in each matching exercise.
2. Indicate clearly the basis on which the matching is to be done.
3. The questions should contain at least 5 and not more than 15 items.
4. The items in the response column should be arranged in systematic order. Dates should be in chronological order, whereas names of people, terms, and so on should be in alphabetical order. This reduces the amount of time needed to search for the correct response.
5. All of the items should be on a single page.
6. Include at least one additional listing in column B so that in a five-item matching, a student who knows four answers doesn't automatically get the fifth item correct.

Pros and Cons

The matching item is most appropriate for assessing associations. It is not readily adaptable for measuring complex levels of learning.

COMPLETION ITEMS

Format

A completion, or fill-in-the-blank, item confronts the students with a statement for which they must supply a missing word or phrase. This type of item emphasizes *recall* of previously learned material rather than recognition.

The Stanford-Binet is an example of a(n) ________ test.

Following are some suggestions for construction of completion items:

1. Omit key words and phrases rather than trivial details.
2. Avoid overmutilated statements, such as "The ________ and ________ were ________ in World War II."
3. If possible, construct items to require a single-word answer.
4. Avoid lifting statements directly from the text.
5. Make the blanks of uniform length.
6. Avoid grammatical clues to the expected answer.
7. Arrange the test with the answers in a column for easier scoring.
8. Prepare a scoring key that contains all acceptable answers.

Pros and Cons

The completion item is relatively easy to construct. It requires recall of information, so it reduces the possibility of guessing the correct answer from the correct response.

The completion item has its limits. Scoring is difficult because constructing items for only one answer is difficult. Second, answers are restricted to a few words, and the items tend to measure recall of specific facts rather than more complex learning outcomes.

TRUE-FALSE ITEMS

Format

The true-false item is a declarative sentence that the test taker must decide is correct (true) or incorrect (false).

T F A table of specifications is used to plan for teacher-made tests.

The following are some suggestions for constructing true-false items:

1. Include only one central idea in each statement.
2. Word the statement so precisely that it is unequivocally true or false.
3. Keep the statements short, and use simple language.
4. Use negative statements sparingly and avoid double negatives.
5. Avoid use of specific terms such as *always, never,* and *seldom.*
6. Attribute statements of opinion to a source.
7. Avoid a disproportionate number of either true or false statements.
8. Explain the desired method of marking before the students begin the test. You may have them write out the words *true* or *false* or circle the correct letter.

Pros and Cons

The advantage of the true-false item is that it tends to be brief. The teacher can ask questions covering a great deal of material and can score the items in a short time. Because true-false items emphasize memorizing facts and are open to guesswork, they have their limits, too.

CLASSROOM Application

WRITING ESSAY TEST QUESTIONS

Essay questions are used to their best advantage in measuring higher-order mental processes—application, analysis, synthesis, and evaluation—and should not be used to measure knowledge of facts or principles. They provide an opportunity for students to use their own words, style, and organization in dealing with the subject matter of a course.

Teachers should be aware of at least three limitations of essay questions:

1. The problem of *content validity*. An adequate sampling of the content and objectives of a unit or course by essay questions is very difficult. These questions take more time to answer than do objective items, limiting the number of questions that can be asked and thus limiting the content coverage of the examination.
2. The problem of *subjective scoring*. Subjectivity makes essay test results lower in reliability than objective tests. A number of extraneous factors can influence a teacher's scoring of an essay question. Poor handwriting, the use of pencil rather than pen, and spelling and grammatical errors negatively influence the teacher. A halo effect (or its opposite), which occurs when a

PERFORMANCE ASSESSMENT

? How might performance assessments provide useful information about student achievement?

In the orientation to this chapter, I introduced performance assessment as a response to the criticism that present measurement instruments don't measure the knowledge and skills that students must perform outside the classroom. For example, students are asked to demonstrate their verbal ability by responding to discrete skills like verbal analogies and vocabulary tasks instead of real-life situations in which verbal ability plays an important role in such activities as debates, discussions, and varied forms of written communication in business. Performance assessment can be achieved through both standardized achievement and teacher-made tests, although many of its advocates call for less formal, more individualized

teacher's general impression of the student affects the evaluation of the paper, is an unfortunate possibility.

3. The problem of *time.* Although essay questions take less time to write than objective questions, this gain is lost in the scoring. For this reason, teachers with large classes often limit essay testing to very specific objectives.

GUIDELINES FOR CONSTRUCTING ESSAY TESTS

1. Use essay items to measure complex learning outcomes only.
2. Relate the questions as directly as possible to the learning outcomes being measured. Gorman (1974, p. 422) suggests some key words that relate to specific types of learning you may wish to measure.

words	define, what is the meaning
facts	state, identify, describe
concepts	explain, distinguish between
relations	explain, giving reasons, examples
structures	explain the interrelationships, show how it is organized
comprehension	give the meaning, summarize
creativity	write a theme, develop a plan, suggest
problem solving	what was the cause
analysis	compare, contrast, distinguish
critical thinking	criticize (on the basis of . . .), evaluate
application, transfer	(given an example or case) explain in terms of . . .

continued

evaluation strategies. Many school districts are involving teachers in the development of performance tests in different academic areas.

Performance-based assessments:

- Tend to use open-ended tasks (i.e., students may respond to the task in many different ways)
- Emphasize higher-order thinking processes
- Require tasks that approximate as closely as possible the situations in which the student ultimately will be expected to perform
- Use varied forms of student products as evidence for assessment, for example, students' essays, journals, or other written work; and they often emphasize group rather than individual performance (Baker, O'Neil, & Linn, 1991).

Students participating in performance assessments might be asked to write an essay, conduct a group science experiment, complete a project, defend in writing how they answered a math problem, or maintain a port-

3. Formulate questions that present a clear, definite task to the students. For example, look at the following questions: (a) Discuss essay tests. (b) Discuss the merits and limitations of essay tests. The first question is too general because it allows the students to write whatever they want. The second question focuses specifically on the particular response requested of the students.
4. Provide ample time for answering, and give suggested time limits for each question.

GUIDELINES FOR SCORING ESSAY QUESTIONS

Because subjectivity in scoring is one of the major limitations of the essay question, the following guidelines for uniform standards in scoring adapted from Gronlund (1985) help reduce (although not totally alleviate) this problem.

1. *Prepare in advance a model answer and the number of credit points allowed for each question.* You have now set a standard against which all students will be judged. By determining the number of points for each question, you can further subdivide the points for various parts of the answer.
2. *Grade all papers without knowledge of the "author."* This procedure attempts to counteract the halo effect (or its opposite). You can implement it in two ways. One method is to ask the students to write their name on the back of the examination booklet so that you will not know which student you are evaluating. A second method is to pass a sheet of paper containing a series of num-

folio of their best work. The California Department of Education, through its California Assessment Program (CAP), is presently developing performance assessments in four major academic content areas—English language arts, mathematics, science, and history–social science—to correspond with new curriculum changes. Writing assessments are already in place at two grade levels. In a study in California most of the teachers surveyed indicated that they now assign more writing tasks than before the writing assessment was introduced (Anderson, 1990). This change is an example of how new assessments can change the curriculum.

A number of performance assessment tasks are currently under development throughout the country. For example, high school students are required to use mathematics and physics concepts to determine whether or not the speed of a car contributed to the death of a pedestrian; or social science students are given a number of artifacts from different civilizations in various time periods and required to make inferences about the extinct cultures (Wiggins, 1989). An assessment procedure for fourth-grade stu-

bers and ask the students to write their name on the sheet opposite one of the numbers. The students then place their number instead of their name on the examination booklet. After all the students have signed the sheet, file it until all the examinations are scored. Only then are the students' names matched with their numbers for recording the grades. Of course, if a teacher is familiar with the handwriting of the students, these procedures would not reduce the halo effect.

3. *Grade only one question at a time for all papers.* By grading the first question for all students before moving on to the next question, you are more likely to use the same standard for every student. When you switch from one model answer to another in grading each question in one paper, you will probably modify the standard. This question-by-question procedure can also limit the halo effect. Suppose a student does poorly on the first three questions of an examination but does very well on the fourth question. If you had graded each student's complete paper, you might be prejudiced by the student's poor start. Your expectations would preclude your adequately crediting the student's response to question 4.
4. *Write comments as well as grades on the paper.* Students frequently hear that examinations are learning experiences. If this is to be true, you should briefly explain deficiencies in the students' responses for their benefit. Students also like to be praised for their good work. If they receive only criticism, they might develop anxiety about writing. Can you remember any personal experiences, bad or good, with teacher evaluations of your essays or term papers?

dents in the state of New York evaluates students' understanding of scientific principles: A science lab is set up with various equipment at different stations, and students are given time to experiment with the appropriate instruments to study and solve a series of questions—for example, at the "water station" students must use their observational skills to first study and then predict what will happen when they immerse various objects in water (Zessoules & Gardner, 1991).

Guide to the Development of Performance Assessments

The measurement procedures for performance assessments are still being developed. You will find many journal articles and books on the topic. An excellent primer in the area is *A Practical Guide to Alternative Assessment* (Herman, Aschbacker, & Winters, 1992) and *Testing for Learning: How New Approaches to Evaluation Can Improve American Schools* (Mitchell, 1992).

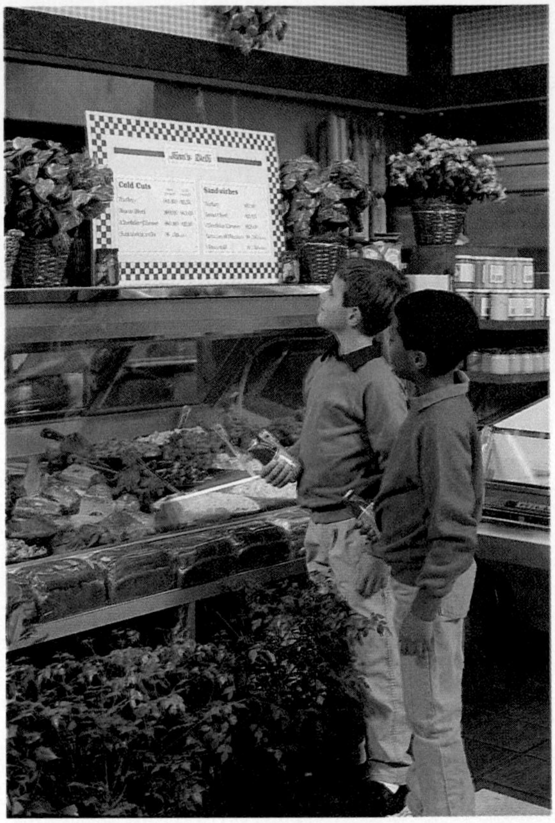

Teachers are encouraged to develop more student assessment in real-life situations.

Keep the following questions in mind in the development of your own performance assessments (Dietz & Moon, 1992):

What do you want students to know and be able to do? Focus on more than the acquisition of knowledge by emphasizing higher levels of thinking. Also, consider personal development objectives such as empathy and tolerance for others in social science and literature courses.

What will count as acceptable performance? You need to consider what students would be able to do if they mastered a specific ability. For example, the following is an example of alternative assignments given to students in an American History course to measure students' ability to demonstrate *empathy* for different periods of history:

- Create a play about a family in the Civil War, where the action revolves around the decision of a member of the family to join the army. Attach a commentary about how the members of this family are like or unlike families you know.
- Write a diary as though you were the mother of two sons during the Civil War, one fighting for the South and one for the North. Attach a statement about what you think was hardest for this mother.

- Create a chart of aspects of the Civil War that affected families. Compare the experiences of families during the recent Persian Gulf War. (p. 38)

One criterion is to determine how well students demonstrate the objective through some comparison with their own experiences, perhaps by asking them to analyze a period of history as to how they might have reacted to a situation had they lived at the time.

How can you ensure expert judgments? Considerable attention needs to be given to the development of fair and objective criteria. Most important, students must be told the criteria used to assess their work. Some criteria for the Civil War assessment might include:

- using accurate information from the historical period
- using sufficient detail to create a sense of what it was like for people who lived at the time under study
- developing relationships or comparisons between that period of history and the present
- using language that captures what it feels like to live in a period of war or turmoil

How can you provide feedback? In addition to providing written and/or personal feedback to each student based on the criteria for each project, you can discuss with students and their parents how well they are learning to make relationships and comparisons. Also consider how the development of these thinking skills might be used at home or in making practical decisions of daily life.

Portfolio Assessment

Another development in performance assessment is the use of portfolios and journals in which students maintain a collection of their writings to document the development of a research project. One of the uses of portfolios is to encourage students to evaluate their own progress as they complete a long-term assignment. Portfolio assessment has been used for years by professionals in the visual arts, music, and writing. Wiggins (1989, p. 42) provides the following example of a portfolio assignment as part of a larger graduation requirement for seniors in Racine, Wisconsin:

> The . . . portfolio, developed in the first semester, is intended to be "a reflection and analysis of the senior's own life and times." The requirements include:
>
> - a written autobiography,
> - a reflection on work (including a resume),
> - an essay on ethics,
> - a written summary of coursework in science,

- an artistic product or a written report on art (including an essay on artistic standards used in judging artwork).

GUIDELINES FOR ESTABLISHING AND USING PORTFOLIOS. When students maintain portfolios of their work, they often become directly involved in evaluating their own learning. This changes the traditional role of the student who, in the past, would wait for the teacher to evaluate his or her work. Now students are asked to become judges of their own work. Some educators believe that this type of assessment can impact student motivation and interest in the assigned task. In addition, the assessment procedure changes the role of the teacher, who now does more than evaluate. Teachers must become more reflective in helping students improve their product as they give advice about strategies they should attempt, raise questions for them to consider, and in general, provide feedback concerning their progress. In other words, teachers become more like coaches!

Although portfolios can be used in any subject area, the most common usage today appears to be in reading and writing. Portfolios consist of large folders placed in the classroom where students have easy access to them. Tierney, Carter, and Desai (1992) recommend the following strategies for using portfolios in the classroom:

- Collect samples of student work (involve students in the decision making).
- Invite parents to be involved in the portfolio process. Students can share their writing with parents to help parents understand the kind of reading and writing that is taking place in the classroom.
- Facilitate class discussion about establishing portfolios. Explain to students that they are to choose pieces that represent their strengths, interests, versatility, and effort.
- Discuss different elements that could be included in their portfolios.
- Assist students in selecting work for their portfolios.
- Ask students to write their reasons for including each piece in their portfolio. These pieces can be dated to help students recall dates completed. Work could be labeled on a 3 × 5 card, stapled to the work, that tells the strengths the piece shows or other reasons for its being included in the portfolio.
- Take time to review the portfolios by yourself. Write a few comments on a portfolio's review record about the strengths and needs you notice about each portfolio. Create checklists to facilitate instructional interventions as well as to keep track of student accomplishments.
- Update portfolios at regular intervals. As collections of student work grow, students will have a more difficult time narrowing their choices for their portfolio.
- Allow students to share their portfolios with other students at a class meeting and with their parents.
- Use portfolios to discuss aspects of student work with parents.

Performance assessment is in its early stages. It requires a new science of educational testing and assessment. A great deal of work needs to be done to develop these new procedures and ensure their validity and reliability. Many problems need to be overcome; for example, how does one evaluate a project in various stages? A portfolio might contain different tasks, some completed at earlier stages of a project and others at later stages. In addition, depending on the topic or area of interest, tasks in a portfolio could vary in length. Some tasks might be completed in an hour while other tasks might take days or weeks. Decisions need to be made about the kinds of materials included, how much of each kind, whether to score separate tasks or the total portfolio, and what criteria to use for evaluating the many different entries in the portfolio.

Most educators believe that the time and attention given to the development of new types of assessment will be worthwhile. Hiebert and Calfee (1989) concisely summarize the needed changes in learning and evaluation: "Citizens in the 21st century will not be judged by their ability to bubble in answers on test forms: Their success both personally and professionally will depend on their capacity to analyze, predict, and adapt—in short, to think for a living" (p. 54).

MEASURING AFFECTIVE OUTCOMES

When teachers need to measure the outcomes of affective objectives or to learn more about the personal concerns and learning strategies of their students, they can use a variety of measurement techniques. Some of these procedures require teachers to develop their own assessments. Open-ended questions, questionnaires, and student journals are useful formats for eliciting useful information from students.

Open-Ended Questions

Open-ended or incomplete sentences require students to complete a statement in any way they choose, thereby revealing what feelings and attitudes the topics arouse in them. The following examples illustrate stimuli that will evoke student responses:

- My teacher . . .
- What I want most . . .
- I am happiest when . . .
- The thing I like most about this class . . .
- The thing I like least about this class . . .
- Other boys [girls] . . .

Questionnaires

Questionnaires can be designed to obtain a wide variety of responses regarding student problems, attitudes, and interests. The following are some of the forms questionnaires can take:

A. On the next social studies unit

1. I want to work alone.
2. I want to work with one or two friends.
3. I want to work with a group.

B. Forty minutes of science is

1. too much.
2. about right.
3. not enough.

	Always	Sometimes	Never
C. Does the teacher give you enough time to finish tests?			
Does the teacher listen to you when you have a problem?			
Does time go quickly in this class?			

D. For each activity listed below, circle the choice that best represents how you feel about the activity in question. SL means "strongly like"; L means "like"; I means "indifferent to"; D means "dislike"; and SD means "strongly dislike."

1. Spending time in a library
   SL L I D SD
2. Listening to the top musical hits of the week
   SL L I D SD

Journals

Journals can provide opportunities for students to express their feelings about personal experiences or classroom activities. Tell students that you will not share the journal with anyone else so that they will feel comfortable about placing entries in it.

Another use of journals is to have students describe and evaluate the learning strategies they are using to learn the material in your course. These entries provide excellent opportunities to discuss effective and ineffective learning strategies with students.

Summary

THE USE OF EVALUATION IN CLASSROOM INSTRUCTION

1. Evaluation is used for various purposes—*placement* (to determine where students should be placed in the proper sequence of instruction), *formative* (to determine student performance during instruction), *diagnostic* (to diagnose learning difficulties during instruction), and *summative* (to evaluate achievement at the end of instruction).

JUDGING STUDENT LEARNING

2. Norm-referenced assessment interprets student performance relative to a group.
3. Criterion-referenced assessment interprets student performance with respect to a specified behavioral criterion of proficiency.

CHARACTERISTICS OF A GOOD TEST

4. Validity and reliability are two important criteria for evaluating the quality of tests.
5. Validity refers to the appropriateness of the interpretation of the test scores with regard to a particular use. A test may be valid for one purpose but not for another. Several approaches are taken to establish validity—content, criterion related, and construct. Validity is a matter of degree and should not be considered an all-or-none characteristic.
6. Reliability refers to the consistency of test scores or other evaluation results from one measure to another. Because there are different types of consistency, different indicators of reliability are used (e.g., test-retest, equivalent form, and split-half).

STANDARDIZED TESTS

7. Standardized tests are commercially prepared by measurement experts, and they measure behavior under uniform procedures.
8. Achievement tests measure a student's knowledge in a particular academic area at some point. Diagnostic and readiness tests are special types of achievement tests.
9. Aptitude tests predict the student's potential for success in various educational programs.
10. Scholastic aptitude tests are group tests for measuring academic potential.
11. Information on standardized tests can be located in *Tests in Print* and *Mental Measurements Yearbooks.*
12. Minimum competency testing is a procedure in which students and teachers must demonstrate mastery of specific skills.

PREPARING STUDENTS FOR TESTS

13. Training in test-taking skills can help students to perform more effectively in testing situations.

NEW DEVELOPMENTS IN TESTING

14. Many educators criticize standardized tests. These criticisms pertain to both the validity and use of the tests.
15. New tests are being developed to measure students' use of learning strategies.

TEACHER-MADE TESTS

16. The main advantage of teacher-made classroom tests over standardized tests is their greater relevance to the local curriculum.
17. The development of a table of specifications (a two-way grid integrating content and behavioral outcomes) can make test development easier for the teacher and ensure greater content validity.
18. The multiple-choice test can be used to measure objectives at all levels of complexity.
19. Essay tests are most appropriate for measuring the higher-order mental processes of application, analysis, synthesis, and evaluation.

PERFORMANCE ASSESSMENT

20. Performance assessment measures attempt to simulate real-life applications of academic knowledge.
21. Performance assessment can be used in both standardized and teacher-made tests.
22. Keep the following questions in mind while developing your own performance assessments: What do you want students to know and be able to do? What will count as acceptable performance? How can you assure expert judgments? How can you provide feedback?
23. Portfolios are used to involve students in self-evaluation.
24. Portfolios provide an alternative measure of student achievement.
25. Journals can provide opportunities for students to express their feelings about personal experiences and classroom activities.

Reflecting on Classroom Assessment

1. Identify Your Position on Standardized Testing

Which of the following statements comes closest to representing your position on standardized testing? Defend the reasons for your selection.

a. Standardized tests serve an important function by helping the school and teacher assess a student's achievement level, assisting in academic and vocational guidance, and determining placement in appropriate classes. Without these tests, teachers and administrators would make greater errors in their decisions.
b. Schools spend too much time testing students. Most tests have little impact on student learning and should be abolished. Better decisions can be made without these tests.

2. Evaluate Teacher-Made Tests

a. What types of teacher-made tests have given you the greatest aggravation in the past? Why? Obtain a copy of a teacher-made test and analyze it for examples of faulty test construction. If you cannot obtain a copy of a test, report on faulty items in a test you have recently taken. Discuss the modifications you would make in the items.
b. Obtain a copy of a teacher-made test, and classify each question according to the *Taxonomy of Educational Objectives: Cognitive Domain* (Bloom et al., 1956). Does one type of thinking dominate the test?

3. Write Exam Questions

Write 10 exam questions on material covered in Chapter 12. Adapt your questions to true-false, completion, four-item multiple-choice, matching, or short-answer formats. Ask a member of your class to answer the test items. Provide your classmate with the correct answers, and allow the person to critique the quality of your test.

4. Use the *Mental Measurements Yearbooks*

Select two or three standardized tests that a school district could use for a subject area or grade level of interest to you. Use the *Mental Measurements Yearbooks* (Mitchell, 1985) to report on the merits and limitations of each test. What are the different uses of evaluation?

Key Terms

assessment, p.549
evaluation, p. 549
performance assessment, p. 550
portfolio, p. 550
standardized test, p. 551
placement evaluation, p. 551
formative evaluation, p. 553
diagnostic evaluation, p. 553
summative evaluation, p. 553
norm-referenced assessment, p. 554
criterion-referenced assessment, p. 554
validity, p. 555
reliability, p. 555
content validity, p. 556
criterion-related validity, p. 556
construct validity, p. 556
test-retest reliability, p. 557
equivalent forms reliability, p. 557
split-half reliability, p. 557
norms, p. 559
aptitude test, p. 560
achievement test, p. 560
teacher-made test, p. 562
minimum competency testing, p. 565
test-wiseness training, p. 567
coaching, p. 568
table of specifications, p. 575

Suggestions for Further Reading

The following references are critical of the use of testing:

Block, N. J., & Dworkin, G. (Eds.). (1976). *The IQ controversy*. New York: Pantheon.
Cohen, A. S. (1988). *Tests: Marked for life?* New York: Scholastic.
Hoffmann, B. (1962). *The tyranny of testing*. New York: Collier.
Houts, P. (Ed.). (1977). *The myth of measurability*. New York: Hart.
Strenio, A. J., Jr. (1981). *The testing trap*. New York: Rawson, Wade.

For a comprehensive review of the minimum competency testing movement in the United States and a discussion of the legal and policy issues, see the following:

Jaeger, R. M. (1989). Certification of student competence. In R. L. Linn (Ed.), *Educational measurement* (3rd ed.). New York: Macmillan.
Jaeger, R. M., & Tittle, C. K. (Eds.). (1980). *Minimum competency and achievement testing: Motives, models, measures, and consequences.* Berkeley, CA: McCutchan.

Useful resources on alternative assessment:

Educational Leadership. (1992, May). A special issue on using performance assessment in school.
Herman, J. L., Aschbacher, P. R., & Winters, L. (1992). *A practical guide to alternative assessment.* Alexandria, VA: Association for Supervision and Curriculum Development.

Mitchell, R. (1992). *Testing for learning: How new approaches to evaluation can improve American schools:*. New York: Free Press.

Perrone, V. (Ed.). (1991). *Expanding student assessment.* Alexandria, VA: Association for Supervision and Curriculum Development.

Tierney, R., Carter, M. A., & Desai, L. E. (1991). *Portfolio assessment in the reading-writing classroom.* Norwood, MA: Christopher-Gordon.

The following are basic tests and measurement books:

Cangelosi, J. S. (1990). *Designing tests for evaluating student achievement.* White Plains, NY: Longman.

Ebel, R. L., & Frisbie, D. A. (1991). *Essentials of educational measurement* (5th ed.). Englewood Cliffs, NJ: Prentice-Hall.

Gronlund, N. E. (1988). *How to construct achievement tests* (4th ed.). Englewood Cliffs, NJ: Prentice-Hall.

Mehrens, W. A., & Lehmann, I. J. (1987). *Using standardized tests in education* (4th ed.). White Plains, NY: Longman.

Payne, D. A. (1992). *Measuring and evaluating educational outcomes.* New York: Merrill.

Sax, G. (1989). *Principles of educational and psychological measurement and evaluation* (3rd ed.). Belmont, CA: Wadsworth.

Chapter 13

Analyzing Test Results and Reporting Student Progress

Summarizing Test Scores
- Frequency Distribution
- Measures of Central Tendency
- Variability

Interpreting Test Scores
- Percentile Rank
- Grade-Equivalent Score
- Standard Score

Normal Distribution

Standard Error of Measurement

Classroom Application: Interpreting Standardized Test Scores

The Cumulative Record

Classroom Application: Analyzing Cumulative Records

Grading and Reporting Student Progress
- Basing Grades on the Normal Distribution
- The Inspection Method
- Basing Grades on Predetermined Levels of Achievement
- The Contract System
- Behavioral Mastery Reports
- Pass-Fail Grading
- Parent-Teacher Conferences

Grades: Help or Hindrance?

Classroom Application: Preparing and Conducting Parent Conferences

Debate Forum: Do Elementary school Students Benefit from Retention?

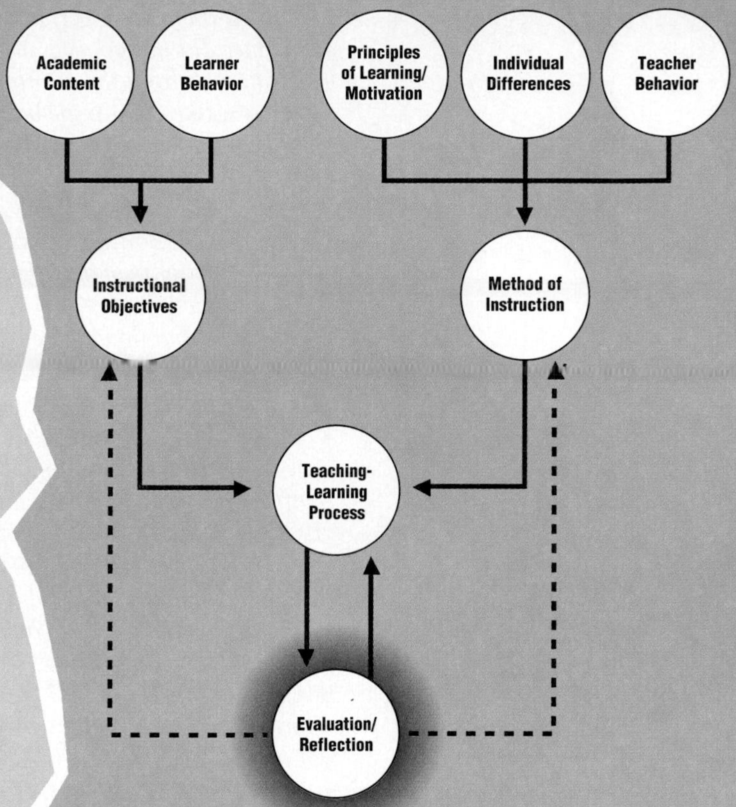

O B J E C T I V E S

After mastering the material in this chapter you will be able to:

- Read and interpret standardized test scores.
- Analyze cumulative records.
- Prepare for and conduct parent conferences.
- Select methods of grading and reporting student achievement.

Orientation

Barry Hanson was very upset after meeting with Javier Ruiz's parents. They had scheduled a parent-teacher conference for that morning, hoping to receive information about their son's performance in Barry's English class. Unfortunately, the conference did not go well, and the Ruizes left the school feeling that they had not learned much from the meeting.

As he walked down the hallway of the school, Barry was stopped by his department chair, Bonnie Miller. The following is an excerpt from their conversation:

Bonnie: *Hi, Barry. What's wrong?*

Barry: *Oh, Bon. I can't believe what just happened. I had a conference with the parents of one of my kids, Javier Ruiz, and I blew it. I mean, I really blew it.*

Bonnie: *What do you mean, you really blew it?*

Barry: *Well, for starters I showed up five minutes late. Fortunately, Alice [the guidance counselor] was able to fill in until I showed up. Then, when they asked me about how Javier was doing, I couldn't remember exactly what his grades were this quarter.*

Bonnie: *Didn't you have a printout of his grades with you?*

Barry: *I know I should have had one to give to the Ruizes, but I was running late today and I didn't have time to print one out. I was going to give them a copy, so I didn't even look at his record before I went into the meeting. All I could tell them was that he was doing "Okay" and that they didn't have to worry about Javier, that he was a great kid.*

Bonnie: *Was that true?*

Barry: *Well, he is a great kid, but there are some areas that need improvement.*

Bonnie: *Well, instead of kicking yourself, it might be wise to contact the Ruizes and reschedule. I had Javier in class last year, and I know his parents care a lot. They are very nice, very understanding people, Barry. When I gave them a complete printout with all of his assignments, including test and quiz scores, they were really thrilled. It gave them something tangible to work with.*

Barry: *What do you mean, tangible?*

Bonnie: *Well, most parents want to be able to support, at home, what's happening in the classroom. Usually, parents ask the teacher how their child is doing, and the response is "Great!" or "Just fine," when actually that teacher doesn't have the foggiest idea about their child. When you give parents something concrete, like a printout of their child's grades or some concrete suggestions about what they can do at home, they feel more in control. As a parent, I know how it feels to want to help your child's performance in school, and to have too little information from the teacher. It's really frustrating. It tells the parent that the child isn't that important.*

Barry: *I don't want the Ruizes to think that I don't consider Javier as important as any of my other students. What should I do?*

Bonnie: *Like I said, call them and ask them if they would like to reschedule another appointment. You might tell them how you felt about today's meeting, and plan another strategy for conducting a more productive conference.*

Now that you are aware of how evaluation works in the classroom, you need to know how to interpret and report test results to students and parents and to make instructional decisions based on the information you collect. In Chapter 1 you learned that beginning teachers find that assessing students' work and establishing relationships with parents are two of the major challenges they face in teaching. My goal in this chapter is to limit the possibility that these tasks will cause you any grief! I believe that lack of information is one of the primary reasons teachers have problems relating to the interpretation of test scores.

One of the factors influencing teachers' sense of efficacy is their relations with parents. Teachers need to develop skills to interact effectively with parents. Conducting productive parent-teacher conferences can be an important step toward developing a greater sense of efficacy.

Remember some of the comments made about parents of exceptional children in Chapter 11. These parents can be under a great deal of pressure in dealing with education and child-rearing problems. If you use the ideas from humanistic psychology (i.e., focus on a person's perceptions), you may better understand the concerns of parents. Also, the humanistic teacher's reliance on genuineness, trust, and empathic understanding, and the active listening skills identified by Gordon, are useful teacher behaviors for interacting with adults as well as children. If you practice these skills during conferences with parents, you may find that you are able to communicate more effectively with them.

Throughout the text I have emphasized the importance of teachers' beliefs. A study by Smith and Shepard (1988) shows how teachers' beliefs influence their decisions regarding student retention. These researchers found that teachers in schools with different retention rates tended to hold different beliefs regarding child development and school policies. The beliefs ranged from assumptions described as "nativist" (the idea that development and learning are strongly influenced by internal processes that cannot be accelerated by teacher involvement) to "remediationist" (the belief that learning and development can be influenced by educational intervention). Schools in which teachers hold nativist beliefs retained a higher proportion of students than schools in which teachers hold remediationist beliefs.

Teachers' decisions regarding evaluation have important influences on student motivation and behavior. In Chapter 4, I first mentioned the link between student motivation and evaluation. Students' self-perceptions of ability, sense of efficacy, and level of test anxiety are influenced by their evaluation experiences. For example, Natriello and Dornbusch (1985) found that student effort can be encouraged and increased by an effective evaluation system. They point out that the lack of frequent and challenging teacher evaluation of students' academic work can lead to low student effort and achievement.

There are other individual differences to consider in developing evaluation systems. For example, Bolocofsky and Mescher (1984) investigated the effects of different standards—individually referenced, criterion referenced, and norm referenced—for students who differed in their self-esteem

frequency distribution. A table that summarizes how often each score on a test occurs.

and locus of control. They found that these students performed differently under different kinds of standards. Individually referenced standards were more effective with students of low self-esteem and internal locus of control. Criterion-referenced standards were more effective with students of low self-esteem and external locus of control. Norm-referenced standards were more effective with students of high self-esteem, regardless of locus of control.

Students who receive unsatisfactory evaluations often misunderstand the criteria by which they are to be evaluated (Natriello, 1982). Therefore, you need to review carefully the criteria used to judge performance and discuss the questions students may have about their work.

Grading is one aspect of an evaluation system that can affect student behavior because grading communicates information to students about their academic and personal competencies. For example, absolute standards can be fine. However, if the standards are perceived as unattainable by some students, they may give up and expend only minimal effort in their academic work (remember information in Chapter 4 about the impact of student attributions). Norm-referenced letter grades can provide students with information as to how well they achieved in relation to their peers, but students who do poorly on early tests often reduce their time and effort in the course when they realize they cannot achieve a high grade.

Suppose your college instructor gives you two exams, each worth 50 percent of your final grade, and you receive a C on the first test early in the semester. Would this grade play any role in your work habits in this course for the rest of the semester? Think about other examples of how grading policies and procedures influence student motivation, attention, and work habits. Remember that grades generally do not motivate low achievers to excel in the classroom. Therefore, consider the issues on grading and evaluation discussed in this book before you develop your own system.

SUMMARIZING TEST SCORES

Frequency Distribution

Suppose you correct a test taken by 35 students and put the scores in your roll book. The highest possible score is 80. The next day you hand out the corrected papers. As students receive their papers, they begin to compare scores because they have no idea how well they did in comparison with others in the class. One student received a 65 on the exam. If the test was hard, a 65 could be a good score, but if the test was easy, a 65 could be a bad score. You cannot easily provide more information for the students as you look at the scores in your grade book, listed alphabetically by student.

You can, however, develop a table that summarizes the frequency with which each score occurs. This table is called a **frequency distribution** of test scores. Using this table, you and your students can get a better picture of how well the class achieved on the test. Table 13.1 is an example of a frequency distribution for 35 students on an 80-item exam. It is an improvement over a disorganized list of scores. You can summarize the

TABLE 13.1 FREQUENCY DISTRIBUTION OF TEST SCORES

Test Score	Frequency	Test Score	Frequency	Test Score	Frequency	Test Score	Frequency
78	1	68	0	58	0	48	1
77	0	67	2	57	0	47	0
76	2	66	3	56	2	46	0
75	2	65	0	55	2	45	0
74	0	64	1	54	0	44	0
73	2	63	0	53	0	43	0
72	0	62	3	52	1	42	0
71	3	61	1	51	1	41	2
70	4	60	0	50	0		
69	0	59	2	49	0		

measures of central tendency. Statistical measures that are intended to describe the typical score of a distribution.

mean. The arithmetic average of a group of scores.

median. The middle score in the distribution.

mode. The most frequently occurring score.

scores in greater detail by developing a *grouped* frequency distribution. In this distribution, you provide intervals of 5 or 10 points and determine the frequency of scores in the assigned intervals. For example, 14 students scored between 70 and 79, and 10 students scored between 60 and 69.

Measures of Central Tendency

? What is the difference between the mean, median, and mode?

As part of the analysis of a distribution of scores, we often need to calculate various measures of the average, or typical, performance of the group as a whole. These calculations are called **measures of central tendency**, the most familiar of these being the **mean**, the **median**, and the **mode**. Let's use the following small distribution of scores to determine the three measures: 8, 10, 12, 13, 16, 16, 23.

MEAN. The *mean* is the arithmetic average of a set of scores, the result of adding the scores and dividing this sum by the total number of scores.

$$\text{Mean} = \frac{\Sigma X}{N} = \frac{98}{7} = 14$$

The symbol Σ signifies "sum" whatever follows. The letter X stands for any score value, and N equals the number of scores. The symbol M is used to denote the mean.

MEDIAN. The *median* is another measure of central tendency representing the middle score in a distribution. The median in the foregoing sample distribution is 13. In a distribution with an even number of scores (8, 10, 20, 32), there are two middle values; in this case, the median is the mean of the two middle scores ([10 + 20] ÷ 2 = 15).

MODE. The third measure of central tendency is the *mode*, the score with the highest frequency of occurrence. The mode in the sample distribution

variability. The spread of scores in a distribution.

range of scores. A measure of dispersion calculated by subtracting the highest and lowest scores in a distribution.

standard deviation. A measure of the spread of scores around the *mean* of the distribution.

is 16. When a distribution has two most frequently occurring scores, it is a *bimodal* distribution.

All three of these measures provide an indication of the central tendency, but their usefulness often hinges on the character of the score distribution. The mean generally gives the best average of test scores. However, when there are extreme scores at one end of the distribution, the median can better describe the average. Look at the following distribution of scores: 90, 43, 40, 30, 22. The mean is 45 and the median is 40. Four of the five scores are less than the mean because of the one extreme score. In this case, the mean gives a less accurate impression of the actual central tendency of scores than does the median. The mode is not used as often as the mean and median, but it is appropriate when there are many identical scores, as in the following distribution: 54, 52, 52, 52, 48, 44, 43, 42, 37.

Variability

Although the measures of central tendency provide helpful information for interpreting test scores, they don't take into consideration an important characteristic of test scores. Look closely at the following distribution:

Group A	Group B
96	82
98	90
100	100
102	110
104	118
Mean = 100	Mean = 100
Median = 100	Median = 100

Although the two distributions exhibit the same mean and median, the variability, or dispersion, of the scores differs. One indicator of the **variability** is the **range of scores**. In group A, the range is 8 (104 – 96); the range for group B is 36 (118 – 82).

? Why is the standard deviation necessary in interpreting test scores?

STANDARD DEVIATION. The range tells us the variability between the highest and lowest scores in a distribution, but it doesn't tell us anything about the variability between the mean and the rest of the distribution. For this reason, the **standard deviation** is the most important measure of variability because it provides a measure of how dispersed, or spread out, the scores are around the mean. The more spread out from the mean, the larger the standard deviation. The more scores cluster around the mean, the smaller the standard deviation. The standard deviations for the scores in group A and group B are 2.8 and 13.0, respectively. This statistic is important in understanding scores in a normal curve (discussed later in this chapter).

The formula for determining the standard deviation is

$$s = \sqrt{\frac{\Sigma (X - M)^2}{N}}$$

It reads like this: "The standard deviation is equal to the square root of the sum of the squared deviation from the mean divided by the number of scores." Figure 13.1 provides a step-by-step illustration for computing the standard deviation.

raw score. A test score that identifies the number of correct responses.

s = standard deviation of a set of scores
Σ = the sum of
X = one score
M = the mean of a set of scores
N = the number of students with scores
$\sqrt{}$ = the square root of

Problem: Compute the standard deviation of the following sources: 4, 6, 8, 14.
Step 1: Prepare four columns of figures as follows: X, M, $(X - M)$, and $(X - M)^2$
Step 2: List the scores under Column X, and determine M. ($M = 8$)
Step 3: Subtract the mean from each score to obtain figures for column $(X - M)$ as follows:

X	M	$(X - M)$	$(X - M)^2$
4	8	-4	16
6	8	-2	4
8	8	0	0
14	8	6	36

Step 4: Square each of the differences in column $(X - M)$ to obtain the figure in column $(X - M)^2$ as shown above.
Step 5: Add column $(X - M)^2$ to obtain $(X - M)^2 = 56$.
Step 6: Substitute the numbers in the formula as follows:

$$s = \sqrt{\frac{56}{4}} = \quad 14$$

Step 7: Find the square root of 14:

$$s = \sqrt{14} = 3.74$$

Figure 13.1 Computational Guide for Standard Deviation.

INTERPRETING TEST SCORES

The number of items answered correctly on a test is the **raw score**. If a test has a number of subtests, each subtest engenders a separate raw score. The teacher cannot interpret the meaning of these scores or compare them with other scores if all they represent is the number of correct items. Suppose Vivian and Doreen each answer 23 items correctly on their French and Spanish examinations, respectively. Who performed better? First, we don't know the number of items on each test. Second, we do not know how Vivian and Doreen performed in relation to other students.

derived score. A raw score that has been converted to another scale.

percentile rank. The percentage of scores equal to or lower than a given score in a distribution.

grade-equivalent score. A score expressed in terms of the school-grade placement of students whose raw scores are typical of students at that particular grade level.

standard score. A score described in terms of standard deviation units from the mean of the distribution.

To simplify the interpretation of test scores, test makers provide ways to make comparisons among test scores by converting raw scores to **derived scores.** The derived scores most frequently used in schools are the **percentile rank, grade-equivalent score,** and **standard score.**

One of the easiest ways to compare an individual's score with others in a group is to rank all the scores. The disadvantage of this method is that it does not make distinctions between the size of groups. A rank of 14 in a group of 14 is quite different from a rank of 14 in a group of 40. In the first case, the rank is the lowest in the group, whereas in the second it is considerably higher.

Percentile Rank

One way to alleviate the problem is to use a *percentile rank*. A percentile rank indicates a person's group rank in terms of the percentage of individuals at or below that person's score. If Bob's score on a science test gives him a rank of 10 in a class of 40, we can say that three-fourths, or 75 percent, of the class made a lower score than Bob on the science test. Thus, 75 is his percentile rank. Another way of stating his performance is that he scored at the 75th percentile. By using a percentile rank, the position of individuals in groups of unequal size can be compared. The designations Q_1 and Q_3 are often used to represent the 25th and 75th percentiles of a distribution, respectively.

? Does a percentile rank have anything to do with the number of items answered correctly?

No! The beginning student in measurement often confuses percentile ranks with the percentage of correct items on the test. These are two entirely different scores. Getting 85 percent of the items correct on an easy test may place a student at the 50th percentile. On a more difficult test, getting 85 percent of the items correct may place the student at the 95th percentile.

Another precaution to take with percentile ranks is not to average or add them, because they do not form equal intervals at all points along the scale. In most distributions, the distance between percentiles is less near the middle and greater at its extremes. More people tend to score in the middle range of a test. Therefore, in terms of actual points scored on a given test, a difference of 4 percentile ranks at the upper extreme—say, percentile 90 to 94—may mean a difference of 15 points on the test. On the other hand, a difference of 4 percentile ranks near the center of a distribution—say, percentile 50 to 54—may mean a difference of only 2 or 3 points.

Grade-Equivalent Score

Another type of derived score is the *grade-equivalent score*. Grade equivalents indicate the average performance of students at different grade

z score. A standard score in a distribution with a mean of 0 and a standard deviation of 1.

levels. A table for grade-equivalent scores is included in the test manual for most standardized achievement tests. If a score of 60 on a reading test has a grade equivalent of 4.9 (read "4 years, 9 months"), 60 would be the average score of students in the ninth month of the fourth grade. Because the school year comprises 10 months, grade-equivalent scores range from .0 to .9. At certain points along the scale, raw scores corresponding to grade equivalents are estimated or extrapolated rather than determined by measurement. This procedure can lead to a misinterpretation of the meaning of the scores.

Grade-equivalent scores have been popular in the elementary grades because of their apparent ease of interpretation. If a sixth-grade student takes a test in September (6.0) and scores 6.3, it is obvious that the student has scored higher than the average student in the first month of the sixth grade. The student's score is the average score obtained by students in the third month of the sixth grade.

? Why do teachers need to be cautious when reporting grade-equivalent scores to parents?

Test specialists have been concerned about the misinterpretations to which grade-equivalent scores are often subject. The units are not equal along the scale, so an increase from 5.5 to 5.6 may very well require more items correct than an increase from 5.8 to 5.9. A second circumstance open to misinterpretation occurs when a student scores two or more grades above the grade level. Can a fourth grader who receives a grade-equivalent score of 6.8 on a mathematics examination do sixth-grade mathematics? Not necessarily, for the student may have received a high grade-equivalent score by successfully completing the easier test items more quickly and accurately than the average fourth-grade student. As a result, the grade-equivalent score of 6.8 may indicate nothing more than a mastery of skills taught in the first four grades. The important point to remember is that a grade-equivalent score is not related to a student's actual ability to perform successfully at any given grade level (Gronlund, 1985a).

Standard Score

? Why do measurement specialists use standard scores?

Another way to interpret raw scores is by the use of a *standard score*, expressed in terms of standard deviation units. These scores indicate how far from the mean of the distribution a given score appears. A big plus in their favor is that they are based on equal units of measurement throughout the distribution. As a result, you can average standard scores.

A typical type of standard score is the **z score**. This score represents the number of standard deviation units a raw score is from the mean. It is based on a mean of 0 and a standard deviation of 1. A negative z score

T score. A standard score in a distribution with a mean of 50 and a standard deviation of 10.

indicates that a student scored below the mean. For example, if Debbie made a raw score of 27 in a distribution with a mean of 30 and a standard deviation of 5, her z score would be –.6. She is 3 raw-score points, or –.6 standard deviations, below the mean. Mathematically, a z score is defined as follows:

$$z = \frac{X - M}{s} = \frac{27 - 30}{5} = \frac{-3}{5} = -.6$$

If Debbie had a score equal to the mean, her z score would be zero:

$$z = \frac{30 - 30}{5} = \frac{0}{5} = 0$$

Because many individuals find negative numbers and decimals troublesome to work with, test publishers often convert the z score to a **T score**. This is done by multiplying by 10 and adding 50:

$$T = 10z + 50$$

By multiplying each z by 10, you eliminate the decimal; by adding 50 points to the product, you eliminate the negatives. The T score scale has a mean of 50 and a standard deviation of 10.

Another of the common standard scores is the College Examination Board (SAT) score. On this scale, z scores are multiplied by 100, and 500 points are added to the product. Thus, a z score of 0 (mean) is equivalent to 500, and a z score of –1 is equivalent to 400 (i.e., the standard deviation is 100).

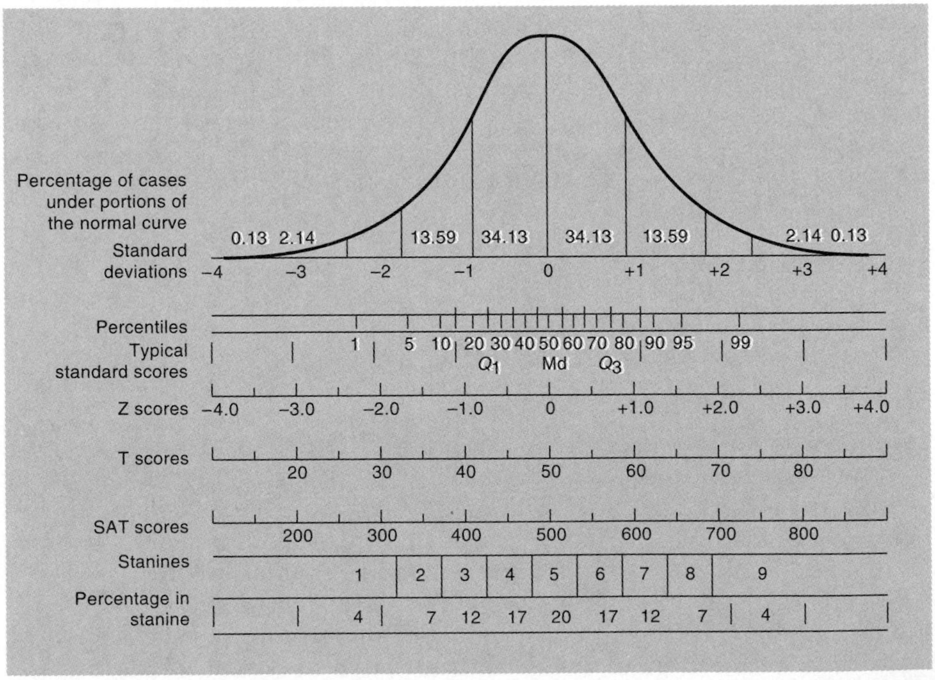

Figure 13.2 The Normal Curve and Various Derived Scores.

Many intelligence tests convert raw scores to **deviation IQ** scores, another type of standard score. Deviation IQs have a mean of 100 and standard deviations of 15 or 16 (depending on the particular test). As a result, a deviation IQ of 130 always represents a score falling 2 standard deviations from the mean (assuming $s = 15$).

To understand the relationship between the various derived scores discussed in this section, examine the normal distribution and related scales in Figure 13.2. In a normal distribution, for example, a z score of –1 is the same as a T score of 40 or a percentile rank of 16.

deviation IQ. An intelligence test score based upon the difference between an individual's score and the average score for persons of the same chronological age.

normal distribution. A symmetric distribution of test scores in which most scores lie in the center, and scores decline in frequency as they move away from the center.

stanines. Intervals on a nine-point scale of standard scores.

NORMAL DISTRIBUTION

A **normal distribution** is a mathematical model that represents the way in which many human characteristics are distributed. It is bell shaped and symmetrical, and the mean, median, and mode all fall at the same point. Because of this precise definition, it is possible to determine the proportion of scores falling under any area of the curve.

Several features of the normal distribution are of special interest in interpreting scores. For example, approximately 34 percent of the scores fall 1 standard deviation above and below the mean. This means that approximately 68 percent of normally distributed scores are within 1 standard deviation of the mean. Approximately 14 percent of the scores fall 1 to 2 standard deviations above and below the mean; approximately 2 percent of the scores fall 2 to 3 standard deviations above and below the mean.

By identifying how far a score is from the mean in a normal distribution, you can determine the percentage of scores above or below any given score. A student who receives a 600 on the Scholastic Assessment Test (SAT) is 1 standard deviation above the mean ($M = 500$). Therefore, the student scored higher than approximately 84 percent of all students taking the test. In other words, an SAT score of 600 is equivalent to a percentile rank of 84.

Many school districts report test scores by **stanines**. This type of scale divides the normal curve into nine parts. Scores are expressed along a scale ranging from 1 (low) to 9 (high), with 5 representing the average performance for students in the reference group. The percentage of students at each stanine level is shown below.

Stanine	1	2	3	4	5	6	7	8	9
Percentage	4	7	12	17	20	17	12	7	4

A stanine represents a percentage of scores; it is not a point. Therefore, in a given distribution of scores, the lowest 4 percent receives a stanine of 1, the next highest 7 percent, a stanine of 2, and so on until the highest 4 percent receive a stanine of 9.

Standardized tests have tables that convert raw scores to derived scores. The teacher must record these scores on a profile sheet for each student and interpret their meaning. In many instances a profile sheet similar to the one presented later, in Figure 13.4, is provided for the teacher.

standard error of measurement. An estimate of the amount of error in a test score.

STANDARD ERROR OF MEASUREMENT

It would suit everyone if a test score were a precise measure of a student's true ability or achievement. Unfortunately, even the best tests have some degree of error in the scores they produce. As a result, measurement experts believe that it is often desirable to record a test score as a band or interval rather than as a single point or score.

? How is the standard error of measurement used in analyzing test scores?

Most standardized test manuals report the **standard error of measurement** of a particular test. This statistic is an estimate of the amount of error in a test score. Suppose the standard error of measurement of a test is 4. If a student who makes a raw score of 40 on the test takes the test many times,

CLASSROOM Application

INTERPRETING STANDARDIZED TEST SCORES

Now that you know about the types of test scores used in reporting test results, I want to show you how these scores are used in interpreting actual results of achievement tests. Each test company provides various options for reporting test results to school districts. The most common reports are student and class profiles that identify scores by subtests and national norms for determining how well the student or class has achieved on the test in comparison with other students in the nation who have taken the test. Narrative reports that describe student performance in words, not numbers, also can be sent to parents to better communicate the meaning of the test results. Additional information that is usually available includes individual and group skill analyses, in which scores are provided for various subskills such as word study skills, reading comprehension, spelling, science, and so forth. This information can be useful in determining the specific strengths and weaknesses of students in the class. In addition, pupil and group item analyses data can be provided so that the teacher can focus more specifically on particular questions that were answered correctly or incorrectly. School committees that decide

about two-thirds of the student's scores will fall between 36 and 44 (40 ± 4). The interested reader can find more information about this statistic in any basic measurement book (see the Suggestions for Further Reading in Chapter 12).

The standard error of measurement keeps us aware of the inaccuracy of test scores and helps us to compare students. A principal who decides to offer a special class for bright students might use an aptitude test to select the composition of the class. Suppose the standard error of measurement of this test is 5. The principal decides that all students who score 70 or above on the test may select the course. Mary scores 68 and wants to take the course. On the basis of her academic record, she appears to be someone who could benefit from such a course. Because the standard error of measurement of the aptitude test is 5, Mary's actual ability is probably between 63 and 73 (68 ± 5). Thus it would be quite possible for Mary to obtain a score above the cutoff score if she were tested again. There is strong support for including Mary in the class. This example illustrates the importance of considering test scores as intervals rather than as static scores.

which test will be used in the district take into consideration the scoring and reporting systems of the published tests.

Figures 13.3 and 13.4 (on pages 610 and 611) present two forms that are used by the Psychological Corporation to report the results of the Stanford Achievement Tests. This company provides more than 15 different reports of test results. Figure 13.3 shows a ranked list of three scores with five different types of information on the fourth-grade students in Ms. Wellens's class (marked *A* through *E*) on the form. *A*—students are ranked from low to high so that administrators of funded programs can easily determine who is eligible for gifted or remedial programs. *B*—three test results are listed for each student: reading comprehension, math computation, and language. *C*—four scores are reported for each student: the raw scores, national percentile ranks (PR), stanines (S), and normal curve equivalents (NCE), which are used by the U.S. Office of Education for the evaluation of federally funded programs. The NCE is a standard score with a mean of 50 and a standard deviation of 21.06. *D*—the number of students tested and the summary statistics for the group. *E*—the number, or percentage, of students in each percentile-rank quarter.

Let's look at the results for Ms. Wellens's class in reading comprehension. Twenty-five students were ranked. They attained an average of 45.4 on the test (based on the number of items on the test). The percentile-rank information tells us that only 9 students scored in the top 50 percent of students taking the exam in the nation, and 16 students scored in the bottom 50 percent of the normative group. The lowest student in reading comprehension was Matt Grover, who received a percentile rank of 11 and a stanine of 3; the highest score was attained by Dennis Blackman, who received a percentile rank of 70 and a stanine of 6. Matt scored higher than 11 percent of the students taking

continued

the test, and Dennis scored higher than 70 percent of the students taking the test.

Figure 13.4 shows the pupil profile report, including four types of information (marked *A* through *D*) that can be sent to parents with a printed narrative report from the test company. The following types of information are provided: *A*—the names of subtests and totals; *B*—national percentile ranks and stanine; *C*—national percentile bands spanning plus or minus 1 standard error of measurement; and *D*—

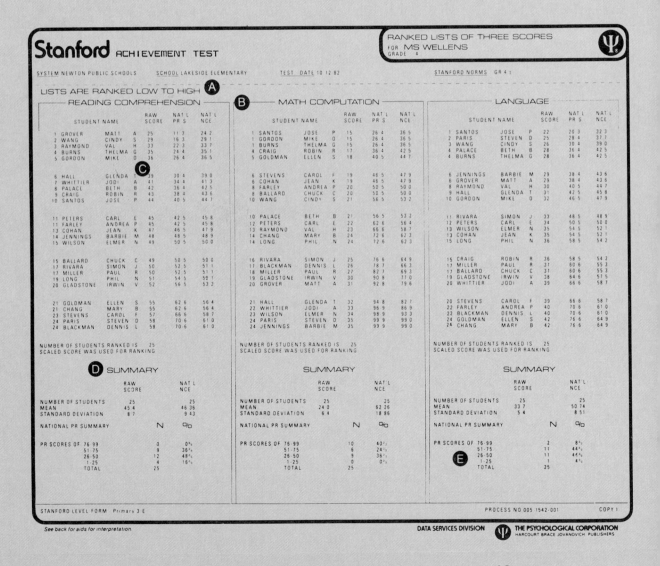

Stanford ACHIEVEMENT TEST

RANKED LISTS OF THREE SCORES
FOR MS WELLENS
GRADE 4

SYSTEM NEWTON PUBLIC SCHOOLS   SCHOOL LAKESIDE ELEMENTARY   TEST DATE 10 12 82   STANFORD NORMS GR 4 1

(A) LISTS ARE RANKED LOW TO HIGH

READING COMPREHENSION

	STUDENT NAME			RAW SCORE	NAT'L PR S	NAT'L NCE
1	GROVER	MATT	A	25	11 3	24 2
2	WANG	CINDY	S	29	16 3	29 1
3	RAYMOND	VAL	H	33	22 3	33 7
4	BURNS	THELMA	G	35	24 4	35 1
5	GORDON	MIKE	O	36	26 4	36 5
6	HALL	GLENDA	T	39	30 4	39 0
7	WHITTIER	JODI	A	41	34 4	41 3
8	PALACE	BETH	B	42	36 4	42 5
9	CRAIG	ROBIN	R	43	38 4	43 6
10	SANTOS	JOSE	P	44	40 5	44 7
11	PETERS	CARL	E	45	42 5	45 8
11	FARLEY	ANDREA	P	45	42 5	45 8
13	COHAN	JEAN	K	47	46 5	47 9
14	JENNINGS	BARBIE	M	48	48 5	48 9
15	WILSON	ELMER	N	49	50 5	50 0
15	BALLARD	CHUCK	C	49	50 5	50 0
17	RIVARA	SIMON	J	50	52 5	51 1
17	MILLER	PAUL	R	50	52 5	51 1
19	LONG	PHIL	N	51	54 5	52 1
20	GLADSTONE	IRWIN	V	52	56 5	53 2
21	GOLDMAN	ELLEN	S	55	62 6	56 4
21	CHANG	MARY	B	55	62 6	56 4
23	STEVENS	CAROL	F	57	66 6	58 7
24	PARIS	STEVEN	D	58	70 6	61 0
24	BLACKMAN	DENNIS	L	58	70 6	61 0

NUMBER OF STUDENTS RANKED IS 25
SCALED SCORE WAS USED FOR RANKING

(D) SUMMARY

	RAW SCORE	NAT'L NCE
NUMBER OF STUDENTS	25	25
MEAN	45 4	46 36
STANDARD DEVIATION	8 7	9 43

NATIONAL PR SUMMARY	N	%
PR SCORES OF 76-99	0	0%
51-75	9	36%
26-50	12	48%
1-25	4	16%
TOTAL	25	

(B) MATH COMPUTATION

	STUDENT NAME			RAW SCORE	NAT'L PR S	NAT'L NCE
1	SANTOS	JOSE	P	15	26 4	36 5
1	GORDON	MIKE	O	15	26 4	36 5
1	BURNS	THELMA	G	15	26 4	36 5
4	CRAIG	ROBIN	R	17	36 4	42 5
5	GOLDMAN	ELLEN	S	18	40 5	44 7
6	STEVENS	CAROL	F	19	46 5	47 9
6	COHAN	JEAN	K	19	46 5	47 9
8	FARLEY	ANDREA	P	20	50 5	50 0
8	BALLARD	CHUCK	C	20	50 5	50 0
10	WANG	CINDY	S	21	56 5	53 2
10	PALACE	BETH	B	21	56 5	53 2
12	PETERS	CARL	E	22	62 6	56 4
13	RAYMOND	VAL	H	23	66 6	58 7
14	CHANG	MARY	B	24	72 6	62 3
14	LONG	PHIL	N	24	72 6	62 3
16	RIVARA	SIMON	J	25	76 6	64 9
17	BLACKMAN	DENNIS	L	26	78 7	66 3
18	MILLER	PAUL	R	27	82 7	69 3
19	GLADSTONE	IRWIN	V	30	90 8	77 0
20	GROVER	MATT	A	31	92 8	79 6
21	HALL	GLENDA	T	32	94 8	82 7
22	WHITTIER	JODI	A	33	96 9	86 9
23	WILSON	ELMER	N	34	98 9	93 3
24	PARIS	STEVEN	D	35	99 9	99 0
24	JENNINGS	BARBIE	M	35	99 9	99 0

NUMBER OF STUDENTS RANKED IS 25
SCALED SCORE WAS USED FOR RANKING

SUMMARY

	RAW SCORE	NAT'L NCE
NUMBER OF STUDENTS	25	25
MEAN	24 0	62 26
STANDARD DEVIATION	6 4	18 86

NATIONAL PR SUMMARY	N	%
PR SCORES OF 76-99	10	40%
51-75	6	24%
26-50	9	36%
1-25	0	0%
TOTAL	25	

LANGUAGE

	STUDENT NAME			RAW SCORE	NAT'L PR S	NAT'L NCE
1	SANTOS	JOSE	P	22	20 3	32 3
2	PARIS	STEVEN	D	25	28 4	37 7
3	WANG	CINDY	S	26	30 4	39 0
4	PALACE	BETH	B	28	36 4	42 5
4	BURNS	THELMA	G	28	36 4	42 5
6	JENNINGS	BARBIE	M	29	38 4	43 6
6	GROVER	MATT	A	29	38 4	43 6
8	RAYMOND	VAL	H	30	40 5	44 7
9	HALL	GLENDA	T	31	42 5	45 8
10	GORDON	MIKE	O	32	46 5	47 9
11	RIVARA	SIMON	J	33	48 5	48 9
12	PETERS	CARL	E	34	50 5	50 0
13	WILSON	ELMER	N	35	54 5	52 1
13	COHAN	JEAN	K	35	54 5	52 1
15	LONG	PHIL	N	36	58 5	54 2
15	CRAIG	ROBIN	R	36	58 5	54 2
17	MILLER	PAUL	R	37	60 6	55 3
17	BALLARD	CHUCK	C	37	60 6	55 3
19	GLADSTONE	IRWIN	V	38	64 6	57 5
20	WHITTIER	JODI	A	39	66 6	58 7
20	STEVENS	CAROL	F	39	66 6	58 7
22	FARLEY	ANDREA	P	40	70 6	61 0
22	BLACKMAN	DENNIS	L	40	70 6	61 0
24	GOLDMAN	ELLEN	S	42	76 6	64 9
24	CHANG	MARY	B	42	76 6	64 9

NUMBER OF STUDENTS RANKED IS 25
SCALED SCORE WAS USED FOR RANKING

SUMMARY

	RAW SCORE	NAT'L NCE
NUMBER OF STUDENTS	25	25
MEAN	33 7	50 74
STANDARD DEVIATION	5 4	8 51

NATIONAL PR SUMMARY	N	%
PR SCORES OF 76-99	2	8%
51-75	11	44%
(E) 26-50	11	44%
1-25	1	4%
TOTAL	25	

STANFORD LEVEL FORM Primary 3 E   PROCESS NO 005-1542-001   COPY 1

See back for aids for interpretation.

DATA SERVICES DIVISION   THE PSYCHOLOGICAL CORPORATION
HARCOURT BRACE JOVANOVICH PUBLISHERS

Figure 13.3 Stanford Achievement Test. Ranked Lists of Scores.
Source: Stanford Achievement Tests, 1982.

explanation and interpretation of scores. Notice how the pictorial representation of Charles Ballard's test performance provides an easy reference to understand his achievement. His weakest areas are concepts of numbers and science, and his strongest areas are social science and using information. The Otis-Lennon School Ability Test is a scholastic aptitude test that allows the teacher to compare a measure of a student's potential to achieve in school with his or her actual achievement test results.

Stanford ACHIEVEMENT TEST
WITH OTIS-LENNON SCHOOL ABILITY TEST

PUPIL PROFILE
CHARLES A BALLARD

TEACHER MS WELLENS
SCHOOL LAKESIDE ELEMENTARY
SYSTEM NEWTOWN PUBLIC SCHOOLS

GRADE 4
TEST DATE 10 12 82
STANFORD NORMS GR 4.1
OLSAT NORMS GR 4 FALL

TESTS	NATIONAL PR	NATIONAL S
WORD STUDY SKILLS (A)	50	5
READING COMPREHENSION	50	5
VOCABULARY	52	5
LISTENING COMPREHENSION	44	5
SPELLING	40	5
LANGUAGE	60	6
CONCEPTS OF NUMBER	32 (B)	4
MATH COMPUTATION	50	5
MATH APPLICATIONS	50	5
SOCIAL SCIENCE	82	7
SCIENCE	34	4
USING INFORMATION	77	7
TOTAL READING	50	5
TOTAL LISTENING	48	5
TOTAL LANGUAGE	52	5
TOTAL MATHEMATICS	44	5
OTIS-LENNON SCHOOL ABILITY TEST	82	7

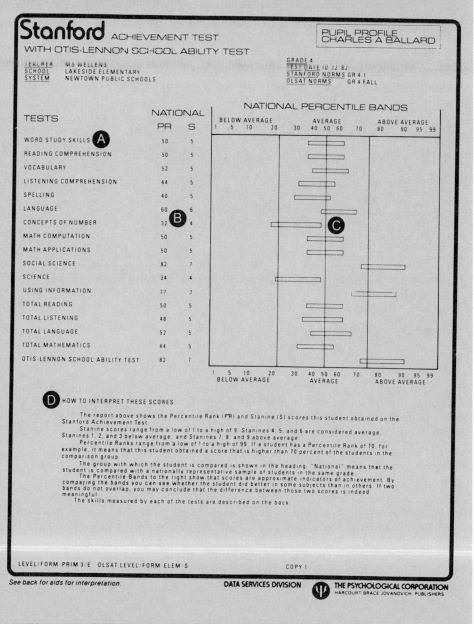

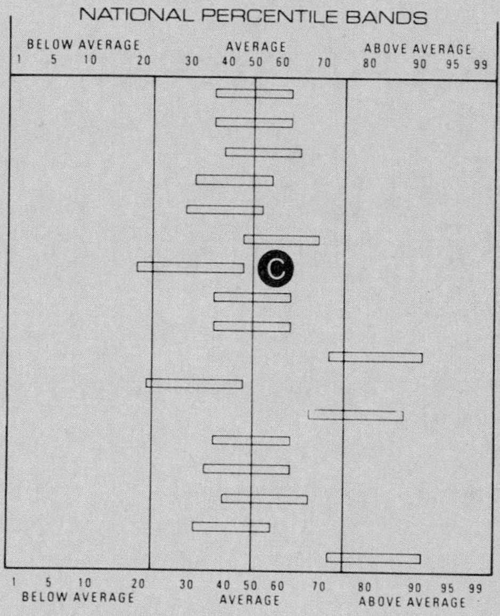

(D) HOW TO INTERPRET THESE SCORES

The report above shows the Percentile Rank (PR) and Stanine (S) scores this student obtained on the Stanford Achievement Test.

Stanine scores range from a low of 1 to a high of 9. Stanines 4, 5, and 6 are considered average, Stanines 1, 2, and 3 below average, and Stanines 7, 8, and 9 above average.

Percentile Ranks range from a low of 1 to a high of 99. If a student has a Percentile Rank of 70, for example, it means that this student obtained a score that is higher than 70 percent of the students in the comparison group.

The group with which the student is compared is shown in the heading. "National" means that the student is compared with a nationally representative sample of students in the same grade.

The Percentile Bands to the right show that scores are approximate indicators of achievement. By comparing the bands you can see whether the student did better in some subjects than in others. If two bands do not overlap, you may conclude that the difference between those two scores is indeed meaningful.

The skills measured by each of the tests are described on the back.

LEVEL/FORM-PRIM 3/E OLSAT LEVEL/FORM-ELEM/S COPY 1

See back for aids for interpretation.

DATA SERVICES DIVISION THE PSYCHOLOGICAL CORPORATION HARCOURT BRACE JOVANOVICH, PUBLISHERS

Figure 13.4 Stanford Achievement Tests. Pupil Profile.
Source: Stanford Achievement Tests, 1982.

cumulative record. A file on a student that includes such information as family data, health, academic grades, standardized test scores, attendance, and teacher comments.

THE CUMULATIVE RECORD

A **cumulative record** is a file on a student that includes such information as family data, health information, academic grades, standardized test results, attendance, and teacher comments. The exact form and the information included vary from one school district to the next. If a student has had an assessment by a school psychologist, a separate file reporting the results of the evaluation usually is kept in the psychological services office with a notation in the cumulative record as to when the assessment was made. The classroom teacher can ask for a consultation with the school psychologist to discuss the results of the assessment.

There is some controversy regarding the use of information in students' cumulative records. A major concern is that the information can lead a teacher to develop expectations about certain students before meeting them. The teacher may then act in ways that produce a self-fulfilling

CLASSROOM Application

ANALYZING CUMULATIVE RECORDS

The following information (Roffman, 1983) will help you evaluate the cumulative record.

FAMILY HISTORY

The size of the family, the number of siblings living in the home, how far the student has to travel to school, and the number of changes in schools since kindergarten can provide important insight into the student's behavior. For example, if there has been some trauma in the family, such as the death of a parent or a divorce, you might check the student's grades over the years to see whether academic performance slipped during this period and whether the student recovered. A student who has attended several schools in a short time may have missed academic content and thus may not have adequate preparation for the present grade. Does the student have to travel far to get to school? If the student is tired, you may want to check with the parents to find out when the student goes to bed at night.

MEDICAL HISTORY

Note whether the student has any hearing, vision, or severe health problems. This information could determine classroom seating or the

prophecy (Dusek & Joseph, 1985). For example, comments by previous teachers regarding attentiveness, obedience, industriousness, and work habits can have a strong impact on expectancies (Willis, 1972). On the other hand, an expert teacher who knows how to evaluate the information in a cumulative record may gain enough insight into a student's problem so that a more effective educational program can be developed.

My personal position on this issue is that teachers need to be aware of the danger of formulating expectations based on the opinions of others. Thus I am not in favor of reviewing cumulative records until after a teacher has worked with students in class for a few weeks, unless it appears to a teacher that a student has an obvious problem that needs immediate attention. I believe that if teachers are trained to evaluate and use the information in the cumulative record, they can gain insight into problems and make changes in the ways they interact with certain students.

type of physical activity allowed in school. In most cases, you would be notified by the school nurse or psychologist if a child had a severe health problem. You may not be notified about minor health problems, however. For example, many students refuse to wear their eyeglasses in class, and, as a result, they cannot see the chalkboard. If the medical history identifies the fact that a child needs to wear eyeglasses, you can then take steps to deal with the situation.

YEARLY ATTENDANCE RECORD

Check the student's attendance record over the years. Notice the number of absences, the time of the year they occurred (if available), and the resulting academic achievement. Winter absences may indicate certain respiratory infections and possibly a subsequent hearing loss. Extended absences in the early grades might have caused a student to miss important basic skills and be affecting present performance. Chronic absences over several years may suggest serious health problems or lack of parental support for ensuring that the student attends school. When there is a constant attendance problem that is not verified or health related, you should notify the school agency responsible for home visitations to ensure student attendance at school.

SCHOOL GRADES

Look for patterns of strengths and weaknesses in various academic areas. Did an academic problem begin from grade 1? Did a problem emerge in junior high school? Could the problem be developmental? For example, perhaps the student has not been prepared to do formal reasoning in algebra. Could biological and social changes at puberty have an impact on the student's adjustment to a new school?

continued

GRADING AND REPORTING STUDENT PROGRESS

? What are the advantages and disadvantages of using different grading systems?

Various methods are used to grade students and report their progress, including letter grades based on comparative and absolute standards, behavioral mastery reports, pass-fail, and parent-teacher conferences. Many schools use combinations of methods, such as letter grades and parent-teacher conferences. This section presents material on the advantages and limitations of these procedures.

INDIVIDUAL AND GROUP TESTING RESULTS

School districts have schedules for certain testing. In addition, special tests may be given to a student to diagnose academic problems. In the preceding Classroom Application, I discussed how to interpret standardized test scores. The following are some additional questions you should be concerned about. Notice the dates for each evaluation, and determine whether you may need to request any special testing. What information do the tests provide? If an individual intelligence assessment or group scholastic aptitude test was given, does the student score differently in the verbal and mathematical areas? Do these scores correlate with grades given in various subject areas? Does the student need special attention in one area? Ask the school counselor or special education teacher to review the meaning of the test scores with you. The information presented earlier in the chapter will help you to read the manual.

TEACHERS' COMMENTS

Teachers are asked from kindergarten on to write a brief evaluation regarding a student's progress or any problems encountered during the school year. Be as concise and objective as possible when you write comments about students and describe their behavior. Remember that other professionals will read your comments and will not know your frame of mind when you made your observations. Does a pattern emerge in the teachers' comments? Be aware of a teacher writing "ditto" to the comments made by a previous teacher. This response *may not* indicate a recurring problem, only that the particular teacher did not put any effort into completing the comments on the cumulative record. Does a problem noted in an early grade

Basing Grades on the Normal Distribution

In *norm-referenced evaluation,* grades are assigned for different levels of achievement. A certain percentage of students get As, Bs, Cs, Ds, and Fs. Letter grades are easily understood by parents and students and are convenient in maintaining school records. These advantages aside, the meaning of letter grades varies from teacher to teacher, and the grades do not indicate a student's learning strengths and weaknesses.

The most rigid form of letter-grade evaluation is grading on the curve. In this procedure the grades are arranged to approximate the shape of a normal distribution. The largest proportion of students receive C grades, and the percentage of A and B grades is matched by an equivalent percentage of D and F grades. When a teacher grades on a curve, the percentage of students receiving each grade is predetermined. The grading is based on

appear to persist with nothing having been done to alleviate it? The following is an example of comments from an actual cumulative record by different teachers who failed to recognize that the student might have a learning disability. This student had problems in the first grade that required special attention. However, he did not receive any special education until the ninth grade, after receiving unsatisfactory evaluation in work habits and Ds and Cs in his academic subjects in the seventh and eighth grades. His cumulative record indicated an IQ of 110.

- *Kindergarten.* "Sufficient growth in areas of cognitive and affective domain; uses materials in a creative manner."
- *First grade.* "Academically capable but has an extremely short attention span."
- *Second grade.* "Very poor work habits, extremely poor handwriting; has difficulty understanding presented material."
- *Third grade.* "Very poor cursive writing; avid reader; poor work habits; must be helped to adhere to room standards. At times capable if he can be motivated to follow and listen."
- *Fourth grade.* "Has learned to sit for longer periods of time. Restless; needs constant supervision. Poor writing skills; avid reader."
- *Fifth grade.* "Has made progress; still rushes through work."

In summary, the cumulative record contains a great deal of information that can help you to learn more about individual students. Do not hesitate to ask more experienced teachers, the school counselor, or the psychologist for help in evaluating any information in the file. Last, be careful in drawing conclusions about cause-and-effect relationships when you come across certain data. Consider possible alternative explanations for behavior before reaching conclusions about student behavior.

the assumption that the students in a typical class will fall into a normal distribution on achievement because they are normally distributed on aptitude.

The assumptions underlying the letter-grading system have been abundantly criticized. The size of many classroom groups is too small to expect a normal distribution, and teachers' achievement tests seldom yield normally distributed scores. The homogeneous grouping system of placing students with similar abilities in classes, used in many schools, negates the assumption of normal distribution from the beginning (Terwilliger, 1971). Finally, even if students were normally distributed in terms of aptitude, would achievement be distributed in the same way? We discussed earlier the notion of mastery learning, which attempts to ensure that almost all students can master the material in a given course. You should think carefully about these criticisms before grading on the curve.

The Inspection Method

Smith and Adams (1972) support a visual inspection method of grading. With this method, the teacher grades students on a norm-referenced system but experiences greater flexibility in the percentages of letter grades assigned.

The procedure is quite simple. After the scores have been obtained, the teacher establishes a frequency distribution (see Figure 13.5). The following are guidelines for determining letter grades:

1. The large group of scores around the median should be assigned C.
2. The lines drawn at Q_1 and Q_3, the 25th and 75th percentiles, can be used to indicate the limits of the C group.
3. The groups just above and below the C group are assigned B and D, respectively. The groups at either extreme are assigned A or F.

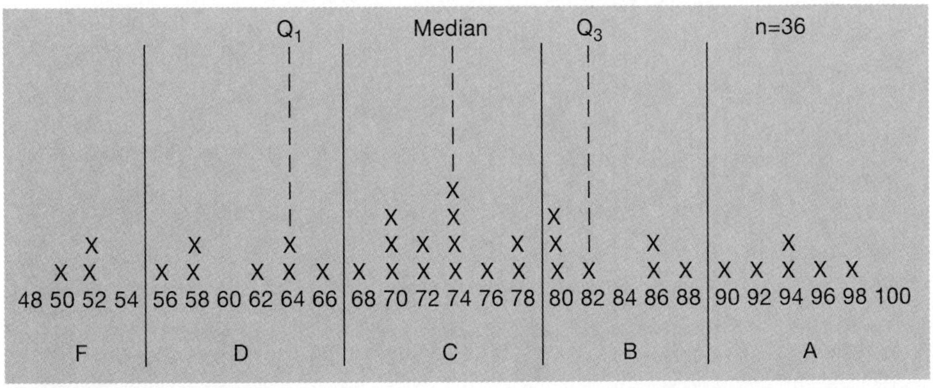

Figure 13.5 Grades Assigned by Visual Inspection of Scores.

If the test is too easy or too difficult, the scores will pile up at one end of the distribution, making a clear separation of achievement levels difficult. If everyone does well, there may be no need to assign Fs. In other distributions, no one may do well enough to receive an A. In distributions with gaps above or below the median, the teacher may not assign any Bs or Ds.

A teacher must be cautious in using this approach because it is subjective and inexact; grades often don't mean the same thing, since the gaps appear by chance.

COMBINING DATA IN ASSIGNING GRADES. When you are faced with the task of combining scores from tests, papers, and projects for a final letter grade, you need to realize that each component carries different weight. This is true even if the assignments and tests have the same number of points. Let's assume that an instructor gives a midterm and final worth 50 points each and says to the class that each exam is worth 50 percent of the final grade. At the end of the semester, the instructor adds the total number of points, ranks the students from highest to lowest, and assigns the final grade.

The procedure I have just described is accurate *only* if the standard deviations, or variability, of the two exams are approximately equal. For example, if Set of Scores A is twice as variable as Set of Scores B, then A is likely to be twice the weight of B when they are totaled. Suppose the range of scores on the midterm was 20 to 45, with most of the scores being spread along the distribution, and the range of the scores on the final was 40 to 50, with most of the scores being between 40 and 45. If the total points for the two tests are to be summed, which test carries the greater weight? If you said the midterm, you would be correct. Because most of the scores on the final are clustered together, the lowest student (40) is only 10 points from the highest student (50). However, on the midterm, the difference between the highest and lowest is 25 points. You also know that the scores are spread out, so it is more difficult to make up lost ground on the final because of the lack of variability of the examination. If the number of points on each exam differs, as in most test situations, the possibility of even greater variability is apparent.

Gronlund (1985a) recommends that the teacher determine the range of scores as an estimate of score variability and equate the set of scores. For example, if the ranges of scores on midterm and final examinations were 80 to 100 and 10 to 50, respectively, the range for the midterm is 20 (100 – 80) and for the final 40 (50 – 10). The teacher then multiplies each midterm examination score by 2 to obtain the equal weight.

This procedure provides a fairly accurate measure of the variability, or standard deviation, if the scores extend across the whole range of scores. If students score along a small part of the range, the difference between the highest and lowest scores (range) can be a poor estimate of the variability of the scores. For this reason, measurement experts find that the most accurate procedure for weighting scores is to compute the actual standard deviation for each test or paper and then change all the scores to a standard score, perhaps a T score. The scores are then based on the same scale. A teacher has five components of a final grade and wants to weight them as follows: Unit test I—20 percent; Unit test II—20 percent; final—30 percent; paper—10 percent; term project—20 percent. The T scores for each component would be multiplied by 2, 2, 3, 1, and 2, respectively, to complete the desired weighting. More detailed information on this procedure can be found in Terwilliger (1971) and most basic texts in measurement.

One final note regarding grading and combining scores: It is not a good procedure to convert test scores to letter grades and then reconvert the grades to numbers (A = 3, B = 2, and so forth) for the purpose of determining a final grade. The problem with this procedure is that information is lost because the same grade is given whether a student is at the top or bottom of a grade range in the reconversion process. A better procedure is to record the test score directly and use the weighting procedure at the end of the semester (Ebel & Frisbie, 1986).

Basing Grades on Predetermined Levels of Achievement

Sometimes grades are assigned on the basis of predetermined levels of achievement, such as the following:

A = 90–100 percent
B = 80–89 percent
C = 70–79 percent
D = 60–69 percent
F = below 60 percent

With this system the student receives a grade based on the percentage of questions answered correctly. There are no limitations on the percentage of letter grades given. At first glance, this system of grading appears fair: No student receives a low grade just because that person is at the bottom of the class distribution. The drawback lies with the teacher, who through the difficulty of the tests can control the percentage of students receiving high or low grades. If scores are too high, the teacher may begin to grade a little tougher to bring them down. If they are too low, the teacher may grade a little easier.

The Contract System

A system of grading that is most appropriate at the junior high and high school levels is to establish individualized contracts with students allowing them to determine how much effort they wish to expend on school tasks. This is done by promising specific grades when certain levels of accomplishments are achieved. For example, a teacher might require a 90 percent on tests and a paper for an A; 85 percent on tests without a paper would earn a B; 80 percent on tests for a C, and so on. Standards can be adjusted according to the ability and interests of the students and the expectations of the teacher. Makeup assignments and extra-credit assignments can be added to the contract so that students can improve their grades by doing extra work. Attendance requirements also can be included in the contract.

The advantage of this system is that students know exactly what is expected of them in order to achieve specific grades. In addition, it can reduce anxiety because students know their performance level and what can be done to increase their grades. It is important that the teacher establish standards that differentiate acceptable from unacceptable work in evaluating student papers and projects. Sometimes there is difficulty judging the appropriate performance level of a class by establishing a system in which it is too difficult or too easy to obtain an A or B. Don't hesitate to modify your standards if you find that they are unfair or inappropriate for the students in your class.

behavioral mastery reports. Reports that measure competency by assessing specific behavior.

Behavioral Mastery Reports

Dissatisfaction with traditional grading and reporting systems has led to the development of **behavioral mastery reports**. These reports consist of a list of behavioral objectives with indications of the extent to which the student has met or mastered each objective. Figure 13.6 is a report card with such a list of objectives.

A behavioral report permits a degree of communication to the parents that is not possible with other systems. By specifically identifying the skills and abilities the student has attained, the report puts the parents in a better position to judge the quality of their child's education.

The use of this approach drives home its limitations. In highly structured subjects like mathematics, it is possible to identify and report student progress in a specific domain of learning outcomes; in loosely defined subjects like social studies, the domain of learning outcomes is difficult to assess and there is no clear hierarchical structure. A second deficiency in behavioral mastery reports is the problem of identifying all instructional objectives in terms of specific student outcomes. Third, it is difficult to specify meaningful standards of performance for many objectives: What is mastery? How does one establish a minimal level of competency (Gronlund, 1974a)?

Pass-Fail Grading

Pass-fail grading removes the competitive pressures of letter grading and permits students to explore new subject areas without fear of receiving low grades. In some pass-fail procedures, the instructor does not know who in the course is on the pass-fail basis and who is on a regular grading system. The instructor submits letter grades for all students to the registrar, who then converts all passing grades to P for the pass-fail students.

This system is limited in that it provides little information about student learning. In addition, students may not do assigned readings or may do just enough to get by in lieu of attempting to attain a high level of competency in the course. Finally, there is no evidence that students are more motivated to learn under this system of grading.

Parent-Teacher Conferences

The parent-teacher conference is most effective for reporting student progress at the elementary school level and for dealing with special problems at the secondary level. It improves the teacher's communication with

Grade Two	
Skill	Date
Concepts	
Understands commutative property of addition (e.g., 4 + 3 = 3 + 4)	________
Understands place value (e.g., 27 = 2 tens + 7 ones)	________
Addition	
Supplies missing addend under 10 (e.g., 3 + ? = 5)	________
Adds three single-digit numbers	________
Knows combinations 10 through 19	________
Adds two 2-digit numbers without carrying	________
Adds two 2-digit numbers with carrying	________
Subtraction	
Knows combinations through 9	________
Supplies missing subtrahend—under 10 (e.g., 6 − ? = 1)	________
Supplies missing minuend—under 10 (e.g., ? − 3 = 4)	________
Knows combinations 10 through 19	________
Subtracts two 2-digit numbers without borrowing	________
Measurement	
Reads and draws clocks (up to quarter hour)	________
Understands dollar value of money (coins up to $1.00 total)	________
Geometry	
Understands symmetry	________
Recognizes congruent plane figures—that is, figures which are identical except for orientation	________
Graph Reading	
Knows how to construct simple graphs	________
Knows how to read simple graphs	________

Figure 13.6 Report Card Based on a System of Criterion-Referenced Measurement.
Source: Millman, 1970.

parents and can provide the teacher with a source of more detailed information about the student. The limitations of the parent-teacher conference are the amount of time needed to conduct the interviews and the special counseling skills required for communicating productively with the parent.

GRADES: HELP OR HINDRANCE?

Hill and Wigfield (1984) have made a number of recommendations for reducing anxiety in school. One of their suggestions entails abolishing letter grades at the elementary school level, substituting instead information on the child's achievement, effort, social development, and specific strengths and weaknesses in each subject area. Concerned over the pressure of grades and the premature labeling of young children as failures, the Board of Education for the Los Angeles Unified School District voted to abolish letter grades in the early elementary grades and replace them with a system that reports whether students performed satisfactorily or need to improve.

Soon after this change, the following article by Robert Butterworth and Daniella Alloro, codirectors of Contemporary Psychology Associates in

Los Angeles, appeared in the opinion section of the *Herald Examiner*, a newspaper in Los Angeles. As you read the article, identify some of the issues regarding grading that need to be discussed.

Changing "F" to "N" Only Disguises the Fact That a Student Is Failing

By Robert Butterworth and Daniella Alloro

The Los Angeles School Board's decision to change the grading structure in the early elementary grades is a smokescreen to disguise reality and carries with it the danger of erupting into a nationwide trend.

The board's decision to eliminate "F," the failing grade, and substitute "N," for needs improvement was made to protect the young child from a loss of self-esteem associated with a failing grade. Yet it is difficult to understand how self-esteem can be enhanced when we disguise the fact that a child is failing in school.

In some respects, the F grade may be the best friend the parents of a failing child have. The early years of school are crucial in educational development. At this time, future academic- and work-performance patterns are established. It is also the best period to correct problems that may exist in the child.

As psychologists who work with children, we understand that a failing grade is only a symptom of other problems. It is essential that parents have a real understanding of the child's academic status so that if difficulties do exist, they can be treated. There are many reasons why children fail at school.

Learning disorders, family difficulties, emotional problems—all can contribute. Yet by just focusing on the self-esteem issue of failing grades, we pretend to cure the symptoms but overlook the disease.

It isn't the failing grade that makes a child feel like a failure; this is accomplished by parents before children start school. Low self-esteem and a feeling of being a failure comes from random, nondirected punishment and criticism. A failing grade in school is the logical consequence of specific behavior.

Has this newly adopted grading system worked before? Remember the '60s, when many universities decided to throw out the letter grades and adopt "pass-fail" grading? Did it work? Ask students who were competing with other students to get into medical school. Many of them were eliminated because they couldn't be academically ranked. Graduate schools need an accurate gauge to pick the best people they can, and this is as much a fact of life in medical schools as it is in any other educational setting.

The school board says that the child suffers at the hands of his or her peers and teachers if he or she gets an F. Yet classmates and teachers know, based on classroom behavior, who the bright and slow pupils are.

By changing F to N, we are using a smokescreen from which children and parents will get the impression that the failure is minimized and not all that important. Not only do the consequences of having failed become a subject not treated, but the underlying deeper problems are avoided as well.

We have a duty and obligation as parents and educators to prepare our children for the contemporary world. Competition and high achievement may not be liked or favored by some, but they exist and will continue to exist. Jobs are getting scarcer. The competition in all areas of life is keener than ever before. Children should be prepared for it. Is it fair to protect our children from the reality of failure in the early years, only to have this reality resurface with a vengeance when they enter the real world?

There is no need to disguise grades. Schools have to develop better methods to screen and evaluate youngsters in the early grades. And schools and parents have to establish rewards for positive academic achievement. But for those students with academic problems, the focus should be on the underlying problems, not the external cosmetics, of the F grade.

CLASSROOM

Application

PREPARING AND CONDUCTING PARENT CONFERENCES

Teachers often find meetings with parents uncomfortable, especially if they have to report unpleasant information about students. Yet an effective conference can provide parents with the information needed to help their child function more effectively in school and to help them work more closely with the classroom teacher. Thus, in the long run, dealing with learning problems in a direct manner can benefit the teacher as much as students and parents.

Conferences with parents are more likely to be successful if teachers adequately prepare for the conference and use effective communication techniques during the conference. The following guidelines should be helpful in making parent-teacher conferences more productive (Gronlund, 1974a).

PLANNING THE CONFERENCE

1. *Send adequate advance notice of the need for a conference with some options on time and date.* Remember that parents have many demands in their lives and may not be available when you want them. Do not jump to the conclusion that they are not interested in their child if they cannot come to the meetings at the time you suggest.
2. *State the purpose of the conference when contacting the parents.* Making such a statement can help to relieve anxiety and give parents an opportunity to think about issues that might be discussed at the conference.
3. *Review the student's records and collect all relevant information related to the purpose of the conference.* Take notes from the student's cumulative record regarding past performance and adjustment in school. Identify the student's strengths and weaknesses.
4. *Provide a folder of the student's present work.* This folder should include tests, completed assignments, and any other information that will give the parents a clearer understanding of their child's achievement.
5. *Make a tentative list of questions to ask the parents.* Because the purpose of a conference is to provide information for both the teacher and the parents, it is important that the teacher ask questions that will offer insight into the student's attitudes, interests, and general development.

6. *Anticipate parents' questions during the conference.* Although it is impossible to anticipate parental reactions to the conference, there may be particular issues that you can expect to be high on the parents' list of questions. For example, if a child has had social behavior problems, the parents may want to know if the child has friends in class, whether any students are annoying the child, and how they might deal with the child's behavior at home. You may not have all the answers to these questions, but you should be able to refer parents to other school personnel or resource materials that would be helpful.
7. *Select a suitable site for the conference.* In most situations the conference will be held in your classroom. To ensure that you will not be interrupted, place a sign outside the door. Provide large enough chairs for the parents to sit on, and arrange the chairs so that you are not sitting behind your desk. It is important that you provide an informal atmosphere so that the parents will feel more comfortable during the conference.

CONDUCTING THE CONFERENCE

You want to accomplish three primary objectives during the conference: Establish and maintain rapport with the parents, share information, and plan a course of action with them. Specific guidelines for these objectives follow (Gronlund, 1974a, pp. 40–43), with comments.

Establishing and Maintaining Rapport

1. "*Create a friendly informal atmosphere.*" This approach gives parents time to overcome their initial anxiety and allows them to see you in a less formal role.
2. "*Maintain a positive attitude.*" It is important that you communicate directly and indirectly that your primary goal is to help their child, not simply to criticize or point out weaknesses. Use language such as "there are some areas that need improvement" when identifying weaknesses. Parents may become defensive if you use statements like, "According to the test results, he is doing about what I would expect." Parents will respond positively or negatively to the type and tone of communication you use.
3. "*Use language that is understandable to parents.*" Stay away from "educationese." Do not assume that parents understand technical words. Be careful in presenting test information, and help parents to understand what the tests measure, what the test scores mean, and how test information is used. Finally, point out that test scores are not exact measures of behavior or ability.
4. "*Be willing to listen to parents.*" Sometimes teachers are so concerned about completing their agenda that they forget about the concerns of the parents. The more you listen, the more credibility you may develop as an individual who is sincerely

continued

interested in helping. Use Gordon's reflective listening techniques discussed in Chapter 7. Some parents may become emotional and wander into areas of concern other than the purpose of the conference. However, as their emotion subsides, you can get them redirected to the main issue of the conference.

5. *"Be honest and sincere with parents and do not betray confidences."* Be tactful but tell parents what you think, and do not promise anything that you cannot deliver. Most important, if parents communicate some confidential information about their personal or family life, you have a responsibility to honor their confidence by not talking about the child or family in the teachers' lounge or with other parents. Also, it is usually best to avoid comparisons with other children when communicating with parents.

Sharing Information

1. *"Begin by describing the student's strong points."* This approach serves two purposes. It helps in developing rapport with the parents and provides information for the parents when their child asks, "What did the teacher say about me?"
2. *"Describe the areas needing improvement in a positive and tactful manner."* At this time you should present information you have prepared from the student's cumulative folder and/or classroom work. Avoid generalizations that cannot be supported by the information available.
3. *"Encourage parents to participate in the conference."* You will not need to worry about the involvement of some parents because they will ask questions, give advice, and offer recommendations without any encouragement by you. There will also, however, be parents who will answer most questions with "yes" or "no." In this situation, you need to ask more open-ended questions such as, "How does Susan feel about social studies?" "How does Henry prepare for tests?"
4. *"Be cautious about giving advice."* A teacher can easily project a know-it-all image and give simple solutions to difficult prob-

This opinion article presented the classic arguments for the use of letter grades in school: the need to report academic progress to parents, to correct problems early in children's educational careers, to prepare children for competition in the real world, and to provide information to schools and institutions of higher learning.

You should be aware of other positions on this issue: First, there are some educators and psychologists (primarily of a humanistic orientation) who are opposed to all external grading standards. They argue that the best evaluation is self-evaluation, because no one knows more about how much the individual learned than that individual. Second, there are individuals who are opposed to letter grades but who are not opposed to any form of external evaluation. These individuals would favor, in addition to

lems. Questions pertaining to correct ways to handle discipline problems at home are commonly raised by parents. In responding, present information in terms of alternative approaches, pointing out that typically there is no one best way to rear children. Suggest different approaches that other parents have used to deal with the situation or problem. If parents want information dealing with educational matters, you can be more specific in offering advice on tutoring and remedial strategies.

The final phase of the conference is summarizing what has been discussed and planning a course of action. Parents should never leave a conference without any idea as to what should be done to help their child.

Planning a Course of Action

1. "*Begin the conclusion phase of the conference with a brief overall summary.*" By beginning the summary, you communicate to the parents that the conference is coming to an end and you set the stage for planning a course of action.
2. "*Have parents participate in planning a course of action.*" Discuss what can be done at home in addition to what you plan to do at school. You might also discuss plans for another conference at some later time to evaluate the progress that will have been made since the first conference.
3. "*Review your conference notes with parents.*" Some school districts require teachers to fill out a form after a conference with parents. If so, review the content covered during the conference. Even if no formal report is required by the school, a summary will help you and the parents to organize notes before the end of the conference.
4. "*End the conference on a positive note.*" At the end of the conference, you should thank the parents for coming and showing interest in their child. Invite them to visit the class when possible or call you if they have further questions.

self-evaluation, such procedures as written evaluation, pass-fail, credit–no credit, and various mastery approaches. The book *Wad-ja-Get: The Grading Game in American Education*, by Kirschenbaum, Simon, and Napier (1971), provides an excellent discussion of alternative grading systems.

Opponents of the letter-grade system raise a number of issues. First, the letters do not mean the same in all classes. A grade of A in one class may be worth a C in another. Thus educators overemphasize the amount of information communicated to the student and parents. Also, letter grades are not objective and do not ensure competency.

Second, there is evidence that self-esteem is affected by evaluation in school. To argue that low self-esteem comes from experiences in the home prior to school is to reject a great deal of social science research.

Third, students can be better prepared for the competition in the real world without experiencing failure and rejection early in school, which, in turn, leads to less learning rather than more learning. Also, there is no evidence that continual failure leads to greater motivation and more success in competition.

Fourth, the fact that letter grades are not used does not mean that the student and the parents cannot receive detailed information about educational achievement (see "Behavioral Mastery Reports" earlier in this chapter). In fact, when you go to a doctor for a physical, you don't receive a grade on your health condition, but you learn a great deal by discussing your condition with the physician. The same can be said about alternative grading systems, which can provide more specific information about strengths and weaknesses without using a letter grade.

Finally, the argument used primarily at higher levels of education is: How will colleges or universities evaluate applicants without letter grades? There are number of responses to this concern. One is that

DEBATE FORUM

Do Elementary School Students Benefit from Retention?

Throughout the history of public education in the United States, various points of view have dominated educational practice. For example, in the early 1900s the average retention rate for all grades was 16 percent, but by the 1930s it had dropped to 4 to 5 percent. In the 1960s the notion of "social promotion" became prevalent. Instead of repeating a grade, the student would be promoted to the next grade and given remedial instruction to help the student acquire the knowledge and skills that were not attained in the previous grade level (Medway, 1985).

Argument: Studies of teachers' beliefs regarding retention indicate that many teachers believe that students will benefit from retention, especially in grades K–3. They believe that retention prevents students from facing daily failure and motivates them to work harder (Tomchin & Impara, 1992) and that the students are too young to be negatively affected by retention (Shepard & Smith, 1988).

Counterargument: The investigations on the effects of retention (especially in kindergarten) indicate that retention *does not* lead to improved achievement and better personal adjustment (Holmes & Shepard, 1989; Mantzicopoulos & Morrison, 1992). When students with similar problems and backgrounds are compared, the students high school grades do not always predict success in college or in the marketplace. Another argument is that students from outstanding alternative schools with no-grades transcripts have had an acceptance rate equal to or better than that of graduates from traditional schools in the same school districts (Bellanca, 1977). Third, institutions of higher learning would also benefit from more detailed information concerning students in terms of written evaluations regarding academic strengths and weaknesses, as well as effort, interests, attitudes, and behaviors. Fourth, there could be a compromise, whereby grades would begin at the junior high or high school level.

What are your beliefs about grading? Do letter grades provide an important standard of communication? Do you think students would achieve more if grades were abolished? Would they be more motivated to learn? Do you think different procedures need to be established at different educational levels—elementary, junior high, and high school? How do these issues relate to your own learning and evaluation experiences?

who are retained appear to do no better than those who are promoted.

Response: By now you may be thinking, "Well, if the research doesn't support retention, why is it used?" First, school districts are under considerable political pressure to demonstrate to the public that they are dealing with the problem of low achievement, and retention is one way to make this point. Second, each student's situation must be analyzed separately. In some situations the evidence indicates more strongly that the student would benefit from retention. Remember that when research investigations are undertaken, the purpose is to make generalizations based on a large sample of individuals. Thus, the general finding that retention is not effective should not lead one to conclude that *no* student will benefit from retention, only that most young students will not benefit.

Most school districts have a committee to make recommendations about retention. This committee may include the school principal, teacher, parent, school psychologist, and counselor. The committee's responsibility is to collect relevant information before a recommendation is made. For example, it is important that the school psychologist evaluate the teacher's instructional effectiveness and whether remedial methods were attempted to improve the student's achievement. If the student has not received the proper instruction, retention would be unfair and unwise (Medway, 1985).

What do you think? Do you know a student who was retained in school? Did the retention help the student? What do you think are the positive and negative aspects of retention? Would your views differ if you were to take the position of a parent rather than that of a teacher?

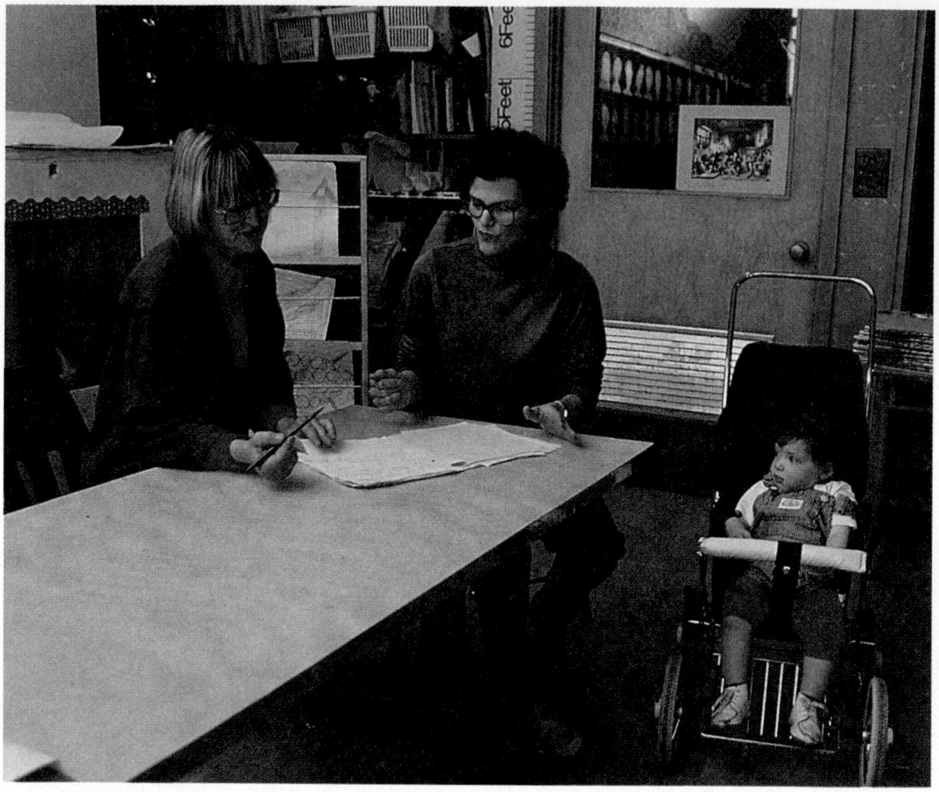

Parent-teacher conferences can be a good method for reporting student progress and working with parents to develop a plan of action to help students achieve at higher levels. It is important that teachers be sensitive to the needs of parents when scheduling these conferences.

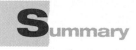

Summary

SUMMARIZING TEST SCORES

1. A frequency distribution for a test is a table summarizing how often each score occurs.
2. The mean is the arithmetic average of a set of scores.
3. The median is the middle score in a distribution.
4. The mode is the score with the highest frequency of occurrence.
5. The standard deviation is a measure of the dispersion, or variability, of the scores from the mean.

INTERPRETING TEST SCORES

6. A raw score is the number of items answered correctly on a test.
7. A percentile rank indicates a person's rank in a group in terms of the percentage of individuals at or below that person's score.
8. Grade-equivalent scores indicate the average performance of students at different grade levels.
9. Percentile ranks and grade-equivalent scores cannot be added or averaged because they do not form equal intervals at all points along the scale.
10. Standard scores represent test scores that have fixed means and standard deviations.

11. The basic standard score is the z score, which is calculated by dividing the standard deviation into the difference between a given raw score and the mean of all the scores.
12. A T score is obtained by multiplying a z score by 10 and adding 50.

NORMAL DISTRIBUTION

13. A normal, or bell-shaped, curve is a mathematical model that symbolically represents the way in which many human characteristics are distributed.
14. Stanines are scores that represent the normal curve divided into nine parts. Each part, or percentage, of the distribution is a stanine.

STANDARD ERROR OF MEASUREMENT

15. The standard error of measurement estimates the amount of error in a test score.

GRADING AND REPORTING STUDENTS' PROGRESS

16. Grades can be based on comparative or absolute standards.
17. The variability of scores on each test can influence the weighting of the test when determining each student's final grade.
18. Preparing and conducting parent conferences are important teaching skills.
19. Educators differ in their beliefs regarding the benefits of student grades.
20. Careful consideration should be given before a student is retained at a particular grade level. Research findings indicate that, in most situations, retention does not lead to improved achievement or better personal adjustment.

Reflecting on Analyzing Test Results and Reporting Student Progress

1. Interpret Achievement Test Scores

Your school system has administered the Elementary Reading Test for grades 3 and 4 from the Elementary Battery of the Metropolitan Achievement Tests to all third-grade students in October, and you now have the scores for each student. A portion of the score sheet is provided on the next page. What does it mean?

Which student does each of the following statements describe?

a. Scored close to the average third grader in the October testing.
b. Was more than a year above third-grade level in Word Knowledge
c. Scored very well in Reading; only 15 percent of the standardization group did better.
d. About 40 percent of the students in the country scored higher in Word Knowledge.
e. With the total score scale divided into nine segments, the student scored the second from the top in Word Knowledge.

		Word Knowledge	Reading
Lidstone, Fred	Grade equivalent	4.8	4.4
	Percentile rank	95	85
	Standard score	55	53
	Stanine	8	7
Simmons, Mary	Grade equivalent	3.2	3.1
	Percentile rank	60	45
	Standard score	44	41
	Stanine	6	5

2. Interpret a Grade Summary Sheet

Given the grade summary sheet that follows for a sample of eighth-grade social studies students, determine the teacher's primary basis for assigning grades. Are there inconsistencies in grading priorities? If so, how would the teacher defend them? What are possible sources of teacher bias? Could the grading system be made more equitable? If so, how?

GRADE SUMMARY SHEET

Grade/Subject: Eighth Grade/Social Studies
Grading Period: First Six Weeks

Name	Pre-test	Post-test	Grades on Group Reports	Individual Project Reports	Student's Self-evaluation	Final Grade
Brooks, Emily	42%	67%	B+	C+	A	B
Colton, Billy	72	82	A–	A+	B	A
Courtes, Lourdes	86	86	B+	B	A	B
Ikada, Akiro	70	80	B	B+	A	B
Javier, Sarita	90	89	A–	A	A	A

Wang, Sam	54	57	B	C	B	C
Williams, Tom	70	80	B	B+	A	B–
Zimmer, Alice	62	72	A–	B+	B	A

3. Evaluate Grading Methods and Procedures

a. What effect do grades have on you? Think about the courses you had in high school or those that you are now taking. Would you have behaved differently had you not been graded in any of them? In which courses would you not have altered your performance, regardless of whether you had been graded?
b. What experiences have you had with pass-fail and absolute standards (A = 90–100 percent, B = 80–90 , and so on)? What do you consider the advantages and disadvantages of each? How did these grading priorities dispose you toward learning?

c. Discuss what you believe was an unfair grading system used by a teacher. Defend your position and point out how the system could be improved.

d. Should a grade represent student achievement only, or should it also include the student's effort and work habits? Explain.

Key Terms

frequency distribution, p. 600
measures of central tendency, p. 601
mean, p. 601
median, p. 601
mode, p. 601
variability, p. 602
range of scores, p.602
standard deviation, p. 602
raw score, p. 603
derived score, p. 604
percentile rank, p. 604
grade-equivalent score, p. 604
standard score, p. 604
z score, p. 605
T score, p. 606
deviation IQ, p. 607
normal distribution, p. 607
stanines, p.607
standard error of measurement, p. 608
cumulative record, p. 612
behavioral mastery reports, p. 619

Suggestions for Further Reading

Kroth, R. L., & Simpson, R. L. (1977). *Parent conferences as a teaching strategy.* Denver: Love. Good suggestions for effective parent-teacher conferences.

Lyman, H. B. (1986). *Test scores and what they mean* (4th ed.). Englewood Cliffs, NJ: Prentice-Hall. A detailed discussion of the interpretation of test scores.

The following references discuss alternative procedures for grading:

Gronlund, N. E. (1974a). *Improving marking and reporting in classroom instruction.* New York: Macmillan.

Kirschenbaum, H., Simon, S., & Napier, R. (1971). *Wad-ja-get? The grading game in American education.* New York: Hart.

Terwilliger, J. S. (1971). *Assigning grades to students.* Glenview, IL: Scott, Foresman.

Part 5 Synthesis

In the last two chapters you learned about different types of classroom assessments and their role in classroom evaluation. You also learned how to develop your own measurement instruments, analyze test scores, and develop different grading systems.

The following exercises provide an opportunity for you to apply your knowledge about student differences from other chapters of the text to the measurement and evaluation issues in Chapters 12 and 13.

1. Discuss how you would deal with each of the following incidents:

   a. You are friends of the Willises, who have a son in a Spanish class in the school where you teach. Al has been identified as learning disabled and has an auditory perception problem. He has difficulty translating Spanish into English when listening to the conversational tapes used to assess the students' knowledge. His parents point out that he likes Spanish but is failing the course. They don't think it is fair that he received an F during the last grading period and want your advice for how they should deal with his teacher. What would you tell them?
   b. You developed a complex system to score students' writing in an English course. During the year you are asked to recommend one student for a writing award given by the school. Based on your criteria, Robert Johnson's essays are poor, but his ideas are well beyond any student in your class. The problem is that Robert includes Nonstandard English in his reports. Do you recommend Bob or another student who meets the criteria for good writing but whose original ideas are limited?
   c. You decide to develop a mastery learning program in your fifth-grade math curriculum and find that the students become highly motivated to learn the material in your program. In fact, you are surprised that even the low-achieving students in your class are responding well to the program. After the first grading period, your principal asks to speak with you about the number of As and Bs you gave during the first grading period. You point out the success of your program, but he mentions that you can't give mostly A and B grades, especially since the other fifth-grade teachers are complaining. The other teachers have received phone calls from parents complaining that they are grading too hard and constantly mention the high grades in your class. How do you defend your program to the principal and other teachers in the school?
   d. You decide to develop a performance assessment in your economics class in which students must complete a community study to apply the principles taught in your class. Jane Cho, an immigrant student who recently joined your class, spends considerable time completing the community study and receives an A on her report. However, on the unit test of economic principles, she receives a C. She is a bright student whose reading skills are not as advanced as her writing

skills. As a result, she has difficulty reading the text and scores low on traditional classroom tests. She comes to see you after school and asks about her grade and general progress in your course. What do you tell her?

2. Interpret Information from a Cumulative Record

In June, Gregory North's parents make an appointment with you, his English teacher, to discuss his academic progress. They want him to become a doctor but are afraid that he will not get into college if his academic work continues to decline. Given the information from a part of his cumulative record that follows, how would you start this meeting? What would you tell his parents about his potential and his academic progress? What recommendations would you make? You may want to consult reference materials for information about the standardized tests used by the school.

CUMULATIVE RECORD
CENTRAL JUNIOR HIGH SCHOOL

Name: Gregory North
Age: 13
Grade: 7

Test Record

Intelligence tests		IQ	Grade Level
Group			
California Test of Mental Maturity	Language	77	6th
	Performance	96	
Individual			
Wechsler Intelligence Scale for Children	Verbal	81	6th
	Performance	99	
	Full Scale	88	
Achievement tests		Grade equivalent scores	
California Achievement Tests (taken in October)	Total reading	5.6	7th
	Total arithmetic	7.3	
	Total language	6.1	

Academic Record

Subject	Final Grades	Grade Level
English	C–	7th
Mathematics	C+	7th
Social Studies	D	7th
Science	B	7th

Work habits: below average.

Glossary

Words set in *italics* are defined elsewhere in the Glossary.

academic learning time (ALT). A subset of *engaged time.* The amount of time a student spends on academic tasks while performing at a high rate of success.

accommodation. Piaget's term for the modification or reorganization of existing cognitive structures (*schemata*) to deal with environmental demands.

achievement test. A test that measures how much a student has learned in a subject area.

acronyms. *Mnemonics* that use the first letter in each word of a list to form a word.

action sequence. A sequence of behaviors or cognitive actions to be taken to reach a goal. Regrouping and borrowing in subtraction are examples of action sequence knowledge.

active listening. A type of communication in which teachers summarize and paraphrase what students have said so that the students feel that they have been understood.

adaptation. Changes in an organism in response to environmental demands. Adaptation comprises *assimilation* and *accommodation.*

advance organizers. Introductory information intended to facilitate a student's learning by providing a framework and organization for the material to be learned.

affective domain. A part of Bloom's *Taxonomy of Educational Objectives* for student attitudes, values, and emotional growth. The affective domain includes five basic categories: receiving, responding, valuing, organization, and characterization by a value.

allocated time. The time that a teacher designates for a particular learning task.

androgyny. A condition that comprises both male and female traits.

anorexia nervosa. An eating disorder in which individuals (primarily females) starve themselves to maintain a slim figure. The illness causes a distortion in one's perceptions of body image.

applied behavior analysis. A scientific method of behavioral change using principles of *operant conditioning* and directed toward clinically or socially significant behavior in a setting such as a hospital or school.

aptitude by treatment interaction (ATI). Research that focuses on how different aptitudes matched with different instructional methods affect learning. The result of this interaction indicates that a particular teaching method may not be equally effective with all students.

aptitude test. A test used to predict how well a student will learn unfamiliar material. A scholastic aptitude test, which measures learning potential, is an example.

assertive discipline. A method of *classroom management* developed by Canter that emphasizes the rights of teachers to teach and the rights of students to learn.

assessment. The processes and procedures used to make decisions about students' progress, both formal and informal measurements.

assimilation. Piaget's term for the process of making sense of experiences and perceptions by fitting them into previously established cognitive structures (*schemata*).

assisted performance. Instructional procedures where the teacher provides certain structure so that students can learn even if they can't complete all aspects of the task by themselves.

associativity. An operation wherein several classes can be combined in any order to produce the same results.

attribution. An individual's perception of the causes of his or her own success or failure.

authoritarian parenting style. A method of child rearing in which parents attempt to control their children's behavior and attitudes to conform to strict rules of conduct. They use punitive measures when their children fail to conform and don't discuss standards with them.

authoritative parenting style. A method of child rearing in which parents direct their children's activities by establishing firm rules and standards but are willing to discuss the reasons behind their regulations. These parents don't threaten their children, and are loving, consistent, and respectful of their children's independent decisions.

automaticity. The result of overlearning behaviors to the point that they can be carried out without conscious thought.

baseline. The natural occurrence of a behavior before intervention.

behavior disordered. A category in special education for students exhibiting one or more of the following behaviors over a substantial period: inability to learn that cannot be explained by intellectual, sensory, or health factors; difficulty in establishing positive interpersonal relationships; frequent inappropriate behavior; a general mood of unhappiness or depression; frequent physical complaints.

behavior modification. Interventions designed to change behavior in a precisely measurable manner.

behavioral learning theories. Theories of learning that focus on external events (e.g., stimuli and responses) and tend to ignore internal (mental) factors in learning.

behavioral mastery reports. Reports that measure competency by assessing specific behavior.

behavioral objectives. Statements regarding the specific changes educators intend to produce in student behavior.

bilingual education. Classroom instruction in two languages (e.g., English and a student's native language).

branching program. Programmed material that, in contrast to a *linear program*, presents a variety of alternative routes through the material.

chunking. Grouping of data so that a greater amount of information may be retained in *working memory*.

classical conditioning. A procedure in which the *conditioned stimulus*, after being paired with the *unconditioned stimulus* often enough, can then be substituted for it. It is often called "stimulus substitution."

classroom management. Teacher behaviors and activities that encourage learning in the classroom.

clustering. The organization of items from a list into groups on the basis of shared characteristics or attributes.

coaching. A program of test preparation to increase scores on specific tests.

cognitive behavior modification. A technique based on behavioral and cognitive theory that changes behavior by modifying an individual's inner, self-directive speech.

cognitive domain. A part of Bloom's *Taxonomy of Educational Objectives*. Bloom divides the objectives in the cognitive domain into six categories: knowledge, comprehension, application, analysis, synthesis, and evaluation.

cognitive learning theories. Explanations for learning that focus on the role of the learner's mental processing of information.

cognitive strategies. Behaviors and thoughts that influence the learning process so that information can be retrieved more efficiently from memory.

cognitive style. The consistent way in which an individual responds to a wide range of perceptual tasks.

combinativity. An operation in which two or more classes are combined into a larger group. It is sometimes called "classification."

computer-assisted instruction (CAI). The use of a computer as tutor to present information, give students opportunities to practice what they learn, evaluate student achievement, and provide additional instruction.

computer-managed instruction (CMI). The use of a computer for managerial purposes in instruction, such as determining error rates, student progress, and class averages and making assignments based on the diagnosis of student weaknesses. In many instruction programs *computer-assisted instruction* (CAI) and CMI are used in an integrated manner.

concept learning. The acquisition of *pattern-recognition knowledge* involving the learning of a rule or rules for classifying a number of objects into mutually exclusive categories based on one or more salient characteristic of the objects.

concrete operations stage. The third of Piaget's four major stages, characterized by children's ability to think logically, but only about concrete problems and objects.

conditioned response. A response elicited by a *conditioned stimulus*. The response is similar but not identical to its associated *unconditioned response*.

conditioned stimulus. A stimulus that does not initially elicit a response but through its pairing with an *unconditioned stimulus* acquires the capability of eliciting the same response as the latter.

connectionism. A term used by Thorndike to explain a type of learning that is concerned with the formation of bonds (connections) between stimuli and responses.

conservation. A Piagetian term for the realization that certain properties of an object (e.g., weight and length) remain the same regardless of changes in its other properties (e.g., shape and position).

construct validity. The degree to which a test measures specific psychological traits or constructs (e.g., intelligence, attitude, anxiety).

content validity. The ability of a test to sample adequately a specific universe of content.

contingency contracting. A document in which a teacher and a student agree that when the student satisfactorily behaves in some specified way or completes some specified work, he or she will be able to engage in a stated amount of some privilege, preferred activity, or other reinforcer. It is sometimes called "behavioral contracting."

continuing motivation. The tendency to return to and continue working on tasks away from the classroom without the supervision or control of the teacher.

control group. A group in an experimental study that receives no special treatment.

convergent thinking. A term used by Guilford to describe the type of thinking in which an individual produces a single response to a specific question or problem.

cooperative learning. Instructional procedures that depend on students helping one another to learn in small groups.

correlation. A measure of the degree of relationship between two variables.

creativity. The capacity of individuals to produce novel or original answers or products.

criterion-referenced assessment; criterion-referenced testing. A testing procedure in which an individual's performance is based on whether specific objectives have been achieved.

criterion-related validity. The extent to which scores on a test are in agreement with (concurrent validity) or predict (predictive validity) some given criterion measure. An example is the Scholastic Assessment Test (SAT), which predicts grade-point average.

critical thinking. Thinking that is focused on deciding what to believe or do. Analyzing an argument in a debate is an example.

culture. The ways in which a group of people think, feel, and react in order to solve problems of living in their environment.

cumulative record. A file on a student that includes such information as family data, health, academic grades, standardized test scores, attendance, and teacher comments.

decenter. The ability to take into consideration two or more details or dimensions (e.g., length and width) at the same time.

declarative knowledge. Knowledge about things.

decoding. The process of translating a symbol back into its original form, such as translating a letter into its sound or a word into its meaning.

dependent variable. A variable in an experimental study that may change as a result of the manipulation of the *independent variable.*

derived score. A *raw score* that has been converted to another scale.

deviation IQ. An intelligence test score based upon the difference, or deviation, between an individual's score and the average score for persons of the same chronological age.

diagnostic test; diagnostic evaluation. Tests and observational techniques designed to assess the skills and abilities that are important in learning a particular subject. Diagnostic tests are widely used in reading and mathematics.

direct instruction. An instructional method that emphasizes the mastery of basic skills by placing a clear focus on academic goals, wide coverage of content, selection of instructional goals, monitoring of student progress, structuring of learning activities, immediate feedback, and creation of an environment that is task oriented but relaxed.

disabled. A term describing children with physical problems that limit their ability to perform certain tasks.

discipline. The degree to which students behave appropriately, are involved in classroom activities, and are task oriented.

discovery learning. The learning of new information largely as a result of the learner's own efforts.

discrimination learning. The restriction of responding to certain stimulus situations but not others.

discriminative stimulus (S^D). A stimulus in the presence of which a given response is likely to be reinforced.

disequilibrium. Piaget's term for the state, or condition, occurring when, in the process of *assimilation*, the individual cannot adapt to the environment. Disequilibrium forces the individual into *accommodation.*

distributed practice. *Learning* trials divided among short and frequent periods.

divergent thinking. A term used by Guilford to describe the type of thinking wherein an individual produces multiple responses or solutions (often nontraditional) to a single question or problem. Divergent thinking is associated with *creativity.*

educable mentally retarded (EMR). A label for mildly retarded children, who are often educated in regular classrooms.

Education for All Handicapped Children Act (P.L. 94-142). A federal law that mandates specific educational procedures and rights for children with disabilities.

egocentrism. Piaget's term for describing children in the *preoperational stage*, who have difficulty in assuming the point of view of others.

elaboration strategies. Integration of meaningful *declarative knowledge* into *long-term memory* through adding detail, creating examples, making associations with other ideas, and drawing inferences.

eliciting effect. A type of imitative behavior in which the observer does not copy the model's responses but simply behaves in a related manner.

empathic understanding. Sensitivity to and awareness of the feelings, motives, attitudes, and values of others.

encoding. The *working memory* process of transforming incoming information into episodic or semantic form and associating it with old knowledge for storage in *long-term memory*.

engaged time. The time students are actively paying attention or learning. Also called time-on-task.

entry behavior. The knowledge, skills, or attitudes that a learner brings into a new learning situation.

episodic memory. Information in *long-term memory* that is stored in the form of images.

equilibration. A motivation principle in Piaget's theory that identifies humans as active and exploratory in attempting to impose order and meaningfulness on experiences. This order or balance occurs through the processes of *assimilation* and *accommodation*.

equivalent forms reliability. Two tests having nearly the same level of difficulty. Two tests are equivalent forms if, for example, the items are different on each test, or form, but all items are representative of the same universe of test items. They are a measure of *reliability*.

evaluation. The process of obtaining information to form judgments so that educational decisions can be made.

exceptional. A term describing children whose performance deviates from the norm—above or below—to the extent that special education is needed.

executive processes. The part of the information-processing system, based on *metacognition*, that controls the flow of information and implements *cognitive strategies* to reach a learning goal.

experimental group. A group receiving special treatment in an experimental study.

experimental research. An investigation that explores cause-and-effect relationships.

expressive objectives. Eisner's approach in which teachers define learning activities for students but do not specify exactly what the students might learn from these activities. Eisner believes that it is not always possible to predict the outcome of activities.

extinction. In *operant conditioning*, the gradual disappearance of reinforcing events that maintain a behavior. In *classical conditioning*, extinction results when a *conditioned stimulus* is no longer paired with an *unconditioned stimulus*.

extrinsic motivation. Motivation influenced by external events such as grades, points, or money.

fading. The gradual removal of *prompting* so that the learner can respond to a *discriminative stimulus* (S^D) without additional assistance.

field-dependent. A *cognitive style* in which the individual operates in a global manner and is distracted by, or sensitive to, background elements.

field-independent. A *cognitive style* in which the individual is capable of overcoming the effects of distracting elements (the field) when attempting to differentiate relevant aspects of a particular situation.

fixed-interval schedule. A *reinforcement* schedule in which a predetermined, fixed-time interval must occur between each reinforced response regardless of the number of responses the subject makes.

fixed-ratio schedule. A *reinforcement* schedule in which a subject is reinforced after a specified number of responses.

formal operations stage. Piaget's final stage of cognitive development, characterized by children's increasing ability to employ logical thought processes.

formative test; formative evaluation. The measurement of student achievement before or during instruction for the purpose of planning instruction or assessing student progress.

frequency distribution. A table that summarizes how often each score on a test occurs.

funds of knowledge. The essential cultural practices and bodies of knowledge that households use to survive, to get ahead, or to thrive.

generative teaching. A method of improving comprehension in which students are trained to generate analogies and images of what they read.

gifted and talented. A category in special education that defines individuals who give evidence of high-performance capability in certain areas.

grade-equivalent score. A score expressed in terms of the school-grade placement of students whose *raw scores* are typical of students at that particular grade level. For example, a grade-equivalent score of 4.5 means that the student's raw score is average for students in the fifth month of the fourth grade.

group contingency. A rule that specifies exactly how a consequence, positive or negative, is applied to a group.

handicapped. A term describing children who have a physical disability or behavioral characteristic so severe that they are hindered in school situations and require special help to profit from instruction.

hearing impaired. Having a hearing loss significant enough to require special education or training. The term includes both deaf and hard-of-hearing persons.

heritability. The extent to which differences in a trait (e.g., intelligence) are attributed to inheritance.

hierarchy of needs. Maslow's classification of human needs.

hypothesis. A statement about the relationship among variables.

hypothetico-deductive reasoning. The ability to formulate many alternative hypotheses in dealing with a problem and to check data against each of the hypotheses to make an appropriate decision.

I-messages. Gordon's strategy for changing student behavior, in which a teacher describes the problem behavior, the concrete effect the behavior is having on the teacher, and the way the behavior makes the teacher feel.

identity. (In Piaget's theory.) An operation involving recognition that physical substances retain their volume or quantity, even when moved or reorganized, as long as nothing is added or taken away.

identity achievement. Described by Marcia as one of the four alternative states during Erikson's identity versus role confusion stage. The adolescent has a strong sense of commitment to life choices after careful consideration of options.

identity diffusion. Described by Marcia as one of the four alternative states during Erikson's identity versus role confusion stage. The adolescent has not made any firm commitments to any ideology, occupation, or interpersonal relationship and is not currently thinking about such commitments.

identity foreclosure. Described by Marcia as one of the four alternative states during Erikson's identity versus role confusion stage. The adolescent selects a convenient set of beliefs and goals without carefully considering the alternatives. An example would be accepting one's parents' choice of life-style and career without considering other options.

identity moratorium. Described by Marcia as one of the four alternative states during Erickson's identity versus role confusion stage. The adolescent considers alternative choices, experiences different roles, but has made no final decision regarding his or her identity.

imaginary audience. The belief that other people are preoccupied with one's appearance and behavior. A form of *egocentrism* in adolescence.

independent variable. A variable that is manipulated or modified in an experimental study.

individual intelligence test. An intelligence test administered to one individual at a time by a trained specialist.

individualized education program (IEP). A document that details a yearly instructional plan for a child with a disability. It is required by federal law.

information processing. The study of specific thinking processes that underlie intelligent behavior or cognition.

information-processing system (IPS). The cognitive structure through which information flows, is controlled, and is transformed during the process of *learning*.

inhibitory-disinhibitory effect. A type of imitative behavior resulting either in the suppression (inhibition) or appearance (disinhibition) of previously acquired behavior.

inquiry learning. A process that is similar to *discovery learning*. Students learn strategies to manipulate and process information, test hypotheses, and apply their conclusions to new content or situations.

instructional objectives. Statements regarding the specific changes educators intend to produce in student behavior. Also called behavioral objectives.

instructional time. The amount of time left for instruction after routine management and administrative tasks are completed.

intelligence. The capacity or set of capacities that allows an individual to learn, to solve problems, and/or to interact successfully with his or her environment.

intelligence quotient (IQ). A term originally defined as an individual's mental age divided by his or her chronological age. It is rarely used in this sense today. The term IQ is still used to mean an intelligence test score.

intrinsic motivation. Motivation influenced by personal factors such as satisfaction or enjoyment.

jigsaw method. A procedure that emphasizes and reinforces cooperation among students.

key-word method. A method of associating new words or concepts with similar-sounding cue words through the use of visual imagery.

Kohlberg's stages of moral reasoning. A theory of moral development based on three levels of moral reasoning, each of which has substages.

language disorder. Difficulties with the linguistic code or rules and conventions for linking symbols and symbol sequences.

latchkey children. Children or adolescents who are without supervision for long periods of time before or after school.

law of effect. Thorndike's finding that the connections between stimuli and responses are strengthened by satisfying outcomes.

law of exercise. Thorndike's finding that the repetition of a learned response strengthens the bond between the stimulus situation and the response.

learned helplessness. A situation in which individuals learn over time, through constant failure, that they cannot control the outcome of events affecting their lives.

learning. A process by which behavior is either modified or changed through experience or training.

learning disabilities. A wide variety of disorders causing learning problems that cannot be attributed to emotional difficulties, retardation, or sensory impairment.

learning strategies. Techniques or methods students use to acquire information.

learning style. Individual differences that influence learning in classroom situations. It is similar to *cognitive style*.

least restrictive educational environment. The educational setting most like the regular classroom in which an individual can succeed.

lesson plan. A detailed outline of the objectives, content, procedures, and evaluation of a single instructional period.

linear program. Programmed material presented in a manner so that all learners progress through the material in the same order.

loci method. A *mnemonic* involving the association of each item to be learned with a particular location in a mental image created by the learner.

locus of control. Individuals' perception of who or what is responsible for the outcome of events and behavior in their lives.

long-term memory (LTM). The part of the *information-processing system* that retains encoded information for long periods.

mainstreaming. The return to the regular classroom, for all or part of the school day, of exceptional children previously educated in self-contained, special classrooms.

mapping. A way of representing ideas in texts in the form of a diagram.

massed practice. Practice that is grouped into extended periods.

mastery goal. Learning as much as possible for the purpose of self-improvement, irrespective of the performance of others.

mastery learning. An instructional strategy that allows students to study material until they master it. It uses alternative instructional materials and *diagnostic tests*.

matrix notes. A system of note taking in which the student fills in information in the cells created by vertical and horizontal headings.

mean. The arithmetic average of a group of scores. The mean can be distorted by extreme scores. It is a *measure of central tendency*.

measures of central tendency. Statistical measures that are intended to describe the typical score of a distribution. The three measures of central tendency are the *mean*, *median*, and *mode*.

median. A *measure of central tendency* defined as the middle score in the distribution. Half of the scores lie above the median and half lie below the median.

mental age. A concept used in intelligence testing as a basis for determining the level of an individual's mental functioning. Mental age is based on the number of questions answered correctly by one individual compared with other individuals of the same age.

mental retardation. A significantly subaverage general intellectual function existing concurrently with deficits in adaptive behavior and manifested during the developmental period.

metacognition. Knowledge of one's own cognitive processes and ability to regulate these processes.

metacognitive strategies. Procedures used to plan, monitor, and regulate one's thinking.

minimal brain damage. A term used by some specialists, who subscribe to the controversial belief that learning disabled children suffer from some form of brain injury.

minimum competency testing; minimum competency standards. A testing program designed to evaluate the mastery of specified academic knowledge before granting promotion to the next grade level or graduation from high school.

mnemonics. Techniques that impose a useful link between new data and visual images or semantic knowledge.

mode. A *measure of central tendency* that is defined as the most frequently occurring score.

modeling. A type of learning in which individuals observe and then imitate the behavior of others.

moral dilemmas. Problem situations that require individuals to make decisions that are used to assess their level of moral development.

motherese. A language used by caretakers who wish to communicate with their children. It involves the simplification of speech by using short, slow, and repetitive phrases.

multicultural education. An educational reform process whose major goal is to change educational institutions so that male and female students, *exceptional* students, and students from all ethnic, cultural, and racial groups have an equal chance to achieve academically in school.

negative reinforcement. The termination of an unpleasant condition following a desired response. The termination serves to reinforce the desired response.

Nonstandard English. An English dialect that deviates from the standard pronunciation, vocabulary, and grammar.

norm-referenced assessment. A rating based on an individual's performance when compared with the performance of others on the same test.

normal distribution. A symmetric distribution of test scores in which most scores lie in the center, and scores decline in frequency as they move away from the center.

norms. Test results from a sample of students similar to those who will take the test. For teachers to compare their students with the norming sample, the students must be similar in background to the normative group.

open education. A type of teaching in which students have a great deal of choice about what work to do and about when and how they do the work. It is also called "open classroom."

object permanence. Piaget's term for children's understanding that objects continue to exist apart from the children's perception of them.

operant. A term used by Skinner to describe responses not elicited by any known stimulus. Such behaviors as walking or writing a letter are operants because no known specific stimulus elicits them. It contrasts with *respondent*.

operant conditioning. A type of learning that involves an increase in the probability that a response will occur as a function of *reinforcement*.

organizational strategies. *Learning strategies* that impose structure on material via hierarchical and other relationships among the material's parts.

overlapping. The ability of a teacher to do two or more things at once.

overlearning. Continuing practice or drill after a student reaches the desired level of performance.

part learning. The process of breaking up a large learning task into smaller segments for easier learning.

pattern-recognition knowledge. *Procedural knowledge* having to do with the recognition of patterns of stimuli. Two important types of pattern-recognition skills are identifying examples of a concept and recognizing the conditions calling for the execution of an *action sequence*.

peg-word method. The formation of a *mnemonic* by the association of a series of cue words and visual images.

percentile rank. The percentage of scores equal to or lower than a given score in a distribution.

performance assessment. Measurement activities that ask students to demonstrate skills similar to those required in real-life settings.

performance goal. An orientation toward learning in which outperforming others is a major concern.

permissive parenting style. A method of child rearing in which parents make few demands on their children, allowing them to regulate their own behavior.

person-centered education. An approach to instruction, favored by Rogers, that focuses on individual feelings, attitudes, and values. Students are given a great deal of choice in deciding what and how they want to learn.

personal fable. The belief in one's immortal and unique existence. A form of egocentrism during adolescence.

Personalized System of Instruction (PSI). An individually based, student-paced form of *mastery learning* developed by Keller. It involves five features: self-pacing, unit mastery, a minimum of lectures, an emphasis on written assignments, and the use of proctors.

placement evaluation. A process of determining performance at the beginning of instruction to decide where a student should begin in the instructional sequence.

portfolio. A file or folder containing a variety of information that documents a student's experiences and accomplishments.

positive reinforcement. A procedure that maintains or increases the rate of a response by presenting a stimulus (a positive reinforcer) following the response.

Premack's principle. A principle that states that contingent access to preferred activities serves as a reinforcer for the performance of low-frequency behaviors. "If you eat your vegetables [low-frequency behavior], you can go out and play [preferred activity]."

preoperational stage. The second stage in Piaget's theory of cognitive development, in which the lack of logical operations forces children to make decisions based on their perceptions.

primary reinforcement. A stimulus, such as food or water, that satisfies a basic need.

proactive inhibition. An explanation for the forgetting that takes place when previous learning interferes with the retention of new information.

problem solving. Finding solutions to problems for which solution methods are not immediately clear. Identifying an unknown chemical in a chemistry class is an example.

procedural knowledge. Knowledge about how to do things, composed of *pattern-recognition* and *action-sequence* knowledge.

programmed instruction. An instructional procedure in which material is arranged in a particular sequence and in small steps, or frames. Programs require the learners to respond, and provide them with immediate knowledge of results.

prompting. The presentation of an additional stimulus (e.g., a cue) to increase the probability that an appropriate response will be made in the presence of a *discriminative stimulus* (S^D).

propositional reasoning. The ability to deal with statements or propositions that describe concrete data. This type of thinking occurs during the *formal operations stage*.

prosocial behavior. The demonstration of positive social behavior such as helping, sharing, and cooperating.

psychometric. An approach to the study of intelligence that uses statistical procedures to identify the factors or mental structures (e.g., reasoning and spatial ability) that are responsible for individual differences on tests.

psychomotor domain. Objectives involving physical ability.

psychosocial crises. Erikson's psychological tasks, or dilemmas, which have their roots in the demands of society and which individuals experience over the course of their lives.

psychosocial moratorium. A period of delay granted by society to someone not ready to meet obligations. The fact that adolescents are not held responsible for all their behavior is an example of a psychosocial moratorium.

puberty. The biological changes that lead to reproductive maturity. Its onset is identified by such factors as the growth of body hair, voice changes in males, and menstruation and breast development in females.

punishment. A procedure in which an aversive stimulus is presented immediately following a response, resulting in a reduction in the rate of response.

range of scores. A measure of dispersion calculated by subtracting the highest and lowest scores in a distribution.

raw score. A test score that identifies the number of correct responses.

Reality Therapy (RT). A counseling approach by Glasser based on the principle that human problems arise when the primary needs of love and worth go unfulfilled.

reciprocal determinism. The mutual influence of the individual and the environment on each other.

reciprocal teaching. Interactive dialogue between teacher and students in which the teacher first models activities, after which the teacher and students take turns being the teacher.

regular education initiative. An attempt to restructure special education so that the regular classroom would serve as the primary setting for special education services. A regular education initiative also attempts to include all special needs students (e.g., economically disadvantaged and non-English-speaking) in one basic program rather than establish separate programs for each type of need.

rehearsal strategies. The process of repeating information over and over in *working memory* in order to retain it.

reinforcement. See *negative reinforcement*; *positive reinforcement*.

reinforcing stimulus (S^R). A stimulus used as a reinforcer. A reinforcer is defined solely by the fact that it increases or maintains the behavior upon which it is contingent.

reliability. The extent to which a test is consistent in measuring what it is supposed to measure.

resource management strategies. Strategies that assist students in managing the environment and the resources available. They include time management, study environment management, effort management, and support of others.

resource room. A special education classroom to which students come from regular classes to receive academic help to remediate their particular learning problems.

respondent. A term used by Skinner in contrast to the term *operant*. A respondent is a response that is elicited by a known stimulus and requires no previous learning.

response cost. The removal of previously earned tokens or points in a *token economy* intervention program.

response generalization. A condition whereby a behavior becomes more probable in the presence of a stimulus or situation as a result of a similar behavior having been strengthened in the presence of that stimulus or situation.

retroactive inhibition. The interference of new material with the retention of previously learned material.

reversibility. In Piaget's theory, the process of performing an action and then restoring the original condition.

reward. An object, stimulus, or outcome that is perceived as being pleasant and may be reinforcing.

scaffolding. Support for learning and problem solving. The support could be clues, questions, prompts, breaking a problem down into steps, and anything else that helps a learner become more successful.

schemata. Cognitive structures created through the abstraction of previous experience. Schemata function in the comprehension and recall of data and can aid learning or be responsible for many types of distortion in recall.

secondary reinforcement. A process that uses a stimulus that is not originally reinforcing but that acquires reinforcing properties when paired with a primary reinforcer. Money is a secondary reinforcer.

self-actualization. Maslow's term for the psychological need to develop one's capabilities and potential in order to enhance personal growth.

self-concept. The total organization of the perceptions individuals have of themselves. See *self-esteem*.

self-efficacy. The belief that one can successfully execute the behavior required to produce a particular outcome.

self-esteem. The value, or judgment, individuals place on their behavior. Self-esteem and *self-concept* are often used interchangeably in educational literature.

self-fulfilling prophecy. A phenomenon in which a teacher's expectations lead to differential behavior by the teacher toward certain students; the teacher's attitude may help produce the "expected" behavior in students.

self-regulated learning. *Learning* in which students are actively involved in motivating themselves and using appropriate learning strategies.

self-reinforcement. A procedure in which individuals reinforce their own behavior.

semantic memory. Verbal information stored in *long-term memory*. Semantic memory is composed of *declarative knowledge* and *procedural knowledge*.

sensorimotor stage. Piaget's first stage of intellectual development, in which the child moves from the reflexive activities of reaching, grasping, and sucking to more highly organized forms of activity.

serial position effect. The process by which the position of material in a list affects the ease with which the material can be recalled. A person is more likely to remember information placed at the beginning (primacy effect) or at the end (recency effect) of a list than information placed in the middle.

serializing. The process of ordering objects in terms of one or more properties (e.g., placing objects in a series from small to large).

set effect. The failure to process important information as a result of the automatic execution of an *action sequence*.

shaping. A technique whereby individuals are taught to perform complex behaviors that were not previously in their repertoire. The method involves analyzing the desired behavior and dividing it into small, easily identifiable behaviors that can be readily reinforced. It is also termed "successive approximations."

short-term sensory store (STSS). The part of the *information-processing system* that briefly stores information from the senses.

signal continuity. The ability of a teacher to move lessons along at a brisk pace and to alert students to what they should attend to.

significant difference. A difference based on a level of probability (e.g., $p < .01$) established before an investigation begins.

social cognitive theory. Bandura's theory to explain learning in naturalistic settings. The theory explains how individuals acquire complex skills and abilities through observing the behavior of others.

socioeconomic status (SES). A ranking to determine social position in a society. In the United States, SES is determined by objective indices such as father's and/or mother's occupation, father's and/or mother's educational background, and the family's material resources (e.g., what the family owns). Sometimes the more subjective term "social class" is used to ascribe high or low status to individuals.

sociolinguistics. The study of language in its social context.

speech disorder. Problems associated with production of the oral symbols of language.

split-half reliability. A measure of *reliability* obtained by correlating the odd and even items on a test.

spontaneous recovery. The re-emergence of behavior after a period of *extinction.*

standard deviation. A measure of the spread of scores around the *mean* of the distribution.

standard error of measurement. An estimate of the amount of error in a test score.

standard score. A score described in terms of *standard deviation* units from the *mean* of the distribution.

standardized test. A test commercially prepared by measurement experts who have carefully studied all test items used in a large number of schools.

stanines. Intervals on a nine-point scale of *standard scores.*

stimulus generalization. A process whereby once a particular *conditioned stimulus* is associated with a response, other similar stimuli are able to elicit the response.

summative test; summative evaluation. The measurement of student achievement at the end of an instructional unit.

T score. A *standard score* in a distribution with a *mean* of 50 and a *standard deviation* of 10.

table of specifications. A two-way chart that relates desired learning outcomes to course content; helps ensure *content validity* in planning test questions.

task analysis. The identification of the subordinate skills and knowledge that learners must acquire in order to achieve an educational objective.

Taxonomy of Educational Objectives. A classification system developed by Bloom that divides objectives into two domains: *cognitive* and *affective.* A third domain—*psychomotor*—has been developed by other individuals.

teacher efficacy. The belief, held by many teachers, that they have the ability to educate all types of students.

teacher expectations. Inferences made by teachers about their students' present and future academic achievement and classroom behavior.

teacher-made test. An *achievement test* constructed by classroom teachers to measure the specific goals or objectives of particular courses.

teaching. A system of actions intended to induce *learning.*

teaching machine. A mechanical device incorporating a programmed *learning* format.

test-retest reliability. A type of *reliability* measure obtained by administering the same test a second time, after a short interval, and correlating the two sets of scores.

test-wiseness training. A program to teach students general test-taking skills for use on any test.

time-out. A behavioral control method that involves removal of a disruptive student from the classroom or to an isolated part of the classroom.

token economy. Reinforcing students through the use of *behavior modification* procedures—specifically, by supplying tokens that can later be exchanged for some reinforcement.

transductive reasoning. Piaget's term to describe thought in the *preoperational stage* when the child moves from the particular to the particular without touching on the general (i.e., the child sees a relationship between particular instances when in fact there is none).

unconditioned response. The unlearned, biological reaction evoked by an *unconditioned stimulus.*

unconditioned stimulus. A stimulus that naturally elicits a particular response.

unit plan. A detailed outline for a series of interrelated *lesson plans* on a particular topic of study that lasts from two to four weeks.

validity. The appropriateness of the interpretation of a test score with regard to a particular use.

values clarification. A humanistic approach to moral education designed to help individuals to understand the relationship between their beliefs and their behavior and to become more aware of their values.

variability. The spread, or dispersion, of scores in a distribution.

variable-interval schedule. A schedule providing *reinforcement* following the first correct response after different lapses of time.

variable-ratio schedule. A schedule of *reinforcement* in which a predetermined number of responses, varied from one time to another, must occur between each reinforced response.

vicarious reinforcement. Observation of positive consequences received by another person or model that leads to matching behavior by the learner. A teacher uses vicarious reinforcement to modify behavior when he or she states to the class: "Look how well row number one has cleaned up their desks" and the rest of the rows begin cleaning their desks.

visual impairment. A difficulty in clearly distinguishing forms or discriminating details by sight at a specified distance, resulting in the need for special methods and materials.

wait-time. The period of time that a teacher waits for a student to respond to a question.

with-it-ness. A teacher's ability to communicate to students that he or she knows what is happening in the classroom.

working memory (WM). A store for the performance of mental operations such as solving math problems; also for temporary storage (sometimes called short-term memory).

z score. A *standard score* in a distribution with a mean of 0 and a *standard deviation* of 1.

zone of proximal development. Vygotsky's description for the difference between an individual's current level of development and his or her potential level of development.

References

Abramson, L., Seligman, M., & Teasdale, J. (1978). Learned helplessness in humans: Critique and reformulation. *Journal of Abnormal Psychology, 87*, 49–74.

Abramson, M., Willson, V., Yoshida, R. K., & Hagerty, G. (1983). Parents' perceptions of their learning disabled child's educational performance. *Learning Disability Quarterly, 6*, 184–194.

Adler, S. (1979). *Poverty children and their language.* New York: Grune & Stratton.

Ahrons, C. R., & Rodgers, R. H. (1987). *Divorced families: A multidisciplinary view.* New York: Norton.

Ainsworth, N. (1984). The cultural shaping of oral discourse. *Theory into Practice, 23*, 132–137.

Airasian, P. W., & Madaus, G. J. (1972). Functional types of student evaluation. *Measurement and Evaluation in Guidance, 4*, 221–233.

Alberto, P., & Troutman, A. C. (1990). *Applied behavior analysis for teachers: Influencing student performance* (3rd ed.). Columbus, OH: Merrill.

Allington, R. L. (1991). How policy and regulation influence instruction for at-risk learners, or why poor readers rarely comprehend well and probably never will. In L. Idol & B. F. Jones (Eds.), *Educational values and cognitive instruction: Implications for reform.* Hillsdale, NJ: Erlbaum.

Almy, M. (1969). *Ways of studying children.* New York: Teachers College Press.

American Association of University Women. (1992). *How schools shortchange girls.* Washington, DC: AAUW.

Ames, C. (1987). The enhancement of student motivation. In M. L. Maehr & D. A. Kleiber (Eds.), *Advances in motivation and achievement: Enhancing motivation* (Vol. 5). Greenwich, CT: JAI Press.

Ames, C. (1990). Motivation: What teachers need to know. *Teachers College Record, 91*, 409–421.

Ames, C. (1992). Achievement goals and the classroom motivational climate. In D. H. Schunk & J. L. Meece (Eds.), *Student perceptions in the classroom.* Hillsdale, NJ: Erlbaum.

Ames, C., & Ames, R. (Eds). (1989). *Research on motiviation in education: Vol. 3. Goals and cognitions.* San Diego: Academic Press.

Ames, C., & Ames, R. (1991). Motivation and effective teaching. In L. Idol & B. F. Jones (Eds.), *Educational values and cognitive instruction: Implications for reform.* Hillside, NJ: Erlbaum.

Ames, C., & Archer, J. (1988). Achievement goals in the classroom: Students' learning strategies and motivation processes. *Journal of Educational Psychology, 80*, 260–267.

Ames, C., & Felker, D. W. (1979). Effects of self-concept on children's causal attributions and self-reinforcement. *Journal of Educational Psychology, 71*, 613–619.

Ames, R., & Ames, C. (Eds.). (1984). *Research on motivation in education: Vol. 1. Student motivation.* Orlando, FL: Academic Press.

Anderson, J. R. (1985). *Cognitive psychology and its implications.* New York: Freeman.

Anderson, L. M., Brubaker, N. L., Alleman-Brooks, J., & Duffy, G. G. (1984). *Making seatwork work* (Research Series No. 142). East Lansing: Michigan State University, Institute for Research on Teaching.

Anderson, L. M., Evertson, C., & Brophy, J. (1979). An experimental study of effective teaching in first-grade reading groups. *Elementary School Journal, 71*, 193–223.

Anderson, R. (1990). *California: The state of assessment.* California Assessment Program. Sacramento, CA: California Department of Education.

Anderson, T. H., & Armbruster, B. B. (1984). Studying. In P. D. Pearson (Ed.), *Handbook of reading research.* White Plains, NY: Longman.

Andre, T., & Phye, G. D. (1986). Cognition, learning, and education. In G. D. Phye & T. Andre (Eds.), *Cognitive classroom learning: Understanding, thinking, and problem solving.* New York: Academic Press.

Arlin, M. (1984). Time, equality, and mastery learning. *Review of Educational Research, 54*, 65–86.

Armbruster, B. B. (1986). Schema theory and the design of content-area textbooks. *Educational Psychologist, 2*, 253–267.

Aronson, E., & Carlsmith, J. (1962). Performance expectancy as a determinant of actual performance. *Journal of Abnormal and Social Psychology, 65*, 178–182.

Ashton, P. T., & Webb, R. B. (1986). *Making a difference: Teachers' sense of efficacy and student achievement.* White Plains, NY: Longman.

Aspy, D. N. (1972). An investigation into the relationship between teachers' actual knowledge of learning theory and their classroom performance. *Journal of Teacher Education, 23*, 21–24.

Atkinson, J. W. (1964). *An introduction to motivation*. Princeton, NJ: Van Nostrand.

Atkinson, J. W., & Feather, N. T. (1966). *A theory of achievement motivation*. New York: Wiley.

Atkinson, R. C. (1975). Mnemotechnics in second-language learning. *American Psychologist, 30*, 821–828.

Au, K. H., & Mason, J. M. (1981). Social organizational factors in learning to read: The balance of rights hypothesis. *Reading Research Quarterly, 17*, 115–152.

Ausubel, D. P. (1968). *Educational psychology: A cognitive view*. New York: Holt, Rinehart & Winston.

Baer, D. M., Peterson, R. F., & Sherman, J. A. (1967). The development of imitation by reinforcing behavioral similarity to a model. *Journal of the Experimental Analysis of Behavior, 10*, 405–416.

Baer, D. M., Wolf, M. M., & Risley, T. R. (1968). Some current dimensions of applied behavior analysis. *Journal of Applied Behavior Analysis, 1*, 91–97.

Bailey, D. B., & Worley, M. (1984). *Teaching infants and preschoolers with handicaps*. Columbus, OH: Merrill.

Baker, E. L., & Linn, R. L. (1992, Spring). Performance based assessments: Early interesting results and complicated futures. *The CRESST Line*. (Newsletter of the National Center for Research on Evaluation, Standards, & Student Testing, Graduate School of Education. University of California at Los Angeles).

Baker, E. L., O'Neil, H. F., Jr., & Linn, R. L. (1991, August). *Policy and validity prospects for performance-based assessment*. Paper presented at the annual meeting of the American Psychological Association, San Francisco.

Bandura, A. (1967, March). Behavioral psychotherapy. *Scientific American*, pp. 78–86.

Bandura, A. (1969). *Principles of behavior modification*. New York: Holt, Rinehart & Winston.

Bandura, A. (1977). *Social learning theory*. Englewood Cliffs, NJ: Prentice-Hall.

Bandura, A. (1982). Self-efficacy mechanism in human agency. *American Psychologist, 37*, 122–147.

Bandura, A. (1986). *Social foundations of thought and action: A social cognitive theory*. Englewood Cliffs, NJ: Prentice-Hall.

Bandura, A., Grusec, J., & Menlove, F. (1967). Vicarious extinction of avoidance behavior. *Journal of Personality and Social Psychology, 5*, 16–23.

Bandura, A., & Kupers, C. J. (1964). The transmission of patterns of self-reinforcement through modeling. *Journal of Abnormal and Social Psychology, 69*, 1–9.

Bandura, A., & Perloff, B. (1967). Relative efficacy of self-monitored and externally imposed reinforcement systems. *Journal of Personality and Social Psychology, 7*, 111–116.

Bandura, A., & Walters, R. H. (1963). *Social learning and personality development*. New York: Holt, Rinehart & Winston.

Bangert-Drowns, R. L., Kulik, J. A., & Kulik, C. C. (1983). Effects of coaching programs on achievement test performance. *Review of Educational Research, 55*, 571–585.

Bangert-Drowns, R. L., Kulik, J. A., & Kulik, C. C. (1985, April). *Effectiveness of computer-based education in secondary schools*. Paper presented at the annual meeting of the American Educational Research Association, Chicago.

Banks, J. A. (1989). Multicultural education: Characteristics and goals. In J. A. Banks & C. M. McGee Banks (Eds.), *Multicultural education: Issues and perspectives*. Boston: Allyn & Bacon.

Bar-Tal, D. (1978). Attributional analysis of achievement-related behavior. *Review of Educational Research, 48*, 259–271.

Barnes, B., & Clawson, E. (1975). Do advance organizers facilitate learning? Recommendations for further research based on the analysis of thirty-two studies. *Review of Educational Research, 45*, 637–659.

Barnett, W. S. (1985). Benefit-cost analysis of the Perry Preschool Program and its policy implications. *Educational Evaluation and Policy Analysis, 7*, 333–342.

Baron, R. M., Tom, D., & Cooper, H. M. (1985). Social class, race, and teacher expectations. In J. Dusek (Ed.), *Teacher expectancies*. Hillsdale, NJ: Erlbaum.

Barrish, H. H., Saunders, M., & Wolf, M. M. (1969). Good behavior game: Effects of individual contingencies for group consequences on disruptive behavior in a classroom. *Journal of Applied Behavior Analysis, 2*, 119–124.

Barth, R. S. (1971). So you want to change to an open classroom? *Phi Delta Kappan, 53*, 97–99.

Bartlett, E. J. (1972). Selecting preschool language programs. In C. B. Cazden (Ed.), *Language in early childhood education*. Washington, DC: National Association for the Education of Young Children.

Bash, M. S., & Camp, B. W. (1980). Teacher training in the think aloud classroom program. In G. Cartledge & J. F. Milburn (Eds.), *Teaching social skills to children*. New York: Pergamon.

Baskin, E. J., & Hess, R. D. (1980). Does affective education work? A review of seven programs. *Journal of School Psychology, 18*, 40–50.

Baumrind, D. (1966). Effects of authoritative parental control on child behavior. *Child Development, 37*, 887–907.

Baumrind, D. (1967). Child care practices anteceding three patterns of preschool behavior. *Genetic Psychology Monographs, 75*, 43–88.

Baumrind, D. (1971). Harmonious parents and their preschool children. *Developmental Psychology, 4*, 99–102.

Beal, C. R. (1989). Children's communication skills: Implications for the development of writing strategies. In C. B. McCormick, G. Miller, & M. Pressley (Eds.), *Cognitive strategy research: From basic research to educational applications.* New York: Springer-Verlag.

Beane, J. R. (1985/1986). The continuing controversy over affective education. *Educational Leadership, 43,* 26–31.

Becker, W. C., & Gersten, R. (1982). A follow-up of Follow Through: The later effects of the direct instruction model on children in fifth and sixth grades. *American Educational Research Journal, 19,* 75–92.

Becker, W. C., Madsen, C. H., Arnold, C. R., & Thomas, D. R. (1967). The contingent use of teacher attention and praise in reducing classroom behavior problems. *Journal of Special Education, 1,* 287–330.

Bee, H. (1989). *The developing child* (5th ed.). New York: Harper & Row.

Bell-Gredler, M. E. (1986). *Learning and instruction: Theory into practice.* New York: Macmillan.

Bellanca, J. A. (1977). *Grading.* NEA Professional Studies. Washington, DC: National Education Association. (ERIC Document Reproduction Service No. ED 143 673).

Belleza, F. S. (1981). Mnemonic devices: Classification, characteristics, and criteria. *Review of Educational Research, 51,* 247–275.

Bem, S. (1974). The measurement of psychological androgyny. *Journal of Consulting and Clinical Psychology, 42,* 155–162.

Bem, S. (1975). Sex-role adaptability: One consequence of psychological androgyny. *Journal of Personality and Social Psychology, 31,* 634–643.

Bem, S. (1981). Gender schema theory: A cognitive account of sex typing. *Psychological Review, 88,* 354–364.

Bem, S. (1984). Androgyny and gender schema theory: A conceptual and empirical integration. In T. B. Sonderegger (Ed.), *Nebraska symposium on motivation: Psychology and gender.* Lincoln: University of Nebraska Press.

Benjamin, M., McKeachie, W. J., Lin, Y. G., & Holinger, D. P. (1981). Test anxiety: Deficits in information processing. *Journal of Educational Psychology, 73,* 816–824.

Bennett, W. J. (1986). *First lessons: A report on elementary education in America.* Washington, DC: U. S. Government Printing Office.

Benninga, J. S. (1988). An emerging synthesis in moral education. *Phi Delta Kappan, 69,* 415–418.

Berdine, W. H., & Blackhurst, A. E. (Eds.). (1985). *An introduction to special education.* Boston: Little, Brown.

Berns, R. M. (1989). *Child, family, community.* New York: Holt, Rinehart & Winston.

Beyer, B. K. (1991). *Teaching thinking skills: A handbook for elementary school teachers.* Boston: Allyn & Bacon.

Biehler, R. F. (1974). *Study guide: Psychology applied to teaching* (2nd ed.). Boston: Houghton Mifflin.

Bjorklund, D. F. (1989). *Children's thinking: Developmental function and individual differences.* Pacific Grove, CA: Brooks/Cole.

Black, K. N. (1979, January). What about the child from a one-parent home? *Teacher,* pp. 24–28.

Blakeslee, T. R. (1980). *The right brain: A new understanding of the unconscious mind and its creative powers.* Garden City, NY: Anchor.

Block, J. H., & Anderson, L. W. (1975). *Mastery learning in classroom instruction.* New York: Macmillan.

Block, J. H., & Burns, R. B. (1976). Mastery learning. In L. Shulman (Ed.), *Review of research in education* (Vol. 4). Itasca, IL: Peacock.

Block, J. H., Efthim, H. E., & Burns, R. B. (1989). *Building effective mastery learning schools.* White Plains, NY: Longman.

Bloom, B. S. (1968). Learning for mastery. *[UCLA-CSEIP] Evaluation Comment, 1,* 1–12.

Bloom, B. S. (1971). Affective consequences of school achievement. In J. H. Block (Ed.), *Mastery learning: Theory and practice.* New York: Holt, Rinehart & Winston.

Bloom, B. S. (1974). An introduction to mastery learning theory. In J. H. Block (Ed.), *School, society and mastery learning.* New York: Holt, Rinehart & Winston.

Bloom, B. S., Englehart, N. D., Furst, E. J., Hill, W. H., & Krathwohl, D. R. (1956). *Taxonomy of educational objectives: Handbook I. Cognitive domain.* New York: Longman.

Bluming, M., & Dembo, M. (1973). *Solving teaching problems: A guide for the elementary school teacher.* Santa Monica, CA: Goodyear.

Blyth, D. A., Simmons, R. G., & Bush, D. (1978). The transition into early adolescence: A longitudinal comparison of youth in two educational contexts. *Sociology of Education, 51,* 149–162.

Bolocofsky, D. N., & Mescher, S. (1984). Student characteristics: Using student characteristics to develop effective grading practices. *The Directive Teacher, 6,* 11–23.

Bond, L. (1989). The effects of special preparation on measures of scholastic ability. In R. L. Linn (Ed.), *Educational measurement* (3rd ed.). New York: Macmillan.

Bondy, E. (1984). Thinking about thinking: Encouraging children's use of metacognitive processes. *Childhood Education, 60,* 234–238.

Borg, W. R., & Gall, M. D. (1993). *Educational research: An introduction* (6th ed.). White Plains, NY: Longman.

Borko, H., & Shavelson, R. J. (1990). Teacher decision making. In B. F. Jones & L. Idol (Eds.), *Dimensions of thinking and cognitive instruction: Implications for educational reform* (Vol. 1). Hillsdale, NJ: Erlbaum.

Bouchard, T. J., Jr., & McCue, M. (1981). Familial studies of intelligence: A review. *Science, 212,* 1055–1059.

Bouvier, L. F., & Agresta, A. J. (1987). The future Asian population of the United States. In J. T. Fawcett & B. V. Carino (Eds.), *Pacific bridges: The new immigration from Asia and the Pacific Islands.* New York: Center for Migration Studies.

Boyer, E. L. (1983). *High school: A report on secondary education in America.* New York: Harper & Row.

Brainerd, C. J. (1978). The stage question in cognitive-developmental theory. *The Behavioral and Brain Sciences, 2,* 173–213.

Bransford, J. D. (1979). *Human cognition: Learning, understanding, and remembering.* Belmont, CA: Wadsworth.

Brodsky, C. M. (1954). *A study of norms for body form: Behavior relationships.* Washington, DC: Catholic University of America Press.

Bronfenbrenner, U. (1974). *Longitudinal evaluations: A report on longitudinal evaluations of pre-school programs: Is early intervention effective?* (Vol. 2, Publication No. OHD 74–25). Washington, DC: U.S. Department of Health, Education, and Welfare.

Brookover, W., Schweitzer, K., Schneider, J., Beady, C., Flood, P., & Wisenbaker, J. (1978). Elementary school social climate and school achievement. *American Educational Research Journal, 15,* 301–318.

Brooks-Gunn, J., & Matthews, W. S. (1979). *He and she: How children develop their sex-role identity.* Englewood Cliffs, NJ: Prentice-Hall.

Brophy, J. E. (1979). Teacher behavior and its effects. *Journal of Educational Psychology, 71,* 733–750.

Brophy, J. E. (1981). Teacher praise: A functional analysis. *Review of Educational Research, 51,* 5–32.

Brophy, J. E. (1985a). Teacher-student interaction. In J. Dusek (Ed.), *Teacher expectancies.* Hillsdale, NJ: Erlbaum.

Brophy, J. E. (1985b). Interactions of male and female students with male and female teachers. In L. C. Wilkinson & C. B. Marrett (Eds.), *Gender influences in classroom interaction.* Orlando, FL: Academic Press.

Brophy, J. E. (1986). On motivating students. (Occasional paper No. 101). East Lansing, MI: Institute for Research on Teaching.

Brophy, J. E., & Evertson, C. M. (1976). *Learning from teaching: A developmental perspective.* Boston: Allyn & Bacon.

Brophy, J. E., & Good, T. L. (1974). *Teacher-student relationships: Causes and consequences.* New York: Holt, Rinehart & Winston.

Brophy, J. E., & Rohrkemper, M. (1981). The influence of problem ownership on teachers' perceptions of and strategies for coping with problem students. *Journal of Educational Psychology, 73,* 295–311.

Brophy, J. E., Rohrkemper, M., Rashid, H., & Goldberger, M. (1983). Relationships between teachers' presentations of classroom tasks and students' engagement in those tasks. *Journal of Educational Psychology, 75,* 544–552.

Brown, A. L. (1980). Metacognitive development and reading. In R. J. Spiro, B. C. Bruce, & W. F. Brewer (Eds.), *Theoretical issues in reading comprehension: Perspectives from cognitive psychology, linguistics, artificial intelligence, and education.* Hillsdale, NJ: Erlbaum.

Brown, A. L., & Smiley, S. S. (1977). Rating the importance of structural units of prose passages: A problem of metacognitive development. *Child Development, 48,* 1–8.

Brown, F. G. (1983). *Principles of educational and psychological testing* (3rd ed.). New York: Holt, Rinehart & Winston.

Brown, H. D. (1987). *Principles of language learning and teaching* (2nd ed.). Englewood Cliffs, NJ: Prentice-Hall.

Bruner, J. (1961). The act of discovery. *Harvard Educational Review, 31,* 21–32.

Buike, S. (1980). *Teacher decision making in reading* (Research Series No. 79). East Lansing: Michigan State University, Institute for Research on Teaching.

Burnham, C. (1986). Portfolio evaluation: Room to breathe and grow. In C. Bridges (Ed.), *Training the teacher of college composition.* Urbana, IL: National Council of Teachers of English.

Buros, O. K., et al. (Eds.). (1938–1978). *Mental measurements yearbook* (Vols. 1–8). Lincoln: University of Nebraska Press.

Butterworth, R., & Alloro, D. (1986, March 21). Changing "F" to "N" only disguises the fact that a student is failing. *Los Angeles Herald Examiner.*

Caldwell, J. H., Huitt, W. G., & Graeber, A. O. (1982). Time spent in learning: Implications from research. *Elementary School Journal, 82,* 471–480.

Canter, L. (1976). *Assertive discipline: A take-charge approach for today's educator.* Seal Beach, CA: Canter &Associates.

Cardenás, J. A. (1986). The role of native-language instruction in bilingual education. *Phi Delta Kappan, 67,* 359–363.

Carin, A. A., & Sund, R. B. (1985). *Teaching science through discovery* (5th ed.). Columbus, OH: Merrill.

Carpenter, R. L., & Apter, S. (1988). Research integration of cognitive-emotional interventions for behaviorally disordered children and youth. In M. C. Wang, M. C. Reynolds, & H. J. Walberg (Eds.), *Handbook of special education: Vol. 2. Mildly handicapped conditions.* New York: Pergamon.

Carroll, J. B. (1963). A model of school learning. *Teachers College Record, 64,* 723–733.

Carter, T. P., & Chatfield, M. L. (1986). Effective bilingual schools: Implications for policy and practice. *American Journal of Education, 95,* 200–234.

Cartwright, G. P., Cartwright, C. A., & Ward, M. E. (1984). *Educating special learners* (2nd ed.). Belmont, CA: Wadsworth.

Casanova, U. (1987). Ethnic and cultural differences. In V. Richardson-Koehler (Ed.), *Educators' handbook: A research perspective*. White Plains, NY: Longman.

Case, R. (1985). *Intellectual development: Birth to adulthood*. New York: Academic Press.

Case, R., & Griffin, S. (1989). Child cognitive development: The role of central conceptual structures in the development of scientific and social thought. In C. A. Hauert (Ed.), *Developmental psychology: Cognitive, perceptual, motor, and neurological perspectives*. Amsterdam: North Holland.

Center for Social Organization of Schools (1984, November). *School uses of microcomputers: Reports from a national survey* (Issue No. 6). Baltimore: Johns Hopkins University.

Chalfant, J. (1989). Learning disabilities: Policy issues and promising approaches. *American Psychologist, 44*, 392–398.

Chapman, J. W. (1989). Learning disabled children's self-concepts. *Review of Educational Research, 58*, 347–371.

Charles, C. M. (1989). *Building classroom discipline: From models to practice* (3rd ed.). White Plains, NY: Longman.

Chase, C. I. (1974). *Measurement for educational evaluation*. Reading, MA: Addison-Wesley.

Chomsky, N. (1965). *Aspects of a theory of syntax*. Cambridge, MA: MIT Press.

Claiborn, W. (1969). Expectancy effects in the classroom: A failure to replicate. *Journal of Educational Psychology, 60*, 377–383.

Clarizio, H. F. (1980). *Toward positive classroom discipline*. New York: Wiley.

Clark, C. M., & Elmore, J. L. (1981). *Transforming curriculum in mathematics, science, and writing: A case study of teacher yearly planning* (Research Series No. 99). East Lansing: Michigan State University, Institute for Research on Teaching.

Clark, C. M., & Peterson, P. L. (1985). Teacher thought processes. In M. C. Wittrock (Ed.), *Handbook of research on teaching* (3rd ed.). New York: Macmillan.

Clark, C. M., & Yinger, R. J. (1979). *Three studies of teacher planning* (Research Series No. 55). East Lansing: Michigan State University, Institute for Research on Teaching.

Clark, R. (1983). *Family life and school achievement: Why poor black children succeed and fail*. Chicago: University of Chicago Press.

Clark, R. E. (1982). Antagonism between achievement and enjoyment in ATI studies. *Educational Psychologist, 17*, 92–101.

Clark, R. E. (1983). Reconsidering research on learning from media. *Review of Educational Research, 53*, 445–459.

Clark, R. E. (1991). When researchers swim upstream: Reflections on an unpopular argument about learning from media. *Educational Technology*, 34–40.

Cohen, E. G. (1982). Expectation states and interracial interaction in school settings. *Annual Review of Sociology, 8*, 209–235.

Cohen, E. G. (1986, April). *Treating status problems in the cooperative classroom*. Paper presented at the annual meeting of the American Educational Research Association, San Francisco.

Cohen, S. (1973). Educational psychology: Practice what we preach! *Educational Psychologist, 10*, 80–86.

Cohen, S. A., Hyman, J. S., Ascroft, L., & Loveless, D. (1989, March). *Comparing effects of metacognition, learning styles, and human attributes with alignment*. Paper presented at the annual meeting of the American Educational Research Association, San Francisco.

Coles, G. S. (1978). The learning-disabilities test battery: Empirical and social issues. *Harvard Educational Review, 48*, 313–340.

Collins, A. M., & Quillian, M. R. (1969). Retrieval time from semantic memory. *Journal of Verbal Learning and Verbal Behavior, 8*, 240–247.

Collins, J. (1982, March). *Self-efficacy and ability in achievement behavior*. Paper presented at the annual meeting of the American Educational Research Association, New York.

Combs, A. W. (1979). *Myths in education*. Boston: Allyn & Bacon.

Combs, A. W. (1981). Humanistic education: Too tender for a tough world? *Phi Delta Kappan, 62*, 446–449.

Combs, A. W. (1982). *A personal approach to teaching: Beliefs that make a difference*. Boston: Allyn & Bacon.

Combs, A. W., & Avila, D. L. (1985). *Helping relationships: Basic concepts for the helping professions* (3rd ed.). Boston: Allyn & Bacon.

Combs, A. W., Avila, D. L., & Purkey, W. W. (1971). *Helping relationships: Basic concepts for the helping professions*. Boston: Allyn & Bacon.

Combs, A. W., Blume, R. A., Newman, A. J., & Wass, H. L. (1974). *The professional education of teachers* (2nd ed.). Boston: Allyn & Bacon.

Congressional Record, October 10, 1978, H-12179.

Cooper, H. (1989). *Homework*. White Plains, NY: Longman.

Cooper, J. O., Heron, T. E., & Heward, W. L. (1987). *Applied behavior analysis*. Columbus, OH: Merrill.

Coopersmith, S. (1967). *The antecedents of self-esteem*. San Francisco: Freeman.

Corno, L. (1987). Teaching and self-regulated learning. In D. C. Berliner & B. V. Rosenshine (Eds.), *Talks to teachers*. New York: Random House.

Corrao, J., & Melton, G. B. (1988). Legal issues in school-based behavior therapy. In J. C. Witt, S. N. Elliott, & F.

M. Gresham (Eds.), *Handbook of behavior therapy in education*. New York: Plenum.

Cortés, C. E. (1986). The education of language minority students: A contextual interaction model. In *Beyond language: Social and cultural factors in schooling language minority students.* Sacramento, CA: Bilingual Education Office, California State Department of Education.

Costa, A. L. (1984). A reaction to Hunter's knowing, teaching, and supervising. In P. L. Hosford (Ed.), *Using what we know about teaching.* Alexandria, VA: Association for Supervision and Curriculum Development.

Costa, A. L. (Ed.). (1985). *Developing minds: A resource book for teaching thinking.* Alexandria, VA: Association for Supervision and Curriculum Development.

Cote, R. W. (1973). Behavior modification: Some questions. *Elementary School Journal, 24,* 45–47.

Cott, A. (1972). Megavitamins: The orthomolecular approach to behavioral disorders and learning disabilities. *Academic Therapy, 7,* 245–258.

Council of State Directors of Programs for the Gifted. (1987). *The 1987 state of the states gifted and talented education report.* Washington, DC: Author.

Covington, M. V. (1983). Motivated cognitions. In S. G. Paris, G. M. Olson, & H. W. Stevenson (Eds.), *Learning and motivation in the classroom.* Hillsdale, NJ: Erlbaum.

Covington, M. V. (1984). The self-worth theory of achievement motivation: Findings and implications. *Elementary School Journal, 85,* 5–20.

Covington, M. V. (1992). *Making the grade: A self-worth perspective on motivation and school reform.* New York: Cambridge University Press.

Covington, M. V., & Beery, R. (1976). *Self-worth and school learning.* New York: Holt, Rinehart & Winston.

Covington, M. V., & Omelich, C. (1979). Effort: The double-edged sword in school achievement. *Journal of Educational Psychology, 71,* 169–182.

Cox, W. F., Jr., & Dunn, T. G. (1979). Mastery learning: A psychological trap? *Educational Psychologist, 14,* 24–29.

Cronbach, L. J., & Snow, R. E. (1977). *Aptitudes and instructional methods: A handbook for research on interactions.* New York: Irvington.

Crooks, T. J. (1988). The impact of classroom evaluation practices on students. *Review of Educational Research, 58,* 438–481.

Cruickshank, D. R., & Callahan, R. C. (1983). The other side of the desk: Stages and problems of teacher development. *Elementary School Journal, 83,* 251–258.

Cummins, J. (1981). The role of primary language development in promoting educational success for language minority students. In *Schooling and language minority students: A theoretical framework.* Los Angeles: State of California, Office of Bilingual Bicultural Education.

Curry, L. (1990). A critique of research on learning styles. *Educational Leadership, 48*(2), 50–52, 54–56.

Curwin, R., & Mendler, A. N. (1988). Packaged discipline programs: Let the buyer beware. *Educational Leadership, 46,* 68–71

Curwin, R., & Mendler, A. N. (1989). We repeat, let the buyer beware: A response to Canter. *Educational Leadership, 46,* 83.

Cziko, G. A. (1992). The evaluation of bilingual education: From necessity and probability to possibility. *Educational Researcher, 21,* 10–15.

D'Amato, J. (1986). *"We cool, tha's why": A study of personhood and place in a class of Hawaiian second graders.* Unpublished doctoral dissertation, University of Hawaii, Honolulu.

Das, J. P., Kirby, J., & Jarman, R. F. (1975). Simultaneous and successive syntheses: An alternative model for cognitive abilities. *Psychological Bulletin, 82,* 87–103.

Davidson, J. E. (1990). Intelligence re-created. *Educational Psychologist, 25,* 337–354.

Davis, E. D. (1984). Should the public schools teach values? *Phi Delta Kappan, 66,* 358–362.

Davis, J. M., Wilson, M., & Sandoval, J. (1988). Strategies for the primary prevention of adolescent suicide. *School Psychology Review, 17,* 559–569.

Day, J. D., Cordon, L. A., & Kerwin, M. L. (1989). Informal instruction and development of cognitive skills: A review and critique of research. In C. B. McCormick, G. E. Miller, & M. Pressley (Eds.), *Cognitive strategy research: From basic research to educational applications.* New York: Springer-Verlag.

deBono, E. (1985). The CoRT thinking program. In J. Segal, S. Chipman, & R. Glaser (Eds.), *Thinking and learning skills: Vol. 1. Relating instruction to research.* Hillsdale, NJ: Erlbaum.

DeCharms, R. (1981). Personal causation and locus of control: Two different traditions and two uncorrelated measures. In H. M. Lefcourt (Ed.), *Research with the locus of control construct: Vol. 1. Assessment methods.* New York: Academic Press.

Deci, E. L. (1975). *Intrinsic motivation.* New York: Plenum.

Deci, E. L., Nezlek, J., & Sheinman, L. (1981). Characteristics of the rewarder and intrinsic motivation of the rewardee. *Journal of Personality and Social Psychology, 40,* 1–10.

Delgado-Gaitan, C., & Trueba, H.T. (1985). Ethnographic study of participant structures in task completion: Reinterpretation of "handicaps" in Mexican children. *Language Disability Quarterly, 8,* 67–75.

Dembo, M. H., & Gibson, S. (1985). Teachers' sense of efficacy: An important factor in school improvement. *Elementary School Journal, 86,* 173–184.

Dembo, M. H., Sweitzer, M., & Lauritzen, P. (1985). An evaluation of group parent education: Behavioral, PET, and Adlerian programs. *Review of Educational Research, 55,* 155–200.

Derry, S. J. (1990). Learning strategies for acquiring useful knowledge. In B. L. Jones & L. Idol (Eds.), *Dimensions of thinking and cognitive instruction.* Hillsdale, NJ: Erlbaum.

Derry, S. J., & Murphy, D. A. (1986). Designing systems that train learning ability: From theory to practice. *Review of Educational Research, 56,* 1–39.

Devin-Sheehan, L., Feldman, R. S., & Allen, V. L. (1976). Research on children tutoring children: A critical review. *Review of Educational Research, 46,* 355–358.

Devine, T. G. (1987). *Teaching study skills: A guide for teachers.* Boston: Allyn & Bacon.

DeVos, G. A., & Lee, C. (1981). *Koreans in Japan.* Berkeley: University of California Press.

Deyhle, D. (1987). Learning failure: Tests as gatekeepers and the culturally different child. In H. T. Trueba (Ed.), *Success or failure? Learning and the language minority child.* Cambridge, MA: Newbury House.

Diener, C. T., & Dweck, C. S. (1978). An analysis of learned helplessness: Continuous changes in performance, strategy, and achievement cognitions following failure. *Journal of Personality and Social Psychology, 36,* 451–462.

Dietz, M. E., & Moon, C. J. (1992). What do we want students to know? . . . and other important questions. *Educational Leadership, 49,* 38–41.

Dinkmeyer, D., & McKay, G. (1976). *Systematic training for effective parenting.* Circle Pines, MN: American Guidance Service.

Divoky, D. (1988). The model minority goes to school. *Phi Delta Kappan, 70,* 219–222.

Dowling, C. (1981). *The Cinderella complex.* New York: Summit.

Doyle, W. (1983). Academic work. *Review of Educational Research,* 53, 159–199.

Doyle, W., & Rutherford, B. (1984). Classroom research on matching learning and teaching styles. *Theory into Practice, 23,* 20–25.

Dreikurs, R., & Soltz, V. (1964). *Children: The challenge.* New York: Hawthorn.

Duckworth, E. (1964). Piaget rediscovered. In R. E. Ripple & V. N. Rockcastle (Eds.), *Piaget rediscovered: A report of the conference on cognitive skills and curriculum development.* Ithaca, NY: Cornell University, School of Education.

Duffy, G. G., & Roehler, L. R. (1987). Improving reading instruction through the use of responsive elaboration. *The Reading Teacher, 40,* 514–520.

Duffy, G. G., & Roehler, L. R. (1989). Why strategy instruction is so difficult and what we need to do about it. In C. B. McCormick, G. E. Miller, & M. Pressley (Eds.), *Cognitive strategy research: From basic research to educational applications.* New York: Springer-Verlag.

Duffy, G. G., & Roehler, L. R. (1990). *Improving classroom reading instruction: A decision-making approach* (2nd ed.). New York: Random House.

Dulay, H., Burt, M., & Krashen, S. (1982). *Language two.* New York: Oxford.

Dunn, R., & Dunn, K. (1972). *Practical approaches to individualizing instruction.* West Nyack, NY: Parker.

Dunn, R., & Dunn, K. (1987). Dispelling outmoded beliefs about student learning. *Educational Leadership, 46,* 55–62.

Dusek, J. B., & Joseph, G. (1985). The bases of teacher expectancies. In J. Dusek (Ed.), *Teacher expectancies.* Hillsdale, NJ: Erlbaum.

Dweck, C. S. (1985). Intrinsic motivation, perceived control, and self-evaluation maintenance: An achievement goal analysis. In C. Ames & R. Ames (Eds.), *Research on motivation in education: Vol. 2. The classroom milieu.* Orlando, FL: Academic Press.

Dweck, C. S. (1986). Motivational processes affecting learning. *American Psychologist, 41,* 1040–1048.

Dweck, C. S., & Goetz, T. (1978). Attributions and learned helplessness. In J. Harvey, W. Ickes, & R. Kidd (Eds.), *New directions in attribution research* (Vol. 2). Hillsdale, NJ: Erlbaum.

Ebel, R. L., & Frisbie, D. A. (1986). *Essentials of educational measurement* (4th ed.). Englewood Cliffs, NJ: Prentice-Hall.

Eccles, J. S. (1991, April). *Motivation: New directions in school-based research: Changing the classroom.* Paper presented at the annual meeting of the American Educational Research Association, Chicago.

Eccles, J. S., & Blumenfeld, P. (1985). Classroom experiences and student gender: Are there differences and do they matter? In L. C. Wilkinson & C. B. Marrett (Eds.), *Gender influences in classroom interaction.* Orlando, FL: Academic Press.

Eccles, J. S., & Jacobs, J. E. (1986). Social forces shape math attitudes and performances. *Signs, 11,* 367–389.

Eccles, J. S., & Midgley, C. (1989). Stage-environment fit: Developmentally appropriate classrooms for young adolescents. In C. Ames & R. Ames (Eds.), *Research on motivation in education: Vol. 3. Goals and cognitions.* San Diego: Academic Press.

Education of the Handicapped (Vol. 12). (1986, January 8). Arlington, VA: Capitol Publications.

Educational Testing Service. (1973). *Making the classroom test: A guide for teachers.* Princeton, NJ: Author.

Edwards, B. (1979). *Drawing on the right side of the brain: A course in enhancing creativity and artistic confidence.* Los Angeles: Tarcher.

Eisner, E. W. (1969). Instructional and expressive educational objectives: Their formulation and use in curriculum. In W. J. Popham, E. W. Eisner, H. J. Sullivan, & L. L. Tyler (Eds.), *Instructional objectives* (AERA Monograph Series on Curriculum Evaluation). Chicago: Rand McNally.

Eisner, E. W. (1983). The art and craft of teaching. *Educational Leadership, 4,* 4–13.

Elawar, M. C., & Corno, L. (1985). A factorial experiment in teachers' written feedback on student homework: Changing teacher behavior a little rather than a lot. *Journal of Educational Psychology, 77,* 162–173.

Electronic Learning's Inservice Workshop. (1983). Part III: Evaluating software. *Electronic Learning, 3,* 1c–8c.

Elkind, D. (1967). Egocentrism in adolescence. *Child Development, 38,* 1025–1034.

Elkind, D. (1968). Adolescent cognitive development. In J. F. Adams (Ed.), *Understanding adolescence: Current developments in adolescent psychology.* Boston: Allyn & Bacon.

Elkind, D. (1974). *Children and adolescents: Interpretive essays on Jean Piaget* (2nd ed.). New York: Oxford.

Elkind, D. (1978). Understanding the young adolescent. *Adolescence, 13,* 127–134.

Elkind, D. (1980). Investigating intelligence in early adolescence. In M. Johnson & K. Rehage (Eds.), *Toward adolescence: The middle school years. Seventy-ninth yearbook of the National Society for the Study of Education* (Part I). Chicago: University of Chicago Press.

Elkind, D. (1986). Formal education and early childhood education: An essential difference. *Phi Delta Kappan, 67,* 631–636.

Elkind, D. (1988). *The hurried child: Growing up too fast too soon* (rev. ed.). Reading, MA: Addison-Wesley.

Ellis, R. (1985). Teacher-pupil interaction in second language development. In S. Glass & C. Madden (Eds.), *Input in second language acquisition.* Rowley, MA: Newbury House.

Ellis, R. (1986). *Understanding second language acquisition.* Oxford: Oxford University Press.

Emery, R. E. (1988). *Marriage, divorce, and children's adjustment* (Vol. 14). Newbury Park, CA: Sage.

Emmer, E. T. (1987). Classroom management and discipline. In V. Richardson-Koehler (Ed.), *Educators' handbook: A research perspective.* White Plains, NY: Longman.

Emmer, E. T., Evertson, C. M., & Anderson, L. M. (1980). Effective classroom management at the beginning of the school year. *Elementary School Journal, 80,* 219–231.

Englemann, S. E. (1977). Sequencing cognitive and academic tasks. In R. D. Kneedler and S. G. Tarver (Eds.), *Changing perspectives in special education.* Columbus, OH: Merrill.

Englert, C. S. (1984). Measuring teacher effectiveness from the teacher's point of view. *Focus on Exceptional Children, 17,* 1–15.

Ennis, R. H. (1985). A logical basis for measuring critical thinking skills. *Educational Leadership, 43,* 44–48.

Enright, R., Lapsley, M., & Levy, M. (1983). Moral education strategies. In M. Pressley & J. R. Levin (Eds.), *Cognitive strategy research: Educational applications.* New York: Springer-Verlag.

Epstein, J. L. (1988). Effective schools or effective students: Dealing with diversity. In R. Haskins & D. MacRae (Eds.), *Policies for America's public schools: Teacher equity indicators.* Norwood, NJ: Ablex.

Epstein, J. L., & McPartland, J. M. (1976). The concept and measurement of the quality of school life, *American Educational Research Journal, 13,* 15–30.

Erikson, E. H. (1963). *Childhood and society* (2nd ed.). New York: Norton.

Erikson, E. H. (1968). *Identity: Youth and crisis.* New York: Norton.

Evertson, C. M., & Emmer, E. (1982a). Effective management at the beginning of the school year in junior high classes. *Journal of Educational Psychology, 74,* 485–498.

Evertson, C. M., & Emmer, E. (1982b). Preventive classroom management. In D. L. Duke (Ed.), *Helping teachers manage classrooms.* Alexandria, VA: Association for Supervision and Curriculum Development.

Evertson, C. M., Emmer, E. T., Clements, B. S., Sanford, J. P., & Worshem, M. E. (1989). *Classroom management for elementary teachers* (2nd ed.). Englewood Cliffs, NJ: Prentice-Hall.

Fearn, L., & McCabe, R. E. (1975). *Human development programs: Supplementary idea guide.* La Mesa, CA: Human Development Training Institute.

Federal Register. (1977, August 23). Washington, DC: U.S. Government Printing Office.

Feingold, B. F. (1975a). Hyperkinesis and learning disabilities linked to artificial food flavors and colors. *American Journal of Nursing, 75,* 797–803(a).

Feingold, B. F. (1975b). *Why your child is hyperactive.* New York: Random House.

Fennema, E. (1983). Success in mathematics. In M. Marland (Ed.), *Sex differentiation and schooling.* London: Heinemann.

Feuerstein, R. (1980). *Instrumental enrichment: An intervention program for cognitive modifiability.* Baltimore: University Park Press.

Field, D. (1987). A review of preschool conservation training: An analysis of analyses. *Developmental Review, 7,* 210–251.

Fischer, K. W. (1980). A theory of cognitive development: The control and construction of hierarchies of skills. *Psychological Review, 87,* 477–531.

Fischer, K. W., & Pipp, S. L. (1984). Process of cognitive development: Optimal level and skill acquisition. In R. J. Sternberg (Ed.), *Mechanisms for cognitive development.* New York: Freeman.

Fisher, C. W., & Berliner, D. C. (Eds.). (1985). *Perspectives on instructional time.* White Plains, NY: Longman.

Fisher, C. W., Filby, N., Marliave, R. S., Cahen, L. S., Dishaw, M. M., Moore, J. E., & Berliner, D. C. (1978). *Teaching behaviors, academic learning time, and student achievement: Final report of Phase III-B, Beginning Teacher Evaluation Study*. San Francisco: Far West Laboratory for Educational Research and Development.

Flavell, J. H. (1963). *The developmental psychology of Jean Piaget*. Princeton, NJ: Van Nostrand.

Flavell, J. H. (1976). Metacognitive aspects of problem solving. In L. Resnick (Ed.), *The nature of intelligence*. Hillsdale, NJ: Erlbaum.

Flavell, J. H. (1985). *Cognitive development* (2nd ed.) Englewood Cliffs, NJ: Prentice-Hall.

Fleming, E., & Anttonen, R. (1971). Teacher expectancy or My Fair Lady. *American Educational Research Journal, 8*, 241–252.

Fogel, A., & Melson, G. (1988). *Child development: Individual, family, and society*. St. Paul: West.

Fowler, R. L., & Barker, A. S. (1974). Effectiveness of highlighting for retention of text material. *Journal of Applied Psychology, 59*, 358–364.

Fraenkel, J. R. (1976). The Kohlberg bandwagon: Some reservations. In D. Purpel & K. Ryan (Eds.), *Moral education . . . It comes with the territory*. Berkeley, CA: McCutchan.

Franco, J. N. (1983). A developmental analysis of self-concept in Mexican-American and Anglo school children. *Hispanic Journal of Behavioral Sciences, 5*, 207–218.

Frase, L. T. (1973). Integration of written text. *Journal of Educational Psychology, 65*, 252–261.

Frazier, B. H. (1969). *Design of a microeconomy system for correcting delinquent behavior patterns in institutionalized children*. Paper presented at the Conference of Behavioral Engineering in Therapeutic Environments, Washington, DC, Walter Reed Army Medical Center.

Friedman, M., & Rosenman, A. H. (1974). *Type A behavior and your heart*. New York: Knopf.

Frymier, J. (1988). Understanding and preventing teen suicide: An interview with Barry Garfinkel. *Phi Delta Kappan, 70*, 290–293.

Fuhrmann, B. S. (1986). *Adolescence, adolescents*. Boston: Little, Brown.

Fuller, F. F., & Bown, O. H. (1975). Becoming a teacher. In K. Ryan (Ed.), *Teacher education: Seventy-fourth yearbook of the National Society for the Study of Education* (Part II). Chicago: University of Chicago Press.

Furth, H. G. (1973). *Deafness and learning: A psychosocial approach*. Belmont, CA: Wadsworth.

Gage, N. L., & Berliner, D. C. (1988). *Educational psychology* (4th ed.) Boston: Houghton Mifflin.

Gagné, E. D. (1985). *The cognitive psychology of school learning*. Boston: Little, Brown.

Gagné, R. M. (1977). *The conditions of learning* (3rd ed.). New York: Holt, Rinehart & Winston.

Gagné, R. M. (1985). *The conditions of learning* (4th ed.). New York: Holt, Rinehart & Winston.

Gall, M. D., & Ward, B. A. (Eds.). (1974). *Critical issues in educational psychology*. Boston: Little, Brown.

Gallagher, J. J. (1975). *Teaching the gifted child* (2nd ed.). Boston: Allyn & Bacon.

Gallagher, J. J. (1989). A new policy initiative: Infants and toddlers with handicapping conditions. *American Psychologist, 44*, 387–391.

García, E. (1992). *Educational practice report: Education of linguistically and culturally diverse students: Effective instructional practices*. Santa Cruz, CA: National Center for Research on Cultural Diversity and Second Language Learning.

Gardner, H. (1983). *Frames of mind: The theory of multiple intelligences*. New York: Basic Books.

Gardner, H., & Hatch, T. (1989). Multiple intelligences go to school: Educational implications of the theory of multiple intelligences. *Educational Researcher, 18*, 4–10.

Gardner, W. I. (1974). *Children with learning and behavior problems: A behavior management approach*. Boston: Allyn & Bacon.

Gasper, K. L. (1980). The student perspective. *Teaching Political Science, 7*, 470–471.

Gaudry, E., & Spielberger, C. D. (1971). *Anxiety and educational achievement*. New York: Wiley.

Gee, J. (1990). *Social linguistics and literacies: Ideology in discourses*. New York: Falmer Press.

Gelardo, M. S., & Sanford, E. E. (1987). Child abuse and neglect: A review of the literature. *School Psychology Review, 16*, 137–155.

Gelman, R., & Gallistel, C. R. (1978). *The child's understanding of number*. Cambridge, MA: Harvard University Press.

Geschwind, N., & Galaburda, A. M. (1985). Cerebral lateralization: Biological mechanisms, associations, and pathology: I and II. A hypothesis and a program for research. *Archives of Neurology, 42*, 428–459; 521–552.

Getzels, J. W., & Jackson, P. W. (1962). *Creativity and intelligence*. New York: Wiley.

Giaconia, R. M., & Hedges, L. V. (1982). Identifying features of effective open education. *Review of Educational Research, 52*, 579–602.

Gibbs, J. C., Arnold, K. D., & Burkhart, J. E. (1984). Sex differences in the expression of moral judgment. *Child Development, 55*, 1040–1043.

Gibson, M. A. (1987). The school performance of immigrant minorities: A comparative view. *Anthropology & Education Quarterly, 18*, 262–275.

Gibson, M. A. (1991). Ethnicity, gender, and social class: The social adaptation patterns of West Indian youths. In M. A. Gibson & J. U. Ogbu (Eds.), *Minority status and schooling: A comparative study of immigrants and involuntary minorities*. New York: Garland.

Gibson, S., & Dembo, M. (1984). Teacher efficacy: A construct validation. *Journal of Educational Psychology, 76,* 569–582.

Gick, M. L., & Holyoak, K. J. (1987). The cognitive basis of knowledge transfer. In S. M. Cormier & J. D. Hagman (Eds.), *Transfer of learning: Contemporary research and applications.* New York: Academic Press.

Gilliam, J. E., & Coleman, M. C. (1981). Who influences IEP committee decisions? *Exceptional Children, 47,* 642–644.

Gilligan, C. (1982). *In a different voice: Psychological theory and women's development.* Cambridge, MA: Harvard University Press.

Gilligan, C., & Attanucci, J. (1988). Two moral orientations: Gender differences and similarities. *Merrill-Palmer Quarterly, 34,* 223–237.

Ginsburg, H. P., & Opper, S. (1988). *Piaget's theory of intellectual development* (3rd ed.). Englewood Cliffs, NJ: Prentice-Hall.

Givner, A., & Graubard, D. S. (1974). *A handbook of behavior modification for the classroom.* New York: Holt, Rinehart & Winston.

Glass, R. M., Christiansen, J., & Christiansen, J. L. (1982). *Teaching exceptional students in the regular classroom.* Boston: Little, Brown.

Glasser, W. G. (1965). *Reality therapy: A new approach to psychiatry.* New York: Harper & Row.

Glasser, W. G. (1969). *Schools without failure.* New York: Harper & Row.

Glasser, W. G. (1972). *The identity society.* New York: Harper & Row.

Glasser, W. G. (1985). *Control theory.* New York: Harper & Row.

Glasser, W. G. (1990). The quality school. *Phi Delta Kappan, 71,* 424–435.

Gleason, J. B. (1985). Studying language development. In J. B. Gleason (Ed.), *The development of language.* Columbus, OH: Merrill.

Glesne, C., & Peshkin, A. (1992). *Becoming qualitative researchers: An introduction.* White Plains, NY: Longman.

Glick, P. C., & Lin, S. (1986). Recent changes in divorce and remarriage. *Journal of Marriage and the Family, 48,* 737–747.

Glickman, C., & Wolfgang, C. (1979). Dealing with student misbehavior: An eclectic review. *Journal of Teacher Education, 30,* 7–13.

Goldenberg, C. N., & Gallimore, R. (1989). Teaching California's diverse student populations: The common ground between educational and cultural research. *California Public Schools Forum, 3,* 41–56.

Goldstein, A. P., Sprafkin, R. P., Gershaw, N. J., & Klein, P. (1980). *Skill-streaming the adolescent.* Champaign, IL: Research Press.

Gollnick, D., Sadker, M., & Sadker, D. (1982). Beyond the Dick and Jane syndrome: Confronting sex bias in instructional materials. In M. P. Sadker & D. M. Sadker (Eds.), *Sex equity handbook for schools.* White Plains, NY: Longman.

Good, T. L. (1979). Teacher effectiveness in the elementary school: What we know about it now. *Journal of Teacher Education, 30,* 52–64.

Good, T. L., & Brophy, J. E. (1978). *Looking in classrooms* (2nd ed.). New York: Harper & Row.

Good, T. L., & Brophy, J. E. (1987). *Looking in classrooms* (4th ed.). New York: Harper & Row.

Good, T. L., & Brophy, J. E. (1990). *Educational psychology: A realistic approach* (4th ed.). White Plains, NY: Longman.

Good, T. L., & Brophy, J. E. (1991). *Looking in classrooms* (5th ed.). New York: HarperCollins.

Good, T. L., & Grouws, D. (1975). *Process-product relationships in fourth-grade mathematics classroom: Final report of National Institute of Education Grant* (NEG-00-3-0125). Columbia: University of Missouri.

Good, T. L., Grouws, D., & Ebmeier, H. (1983). *Active mathematics teaching.* White Plains, NY: Longman.

Good, T. L., & Marshall, S. (1984). Do students learn more in heterogeneous or homogeneous groups? In P. Peterson, L. C. Wilkinson, & M. Hallinan (Eds.), *The social context of instruction: Group organization and group processes.* New York: Academic Press.

Goodlad, J. (1984). *A place called school: Prospects for the future.* New York: McGraw-Hill.

Goodlad, J., & Klein, M. F. (1970). *Behind the classroom door.* Worthington, OH: Jones.

Gordon, C. J., & Braun, C. (1985). Metacognitive processes: Reading and writing narrative discourse. In D. L. Forrest-Pressley, G. E. Mackinnon, & T. G. Waller (Eds.), *Metacognition, cognition, and human performance: Vol. 2. Instructional practices.* Orlando, FL: Academic Press.

Gordon, T. (1974). *T.E.T.: Teacher effectiveness training.* White Plains, NY: Longman.

Gordon, T. (1975). *P.E.T.: Parent effectiveness training.* New York: Hawthorn.

Gorman, R. M. (1974). *The psychology of classroom learning.* Columbus, OH: Merrill.

Greenberg, S. (1985). Educational equity in early education environments. In S. Klein (Ed.), *Handbook for achieving sex equity through education.* Baltimore: John Hopkins University Press.

Greenberger, E., & Steinberg, L. (1986). *When teenagers work: The psychological and social costs of adolescent employment.* New York: Basic Books.

Greenwood, G. E., & Parkay, F. W. (1989). *Case studies for teacher decision making.* New York: Random House.

Gresham, F. M. (1984). Social skills and self-efficacy for exceptional children. *Exceptional Children, 51,* 253–261.

Gresham, F. M. (1988a). Social competence and motivational characteristics of learning disabled students. In M. C. Wang, M. C. Reynolds, & H. J. Walberg (Eds.), *Handbook of special education: Vol 2. Mildly handicapped conditions.* New York: Pergamon.

Gresham, F. M. (1988b). Social skills: Conceptual and applied aspects of assessment, training, and social validation. In J. C. Witt, S. N. Elliott, & F. M. Gresham (Eds.), *Handbook of behavior therapy in education.* New York: Plenum.

Gronlund, N. E. (1974a). *Improving marking and reporting in classroom instruction.* New York: Macmillan.

Gronlund, N. E. (1974b). *Individualizing classroom instruction.* New York: Macmillan.

Gronlund, N. E. (1985). *Measurement and evaluation in teaching* (5th ed.). New York: Macmillan.

Gronlund, N. E. (1991). *How to write and use instructional objectives* (4th ed.). New York: Macmillan.

Gross, T. (1985). *Cognitive development.* Monterey, CA: Brooks/Cole.

Grossman, H. J. (Ed.). (1983). *Classification in mental retardation.* Washington, DC: American Association of Mental Deficiency.

Guilford, J. P. (1959). Three faces of intellect. *American Psychologist, 14,* 469–479.

Guilford, J. P. (1988). Some changes in the structure-of-intellect model. *Educational and Psychological Measurement, 48,* 1–4.

Guskey, T. R. (1985). *Implementing mastery learning.* Belmont, CA: Wadsworth.

Guskey, T. R., & Gates, S. L. (1986). Synthesis of research on the effects of mastery learning in elementary and secondary classrooms. *Educational Leadership, 43,* 73–80.

Hackett, G. (1985). Role of mathematics self-efficacy in the choice of math-related majors of college women and men: A path analysis. *Journal of Counseling Psychology, 32,* 47–49.

Haertel, E. H. (1991a). *Issues of validity and reliability in assessment center exercises and portfolios.* Unpublished manuscript. Stanford University, School of Education.

Haertel, E. H. (1991b). New form of teacher assessment. In G. Grant (Ed.), *Review of research in education* (Vol. 17). Washington, DC: American Educational Research Association.

Hakuta, K. (1986). *Mirror of language: The debate on bilingualism.* New York: Basic Books.

Hakuta, K., & Garcia, E. E. (1989). Bilingualism and education. *American Psychologist, 44,* 374–379.

Hall, E. T. (1959). *The silent language.* Garden City, NY: Doubleday.

Hall, E. T. (1966). *The hidden dimension.* Garden City, NY: Doubleday.

Hall, E. T. (1969). Listening behavior: Some cultural differences. *Phi Delta Kappan, 50,* 379–380.

Hall, E. T., & Hall, M. R. (1987). Nonverbal communication for educators. *Theory into Practice, 26,* 364–367.

Hallahan, D. P., & Kauffman, J. M. (1988). *Exceptional children: Introduction to special education* (4th ed.). Englewood Cliffs, NJ: Prentice-Hall.

Hallahan, D. P., & Kauffman, J. M. (1991). *Exceptional children: Introduction to special education* (5th ed.). Englewood Cliffs, NJ: Prentice-Hall.

Hamachek, D. E. (1978). *Encounters with the self* (2nd ed.). New York: Holt, Rinehart & Winston.

Hamachek, D. E. (1985). *Psychology in teaching, learning, and growth* (3rd ed.). Boston: Allyn & Bacon.

Hamaker, C. (1986). The effects of adjunct questions on prose learning. *Review of Educational Research, 56,* 212–242.

Hamilton, R. J. (1985). A framework for the evaluation of the effectiveness of adjunct questions and objectives. *Review of Educational Research, 55,* 47–85.

Hammond, J. M. (1981, February). Children, divorce, and you. *Learning,* pp. 83–91.

Hamner, T. J., & Turner, P. H. (1985). *Parenting in contemporary society.* Englewood Cliffs, NJ: Prentice-Hall.

Haney, W., & Madaus, G. (1978). Making sense of the competency testing movement. *Harvard Educational Review, 48,* 462–484.

Hanson, S. L., & Ginsburg, A. L. (1988). Gaining ground: Values and high school success. *American Educational Research Journal, 25,* 334–365.

Hare, B. (1985). Stability and change in self-perception and achievement among black adolescents: A longitudinal study. *Journal of Black Psychology, 11,* 29–42.

Harley, R. K. (1973). Children with visual disabilities. In L. M. Dunn (Ed.), *Exceptional children in the schools* (2nd ed.). New York: Holt, Rinehart & Winston.

Harris, L. J. (1985). Teaching the right brain: Historical perspectives on a contemporary educational fad. In L. J. Harris (Ed.), *Hemispheric function and collaboration in the child.* New York: Academic Press.

Harrow, A. J. (1972). *A taxonomy of the psychomotor domain: A guide for developing behavioral objectives.* New York: McKay.

Harter, S. (1981). A new self-report scale of intrinsic versus extrinsic orientation in the classroom: Motivational and informational components. *Developmental Psychology, 17,* 300–312.

Haskins, R. (1989). Beyond metaphor: The efficacy of early childhood education. *American Psychologist, 44,* 274–282.

Hathaway, W. E. (1980). Testing teachers. *Educational Leadership, 38,* 210–215.

Havighurst, R. J. (1970). Minority subcultures and the law of effect. *American Psychologist, 25,* 313–322.

Hawkins, J., Pea, R. D., Glick, J., & Scribner, S. (1984). "Merds that laugh don't like mushrooms": Evidence for deductive reasoning by preschoolers. *Developmental Psychology, 20,* 584–594.

Hearold, S. (1986). A synthesis of 1043 effects of television on social behavior. In G. Comstock (Ed.), *Public communications and behavior* (Vol. 1). New York: Academic Press.

Hellige, J. B. (1990). Hemispheric asymmetry. *Annual Review of Psychology, 41,* 55–80.

Hembree, R. (1988). Correlates, causes, effects, and treatment of test anxiety. *Review of Educational Research, 58,* 47–77.

Henshaw, S., Kenny, A., Somberg, D., & Van Vort, L. (1989). *Teenage pregnancy in the United States: The scope of the problem and state responses.* New York: Alan Guttmacher Institute.

Herman, J. L. (1991). Research in cognition and learning: Implications for achievement testing practice. In M. C. Wittrock & E. Baker (Eds.), *Testing and cognition.* Englewood Cliffs, NJ: Prentice-Hall.

Herman, J. L., Aschbacher, P. R., & Winters, L. (1992). *A practical guide to alternative assessment.* Alexandria, VA: Association for Supervision and Curriculum Development.

Hersh, R. H., Miller, J. P., & Fielding, G. D. (1980). *Models of moral education: An appraisal.* White Plains, NY: Longman.

Hersh, R. H., Paolitto, D., & Reimer, J. (1979). *Promoting moral growth.* White Plains, NY: Longman.

Hetherington, E. M., & Anderson, E. R. (1988). The effects of divorce and remarriage on early adolescents and their families. In M. D. Levine & E. R. McAnarney (Eds.), *Early adolescent transitions.* Lexington, MA: Heath.

Hetherington, E. M., Cox, M., & Cox, A. (1982). Effects of divorce on parents and children. In M. Lamb (Ed.), *Nontraditional families.* Hillsdale, NJ: Erlbaum.

Heward, W. L., & Orlansky, M. D. (1992). *Exceptional children: An introductory survey of special education* (4th ed.). Columbus, OH: Merrill.

Hiebert, E., & Calfee, R. C. (1989). Advancing academic literacy through teachers' assessments. *Educational Leadership, 46,* 50–54.

Higgs, T., & Clifford, R. (1982). The push toward communication. In T. Higgs (Ed.), *Curriculum, competence, and the foreign language teacher. ACTFL Foreign Language Education Series* (Vol. 13). Lincolnwood, IL: National Textbook.

Hill, K. T., & Wigfield, A. (1984). Test anxiety: A major educational problem and what can be done about it. *Elementary School Journal, 85,* 105–126.

Hirsch, E. D. (1987). *Cultural literacy: What every American needs to know.* Boston: Houghton Mifflin.

Hirsch, E. D. (1989). *A first dictionary of cultural literacy: What our children need to know.* Boston: Houghton Mifflin.

Hittleman, D. R., & Simon, A. J. (1992). *Interpreting educational research: An introduction for consumers of research.* Merrill: New York.

Hocevar, S. P., & Arnold, D. (1979). In S. P. Hocevar and C. L. Fox (Eds.), *Trainer's manual for: Module one: Understanding handicapping conditions: Strategies for improving awareness and acceptance of handicapped students in the regular classroom.* Los Angeles: University of Southern California, California Regional Resource Center, School of Education.

Hoffman, L. W. (1989). Effects of maternal employment in the two-parent family. *American Psychologist, 44,* 283–292.

Hoge, R. D. (1988). Issues in the definition and measurement of the giftedness construct. *Educational Researcher, 17,* 12–16, 22.

Holmes, C. T., & Shepard, L. A. (1989). Repeating and dropping out of school. In L. A. Shepard & M. L. Smith (Eds.), *Flunking grades: Research and policies on retention.* Philadelphia: Falmer Press.

Holt, J. (1982). *How children fail* (rev. ed.). New York: Delta.

Homme, L., Csanyi, A. P., Gonzales, M. A., & Rechs, J. R. (1979). *How to use contingency contracting in the classroom.* Champaign, IL: Research Press.

Hops, H., & Cobb, J. A. (1973). Survival behaviors in the educational setting: Their implications for research and intervention. In L. A. Hammerlynk, L. C. Handy, & E. J. Mash (Eds.), *Behavior change.* Champaign, IL: Research Press.

Howe, L., & Howe, M. M. (1975). *Personalizing education: Values clarification and beyond.* New York: A & W Visual Library.

Hoy, W. K. (1967). Organizational socialization and student teacher and pupil control ideology. *Journal of Educational Research, 61,* 153–155.

Hoy, W. K., & Woolfolk, A. E. (1990). Socialization of student teachers. *American Educational Research Journal, 27,* 279–300.

Hudgins, B. B., Phyl, G. D., Schau, C. G., Theisen, G. L., Ames, C., & Ames, R. (1983). *Educational psychology.* Itasca, IL: Peacock.

Humphrey, J. H., & Humphrey, J. N. (1985). *Controlling stress in children.* Springfield, IL: Thomas.

Hunt, J. McV. (1961). *Intelligence and experience*. New York: Ronald Press.

Hunt, J. McV. (1964). The psychological basis for using preschool enrichment as an antidote for cultural deprivation. *Merrill-Palmer Quarterly, 10*, 209– 248.

Hunter, M. C. (1971). *The teaching process*. In D. Allen & E. Seifman (Eds.), *The teacher's handbook*. Glenview, IL: Scott, Foresman.

Hunter, M. C. (1973). Appraising teaching performance: One approach. *National Elementary Principal, 52*, 60–62.

Hunter, M. C. (1982). *Mastery teaching*. El Segundo, CA: TIP Publications.

Hunter, M. C. (1986). Comments on the Napa County, California, Follow Through Project. *Elementary School Journal, 87*, 173–179.

Hunter, M. C. (1988/1989). "Well acquainted" is not enough: A response to Mandeville and Rivers. *Educational Leadership, 46*, 67–68.

Huston, A. C., Watkins, B. A., & Kunkel, D. (1989). Public policy and children's television. *American Psychologist, 44*, 424–433.

Hutton, L. A., & Levitt, E. E. (1987). An academic approach to the remediation of mathematics anxiety. In R. Schwarzer, H. M. van der Ploeg, & C. D. Spielberger (Eds.), *Advances in test anxiety research* (Vol. 5). Lisse: Swets & Zeitlinger.

Hyde, A. A., & Bizar, M. (1989). *Thinking in context: Teaching cognitive processes across the elementary school curriculum*. White Plains, NY: Longman.

Inhelder, B., & Piaget, J. (1958). *The growth of logical thinking from childhood to adolescence*. New York: Basic Books.

Jackson, N. E., Robinson, H. B., & Dale, P. S. (1977). *Cognitive development in young children*. Monterey, CA: Brooks/Cole.

Jackson, P. (1968). *Life in classrooms*. New York: Holt, Rinehart & Winston.

Jacobsen, D., Eggen, P., & Kauchak, D. (1989). *Methods for teaching: A skills approach* (3rd ed.). Columbus, OH: Merrill.

Jaeger, R. M. (1989). Certification of student competence. In R. L. Linn (Ed.), *Educational measurement* (3rd ed.). New York: Macmillan.

Jaynes, J. (1975). Hello, teacher . . . A review of Fred S. Keller, "The history of psychology: A personalized system of instruction" and Fred S. Keller, "Selected readings in the history of psychology: A PSI companion." *Contemporary Psychology, 20*, 629–631.

Jensen, A. R. (1969). How much can we boost IQ and scholastic achievement? *Harvard Educational Review, 39*, 1–123.

Jensen, A. R. (1980). *Bias in mental testing*. New York: Free Press.

Jensen, A. R. (1985). Compensatory education and the theory of intelligence. *Phi Delta Kappan, 66*, 554–558.

Jenson, W. R., Sloane, H. N., & Young, K. R. (1988). *Applied analysis in education: A structured teaching approach*. Englewood Cliffs, NJ: Prentice-Hall.

Johnson, D. I., & Spielberger, C. D. (1968). The effects of relaxation training and passage of time on measures of state- and trait-anxiety. *Journal of Clinical Psychology, 24*, 20–23.

Johnson, D. W. (1979). *Educational psychology*. Englewood Cliffs, NJ: Prentice-Hall.

Johnson, D. W., & Johnson, R. T. (1989). Cooperative learning. In L. W. Anderson (Ed.), *The effective teacher*. New York: Random House.

Johnson, D. W., & Johnson, R. T. (1991). *Learning together and alone: Cooperation, competition, and individualization* (3rd ed.). Englewood Cliffs, NJ: Prentice-Hall.

Johnson, D. W., Johnson, R. T., Holubec, E. J., & Roy, P. (1984). *Circles of learning: Cooperation in the classroom*. Arlington, VA: Association for Supervision and Curriculum Development.

Johnson, G. R., et al. (1991). *Teaching tips for users of the Motivated Strategies for Learning Questionnaire*. School of Education, University of Michigan: National Center for Research to Improve Postsecondary Teaching and Learning.

Johnson, K. R., & Ruskin, R. S. (1977). *Behavioral instruction: An evaluative review*. Washington, DC: American Psychological Association.

Johnson, R. T., Johnson, D. W., & Holubec, E. (Eds.). (1987). *Structuring cooperative learning: Lesson plans for teachers*. Edina, MN: Interaction.

Jones, B. F., Palincsar, A. S., Ogle, D. S., & Carr, E. G. (Eds.). (1987). *Strategic teaching and learning: Cognitive instruction in the content areas*. Elmhurst, IL: North Central Regional Educational Laboratory.

Jones, M. C., & Bayley, N. (1950). Physical maturing among boys as related to behavior. *Journal of Educational Psychology, 41*, 129–148.

Jones, M. C., & Mussen, P. H. (1958). Self-conceptions, motivations, and interpersonal attitudes of early- and late-maturing girls. *Child Development, 29*, 491–501.

Josephson, M. (1992). *Ethical values, attitudes and behaviors in American schools*. Marina del Rey, CA: Joseph & Edna Josephson Institute of Ethics.

Jourard, S. M., & Secord, P. F. (1955). Body-cathexis and the ideal female figure. *Journal of Abnormal and Social Psychology, 50*, 243–246.

Joyce, B., & Weil, M. (1972). *Models of teaching*. Englewood Cliffs, NJ: Prentice-Hall.

Joyce, B., Weil, M., & Showers, B. (1992). *Models of teaching* (4th ed.). Needham Heights, MA: Allyn & Bacon.

Kagan, S. (1984). Interpreting Chicano cooperativeness: Methodological and theoretical considerations. In J. L. Martinez, Jr., & R. H. Mendoza (Eds.), *Chicano psychology* (2nd ed.). New York: Academic Press.

Kamp, S. H., & Chinn, P. C. (1982). *A multiethnic curriculum for special education students.* Reston, VA: Council for Exceptional Children.

Kampwirth, T. J., & Bates, M. (1980). Modality preference and teaching methods: A review of the research. *Academic Therapy, 15,* 597–605.

Kaplan, P., Kohfeldt, J., & Sturla, K. (1974). *It's positively fun: Techniques for managing learning environments.* Denver: Love.

Kauffman, J. M., Pullen, P. L., & Akers, E. (1986). Classroom management: Teacher-child-peer relationships. *Focus on Exceptional Children, 19,* 1–10.

Kaufman, A. S., & Kaufman, N. L. (1983). *Kaufman Assessment Battery for Children (K-ABC).* Circle Pines, MN: American Guidance Service.

Kavale, K., & Forness, S. R. (1983). Hyperactivity and diet treatment: A meta-analysis of the Feingold hypothesis. *Journal of Learning Disabilities, 16,* 165–173.

Kaye, E. (1979). *The ACT guide to children's television.* Boston: Beacon Press.

Kazdin, A. E. (1978). Methodology of applied behavior analysis. In A. C. Catania & T. A. Brigham (Eds.), *Handbook of applied behavior analysis: Social and instructional processes.* New York: Irvington.

Kazdin, A. E. (1987). Treatment of antisocial behavior in children: Current status and future directions. *Psychological Bulletin, 102,* 187–203.

Keat, D. B. (1972). Broad spectrum behavior therapy with children: A case presentation. *Behavior Therapy, 3,* 454–459.

Keller, F. S. (1968). Goodbye teacher . . . ! *Journal of Applied Behavior Analysis, 1,* 79–89.

Kelley, M. L., & Carper, L. B. (1988). Home-based reinforcement procedures. In J. C. Witt, S. N. Elliott, & F. M. Gresham (Eds.), *Handbook of behavior therapy in education.* New York: Plenum.

Kellogg, J. B. (1988). Forces of change. *Phi Delta Kappan, 70,* 199–204.

Kendall, P., & Braswell, L. (1985). *Cognitive-behavioral therapy for impulsive children.* New York: Guilford.

Kerr, D. (1990). Ryan White's death: A time to reflect on schools' progress in dealing wih AIDS. *Journal of School Health, 60,* 237–238.

Kersh, M. E. (1972). *A study of mastery learning in elementary mathematics.* Paper presented at the annual convention of the National Council of Teachers of Mathematics, Chicago.

Kershner, J., Hawks, W., & Grekin, R. (1977). *Megavitamins and learning disorders: A controlled double-blind experiment.* Unpublished manuscript, Ontario Institute of Studies in Education.

Kiewra, K. A. (1985). Investigating notetaking and review: A depth of processing alternative. *Educational Psychologist, 20,* 23–32.

Kiewra, K. A. (1989a). Matrix notes. *Educational Technology, 29,* 55–56.

Kiewra, K. A. (1989b). A review of note-taking: The encoding-storage paradigm and beyond. *Educational Psychology Review, 1,* 147–172.

Kirby, D. (1989). Sex education programs and their effects. *The world & I: A chronicle of our changing era, 4,* 590–603.

Kirp, D., & Epstein, S. (1989). AIDS in America's school houses: Learning the hard lessons. *Phi Delta Kappan, 70,* 584–603.

Kirschenbaum, H. (1992). A comprehensive model for values education and moral education. *Phi Delta Kappan, 73,* 771–776.

Kirschenbaum, H., Simon, S., & Napier, R. (1971). *Wad-ja-get? The grading game in American education.* New York: Hart.

Kitano, H. H. (1980). *Race relations.* Englewood Cliffs, NJ: Prentice-Hall.

Klausmeier, H. J. (1976). Instructional design and the teaching of concepts. In J. R. Levin & V. L. Allen (Eds.), *Cognitive learning in children.* New York: Academic Press.

Klein, S. (Ed.). (1985). *Handbook for achieving sex equity through education.* Baltimore: Johns Hopkins University Press.

Kline, D. F. (1977). *Child abuse and neglect: A primer for school personnel.* Reston, VA: Council for Exceptional Children.

Knight, G. P., & Kagan, S. (1977). Acculturation of prosocial and competitive behaviors among second- and third-generation Mexican-American children. *Journal of Cross-Cultural Psychology, 8,* 273–284.

Kohlberg, L. (1964). Development of moral character and moral ideology. In M. L. Hoffman & L. W. Hoffman (Eds.), *Review of child development research.* New York: Russell Sage Foundation.

Kohlberg, L. (1976). Moral stages and moralization. In T. Lickona (Ed.), *Moral development and behavior: Theory, research, and social issues.* New York: Holt, Rinehart & Winston.

Kohn, A. (1991). Caring kids: The role of the schools. *Phi Delta Kappan, 72,* 496–506.

Kolesnik, W. B. (1975). *Humanism and/or behaviorism in education.* Boston: Allyn & Bacon.

Komarovsky, M. (1953). *Women in the modern world: Their education and their dilemmas.* Boston: Little, Brown.

Kopp, C. B., & McCall, R. B. (1982). Predicting later mental performance for normal, at-risk, and handicapped infants. In P. B. Baltes & O. G. Brim, Jr. (Eds.), *Life-span development and behavior* (Vol. 4). New York: Academic Press.

Kounin, J. (1970). *Discipline and group management in classrooms*. New York: Holt, Rinehart & Winston.

Kozma, R. B. (1991). Learning with media. *Review of Educational Research, 61*, 179–211.

Kozol, J. (1972). *Free schools*. Boston: Houghton Mifflin.

Krashen, S. (1982). *Principles and practice of second language acquisition*. Oxford: Pergamon.

Krashen, S., & Biber, D. (1988). *On course: Bilingual education success in California*. Sacramento: California Association for Bilingual Education.

Krashen, S., & Terrell, T. (1983). *The natural approach: Language acquisition in the classroom*. Oxford: Pergamon.

Krathwohl, D. R., Bloom, B. S., & Masia, B. (1964). *Taxonomy of educational objectives: Handbook II. Affective domain*. New York: Longman.

Kuhn, D., Langer, J., Kohlberg, L., & Haan, N. S. (1977). The development of formal operations in logical and moral judgment. *Genetic Psychology Monographs, 95*, 97–188.

Kulik, J. A., Kulik, C. C., & Bangert-Drowns, R. L. (1985, April). *Effectiveness of computer-based education in elementary schools*. Paper presented at the annual meeting of the American Educational Research Association, Chicago.

Kulik, J. A., Kulik, C. C., & Cohen, P. A. (1979). A meta-analysis of outcome studies of Keller's personalized system of instruction. *American Psychologist, 34*, 307–318.

Laboratory of Comparative Human Cognition. (1982). Culture and intelligence. In R. J. Sternberg (Ed.), *Handbook of human intelligence*. New York: Cambridge University Press.

Labov, W. (1969). Some sources of reading problems for Negro speakers of Nonstandard English. In J. C. Baratz & R. W. Shuy (Eds.), *Teaching black children to read*. Washington, DC: Center for Applied Linguistics.

Labov, W. (1970). *The study of Nonstandard English*. Champaign, IL: National Council of Teachers of English.

Labov, W. (1974). Academic ignorance and black intelligence. In M. D. Gall & B. A. Ward (Eds.), *Critical issues in educational psychology*. Boston: Little, Brown.

Landesman, S., & Ramey, C. (1989). Developmental psychology and mental retardation: Integrating scientific principles with treatment practices. *American Psychologist, 44*, 409–415.

Lareau, A. (1990). *Home advantage: Social class and parental intervention in elementary education*. New York: Falmer Press.

Larkins, A. G. (1981). Minimum competency tests: A negative view. In H. D. Mehlinger & O. L. Davis (Eds.), *The social studies: Eightieth yearbook of the National Society for the Study of Education* (Part II). Chicago: University of Chicago Press.

Larrivee, B. (1985). *Effective teaching behaviors for successful mainstreaming*. White Plains, NY: Longman.

Lawton, J. P., & Wanska, S. K. (1977). Advance organizers as a teaching strategy: A reply to Baines and Clawson. *Review of Educational Research, 47*, 233–244.

Lazar, I., Darlington, R., Murray, H., Royce, J., & Snipper, A. (1982). Lasting effects of early education: A report from the Consortium for Longitudinal Studies. *Monographs of the Society for Research in Child Development, 47* (Serial No. 195).

Lefcourt, H. M. (1966). Internal versus external control of reinforcement: A review. *Psychological Review, 65*, 206–220.

Leinhardt, G., Seewald, A., & Engel, M. (1979). Learning what's taught: Sex differences in instruction. *Journal of Educational Psychology, 71*, 432–439.

Leming, J. S. (1981). Curriculum effectiveness in moral/values education: A review of research. *Journal of Moral Education, 10*, 147–164.

Lemlech, J. K. (1988). *Classroom management* (2nd ed.). New York: Harper & Row.

Lemlech, J. K., & Hertzog-Foliart, H. (1992, April). *Restructuring to become a professional practice school: Stages of collegiality and the development of professionalism*. Paper presented at the annual meeting of the American Educational Research Association, San Francisco.

Lepper, M. R., & Gurtner, J. (1989). Children and computers: Approaching the twenty-first century. *American Psychologist, 44*, 170–179.

Lepper, M. R., & Hodell, M. (1989). Intrinsic motivation in the classroom. In C. Ames & R. Ames (Eds.), *Research on motivation in education: Vol. 3. Goals and cognitions*. San Diego: Academic Press.

Lerner, J. W. (1984). *Learning disabilities: Theories, diagnosis, and teaching strategies* (4th ed.). Boston: Houghton Mifflin.

Lerner, R. M., & Gillert, E. (1969). Body build identification, preference, and aversion in children. *Developmental Psychology, 1*, 456–463.

Lester, F. K., & Garofalo, J. (1986, April). *An emerging study of sixth-graders' metacognition and mathematical performance*. Paper presented at the annual meeting of the American Educational Research Association, San Francisco.

Levy, J. (1982). Children thinking with whole brains: Myth and reality. In *Student learning styles and brain behavior*. Reston, VA: National Association of Secondary School Principals.

Levy, J. (1983). Research synthesis on right and left hemispheres: We think with both sides of the brain. *Educational Leadership, 40,* 66–71.

Lewellen, A. (1980). *The use of quiet rooms and other time-out procedures in the public school: A position paper.* Matton, IL: Eastern Illinois Area of Special Education.

Lewis, L. (1990). *Education of the Handicapped Act Amendments of 1990 (P.L. 101-476): Summary of major changes in Parts A through H of the act.* Washington, DC: National Association of State Directors of Special Education.

Liben, L. S., & Signorella, M. L. (Eds.). (1987). *Children's gender schemata.* San Francisco: Jossey-Bass.

Lickona, T. (1988). Educating the moral child. *Principal, 68,* 6–10.

Liebert, R. M., & Sprafkin, J. (1988). *The early window: Effects of television on children and youth.* New York: Pergamon.

Lillie, D. L., Hannum, W. H., & Stuck, G. B. (1989). *Computers and effective instruction.* White Plains, NY: Longman.

Linn, M. C., & Hyde, J. S. (1989). Gender, mathematics, and science. *Educational Researcher, 18,* 17–19, 22–27.

Linn, M. C., & Petersen, A. C. (1985). Facts and assumptions about the nature of sex differences. In S. Klein (Ed.), *Handbook for achieving sex equity through education.* Baltimore: Johns Hopkins University Press.

Lipman, M. (1985). Thinking skills fostered by Philosophy for Children. In J. W. Segal, S. F. Chipman, & R. Glaser (Eds.), *Thinking and learning skills: Vol. 1. Relating instruction to research.* Hillsdale, NJ: Erlbaum.

Lips, H. M. (1988). *Sex and gender: An introduction.* Mountain View, CA: Mayfield.

Lloyd, J. W. (1988). Direct instruction. In M. C. Wang, M. C. Reynolds, & H. J. Walberg (Eds.), *Handbook of special education: Vol 2. Mildly handicapped conditions.* New York: Pergamon.

Lockheed, M. E., & Hall, K. P. (1976). Conceptualizing sex as a status characteristic: Application to leadership training strategies. *Journal of Social Issues, 32,* 111–124.

Lockheed, M. E., & Klein, S. S. (1985). Sex equity in classroom organization and climate. In S. Klein (Ed.), *Handbook for achieving sex equity through education.* Baltimore: Johns Hopkins University Press.

Lockwood, A. (1978). The effects of values clarification and moral development curriculum on school age subjects: A critical review of recent research. *Review of Educational Research, 48,* 325–364.

Loeber, R., & Dishion, T. J. (1983). Early predictors of male delinquency: A review. *Psychological Bulletin, 102,* 187–203.

London, P. (1987). Character education and clinical intervention: A paradigm shift for U.S. schools. *Phi Delta Kappan, 68,* 667–673.

Long, L., & Long, T. (1983). *The handbook for latchkey children and their working parents.* New York: Arbor House.

Long, L., & Long, T. (1989). Latchkey adolescents: How administrators can respond to their needs. *NASSP Bulletin, 73,* 102–108.

Los Angeles Unified School District. (1981). *Individualized education program* (Form 27.808–2). Los Angeles: Author.

Lovitt, T. C. (1978). The learning disabled. In N. G. Haring (Ed.), *Behavior of exceptional children* (2nd ed.). Columbus, OH: Merrill.

Ludwig, D. J., & Maehr, M. L. (1967). Changes in self-concept and stated behavioral preferences. *Child Development, 38,* 453–467.

Luria, A. (1961). *The role of speech in the regulation of normal and abnormal behaviors.* New York: Liveright.

Lynch, D. O., & Smith, B. C. (1972, April). *To change or not to change item responses when taking tests: Empirical evidence for test takers.* Paper presented at the annual meeting of the American Educational Research Association, Chicago.

Lynn, R. (1982). IQ in Japan and the U.S. shows a growing disparity. *Nature, 297,* 222–223.

Maccoby, E. E., & Jacklin, C. N. (1974). *Sex differences revisited: Myth and reality.* Paper presented at the annual meeting of the American Educational Research Association, Chicago.

Mace, F. C., & Kratochwill, T. R. (1988). Self-monitoring. In J. C. Witt, S. N. Elliott, & F. M. Gresham (Eds.), *Handbook of behavior therapy in education.* New York: Plenum.

Maclure, S., & Davies, P. (Eds.). (1991). *Learning to think: Thinking to learn.* Oxford: Pergamon Press.

Madaus, G. F. (1981). NIE clarification hearing: The negative team's case. *Phi Delta Kappan, 63,* 92–94.

Madaus, G. F. (1992, October). *The influence of testing on teaching math and sciences in grades 4–12.* Report of a study funded by the National Science Foundation (SPA 8954759). Center for the Study of Testing, Evaluation, and Educational Policy. Boston: Boston College.

Madden, N. A., & Slavin, R. E. (1983). Mainstreaming students with mild handicaps: Academic and social outcomes. *Review of Educational Research, 55,* 519–659.

Madsen, C. H., Becker, W. C., Thomas, O. R., Koser, L., & Plager, E. (1968). An analysis of the reinforcing function of "sit down" commands. In R. K. Parker (Ed.), *Readings in educational psychology.* Boston: Allyn & Bacon.

Maehr, M. L. (1976). Continuing motivation: An analysis of a seldom considered educational outcome. *Review of Educational Research, 46,* 443–462.

Maehr, M. L. (1978). Sociocultural origins of achievement motivation. In D. Bar-Tal & L. Saxe (Eds.), *Social psychology of education: Theory and practice*. Washington, DC: Hemisphere.

Maehr, M. L.(1984). Meaning and motivation: Toward a theory of personal investment. In R. E. Ames & C. R. Ames (Eds.), *Research on motivation in education: Vol. 1. Student motivation*. Orlando, FL: Academic Press.

Maehr, M. L. (1992, April). *Transforming school culture to enhance motivation*. Paper presented at the annual meeting of the American Educational Research Association, San Francisco.

Maehr, M. L., & Anderman, E. M. (1993) Reinventing schools for early adolescents: Emphasizing task goals. *Elementary School Journal, 93,* 593–610.

Mager, R. F. (1978). *Preparing instructional objectives.* Belmont, CA: Fearon.

Mager, R. F. (1984). *Preparing instructional objectives.* Belmont, CA: Lake.

Mandeville, G. K., & Rivers, J. L. (1988/1989). Effects of South Carolina's Hunter-based PET program. *Educational Leadership, 46,* 63–66.

Mantzicopoulos, P., & Morrison, D. (1992). Kindergarten retention: Academic and behavioral outcomes through the end of second grade. *American Educational Research Journal, 29,* 182–198.

Marcia, J. E. (1967). Ego identity status: Relationship to change in self-esteem, "general maladjustment," and authoritarianism. *Journal of Personality, 35,* 118–133.

Marcia, J. E. (1980). Identity in adolescence. In J. Adelson (Ed.), *Handbook of adolescent psychology*. New York: Wiley.

Marland, M. (1983). School as sexist amplifier. In M. Marland (Ed.), *Sex differentiation and schooling*. London: Heinemann.

Marland, S. P. (1972). *Education of the gifted and talented.* Washington, DC: U.S. Office of Education.

Marsh, H. W. (1989). Age and sex effects in multiple dimensions of self-concept: Preadolescence to early adulthood. *Journal of Educational Psychology, 81,* 417–430.

Marsh, H. W. (1990). A multidimensional, hierarchical model of self-concept: Theoretical and empirical justification. *Educational Psychology Review, 2,* 77–172.

Marsh, H. W. (1992, April). *The content specificity of relations between academic self-concept and achievement: An extension of the Marsh/Shavelson model.* Paper presented at the annual meeting of the American Educational Research Association, San Francisco.

Marsh, H. W., Byrne, B. M., & Shavelson, R. J. (1988). A multifaceted academic self-concept: Its hierarchical structure and its relation to academic achievement. *Journal of Educational Psychology, 80,* 366–380.

Marsh, H. W., & Parker, J. (1984). Determinants of student self-concept: Is it better to be a relatively big fish in a small pond even if you don't learn to swim as well? *Journal of Personality and Social Psychology, 47,* 213–237.

Marsh, H. W., & Peart, N. (1988). Competitive and cooperative physical fitness training programs for girls: Effects on physical fitness and on multidimensional self-concepts. *Journal of Sport and Exercise Psychology, 10,* 390–407.

Marsh, H. W., & Shavelson, R. J. (1985). Self-concept: Its multifaceted, hierarchical structure. *Educational Psychologist, 20,* 107–125.

Martin, G., & Pear, J. (1988). *Behavior modification: What it is and how to do it* (3rd ed.). Englewood Cliffs, NJ: Prentice-Hall.

Martinez, M. E., & Mead, N. A. (1988). *Computer competence: The first national assessment*. Princeton, NJ: Educational Testing Service.

Maslow, A. H. (1968). *Toward a psychology of being* (2nd ed.). New York: Van Nostrand.

Mattox, B. A. (1975). *Getting it together: Dilemmas for the classrom.* San Diego: Pennant Press.

Mayer, G. R., Butterworth, T. W., Spaulding, H. L., Hollingsworth, P., Amorim, M., Caldwell-McElroy, C., Nafpaktitis, M., & Perez-Osorio, X. (1983). *Constructive discipline: Building a climate for learning*. Downey, CA: Office of the Los Angeles County Superintendent of Schools.

Mayer, R. E. (1979a). Can advance organizers influence meaningful learning? *Review of Educational Research, 49,* 371–383.

Mayer, R. E. (1979b). Twenty years of research on advance organizers: Assimilation theory is still the best predictor of results. *Instructional Science, 8,* 133–167.

Mayer, R. E. (1985a, April). *Recent research on teacher beliefs and its use in the improvement of instruction*. Paper presented at the annual meeting of the American Educational Research Association, Chicago.

Mayer, R. E. (1985b). Mathematical ability. In R. J. Sternberg (Ed.), *Human abilities: An information-processing approach*. New York: Freeman.

Mayer, R. E. (1987). Instructional variables that influence cognitive processes during reading. In B. K. Britton & S. M. Glynn (Eds.), *Executive control processes in reading.* Hillsdale, NJ: Erlbaum.

Mayer, R. E. (1988). Learning strategies: An overview. In C. E. Weinstein, E. T. Goetz, & P. A. Alexander (Eds.), *Learning and study strategies: Issues in assessment, instruction, and evaluation*. San Diego: Academic Press.

McCaslin, M., & Good, T. L. (1992). Compliant cognition: The misalliance of management and instructional goals in current school reform. *Educational Researcher, 21,* 4–17.

McClelland, D. C. (1965). Toward a theory of motive acquisition. *American Psychologist, 20,* 321–333.

McCord, W., McCord, J., & Howard, A. (1963). Familial correlates of aggression in nondelinquent male children. *Journal of Abnormal and Social Psychology, 62,* 79–93.

McCormack, S. (1989). Response to Render, Padilla, and Frank: But practitioners say it works! *Educational Leadership, 46,* 77–79.

McDonald, F. (1965). *Educational psychology* (2nd ed.). Belmont, CA: Wadsworth.

McDonald, F., & Elias, P. (1976). *The effects of teacher performance on pupil learning, beginning teacher evaluation study: Phase II* (Final report: Vol. I). Princeton, NJ: Educational Testing Service.

McGinnis, E., Goldstein, A. P., Sprafkin, R. P., & Gershaw, N. J. (1984). *Skill-streaming the elementary school child.* Champaign, IL: Research Press.

McGinnis, E., Sauerbry, L., & Nichols, P. (1985). Skill-streaming: Teaching social skills to children with behavioral disorders. *Teaching Exceptional Children, 17,* 160–167.

McKeachie, W. J., Pintrich, P. R., Lin, Yi-Guang, Smith, D. A., & Sharma, R. (1990). *Teaching and learning in the college classroom: A review of the research literature* (2nd ed.). National Center for Research in Postsecondary Teaching and Learning. Ann Arbor: University of Michigan.

McKeough, M. (1991). Three perspectives on learning and instruction. In A. McKeough & J. L. Lupart (Eds.), *Toward the practice of theory-based instruction: Current cognitive theories and their educational promise.* Hillsdale, NJ: Erlbaum.

McKey, R. H., Condelli, L., Ganson, H., Barrett, B., McConkey, C., & Plantz, M. (1985). *The impact of Head Start on children, families, and communities: A final report of the Head Start Evaluation, Synthesis, and Utilization Project.* Washington, DC: CSR.

McLaughlin, B. (1978). The monitor model: Some methodological considerations. *Language Learning, 28,* 309–332.

McLaughlin, T. F., & Malaby, J. E. (1972). Intrinsic reinforcers in a classroom token economy. *Journal of Applied Behavior Analysis, 5,* 263–270.

McNeese, M. C., & Hebeler, J. R. (1977). The abused child: A clinical approach to identification and management. *Clinical Symposia, 29,* 1–36.

McWhorter, K. T. (1992). *Study and thinking skills in college* (2nd ed.). New York: HarperCollins.

Medway, F. J. (1985). To promote or not to promote? *Principal, 64,* 22–25.

Meece, J. L., Blumenfeld, P. C., & Hoyle, R. H. (1988). Students' goal orientation and cognitive engagement in classroom activities. *Journal of Educational Psychology, 80,* 514–523.

Mehan, H. (1991). *Sociological foundations supporting the study of cultural diversity.* Washington, DC: National Center for Research on Cultural Diversity and Second Language Learning.

Mehrens, W. A., & Lehmann, I. J. (1984). *Measurement and evaluation in education and psychology* (3rd ed.). New York: CBS College Publishing.

Meichenbaum, D., & Asarnow, J. (1979). Cognitive-behavioral modification and metacognitive development: Implications for the classroom. In P. C. Kendall & S. D. Hollon (Eds.), *Cognitive-behavioral interventions: Theory, research, and procedures.* New York: Academic Press.

Meichenbaum, D., & Goodman, J. (1971). Training impulsive children to talk to themselves: A means of developing self-control. *Journal of Abnormal Psychology, 77,* 115–126.

Mercer, J. R. (1971). Sociocultural factors in labeling mental retardates. *Peabody Journal of Education, 48,* 188–203.

Mercer, J. R. (1973). *Labelling the mentally retarded.* Berkeley: University of California Press.

Mercer, J. R., & Lewis, J. F. (1978). *System of multi-cultural pluralistic assessment: Conceptual and technical manual.* Riverside, CA: Institute for Pluralistic Assessment Research and Training.

Merrill, M. D. (1983). Component display theory. In C. M. Reigeluth (Ed.), *Instructional-design theories and models: An overview of their current status.* Hillsdale, NJ: Erlbaum.

Messick, S. (1976). *Individuality in learning: Implications of cognitive styles and creativity for human development.* San Francisco: Jossey-Bass.

Messick, S. (1981). Evidence and ethics in the evaluation of tests. *Educational Researcher, 10,* 9–20.

Messick, S. (1982). Issues of effectiveness and equity in the coaching controversy: Implications for educational and testing practice. *Educational Psychologist, 17,* 67–91.

Messick, S., & Jungeblut, A. (1981). Time and method in coaching for the SAT. *Psychological Bulletin, 89,* 191–216.

Meyen, E. L. (1988). A commentary on special education. In E. L. Meyen & T. M. Skrtic (Eds.), *Exceptional children and youth* (3rd ed.). Denver: Love.

Midgley, C., Feldlaufer, H., & Eccles, J. S. (1988). Transition to junior high school: Beliefs of pre- and posttransition teachers. *Journal of Youth and Adolescence, 17,* 543–562.

Miller, B. C., Card, J. J., Paikoff, R. L., & Peterson, J. L. (Eds.). (1992). *Preventing adolescent pregnancy.* Newbury Park, CA: Sage.

Miller, G. A. (1956). The magical number seven, plus or minus two: Some limits on our capacity to process information. *Psychological Review, 63,* 81–97.

Miller, H. L., & Woock, R. R. (1970). *Social foundations of urban education.* Hinsdale, IL: Dryden Press.

Miller, N. E., & Dollard, J. (1941). *Social learning and imitation.* New Haven, CT: Yale University Press.

Miller-Jones, D. (1989). Culture and testing. *American Psychologist, 44,* 360–366.

Millman, J. (1970). Reporting student progress: A case for a criterion-referenced working system. *Phi Delta Kappan, 52,* 226–231.

Millman, J., Bishop, C., & Ebel, R. (1965). An analysis of test-wiseness. *Educational and Psychological Measurement, 25,* 707–726.

Mitchell, J. V., Jr. (Ed.). (1983). *Tests in print III.* Lincoln: University of Nebraska Press.

Mitchell, J. V., Jr. (Ed.). (1985). *The ninth mental measurements yearbook.* Lincoln: University of Nebraska Press, Buros Institute of Mental Measurements.

Mitchell, R. (1992). *Testing for learning: How new approaches to evaluation can improve American schools.* New York: Free Press.

Moll, L. C. (1992). Bilingual classroom studies and community analysis: Some recent trends. *Educational Researcher, 21,* 20–24.

Moores, D. F. (1987). *Educating the deaf: Psychology, principles, and practices* (3rd ed.). Boston: Houghton Mifflin.

Moran, M. R. (1978). *Assessment of the exceptional learner in the regular classroom.* Denver: Love.

Morgan, S. R. (1987). *Abuse and neglect of handicapped children.* Boston: Little, Brown.

Moroney, R. M. (1981). Public school policy: Impact on families with handicapped children. In J. L. Paul (Ed.), *Understanding and working with parents of children with special needs.* New York: Holt, Rinehart, & Winston.

Morris, J. (1968). Diary of a beginning teacher. *National Association of Secondary School Principals, 52,* 6–15.

Mowrer, O. H. (1960). *Learning theory and the symbolic processes.* New York: Wiley.

Moynihan, D. P. (1986). *Family and nation.* New York: Harcourt Brace Jovanovich.

Muller, T., & Espenshade, T. (1985). *The fourth wave.* Washington, DC: Urban Institute Press.

Mussen, P. H., & Jones, M. C. (1957). Self-conceptions, motivations, and interpersonal attitudes of late and early maturing boys. *Child Development, 28,* 243–256.

National Assessment of Educational Progress. (1986). *The writing report card: Writing achievement in American schools.* Princeton, NJ: Educational Testing Service.

National Center for Health Statistics. (1985, September). *Monthly Vital Statistics Report.* Washington, DC: Author.

National Commission on Excellence in Education. (1983). *A nation at risk.* Washington, DC: U.S. Department of Education.

National Education Association. (1961). *Central purposes of American education.* Educational Policies Commission of the National Education Association. Washington, DC: Author.

National Education Association. (1983). *Academic preparation for college.* Educational Policies Commission of the National Education Association. Washington, DC: Author.

National Society to Prevent Blindness. (1977). *Signs of possible eye trouble in children* (Publication No. G-112). New York: Author.

Natriello, G. (1982). *Organizational evaluation systems and student disengagement in secondary schools: Final report to the National Institute of Education.* St. Louis, MO: Washington University.

Natriello, G., & Dornbusch, S. (1985). *Teacher evaluative standards and student effort.* White Plains, NY: Longman.

Nelson, C. M., & Rutherford, R. B. (1988). Behavioral interventions with behaviorally disordered students. In M. C. Wang, M. C. Reynolds, & H. J. Walberg (Eds.), *Handbook of special education: Vol 2. Mildly handicapped conditions.* New York: Pergamon.

Newman, R. S. (1991). Goals and self-regulated learning: What motivates children to seek academic help. In M. L. Maehr & P. L. Pintrich (Eds.), *Advances in motivation and achievement* (Vol. 7). Greenwich, CT: JAI Press.

Newman, R. S., & Schwager, M. T. (1992). Student perceptions and academic help-seeking. In D. H. Schunk & M. T. Meece (Eds.), *Student perceptions in the classroom.* Hillsdale, NJ: Erlbaum.

Nicholls, J. G. (1984). Conceptions of ability and achievement motivation. In R. E. Ames & C. R. Ames (Eds.), *Research on motivation in education: Vol. 1. Student motivation.* Orlando, FL: Academic Press.

Nichols, P. L., & Chen, T. C. (1981). *Minimal brain dysfunction: A prospective study.* Hillsdale, NJ: Erlbaum.

Nickerson, R . S. (1988). On improving thinking through instruction. *Review of Research in Education, 15,* 3–57.

Nickerson, R. S., Perkins, D. N., & Smith, E. E. (1985). *The teaching of thinking.* Hillsdale, NJ: Erlbaum.

Nieto, S. (1992). *Affirming diversity: The sociopolitical context of multicultural education.* White Plains, NY: Longman.

Nolan, C. Y. (1961). Legibility of ink and paper color combinations for readers of large type. *International Journal for the Education of the Blind, 10,* 82–84.

Nolan, J. D. (1974). The true humanist: The behavior modifier. *Teachers College Record, 76,* 335–343.

Nolan, S. B. (1988). Reasons for studying: Motivational orientations and study strategies. *Cognition and Instruction, 5,* 269–287.

Oakes, J. (1987). Tracking in secondary schools: A contextual perspective. *Educational Psychologist, 22,* 129–153.

Ogbu, J. U. (1987). Variability in minority school performance: A problem in search of an explanation. *Anthropology & Education Quarterly, 18,* 312–334.

Ogbu, J. U. (1992). Understanding cultural diversity and learning. *Educational Researcher, 21,* 5–14.

Olsen, L. (1988). Crossing the school house border: Immigrant children in California. *Phi Delta Kappan, 70,* 211–218.

Orlich, D. C., Harder, R. J., Callahan, R. C., Kravas, C. H., Kauchak, D. P., Pendergrass, R. A., & Keogh, A. J. (1985). *Teaching strategies: A guide to better instruction* (2nd ed.). Lexington, MA: Heath.

Packard, R. G. (1975). *Psychology of learning and instruction.* Columbus, OH: Merrill.

Palincsar, A. S. (1986). Metacognitive strategy instruction. *Exceptional Children, 53,* 118–124.

Palincsar, A. S., & Brown, A. L. (1986). Interactive teaching to promote independent learning from text. *The Reading Teacher, 39,* 771–777.

Pallas, A. M., Natriello, G., & McDill, E. L. (1989). The changing nature of the disadvantaged population: Current dimensions and future trends. *Educational Researcher, 18,* 16–22.

Palomares, V. H., & Ball, G. (1974). *Human development program.* La Mesa, CA: Human Development Training Institute.

Paris, S. G., & Byrnes, J. P. (1989). The constructivist approach to self-regulation and learning in the classroom. In B. J. Zimmerman & D. H. Schunk (Eds.), *Self-regulated learning and academic achievement: Theory, research, and practice.* New York: Springer-Verlag.

Paris, S. G., Lipson, M. Y., & Wixson, K. K. (1983). Becoming a strategic reader. *Contemporary Educational Psychology, 8,* 293–316.

Paris, S. G., & Newman, R. S. (1990). Developmental aspects of self-regulated learning. *Educational Psychologist, 25,* 87–102.

Paris, S. G., & Oka, E. (1986). Children's reading strategies, metacognition, and motivation. *Developmental Review, 6,* 25–86.

Pascarella, E. T., Walberg, H. J., Junker, L. K., & Haertel, G. D. (1981). Continuing motivation in science for early and late adolescents. *American Educational Research Journal, 18,* 439–452.

Pascual-Leone, J. (1970). A mathematical model for the transition rule in Piaget's developmental stages. *Acta Psychologica, 32,* 301–345.

Pascual-Leone, J. (1989). Organismic processes for neo-Piagetian theories: A dialectical causal account of cognitive development. In A. Demetriou (Ed.), *The neo-Piagetian theories of cognitive development: Toward an integration.* Amsterdam: North Holland.

Patten, J. V., Chao, C. I., & Reigeluth, C. M. (1986). A review of strategies for sequencing and synthesizing instruction. *Review of Educational Research, 56,* 437–471.

Patterson, G. R., DeBaryshe, B. D., & Ramsey, E. (1989). A developmental perspective on antisocial behavior. *American Psychologist, 44,* 329–335.

Patterson, G. R., & Guillion, M. E. (1971). *Living with children.* Champaign, IL: Research Press.

Patterson, J. H., & Smith, M. (1986). The role of computers in higher-order thinking. In J. A. Culbertson & L. L. Cunningham (Eds.), *Microcomputers and education: Eighty-fifth yearbook of the National Society for the Study of Education* (Part I). Chicago: University of Chicago Press.

Peresich, M. L., Meadows, J. D., & Sinatra, R. (1990). Content area cognitive mapping for reading and writing proficiency. *Journal of Reading, 33,* 424–432.

Peters, R. S. (1975). Why doesn't Lawrence Kohlberg do his homework? *Phi Delta Kappan, 56,* 678.

Peterson, N. L., & Cooper, C. S. (1989). Parent education and involvement in early intervention programs for handicapped children. In M. J. Fine (Ed.), *The second handbook on parent education: Contemporary perspectives.* San Diego: Academic Press.

Peterson, P. (1979). Direct instruction reconsidered. In P. Peterson & H. J. Walberg (Eds.), *Research in teaching.* Berkeley, CA: McCutchan.

Peterson, P., Marx, R., & Clark, C. (1978). Teaching planning, teacher behavior, and student achievement. *American Educational Research Journal, 15,* 417–432.

Philips, S. U. (1983). *The invisible culture: Communication in classroom and community on the Warm Springs Indian Reservation.* White Plains, NY: Longman.

Phillips, J. L., Jr. (1969). *The origins of intellect: Piaget's theory.* San Francisco: Freeman.

Piaget, J. (1952). *The child's conception of number.* London: Humanities Press.

Piaget, J. (1964). Development and learning. In R. E. Ripple & V. N. Rockcastle (Eds.), *Piaget rediscovered: A report of the conference on cognitive skills and curriculum development.* Ithaca, NY: Cornell University, School of Education.

Piaget, J., & Szeminska, A. (1952). *The child's conception of number* (C. Gattegno & F. M. Hodgson, Trans.). New York: Humanities Press.

Pintrich, P. R., Cross, D. R., Kozma, R. B., & McKeachie, W. J. (1986). Instructional psychology. *Annual Review of Psychology, 37,* 611–651.

Pintrich, P. R., & DeGroot, E. V. (1990). Motivational and self-regulated learning components of classroom academic performance. *Journal of Educational Psychology, 82,* 33–40.

Pintrich, P. R., & Garcia, T. (1992, April). *An integrated model of motivation and self-regulated learning.* Paper presented at the annual meeting of the American Educational Research Association, San Francisco.

Pintrich, P. R., & Schrauben, B. (1992). Students' motivational beliefs and their cognitive engagement in classroom academic tasks. In D. Schunk & J. L. Meece (Eds.), *Student perceptions in the classroom.* Hillsdale, NJ: Erlbaum.

Pintrich, P. R., Smith, D. A., Garcia, T., & McKeachie, W. J. (1991). *A manual for the use of the Motivated Strategies for Learning Questionnaire (MSLQ).* National Center for Research to Improve Postsecondary Teaching and Learning. Ann Arbor: University of Michigan, School of Education.

Plowden Report. (1967). *Children and their primary schools: A report of the Central Advisory Council for Education.* London: H.M. Stationery Office.

Plowman, P. D. (1971). *Behavioral objectives.* Chicago: Science Research Associates.

Popham, W. J., & Baker, E. L. (1970). *Systematic instruction.* Englewood Cliffs, NJ: Prentice-Hall.

Poteet, J. A. (1973). *Behavior modification: A practical guide for teachers.* Minneapolis: Burgess.

Premack, D. (1959). Toward empirical behavior laws: I. Positive reinforcement. *Psychological Review, 66,* 219–233.

Pressley, M., Goodchild, F., Fleet, J., Zajchowski, R., & Evans, E. D. (1989). The challenges of classroom strategy instruction. *Elementary School Journal, 89,* 301–342.

Ramirez, J. D., Yuen, S. D., Ramey, D. R., & Pasta, D. J. (1990). *Final report: Longitudinal study of immersion strategy, early-exit and late-exit transitional bilingual education programs for language-minority children* (2 vols.). San Mateo, CA: Aguirre International.

Reigeluth, C. M., & Stein, F. S. (1983). The elaboration theory of instruction. In C. M. Reigeluth (Ed.), *Instructional-design theories and models: An overview of their current status.* Hillsdale, NJ: Erlbaum.

Reiling, E., & Taylor, R. (1972). A new approach to the problem of changing initial responses to multiple-choice questions. *Journal of Educational Measurement, 9,* 67–70.

Render, G., Padilla, N. M., & Frank, H. M. (1989a). Assertive discipline: A critical review and analysis. *Teachers College Record, 90,* 607–630.

Render, G., Padilla, N. M., & Frank, H. M. (1989b). What research really shows about assertive discipline. *Educational Leadership, 46,* 72–75.

Renzulli, J. S. (1982). What makes giftedness? *Phi Delta Kappan, 60,* 180–184, 261.

Report of the Ad Hoc Committee to Define Deafness and Hard-of-Hearing. (1975). *American Annals of the Deaf, 120,* 509–512.

Reppucci, N. D., & Haugaard, J. J. (1989). Prevention of child sexual abuse: Myth or reality. *American Psychologist, 44,* 1266–1275.

Resnick, L. B., & Klopfer, L. E. (Eds.). (1989). *Toward the thinking curriculum: Current cognitive research: 1989 yearbook of the Association for Supervision and Curriculum Development.* Alexandria, VA: Association for Supervision and Curriculum Development.

Rest, J. R. (1983). Morality. In J. Flavell & E. Markman (Eds.), *Cognitive development* (Vol. 4), (P. H. Mussen, General Ed.), *Manual of child psychology.* New York: Wiley.

Reynolds, C. R., & Jensen, A. R. (1983). WISC-R subscale patterns of abilities of blacks and whites matched on full scale IQ. *Journal of Educational Psychology, 75,* 207–214.

Richard-Amato, P. A. (1988). *Making it happen: Interaction in the second language classroom: From theory to practice.* White Plains, NY: Longman.

Richardson, J. L., et al. (1989). Substance use among eighth-grade students who take care of themselves after school. *Pediatrics, 84,* 556–566.

Richardson, V., Anders, A., Tidwell, D., & Lloyd, C. (1991). The relationship between teachers' beliefs and practices in reading comprehension instruction. *American Educational Research Journal, 28,* 559–586.

Rickards, J. P., & August, G. J. (1975). Generative underlining strategies in prose recall. *Journal of Educational Psychology, 67,* 860–865.

Robinson, F. (1970). *Study guide for Ausubel/Robinson: School learning.* New York: Holt, Rinehart & Winston.

Roehler, L. R., & Duffy, G. G. (1984). Direct explanation of comprehension processes. In G. G. Duffy, L. R. Roehler, & J. Mason (Eds.), *Comprehension instruction: Perspectives and suggestions.* White Plains, NY: Longman.

Roffman, A. J. (1983). *The classroom teacher's guide to mainstreaming.* Springfield, IL: Thomas.

Rogers, C. R. (1969). *Freedom to learn.* Columbus, OH: Merrill.

Rogers, C. R. (1983). *Freedom to learn for the 80's.* Columbus, OH: Merrill.

Romberg, T. A., & Carpenter, T. P. (1986). Research on teaching and learning mathematics. In M. C. Wittrock (Ed.), *Handbook of research on teaching* (3rd ed.). New York: Macmillan.

Rosenholtz, S. J. (1989). Workplace conditions that affect teacher quality and commitment: Implications for teacher induction programs. *Elementary School Journal, 89,* 421–439.

Rosenholtz, S. J., & Simpson, C. (1984). The formation of ability conceptions: Developmental trend or social construction? *Review of Educational Research, 54,* 31–63.

Rosenshine, B. V. (1980). How time is spent in elementary classrooms. In C. Denham & A. Lieberman (Eds.), *Time to learn.* Washington, DC: U.S. Department of Education.

Rosenshine, B. V. (1983). Teaching functions in instructional programs. *Elementary School Journal, 83,* 335–351.

Rosenshine, B. V. (1986). Synthesis of research on explicit teaching. *Educational Leadership, 43,* 60–69.

Rosenshine, B. V., & Berliner, D. (1978). Academic engaged time. *British Journal of Teacher Education, 4,* 3–16.

Rosenthal, R. (1985). From unconscious experimenter bias to teacher expectancy effects. In J. Dusek (Ed.), *Teacher expectancies.* Hillsdale, NJ: Erlbaum.

Rosenthal, R., & Jacobson, L. (1968). *Pygmalion in the classroom.* New York: Holt, Rinehart & Winston.

Rossel, C., & Ross, J. M. (1986). *The social science evidence on bilingual education.* Boston: Boston University Press.

Rothenberg, J. (1989). The open classroom reconsidered. *Elementary School Journal, 90,* 69–86.

Rothkopf, E. Z., & Billington, M. J. (1979). Goal-guided learning from text: Inferring a descriptive processing model from inspection times and eye movements. *Journal of Educational Psychology, 71,* 310–327.

Rothrock, D. (1982). The rise and decline of individualized instruction. *Educational Leadership, 39,* 528–531.

Rotter, J. (1966). Generalized expectancies for internal versus external control of reinforcement. *Psychological Monographs, 80* (1, Whole No. 609).

Rowe, M. B. (1974). Wait-time and rewards as instructional variables: Their influence on language, logic, and fate control: Part 1. Wait-time. *Journal of Research in Science Teaching, 11,* 81–97.

Rudner, L. (1988). Teacher testing—An update. *Educational Measurement: Issues and Practices, 7,* 16–19.

Ryan, K. (1970). The first year of teaching. In K. Ryan (Ed.), *Don't smile until Christmas.* Chicago: University of Chicago Press.

Ryan, K. (1986). The new moral education. *Phi Delta Kappan, 68,* 228–233.

Ryan, R. M., Connell, J. P., & Deci, E. (1985). A motivational analysis of self-determination and self-regulation in education. In C. Ames & R. Ames (Eds.), *Research on motivation in education: Vol. 2. The classroom milieu.* Orlando, FL: Academic Press.

Ryan, R. M., & Grolnick, W. (1984). *Origins and pawns in the classroom: A self-report and projective assessment of children's perceptions.* Unpublished manuscript, University of Rochester, Rochester, NY.

Sadker, M., & Sadker, D. (1986). Sexism in the classroom: From grade school to graduate school. *Phi Delta Kappan, 67,* 512–515.

Sadker, M., Sadker, D., & Klein, S. (1991). The issues of gender in elementary and secondary education. In G. Grant (Ed.), *Review of research in education* (Vol. 17). Washington, DC: American Educational Research Association.

Salomon, G. (1979). *Interaction of media, cognition, and learning.* San Francisco: Jossey-Bass.

Samson, G. E. (1985). Effects of training in test-taking skills on achievement test performance: A quantitative synthesis. *Journal of Educational Research, 78,* 261–266.

Sarason, S. B., Davidson, K. S., Lighthall, F. F., Waite, R. R., & Ruebrush, B. K. (1960). *Anxiety in elementary school children.* New York: Wiley.

Sarnacki, R. E. (1979). An examination of test-wiseness in the cognitive test domain. *Review of Educational Research, 49,* 252–279.

Sattler, J. M. (1988). *Assessment of children* (3rd ed.). San Diego: Sattler.

Sattler, J. M., & Gwynne, J. (1982). White examiners generally do not impede the intelligence performance of black children: To debunk a myth. *Journal of Consulting and Clinical Psychology, 50,* 196–208.

Scarr, S., & Kidd, K. K. (1983). Developmental behavior genetics. In M. M. Haith & J. J. Campos (Eds.), *Handbook of child psychology: Infancy and developmental psychobiology* (Vol. 2). (P. H. Mussen, General Ed.). New York: Wiley.

Scarr, S., & Weinberg, R. A. (1976). IQ test performance of black children adopted by white families. *American Psychologist, 31,* 726–739.

Scarr, S., & Weinberg, R. A. (1983). The Minnesota adoption studies: Genetic differences and malleability. *Child Development, 54,* 260–267.

Schiedel, D. G., & Marcia, J. E. (1985). Ego identity, intimacy, sex role orientation, and gender. *Developmental Psychology, 18,* 149–160.

Schlaefli, A., Rest, J. R., & Thoma, S. J. (1985). Does moral education improve moral judgment? A meta-analysis of intervention studies using the Defining Issues Test. *Review of Educational Research, 55,* 319–352.

Schneider, W., & Pressley, M. (1989). *Memory development between 2 and 20.* New York: Springer-Verlag.

Schoenfeld, A. H. (1983). The wild, wild, wild, wild, wild world of problem solving. *For the Learning of Mathematics, 3,* 40–47.

Schoenfeld, A. H. (1985). Metacognitive and epistemological issues in mathematical understanding. In E. A. Silver (Ed.), *Teaching and learning mathematical problem solving: Multiple research perspectives*. Hillsdale, NJ: Erlbaum.

Schoenfeld, A. H. (1989). Teaching mathematical thinking and problem solving. In L. B. Resnick & L. E. Klopfer (Eds.), *Toward the thinking curriculum: Current cognitive research*. Washington, DC: Association for Supervision and Curriculum Development.

Schubert, W. H., & Ayers, W. C. (1992). *Teacher lore: Learning from our own experience*. White Plains, NY: Longman.

Schumacker, J. B., Deshler, D. D., Alley, G. R., & Warner, M. M. (1983). Toward the development of an intervention model for learning disabled adolescents: The University of Kansas Institute. *Exceptional Education Quarterly, 4*, 45–74.

Schumacker, J. B., Deshler, D. D., & Ellis, E. S. (1986). Intervention issues related to the education of LD adolescents. In J. K. Torgeson & B. Y. L. Wong (Eds.), *Learning disabilities: Some new perspectives*. New York: Academic Press.

Schunk, D. H. (1986, April). *Self-regulation through overt verbalization during cognitive skill learning*. Paper presented at the annual meeting of the American Educational Research Association, San Francisco.

Schunk, D. H. (1989). Self-efficacy and cognitive skill learning. In C. Ames & R. Ames (Eds.), *Research on motivation in education: Vol. 3. Goals and cognitions*. San Diego: Academic Press.

Schunk, D. H. (1991a). Goal setting and self-evaluation: A social cognitive perspective on self-regulation. In M. L. Maehr & P. R. Pintrich (Eds.), *Advances in motivation and achievement* (Vol. 7). Greenwich, CT: JAI Press.

Schunk, D. H. (1991b). *Learning theories: An educational perspective*. New York: Macmillan.

Schunk, D. H., & Meece, J. L. (Eds.). (1992). *Student perceptions in the classroom*. Hillsdale, NJ: Erlbaum.

Schwebel, M. (1975). Formal operations in the first year college student. *Journal of Psychology, 91*, 133–141.

Seaberg, D. I. (1974). *The four faces of teaching: The role of the teacher in humanizing education*. Santa Monica, CA: Goodyear.

Seifert, K. L. (1991). *Educational psychology* (2nd ed.). Boston: Houghton Mifflin.

Semmel, M. I., Gottlieb, J., & Robinson, N. M. (1979). Mainstreaming: Perspectives on educating handicapped children in the public school. In D. C. Berliner (Ed.), *Review of research in education* (Vol. 7). Washington, DC: American Educational Research Association.

Serbin, L. A. (1983). The hidden curriculum: Academic consequences of teacher expectations. In M. Marland (Ed.), *Sex differentiation and schooling*. London: Heinemann.

Shapiro, J., Kramer, S., & Hunerberg, C. (1981). *Equal their chances: Children's activities for non-sexist learning*. Englewood Cliffs, NJ: Prentice-Hall.

Sharon, S., et al. (1984). *Cooperative learning in the classroom: Research in desegregated schools*. Hillsdale, NJ: Erlbaum.

Shavelson, R. J. (1973). What is the basic teaching skill? *Journal of Teacher Education, 14*, 144–151.

Shavelson, R. J., Hubner, J., & Stanton, G. (1976). Self-concept: Validation of construct interpretations. *Review of Educational Research, 46*, 407–441.

Shepard, L. A., & Smith, M. L. (1988). Escalating academic demand in kindergarten: Counterproductive policies. *Elementary School Journal, 89*, 135–145.

Short, E. J., & Weissberg-Benchell, J. A. (1989). The triple alliance for learning: Cognition, metacognition, and motivation. In C. B. McCormick, G. E. Miller, & M. Pressley (Eds.), *Cognitive strategy research: From basic research to educational applications*. New York: Springer-Verlag.

Sieber, J., O'Neil, H., & Tobias, S. (1977). *Anxiety, learning, and instruction*. Hillsdale, NJ: Erlbaum.

Siegel, I. E. (1969). The Piagetian system and the world of education. In D. Elkind & J. H. Flavell (Eds.), *Studies in cognitive development: Essays in honor of Jean Piaget*. New York: Oxford University Press.

Silverman, S., & Kimmel, D. (1972). The effects of immediate feedback on the behavior of teachers in training. *School Application of Learning Theory, 4*, 16–23.

Simmons, R. G., Blyth, D. A., Van Cleave, E. F., & Bush, D. M. (1979). Entry into early adolescence: The impact of school structure, puberty and early dating on self-esteem. *American Sociological Review, 44*, 948–967.

Simmons, R. G., Rosenberg, F., & Rosenberg, M. (1973). Disturbance in the self-image at adolescence. *American Sociological Review, 38*, 553–568.

Simon, S. B., Howe, L. W., & Kirschenbaum, H. (1972). *Values clarification: A handbook of practical strategies for teachers and students*. New York: Hart.

Simpson, A. W., & Erickson, M. T. (1983). Teachers' verbal and nonverbal communication patterns as a function of teacher race, student gender, and student race. *American Educational Research Journal, 20*, 183–198.

Skinner, B. F. (1948). *Walden two*. New York: Macmillan.

Skinner, B. F. (1953). *Science and human behavior*. New York: Macmillan.

Skinner, B. F. (1954). The science of learning and the art of teaching. *Harvard Educational Review, 24*, 86–97.

Skinner, B. F. (1958, October). Teaching machines. *Science 128*, 969–977.

Skinner, B. F. (1973). The free and happy student. *Phi Delta Kappan, 55*, 13–16.

Skinner, B. F. (1986). Programmed instruction revisited. *Phi Delta Kappan, 68*, 103–110.

Skodak, M., & Skeels, H. M. (1945). A follow-up study of children in adoptive homes. *Journal of Genetic Psychology, 66,* 21–58.

Slater, A. M., & Kingston, D. J. (1981). Competence and performance variables in the assessment of formal operational skills. *British Journal of Educational Psychology, 51,* 163–169.

Slavin, R. E. (1983). *Cooperative learning.* White Plains, NY: Longman.

Slavin, R. E. (1985). Team-assisted instruction: A cooperative learning solution for adaptive instruction in mathematics. In M. C. Wang & H. J. Walberg (Eds.), *Adapting instruction to individual differences.* Berkeley, CA: McCutchan.

Slavin, R. E. (1987). Mastery learning reconsidered. *Review of Educational Research, 57,* 175–213.

Slavin, R. E. (1988). *Educational psychology: Theory into practice* (2nd ed.). Englewood Cliffs, NJ: Prentice-Hall.

Slavin, R. E. (1989). Class size and student achievement: Small effects of small classes. *Educational Psychologist, 24,* 99–110.

Slavin, R. E. (1990). *Cooperative learning: Theory, research and practice.* Needham Heights, MA: Allyn & Bacon.

Slavin, R. E. (1991). *Educational psychology: Theory into practice* (3rd ed.). Englewood Cliffs, NJ: Prentice-Hall.

Slavin, R. E., & Karweit, N. (1984). Mastery learning and student teams: A factorial experiment in urban general mathematics classes. *American Educational Research Journal, 21,* 725–736.

Slavin, R. E., Karweit, N. L., & Madden, N. A. (1989). *Effective programs for students at risk.* Boston: Allyn & Bacon.

Sloane, H. N., Gordon, H. M., Gunn, C., & Mickelsen, V. G. (1989). *Evaluating educational software: A guide for teachers.* Englewood Cliffs, NJ: Prentice-Hall.

Smart, K. L., & Bruning, J. L. (1973, August). *An examination of the practical import of the Von Restorff effect.* Paper presented at the annual meeting of the American Psychological Association, Montreal. (ERIC Document Reproduction Service No. ED 102 502)

Smith, B. O. (1960). A concept of teaching. *Teachers College Record, 61,* 229–241.

Smith, C. R., Wood, F. H., & Grimes, J. (1988). Issues in the identification and placement of behaviorally disordered students. In M. C. Wang, M. C. Reynolds, & H. J. Walberg (Eds.), *Handbook of special education: Vol 2. Mildly handicapped conditions.* New York: Pergamon.

Smith, D. D., & Luckasson, R. (1992). *Introduction to special education.* Boston: Allyn & Bacon.

Smith, E. L., & Sendelbach, N. B. (1979, April). *Teacher intentions for science instruction and their antecedents in program materials.* Paper presented at the annual meeting of the American Educational Research Association, San Francisco.

Smith, F. M., & Adams, S. (1972). *Educational measurement for the classroom teacher* (2nd ed.). New York: Harper & Row.

Smith, M. L., & Glass, G. V. (1980). Meta-analysis of research on class size and its relationship to attitudes and instruction. *American Educational Research Journal, 17,* 419–433.

Smith, M. L., & Shepard, L. A. (1988). Kindergarten readiness and retention: A qualitative study of teachers' beliefs and practices. *American Educational Research Journal, 25,* 307–333.

Smith, R. M. (1982). *Learning how to learn: Applied theory for adults.* New York: Cambridge University Press.

Snider, V. (1990). What we know about learning styles from research in special education. *Educational Leadership, 48*(2), 53.

Snowman, J. (1984). Learning tactics and strategies. In G. D. Phye & T. Andre (Eds.), *Cognitive instructional psychology.* Orlando, FL: Academic Press.

Sosniak, L. A. (1987). Gifted education boondoggles: A few bad apples or a rotten bushel? *Phi Delta Kappan, 68,* 535–538.

Spaulding, C. L. (1992). *Motivation in the classroom.* New York: McGraw-Hill.

Spearman, C. (1927). *The abilities of man: Their nature and measurement.* New York: Macmillan.

Spears, H. (1973). Kappans ponder the goals of education. *Phi Delta Kappan, 55,* 29–32.

Spence, J., & Helmreich, R. (1978). *Masculinity and femininity.* Austin: University of Texas.

Spindler, G. (Ed.) (1982). *Doing the ethnography of schooling.* New York: Holt, Rinehart & Winston.

Staffieri, J. R. (1967). A study of social stereotype of body image in children. *Journal of Personality and Social Psychology, 7,* 101–103.

Stallings, J., & Krasavage, E. M. (1986). *Peaks, valleys, and plateaus in program implementation: A longitudinal study of a Madeline Hunter follow-through project.* Nashville, TN: Vanderbilt University, Peabody Center for Effective Teaching.

Stallings, J., Robbins, M., Presbrey, L., & Scott, J. (1986). Effects of instruction based on the Madeline Hunter model on students' achievement: Findings from a follow-through project. *Elementary School Journal, 86,* 571–587.

Standards for educational and psychological testing. (1985). Washington, DC: American Psychological Association.

Stanford Achievement Tests (7th ed.). (1982). San Diego: Harcourt Brace Jovanovich.

Steele, C. M. (1988). The psychology of self-affirmation: Sustaining the integrity of the self. In L. Berkowitz

(Ed.), *Advances in experimental social psychology* (Vol. 21). New York: Academic Press.

Steele, C. M. (1992, April). Race and the schooling of black Americans. *The Atlantic Monthly*, 69–78.

Steinberg, C. (1985). *TV facts*. New York: Facts on File.

Steinberg, L., & Dornbusch, S. M. (1991). Negative correlates of part-time employment during adolescence: Replication and elaboration. *Developmental Psychology, 27*, 304–313.

Stern, P., & Shavelson, R. (1981). *The relationship between teachers' grouping decisions and instructional behaviors: An ethnographic study of reading instruction*. Resources in Education. (ERIC Document Reproduction Service No. ED 210 971).

Sternberg, R. J. (Ed.). (1985). *Human abilities: An information-processing approach*. New York: Freeman.

Sternberg, R. J. (1986). *Intelligence applied: Understanding and increasing your intellectual skills*. New York: Harcourt Brace Jovanovich.

Sternberg, R. J. (1987a). A day at developmental downs: Sportscast for race #2—Neo-Piagetian theories of cognitive development. *International Journal of Psychology, 22*, 507–529.

Sternberg, R. J. (1987b). Teaching intelligence: The application of cognitive psychology to the improvement of intellectual skills. In J. B. Baron & R. J. Sternberg (Eds.), *Teaching thinking skills: Theory and practice*. New York: Freeman.

Sternberg, R. J. (1988). *The triarchic mind: A new theory of human intelligence*. New York: Viking.

Sternberg, R. J., & Bhana, K. (1986). Synthesis of research on the effectiveness of intellectual skills programs: Snake-oil remedies or miracle cures? *Educational Leadership, 44*, 60–67.

Sternberg, R. J., & Davidson, J. E. (Eds.). (1986). *Conceptions of giftedness*. New York: Cambridge University Press.

Sternberg, R. J., & Suben, J. G. (1986). The socialization of intelligence. In M. Perlmutter (Ed.), *Minnesota symposia on child psychology: Perspectives on intellectual development*. Vol. 19. Hillsdale, NJ: Erlbaum.

Stipek, D. J. (1988). *Motivation to learn: From theory to practice*. Englewood Cliffs, NJ: Prentice-Hall.

Strain, P. S., & Kerr, M. M. (1981). *Mainstreaming of children in schools: Research and programmatic issues*. New York: Academic Press.

Strein, W. (1988). Classroom-based elementary school affective education programs: A critical review. *Psychology in the Schools, 25*, 288–296.

Sue, S., & Padilla, A. (1986). Ethnic minority issues in the United States: Challenges for the educational system. In *Beyond language: Social and cultural factors in schooling language minority students*. Los Angeles: California State University, Evaluation, Dissemination, and Assessment Center.

Sullivan, E. V. (1967). *Piaget and the school curriculum: A critical appraisal* (Bulletin No. 2). Toronto: Ontario Institute for Studies in Education.

Summers, M. (1977). Learning disabilities . . . A puzzlement. *Today's Education, 66*, 42.

Suran, B. G., & Rizzo, J. (1979). *Special children: An integrative approach*. Glenview, IL: Scott, Foresman.

Sutherland, K. (1979). Accuracy vs. fluency in the second language classroom. California Association of Teachers of English to Speakers of Other Languages. *CATESOL Occasional Papers, 5*, 25–29.

Tarver, S. G., & Hallahan, D. P. (1976). Children with learning disabilities: An overview. In J. M. Kauffman & D. P. Hallahan (Eds.), *Teaching children with learning disabilities: Personal perspectives*. Columbus, OH: Merrill.

Taylor, M. J., & Hegarty, S. (1985). *The best of both worlds: A review of research into the education of pupils of South Asian origin*. Windsor, UK: National Foundation for Educational Research–Nelson.

Tenbrink, T. D. (1974). *Evaluation: A practical guide for teachers*. New York: McGraw-Hill.

Tennyson, R. D., & Park, O. (1980). The teaching of concepts: A review of instructional design literature. *Review of Educational Research, 50*, 55–70.

Terman, L. M., & Oden, M. (1925). *Genetic studies of genius: Mental and physical traits of a thousand gifted children*. Stanford, CA: Stanford University Press.

Terman, L. M., & Oden, M. (1954). *Genetic studies of genius: The gifted group at mid-life. Thirty-five years' follow-up of the superior child*. Stanford, CA: Stanford University Press.

Terwilliger, J. S. (1971). *Assigning grades to students*. Glenview, IL: Scott, Foresman.

Test, D. W., Heward, W. L., & Orlansky, M. D. (1980). *A teacher's guide to Heward and Orlansky's exceptional children*. Columbus, OH: Merrill.

Tharp, R. G. (1989). Psychocultural variables and constants: Effects on teaching and learning in schools. *American Psychologist, 44*, 349–359.

Tharp, R. G., & Gallimore, R. (1988). *Rousing minds to life: Teaching, learning, and schooling in social context*. New York: Cambridge University Press.

Tharp, R. G., & Gallimore, R. (1991). *The instructional conversation: Teaching and learning in social activity*. Washington, DC: National Center for Research on Cultural Diversity and Second Language Learning.

Thorndike, E. L. (1913). *Educational psychology*. New York: Columbia University, Teachers College Press.

Thorndike, E. L. (1927). *The measurement of intelligence*. New York: Columbia University, Teachers College Press.

Thorndyke, P. W., & Stasz, C. (1980). Individual differences in procedures for knowledge acquisition from maps. *Cognitive Psychology, 12,* 137–175.

Thurstone, L. L. (1938). *Primary mental abilities.* Chicago: University of Chicago Press.

Tiedemann, J. (1989). Measures of cognitive styles: A critical review. *Educational Psychologist, 24,* 261–275.

Tierney, R. J., Carter, M. A., & Desai, L. E. (1991). *Portfolio assessment in the reading-writing classroom.* Norwood, MA: Cristopher-Gordon.

Tobias, S. (1979). Anxiety research in educational psychology. *Journal of Educational Psychology, 71,* 573–582.

Tobias, S. (1980). *Paths to programs for intervention: Math anxiety, math avoidance, and reentry mathematics.* Washington, DC: Institute for the Study of Anxiety in Learning.

Tobias, S. (1985). Computer-assisted instruction. In M. C. Wang & H. J. Walberg (Eds.), *Adapting instruction to individual differences.* Berkeley, CA: McCutchan.

Tobin-Richards, M. H., Boxer, A. H., & Petersen, A. C. (1983). The psychological significance of pubertal change: Sex differences in perception of self during early adolescence. In J. Brooks-Gunn & A. C. Petersen (Eds.), *Girls at puberty: Biological and psychological perspectives.* New York: Plenum.

Tomás Rivera Center. (1991). *(Almost) 8 million and counting: A demographic overview of Latinos in California with a focus on Los Angeles County.* Claremont, CA: Author.

Tomchin, E. M., & Impara, J. C. (1992). Unraveling teachers' beliefs about grade retention. *American Educational Research Journal, 29,* 199–223.

Torrance, E. P. (1962). *Guiding creative behavior.* Englewood Cliffs, NJ: Prentice-Hall.

Troike, R. C. (1978). Research evidence for the effectiveness of bilingual education. *National Association for Bilingual Education Journal, 3,* 13–24.

Trojcak, D. A. (1977). Implementing the competency of sequencing instruction. In J. Weigand (Ed.), *Implementing teacher competencies.* Englewood Cliffs, NJ: Prentice-Hall.

Underwood, B. J. (1961). Ten years of massed practice on distributed practice. *Psychological Review, 68,* 229–247.

Underwood, B. J., & Ekstrand, B. R. (1966). An analysis of some shortcomings in the interference theory of forgetting. *Psychological Review, 73,* 540–549.

United States Department of Education. (1992). *Fourteenth annual report to Congress on the implementation of the Education of the Handicapped Act.* Washington, DC: U. S. Government Printing Office.

United States Office of Education (1977). *Procedures for evaluating specific learning disabilities. Federal Register* 42, 65082–65085.

Urman, H. N. (1982). *Ethnic differences and the effects of test-wiseness training on verbal and math achievement.* Unpublished doctoral dissertation, University of Southern California, Los Angeles.

Values in the classroom. (1992, June 8). *Newsweek,* pp. 26–27.

Van Patten, J., Chao, C., & Reigeluth, C. M. (1986). A review of strategies for sequencing and synthesizing instruction. *Review of Educational Research, 56,* 437–471.

Van Riper, C. (1978). *Speech correction: Principles and methods* (6th ed.). Englewood Cliffs, NJ: Prentice-Hall.

Vargas, J. S. (1986). Instructional design flaws in computer-assisted instruction. *Phi Delta Kappan, 67,* 738–744.

Veenman, S. (1984). Perceived problems of beginning teachers. *Review of Educational Research, 4,* 143–178.

Verhovek, S. H. (1990, March 4). Girls win 51.3% in Regents series. *New York Times,* p. 28.

Vogt, L. A., Jordan, C., & Tharp, R. G. (1987). Explaining school failure, producing school success: Two cases. *Anthropology & Education Quarterly, 18,* 276–286.

Vygotsky, L. S. (1962). *Thought and language.* Cambridge, MA: MIT Press.

Vygotsky, L. S. (1978). Interaction between learning and development. In M. Cole, S. Scribner, V. John-Steiner, & E. Sonberman (Eds.), *Mind in society: Development of higher psychological processes.* Cambridge, MA: Harvard University Press.

Wadsworth, B. (1989). *Piaget's theory of cognitive and affective development* (4th ed.). White Plains, NY: Longman.

Wagner, R., & Sternberg, R. J. (1984). Alternative conceptions of intelligence and their implications for education. *Review of Educational Research, 54,* 179–223.

Walberg, H., & Thomas, S. (1972). Open education: An operational definition and validation in Great Britain and the U.S. *American Educational Research Journal, 9,* 197–208.

Walker, J. E., & Shea, T. (1988). *Behavior management: A practical approach for educators* (4th ed.). Columbus, OH: Merrill.

Walker, L. J. (1984). Sex differences in the development of moral reasoning: A critical review. *Child Development, 55,* 677–691.

Walker, L. J. (1989). A longitudinal study of moral reasoning. *Child Development, 60,* 157–166.

Wallach, M. A., & Kogan, N. (1965). *Modes of thinking in young children: A study of the creativity-intelligence distinction.* New York: Holt, Rinehart & Winston.

Wallerstein, J. S., Corbin, S. B., & Lewis, J. M. (1988). Children of divorce: A ten-year study. In E. M. Hetherington & J. Arasteh (Eds.), *Impact of divorce, single-parenting, and stepparenting on children.* Hillsdale, NJ: Erlbaum.

Wallerstein, J. S., & Kelly, J. B. (1980). *Surviving the breakup.* New York: Basic Books.

Walters, R. H., Parke, R. D., & Cane, V. A. (1965). Timing of punishment and the observation of consequences to others as determinants of response inhibition. *Journal of Experimental Child Psychology, 2,* 10–30.

Wang, M. (1980). Adaptive instruction: Building on diversity. *Theory into Practice, 19,* 122–128.

Wang, M. C., Reynolds, M. C., & Walberg, H. J. (1988). Integrating the children of the second system. *Phi Delta Kappan, 70,* 248–251.

Waterman, A. S. (1982). Identity development from adolescence to adulthood: An extension of theory and a review of research. *Developmental Psychology, 18,* 341–358.

Webb, N. (1982). Peer interaction and learning in cooperative small groups. *Journal of Educational Psychology, 74,* 642–655.

Webb, N. (1985). Verbal interaction and learning in peer-directed groups. *Theory into Practice, 24,* 32–38.

Webb, N. (1987, April). *Helping behavior to maximize learning.* Paper presented at the annual meeting of the American Educational Research Association, Washington, DC.

Webb, N. M., & Kenderski, C. M. (1985). Gender differences in small-group interaction and achievement in high- and low-achieving classes. In L. C. Wilinson & C. B. Marrett (Eds.), *Gender influences in classroom interaction.* Orlando, FL: Academic Press.

Weiner, B. (1972). *Theories of motivation.* Chicago: Rand McNally.

Weiner, B. (1990). History of motivational research in education. *Journal of Educational Psychology, 82,* 616–622.

Weiner, B., Frieze, I., Kukla, A., Reed, L., Rest, S., & Rosenbaum, R. (1971). Perceiving the causes of success and failure. In E. E. Jones (Ed.), *Attribution: Perceiving the causes of behavior.* Morristown, NJ: General Learning Press.

Weiner, B., & Kukla, A. (1970). An attributional analysis of achievement motivation. *Journal of Personality and Social Psychology, 15,* 1–20.

Weinstein, C. E., & Mayer, R. E. (1986). The teaching of learning strategies. In M. Wittrock (Ed.), *Handbook of research on teaching* (3rd ed.). New York: Macmillan.

Weinstein, C. E., & Stone, G. (1993). Broadening our conception of general education: The self-regulated learner. In N. Raisman (Ed.), *New directions for community colleges: Directing general education outcomes.* San Francisco: Jossey-Bass.

Weinstein, C. L., & Palmer, D. R. (1990). *The learning and study strategies inventory: High school version.* Clearwater, FL: H & H Publishing.

Weinstein, R. (1989). Perceptions of classroom processes and student motivation: Children's views of self-fulfilling prophecies. In C. Ames & R. Ames (Eds.), *Research on motivation in education: Vol. 3. Goals and cognitions.* San Diego: Academic Press.

Wentzel, K. R. (1991). Social and academic goals at school: Motivation and achievement in context. In M. L. Maehr & P. R. Pintrich (Eds.), *Advances in motivation and achievement* (Vol. 7). Greenwich, CT: JAI Press.

Wertsch, J. V. (1991). The problem of meaning in a sociocultural approach to mind. In E. McKeough (Ed.), *Toward the practice of theory-based instruction.* Hillsdale, NJ: Erlbaum.

Whelan, R. J. (1981). Prologue. In G. Brown, R. L. McDowell, & J. Smith (Eds.), *Educating adolescents with behavior disorders.* Columbus, OH: Merrill.

Whelan, R. J., & Gallagher, P. A. (1972). Effective teaching of children with behavior disorders. In N. G. Haring & A. H. Hayden (Eds.), *The improvement of instruction.* Seattle: Special Child Publications.

Wherry, J. N. (1983). Some legal considerations and implications for the use of behavior modification in the schools. *Psychology in the Schools, 20,* 46–51.

White, S., & Tharp, R. G. (1988, April). *Questioning and wait-time: A cross-cultural analysis.* Paper presented at the annual meeting of the American Educational Research Association, New Orleans.

Wigfield, A., & Eccles, J. S. (1989). Test anxiety in elementary and secondary students. *Educational Psychologist, 24,* 159–183.

Wiggins, G. (1989). Teaching to the (authentic) test. *Educational Leadership, 46,* 41–46.

Willig, A. C. (1985). A meta-analysis of selected studies on the effectiveness of bilingual education. *Review of Educational Research, 55,* 269–317.

Willis, S. (1972). *Formation of teachers' expectations of students' academic performance.* Unpublished doctoral dissertation, University of Texas, Austin.

Winograd, P., & Hare, V. C. (1988). Direct instruction of reading comprehension strategies: The nature of teacher explanation. In C. E. Weinstein, E. T. Goetz, & P. A. Alexander (Eds.), *Learning and study strategies: Issues in assessment, instruction, and evaluation.* San Diego: Academic Press.

Witkin, H. A., Moore, C., Goodenough, D., & Cox, P. (1977). Field-dependent and field-independent cognitive styles and their educational implications. *Review of Educational Research, 47,* 1–64.

Wittrock, M. C. (1991). Generative teaching of comprehension. *Elementary School Review, 92,* 169–184.

Wolfe, P. (1984). *Instructional skills trainers' manual.* Napa, CA: Napa County Office of Education.

Wood, P., Bruner, J., & Ross, G. (1976). The role of tutoring in problem solving. *Journal of Child Psychology and Psychiatry, 17,* 89–100.

Woolfolk, A. E., Rosoff, B., & Hoy, W. K. (1990). Teachers' sense of efficacy and their beliefs about managing students. *Teaching & Teacher Education, 6,* 137–148.

Workman, E. A. (1982). *Teaching behavioral self-control to students.* Austin, TX: PRO-ED.

Workman, E. A., & Hector, M. (1978). Behavior self-control in classroom settings: A review of the literature. *Journal of School Psychology, 16,* 227–236.

Wrightsman, L. S. (1962). The effects of anxiety, achievement, motivation, and task importance upon performance on an intelligence test. *Journal of Educational Psychology, 53,* 150–156.

Wynne, E. A. (1988). Balancing character development and academics in the elementary school. *Phi Delta Kappan, 69,* 424–426.

Youngs, B. B. (1985). *Stress in children: How to recognize, avoid, and overcome it.* New York: Arbor House.

Ysseldyke, J. E., Algozzine, B., & Thurlow, M. L. (1992). *Critical issues in special education* (2nd ed.). Boston: Houghton Mifflin.

Zahorik, J. A. (1975). Teachers' planning models. *Educational Leadership, 33,* 134–139.

Zessoules, R., & Gardner, H. (1991). Authentic assessment: Beyond the buzzword and into the classroom. In V. Perrone (Ed.), *Expanding student assessment.* Alexandria, VA: Association for Supervision and Curriculum Development.

Zeuli, J. S., & Floden, R. E. (1987). Cultural incongruities and inequities of schooling: Implications for practice from ethnographic research. *Journal of Teacher Education, 38,* 9–15.

Zigler, E., & Valentine, J. (Eds.). (1979). *Project Head Start: A legacy of the war on poverty.* New York: Free Press.

Zimmerman, B. J. (1989). Models of self-regulated learning and academic achievement. In B. J. Zimmerman & D. H. Schunk (Eds.), *Self-regulated learning and academic achievement: Theory, research, and practice.* New York: Springer-Verlag.

Zimmerman, B. J., & Martinez-Pons, M. (1986). Development of a structured interview for assessing student use of self-regulated learning strategies. *American Educational Research Journal, 23,* 614–628.

Zimmerman, B. J., & Schunk, D. H. (Eds.). (1989). *Self-regulated learning and academic achievement: Theory, research, and practice.* New York: Springer-Verlag.

Author Index

Subject Index

COPYRIGHT ACKNOWLEDGMENTS

Photo Credits

Bob Backman/Leo de Wys, Inc.: pages 10, 504

Bas Van Beek/Leo de Wys, Inc.: page 86

Jodi Buren/Woodfin Camp: page 340

Elizabeth Crews: pages 60, 69, 207, 226, 546, 558, 621

Bob Daemmrich: pages 2, 8, 175, 296, 411, 417

Daniel DeWilde: pages 19, 173, 257, 492, 567, 596

Paul Gerda/Leo de Wys, Inc,: page 478

Bob Krist:/Leo de Wys, Inc.: page 434

Lorne/Photo Researchers, Inc.: 1, 36, 235, 339, 545

Lawrence Migdale: pages 38, 45, 131, 144, 149, 198, 247, 262, 282, 292, 320, 375, 378, 402, 413, 441, 446, 486, 509, 586

Jeff Sedlik: pages 52, 91, 98, 110, 163, 168, 212, 241, 287, 302, 317, 322, 358, 359, 361, 449, 461, 500, 552

Sepp Seitz/Woodfin Camp: page 236

Curtis Willocks/Brooklyn Image Group: pages 209, 388

Figure and Table Credits

Figure 1.1 Adapted from *Preparing Instructional Objectives*. Copyright 1984 by Lake Publishing Company, Belmont, CA 94002.

Figure 2.4. From *Science* by B. F. Skinner. Copyright 1958 by the AAAS.

Figure 2.5. From *Preparing Instructional Objectives* by Robert F. Mager. Copyright 1984 by David S. Lake Publishers, Belmont, CA 94002.

Table 2.4. Reprinted with the permission of Macmillan Publishing Company from *Mastery Learning and Classroom Instruction* by James Block and Lorin Anderson. Copyright 1975 by Macmillan Publishing Company.

Table 3.1. From *Teaching and Learning in the College Classroom* by McKeachie, W., et al., copyright 1990 by NCRIPTAL, the University of Michigan. Reprinted with permission.

Figure 3.3. From *Study and Thinking Skills in College*, 2/e, by Kathleen T. McWhorter. Copyright 1992 by Kathleen T. McWhorter. Reprinted by permission of HarperCollins Publishers.

Figure 3.6. From "Content area cognitive mapping for reading and writing proficiency," in the *Journal of Reading*. Reprinted with permission of Mark Lee Peresich and the International Reading Association.

Figure 3.7. From the Study Guide for *School Learning* by Floyd G. Robinson, copyright 1970. Reprinted with permission.

Table 4.1. From *Transforming School Culture to Enhance Motivation* by Martin Maehr, copyright 1992 by AERA. Reprinted with permission.

Table 4.3. From *Teaching and Learning in the College Classroom* by McKeachie, W., et al., copyright 1990 by NCRIPTAL, the University of Michigan. Reprinted with permission.

Figure 5.1. From *Helping Relationships: Basic Concepts for the Helping Professions* by Combs et al., copyright 1971 by Allyn and Bacon. Reprinted with permission of Allyn and Bacon.

Table 5.1. From *Kohlberg's Stages of Moral Development*, copyright 1979 by David Johnson. Reprinted with permission.

Figure 6.1. From Doris A. Trojcak, "Implementing the Competency of Sequencing Instruction," in *Implementing Teacher Competencies*, Weigand ed., copyright 1977, p. 200. Reprinted by permission of Prentice-Hall, Inc., Englewood Cliffs, New Jersey.

Figure 6.3. From *Lesson Plan Outline* by Patricia Wolfe. Reprinted by permission of the author.

Table 7.1. From Emerle and Anderson, *ESJ 80* (1980), p. 224, 1 Table. Reprinted with permission of the University of Chicago Press.

Table 7.2. From Caldwell, Huitt, Braeber, *ESJ 82* (1980), 1 Table. Reprinted with permission of the University of Chicago Press.

Table 7.3. From "Measuring Teacher Effectiveness from the Teacher's Point of View" by C. S. Englert, 1984, *Focus on Exceptional Children,* 17, pp. 1–15. Copyright 1984 by Love Publishing Company. Adapted by permission.

Figure 7.2. From *It's Positively Fun! Techniques for Managing Learning Environments* (pp. 38–39) by P. Kaplan, J. Kohfeldt, and K. Sturla, 1974, Denver, Love Publishing. Reprinted with permission.

Figure 7.3. From *Handbook of Behavior Therapy in Education.* Edited by J. C. Witt et al. Copyright 1988 by Plenum Press. Reprinted by permission.

Table 8.1 From *Piaget's Theory of Cognitive and Affective Development,* Fourth Edition, by Barry J. Wadsworth. Copyright 1989 by Longman Publishing Group. Reprinted with permission.

Table 8.2 From *Human Abilities: An Information-Processing Approach,* edited by Robert J. Sternberg. Copyright 1985 by W. H. Freeman and Company. Reprinted by permission.

Table 8.3. From "Multiple Intelligences Go to School..." Copyright 1989 by the American Educational Research Association. Reprinted by permission of the publisher.

Figures 9.1. and 9.2. "The Changing Nature of the Disadvantaged Population: Current Dimensions and Future Trends" by A. M. Pallas, G. Natriello, and E. L. McDill, 1989, *Educational Research, 18.* Copyright 1989 by the American Educational Research Association. Reprinted by permission of the Publisher.

Table 10.1. From *Educational Psychology* by Thomas Good and Jere Brophy. Copyright 1986 by Longman Publishing Group. Reprinted with permission.

Figure 10.2. From "A Developmental Perspective on Antisocial Behavior" by G. R. Patterson, B. D. DeBaryshe, and E. Ramsey, 1989, *American Psychologist, 44.* Copyright 1989 by the American Psychological Association. Reprinted by permission.

Table 10.3. From "Achievement Goals in the Classroom: Students' Learning Strategies and Motivation Processes" by C. Ames and J. Archer, 1988. *Journal of Educational Psychology, 80.* Copyright 1988 by the American Psychological Association. Reprinted by permission.

Table 10.4. From David Elkind, *The Hurried Child,* Copyright 1981 by David Elkind. Reprinted with permission of Addison-Wesley Publishing Company, Inc.

Table 11.2. From "Learning Disabilities...A Puzzlement" by M. Summers, 1977, *Today's Education, 66* (4), p. 42. Copyright 1977 by the National Educators Association. Reprinted by permission.

Table 11.3. From *Teaching for Learning* by Bernice Sedlik. Reprinted by permission from the author.

Table 11.4. From *Special Children: An Integrative Approach* by Bernard G. Suran and Joseph V. Rizzo. Copyright 1979 by Scott, Foresman and Company. Reprinted by permission of HarperCollins Publishers.

Table 11.5. From *An Introduction to Special Education,* 2/e, by William H. Berdine and A. Edward Blackhurst. Copyright 1985 by William H. Berdine and A. Edward Blackhurst. Reprinted by permission of HarperCollins Publishers.

Figure 11.1. From "Individualized Education Program" page 2—form 27.808-2 (revised 6/81) by the Los Angeles Unified School District, copyright 1981. Reprinted with permission.

Table 12.2. From *Making the Classroom Test: A Guide for Teachers.* Copyright 1959, 1961, 1973 by Educational Testing Service. All rights reserved. Reprinted by permission.

Table 12.3. From *Measurement and Evaluation in Education and Psychology,* 3rd edition, by William A. Mehrens and Irvin J. Lehman. Copyright 1978 by Holt, Rinehart, & Winston. Copyright 1973 by Holt, Rinehart & Winston, Inc. Reprinted by permission of CBS College Publishing.

Figure 13.3. From the Stanford Achievement Test: 7th Edition. Copyright 1982, 1983, 1984, 1986 by Harcourt Brace Jovanovich, Inc. Reproduced by permission. All rights reserved.

Figure 13.4. From the Stanford Achievement Test: 7th Edition. Copyright 1982, 1983, 1984, 1986 by Harcourt Brace Jovanovich, Inc. Reproduced by permission. All rights reserved.

Figure 13.6. From "Reporting Student Progress: A Case for a Criterion-Referenced Working System" by J. Millman, 1970, *Phi Delta Kappan, 52,* 55. 226–231. Copyright 1970 by Phi Delta Kappa. Reprinted by permission.

3332

The purpose of this suggestion sheet is to solicit student feedback that can be used to improve the next edition of *Applying Educational Psychology.* The first three questions are aimed at learning more about the students who, like you, are using this book. The remaining questions will allow Myron Dembo to know your reactions to this text, so please be as specific as possible. When you complete this sheet, simply cut along the dotted line, fold and tape or staple closed, and place a stamp in the appropriate place.
Thank you!

Dembo, *Applying Educational Psychology* 5E

SUGGESTION SHEET

(1) Degree you are seeking (circle one): **BA, BS, MA, MS, MEd, EdD, PhD, Other** __________

(2) Your major (circle one): **Elem Ed, Sec Ed, Spec Ed, Ed Psych, Psych, Other** __________

(3) *Optional*

Name ____________________

School ____________________

Address ____________________

____

(4) Did you find this textbook appropriate for your course in terms of:

Content: Yes No

Comments: ____________________

Writing Level: Yes No

Comments: ____________________

Organization: Yes No

Comments: ____________________

Pedagogical Aids: Were these useful?

Advance Organizers	**Yes**	**No**
Focus Questions	**Yes**	**No**
Debate Forums	**Yes**	**No**
Classroom Applications	**Yes**	**No**
Reflecting On. . .	**Yes**	**No**
Part Syntheses/Questions	**Yes**	**No**

Comments on Pedagogical Aids:

Other Comments:

Myron H. Dembo
600 Phillips Hall
University of Southern California
Los Angeles, CA 90089-0031